Business Communication
Principles and Applications

Business Communication

Principles and Applications

Zane K. Quible
Department of Management
Oklahoma State University

Margaret H. Johnson
emerita
University of Nebraska

Dennis Mott
Department of Management
Oklahoma State University

Prentice Hall
Upper Saddle River, New Jersey 07458

Library of Congress Cataloging-in-Publication Data

Quible, Zane. K., 1942–
Business communication : principles and applications / Zane K. Quible, Margaret H. Johnson, Dennis Mott.
p. cm.
Includes index.
ISBN 0-13-304429-7 (alk. paper)
1. Business communication. 2. Business writing. I. Johnson, Margaret, 1920– . II. Mott, Dennis L. III. Title.
HF5718.Q528 1995
808′.06665—dc20 95-9246
CIP

Acquisitions Editor: Don Hull
Production Management: Impressions, a Division of Edwards Brothers, Inc.
Project Manager: Cathi Profitko
Managing Editor: Joyce Turner
Buyer: Vincent Scelta
Editorial Assistant: John Larkin
Production Assistant: Florrie Gadson
Cover art: *Space Visions* by Myrle Krumper

Printed in the United States of America

10 9 8 7 6 5

ISBN 0-13-304429-7

PRENTICE-HALL INTERNATIONAL (UK) LIMITED, *LONDON*
PRENTICE-HALL OF AUSTRALIA PTY. LIMITED, *SYDNEY*
PRENTICE-HALL CANADA INC., *TORONTO*
PRENTICE-HALL HISPANOAMERICANA, S.A., *MEXICO*
PRENTICE-HALL OF INDIA PRIVATE LIMITED, *NEW DELHI*
PRENTICE-HALL OF JAPAN, INC., *TOKYO*
PEARSON EDUCATION ASIA PTE. LTD., *SINGAPORE*
EDITORA PRENTICE-HALL DO BRASIL, LTDA., *RIO DE JANEIRO*

To: Patricia and Chris
Carolyn and Greg
Karen, Nicole, and Bryan

Contents

Preface

Employers today are demanding better writing skills of their employees than ever before. Evidence to support this claim is found in the ever-increasing number of job vacancy notices, in general, that indicate the need for applicants to possess effective written and oral communication skills. Likewise, the number of higher-level positions in many organizations that mention communication skills in their job vacancy notices also has steadily increased. Clearly, outstanding communication skills will give today's college students the competitive edge when they begin their job-searching efforts.

Business Communication: Principles and Applications was written and designed to help current and future employees of all types of organizations improve their ability to communicate more effectively, primarily in writing, but also orally. The portion of this text that focuses on writing is concerned with two important aspects: (1) writing essentials for all types of business documents and (2) appropriate content and structure for various types of business documents. The content that focuses on oral communication is concerned primarily with how employees can make more effective presentations in both small and larger groups.

In addition, to address the contemporary issues of today's global business environment, aspects of effective and appropriate international business communication skills are discussed.

This text's general features include the following:

1. Well-written, easy-to-understand, interesting content
2. Comprehensive, up-to-date coverage of important business topics
3. Abundant examples that show the reader both the incorrect and the correct ways to prepare a number of different types of written business documents
4. Detailed analysis of a variety of written business documents

A number of pedagogical devices have also been created for this text. Among these devices are the following:

1. Marginal notations (set in a question format that helps students in mastering important concepts)
2. End-of-chapter review questions

3. Application problems that give students an opportunity to apply their knowledge of important concepts discussed in the various chapters. (The vast majority of these problems require the writing of a business document.)
4. Clear illustrations that help students quickly master important chapter concepts
5. Appendices that focus on grammar, punctuation, document format, legal aspects of writing, and technology

In deciding which features to incorporate, the authors were always mindful of how these features would influence learner mastery of content covered throughout the text. We believe students will find these additional features beneficial in their study of business communication:

1. Checklists for a variety of business documents that students will be able to use in assessing how well various documents they write conform with accepted practices
2. Many illustrated documents presented in formats (primarily letters and memoranda) commonly used in the business world
3. Communication capsules in each chapter that focus on specific content relevant to the chapter
4. Ethics episodes in a number of chapters that are designed to help readers avoid creating serious ethics dilemmas
5. A variety of application problems, some of which present alternative assignments requiring that the learner demonstrate knowledge acquisition in ways other than writing a business document
6. More attention than many other texts focused on the proper content and structure for a variety of types of business memos
7. Nearly 50 exercises at the end of the text, designed to help students improve their basic writing skills. These exercises will help learners improve writing proficiency using assignments other than those that require the preparation of a complete business document. Included in the exercises are
   a. editing exercises that require the learner to correct focused writing errors in a variety of paragraphs (subject-verb disagreement, pronoun-antecedent disagreement, lack of "you-attitude," use of expletives, etc.).
   b. exercises (involving primarily letters) that present the learner with poorly written paragraphs comprising various business letters; the learner is asked to revise each paragraph, paying particular attention to specified deficiencies as well as general deficiencies.
   c. critiquing exercises focusing on various types of business letters that contain both specific and general errors; the learner is asked to provide a line-by-line critique of each letter and then rewrite each paragraph to remove the weaknesses.
   d. sentences which contain errors that the learner is asked to correct in the rewriting process.
   e. sentence-combining exercises that require the writing of one, two, or three sentences to combine the ideas presented in each sentence set.

The *Teacher's Manual* accompanying *Business Communication: Principles and Applications* contains a wealth of helpful information. Included in the manual are the following types of information:

- Course structure
- Course content and organization
- Sample course outlines
- General class procedures and suggestions
- Grading suggestions and systems

- Answers to review questions
- Answers to selected application problems
- Solutions to exercises found at end of text
- Test bank comprised of multiple-choice and true-false questions

The authors wish to acknowledge the following individuals for their assistance during the various stages of this project:

Don Hull, acquisitions editor, who provided helpful advice in the conceptualizing of various sections of this text.
Cathi Profitko, project manager, who was always readily available to answer any questions the authors had.
Sarah Putzer, production editor, whose patience and expertise enabled this project to run smoothly.

Zane K. Quible
Margaret H. Johnson
Dennis L. Mott

Business Communication
Principles and Applications

1

The Nature of Communication

After studying this chapter, you should be able to

1. Identify the differences among organizational communications that are directed downward, upward, and laterally.
2. Recognize the different types of media commonly found within each of the directions of communication flow.
3. Outline differences between internal and external communication.
4. Identify and describe the essential types of communication skills needed by individuals in business.
5. Discuss the ways in which effective communication benefits the entire organization.

In what types of communication activities do employees engage?

Communication, or the sending and receiving of information through messages, is an essential process of organizational life that occurs in a variety of ways and circumstances. Whatever organization you work for, you receive and send many types of messages—written, verbal, and nonverbal communications. Communication was once considered simply as a response to a stimulus. Now it is viewed as a more complex process. Today, to understand the process of *business communication,* or the internal and external communication of an organization, we need to focus on the sender and the receiver and, especially, on the clarity of the message that is sent.

We communicate every moment we say or do something. In business the amount of time people spend communicating ranges from 50 percent to 75 percent of their waking hours. Listening and speaking consume more time than reading and writing, but all four activities are important in business careers.

In what way are communication skills beneficial?

Effective communication skills benefit not only employees but also their employers. Effective communicators become more visible within the organization, which usually has a positive impact on their career progression. In contrast, poor communicators cause personal and organizational problems, often reflected in a lack of motivated employees, ineffective coordination of activities, negative attitudes among employees, and ineffective leadership. Employees who cannot make their points quickly and effectively will cost their organization millions of dollars of lost business.

THE NATURE OF COMMUNICATION IN THE MODERN ORGANIZATION

Nearly every task a manager performs—whether it is planning, organizing, staffing, directing, or controlling—requires the use of communication in one form or another. The direction of communication along communication pathways is known as the *communication flow.* One method of studying the nature of communication in the modern organization is to examine the direction of the communication flow and the intended destination of the message. A communication message can flow downward, upward, and laterally. *Internal communication* stays within the organization. *External communication* moves outside the organization.

Communication Flow

What media are used in the communication process?

A variety of formal and informal transmission media, or *communication channels,* are used in the communication process. Some are employed in all three directions of communication flow, but others are limited to one direction. For example, downward, upward, and lateral communication often occurs via interoffice memos and reports. Bulletin boards are a common downward communication medium, but they are rarely used for upward or lateral communication. In contrast, suggestion systems and attitude surveys represent common upward communication media that are unsuitable for downward communication.

Downward-Directed Communication

What is the primary purpose of downward communication?

Downward communication, or communication from a superior to subordinates, informs employees about important situations, such as information about their jobs, organizational policies and procedures, performance feedback, and organizational or unit goals and objectives. Lack of information in one or more of these areas tends to have a negative effect on employees' productivity, attitudes, and job satisfaction.

What types of downward communication media are used?

Types of media used in downward communication are interoffice memos, reports, bulletin boards, company newsletters and magazines, staff meetings, audiovisual programs, public address systems, manuals, pay-envelope inserts, and conferences. Some of these media are in the form of written communication; others are primarily oral communication.

Interoffice memos are the most common written communication medium and are frequently used to communicate within an organization. But their informality makes them unsuitable for extensive use in external communication. That is, memos not only lack many of the formal parts of a business letter (inside address, salutation, and complimentary close), but also they are written in a more informal style than business letters.

Reports are used to transmit a variety of different types of downward-directed internal information to employees. The various types of informal reports discussed in Chapter 12 are appropriate for this application. Formal reports (see Chapters 13 and 14) can also be used internally, although they are more likely to be used externally.

Bulletin boards provide a valuable communication link, but they should be used with discretion. Employees rarely read the information posted on bulletin boards. Therefore, another medium may be more effective when communicating important information. The location of bulletin boards often determines whether their contents are likely to be read. For that reason, they are generally installed in highly visible locations such as near water fountains and around elevators. Important information has a better chance of being read if it is always posted in the same location and identified as "important."

Company newsletters and *magazines* are used by top management to keep lower-level employees informed about significant events, activities, operations, and issues. Information typically contained in these publications that is of greatest interest to employees is news about themselves—promotions, retirements, transfers, and marriages.

Company newsletters and magazines also help persuade employees to accept managerial decisions and initiate actions desired by management.

Staff meetings depend heavily on oral communication, although some written communication, such as agendas, minutes, and reports, usually circulate at meetings as well. Although management can use staff meetings to inform employees about important matters, meetings can also be effective forums for persuading employees to complete specific tasks. Staff meetings will also assist managers in situations where a change or modification of attitude is desired.

The information employees receive at staff meetings can also be presented through a written medium. Many managers prefer to use the staff meeting to convey a more personal concern for how information affects their subordinates or to stress its importance. Organizations that solicit extensive employee input into the decision-making process (known as *participative decision making*) also commonly use staff meetings.

Audiovisual programs inform employees about new programs (such as a new fringe benefit) or work units (such as a new child-care center) or changes in operating procedures (such as a change in the process for submitting travel reimbursement claims). These programs are more useful as an information-presentation medium than as a medium of persuasion. Information in audiovisual programs can be presented by slides and audiotapes as well as by videotapes. The main advantage of audiovisual programs is their ability to transmit information to large numbers of people in a relatively short time. Their primary disadvantage is their failure to convey the significance of that information.

Public address systems provide a medium for public announcements and emergency-type messages. Employees *do* listen to information transmitted through the public address system, making this medium an effective way of communicating.

In addition, communication is enhanced through *manuals,* such as orientation manuals and functional manuals. These manuals cover such areas as the organization's records management, procedures, policies, and operations. Much of their success is attributed to the skill and care given to each phase of their development. Their ease of use and their understandability are special communication assets.

Some organizations use *pay-envelope inserts* to deliver important messages to employees. The information contained on inserts is typically brief and important. Overuse of this medium diminishes the significance that employees attach to the information the inserts provide.

Conferences are conversations between a supervisor and subordinate. Supervisors use them to mobilize support, provide information, take disciplinary action, and communicate performance appraisal results. Although most conferences are oral, some written materials may be distributed during them. The supervisor's skill in conducting a conference significantly affects the employee in the achievement of desired objectives.

Upward-Directed Communication

What is the purpose of upward communication?

The purpose of downward-directed internal organizational communication is to inform employees. The purpose of *upward-directed communication,* or communication from a subordinate to a superior, is to provide managers with essential feedback required for making decisions. The better the quality of information received, the more useful and effective will be its role in the decision-making process. A potential problem associated with upward-directed communication is the reluctance of employees to convey to their superiors the negative aspects of such messages.

What types of upward communication media are used?

The media relied on to direct information upward are reports, interoffice memos, suggestion systems, attitude surveys, supervisor-subordinate conferences, management-employee councils, and grievance procedures.

Reports provide a medium for transmitting information upward in the same manner that they transmit information downward. Upward-directed reports are prepared periodically or regularly as well as when the need arises. Periodic reports emerge from assigned job responsibilities of a particular employee or department. Some organizations request reports on an ad hoc basis. Most reports are requested by a person who holds a higher position or rank than the preparer, but some reports are written at the preparer's discretion and then transmitted upward.

Upward-directed *interoffice memos* provide managers with facts and information essential to the decision-making process. In addition, they give documentation for activities and personal requests, such as permission to engage in a certain activity or approval for vacation or annual leave time.

Suggestion systems offer many benefits to the organizations that have them as a communication medium. Employees are invited to submit their suggestions for improving the efficiency of certain organizational operations. They typically possess valuable information about various job activities; in fact, their input is often more valuable than that of managers. The most effective suggestion system gives employees material rewards, such as cash, stock certificates, or coupons for discounted purchases. The value of a reward relates directly to the perceived value of the suggestion to the company, department, or work group.

Attitude surveys enable top management to identify areas in which employees believe managerial or operational effectiveness can improve. These surveys usually include a questionnaire as the input medium. Sometimes the nature of the survey topic is quite general, such as an evaluation of the organization's fringe benefits. In other instances, the survey topic may be specialized, such as an evaluation of a specific type of fringe benefit. Survey information is tabulated and used as important input by managers in their decision-making process.

Employer-employee conferences represent a valuable medium for conveying information upward, whether they are conducted face-to-face or by telephone. Conferences have a variety of uses: to discuss problem situations with superiors, to provide input to superiors that will enhance their decision making, and to discuss employee ideas and suggestions for improving organizational efficiency. The effectiveness of these conferences is largely determined by the nature of the superior-subordinate relationship. Conferences are more effective when the participants are open with one another and willingly share information.

Success of *management-employee councils* depends on two-way communication. Because councils are basically designed to serve the interests of employees rather than employers, they are classified as an upward-communication medium. Council members are usually elected by peers in their various work units because they are viewed as the people best able to represent their constituents. Council meeting agenda topics include a wide range of concerns, interests, and irritations; but in unionized organizations, union-management topics may be excluded from formal discussion.

Unionized organizations have a formal *grievance* procedure, and an increasing number of nonunionist organizations have followed this practice. Employees file grievances when they believe they have been treated unfairly by their supervisor or by someone else in the organization. Unionized organizations choose a member to be their union steward. The steward then assumes a major part of the responsibility for filing the grievance. In nonunion organizations, an employee has virtually no assistance in filing and processing a grievance. Resolution of grievances involves the use of both written and oral communication media.

Lateral Communication

What is the function of lateral communication?

The operating efficiency of the modern organization is enhanced through effective *lateral communication* (sometimes called *horizontal communication*)—the communication between individuals of equal hierarchical rank. Employees use lateral communication to exchange ideas and information, solve problems, perform job duties, and coordinate work on projects. Lateral communication is equally valuable for employees in the same or different departments. Most lateral communication is oral, so the use of clear language and terminology understandable to each participant is necessary. Sometimes a lateral communication conference is conducted by telephone.

Another common type of horizontal communication is the *grapevine,* an informal communication medium that depends on unofficial or social interrelationships among employees. The grapevine is informal because the communicators and the direction of communication pattern changes from situation to situation. For example, an employee may convey one type of information during lunch with two fellow employees but different information when taking a break with another group of employees. Information transmitted through the grapevine typically travels faster than information sent through formal organizational channels.

The grapevine is sometimes mistakenly perceived as a medium for passing along gossip or rumors and for transmitting inaccurate information. More often, the grapevine is an excellent source of accurate information. In most cases, grapevine information eventually becomes accessible to management, which will, if wise, seriously assess it. If the information about an organizational matter is inaccurate, management may then attempt to correct the inaccuracy by transmitting the correct information to an appropriate individual for transmission through the grapevine.

Managers frequently consider all types of upward-directed information as input into their decision-making processes, but wise managers use the downward-directed grapevine as a barometer to assess employee acceptance or rejection of an anticipated action.

COMMUNICATION DESTINATION

What types of communication destinations are found?

The ratio between internal and external communication varies from organization to organization. As the size of the organization expands, the amount of internal communication increases at a faster rate than the amount of external communication.

Internal Communication

What types of internal media are found?

Each of the communication media discussed previously is also classified as an internal communication medium. Interoffice memos, reports, and conferences are the most commonly used internal media in the modern organization. Because we previously discussed the various internal media, they will not be discussed in this section.

External Communication

What types of external media are found?

Modern organizations maintain close ties with various constituencies and publics. They often depend, in fact, on these publics for economic survival; therefore, external communication plays a significant role in their operations. Examples of publics that organizations communicate with are consumers, stockholders, contributors, governmental agencies, news media, suppliers, wholesalers, and retailers. Types of media used to communicate externally are letters, reports, stockholder reports, proposals, news releases, stockholder meetings, telephone conversations, and conferences.

Letters are a more formal communication medium than interoffice memos. The variety of letters organizations use to communicate externally include the following kinds: request, acknowledgement, order, claim, adjustment, sales, credit, and collection letters. Much of the success of these letters depends on the care and skill with which they are prepared. Ineffective letters cost American organizations millions of dollars each year—a waste that may greatly diminish if employees improve their letter-writing skills.

Although *informal reports* are sometimes used for external purposes, *formal reports* are more commonly used externally. The formality of the situation the report addresses determines whether the report will be formal or informal. Formal reports are often longer than informal reports, although not necessarily so. Currently, employees in many organizations are finding that their responsibility for report preparation is increasing.

Stockholder reports convey information vital to the organization's stockholders. These reports are prepared annually. Less extensive reports are often prepared and relayed to the stockholders on a quarterly or as-needed basis. Stockholder reports include financial information and data about products, services, employees, plants, research and development, as well as community activities.

Some organizations use *proposals* for communications about contract-type research and development activities. For example, assume a company is interested in installing a management information system. The complexity of the project requires the company to seek outside assistance in the design and installation of the new system. A request for a proposal (RFP) that outlines the company's plans and expectations is prepared and distributed to organizations specializing in developing such systems. Organizations receiving the RFP then prepare and submit a proposal to the company. After reviewing the proposals, the company contracts with the organization that submitted the most effective proposal for the installation of the new system.

News releases offer news media agencies—broadcast and print—organizational information of interest to the public. Most organizations try to capitalize on favorable information by keeping the public well informed and up-to-date. Organizations also submit news releases to minimize the impact of negative situations that may create a poor public image.

Organizations responsible to stockholders schedule annual *stockholder meetings* to conduct official business, such as electing new members to the board of directors and to present information of interest to the stockholders. Although these meetings naturally depend heavily on verbal communication, they include written communication.

An increasing amount of organizational business is conducted over the *telephone.* If the telephone is the single best invention for the effective use of time, it is also one of the greatest time wasters for an organization. When several calls have to be placed before the person is reached, the time and organizational expense is very high. Excessive amounts of small talk during phone conversations are also time wasters. Furthermore, the practice of providing a written document to confirm the substance of the phone conversation is especially wasteful of time, human resources, and monetary resources. When this occurs, the basic reason for using the phone—to save time—actually consumes more time because of the duplicate effort in making the phone call and in subsequent written documentation.

Employees spend part of their time in face-to-face *conferences* with individuals from outside the organization, including purchasing agents, sales representatives, upper-level managers, and department managers. Goodwill is essential for organizational relationships; therefore, both parties must treat each other with courtesy and respect.

HOW EFFECTIVE COMMUNICATION SKILLS BENEFIT EMPLOYEES

Communication skill continues to rate as one of the key personal skills that employees need. The increasing number of organizations that list "effective written and verbal communication skills" as a main job qualification in their job vacancy notices illustrates the need for these skills. Exhibit 1-1 shows some examples.

What types of job-entry communications skills are needed?

Obviously, specific communication skills employees are expected to have vary from job to job; but if they possess highly developed communication skills, these will pay rich career dividends. Effective communication skills lead to a more satisfying initial employment experience and also contribute to more rapid promotions throughout a person's working life. Communication Capsule 1-1 identifies common job-entry communication and related skills that are important and beneficial to new employees.

```
. . . excellent communication skills.
. . . effective communicator, both orally and in writing.
. . . well-developed oral and written communication skills.
. . . excellent communicator.
. . . excellent communication skills are especially important in making
      presentations.
. . . verbal and written communication skills are crucial.
. . . skill in writing reports is essential.
. . . outstanding communication skills required.
. . . excellent communication skills essential.
. . . must have excellent communication skills.
. . . excellent verbal and written communication skills required.
. . . must have excellent communication and follow-up skills.
. . . must be able to communicate results clearly to clients and coworkers.
. . . must have ability to communicate orally.
```

Exhibit 1-1 Examples of required communication skills found listed in job vacancy notices.

Communication Capsule 1-1 Communication Competence: An Important Skill for Success

You have been communicating with others around you since the moment you were born. You are well aware of the important role communication plays in your personal life. Upon entering your chosen field, you will rapidly discover the important role communication plays in your work life.

Conflict is an inevitable aspect of organizational life. Therefore, skill in recognizing and maintaining control over both minor and serious conflict situations is a basic part of professional growth and development. Conflict resolution is not always as clear-cut as it might appear. Seldom do winners and losers exist in long-term conflicts. Rather, all parties must be willing to endorse the win-win concept of conflict resolution. A hands-off style of conflict resolution encourages a hostile environment, whereas a higher-level management mandate seriously erodes organizational communication improvement efforts.

Decision making is a learned skill, not an innate trait. The most highly regarded leaders share a common trait that assists them in their managerial responsibilities—they make decisions only after they have available the essential facts they need to support their decision-making efforts. Deciding too quickly impinges on the quality of their decisions, whereas not making decisions until all facts are available renders the final decisions virtually useless.

Listening is another basic communication skill that is rarely fully developed. Too often employees listen for facts at the expense of a broader analysis. The good news, however, is that listening skill can grow and improve throughout a person's professional life. Practice and professional assistance provide valuable experience and tips. Improved listening enables you to become sensitive about facts, emotions, and broad-based application possibilities.

The art of managerial persuasion depends on highly developed communication skills. Although initial employment may not require such skills, when people are promoted into managerial positions, they will quickly become aware of the value of convincing and understandable persuasive messages.

Presentation skills are a visible sign of professional competence. Persons possessing them must continually communicate their expertise to others. Waiting for peers and superiors to recognize specific personal skills will slow and limit movement up the corporate ladder.

Writing is an essential communication skill. Like listening, persuading, and presenting, a carefully developed ability to use the written word is essential for ultimate success in business careers. Although other communication skill areas rely on interpersonal interpretation, the written word depends on the writer. In the end, the writer's words must clarify the overall intent and meaning of the message.

Business success requires an ability to communicate effectively with all levels of management. Such ability includes effective writing skills, effective job-related technical skills, and an awareness of the value of oral and interpersonal communication. The ability to prepare and deliver persuasive messages is necessary to employees at all career levels, whether they must sell an idea, create positive customer relations, or interpret research data.

During the initial stages of employment, newcomers who possess well-developed communication skills are identified as "better performers" than peers whose communication skills are average or below. Consequently, effective communicators are likely to receive immediate positive recognition of their performance.

Although effective communication skills are the most critical requirement in some jobs, they are valuable to any job in the modern organization. Types of jobs in the business world requiring substantial communication skills are management, marketing, accounting, public relations, sales, customer relations, labor relations, research, and training. Other fields, such as visual and print media, science, politics, medicine, teaching, and engineering, also require effective communication skills. The amount of mental effort required in a job is directly related to the overall need for effective communication skills.

Promotability in an organization depends largely on effective communication skills. Many executives possess technical ability, but an inability to communicate effectively may hinder their career progression. In addition, as the amount of time spent communicating on the job increases, so does the importance of communication.

HOW EFFECTIVE COMMUNICATION BENEFITS THE ORGANIZATION

Effective communication enhances the organization in several ways: providing a more positive image to outsiders, reducing costs, improving employee morale, and raising employee productivity. In many instances, putting a little more effort into the communication process provides rich dividends for the organization.

Essential for Positive Image

What impact does communication have on an organization's image?

The image outsiders have of many organizations is negative because of ineffective communication by employees. Because employees in some organizations are dissatisfied with their jobs, they do not care that what they say or write produces damaging results. Employees, when using either a written or verbal communication medium, have an almost infinite number of opportunities for tarnishing the organization's image. Damaging outcomes may range from failing to answer a question to the outsider's satisfaction to knowingly communicating inaccurate information.

Effective communicators are concerned about the impact of what they say or write on the listener or reader. Often the *implication* of what was said, rather than what was actually said, produces negative results. An incorrect perception is unfortunate when the listener or reader depends on the overall accuracy of the communication process. Consider, for example, the cost to an organization of preparing a typical business letter. By the mid-1990s, the cost exceeded \$15. If an employee prepares an ineffective letter—one that causes unnecessary additional correspondence—the organization's profitability is decreased.

Communication Capsule 1-2 Time Is Money

Personal organization and time management are becoming as necessary to successful job applicants as the more obvious technical and quantitative skills. The new employee must be able to contribute to the organization almost immediately. Gone are the days when employees could leisurely learn a new job at their own pace. International markets, harsh competition, and net profit orientation of business organizations demand people who can instantly perceive, learn, and remember critical information and procedures.

Time is money in the view of corporate executives. Employees who need to be constantly reminded about pending deadlines or reprimanded for excessive socializing are too expensive to maintain. The following data reveal the perceived cost of wasting an hour a day at various monthly salaries.

Mini-Mini Time Cost Scenario

Employee	*Monthly Salary*	*Monthly Cost of Wasting an Hour a Day*
Joan J. Jones	$4,500	$562.50
Frank F. Frank	$4,000	$500.00
Jill W. Wills	$3,000	$375.00
Glen G. Glenn	$2,500	$312.50
Paula P. Pauls	$2,250	$281.25

Mini Time Cost Scenario

As you consider the preceding figures, remember that the five individuals are avid sports fans, often spending many minutes every day discussing various sporting events. If each person wastes an hour a day, the combined cost of their negligent time use would be a continuing cost of $2,031.25 per month.

Mini-Macro Time Cost Scenario

Consider an organization that employs three hundred people, divided into social groups of five like that shown in the time cost scenario data. This would mean sixty groups. In such a situation, the organizational cost of one-hour wasted each day per month is

$2,031.25 time cost per month x 60 groups = $121,875.00 per month.

Macro Time Cost Scenario

An organization of three hundred employees at various salary levels, each of whom wastes one hour a day, will cost an organization millions of dollars a year as shown in the following:

$121,875.00 time wasting cost per month x 12 = $1,462,500.00 per year.

The analysis becomes even more frightening when one contemplates the possibility that many employees may waste more than one hour per day! Do you see the picture? Businesses need workers who are skilled technicians and also effective time managers because . . . time is money.

Communication Capsule 1-2 illustrates the value of time to an employee and also to an organization. Effective communication skills increase the probability of efficient time use while decreasing the amount of wasted effort. This translates into decreased costs and increased profits for the organization.

Essential for Employee Morale

How does communication affect morale?

Managers often unknowingly contribute to employee morale problems because they fail to communicate effectively with subordinates. They frequently underestimate the amount of communication employees desire. Therefore, information useful to employees simply does not get communicated. This, in turn, makes employees believe that their managers are not concerned about them or the positions they hold. When such an impression is created, employee morale deteriorates.

Managers and supervisors need to determine the types and quantities of information their subordinates desire. Because this tends to vary from work group to work group, prescribing a predetermined quota of what constitutes an adequate amount of communication for a given group is impossible. However, if employees desire more information than they are currently receiving from management, every effort should be made to increase the available information.

Essential for Employee Productivity

How does communication affect productivity?

Many organizations are concerned about their inability to improve their productivity, a necessity for their economic well-being. A variety of factors can be identified that impact negatively on organizational productivity, including ineffective communication. For example, in some organizations, employees are not as productive as possible because management fails to communicate its goals and expectations to them.

COMMUNICATION IN SMALL GROUPS

An organization is a combination of small groups of individuals who seek to satisfy both their individual goals and the collective goals of the group. Every organization employs the small group to collect, process, and produce information, solve problems, and make decisions.

The Nature of a Group

What is the nature of a group?

According to an operational view, a small group is a combination of individuals who are interdependent on one another. Viewing small groups from an operational perspective separates the operational small group from a collection of people who might be waiting for the subway or a taxi. Whereas the members of the small group are interdependent on one another, the collection of people waiting for the subway, for example, are independent of one another.

Groups created by the organization include functional groups, project groups, and committees. A *functional group* is a combination of individuals who perform the same job or task within the organization. A *project group* includes people from a cross section of the organization's functional areas who come together to work on a specific task. After the task is accomplished, the group is dissolved. A *committee group* operates in an ad hoc or advisory capacity to examine, analyze, and evaluate the various areas of organizational operations. Some standing committees, however, continue to exist indefinitely.

The small group is a group of individuals who distinguish themselves in some manner—common dress, equipment, and demeanor, for example—from nonmembers. Examples of identification through dress are suits, uniforms, and labels. Examples of identification through equipment are calculators, beepers, and stethoscopes. Examples of identification through demeanor usually refer to communication characteristics, such as voice inflection, listening, and posture.

Communication both within and outside the organizational small group typically follows the chain of command present in the group structure. Downward flow carries facts and information related to objectives, assignments, rules, policies, and procedures. Upward flow conveys information related to periodic updates, requests for data, clarification of directives, and requests for additional financial support or assistance. Horizontal communication coordinates members' efforts.

SUMMARY

In a business organization, information flows in three directions: downward, upward, and laterally. Examples of written information flowing downward are interoffice memos, reports, and newsletters. Examples of written information flowing upward are memos, reports, suggestion system ideas, and attitude surveys. In lateral communication, the exchange of information occurs between two or more employees at the same level.

Business communication is characterized as being either internal or external to the organization. Internal communication occurs through the downward, upward, and lateral media previously described. A variety of media are used in external communication, including letters, reports, proposals, news releases, and phone conversations.

Regardless of the jobs a person may eventually hold, the ability to communicate effectively will be extremely valuable, usually paving the way for systematic career progression. All communication skills are needed; however, depending on the job, some may prove more essential than others.

Effective communication benefits the organization by enhancing its image, improving cost effectiveness, raising employee morale, and increasing employee productivity.

REVIEW QUESTIONS

1. What communication activities are likely to consume most of the typical business employee's workday?
2. Explain the primary function of downward-directed communication.
3. What types of media are typically used in downward communication?
4. Describe the primary purpose of upward-directed communication.
5. What types of media are typically used in upward communication?
6. How do business organizations use attitude surveys?
7. Explain how lateral communication differs from downward and upward communication.
8. What types of media are used in lateral communication?
9. Explain the nature, function, and importance of news releases in the modern organization.
10. New employees are expected to possess effective communication skills. Describe in descending order of importance the five job-entry communication skills you view as most important.
11. Explain how effective communication benefits the modern business organization.

APPLICATION PROBLEMS

1. Select someone you consider to be a good communicator. Now explain in writing the specific skills this person possesses that make him or her effective.
2. Examine both a business letter and an interoffice memorandum to determine their direction, formality, and effectiveness. Explain what you consider to be the major difference between these two types of written communication.
3. Read a stockholder report from a major corporation. Describe the types of information included and evaluate the report's overall effectiveness.
4. As shown in this chapter, the efficient use of time is essential in business. Prepare a list of suggestions to help employees decrease the unnecessary time spent on telephone calls.
5. Examine the "Help Wanted" section of a metropolitan newspaper or the job listing section of a magazine. How many of the positions list effective communication skills as a job qualification? What types of jobs emphasize effective communication skills the most?
6. Draft a letter requesting additional information about one of the positions you reviewed in application problem 5.
7. Review the list of common job-entry communication skills in Communication Capsule 1-1 that are beneficial to new employees. Do a self-appraisal to determine how well developed each communication skill is.
8. Interview five currently employed people about their perception of the value of communication skills for job success.
9. Read several newspapers and magazines to collect evidence that reveals how effective communication (a) influences the overall image of the company, (b) is essential for cost reduction, (c) improves employee morale, and (d) increases productivity.
10. Examine a company newsletter to identify the type of material it contains. Evaluate the information for overall effectiveness and suggest why it was included.

2

The Elements of Communication in the Modern Organization

After studying this chapter, you should be able to

1. Describe how the functions of communication in the modern organization differ from one another.
2. Explain the characteristics of the communication process.
3. Discuss the elements of the communication model presented in this chapter.
4. Identify the types of nonverbal communication affecting the communication process.
5. Outline the barriers to effective communication.

A complex—and pervasive—element of modern organizations is the communication that occurs inside. Communication is essential to virtually all employees as they perform assigned job duties. Varying in their complexity, communication activities range from a simple information request by one employee to another to the negotiation of a new labor contract by management and union representatives.

Chapter 2 provides you with an excellent understanding of the communication process. The functions of communication in the modern organization, the characteristics of the communication process, and the types of communication are discussed. Also included are a model of the communication process, examples of nonverbal communication, and several of the major personal and organizational barriers to effective communication.

THE FUNCTIONS OF COMMUNICATION IN THE MODERN ORGANIZATION

Communication in the modern organization fulfills the functions of informing, controlling, persuading, and coordinating. Each of these functions is essential to organizations and to their managers and employees.

The Informing Function

The modern organization requires a vast amount of information if the various components are to function properly. Managers must constantly make effective decisions based on accurate, timely, and well-organized information. Similarly, employees also need accurate, timely, and well-organized information to perform their jobs effectively.

What functions does communication fulfill?

Letters, memos, reports, manuals, staff meetings, conferences, and interviews perform the *informing function* of modern organizations. A weakness in any of these communication skill areas will negatively impact the overall information flow. The result will be time problems and increased cost of operations for the organization.

The Controlling Function

Naturally, daily activities do not always proceed according to plan. Organizations must determine how well actual results match anticipated ones. The *controlling function* provides the means by which to undertake corrective action.

What types of communication media are used in the controlling function?

Many of the activities of the controlling function depend on communication. Examples of communication media used in the controlling function are operations manuals, policies and procedures statements, and daily instructions. The controlling function becomes less time-consuming when communication efforts improve in each medium.

Communication effectiveness determines whether those being controlled in an organization will respond to the authority and power of the individual responsible. The sender's communication skills have a definite effect on whether the receiver perceives the control process as legitimate. Whether the receiver perceives the sender to have the credibility and power to exert that amount of control over him or her also depends on the sender's communication skills.

The Persuading Function

Many managers believe that persuading is preferable to forcing subordinates to take a certain course of action. Persuasion often results in voluntary compliance, which usually produces greater commitment than does forced compliance. The communication medium well suited to the *persuading function* is one-on-one communication.

What communication medium is well suited for the persuading function?

The Coordinating Function

The *coordinating function* provides the unity and cohesion an organization needs to operate smoothly. Activities common to the coordinating function are developing and defining goals and objectives, determining work schedules for departments and individuals, communicating task assignments, and providing feedback. The coordinating function also assists employees to identify more with the organization. Ineffectiveness within the coordinating function is reflected in decreased organizational productivity and dissatisfied employees.

Types of communication media used in the coordinating function are one-on-one and small-group conferences, as well as written memos, reports, performance-evaluation summaries, job descriptions, and manuals.

CHARACTERISTICS OF THE COMMUNICATION PROCESS

Identifiable characteristics of the communication process are the following: (1) It uses symbols, (2) it is dynamic, (3) it is understandable, and (4) it involves two or more individuals with unique backgrounds and experiences. The absence of any of these characteristics results in something other than communication.

Symbolic

Communication involves the use of symbols, such as words (both spoken and written) and nonverbal cues (gestures, facial expressions, and tone of voice). Symbols by themselves have no meaning; however, the context in which they are used transmits a meaningful and understandable message. The communication process is effective

In what way is communication symbolic?

when the sender and receiver attach the same meaning to the words and the nonverbal cues in the message. If the receiver interprets a word differently than the sender intends, the communication process may break down. When individuals communicate, the use of symbols should transmit uniform meaning to both the sender and the receiver.

Dynamic

In what way is communication dynamic?

The communication process is dynamic because it continually changes. This characteristic is at the core of effective communication, permitting continuous adaptation of the message for more effective understanding. In addition, the interaction between sender and receiver will allow changes in the message as circumstances alter. One minute may require persuasion—for example, when writing a sales letter—and the next minute may require a more direct and commanding tone—for example, when encouraging a subordinate to change an unacceptable behavior pattern.

Understandable

Effective communication is understood by the receiver. Ineffective communication, on the other hand, is frequently misunderstood by the receiver. One of the distinct advantages of oral communication, when contrasted with written communication, is that it is easier to modify your message to obtain greater understanding. When receivers are unsure about the intended meaning, they can ask questions to increase their level of comprehension. Written communication includes questions about the intended meaning, too, but the clarification (even if you are both using faxes) will not be immediate.

Unique

In what way is communication unique?

Communication is a process that involves two or more unique individuals. Effectiveness in communication is enhanced when the messages sent match the expectations of their intended receivers. The majority of our business messages are designed to persuade a receiver to do something—to buy a product, accept a viewpoint, or change unacceptable behavior. Communication, then, is not an end in itself; it is a means to an end. The probability of eliciting specific action from the receiver depends on the overall effectiveness of the communication. Failing to visualize the receiver when sending a message increases the likelihood of communication failure.

TYPES OF COMMUNICATION IN THE MODERN ORGANIZATION

Modern organizations use different types of communication: oral, written, oral and written, visual, and nonverbal. Examples of the kinds of communication in each of these categories include the following:

What types of communication are found in the modern organization?

Oral Communication

- Conferences
- Interviews
- Orientation sessions
- Sales presentations
- Staff meetings
- Task assignments
- Training sessions

Written Communication

- Advertisements
- Bulletins

Electronic mail
Letters
Magazine and newspaper articles
Manuals
Memoranda
Newsletters
Policy statements
Reports

Oral and Written Communication
Closed circuit television
Film presentations
Slide-tape presentations
Television presentations
Videotape presentations

Visual Communication
Building design
Clothing
Drawings
Illustrations
Office design
Photographs
Signs

Nonverbal Communication
Body movement
Facial expressions
Gestures
Odors
Space utilization
Time

Each of these types of communication media is effective because each is capable of conveying a message. The ability to write an effective message, deliver an effective presentation, prepare effective illustrations, or use gestures consistent with the spoken message significantly impact on a person's job effectiveness.

MODEL OF THE COMMUNICATION PROCESS

What are the elements of the communication process?

Exhibit 2-1 shows a model of the communication process. As the model shows, the communication process is always affected by the external environment in which the communication occurs.

In every communication situation is a sender and a receiver. *Senders* communicate messages to their *receivers,* or audience. This process begins when a sender creates a message, which is then transmitted through a channel to the intended receiver. The person receiving the message interprets, or decodes, the message and reacts by providing feedback. At this point the communication process restarts, with the receiver as the new sender and the sender as the new receiver. Noise can infiltrate the communication process at any point. A detailed discussion of each component of the communication process—external environment, sender, message, channel, receiver, feedback, and noise—follows.

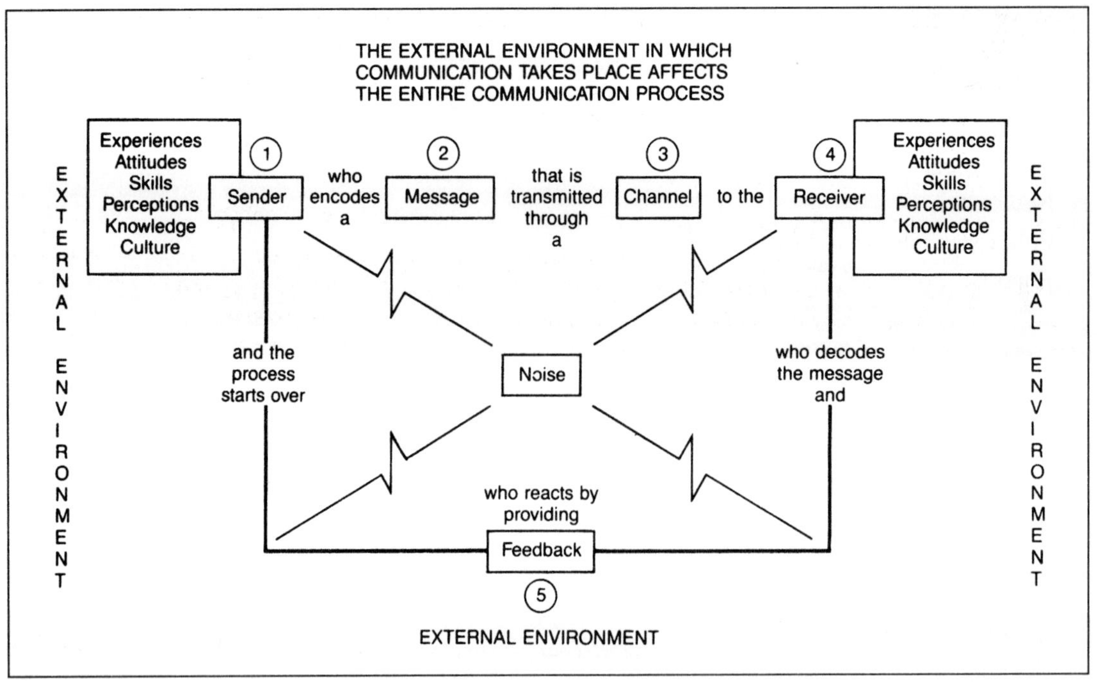

Exhibit 2-1 Communication model.

External Environment

The communication environment obviously affects the success of the interaction between the sender and receiver. Care should be exercised to ensure that the environment enhances rather than impedes the process. Overall, the nature of the situation determines what constitutes an appropriate or inappropriate environment. An inappropriate environment can have a disastrous effect on the process, especially when it results in either communication breakdown or miscommunication.

In contrast, a proper environment ensures that the communication occurs in a location that incorporates the necessary amount of privacy, the level of formality the situation requires, and the appropriate distance between the sender and receiver. Disregarding any of these elements in the communication environment increases the opportunity for miscommunication.

Several types of communication situations common to modern organizations require privacy. For example, when a supervisor (sender) must reprimand a subordinate (receiver), the encounter should be conducted in a private setting. Privacy is also needed during performance appraisal interviews. If a supervisor chooses a public location to discuss such situations, the subordinate will not only lose respect for the supervisor but also will be less receptive to the supervisor's comments.

Some communication situations in the modern organization call for an informal environment, but others require a formal environment. An inappropriate level of formality or informality reduces the effectiveness of the communication process. Common sense is valuable in determining the appropriate level of environmental formality for the situation. For instance, negotiating a multimillion dollar contract in a neighborhood pub is probably not as appropriate as using a board or conference room for the same purpose.

The nature of the situation determines what constitutes an appropriate distance between the sender and receiver. The greater the distance, the less personal and private the situation will be. Increased distance can interfere with hearing and add to the difficulty of observing the nonverbal cues used by the sender and receiver. When the distance between the sender and receiver becomes too great, a mechanical device—such as a telephone—is required. Face-to-face communication, which enables the sender and receiver to "read" each other's nonverbal communication, is considered more personal than a telephone conversation.

Sender

What factors affect the sender's encoding of the message?

The sender begins the communication process by encoding the message he or she wishes to transmit to the receiver. Factors that influence the sender's encoding of the message include experiences, attitudes, skills, perceptions, knowledge, and culture. The sender must select symbols—written words, spoken words, gestures, facial expressions, and illustrations—that the receiver understands.

The sender not only needs to choose appropriate symbols and provide an appropriate environment, but also he or she must select an appropriate channel for the situation. To use a verbal channel when a written channel is more appropriate reduces the effectiveness of the communication process. *Feedback,* another element in the process, helps the sender determine how effectively he or she has communicated with the receiver. Feedback occurs when the receiver sends a message—written, oral, or nonverbal—back to the sender.

Message

In modern organizations, as elsewhere, people communicate because they have a message they wish to share with at least one other person. Thus, the desire to transmit a message is the sole reason for entering the communication process.

What categories of messages are used in the communication process?

Two categories of messages are used in today's organization: verbal and nonverbal. *Verbal symbols* include both written and spoken words. *Nonverbal symbols* include facial expressions, gestures, body movement, drawings, and pictures.

Senders must remember that symbols they select to convey the message do not have uniform meaning. Indeed, symbols have no meaning until the individuals involved in the communication process attach meaning to them. In the encoding process, the sender should strive to select symbols that mean the same thing to the receiver. The sender should prepare a message that contains the necessary content and communicate this content with clarity and accuracy.

Channel

For each message, senders need to select carefully the channel that is most effective. Even when both an oral and a written channel appear to be appropriate for transmission of a particular message, one medium may still be more effective than the other. For example, assume that a supervisor desires an immediate reply to a question. Although the message, both from and back to the supervisor, could be in either an oral or a written form, the oral medium will be more effective because of its immediacy.

What factors need to be considered in selecting an appropriate channel?

Selection of an appropriate channel requires the sender to assess the following factors as they relate to the situation: need for immediate transmission of message, probable need for immediate feedback, need for permanent record of the message, degree of negotiation and persuasion required, destination of the message, and content of the message. In addition, the sender should consider his or her skill in using the various channels, as well as the receiver's in using each of them.

Receiver

The *receiver,* attaches meaning to the message that has been transmitted through the process of decoding, which is essentially an interpretation. Just as the encoding process the sender uses is influenced by numerous factors, so is the receiver's decoding process. The receiver's experiences, attitudes, skills, perceptions, knowledge, and culture will affect the decoding of the message.

Critical to the success of a message is the receiver's interpretation of its content and meaning. The sender, when encoding the message, considers the receiver's background, knowledge of the subject, and attitudes as a means of designing an appropriate message. Senders who fail to consider these factors may create ineffective messages. The greater the common understanding between the sender and the receiver, the more effective the communication process probably will be. Similarly, the greater the commonality of experiences between the sender and the receiver, the more easily they will be able to communicate with each another.

Feedback

In the communication process, feedback is a key element because in its absence, senders cannot be sure that they have communicated effectively with receivers. Feedback enables senders to become receivers and receivers to become senders. In addition, feedback is the element of the process that provides two-way communication. Its absence results in one-way communication.

What fine-tuning function does feedback perform?

Feedback provides an important fine-tuning function for the communication process. When senders realize through feedback that they are not being understood, they can include additional information to create greater comprehension. Feedback is also used to confirm agreement, clarify viewpoints and positions, and assess understanding to determine the necessity for additional information.

The various communication channels are not equally suited to obtaining feedback. When selecting an appropriate channel for the situation, the astute sender considers the desired type and amount of feedback. As the need for feedback increases, the use of an oral communication channel, instead of a written channel, becomes more attractive.

An original message is communicated in a variety of ways, and so is feedback. Besides verbal and written feedback types, feedback may come in the form of gestures, facial expressions, and body movement. Obviously, feedback need not be in the same form as the original message.

Feedback is either intentional or unintentional. Even when the receiver does not react to the sender's message, feedback is provided. By sitting motionless in a chair, a receiver may provide as much feedback to the sender as he or she does with a verbal response.

Feedback helps those communicating avoid the turmoil described in Communication Capsule 2-1.

Communication Capsule 2-1 Communication: Harmony or Turmoil?

The English language includes approximately 650,000 words. Obviously a communicator thus has several thousand opportunities to select a combination of words that may not be interpreted in the same manner by the person who receives the message. In addition, the average person's vocabulary is estimated to range from 15,000 to 20,000 words. Philologists and lexicographers estimate that this same average person possesses a working understanding of approximately 25,000 words for use in proper interpretation of daily communication situations. In other words, the person may have a substantially greater understanding of word meanings when they are used in context.

A major source of misunderstanding stems from the use of words that are too technical or too uncommon for proper interpretation by the intended audience. Each profession, whether medicine, engineering, or music, uses words and phrases that are unique to it. These words contain meaning and transmit understanding far beyond the traditional dictionary meaning. For example, AACSB is an acronym for the American Assembly of Collegiate Schools of Business, a blue book (for course examinations) is uniquely understood by college students, and the quarterback's message (123, Left, Wide, Sprint on two) identifies a plan of action that is understood by the players but is rather nonsensical when spoken to the general public.

Turmoil within organizations and among people primarily occurs when individuals or groups do not understand what is being said or implied. Careless use of a word or phrase creates an environment of fear, distrust, and perhaps anger. The word or phrase that evokes a negative emotional reaction is usually not perceived as negative by the sender. But damage to personal and professional relationships from the careless use of words and phrases remains as a residue of distrust for weeks, months, and even years.

Harmony within organizations and among individuals is an essential ingredient for ultimate professional success. People who work well with others, who say and do what is right, and who earn the respect and trust of peers and associates more often than not enjoy steady and progressive movement up the corporate ladder.

Noise

What is noise?

Noise is the perception of anything not part of the original message that the sender intended to transmit to the receiver. The impact of noise on the communication process can result in significant problems in content and understanding. Noise in the channel may alter the intended meaning, which in turn creates an environment for miscommunication.

Many types of noise can have a negative impact on the communication process, including physical noise that prevents the receiver from hearing and/or concentrating totally on the message being transmitted by the sender. Another category includes a variety of such inaudible signals as typographical errors, poor quality illustrations, annoying speaking mannerisms, distasteful dress, and grammatical errors. Other forms of noise in the channel include physical pain in the form, for example, of a headache or backache or failure to maintain eye contact, which is apparent when one stares at the floor or ceiling when listening to an oral message. Unintentional noise in the channel will seriously hinder reading and properly interpreting both verbal and nonverbal communication cues.

Senders and receivers who wish to improve the effectiveness of their communications will limit distractions and other noise in the channel. This can be accomplished in several ways, but the most effective way is to communicate in a noise-free environment. If uncontrollable noise does occur, then communicators need to minimize its impact by concentrating on the message rather than on the environment.

NONVERBAL COMMUNICATION

Nonverbal communication plays an important role in the communication process. *Nonverbal communication* is an intentional or unintentional message that is neither written nor spoken. Most people associate nonverbal communication solely with the verbal communication process; however, nonverbal messages can be understood without a verbal counterpart. For example, police officers direct traffic with motions; drivers communicate movement from lane to lane or turns with arm signals; and referees communicate with officials and fans with motions and signals.

To use a combination of nonverbal and verbal communication requires consistency between both messages. When they conflict, the nonverbal message is usually viewed as the more accurate expression of the person's true feelings.

What types of nonverbal factors affect the communication process?

The types of nonverbal communication seem almost limitless. But those most common to business communications are appearance, facial expressions, gestures, touch, posture, voice, silence, personal space, and time. Nowhere is nonverbal communication more important than in job interviews; the interviewee's nonverbal communication is often the critical factor that determines whether he or she receives a job offer.

Appearance

In what way does appearance affect the communication process?

Some aspects of nonverbal communication that influence communication success are the quality of written messages, a person's physical appearance, and the appearance of the personal work area. For example, messages with obvious corrections, strikeovers, faint printing, grammatical errors, or illegible handwriting make a negative impression on the reader. Material that contains any of these flaws tends to transmit a nonverbal message that discredits the originator.

For written material, the originator, when wishing to emphasize certain words or points, can underline, put in all caps, or use bold print for the parts that need emphasis. Material so presented carries a different nonverbal message than material that is not emphasized through the available mechanical means.

In addition, elements such as clothing, hair style, cleanliness, jewelry, cosmetics, body size, and body shape transmit messages. Any of these that are outside the range considered acceptable, normal, or standard for the situation may negatively affect the process. In extreme cases, these elements may inject so much "noise" into the communication process that the clarity of the message becomes distorted. Individuals' physical appearance can affect the impression others receive of their credibility, honesty, trustworthiness, competence, judgment, or status.

The physical appearance of one's work area also sends nonverbal messages. Objects on a person's walls, shelves, and desk transmit messages as does the overall cleanliness of the office area. Cluttered work areas tend to send nonverbal messages that the office holder is unorganized and may have inefficient work habits.

Facial Expressions

What nonverbal messages is the facial area capable of sending?

Research findings estimate that the human face can transmit more than 250,000 different expressions. Therefore, your facial area (eyes, eye brows, forehead, mouth, and chin) is probably more capable of communicating nonverbally than any other part of your body. Although you may be unable to perceive or interpret the vast array of facial expressions, such actions as raising or lowering the eyebrows, a nervous tic, unusual swallowing, clenching the teeth, or tensing the lips can give clues to another person's feelings. Messages about a person's happiness, sadness, anger, frustration, disgust, fear, or surprise are transmitted through facial expressions. In fact, often we do not need to ask our colleagues whether they are happy or sad—their face will reveal their emotional state.

Business communicators who wish to control their facial cues will consciously select expressions that complement their verbal messages. When you are trying to communicate happiness, a happy facial expression is just as important as the words you choose to convey your feeling. Individuals whose verbal message and nonverbal facial expressions contradict each other add confusion to the communication process. So do individuals whose facial expressions appear false to the receiver.

Eye Contact

What nonverbal messages does eye contact signal?

Because the eyes are the most expressive part of the face, they have a considerable effect on the communication process. Establishing and/or maintaining eye contact signals that a person desires to communicate—the communication channel is open. Eye contact can also signal a person's desire to be included in a conversation or to make another person somewhat uncomfortable by focusing intently on him or her.

Breaking eye contact sends several signals, such as some discomfort with the topic or situation, a desire for the communication encounter to end, an acknowledgement of status differences between the sender and the receiver, or an indication that all or part of a message is untrue. In addition, lack of eye contact can control the flow of the communication because it signals that it is time for the conversation to end. Eye contact is a powerful communication tool; speakers with a tendency to face one way or the other will discover that only those with whom they have made eye contact will ask them questions.

Gestures

What nonverbal messages are communicated by gestures?

The use of gestures in the verbal communication process is another way to add meaning to the sender's message. Some gestures (clenched fist, foot stomping) indicate anger; others (foot tapping, finger tapping) suggest nervousness. Head nodding may indicate agreement, but head shaking usually suggests disagreement. A nod of the head may also signal the receiver's desire for the sender to continue talking. Keeping your arms folded over the chest signals uncomfortableness or nonacceptance, but open arms tend to convey openness and acceptance.

Gestures do not have universal meaning. For example, an "A-OK" gesture (circle made with the thumb and forefinger) is considered by Latin Americans to be a sign of contempt. People whose jobs involve interaction with peoples of other cultures must identify which gestures are acceptable and unacceptable in those cultures. This will allow communicators to avoid offending those with whom they communicate.

Touching

What nonverbal messages are transmitted by touching?

Even during the communication process, touching can transmit significant messages, such as decisiveness, solidarity, or reassurance. The amount and nature of touching considered appropriate for the situation varies from culture to culture. An embrace between business associates in some cultures is appropriate and expected. But Americans typically consider such an embrace distasteful and inappropriate.

In business, a handshake not only transmits greetings but also a feeling of solidarity and assurance. Many people assess the firmness of the handshake, believing that a firm handshake sends a message of decisiveness and strength and that a limp handshake indicates weakness and a lack of vitality. Other forms of touching also communicate; for example, grasping a person's left elbow during a handshake communicates solidarity, whereas patting a person on the back conveys assurance or reassurance.

Posture

What nonverbal messages are transmitted by posture?

A person's posture transmits signals about a variety of feelings and emotions, such as status, confidence, interest, and openness. Higher-status people often stand more erect and hold their heads higher than lower-status people do. But in a sitting position, higher-status people are likely to reveal a more relaxed posture than lower-status people, who tend to sit in a rather rigid, erect position.

Self-confident individuals usually stand more erect than those lacking confidence. Persons interested in a conversation will lean forward toward those with whom they are communicating, but persons lacking interest may slump down. Finally, the posture of several individuals talking with one another, as in a functional group, sends a message about their willingness to allow other people into their group. Persons turned inward toward one another convey the impression that they are not willing to accept others, but those turned outward are willing to accept others.

Voice

The manner in which individuals express themselves communicates an additional message that is transmitted simultaneously. Often, voice mannerisms—pitch, rhythm,

What voice mannerisms transmit signals?

range, rate, nonwords (such as *ah, um, uh*), and pauses—communicate more than the actual words.

Voice mannerisms also communicate messages about the sender's emotional state. For example, the excitement at the close of a business agreement may be communicated by a high-pitched voice and a rapid rate of speaking. Messages sent in anger are often accompanied by a loud speaking voice, but seriousness and sadness are communicated by a low-pitched voice. Unexpected pauses may indicate the sender's uncertainty.

Silence

As a type of nonverbal communication, silence has implications for written and verbal messages. A lack of immediate response to a letter stressing the urgency of a business situation or to a letter that requests an immediate reply indicates the receiver is either unwilling or unable to respond favorably. The old adage of "no news is good news" may be inappropriate because many letter writers delay preparing a response to a negative situation. When positive public relations is important—and for an organization it nearly always is—an individual who receives a letter requesting an immediate response should respond if at all possible. If for some reason an immediate response is impossible, the recipient should consider acknowledging receipt of the letter and explain that a decision will be forthcoming.

In verbal encounters, the receiver's silence can transmit several types of messages. Silence can communicate that the receiver wishes the sender to continue talking or that the receiver outranks the sender and is using silence to make the sender feel uncomfortable. In addition, a receiver's silence can signal that the person is contemplating a response before putting it into words.

Physical Space

How does space affect the communication process?

The physical space assigned to an employee by an organization and how this space is used communicates values and interests to others. A person's hierarchical rank in an organization typically determines assigned office space. Higher-ranking individuals generally have a greater amount of space with more luxurious furniture than lower-ranking employees. In addition, the building floor, the location on that floor, and the assistance of support personnel permit higher-ranking employees to control their space more effectively than lower-level employees. Employees able to control their space can make it temporarily off-limits to virtually everyone of a lesser rank.

Employees take possession of their assigned space, and they become uncomfortable when others invade their territory. For example, the area in an office and behind a desk is considered to be off-limits to others. Most employees prefer that others not invade this space, and they consider it inappropriate if it is done, especially for persons below them in the corporate hierarchy.

Many people believe that staying behind their desk during a conversation sends a message that they are in control of their space and of the most powerful area in the office. This sense of control permits them to believe that they can use their space to assert authority or enhance competitiveness. During conversations in which the office occupant does not wish to create or maintain an authoritative or powerful position, the person should move to more neutral territory, such as a conference room.

Time

The time of day that people communicate sends signals about the importance they attach to their message. For example, a message received from a supervisor during a midnight telephone call is typically perceived as more important than an identical telephone message received during regular working hours.

The way people use their time is another nonverbal communication. For example, forcing subordinates to wait unnecessarily for a scheduled appointment is often interpreted by them as a nonverbal indication that they are unimportant. In addition, taking telephone calls during a meeting with a subordinate transmits a feeling of unimportance to the subordinate.

How does time affect the communication process?

Various cultures differ in the way they attach meaning to the use of time. Americans believe in arriving on time for an appointment. In other cultures, a manager, for example, may not be offended by a person who arrives an hour late for an appointment.

BARRIERS TO EFFECTIVE COMMUNICATION

A variety of barriers hamper—sometimes quite seriously—the communication process. Common communication barriers are language, semantics, insufficient information, excessive information, perception, and defensiveness. Effective communicators learn to recognize and also to minimize the effects of these communication barriers.

What barriers affect the communication process?

Language

All human languages have the same basic purpose—to communicate thoughts. Nearly 300 million of the world's people speak English. Many of them use poor grammar, spell incorrectly, or pronounce words wrong. Each of these barriers represents formidable communication problems. Receivers who are aware of errors committed by a sender may be distracted, which causes, at the least, a momentary loss of their ability to concentrate on the message. If a key part of the message is sent during such a lapse, this will negatively affect the communication process.

Semantics

Semantics refers to the meaning of words. Significant communication problems arise when the meaning the sender attaches to a word differs from the meaning the receiver attaches to it. Communication problems caused by semantics can be reduced by using words as precisely as possible, substituting concrete for abstract words, defining words that the receiver may misinterpret, and using the simplest words the communication situation will allow.

What is semantics?

Insufficient Information

Communication problems may arise when a sender fails to give sufficient information to the receiver. In some cases, however, senders may purposely select words that are evasive. In most cases, however, senders simply miscalculate the amount of information receivers need for proper understanding. When the gap between sender intent and receiver comprehension becomes too wide, significant communication problems are created. To overcome such problems, the sender must try to determine the information that the receiver will find helpful—and then provide the desired type and amount of information. Sometimes, depending on their relationship, the receiver may be too intimidated by the sender to ask appropriate questions. Then very little can be done to salvage the communication process.

Excessive Information

Providing the receiver with too much information, either oral or written, can create communication problems. When receivers have an excessive amount of written information to digest in a limited period, they do not have the time to read it carefully and completely. Either way, they will miss significant information. In oral communication, excessive information may result either in the receivers' being unable to sort out the important data from the unimportant or in their forgetting significant information.

In what way is excessive information a barrier?

Perception

How does perception affect the communication process?

Perception refers to one's awareness of a message. Numerous business messages bombard a receiver each day. Because they occur simultaneously, perceiving all of them is difficult. In some instances, the messages are so frequent that the receiver can perceive only one or two. In other instances, the vast number of messages makes it impossible to perceive a particular message fully and accurately. People perceive messages through mental, emotional, and psychological filters; that is, the meanings they attach to simultaneous messages are not contained in the words but in the full scope of understanding that the receiver has developed through education, experience, and exposure.

The rate at which people receive messages requires them to be selective, a communication phenomenon known as *selective perception.* Because ineffective selection impedes our ability to use communication processes, it may create communication barriers. Finally, sometimes, for one reason or another, a receiver is even unaware that a message has been transmitted. In such circumstances, we might say that these unreceived messages are simply not received.

Defensiveness

A defensive attitude on the part of the sender or the receiver can also create a communication barrier. One form of defensiveness is closed-mindedness—mentally forming a reply to the sender rather than concentrating on the message—thereby protecting the receiver's own ego rather than being receptive to suggestions or new ideas.

SUMMARY

Communication in the modern organization performs the functions of informing, controlling, persuading, and coordinating. Each function is critical to the organization's success.

Communication in the modern organization has several characteristics: (1) It uses symbols; (2) it is dynamic; (3) it must be understandable; and (4) it involves at least two unique individuals.

Elements that compose the model of the communication process include external environment, sender, receiver, channel, feedback, and noise. Problems with any of the elements can seriously impede the effectiveness of the communication process.

Nonverbal communication affects oral communication. Appearance, facial expressions, eye contact, gestures, touching, posture, tone of voice, silence, space, and time are nonverbal elements that influence the communication process.

Several types of barriers impede communication success. Inappropriate language can be a barrier, as can poor semantics. Others barriers are insufficient information, excessive information, lack of or limited perception, and defensiveness.

REVIEW QUESTIONS

1. Identify the various functions that communication fulfills in the modern business organization.
2. Explain the value of communication to the controlling function of an organization.
3. Select three recent articles about company communications, and describe how they illustrate the main characteristics of the communication process.
4. "Dynamic" is a term often used to describe effective communications. Explain dynamic communications.
5. What different categories of communication occur in the modern organization?
6. What are the factors affecting a sender's ability to encode a message?
7. Explain the importance of selecting an appropriate communication channel for transmission of your messages.
8. Describe the significance of feedback in the communication process.

9. Noise is always present during the communication process. Identify some and explain why both the sender and receiver should be aware of noise in the communication channel.
10. List the types of emotions a person's facial expressions can transmit.
11. Explain how posture, semantics, and perception impact the overall effectiveness of communication.

APPLICATION PROBLEMS

1. Prepare a list of your communication strengths and weaknesses. How have the strengths benefited you in a professional situation? Identify and describe how the absence of a particular communication skill contributed to a communication breakdown.
2. Explain the preparation of a business letter in terms of the various steps shown in Exhibit 2-1.
3. Prepare a list of five situations you experienced in which lack of feedback resulted in communication breakdown.
4. Watch two or more individuals who are conversing with one another. What kinds of emotions were displayed? What types of nonverbal communications did they employ? What types of feedback did you observe?
5. Prepare a list of several situations you have experienced in which the presence of noise in the communication process caused a communication breakdown.
6. Prepare a report that explains a plan for improving an organization's nonverbal communications.
7. During a three-day period, observe and record the various facial expressions used when two or more individuals are conversing with one another. What did the expressions mean in relation to the entire message?
8. Although language is essential for effective communication, it can also become a communication barrier. Explain.
9. Explain "semantics" as it impacts the communication process.
10. List and describe several situations in which your perceptions or the perceptions of those with whom you were communicating became a communication barrier.

3

Elements of Effective Written Communication

After studying this chapter, you should be able to

1. Discuss ways in which you can incorporate courtesy into your business messages.
2. Discuss how to ensure you write at a correct language level for your audience.
3. Describe ways to make your business writing more concise.
4. Outline ways to achieve unity, coherence, proper emphasis, and pace in the messages you write.
5. Identify ways to make your messages more concrete.
6. Discuss why your messages need to be complete.

Understanding the essentials of written communication is critical because of its significant role in the daily routines of the vast majority of organizations. Knowing *what* you want to say and *how* you want to say it are equally significant. In addition, you must design your messages so the meaning is exact and the impression you create is favorable. Not only do well-worded messages bring you and your reader closer together mentally, but also they make you appear friendly, helpful, and interested.

What are the characteristics of effective written communication?

To choose the right words and sentences for your letters, you need to be familiar with the characteristics of effective written communication shown in Communication Capsule 3-1.

Communication Capsule 3-1 Characteristics of Effectively Written Business Documents

Effectively written business documents possess certain characteristics, including the following:

Courtesy—You use courtesy to enhance the relationship between you and the reader and to increase the reader's self-esteem. The consideration you show your reader in your documents also enhances your company's quality and prestige image. Courtesy is a key ingredient of the goodwill so essential in developing an effective relationship with customers or clients.

Correctness—You are being concerned with correctness when you ensure that your documents are properly written and formatted and that they are free of errors in punctuation, word usage, spelling, and grammar. The documents you prepare should also be neat and attractive in their appearance. The presence of an error in what you write will distract the reader from focusing on your message.
Conciseness—You use the fewest number of words in presenting the information. Words that can be omitted, even as few as one or two per document, result in a sizable cost savings over a year's time.
Clarity—You tell readers exactly what they want and need to know, using words and a format that make your communication totally understandable after just one reading. Lack of clarity is likely to either confuse or frustrate readers, possibly resulting in a lack of compliance with your request.
Concreteness—You present information that is as specific and as definite as possible. Concrete writing does not contain words capable of misinterpretation.
Completeness—You tell the reader all that he or she wants and needs to know. Every question the reader asks should be answered. Sometimes, you may want to include answers to other questions you believe the reader had but did not ask.

COURTESY

Special attention is necessary to ensure the courtesy of written business communication. *Courtesy,* which involves showing consideration of the reader's feelings, position, and concerns, does not automatically result from the inclusion of such words as *please* and *thank you*, although the use of these words certainly helps. For example, before replying to a supervisor's request for a memo on how to reduce in-office noise, you will want to consider the reader's desires, circumstances, emotions, and probable reaction to your response. This will enable you to develop your communication from the reader's point of view. Indeed, a courteous message builds goodwill with both previous and new customers/clients. Courteous writing, in other words, is empathetic writing.

You-Attitude

What is you-attitude?

Evoking a *you-attitude*—which emphasizes the reader's viewpoint rather than your own—in the material you write enables you to focus on your reader rather than on yourself. Its use shows genuine concern for the reader and demonstrates your sincerity. But merely replacing the words *I, we, our,* and *my,* with *you* and *your* throughout a letter will not guarantee the presence of you-attitude. Instead, you must create a positive state of mind through your suggestions and decisions.

A you-attitude, then, is more than simple courtesy or politeness. It demonstrates a clear understanding of the reader's problem or question. If readers are convinced of your genuine concern about their situation or question, this will greatly increase the overall impact of your message.

Note how the first sentence in each of the following sets lacks you-attitude, whereas the second sentence repairs the omission.

Change:	I am glad to welcome you as a new charge customer.
To:	Welcome as a new charge customer.
Change:	I want to take this opportunity to thank you for the time you spent with me yesterday.
To:	Thank you for spending time with me yesterday.
Change:	I hope you will contact me if you have additional questions about the Model 80 computer.
To:	Please contact me if you have additional questions about the Model 80 computer.

Reader-Benefit Material

How can reader benefit be expressed?

Including *reader-benefit material* in your business documents enables you to outline for the reader the positive effects of agreeing or complying with your request or announcement. Readers are more likely to comply if the benefits appear to be worth their time, effort, or cost. When the advantages are obvious to your reader, the amount of reader-benefit material you include is likely to be brief. On the other hand, when the advantages of compliance may not be as readily apparent, a greater amount of reader benefit is advised.

You may express reader-benefit material in several ways, including the following:

1. Assuring readers that purchases they made or may make are wise ones
2. Assuring readers that you can effectively accommodate their needs
3. Assuring readers that you have something of value to offer, as in a letter of application
4. Assuring readers that their needs are of concern to you

The first sentence in each of the following pairs elicited little response when it was used in a collection letter. When the sentence was revised to include reader-benefit material, the letter was more successful.

Change:	Please send your check for the amount you owe.
To:	By sending your check for $298.87 today, you will be able to maintain your good credit reputation.
Change:	You will be glad to know that we are now open until 9 on Friday nights.
To:	For your shopping convenience, Bartles is now open until 9 on Friday nights.

Why should readers be given in the opening of the message the information of greatest interest?

The opening paragraph of a letter is in a position of emphasis; therefore, incorporating you-attitude requires special care and, if appropriate, reader-benefit material. You can also make your opening paragraphs more effective by immediately giving readers the information in which they are most interested. Note how the first two sentences in the following set, although courteous, lack you-attitude and reader-benefit material. The revised version is much more effective because it immediately tells the reader what she wants to know and reassures her that she made a wise purchase. Appreciation for the order can be expressed later in the letter—perhaps in the closing.

Change:	I want to thank you for your recent order for a new set of Continental luggage.
Change:	We appreciate your recent order for a new set of Continental luggage.
To:	Your Continental luggage was shipped today and should reach you early next week. The quality of this luggage will give you many years of satisfied service.

Tone

How does tone affect the message?

Although a business document may be grammatically correct and in proper form, the *tone* conveyed by the sender—how he or she views the reader and/or the subject of the message—may make the difference between the reader's accepting or rejecting the message. Improper tone is most likely to occur in negative messages. Because the reader wants to receive a *yes* response and you have to say *no,* the reader will probably react to what you say as well as to how you say it. An improper tone is reflected in material that belittles the reader, is curt, or shows insensitivity.

You may have little or no control over the content of the letters you prepare, but you do have control over their tone. For example, the use of negative tone in a letter concerned with a negative situation will probably worsen conditions. Other factors related to tone over which you have no control that may perpetuate a negative reaction are

1. The authority relationship between you and the reader.
2. The reader's frame of mind.
3. The reader's attitude toward you.
4. The circumstances impacting the reader at the time the message is received.
5. The reader's disposition at the time of receiving the message.

Although you have limited or no control over these factors, you can write your messages with a natural, courteous, and friendly tone. Visualizing the reader and the reader's position—as well as writing to the reader as you would speak to that person—will enable you to prepare more effective written communication.

A pleasant tone in written communication, by showing courtesy for the reader, builds goodwill—the foundation of the business relationship. No company or individual can thus afford to dispense with courtesy in written communication.

Our daily lives are filled with disappointing and exasperating situations. We have plenty of opportunities to be discourteous in the messages we write, especially when preparing collection, claim, and adjustment letters. The effective writer never gives way to anger or indulges in sharp insinuations bound to arouse resentment. Consider the following sentences that contain a negative tone and their positive-tone revisions.

Change:	It is absurd for you to think that you will be able to get away without paying your long overdue account.
To:	So that you are able to maintain your good credit reputation, we are certain you plan to pay your overdue account.
Change:	You failed to specify the color of coat you wanted.
To:	The coat you ordered is available in the following colors: rust, maize, and tan. Your returning the enclosed card after you have marked your color choice will enable us to ship your coat immediately.

The negative examples are demeaning and show insensitivity toward their recipients. They are bound to create ill feelings. The rewritten versions treat the reader in a more sensitive (and sensible) manner.

When should the subjunctive mood be used?

One way of improving tone is to employ the subjunctive mood when expressing a negative idea. *Subjunctive mood*, which is used following clauses of necessity, demand, or wishing, is especially useful for improving the tone of negative information that you cannot make positive. Because the subjunctive mood enables you to express what you wish you could do rather than what you can do, the result is more diplomatic. Each of the following revised versions uses the subjunctive mood.

Change:	I cannot attend the budget committee scheduled for Thursday morning.
To:	I would like to attend the budget committee meeting scheduled for Thursday morning, but I will be in Los Angeles.
Change:	We cannot accept your recommendation.
To:	I wish we were able to accept your recommendation.

Whenever possible, you can also improve the tone of a sentence by including a positive idea with the negative idea. The positive idea helps offset the negative idea, as the revised sentences in the following example illustrates.

Change:	We cannot open a credit account with a $500 limit as you requested.
To:	Even though we are unable to open a credit account for you at this time, we thought you would be pleased to know your references commented favorably about your bill-paying habits.

Negative words or phrases are not the only causes of tone problems in documents. Unnecessary facts can cause the same effect. This problem usually is found in inexperienced writers who often think that the more important their readers are, the more facts and details they need in their message. Or they believe that an abundance of facts and details shows their superior how conscientious and hardworking they are. Some inexperienced writers also believe they can be more convincing by presenting a wealth of facts and details. Unfortunately, inexperienced writers too often forget that their superiors are extremely busy so will probably not have time to read through a wordy message.

How does excessive flattery affect messages?

Flattery, bragging, and preaching also cause tone problems. For example, messages that excessively flatter the reader are generally considered to lack sincerity. Although the reader should receive credit where it is due, the praise should never be too lavish. The first sentence in the following example illustrates the kind of excessive flattery that is likely to produce an offensive tone. The revision, in contrast, is sincere and genuine.

Change:	Your phenomenal contribution to our understanding of tax laws is remarkable.
To:	Thanks to you, we all have a better understanding of tax laws.

How does a bragging tone affect messages?

Although some writers believe that a bragging tone can be effective, it tends to offend the reader. Skilled writers take special effort to avoid or delete words that connote superiority. Bragging is often interpreted by the reader as arrogance, and thus it can destroy any goodwill that may have existed. The following sentences illustrate how bragging can be effectively deleted.

Change:	It is difficult for us to understand how you could have been overcharged because we pay meticulous attention to detail.
To:	For the overcharge on your account, we apologize. Your account balance has been corrected.
Change:	The numerous quality-control measures we have implemented make it difficult for us to understand how you could have received a garment as poorly sewn as you claim.
To:	Your satisfaction with our garments is important. Therefore, we are sending you another dress identical to one you purchased from us earlier. At your convenience, please return the earlier-purchased dress.

What does a preaching tone do to messages?

A *preaching tone*, also offensive to the reader, is based on commands, forceful suggestions, and claims that "you should" or "you must," all of which are best avoided. Effective writers do not advise readers how to conduct or manage their affairs unless their advice is solicited. Note the preaching tone in the following sentence and its omission in the revised version.

Change: If you expect to have an ample supply of Royal soil tillers on hand for the upcoming spring planting season, you must replenish your inventory right now.

To: By replenishing your inventory of Royal soil tillers now, you can be sure of having an ample supply to meet your customers' needs during the upcoming spring planting season.

Why should you avoid thanking readers in advance?

Another habit that negatively impacts the tone of a message is *thanking in advance*, which results when you thank the reader before he or she actually does something for you. Doing so conveys the impression that you are taking the reader for granted, an insinuation you surely will want to avoid. You can still show courtesy when making a request by expressing your appreciation. After the reader has complied with your request, the extension of thanks is appropriate.

What words and phrases are irritating?

Many words and phrases used effectively in oral and interpersonal communication are inappropriate in written communication. Exhibit 3-1 presents a list of words and phrases generally considered discourteous because they typically anger, irritate, or belittle the reader.

We tend to react negatively to words and phrases implying that we are lying or dishonest. Yet that is the implication you are likely to receive from such phrases as "You claim that . . ." or "You state that . . . ," or "According to your letter. . . ." Writers can belittle and make readers feel awkward by statements such as the following: "As we have explained to you many times . . ." or "Why can't you understand our position?"

Most readers are likely to be irritated by the following opening sentence: "I regret you are having problems with the S-20 lawn mower you recently purchased from us."

Exhibit 3-1 Words and phrases that anger, irritate, or belittle.

We deny your claim	complaint
We do not believe	confusion
We are not sure	contrary
We find it difficult to understand	contrivance
We expect	delinquent
We insist	deny
We are forced	disagreeable
We take issue	exasperate
We did not	failure
You neglected	ignorance
You failed to	impatience
You misunderstood	incompetent
You must	incredible
You should know	inexcusable
You do not have	inference
You are delinquent	insincere
You insist that	insinuate
You did not say	insulting
You forgot	intolerable
Your credit refusal	irresponsible
Your recent complaint	irritated
Your failure to	lack
Your misunderstanding	neglect
Your neglectful attitude	objection
Your disregard for	obnoxious
Your insinuation	offensive
Your lack of communication	unbelievable
Your delinquent account	uncooperative
Your ignoring	

	Blunt, Harsh Wording	Tactful Wording
1.	You did not read my recent letter.	Please refer to my June 10 letter.
2.	The Executive Board did not receive notification.	Several members of the Executive Board inquired about the time of our December meeting. Will you please send them a follow-up?
3.	Your letter was not clear.	I would appreciate an outline of our marketing differences that you mentioned in your October 14 letter.
4.	John, I suggest you read the Constitution and By-Laws to clarify our position.	John, our Constitution and By-Laws and Section IV on page 9 should answer our questions concerning silent members. Let me know if you believe we should discuss this matter before the meeting.

Exhibit 3-2 Comparisons between blunt, harsh, and tactful wording.

(The reader is probably more interested in learning how the writer is going to help with the lawnmower dilemma than in the acknowledgment of the problem.) As a writer, you need to be aware of such trouble spots to avoid using words or phrases that may provoke a negative reaction.

Omitting words or phrases that contribute to a discourteous tone does not necessarily guarantee courteous messages. Although some messages are void of discourteous words, they can nevertheless be overly harsh or blunt. Note how the harsh wording on the left side in Exhibit 3-2 is revised to be more pleasant on the right side.

Positive Wording

In written communication, *positive wording,* which eliminates words with negative connotations, will increase the possibility of forming a pleasing and comfortable link with the reader. Examples of positive and negative wording are shown in Exhibit 3-3.

Certain questions in a message are bound to evoke a negative response. In such instances, careless wording may be the culprit, even though negative wording is not used. Note the differences between the first and second versions of the following questions.

Change:	Wouldn't you rather drive a Johnson cycle? (causes the reader to seriously consider all of the options, including cycles made by other manufacturers)
To:	A Johnson cycle can be delivered to your home tomorrow morning.
Change:	Why not try our facial products? (encourages the reader to think of reasons why other facial products might be better)
To:	Amour facial products will add to your beauty and mystique.

Of course, positive writing also involves a conscious effort to exclude words readers normally consider as being negative. You cannot use such words as *sorry* or *unfortunately* without conveying to the reader that the situation is going to end with somewhat-less-than-desired results. In addition, some words cannot be employed without causing the reader to react to the *word* itself rather than to the *intention* of the writer. Use of the following words in business communication tends to convey a negative tone: *disappointment, inconvenience, delay, broken, lost, cannot, unable,* and *deny*.

What is the result of emphasizing what the writer can do?

Writing in a positive tone also requires emphasizing what can be done (positive) rather than what cannot be done (negative). Nearly every business situation contains both positive and negative features—your task is to emphasize the positive features

	Negative Wording	Positive Wording
1.	You do not qualify for the free gift because you did not respond within ten days.	You probably did not notice that your order was mailed after our special gift offer had expired.
2.	I expect you to send the order immediately.	Can you assist us in our special sale of your products by rushing the merchandise to us?
3.	Naturally, you have not received your order because, as you should remember, we had to special-order the material from London.	Your special order of London fashions will be shipped as soon as it arrives at our Houston store.
4.	Circumstances will not allow us to send final analysis of your results.	When our extensive analyses are completed, we will send you a copy of the results.

Exhibit 3-3 Negative versus positive wording.

and deemphasize the negative features. Note the difference in the tone of the following examples.

Change:	Your order cannot be shipped until August 23.
To:	Your order will be shipped on August 23.
Change:	I will not be able to speak to your group on January 15 because I will be out of the country.
To:	Although I will be out of the country on January 15, I will appreciate your asking me to speak to your group at another time.

Written messages are extensions of company policy and concern. Large sums of money are spent for advertising to keep existing customers and to attract new ones. Yet this money is wasted if the written messages prepared by the company are discourteous, causing customers to take their business elsewhere.

Perception

Even when you select what you consider to be appropriate words, eliminate vague and abstract words, and write positively and concisely, your messages may not accomplish what you intend. This is especially true when readers form a *perception*, or a mental image, of a word with a meaning that differs from yours. To illustrate, ask a friend to recommend a decent place to eat. You may regret heeding her advice because of a difference of opinion or perception. To her, a decent restaurant has good food, fast service, and inexpensive prices. To you, a decent restaurant has excellent food, leisurely dining, elegant ambiance, and reasonable prices.

How is a word given meaning?

In written communication, a word is a written symbol given meaning by its use. Readers who apply emotions to words that affect their understanding of these words may by this create an inappropriate or unusual meaning.

Because of varying perceptions, use in a business message of the following words may cause a misunderstanding between the writer and reader:

vivacious date	immature
liberal teacher	crooked
honest student	biased
great teacher	premature
family man	careless

In other words, what you think you are saying may not coincide with what the reader perceives you are saying. For this reason, you need to use words that convey exact meanings or that ask questions or explain purpose precisely.

Gender-Neutral Terminology

How can you make sexist terms gender neutral?

Your writing should be *gender neutral,* which means it is void of any words with either a male or female connotation unless the situation about which you are writing calls for such a connotation. Sexist language is offensive to at least half of the country's population. You can sometimes eliminate sexist language by using the word *person* rather than a third-person singular pronoun, as in the following example.

Change: Please share this report with your supervisor. He will find it interesting.
To: Please share this report with your supervisor, who is sure to find it interesting.

You can also eliminate sexist language by using plurals and by employing the words *you* and *your,* as the following examples illustrate.

Change: The attitude of an employee is important if he expects to be promoted.
To: The attitudes of employees are important if they expect to be promoted.
Change: An employee should plan to attend the meeting if he is interested in learning more about the program.
To: You should plan to attend the meeting if you are interested in learning more about the program.

One aspect of courtesy is avoidance of words with a sexist tone. For example, even today a number of terms used in the business world lack a gender-neutral tone. The following list suggests replacements for some of the more common of such terms.

Change	*To*
businessman	businessperson
businessmen	business employees
chairman	chairperson
foremen	supervisors
salesman	sales representative or sales person
spokesman	spokesperson
stockboy	stock clerk
workman	employee or worker

Sometimes you may have to use *him/her* or *he/she* when a singular pronoun of either gender is unavoidable. Although *him/her* and *he/she* tend to be awkward constructions, they can be incorporated if used with restraint.

Meaningful Apologies

The wording of any apology you have to include in the document may affect the courtesy of your writing. An apology that seems insincere to the reader can be especially damaging. One of the best ways to apologize courteously is to use the direct approach by presenting the good news first and then following with a sincere explanation or apology, if needed.

When you receive a discourteous letter, for example, one that incorrectly accuses you, the best procedure is to devise a courteous reply. This response may win a lifelong customer. Another effective way to enhance goodwill is to apologize for a mistake or error before the customer even discovers it. For less serious mistakes or errors, a printed form may be suitable. For more serious mistakes or errors, a personalized letter is the only appropriate communication medium.

Timely Response

Why should you respond to the reader as soon as possible?

Although one person's priority may be another person's time waster, prompt attention to customer questions and needs is always imperative. Think of your own reaction when you do not receive an answer to a letter within a reasonable time. Usually you believe you have been treated discourteously because your concerns are apparently not all that important to the person to whom you wrote. Delaying a response can severely damage the writer-reader relationship.

When the action requested by customers cannot be completed within a reasonable time, they should be notified of the delay. Sending a brief note similar to the following shows courtesy to readers.

> A service technician will immediately examine your camera to determine the nature of the shutter-response problem. Therefore, you should have use of your camera within three weeks. If repairs are needed, I will call you on Friday, January 11, for approval to make the repairs.

When the person to whom a business letter is addressed is out of town for an extended period, the following is a suitable response.

> Mr. Nettleton is out of the office until next Wednesday. I am sure he will be able to provide you with all of the information you requested when he returns.

Many companies have found that prompt answers to questions result in satisfied customers and in fact generate additional business. Courteous writing, then, is more than words and sincerity. Demonstrating sincerity through positive writing and prompt attention to customer questions and inquiries is part of the total effort.

CORRECTNESS

In the broadest sense, the term *correctness* means that the writer should (1) write at a level the reader understands; (2) ensure the accuracy of the words, information, and data; (3) apply principles of grammar and punctuation; and (4) spell words correctly.

Correct Level of Language

The reader's level of understanding of written communication ultimately determines whether your writing is effective. Obviously, that understanding is affected by the reading level of the material you compose.

What does the Fog Index^{SM} scale determine?

Robert Gunning developed the Fog Index^{SM} scale, a measure used to determine the readability level of written communication. To use this index, follow these steps:[1]

[1]Robert Gunning and Richard A. Kallan, *How To Take the Fog Out of Business Writing*, Dartnell, 1994. (The Fog Index^{SM} scale is a service mark licensed exclusively to RK Communication Consultants by D. and M. Mueller.)

1. Count the number of words in a group of sentences. Then divide the total number of words by the number of sentences. This gives you the average sentence length of the passage.
2. Count the number of hard words (those containing three or more syllables) in the passage. Do not count words that are (a) capitalized, such as *Virginia,* (b) combinations of short words, such as *bookkeeper, butterfly,* or (c) verb forms made into three syllables by adding *ed* or *es*, such as *created* or *trespasses*. Divide the number of hard words by the total number of words in the passage. Then multiply this result by 100. This gives you the percentage of difficult words in the passage.
3. Add the average sentence length to the percentage of hard words. Multiply your total by 0.4. Your answer corresponds to the number of years of education needed to understand the passage.

The following passage shows how the Fog Index^{SM} score is calculated. Note that the hard words have been capitalized.

> Three types of APPLICATION letters are used. An UNSOLICITED letter is used when an INDIVIDUAL applies to a COMPANY, not knowing whether an opening exists. The blind-ad letter is sent to a post office box number without knowing the IDENTITY of the COMPANY in which the opening exists. The SOLICITED is used when the person writing the letter knows of an opening in the COMPANY to which the letter is being sent.

Step 1: 72 words divided by 4 sentences equals 18.00 words per sentence
Step 2: 8 hard words divided by 72 words multiplied by 100 equals 9.00 percent
Step 3: 18.00 plus 9.00 multiplied by 0.4 equals the Fog Index^{SM} score (10.80)

Some examples of the Fog Index^{SM} score for general-purpose magazines and grade levels are shown in Table 3-1.

Writing at a level appropriate for your reader is crucial. The words you choose and the way you use them to form sentences affect comprehension. In some cases, the words you select and how you use them convey an unwritten message of their own. If you write in a stiff, formal manner, you will probably give the impression of being formal, whether or not that is your intention. On the other hand, if you write as casually as you speak when talking to your friends, you may create an impression of informal-

Table 3-1 Fog Index^{SM} Scores for General-Purpose Magazines and Grade Levels

	Fog Index^{SM} score	Reading level by grade	By magazine
	17	College graduate	None
	16	College senior	None
	15	College junior	None
	14	College sophomore	None
Danger line			
	13	College freshman	This is difficult
	12	High school senior	*Atlantic, Harper's*
	11	High school junior	*Time, Newsweek*
	10	High school sophomore	*Reader's Digest*
Easy-reading range	9	High school freshman	*Better Homes and Gardens*
	8	Eighth-grade level	*Ladies' Home Journal*
	7	Seventh-grade level	*People, TV Guide*

ity. *Formal English,* embodying precise and graceful word usage, sentence structure, and grammar, is appropriate for formal reports, research papers, and addresses delivered on serious or solemn occasions.

Informal English, a variety of writing that uses less rigid conventions than those of formal English, is the language of business correspondence written for a general readership. Sentences may be long or short, and they tend to sound more conversational than formal English. For example:

Formal	*Informal*
Please inform me of the manner in which you intend to liquidate this balance.	Please let me know when you plan to pay the outstanding balance of your account.

The vocabulary of informal writing is also at a lower level than what you use for formal writing. Compare the following lists, noting the differences between the formal and informal (or business) usage:

Formal	*Informal*	*Formal*	*Informal*
approximately	about	inquire	ask
ascertain	find out	obtain	receive
assist	help	participate	share
construct	build	purchase	buy
contribute	give	sufficient	enough
difficult	hard	utilize	use

Note too that the majority of the words classified as formal are "hard" words when calculating material according to Gunning's Fog Index.SM This is another reason to avoid using formal words whenever possible.

Although we can write generally about both formal and informal standard English as well as substandard English, the distinction among them is not always clear as one level of usage shades into another. *Standard English* is the English of choice for educated individuals; *substandard English* is the type of English typically used by uneducated individuals because they are not aware its use should be avoided. In fact, the great majority of our words and our ways of expressing them are common to all three levels. An expression generally considered to be informal may appear in a formal address, whereas a slang word that originated in substandard English may be acceptable only in an informal vocabulary.

What is the crucial test in word usage?

The crucial test of any word usage is whether you will be understood. If the communication is directed to the public, a customer, or a vendor, your wording should help maintain and encourage goodwill as well as ensure that the average reader understands your message.

As an effective writer, you should develop a vocabulary that enables you to exchange thoughts and feelings with people whose vocabulary may be at different levels than yours. Carefully choosing your words with your readers in mind will help them understand your message.

Word, Information, and Data Accuracy

Effective business communication requires the use of accurate words, information, and data. Even a minor error may destroy goodwill that perhaps required years to develop. A single error in a letter, a figure, or a digit can make a big difference in the meaning intended. To ensure the accuracy of your facts, recheck before signing a document.

Because of the increasing speed of change in laws, technical developments, and other conditions that influence business, the effective business writer must keep abreast of current language usage. The writer should also be sensitive to troublesome words—those that people often confuse with each other—and develop skills in correct usage. Following is a list of the words and phrases frequently confused. Make a special effort to become familiar with their correct use.

a lot/alot (no such word as alot): Unless you are using the expression *a lot* to refer to a parcel of land, avoid its use in business writing because many consider it a substandard English expression.

all right/alright (no such word as alright): The expression *all right* means total correctness. Do not use it to mean *good* or *acceptable.*

believe/feel: Avoid *feel* when you can substitute for it either *believe* or *think.* Restrict the use of *feel* to situations involving *a sense of touch.*

cannot/can not: Because *can not* is so rarely used as two words, you may generally be sure that you are employing correct usage when you use *cannot* as one word. In fact, try to avoid using *cannot* when you are able to tell your reader what you can do rather than what you cannot do.

different from/different than: *Different from* is more formal than *different than.* However, use *different than* after a clause.

due to/because of/since: Avoid using the phrase *due to* as the first two words of a sentence because a linking verb must always precede this phrase. Instead, use *since* when referring to time and *because* when referring to a cause-effect relationship.

effect/affect: The word *effect* is used as a noun (to mean "result") or as a verb (to mean "bring about"). *Affect* is used only as a verb (to mean "influence").

fewer/less: The word *fewer* is used with plural nouns, whereas *less* is employed with singular nouns.

lie/lay: *Lie* and its principal parts (*lie, lay, has/have lain,* and *lying*) are used to mean "rest," "recline," "stay." *Lay* and its principal parts (*lay, laid, has/have laid,* and *laying*) are used to mean "place" or "put." Knowing the proper meaning will help you determine whether *lie* or *lay* is appropriate.

principal/principle: When used as a noun, the word *principal* refers to an amount of money or to a high-level official. Used as an adjective, *principal* means "main" or "primary." *Principle* refers to "beliefs" or "truths."

that/which: The word *that* introduces essential, or restrictive, clauses (clauses that change the intended meaning of the sentence if they are removed). The word *which* is used to introduce nonessential, or nonrestrictive, clauses (clauses that do not change the intended meaning of the sentence if they are removed).

their/there/they're: *Their* is the possessive form of the word *they*; *there* is an adverb. *They're* is the contraction of *they are.*

whether/if: If you can insert the words *or not* after the word *whether,* then the use of *if* rather than *whether* or *whether or not* is incorrect. Note that you need not use *or not* after the word *whether.* If you cannot insert *whether or not* in the sentence, then *if* is the correct choice.

while/whereas/although: The word *while* is appropriately used when a reference to time is being made. If you can replace the word *while* with the word *whereas* or the word *although* in a sentence, *while* is being incorrectly used.

who/whom: The word *who* is the subjective case form and is used as the subject of the sentence. *Whom* is the objective case form and is used as the object of the sentence.

Correct Grammar and Punctuation

Many people in business organizations incorrectly apply principles of grammar and punctuation. The proper use of these two language fundamentals is crucial. Even if the content of the document is appropriate and contains the essential qualities of written communication, incorrect grammar and punctuation will have a negative impact on the message. Mistakes generally fall into the following categories:

What types of grammar errors are commonly made in written business communication?

Grammar

Lack of agreement between the subject and verb

Incorrect:	John, as well as his two brothers, are here today.
Correct:	John, as well as his two brothers, is here today.

Lack of agreement between a pronoun and the noun to which it refers

Incorrect:	Every company needs to be concerned about their employees.
Correct:	Every company needs to be concerned about its employees.

A dangling modifier

Incorrect:	Jogging down the street, a truck passed him.
Correct:	Jogging down the street, John noticed the truck that passed him.

A modifier that is misplaced

Incorrect:	Only he is 23 today.
Correct:	He is only 23 today.

An illogical sequencing of ideas, resulting in an incoherent, illogically organized paragraph

Pronouns with unclear referents

Incorrect:	John asked Bill if his report was acceptable.
Correct:	John asked Bill if Bill's report was acceptable.

Punctuation

Misuse of commas

Misuse of apostrophes

Misuse of punctuation, resulting in fragmentary sentences or run-together sentences

Appendix A contains a condensed guide of correct grammar usage. Writers who need an extensive review of grammar rules and procedures should consider taking a grammar course or studying one of the many excellent texts on business English and grammar. Appendix B contains a list of punctuation rules.

Correct Spelling

Administrative assistants perform a valuable function for many supervisors, managers, and executives by double-checking the correct spelling of words. Some word processing software programs also have spelling subprograms that help identify incorrectly spelled words. Although the first draft of a written message is the responsibility of the typist or word processing specialist, the final document is the responsibility of the person signing it. Errors in the final draft, in other words, are ultimately the responsibility of the person who originated the document. When you are uncertain about correct spelling or word usage, consult a dictionary.

CONCISENESS

What is concise writing?

Effective writing is *concise*, which means that it includes only the words, sentences, or paragraphs necessary to convey a message. Conciseness does not simply mean brevity, for this may result in an incomplete message. A two-page letter that cannot be shortened without a loss in meaning is concise. But compacting a two-page letter into one page by eliminating important content creates brevity—without communicating.

Concise communication does the following:

1. Omits trite expressions
2. Avoids wordy expressions and unnecessary repetition
3. Uses active voice rather than passive voice and imperative mood rather than indicative mood

Trite Expressions

What is a trite expression?

Trite expressions are overused, worn-out words or phrases. Such expressions, which you should avoid, are also referred to as hackneyed words, clichés, and stereotyped expressions. Note how the following paragraph contains several trite expressions, which have been removed in the revised version, leaving only the essential information.

Change: Please be advised that it has come to my attention that you need your order for a trash compactor filled at the earliest possible time. Your position is relevant to our situation, and we will act in accordance with your request.

To: Your R600 trash compactor will arrive by rush delivery on or before January 16.

The following are common trite expressions to avoid and what you may substitute for them:

Avoid	*Use*
according to our records	our records indicate
acknowledge receipt of	have received
are in receipt of	have
as a matter of fact	(omit)
as soon as possible	by January 15

Avoid	*Use*
as the case may be	(omit)
at an early date	by June 10
at this point in time	now
at this time	currently
at your earliest possible convenience	by August 12
avail yourself of the opportunity	(omit)
crack of dawn	at dawn
due to the fact that	because of
enclosed herein	are enclosed
enclosed please find	are enclosed
feel free to call me	please call me
hoping to hear from you	please let me know
I look forward to	(omit)
I wish to state	(omit)
in accordance with	consistent with
in due course	(omit)
in reference to your letter	(omit)
in regard to	(omit)
in terms of	regarding
in the event that	if
in the near future	by June 10
it has come to my attention	I am aware that
kindly advise	please inform me
more than happy	happy
permit me to say	(omit)
please be advised	please be aware that
please don't hesitate to call me	please call me
previous to	before
pursuant to your request	regarding your request
take the liberty to	(omit)
thanking you in advance	(omit)
this is to inform you	(omit)
under separate cover	mailed separately
we regret to inform you	(omit)
with kindest regards	(omit)
with reference to	about

The number of trite expressions is ever-growing. Your messages will be more effective if you eliminate trite expressions.

Wordy Expressions and Unnecessary Repetition

Using unnecessary words or wordy expressions increases the length of sentences and forces readers to remember an excessive number of words. In the first of the following two paragraphs, the writer needs to be more careful in selecting words and phrases and in eliminating trite expressions. Notice how much more concise the revised paragraph is.

Change: We would like to ask you to return the form enclosed herein at your earliest possible convenience. In accordance with your request, we have a consensus of opinion that the washing machine you purchased when you were in our store is at this time still under warranty.

To: The warranty on your washing machine continues in effect. As soon as you return the enclosed form, we will send our repair technician to your home.

How does concise writing affect clarity?

Unless your message is clear to the reader, you have wasted the time you spent writing. Concise writing enhances clarity because the reader is relieved of the difficult task of separating important facts from unessential information.

Wordiness often results from using modifiers that repeat an idea or fact. Several examples of words, phrases, and unnecessary modifiers follow. The correct usage is shown in a nonitalics format.

1. *Could be heard* by ear
2. *Light* in weight
3. *Join* together
4. *Round* circles
5. *Alone* by himself
6. *Each* and every person
7. Fair, *just*, and equitable
8. Silently *think* to yourself
9. *Merge* together
10. *Modern* up-to-date *equipment*

A cautionary note: When eliminating unnecessary words, do not sacrifice meaning to obtain brevity. If your message is clear after revision, then you have achieved conciseness.

What should be done with facts that serve no purpose in a message?

By including only needed facts—those that serve a purpose—you can eliminate the wordiness that destroys your message's conciseness. Including unneeded facts confuses the reader because the added words do not enhance the meaning of the message. Unneeded facts may also cause the reader to experience memory overload.

The following examples show how removing unneeded facts from sentences makes them more concise.

Change: This is to acknowledge receipt of your letter of January 10 in which you ordered sixteen cases of Jones Applesauce. I am answering your letter at this time to hereby let you know that your order has been packaged and sent according to the specified directions in your letter.

To: Sixteen cases of Jones Applesauce have been shipped to your Dallas office via Nord Delivery Services.

Exhibit 3-4 illustrates some common wordy expressions and their more concise alternatives.

Active/Passive Voice and Indicative/Imperative Mood

Conciseness can also be achieved by changing sentences from passive to active voice. In *active-voice sentences,* the subject is the doer of the action. In other words, active

	Wordy	Concise
1.	We would like to ask	Please
2.	For the month of August	For August
3.	Pursuant to the end of this week	Now
4.	A long period of time	A long time
5.	At this time	Now
6.	Is at this time	Is
7.	The weight was higher than I expected it to be	The weight was greater than expected
8.	During the year of 1993	During 1993
9.	For the development of	For developing
10.	In the city of Dallas	In Dallas
11.	The problem was that the car would not start	The car would not start
12.	Square in shape	Square
13.	In accordance with your request	As you requested
14.	Sign on the front of this form	Sign this form
15.	During the time that	While
16.	Consensus of opinion	We agree
17.	Remember the fact that	Remember
18.	Held a meeting	Met
19.	This is the situation at this time	Now
20.	As soon as possible	By July 10
21.	As you indicated in your letter	As you indicated
22.	At all times	Always
23.	Continue to utilize the old form until such time as the new form is available	Start using the new form on May 1
24.	Despite the fact that	Despite
25.	For the obvious reason that	Because
26.	I would ask that you	Please
27.	In conjunction with	With
28.	In the more recent past	Recently
29.	In the unlikely event that	If
30.	In the unlikely event that I am unable to be on time, please	If I am late, please delay the meeting
31.	In view of the fact that	Because
32.	It will be greatly appreciated if you	Please
33.	Our production of the new product will commence on July 1	Production will begin on July 1
34.	Please be advised that we expect you to review the enclosed contract	Please review the contract

Exhibit 3-4 Wordy versus concise writing.

voice uses a verb with a direct object. Furthermore, active voice focuses attention on the subject, is more forceful, and is more emphatic.

How do active and passive voice differ from one another?

In *passive-voice sentences,* the subject is acted upon. Passive verbs always require a verb phrase consisting of a form of the verb *be* (or sometimes *get*), followed by a past participle. Passive voice focuses attention on the verb—what is being done to the subject.

In the following examples, note the differences between active and passive voice.

Change:	The paper was presented by John. (passive)
To:	John presented the paper. (active)
Change:	The data were gathered by the sales staff. (passive)
To:	The sale staff gathered the data. (active)
Change:	The report was typed by Mary. (passive)
To:	Mary typed the report. (active)

Of the two types of voice, sentences written in active voice are generally preferred for the reasons already suggested. This does not mean, however, that you should never use passive voice. In fact, passive voice is especially useful in the following situations, although it may be less concise than the active voice:

1. When you want to avoid being accusatory or blunt
2. When, because of the situation, you want to emphasize the object of the sentence rather than the subject

The following sentences illustrate both situations:

a. Purchasing the materials on the following list is required by each student. (This sentence is more diplomatic than "You must purchase the materials on the following list.")
b. The effort put forth by you this semester resulted in your earning the best grades you have ever had. (This example puts emphasis on *effort;* the following sentence puts emphasis on *we,* the subject of the sentence: "We have been made aware that your grades this semester, because of the effort you put forth, are the best they have ever been.")

3. When you want to break up the monotony resulting from the consistent use of active voice. One way to do this is to switch from the indicative to the imperative mode whenever possible.

How do indicative and imperative mood differ from one another?

The *indicative mood* refers or "indicates" that a certain action or a particular state of something is perceived as fact. *Imperative mood*, on the other hand, expresses a suggestion, command, or request. Note the difference between the two types of mood as the following examples illustrate.

Change:	Data are normally processed only after it is possible to assure their accuracy. (indicative)
To:	Process data only after their accuracy can be assured. (imperative)
Change:	The vacation schedule desired by each employee needs to be cleared by the Personnel Department. (indicative)
To:	Please clear your vacation schedule with the Personnel Department. (imperative)

CLARITY

How can you improve the clarity of the material you write?

Clarity, or clearness, in writing is achieved in several ways. Two of these ways have already been discussed: using words the reader is certain to understand and writing at a level appropriate for the reader.

Logical development, the use of effective sentences and paragraphs, and the pace with which you present your ideas all affect clarity. Other ways to enhance clarity are maintaining a consistent point of view (first person or third person), using clear transitions, and maintaining parallel construction. Avoiding jargon—words common to your field but unlikely to be understood by others—will also help you achieve clarity.

Logical Development

Unless you use logical development—the manner in which you structure your material—you risk confusing the reader. Methods to develop logical written communication are as follows:

Cause and Effect: To present information about a problem and its solution.

Chronological: To present information with an important time sequence. Good for presenting information about a problem.

Comparison: To present information about several alternatives and their comparative advantages and disadvantages. Good for presenting information about recommended action.

General to Specific: To present information that ends with specific details. Good for certain types of reports.

Specific to General: To present information that begins with specific details. Good for certain types of reports.

Sequential: To present information that has an ordered, sequenced nature. Good for instructions.

Clear Expression of Ideas

Effective sentences and paragraphs are easy for the reader to understand. Although the content of a sentence or paragraph may be beyond the reader's comprehension level, the way you express your ideas should, nevertheless, enhance the comprehension process. When the expression of an idea rather than something about the idea itself confuses the reader, you are not communicating effectively.

The first of the following two paragraphs illustrates that how you express your ideas (rather than the ideas themselves) can confuse the reader. The second paragraph shows the same ideas expressed with greater clarity.

Change:	When you have to purchase your next suit, please be aware that although an increase in labor costs is forcing all suit manufacturers to increase their prices, some stores did purchase their spring inventory before the price increases took effect and, therefore, they may be willing to sell their earlier-purchased stock for less than the current prices.
To:	Rising labor costs within the clothing manufacturing industry have resulted in increased prices of men's suits. Stores that still have a supply of suits purchased before the price increases may be offering this stock at the original price.

The first paragraph is confusing for two primary reasons: Written as one sentence, the paragraph contains too many words; and the ideas are not communicated directly.

Modifiers

Modifiers are words or phrases that expand or limit other elements within a sentence. Incorrect use of modifiers destroys sentence clarity, sometimes resulting in humorous writing and/or confusion. An example of unintentional humorous writing, because of the use of incorrect modifiers, is found in the following example: "Your desk should be cleared of all confidential materials before leaving work at the end of the day." Read literally, this sentence sounds as if the desk leaves work at the end of the day.

Among the troublesome modifiers are misplaced modifiers and dangling modifiers. A *misplaced modifier*, occurring when the modifier is placed too far from the word it modifies, often causes confusion. The following example illustrates how to correct misplaced modifiers in a sentence:

Change:	Competent in work measurement, the productivity of the company was improved considerably by Mr. Jones, who implemented the PRO-IM Program. (This sentence reads as if productivity is competent in work measurement.)
To:	The productivity of the company improved considerably after Mr. Jones, who is competent in work measurement, implemented the PRO-IM Program.

Dangling modifiers are expressions that do not clearly refer to the proper noun or pronoun in a sentence and usually occur when the sentence begins with a participle, infinitive, or a gerund. To correct dangling modifiers, (1) add the proper subject to the independent part, or (2) make the dependent part agree with the main clause and the main subject. The first sentence in each set of the following examples contains a dangling modifier; the second sentence is a corrected version.

Change:	Having read your report, a few questions come to mind.
To:	Having read your report, I have a few questions. (The sentence was corrected by adding the proper subject to the independent clause.)
Change:	At the age of seven, Mary's family toured Europe.
To:	When Mary was seven, her family toured Europe. (The dependent part agrees with the main clause.)

Misinterpretation often results from misplacing the following adverbs: *almost, hardly, merely, scarcely,* and *only.* Of these, *only* is the most troublesome because it is both an adverb and an adjective. Therefore, *only* can modify nearly anything and so fits into a sentence at almost any point. Note how each of the following sentences changes as the word *only* is relocated:

Only I urged him to try.

I *only* urged him to try.

I urged *only* him to try.

I urged him *only* to try.

I urged him to *only* try.

I urged him to try *only.*

Parallel Construction

The presence of *parallel construction*—the quality of presenting like sentence elements using like construction—will also enable you to improve the clarity of your sentences. Here is how parallel construction works: If you employ a gerund (verb ending in *-ing* used as a noun) to express an idea in a sentence, other related ideas should also be expressed by a gerund. Or if you use an infinitive phrase to express an idea, other related ideas should also be expressed in the infinitive form. The first sentence in each of the following sets violates the parallel-construction rule; the second sentence corrects the problem.

Change:	Selling subscriptions, buying supplies, and the collection of money are important activities.
To:	Selling subscriptions, buying supplies, and collecting money are important activities.
Change:	To order flowers, to greet new members, and helping plan the annual banquet are functions of the hospitality committee.
To:	To order flowers, to greet new members, and to help plan the annual banquet are important functions of the hospitality committee.

Sentence/Paragraph Length

Why should a long series of equal-length sentences be avoided?

A long series of sentences of approximately the same length is monotonous; it also increases the reading difficulty of written material. Stringing together a series of short independent clauses is one cause of this problem. Therefore, try to connect these clauses with subordinating connectives, or make separate sentences out of some of the clauses that are related to one another. The following example illustrates the problem resulting from stringing together a series of independent clauses and how to correct it.

Change:	The Marshall Corporation was founded forty years ago, and it now has branch offices in four states, and it employs nearly four hundred individuals.
To:	The Marshall Corporation was founded forty years ago. With branch offices in four states, it now employs nearly four hundred individuals.

Although long sentences lack clarity, too many short sentences in a paragraph make writing sound choppy and immature. Sentence length averaging between fifteen and twenty words is typically recommended. Paragraph length in letters should average around four to six lines, with a maximum of ten lines. For reports, paragraph length can extend to a maximum of fourteen to sixteen lines. To enhance clarity and reading ease, use shorter sentences (but not too many of them) and shorter paragraphs in presenting complex ideas.

Unity

What is unity?

Your sentences and paragraphs should have *unity*, which means that each unit of writing presents only one main idea and information closely related to it. Because sentences and paragraphs containing unrelated information are difficult to comprehend, they are likely to interfere with reader understanding. Furthermore, when sentences and paragraphs contain irrelevant ideas, the reader has more difficulty separating important ideas from less important ideas. In Example A, that follows, the sentence lacks unity; in Example B, the paragraph is disjointed.

A.	We do have the VCR in stock about which you inquired, and we are planning to double the size of our electronics department in the near future.
B.	No other computer manufacturer currently offers a warranty as favorable as the one offered by Electro Computer Corporation. We offer an unlimited warranty for one year after the date of purchase and a limited warranty for the next four years. Our company is growing by leaps and bounds. Much of our success has to be attributed to the creative advertising of our products.

Note how removing the irrelevant ideas in the first version of the following sentences improves the revised version.

Change:	John Jones, who has a car like mine, was extremely helpful in solving the problem with the computer program.
To:	John Jones was extremely helpful in solving the problem with the computer program. (The clause, "who has a car like mine," is irrelevant to the problem and its solution as it is stated in the sentence.)
Change:	Even though our company was not as profitable as we had forecast, the employees seem to enjoy working here.
To:	Our company was not as profitable as we had forecast.

Paragraph unity is achieved by expressing the main idea in a *topic sentence* and the supporting ideas in the other sentences. The topic sentence should appear in a position of emphasis; typically, this is at the beginning of the paragraph. The sentences that follow the topic sentence offer supporting information.

To break the monotony of always placing the topic sentence first, you can include it as the last sentence of a paragraph. In this case, it becomes a summary rather than an introduction or overview. When you must state refusals in letters, like those presented in Chapter 7, including the topic sentence as the last sentence of the paragraph may be psychologically advantageous. When using this approach, supporting details leading up to the refusal are then presented first.

The first version of the following paragraph lacks unity because the topic sentence does not clearly stand out. The revised version has unity.

Change: When compared with last year, our sales this year have increased approximately 20 percent. Coupling this with the fact that the achievements of our newly installed employee productivity program are exceeding expectations makes this one of Howerton's most profitable years in recent history. The full impact of the new employee training program, which has undoubtedly contributed to our success, is also just now being realized.

To: Howerton is currently experiencing its most profitable year in recent history. Several contributing factors can be identified: Sales are 20 percent higher this year than last; and the success of two new programs—the employee productivity program and the employee training program—is being felt.

Coherence

What is coherence?

To sharpen the clarity of your writing, your sentences and paragraphs need to possess *coherence,* the writing quality that enables ideas to hang together in a logical manner. Without coherence, the ideas presented in the material will seem disjointed. When the reader is unable to determine how various ideas in a sentence or paragraph relate to one another, the unit of writing becomes incoherent.

How can coherence be attained?

Coherence is achieved by making the relationships between parts of sentences and paragraphs clear to the reader, by ensuring that one idea leads to another throughout the sentence or paragraph, and by placing modifiers in the correct location in each sentence.

Observe how the first sentence in each of the following sets lacks coherency and the second sentence in each set is an improved version.

Change: Lack of unity destroys the effectiveness of sentences, and well-written paragraphs are critical to the success of your message.

To: Sentence unity and well-written paragraphs are two of the critical elements that will affect the success of your message.

Change: Our company has been a leader in this field since it was founded, and it is now in its sixty-seventh year.

To: Our company, which was founded sixty-seven years ago, has always been a leader in its field.

The following list of suggestions can help you achieve coherence:

1. Use parallel construction when presenting a series of facts or ideas of equal emphasis or significance.
2. Use repeating construction to tie a series together. Example: These are the things I most enjoy doing: attending concerts, attending ballet performances, traveling in foreign countries, and reading good books.

3. Use conjunctions (*and, but, or, nor*) and transitional phrases (*in addition to, as well as*) to achieve smoothness between phrases, clauses, and sentences.

Closely related to content coherence is reading coherence, or the ease with which your material can be read. You can achieve reading coherence through the following techniques: using transitional words, repeating key words, employing pointing words, providing explanatory statements, and enumerating numbers or letters to indicate a series. The following examples illustrate each of these techniques.

Using transitional words includes the utilization of such words or phrases as *therefore, for example, in addition,* and *in contrast.*

> The new president is interested in enhancing the firm's public image. In addition, she is interested in diversifying the product line. Therefore, I think you will see more emphasis placed than ever before on the public relations and marketing units.

Repeating key terms includes the repetition of key terms.

> As children, we were taught to take responsibility for our actions. We were taught to respect the views of others. Our parents also taught us the virtues of hard work and the necessity for relaxation.

Employing pointing words includes the use of such words as *this, that, those, these, such, some,* and *a few.*

> I will be in Philadelphia on May 18. Thus, I will be able to discuss with you your ideas for the marketing strategy you have been working on for our new paint line. These ideas, which many of us are looking forward to receiving, are critical to our financial future.

Providing explanatory statements includes the use of statements to support a previously stated idea.

> John's performance the last few weeks has deteriorated. For example, he rarely submits reports on time now, nor does he seem to care about the direction of the marketing department. Furthermore, he regularly arrives late to work and leaves early several times each week.

Utilizing enumerations includes the use of either letters or numbers to identify the series of ideas that can be presented in either tabular form or paragraph form.

> The following outlines the reasons for my beliefs:
>
> 1. We can now afford to purchase a new word processor.
> 2. We can now afford to hire more employees.
> 3. We can now afford to expand the size of the word processing center.

Emphasis

What are the two positions of emphasis?

The technique of *emphasis* is useful when you want certain words, phrases, clauses, sentences, or paragraphs to stand out. Emphasis techniques include position, repetition, quantity, and mechanics. A note of caution: Overuse of any of these techniques tends to deemphasize the information you want to emphasize.

Emphasis of material is accomplished by placing it in either of two positions: the beginning or the ending. The beginning of a sentence is generally the preferred location unless you are presenting negative information. Knowing which idea you want to emphasize will enable you to place it in the most prominent location.

In sentences that contain both independent and dependent clauses, a recommended technique is to use the independent clauses for ideas you want to emphasize and the dependent clauses for the ideas you want to deemphasize. If a sentence contains both positive and negative information, the positive information should be placed in the emphasized position; and the negative information should be placed in the deemphasized position, which is the middle of the sentence.

The importance of a major idea in a paragraph is emphasized when it appears in either the first or last sentence. The beginning position, however, is more emphatic than the ending position is. The middle of the paragraph generally discusses ideas of secondary importance.

In each of the following sentence sets, the first sentence improperly emphasizes the main idea, whereas the second sentence corrects this problem.

Change: Our new employee, Mary Johnson, is a specialist in labor relations.
To: Mary Johnson, who is a new employee, is a specialist in labor relations. (That Mary Johnson is a new employee is relatively unimportant; therefore, that fact either can be omitted or included in the middle of the sentence.)
Change: One of the essential characteristics of effective writing, which is clarity of expression, is often overlooked by many inexperienced writers. ("Clarity of expression" is an important idea; therefore, it needs to be moved from the middle of the sentence.)
To: Clarity of expression, which is an essential characteristic of effective writing, is often overlooked by many inexperienced writers.

In using the repetition technique, you simply repeat the words you want to emphasize. Furthermore, you can emphasize an idea by expanding your discussion of it.

Another technique is to introduce a key idea in a short paragraph and then present information about it in the following paragraphs. Several mechanical means of emphasizing ideas are also available, including underlining, using all capitals, using a boldface type graphical font, and using a different ink color.

The first of the following two sentences illustrates how overuse of the repetition technique can have a boring and, hence, negative impact, whereas the second sentence corrects this problem.

Change: I enjoy playing football, playing soccer, and playing baseball and watching the sports of basketball and rugby.
To: Playing football, soccer, and baseball and watching basketball and rugby are activities I enjoy most.

Effective paragraphs, like effective sentences, have unity, coherence, and emphasis. Paragraphs have unity when each sentence contributes to the development of the main, or core, idea. Coherence gives sentences one point of view and one tense.

Coherence is also achieved by carefully choosing transitional words so ideas are tied together as you develop them. Emphasis enables you to put maximum attention on the primary idea within a sentence and minimum attention on the secondary idea.

Pace

Clarity is also affected by *pace*, which refers to the rate at which you present ideas in your writing. The pace needs to be appropriate for your reader. Presenting ideas at too fast a pace tends to affect clarity. The pace appropriate for your writing depends on the level of knowledge the reader has about the subject as well as the technical nature of the subject. When you are in doubt about the reader's knowledge of the subject, slow the pace of your ideas as they appear on paper.

What happens when you present material at too fast a pace?

To slow the pace of your writing, you can use different types of sentence structure and incorporate transitional words and phrases. In the following first paragraph, the pace is too fast. The revision uses transitional phrases and a different sentence structure to slow the pace.

How can you slow the pace of your writing?

Change: The equipment had been malfunctioning for two days. We were not aware of it. It became inoperable on the third day.
To: Although we were not aware of it, the equipment had been malfunctioning for two days. On the third day, it became inoperable.

CONCRETENESS

Business communication should be concrete rather than abstract. *Concrete writing* involves the preparation of material that makes specific references to persons, places, objects, and actions; *abstract writing* involves material that makes general references to these items. Perhaps the best way to distinguish between the two is to ask whether you give the reader "something on which to hold." If not, you are probably being too abstract, a position that allows your reader to "dangle from thin air."

What is concrete writing?

To make your writing more concrete,

How can you make your writing more concrete?

1. Include as much specific information as possible.
2. Use words that provide exacting detail rather than fuzzy meaning.

Include As Much Specific Information As Possible

What is concrete to you may not be concrete to your readers. An effective way to overcome this difficulty lies in offering specific information rather than general information. For example, for the reader to learn how fast "fast" is in the first of the following sentences is impossible. But additional information makes possible such an understanding.

Change: She is a fast typist.
To: Her typing rate is 85 words per minute.

Another example of a general statement and a more concrete revised version follows.

Change: She lives nearby.
To: She lives in Orange County, which is about 20 miles from here.

General words or phrases are often used by the reader differently than you intended them to be. A partial list of particularly troublesome words follows:

a great deal of time	less
large	bad
small	good
old	around
young	convenient
majority	little
minority	most

A cautionary note: You may wish to use general words rather than specific words when you need to be diplomatic or when the situation does not require specificity, as the following examples illustrate.

Specific: The data analysis section of this report is very weak.
General: Certain sections of this report are stronger than others.

Choose Words That Provide Exact Meaning Rather Than Fuzzy Detail

Using words that convey exact meaning also improves your writing clarity. Otherwise, your thinking may seem fuzzy. Fuzzy words or expressions are those that open the door for readers to infer whatever meaning they desire. Whenever the reader can either "read in" or "read out of" your message, the opportunity for miscommunication greatly increases—sometimes to the writer's disadvantage.

Examples of sentences containing fuzzy detail and more precise revised versions follow.

Change: John is a good worker.
To: John, who is a good worker, is conscientious about meeting deadlines, is a loyal employee, and can always be counted on to do his fair share of the work.
Change: This report is weak.
To: The following flaws weaken the quality of this report: the numerous grammatical errors, the inaccurate information that is presented, and the absence of feasible recommendations.

COMPLETENESS

In what ways are incomplete messages costly?

Incomplete messages quickly increase the organization's communication costs. When a message is prepared requiring the preparation of another message, the cost of communicating about this specific situation has doubled. Incomplete messages are costly in other ways, because they can also result in the following:

1. Loss of goodwill
2. Loss of valued customers
3. Loss of sales
4. Cost of returning merchandise because of an incomplete order
5. Waste of time trying to make sense out of an incomplete message

In business writing, an appropriate strategy is to include information unless you are reasonably certain the reader already knows it. In too many instances, when you fail to inform them adequately, readers receive the impression they are not very important to you.

When responding to an inquiry, you need to answer all the questions you were asked. Sometimes you may even have to "read between the lines" to determine what the inquiry is. Most readers will be favorably impressed when they are given relevant information in addition to that for which they specifically asked.

What test can you use to determine whether your message is complete?

Perhaps the best test to determine whether you have relayed essential information is to evaluate your writing with the following questions: Who? What? When? Where? Why? and How? If your message clearly answers these questions (assuming they are asked), then it is complete. If, after reading your message, you cannot answer these questions, consider adding additional information.

SUMMARY

One of the important elements of written communication is courtesy. Courteous communications possess a you-attitude, an appropriate tone, positive wording, and gender-neutral language.

Written communication should also be correct. This means that it has an appropriate level of language for the reader, that words are used correctly, and that data and information are accurate. Other attributes of correctness are proper spelling, grammar, and punctuation.

Conciseness is another key element of written communication. To write concisely, avoid trite expressions, wordiness, and unnecessary repetition. In addition, eliminate unneeded facts.

Written communication should have clarity. This means material is developed logically, sentences and paragraphs are well written, and the whole possesses unity and coherence. Proper emphasis and pacing are two other elements of clarity.

Concrete material is specific. It also tends to be written with active verbs rather than passive verbs. In addition, to be concrete, words must have exact meaning. The final element of effective written communication presented is completeness.

REVIEW QUESTIONS

1. Describe reader benefit and explain why this quality should be included in business correspondence.
2. What are some of the ways reader-benefit material can be incorporated into business correspondence?
3. Besides using negative words or phrases, what are some of the other types of tonal problems that occur in business correspondence?
4. What impact does perception have on business correspondence?
5. How do you achieve correctness in the material you write?
6. How do you achieve conciseness in the material you write?
7. What is a trite expression?
8. What alternatives are available for logically developing the material you write?
9. What is meant by unity?
10. What is meant by coherence?
11. How can you make your writing more coherent?
12. How can you make your writing more concrete?
13. How are incomplete messages expensive to business organizations?

APPLICATION PROBLEMS

1. Using the Fog Index,^{SM} calculate the readability level of a message you have written; a story in your local newspaper; and an article in a weekly news magazine, such as *Time* or *Newsweek*.
2. Rewrite the following sentences to eliminate the negative tone.
    a. I am sure you will see, once you examine the attached price list, that our prices are no higher than our competitor's prices.

b. I am sorry that I cannot amend Policy No. 34543 without your wife's signature.
c. Because one of our major suppliers is on strike, we will not be able to ship your order until we find another supplier.
d. We are informing you of this change in our operating procedure so that we will not have a misunderstanding later on.
e. We will delay shipping your order until we learn which color of coat you wish.
f. To avoid damaging your credit rating, please send your check for $129.54 immediately.

3. Rewrite the following sentences to improve the you-attitude.
   a. We will honor your request.
   b. To help us best accommodate our customers' needs, we ask that all our customers begin making appointments when they need their cars worked on.
   c. We will give you a cash discount of 6 percent on purchases made before November 15.
   d. We hope to have the pleasure of serving you in the near future.
   e. We quit providing receipts two months ago because most customers said that they use their canceled check as a receipt.
   f. I wish to inform you about our midsummer sale that begins next week.
4. Rewrite the following sentences to eliminate the weakness that each contains.
   a. Allow me to take this opportunity to extend to you a cordial invitation to join us on our ten-year anniversary celebration.
   b. Your letter of January 14 has arrived in which you requested that we give you a cash refund of $13.98 purchase price of two LP records, which we are going to do.
   c. A careful study has been made by the finance committee.
   d. Your tape deck has been repaired and it is our hope that you will experience no further trouble with it.
   e. Please be assured that we are doing everything in our power to accommodate your wishes even if it does not seem that we are.
   f. For your information and enlightenment, attached hereto is a carbon copy of the letter I received nearly three weeks ago on January 14 about the proposed changes and amendments to their operating policy.
5. Rewrite the following letter to eliminate the weaknesses.

Dear Mrs. Mathison:

In accordance with your request recently transmitted to us that we send you a service manual to replace the one you did not receive when you purchased your new Sanger sewing machine, I am all to happy to do so.

We are convinced that you certainly made a wise choice when you purchased your new machine. Believe it or not, sales of this machine are exceeding our expectations by a significant margin. Obviously, that is good news for us.

I would like to thank you for your graciousness and understanding in this situation.

4

The Process of Writing Business Documents

After studying this chapter, you should be able to

1. Identify the steps in each stage of writing a business document.
2. Discuss how to determine the appropriate content for a business document.
3. Identify the differences between the direct and the indirect methods of organizing a document.
4. Identify the characteristics of effective sentences and paragraphs in a document.
5. Explain how to increase the effectiveness of paragraph beginnings and endings in a document.
6. Identify several questions to ask yourself during the editing process for a document.
7. Identify methods to help you proofread a document more accurately.
8. Describe the steps involved in dictating a business document.

Effective business writers prepare for writing. In fact, much of their writing success stems from the effort they put into preparation. Indeed, preparing to write may occasionally be as time consuming as the actual writing process itself.

Preparing to write a document is a multifaceted activity that includes the planning and organizing stages, followed by the drafting or dictating stage. Most business writers, especially inexperienced ones, also consider it necessary to edit at least their first draft—and, in some cases, several drafts—before they are satisfied with their message.

This chapter discusses the following methods for converting your original idea into a business document: planning, organizing, drafting, editing, dictating, and proofreading. We include the process of dictating because of the increasing number of business writers who choose dictating over drafting.

Several steps compose each of the stages. The following outlines these steps:

What stages are included in the writing process?

Planning Stage

1. Determine your purpose.
2. Consider your reader.
3. Determine the appropriate content for your message.

Organizing Stage

1. Outline the topics you plan to include in your message.
2. Determine the appropriate order of your topics.

Drafting/Dictating Stage

1. Develop an appropriate beginning paragraph.
2. Compose the body.
3. Develop an appropriate ending paragraph.

Editing Stage

1. Review and assess how well your message conforms with
    a. principles of effective communication,
    b. appropriate content,
    c. appropriate organizational structure,
    d. logical sentence and paragraph construction,
    e. correct grammar, punctuation, spelling, and word usage fundamentals.
2. Make needed changes.

Proofreading Stage

1. Check for the accuracy of dates, figures, amounts, numbers, and so forth.
2. Check for misspelled words.
3. Check for typographical errors.
4. Check for omissions and additions of material.
5. Check for proper sequence of material.

As you prepare business documents, keep in mind that the types of situations discussed in the following Ethics Episode can create difficulties.

ETHICS EPISODE

As a business writer, you have to guard against preparing business documents that either mislead the reader or that enable him or her to manipulate the interpretation of your work. Whether you knowingly or unknowingly permit the occurrence of either of these situations, the result is the same: The ethics of your actions can be challenged. These two situations are likely to result in the following negative consequences:

1. Your credibility as a business writer is severely damaged.
2. Your employer becomes the target of allegations that it employs individuals who engage in unethical behavior.
3. Your employer experiences a costly situation, resulting from flawed managerial decision making that was based on business documents that either misled the reader or that allowed the reader to manipulate his or her interpretation of your work.

Consider the following examples that can create an ethical dilemma for the business writer:

1. Suppose you have been assigned the responsibility of investigating the feasibility of your employer's implementing an in-house training program. Also suppose you believe that you have an excellent opportunity of becoming its director should one be implemented. Furthermore, suppose the results of your investigation revealed that rarely can an organization the size of the one for which you work financially justify the implementation of an in-house training program. Rather, contracting with outside trainers on an as-needed basis is more economical. In the report you prepare for your superiors, you will be acting unethically if you overstate the advantages and understate the disadvantages of an in-house training program or if you fail to mention that rarely can an organization of the size of the one for which you work financially justify the implementation of an in-house training program. (You will also be acting unethically if you cleverly word the report in such a way that the reader can manipulate his or her interpretation of your writing.)

2. Suppose you are sending a memo to your superior to justify the implementation of a tuition-reimbursement program for employees who take college-level courses that would enable them to perform better in their jobs. You believe this is an excellent idea because you are working on your bachelor's degree and you believe your employer benefits by what you are learning and, therefore, should help pay the tuition. When you discussed the implementation of such a program with a number of your coworkers, you found that 60 percent favored your proposal. Among your coworkers against the implementation of a reimbursement program, three reasons were common: They were not working on a bachelor's degree, they already had a bachelor's degree for which they paid their own tuition, and they would rather have the money that would be allocated for tuition reimbursement earmarked for a larger salary increase that would benefit everyone. You will be engaging in unethical behavior as a business writer if you state in the memo to your superior that the "vast majority" of those whom you surveyed favored the implementation of a tuition-reimbursement program. Generally, "60 percent" does not constitute a "vast majority."

To help eliminate either of these two situations mentioned, you need to

1. Be as objective as you can in presenting information.
2. Avoid allowing your biases to contaminate the content of your documents.
3. Define or quantify any terms or words you believe the reader may misinterpret differently from what you intended.

PLANNING

The more time you devote to *planning* your business message, the more likely it will be effective. Effective planning will help you determine what material to include in your message, given the nature of the situation and the reader. The planning stage, as indicated, includes these sequential steps: (1) determine your purpose, (2) consider your reader, and (3) determine the content appropriate for your message.

What steps are included in the planning stage?

Determine Your Purpose

Before you actually begin the composing process, you need to determine your *purpose*, which is your reason for writing. The following questions will help you discover it:

What is involved in determining message purpose?

1. Is your message to be sent in response to a message you received from the reader?
2. Does your message have to be persuasive?
3. Is the situation positive or negative?

The general purpose, or goal, of your message determines the content that you include as well as the order in which you present the material.

Becoming familiar with your purpose early will help you avoid wasting time because you know what you need to accomplish. Such familiarity enables you to focus more specifically on your reader's needs—it will keep you from "wandering"—and thus enable you to prepare a more effective message.

What three levels of writing objectives are found?

Becoming familiar with your purpose allows you to formulate your writing objectives or outcomes. That is, you typically need to be clear about your broad, specific, and desired outcomes. A broad objective states in general terms the problem you are attempting to solve or what you hope to achieve. A specific objective outlines the suggested action you are proposing to accomplish your broad objective. A desired outcome refers to what you perceive to be the results of your efforts.

The following example illustrates these three levels of writing objectives:

Broad	*Specific*	*Desired Outcome*
Increase employee motivation.	Implement flextime plan.	As a result of my report, a flextime program will be installed.

Broad	*Specific*	*Desired Outcome*
Hire better qualified employees.	Improve employee quality.	As a result of my report, managers will have a better idea of how to identify the best qualified applicants.

Consider Your Reader

An effectively written document must be understood by your reader. Unless you are familiar with your reader and have considered or analyzed the person's background and knowledge, you may have difficulty focusing on him or her. Clearly, the approach and content you use in writing for one reader may be inappropriate for another reader.

What determines how much you need to know about your reader?

The purpose of your message will probably determine how much you need to know about your reader. The amount of background information needed to communicate effectively with your reader will vary from situation to situation. For example, in preparing a reply to an invitation to speak at a convention, you will need to know less about your reader than in preparing a sales letter designed to promote the computer supplies distributed by your company. For the response to the invitation, you will want to write in a concise, courteous, and straight forward manner. For your sales letter, you will want to know the type of computer supplies the "typical" reader buys, in what quantity, for what popular brands of equipment, and so forth. Knowing this information will enable you to "pitch" your message to the reader.

To give full consideration to your reader, you will want to have answers to a number of questions about him or her. Communication Capsule 4-1 lists some of the most common questions.

Communication Capsule 4-1 Questions to Help You Better Understand Your Reader

The following questions should elicit answers that will help you better understand the reader of your message:

1. *How much technical background does your reader have?* Unless the reader has a technical background in the subject of the document you are preparing, do not include technical material.
2. *Are you preparing material for one reader or multiple readers?* Writing for multiple readers becomes a more complex task because you need to meet the needs of several individuals, not just one. For multiple readers, you have to simplify the message while simultaneously making it more interesting.
3. *Is your reader from inside the organization or outside the organization?* The answer to this question will generally help you determine how much background information you may need to include. Employees are apt to be more familiar with the situation about which you are writing than are outsiders.
4. *What is your reader's occupation, age, and income level?* Some types of business documents, especially sales messages, are intricately tied to the reader's occupation, age, and income level. These factors help determine what types of appeals are appropriate for different types of readers.
5. *What important characteristics of your reader should be considered?* Several of the reader's characteristics, including habits and attitudes, tend to affect how the reader will react to your message. Frequently, habits and attitudes will determine what you need to do to attract the reader's attention—and then keep it.

6. *What is the educational level of your reader?* Generally, the more education the reader has, the less likely you will have to "write down" as a means of ensuring reader understanding.
7. *What is your reader's geographical location?* Because people living in different parts of the country have different needs, wants, interests, customs, and habits, you may need to become familiar with these specific characteristics, especially if they are likely to affect the reader's acceptance of your message.
8. *Is your message likely to be read as part of your reader's routine?* When you prepare messages that are unlikely to be read by your readers as part of their daily routine, you will need to be more concerned about attracting and keeping their attention. An example is direct-mail advertising, which many individuals discard without opening.
9. *What do you expect your reader to do with the information contained in your message?* Knowing reader expectations will enable you to focus your message more readily on reader needs.

Once you are familiar with your reader, you then have to decide how to work effectively with that person. On the basis of what you know, is your reader likely to be interested or uninterested in your message? Is your reader likely to react positively or negatively? Is your reader likely to trust or distrust you? Is your reader likely to comply with your wishes readily, reluctantly, or not at all?

Some situations that you write about will not be well received by your reader. In these instances, you will have to work especially hard to increase reader receptivity to your message. The more writing experience you have, the easier it will be to determine which techniques will probably work best in various types of business situations.

How can you increase the receptivity of your writing?

To increase your reader's receptivity, you can clearly relate your message to the reader's interests. This is what we called *reader benefit* in Chapter 3. Relating the message to the reader's knowledge level and specific interests is important.

Besides relating your message to your reader's needs, you can enhance message receptivity by "putting your best foot forward." That is, you try to convey the impression that you are knowledgeable. All too often, inexperienced business writers diminish their communicating effectiveness because they do not express themselves clearly. They hedge in developing their messages; their messages contain grammatical, punctuation, spelling, or word usage errors. In one way or another, their messages lack the basic elements of effective business communication.

Determine the Appropriate Content

How can you determine the appropriate content of a message?

The extent to which you effectively determine the content appropriate for your document obviously impacts on its success. Inappropriate content is sure to produce a communication disaster. But determining the content appropriate for some situations is easier than for others. For example, deciding on the content appropriate for a letter in response to an inquiry is often easier than deciding on the content appropriate for preparing an adjustment request. In responding to an inquiry, you simply answer the questions asked in the originating letter, adding any information helpful to your reader. In preparing an adjustment request, because you have no prior communications to guide you in deciding what material is appropriate to include, the process is harder.

Nevertheless, once you have determined the broad topics to include in your message, the planning stage is completed. You are now ready to begin the next stage, which involves organizing the material.

ORGANIZING

In the *organizing stage,* you build on the steps you followed in the planning stage. First you outline the topics you plan to include in your message. Then you determine the appropriate order of these topics.

Outline the Topics

Outlining, which consists of identifying the various subtopics to discuss within each broad topic, is a critical task. Following the various plans presented in subsequent chapters will aid you in outlining broad topics.

For example, assume you are composing a letter to a client whose credit account has had a past-due balance for the past four months. One of the broad topics you decide to discuss is the need for the client to pay you the amount of the past-due balance. The following partial outline summarizes the information you plan to include in your discussion of this broad area:

A. Need to have account paid in full by January 20.
   1. The customer can protect his or her credit reputation by paying now.
   2. Receipt of payment now will help you avoid having to borrow short-term money, which will benefit the customer in the long run because you will not have to increase your prices.
   3. The customer can avoid paying additional finance or interest charges on his or her account.

In what way is careful outlining helpful?

Careful outlining is useful for several reasons. Besides improving the clarity of your message, it can save you writing time later on. This is because, as you will discover, altering your ideas before a document is actually written is much easier than making changes after it has been composed. Furthermore, careful outlining improves the chances of your fulfilling your communication objective. Your outline is merely a "road map" that you can readily adjust before you begin writing. The use of an outline is especially helpful when you are dealing with a complex situation.

Careful outlining also enables you to give proper emphasis to the various topics in your message. Although exceptions do occur, the topics you decide to emphasize are most likely to elicit the greatest amount of discussion. Including a discussion of the most important positive points at the beginning or end of a paragraph is more emphatic than presenting them in the middle.

What three methods are used in developing your message?

Several methods are useful in developing written business communication. Among the most common are topical, direct, and indirect. By specifically determining which of these to employ before actually beginning the outlining process, you greatly enhance the chances of your preparing a well-developed message. Because different methods are useful for different situations, being aware of the various uses of each method will enable you to prepare more effective outlines.

Exhibit 4-1 illustrates a preliminary draft of a *topical* outline.

When is the direct method preferred?

The *direct* method presents a general statement first, followed by specific supporting statements. This method is generally used to transmit positive or good-news information because the reader immediately learns the information of greatest interest. The supporting information, which is of less interest, is presented next. This method is consistent with the reader-benefit concept discussed in Chapter 3.

Exhibit 4-2 shows a sample direct outline, and Exhibit 4-3 shows the letter that was written, based on it.

The *indirect* method, which is more appropriate for negative-news messages, presents the specific information first, followed by the conclusion. Therefore, by the time the reader reads the conclusion, you have presented the reasons that you cannot accommodate him or her. This approach gives you psychological control over your message.

Exhibit 4-4 shows an indirect outline.

The letter that emerged from the indirect outline is shown in Exhibit 4-5. Although outlining may seem difficult initially, the process will definitely become easier with practice.

```
 I.  Health insurance
     A. Mutual of Lincoln
     B. HMO
     C. Federal plan
     D. Dependent coverage
II.  Life insurance
     A. Basic life insurance
        1. Option I
        2. Option II
     B. Federal plan
III. Long-term disability
     A. Mutual of Lincoln
     B. Federal plan
IV.  Dental insurance
     A. American Dental plan
     B. Green Cross plan
     C. Dependent coverage
V.   Retirement
     A. Social security
     B. State retirement
     C. TIBB/GREF
```

Exhibit 4-1 Preliminary draft of topical outline.

```
A. Mention that replacement scanner is on its way.
B. Discuss that examination of scanner revealed two defects.
   1. Weak transistor
   2. Short circuit in one of the electronic components
C. Mention that quality control does not find all defects; incorporate resale material.
D. Discuss warranty on new scanner.
E. Express "satisfaction guaranteed" in courteous closing.
```

Exhibit 4-2 A sample direct outline.

Dear Mr. Jones:

A HD-40 Reliable Scanner was sent to you this morning to replace the scanner you recently sent us for repair.

An examination of your scanner revealed a weak transistor and a short circuit in one of the electronic components. Because your scanner was still under warranty, we prefer—and I am sure you will agree with our decision—to replace the scanner with a new one.

Reliable's electronic equipment is subjected to rigid quality control tests during several stages of its manufacture. These tests find nearly 99 percent of the defective components—which is the best performance record in the industry. The reliability of our products is responsible for the feeling shared by many of our customers that "If you want reliability, buy Reliable."

The 120-day warranty on your replacement scanner will take effect upon its receipt. Please complete and return the warranty card enclosed with the scanner.

You are sure to have many hours of listening enjoyment provided by your scanner. Remember, your satisfaction is guaranteed.

Exhibit 4-3 Example of letter, based on a direct outline.

```
A. Use a neutral opening that compliments the reader for having good credit references.
B. Discuss the reasons that the credit account cannot be approved for $1,000.
   1. Company requires minimum yearly income of $30,000 for this credit limit.
   2. Is advantageous to applicant by helping him avoid assuming a potentially greater
      financial burden than can be effectively handled on this income level.
C. Mention that the credit account can be opened for $750 but not for the $1,000 that was
   requested.
```

Exhibit 4-4 A sample indirect outline.

```
Dear Mr. Quigley:

Each of the individuals you listed as credit references on your charge account
application spoke favorably about your bill-paying habits. You can be proud of
this record.

A minimum yearly income of $30,000 is required to open an account for the
$1,000 maximum that you requested. Your present yearly income is listed as
$24,000. We find this limit actually benefits many of our customers because it
helps them avoid assuming a greater financial burden than they might be able to
handle on incomes of less than $30,000.

Your income level qualifies you for a charge account with a credit limit of
$750. If you would like for us to open an account with this credit limit,
please sign and return the enclosed card, which we need as authorization to
open an account for you.

If you wish, we will review your account after one year to determine whether
the maximum limit can be increased to $1,000. All you need do is request the
review.

A Bailey's charge account can enhance the convenience of your shopping in our
store.
```

Exhibit 4-5 Example of letter, based on an indirect outline.

After preparing your outline, you need to review it for completeness (does the outline contain all the needed information?), logical order (is the information presented in the correct order?), proper emphasis of topics (are important topics more prominent than the less important topics?), and so on. Determining the appropriate order of the topics, discussed in the next section, is the last step in the organizing stage.

Determine the Appropriate Order of the Topics

In some instances, business writers find it wise to delay determining the appropriate order of the topics until after the outline has been completed. This approach is especially true when the ideas are being generated at a fast rate. In fact, you most likely will find the process of determining the appropriate order of the topics easier once you are certain which ones you plan to include in your message. You can also add additional topics to your outline during this step.

How can you determine the appropriate order of the topics for an outline?

The following questions should help you determine whether you have appropriately ordered the topics in your outline:

1. Are my ideas of equal importance presented in a parallel manner?
2. Is my topic sentence appropriate for the development method I'm using (topical, direct, indirect)?

3. Does my topic sequence make my message clear?
4. Are related topics properly sequenced?
5. Is my topic sequence appropriate for the type of message I'm preparing?

To illustrate how changing the order of topics can improve message clarity, consider the outline in Exhibit 4-1. After reviewing this preliminary draft of the outline, the writer decided to describe employee and dependent coverage separately because they are two separate issues. In addition, by changing the order of the benefits, she decided it logical to discuss the insurance benefits before the noninsurance benefits. She also saw that dealing with dental insurance immediately after health insurance was more logical because these two types of benefits are more closely related to each other than are the topics of dental insurance and retirement. Clearly, changing the order of the discussion of these topics in the outline improves the clarity of the final message. Exhibit 4-6 shows the revised outline.

The checklist illustrated in Exhibit 4-7 will help you evaluate how well you have determined the purpose of your message, analyzed the reader, and determined the appropriate content for the message you are developing.

DRAFTING

After completing the planning and organizing stages, you are ready to draft (or dictate) your message. Because *drafting* (composing either in longhand or at a computer/typewriter keyboard) and *dictating* (composing using your voice) are different processes—although their result is the same—each is discussed in a separate section in this chapter. As you are probably more familiar with the drafting process, it is described first. We discuss sentence construction, paragraph construction, including construction of beginning paragraphs, development of the body of the message, and construction of ending paragraphs.

Sentence Construction

What are the characteristics of effective sentences?

The *sentence*—the fundamental unit of thought—is a perfect vehicle for transmitting one or more ideas thoroughly and easily. Indeed, problems in construction destroy the

Exhibit 4-6 Revised topical outline.

```
I. Types of employee benefit plans and coverage
   A. Health insurance
      1. Mutual of Lincoln
      2. HMO
      3. Federal plan
   B. Dental insurance
      1. American Dental plan
      2. Green Cross plan
   C. Life insurance
      1. Basic life insurance
         a. Option I
         b. Option II
      2. Federal plan
   D. Long-term disability insurance
   E. Retirement
      1. Social security
      2. State retirement
      3. TIBB/GREF
      4. Civil service
II. Dependent coverage
   A. Health insurance
      1. Mutual of Lincoln
      2. HMO
      3. Federal plan
   B. Dental insurance
      1. American Dental plan
      2. Green Cross plan
```

A. Purpose
   1. Does the message begin a communication encounter, or does it reply to a message you received earlier?
   2. Is the message designed to inform, persuade, or request?
   3. Is the situation positive or negative?
   4. What are the reader's needs, concerns, desires, and so forth?
   5. What do you want to accomplish through the message you are about to prepare?
   6. What medium best accomplishes your purpose?
B. Reader Analysis
   1. What is the nature of the reader's background?
   2. How familiar is the reader with the situation about which you are communicating?
   3. Will the reader react positively or negatively to your message?
   4. What is your relationship with the reader?
   5. Is the reader likely to be interested in what you have to say?
   6. Is the approach you are using appropriate for your reader?
C. Content
   1. What content needs to be included in your message to cause the reader to respond in the way you intend?
   2. What content needs to be included in your message to satisfy the reader's needs, wants, and desires?
   3. What content is relevant for this situation, given the purpose of the message?
   4. What content needs to be included to make the message conform with that typically included in the type of letter you are preparing?

Exhibit 4-7 Checklist for planning your message.

effectiveness of many sentences. Among the important characteristics of effective sentences are variety, conciseness, personalization, and the absence of expletives.

Why is sentence variety important?

Variety is among the more important elements to incorporate when drafting your message. You need to be concerned about variety in sentence type, in sentence length, and in internal structure. Consistent use of the same type of sentence throughout a message becomes monotonous and boring. Messages that contain consecutive sentences of equal length are also uninteresting. So are messages whose sentences have the same internal structure throughout. For example, using introductory prepositional clauses or phrases in several consecutive sentences is monotonous.

The basic types of sentences in the English language are simple sentences, compound sentences, complex sentences, and compound-complex sentences. You can make your writing more exciting when you use at least several of these sentence types in your message. The following sections identify the differences between the four types of sentences and present examples of each.

Simple Sentence

What is a simple sentence?

A *simple sentence* contains only one independent (main) clause and no dependent (subordinate) clauses.

He went home after the meeting.
Please return the form as soon as possible.
Your order was mailed today.

Compound Sentence

What is a compound sentence?

A *compound sentence* contains two or more independent clauses usually joined by one of the coordinating conjunctions (*and, but, or, nor, for*, or *yet*). Note that some compound sentences omit the coordinating conjunction.

Our business offices are located in California, and our plant is located in New Jersey.
John will be out of the office next week, but he will be here the rest of this week.
The report has been typed; it has not been photocopied.

Complex Sentence

A *complex sentence* contains an independent clause and at least one dependent (or subordinate) clause. The main idea is expressed in the independent clause and is expanded in the dependent clause.

What is a complex sentence?

If you would like to receive our illustrated catalog, just sign and return the enclosed card. (one dependent and one independent clause)

When you read Chapter 2, please pay particular attention to the section on punctuation. (one dependent and one independent clause)

Compound-Complex Sentence

A *compound-complex sentence* contains two or more independent clauses (joined by *and, but, or, nor, for*, or *yet*) and at least one dependent clause.

What is a compound-complex sentence?

If we have good weather, we will complete construction of the building by September 1; and landscaping crews can move in any time after that date.

I thought he told me that he was to leave tomorrow; but when I arrived at work this morning, I discovered he left yesterday.

John Jones, our last president, no longer works full time; but he still has considerable influence here.

To enliven your writing, you can also vary sentence length. Note how much more exciting the variable length sentences make the following revised example.

Change:	The first thing you do in writing a letter is to determine your purpose. After this, you consider the background and needs of your reader. Then you determine the appropriate content, given the letter's purpose and reader's background.
To:	Writing a letter consists of several steps. First, you determine your purpose and then consider the reader's background and needs. Next, you determine the appropriate content for your message, given its purpose and the reader's background.

In using a variety of sentence types, you will probably automatically vary sentence length. Although exceptions do exist, simple sentences generally tend to be the shortest type, whereas compound-complex sentences tend to be the longest. The length of compound and complex sentences often falls somewhere between the length of simple and compound-complex sentences.

Some writers tend to overuse a certain type of internal structure, a practice that reduces their writing effectiveness. The first paragraph in the following message indicates what happens when the writer starts each sentence with an infinitive phrase. Note how much more exciting the revision is to read.

Why is variety in the internal structure of a sentence important?

Change: To work hard is a quality I have always admired. To be on time, whether arriving at work or submitting a report, is another quality I have always admired. To continue to learn is another trait I appreciate among employees.
To: The following outlines desirable employee characteristics I have always admired: (1) working hard; (2) arriving at work and submitting work on time; and (3) continuing to learn.

How can you attain sentence conciseness?

Another characteristic of effective sentences is *conciseness,* which is achieved by economizing on the words you include in your messages. Conciseness is attainable in several ways, including the following: (1) using enumerations to avoid repetitively stating an idea common to a series of sentences, (2) avoiding the direct statement of ideas that can be implied, (3) shortening modifying phrases, and (4) choosing compound adjectives.

The following revised example shows how using enumerations results in conciseness.

Change: One of the main duties of this job is maintaining the departmental budget. The holder of this job is also responsible for preparing the year-end reports. Another important responsibility involves the supervision of other employees. In addition, the holder of this job is expected to prepare periodic employee performance appraisals.
To: Among the important duties of this job are the following:
1. Maintaining the departmental budget
2. Preparing year-end reports
3. Supervising other employees
4. Preparing periodic employee performance appraisals

Lack of conciseness often occurs because the writer states what is clearly implied. For example, if a later action implies an earlier action, you can probably delete any discussion of the earlier action without destroying the clarity of the sentence. Note how the following sentences are made more brief by using an implied rather than an explicit reference to the earlier action.

Change: Mary rode the train and enjoyed her ride.
To: Mary enjoyed her train ride. (Mary had to ride the train if she enjoyed riding it; therefore, let the "rode the train" be implied.)
Change: She proofread the letter and found three typographical errors.
To: She found three typographical errors in the letter. (Let the proofreading task be stated by implication.)

Sentence conciseness can be achieved also by shortening modifying phrases—phrases that can frequently be shortened to one word, as in the following examples.

Change: He spoke in a hesitating manner.
To: He spoke hesitatingly.
Change: This is the machine that is malfunctioning.
To: This is the malfunctioning machine.
Change: Omit the material for which you have no use.
To: Omit the useless material.

Converting a modifying phrase into a compound adjective and placing it before the word it modifies will also trim the fat off sentences. The modifying phrase is converted to a compound adjective and placed before the word it modifies. The following examples illustrate this technique.

Change: These imports that are duty free are selling well.
To: These duty-free imports are selling well. (Note that compound adjectives are hyphenated.)
Change: This book that is up to date has been helpful.
To: This up-to-date book has been helpful.

What is the impact of personalizing sentences?

Another characteristic of successful sentences is to personalize them with your reader's name. By doing so, you attract the reader's attention. For personalizing to be effective, rather than distracting, the reader's name has to fit naturally and not be overused. By directly addressing the reader by name in the first word or two in your sentence, you can also avoid using a self-referential. The following examples illustrate the advantages of personalizing.

Mr. Jones, members of the Citizens Club enjoyed your excellent talk.
John, I look forward to meeting you next week.

An increasing number of people now omit the salutation of letters (Dear John) and personalize the first sentence of the letter, as the following example illustrates.

John, will you please sign and return by next week the enclosed card?

What are expletives?

Avoiding the use of *expletives*—meaningless phrases that simply fill up space—will also improve the effectiveness of your writing. In business communication, expletives commonly appear as the first several words in a sentence, although they can crop up elsewhere in the sentence. Among the more common expletives are the following:

there is (are) (will be)
there was (were) (will be)
there can (could) be
it is (was) (will be)
it has been

The use of expletives as the first two or three words of the sentence is not recommended for the following reasons:

1. The expletive becomes the subject (*It/there*) and verb (*was/were*) of the sentence. Consequently, you have to read beyond the expletive to determine what the sentence is about.
2. The expletive destroys the conciseness of your sentence. Notice in the original version of the following examples that sentences—the ones containing the expletives—are not as concise as in the rewritten version.
3. In the English language, readers are used to a subject-verb-complement pattern, with the subject often being the first word or two of the sentence. Expletives

disrupt this pattern because the "real" subject is found buried elsewhere in the sentence.

Note how removing the expletives in the first sentence of each of the following sets improves the second, or revised, sentence in each set:

Change:	There are three errors on page 23.
To:	Page 23 contains three errors.
Change:	It is most likely that he will not be here.
To:	He most likely will not be here.

Paragraph Construction

Just as effective sentences possess certain qualities, so do effective paragraphs. But the presence of grammatically correct sentences does not ensure effective written paragraphs. Other essential qualities of paragraphs include the following: topic sentence, variety, and sequence.

What is a topic sentence?

As mentioned in Chapter 3, the topic sentence expresses the main idea of the paragraph. The first sentence of a paragraph is usually the topic sentence. Less frequently, the last sentence of the paragraph can also be the topic sentence. Very rarely will a writer place the topic sentence in the middle of the paragraph.

When the topic sentence is the first sentence of the paragraph, it serves to tell the reader immediately what the paragraph is about. Each sentence that follows it, then, provides supporting information. When placed at the end of the paragraph, the topic sentence performs a concluding, or summarizing, function. The following three paragraphs show topic sentences (in italics) located in the three possible positions.

Opening:	*The role of the chief executive officer in negotiations is a complex one that demands many executive skills.* The CEO's responsibilities include providing the necessary overview and conceptual framework, organizing staff and team, planning and making decisions regarding priorities and objectives, and motivating negotiators to achieve their objectives.
Closing:	The personnel manager is responsible for determining which recruitment techniques attract the best-qualified applicants. Another important responsibility is the interview, which allows the manager to identify the most desirable applicants. The manager is also responsible for designing an effective testing program that helps identify those applicants who are best qualified for the positions for which they are being considered. *These responsibilities give the personnel manager a vital role in improving the quality of an organization's workforce.*
Middle:	The personnel manager is responsible for determining which recruitment techniques attract the best-qualified applicants. Another important responsibility is the interview, which allows the manager to identify the most desirable applicants. *These responsibilities give the personnel manager a vital role in improving the quality of an organization's workforce.* In addition to the responsibilities already mentioned, the personnel manager is also responsible for designing an effective testing program that helps identify those applicants who are best qualified for the positions for which they are applying.

Variety in the construction of paragraphs is achieved by varying their length. A business document composed of a series of equal-length paragraphs is less interesting than a document with a number of variable-length paragraphs. Your writing will be more inviting to read if you include some paragraphs that are shorter than average length and others that are longer. In business letters, the average length is six to eight lines; but in reports, ten to twelve lines are standard. Enumerating a series of ideas creates variety, as does using a variety of different types of sentences in each paragraph.

The sequence of the material in a message affects its understandability. In some of the material you write, the ideas must follow in a certain sequence because of their relationship to time or to importance. Or a relationship between components occasionally determines the sequence, as in the case of presenting information about various work units in the company's auditing department. Presenting the material in a logical sequence apparent to readers will enhance their understanding and comprehension. Using transitional words and phrases, pointing words, and repeating key terms will also make the logical sequence of the material more apparent.

For example, note how the illogical sequence in the first of the following two paragraphs (ideas not presented in order) is remedied in the second paragraph.

Change: Once the appraisal process has been completed, an appraisal interview should be conducted. However, before you conduct the appraisal interview, you should do a background check to make sure the applicant is suitable for the position for which he or she is being interviewed. Following the interview, the selection tests should be administered.

To: You should begin the applicant appraisal process by undertaking a background check that will help you determine whether the applicant is suitable for the position for which he or she is being considered. If the background check reveals no significant weaknesses, an appraisal interview should be conducted. Following the interview, the selection tests should be administered.

Beginning and Ending Paragraphs

The beginning and ending paragraphs of the message are critical to its effectiveness. Because beginning and ending paragraphs occupy positions of emphasis, the reader often scrutinizes them with special care.

Beginning Paragraphs

How can you improve the effectiveness of beginning paragraphs?

The beginning paragraph may determine whether the reader reads your message in its entirety. Because your goal is to entice the reader to read the entire message without putting it aside, the wording in the beginning paragraph is particularly critical. The following suggestions should help you improve the effectiveness of your beginning paragraphs:

1. Check that the beginning is appropriate for the reader.
2. Check that the beginning is appropriate for the situation. Normally, in good-news letters, begin with the good news; in neutral or request letters, begin with the main idea or request; in disappointing-news letters, buffer the beginning with neutral information or information with which the reader will agree; and in persuasive messages, begin with information that will catch the reader's attention.
3. Avoid including negative information or discourteous wording. Do this by emphasizing what can be accomplished rather than what cannot be accomplished.
4. Use a you-viewpoint (rather than an I-viewpoint) in the opening.
5. Use a fast-start beginning rather than a slow-start beginning in which you provide obvious information to the reader.
6. Keep the beginning paragraph fairly short.
7. Make sure the beginning paragraph possesses unity and coherence.

Note how the first of the following two paragraphs fails to present good news in the beginning of a good-news letter. In contrast, observe how the reader's curiosity about the status of his or her order is quickly satisfied by the revised paragraph.

Change:	We appreciate your recent order for a variety of decorating accessories for your interior design studio. The items you ordered are sure to be popular among your clients. (This beginning paragraph fails to convey the good news first.)
To:	Your order for a variety of decorating accessories was shipped by UPS this morning. The items you ordered are sure to be popular among your clients. (The good news is now first.)

In a request letter, the opening sentence can present the request. In the first of the following two paragraphs, the reader has to read more than the opening to learn why she received a letter. In the revised paragraph, note how much more quickly the reader learns its purpose.

Change:	I am a student at Iowa College and am currently enrolled in a business finance course. One of the projects in the class is to make an in-depth financial analysis of a *Fortune* 500 company. I have selected your company for this project. (The main idea—which was to request an annual report from the selected company—is not even presented in the beginning paragraph.)
To:	Will you please send me an annual report for use in making a financial analysis of your company? Making a thorough analysis of the financial condition of a *Fortune* 500 company is one of the requirements for a business finance course I am enrolled in at Iowa College.

To open a disappointing-news letter with negative information intensifies a negative situation, as the first of the following two paragraphs illustrates. Psychological advantages result from delaying negative news until later in the letter as the following revision shows.

Change:	We are sorry to have to inform you that we are unable to open a charge account for you at Kelsey's Department Store. Unfortunately, you have too many liabilities in relation to your assets for you to qualify for a charge account. (A beginning like this will surely irritate the reader.)
To:	You will be pleased to learn that the credit references you listed on your credit application commented favorably on your bill-paying record. Several were also impressed with your promptness that has enabled you on numerous occasions to avoid interest charges. (A beginning like this will help put the reader in a more positive frame of mind before reading the disappointing news.)

We are not always inclined to read unsolicited mail unless something in it attracts our attention. For this reason, in persuasive messages, attention-getting beginnings are especially desirable. Note how the first of the following two paragraphs, which does nothing out of the ordinary, fails to capture the reader's attention, whereas the revised paragraph creates initial interest.

Change:	We are soliciting volunteers to donate an hour or two of their time each month to work at the information desk in Portsmouth Art Museum. We hope you will consider volunteering.
To:	What could be more exciting than helping direct visitors at the Portsmouth Art Museum to the location of the work of their favorite artist? You can share the excitement of our visitors by volunteering to work at the information desk in Portsmouth Art Museum an hour or two each month.

One of the most effective ways to ensure that your message will be read is to focus on the reader's needs, concerns, and questions. This prescription is violated when the pronoun *I* is used extensively. Although the pronoun *you* does not by itself guarantee the you-viewpoint, using it is a step in the right direction, as the second of the following two paragraphs indicates.

Change:	I will appreciate your signing the enclosed card and returning it to me as soon as possible. Once I have the signed release, I can begin the process of modifying your insurance policy. (The excessive usage of the I pronoun in this paragraph focuses attention on the writer rather than on the reader.)
To:	Will you please sign the enclosed card and return it to me as soon as possible? Doing so will enable me to change your insurance policy as you asked.

Slow-start beginnings also get in the way of your message being read. A paragraph that contains information obvious to the reader is, as indicated, an example of a slow-start beginning. Note how much more effective the second of the following two paragraphs is because it tells the reader something he or she does not already know.

Change:	We have received your letter of October 15 in which you asked for the name of the Arnson lawnmower dealer located closest to you. Bill's Hardware in Eli is our closest dealer to you. (This is a slow-start beginning because it provides information that is obvious to the reader—that his/her letter of October 15 has been received. If the letter had not been received, you would not be responding.)
To:	Bill's Hardware in Eli is your nearest Arnson lawnmower dealer. This dealer carries our complete line of Arnson lawn mowers.

Body Composition

The body of the message should be composed after the beginning paragraph is written but before the ending paragraph is completed.

Besides the elements of effective sentence and paragraph construction, correct grammar, and other aspects of good business communication that we described, you also need to focus on the content of your message. In the end, *what* you say is at least as important as *how* you say it. Each of the following chapters that refer to specific types of written business communication contains information to help you determine what material to include. Omitting the kinds of information suggested in these chapters may reduce the effectiveness of your messages.

Ending Paragraphs

The ending paragraph of your messages is apt to determine whether your reader complies with your wishes. In the ending, you have an opportunity to do two things: (1) concentrate on the action you want the reader to take (if appropriate); and (2) show courtesy toward the reader.

How can you improve the effectiveness of ending paragraphs?

Suggestions for improving the effectiveness of the ending paragraph of your messages are

1. State the desired action clearly and completely.
2. State who is to perform the desired action if it is to be performed by someone other than the reader.
3. State how the action is to be performed.
4. Make the action seem easy to perform.
5. State when the action is to be performed, if appropriate.
6. Include reader-benefit material, if appropriate.
7. Show appreciation to the reader, if appropriate. Remember, until the reader does something for you, thanking the reader is inappropriate.
8. Avoid the inclusion of negative information in the ending.
9. Offer to be of assistance, if appropriate.
10. Keep the ending paragraph as brief as realistically possible.

Note how the first of the following paragraphs avoids specifying clearly and completely the action the reader desires. The revised version removes any doubts the reader may have about what is the desired action.

Change:	Please let us hear from you.
To:	Just as soon as you sign and return to us the enclosed authorization card, we will be able to make the requested modifications to your retirement plan. (This paragraph is effective because it tells when, who, what, how, and why; in addition, it contains reader-benefit material.)

Note how the first of the following two paragraphs violates several of the suggestions for writing effective ending paragraphs. The revision corrects these problems.

Change:	Let me know when you would like to come for an interview.
To:	Please call me at 654-2347 early next week to let me know when you will be able to come for an interview. (This paragraph identifies who, what, where, when, and why.)

The negative information in the first of the following two ending paragraphs does not appear in the revision.

Change:	We regret that we do not have the information you requested. Best wishes for the successful completion of your project.
To:	Best wishes for the successful completion of your project. Your effort to obtain actual material for inclusion in your project is commendable. (The refusal, which was stated earlier in the letter, is not repeated in the closing paragraph.)

The premature statement of thanks in the first of the following two paragraphs is revised in the second paragraph to include a statement of appreciation.

> Change: Thank you for sending me the requested material.
> To: Your sending the requested material will be appreciated as I will be able to include more helpful information in the feasibility study you commissioned me to undertake. (This paragraph also shows reader benefit.)

The first of the following two paragraphs lacks courtesy as well as some of the other elements of effective ending paragraphs; the second paragraph is much improved.

> Change: Send your check to us today. Otherwise, you will lose your good credit rating.
> To: To maintain your good credit standing, please send us your check for $323.23 today. We appreciate your being our client. (Besides showing courtesy, this sentence contains reader-benefit material and tells the reader how much and when.)

An offer to be of assistance is appropriate in some closing paragraphs. In the first of the following two paragraphs, such an offer is missing. Note how much more effective the revised paragraph is because it corrects this omission.

> Change: Enclosed you will find the two reports you requested. (The writer should have notified the reader in the opening paragraph that he was sending the requested material. If the writer mentioned earlier in the letter that the material was being sent, he need not mention it again in the closing.)
> To: If you have any questions after reading the enclosed material, please phone me at (407) 377-2999.

EDITING

After you have completed the initial draft of your message, ideally you should put it aside for several hours before you begin its *editing,* which is the process of making needed changes in sentence structure and organization, content, and the mechanics (grammar, punctuation, and spelling) in your document. This pause allows you to look at your message with a fresh perspective. But a time limitation may not permit this. As you gain more writing experience, however, you will find the time lapse between initial drafting and editing usually grows shorter. Still, you may want some time between drafts when the complexity of your message increases or when the nature of the communication situation becomes more unpleasant.

The editing process is simplified if you evaluate your work, keeping in mind the following:

What questions should you evaluate your work against in the editing process?

1. Evaluate the message for effectiveness of communication.
   a. Have you accomplished your purpose for writing the message?
   b. Have you shown courtesy for the reader, regardless of the communication situation?
   c. Is the information in your message correct?
   d. Can you verify the accuracy of all facts and figures?

e. Is each word in your message necessary?
f. Is the information in your message clear?
g. Will your reader be able to understand your message?
h. Is the information in your message presented with as much specificity and concreteness as possible?
i. Is your message complete?
j. Have you answered all the questions asked by the reader?
k. Have you provided additional information that you believe the reader will appreciate having?

2. Evaluate for appropriate content.
   a. Have you followed the recommended plan for the type of message you are preparing?
   b. Have you included all of the information appropriate for the type of message?
   c. Can you justify the inclusion of each part of your message?
   d. Is the content appropriate for the reader?
3. Evaluate for the organizational structure.
   a. Are your ideas presented in a logical sequence?
   b. In a disappointing-news message, does the negative information appear *after* the beginning paragraph?
   c. In a good-news message, is the good news presented in the beginning?
   d. In a request message, is the request presented in the beginning?
   e. Is the ending paragraph appropriate for the message?
   f. Are related ideas grouped together?
   g. Is the material presented in a sequence appropriate for the type of message?
4. Evaluate for the effectiveness of the sentences and paragraphs.
   a. Is the construction of each sentence consistent with the principles of effective sentences?
   b. Is the construction of each paragraph consistent with the principles of effective paragraphs?
5. Evaluate for the correctness of grammar, punctuation, spelling, and word usage fundamentals.
   a. Is the grammar in each sentence correct?
   b. Is each sentence punctuated correctly?
   c. Is each word spelled correctly?
   d. Is each word used appropriately?

PROOFREADING

What should be checked during the proofreading process?

Uncorrected errors in their messages are costly to writers not only in terms of dollars but also in terms of image and respect. Errors are found during *proofreading,* which involves checking the document for omissions or inconsistencies in content as well as in spelling, grammar, and punctuation. Many readers think less of writers whose work contains errors. Even though you—the writer—may not type the final draft of a message, you—not the typist—are responsible for ensuring its accuracy.

As you proofread, you should check for the following:

1. Accuracy of dates, figures, amounts, and numbers
2. Misspelled words
3. Typographical errors
4. Omissions and additions of material
5. Proper sequencing of material
6. Correct format

In checking the accuracy of numerical information, comparing your numbers against the original numbers is wise. If messages are revised several times, errors can slip in during one of the revisions. Therefore, checking the accuracy of the numerical information of the final draft only against the numbers in the next-to-last draft may be inviting trouble. If the message contains considerable numerical information, having someone read the numbers in the final draft aloud as you compare these numbers against the original numbers is suggested. When the message contains mathematical calculations, recalculating the numbers to check their accuracy is also recommended.

Verifying the correct spelling of words is especially useful when (1) you dictated your message; (2) the typist is not a good speller; or (3) you are not a good speller. Programs that electronically check the spellings of words are available for most word processing equipment and other devices capable of performing word processing functions. These programs, however, are unable to differentiate between words with similar pronunciation but different spelling. An example is *principle* and *principal.*

The presence of typographical errors in your written messages also detracts from their effectiveness. Typographical errors, which are usually accidentally misspelled words, occur in the typing/keyboarding process because the typist depressed incorrect keys. For example, *receivef* is a typographical error, whereas *reciever* is more likely to be considered a misspelled word. Spelling checks are also helpful in locating typographical errors. When checking manually for typographical errors, you use the same process that you use for locating misspelled words.

Checking the context of material is also necessary because of the possibility that words are either omitted or added. An interruption in the typing/transcription process may result either in the omission or addition of words. To check the context, read the material word by word, comparing the last draft with the next-to-last draft.

You may decide to proofread a document twice: once for spelling and accuracy of numbers and another time for context. To try to accomplish both goals in one reading may result in your overlooking errors. Proofreading for accuracy is often best accomplished by examining the words or numbers character by character, although proofreading for context is done by reading the material word by word.

Interruptions in the typing/transcription process may also cause changes in the sequence of the material in the document. Proofreading for context may or may not enable you to locate such errors. This proofreading task is also best accomplished by comparing the last version of the document against the next-to-last version.

Material typed/keyboarded on word processing equipment greatly simplifies the proofreading process. Because the unchanged material prepared on such equipment is not rekeyboarded during each revision, the unchanged material will continue to be printed in the same way during each revision. Therefore, material correct in one version will be correct in subsequent versions. When material is typed on conventional typewriters, each revised draft has to be proofread as carefully as the first draft.

Exhibit 4-8 shows the standard proofreading marks that you should use in revising and/or proofreading your work.

DICTATING

One of the most effective ways for increasing the amount of time available to devote to other duties is to dictate rather than handwrite or compose at the keyboard during the origination process. Executives with efficient dictating skills find they can dictate much faster than they can write by hand and perhaps faster than they can compose at the keyboard.

Although dictation systems vary, the process is the same, regardless of the type of system used. In some systems, dictators input their dictation into the system via their office telephones; in others, a special dictation microphone is used. In some systems, the dictation is recorded in a centralized dictation system located in the word processing center; in other systems, the magnetic medium on which the dictation is recorded is hand carried to the individual responsible for transcribing the material.

To increase the efficiency of the dictation process, you will have to follow a set of instructions that all other dictators in the organization are also expected to follow. The

These standard proofreader's marks are helpful when you are revising and proofreading.

[delete mark]	Delete, omit word.
[close-up mark]	Close up.
#	Leave space.
¶	New paragraph.
No ¶	No paragraph.
[arrow] or [run-on mark]	Run on. Connects words when space has been left out or you have crossed out several lines of text.
(more)↑	Rest of paragraph continues on next page.
] [	Center.
(tr)	Transpose letters or words.
(10)	Spell out; don't abbreviate.
Stet	Let it stand — Let it stand (when copy appears to be deleted but you want it to remain).
lc or ¢	Lowercase capital letter.
C (triple underline)	Capitalize lowercase letter.
^,	Insert comma.
' V	Insert apostrophe (for single quotation mark).
" V	Insert quotation marks.
; V	Insert semicolon.
: V	Insert colon.
= V	Insert hyphen.
⊙	Insert period.
organization (triple underline)	Make all capitals.

Exhibit 4-8 Commonly used proofreading marks.

uniformity resulting from these instructions helps the individuals responsible for transcribing the material. An example of such instructions, presented in the form of a checklist, is illustrated in Exhibit 4-9.

If you are dictating a response to a letter you received, you may find marginal notes to be helpful, as illustrated in Exhibit 4-10. These notes can "jog" your memory about points or information you want to include in your response. Referring to notes is also helpful in the dictation of originating correspondence. Exhibit 4-11 shows notes used to dictate a letter of request.

What is the purpose of marginal notes?

Some of the errors found in the first transcribed draft of a dictated message result from carelessness in the dictation process. Exhibit 4-12a shows what the dictator intended to say in his letter; but carelessness resulted in the letter shown in Exhibit 4-12b.

A major portion of the material dictated in most organizations is in the form of letters, memos, and tables. You may find the following instructions helpful in dictating for each of these three categories:

BEFORE DICTATION

1. Identify yourself—name, position, and department.
2. State type of document dictation:
   Letter
   Memo
   Report
   Proposal
   Contract
   Form number
3. State number of copies.
4. State type of transcription.
   Rough draft
   Revision
   Final draft
5. State type of stationery to be used (letterhead, plain, and so forth).
6. State special instructions—format, spacing, and so forth.
7. State name and address of recipient—spell out.
8. State any mailing instructions.

DURING DICTATION

1. Spell
   All names and addresses
   Technical/unusual words
   Words commonly confused
2. Describe special punctuation and format, such as
   Underscoring
   Capitals
   Tabulations
   Indentations
   Paragraphing
3. Dictate closing, only if differing from Item 1, "Before" section.

AFTER DICTATION

1. Dictate names and addresses of persons receiving copies.
2. List enclosures.
3. Provide instructions for retention of magnetic medium.

Exhibit 4-9 Dictator's checklist.

Yes; Clear Schedule

Dear Ms. Leland:

Are you interested in speaking on the topic of your choice at the 45th Annual Convention of the Business Communication Association to be held in St. Louis on May 25? Your name was suggested to me by several individuals who have heard you make excellent presentations at other meetings.

1:30 Nonverbal Communication

The following session times are available: 10:30, 1:30, and 3:30. If you will be able to speak, please select whichever time best fits into your schedule, as well as choose the topic of your presentation.

Will not be able to stay for meal functions

Convention speakers are given a $200 honorarium, in addition to the reimbursement of travel expenses. Complimentary tickets are also given to speakers who are available to attend the various meal functions during the convention.

Your being able to speak at our convention will be greatly appreciated. Please let me know your decision as soon as possible.

Exhibit 4-10 Marginal notations.

Wood-Tone Computer Desk
- how much assembly required?
- adjustable height for Key board?
- freight charges from St. Louis to Chicago?
- Wood finishes?

answers needed in 3 weeks

Exhibit 4-11 Dictation notes.

How to Dictate a Standard Letter

1. This is (your name) of (office/division/department).
2. This letter is to be typed on letterhead, and (number) copies are required.
3. It is addressed to (spell proper names and give full addresses).
   For example:
   Mr. John Winchell (W-I-N-C-H-E-L-L)
   The Brownlee (B-R-O-W-N-L-E-E) Corporation
   2457 (two-four-five-seven) Enterprise (E-N-T-E-R-P-R-I-S-E)
   Avenue, Omaha, Nebraska 68540 (six-eight-five-four-zero)
4. Dear John.
5. Dictate the body of the letter, including paragraphs and punctuation, when possible.
6. Dictate the complimentary closing and your name and title.
7. (Number) enclosures that will be included.
8. Please send a copy of the letter to (name, title, and address).

a. Dictated

```
Ms. M. R. Pierre
7510 Hale
St. Louis, Missouri 67890

Dear Melissa:

Your belief that effective communication is one of the biggest problems of
business today is one I heartily share.

A great deal of effectiveness is lost in the simple mechanics of dictation.
Perhaps a good communications training program would have some value in your
organization.

Mr. Pitt of the X-L Company has developed an excellent dictation training
course. If you will contact him at MU-7-8018, he will be happy to give you some
suggestions.

How you approach this problem in your company is something about which I'm
anxious to learn.

Sincerely,

Jack Fiden
```

b. Transcribed

```
Dear Ms. Peer:
75 Tin Hall
St. Louis, Missouri 67890

Dear Ms. Peer:

Your belief that effective communication is one of the biggest problems of
business today is one I hardly share. A great deal of effectiveness is lost in
the simple mechanics of dictation. Perhaps a good communications training
program would have some value in your organization. Mr. Pit of the Excell
Company has developed an excellent dictation training course. If you call him
at MU 7-8810, he will be happy to give you some suggestions. How you approach
this problem in your company is something about which I am anxious to learn.

Sincerely,

Jack Fiden
```

Exhibit 4-12 Illustration of how errors are made.

How to Dictate a Memorandum

1. This is (your name) in (office/division/department).
2. This is a memorandum, and I will need (number) copies.
3. It is to be addressed to (name/title/department).
4. It is from (your name and title).
5. Dictate the subject and message, indicating paragraphs and punctuation when possible.
6. This memo will be accompanied by (number of) enclosures (or attachments).
7. Address an envelope to (name(s) and address(es) of recipient(s)).

How to Dictate a Table

1. This is (your name) in (office/division/department).
2. This is a table.
3. The title of the table is (title of table).
4. This table contains (number of) column headings. They are (name of column headings).

5. The longest line in each column contains (number of) spaces, respectively.
6. The first row of the table contains these numbers: (dictate numbers). The second row contains these numbers: (dictate numbers). The third row contains these numbers: (dictate numbers), and so on.

Many business writers find it useful to dicate draft copy that will be revised rather than final copy that cannot be revised. And most transcriptionists prefer to type from a recording than decipher an illegibly written draft. Reading and correcting each of your dictated messages is, therefore, important. You, not the transcriptionist, are responsible for ensuring the final copy is correct.

Proper use of the specialized dictation system within an office contributes immeasurably to the efficiency of the word processing system and, ultimately, to the effectiveness of the dictator. Well-developed skills in speaking clearly and giving understandable instructions to the transcriptionist also greatly enhance the efficiency of the word processing system.

SUMMARY

In planning to write, you must first determine your purpose and then consider your reader. You must also determine appropriate content.

Once you have planned your writing, your next step is to organize your material by outlining the topics. Then you detemine the appropriate order or sequence of topics.

The next step is the drafting process. During the actual writing, you need to be concerned about sentence and paragraph construction, as well as beginning and ending paragraphs and body composition.

Once the drafting is completed, you must edit your work. A number of suggestions are presented in this chapter that will enable you to edit more effectively. Once the final draft is prepared, proofreading is critical.

The development of good dictation skills will also help you save considerable origination time and enable you to originate work at times when a secretary is unavailable to take your dictation.

REVIEW QUESTIONS

1. In considering the reader of the message you are preparing to write, what factors should you take into consideration?
2. How can you increase your reader's receptivity to your message?
3. Why is the careful outlining of your message before beginning to write important?
4. To help determine the appropriate order of the topics you plan to discuss in your message, what questions should you ask yourself?
5. What is the most emphatic position of a complex sentence? A compound-complex sentence?
6. What is an expletive?
7. What are the two most common locations of topic sentences in paragraphs?
8. Identify several ways to improve the effectiveness of the beginning paragraph of a business letter.
9. Identify several ways to improve the effectiveness of the ending paragraph of a business letter.
10. In editing your document, what elements should you especially evaluate?
11. In the dictation process, how should you use marginal notes?

APPLICATION PROBLEMS

1. Assume you are about to write a letter requesting information about a new electronic stereo system you saw advertised. In the letter to the manufacturer of the system (Model No. K-80), you ask for answers about the following: the wattage and size of the speakers, the special features of the compact disk player, whether

the system has a tape deck, and the cost of the system. Prepare an outline of the material you plan to include in your letter.

2. Revise the following material into a paragraph, making sure to include a variety of sentence structures.

> James Vickers is president of Vickers, Inc. W. A. Jones is vice-president in charge of investments. I. A. Evans is vice-president in charge of systems. T. V. Pickens heads purchasing. J. M. Stewart runs the legal department. Their investment portfolio totals more than ten million dollars. A new computerized system has contributed to a streamlined operation. The purchasing department has been divided into five divisions under Pickens' leadership. Stewart's skill in negotiation has been beneficial in the company's efforts to buy out some of their suppliers.

3. Revise the following opening paragraph of a letter acknowledging the shipment of the customer's order.

> Your order of October 3 is appreciated. It will be sent tomorrow. I am sure you will find that the Christmas ornaments you ordered will sell quickly in the upcoming Christmas season.

4. Revise the following closing paragraph of a letter informing a credit applicant that her application is being denied.

> We regret that we cannot open a credit account for you at this time.

5. Compose a paragraph to accompany the following topic sentence, which you will use as the first sentence.

> Our Model 80, which is a new product in our television line, has become an instant success.

6. Compose a paragraph to accompany the following topic sentence, which you will use as the last sentence.

> Now you can see why we are so excited about our new Model 80 television set.

7. Using the proofreader's marks found in Exhibit 4-8, correct the following sentences:
   a. The Annual management confernce of ABC, Inc., being scheduled for December and you hotel is being considered for the cite.
   b. We are planing to use your the confernce facilities.
   c. The conference is tentatively scheduled for Dec. 10-14.
   d. Do think you that your facilities will accomodate 1200 participants?
   e. There is a banquet scheduled for the evening of December 12.

f. Your well known catering service has been highly recommended to us by others who have attended conferences at your facility.

g. I will appreciate your responding by July 1.

8. The following topics are to be included in a paper about word processing. Prepare a topical outline, paying particular attention to the proper sequencing of the topics. If it is useful, edit the wording of the topics.

The personnel component of word processing
The administrative support concept
The equipment component of word processing
Word processing defined
The cost-reduction advantage of word processing
The procedures component of word processing
Text-editing equipment
Early developments in word processing
The faster-turnaround advantage of word processing
The centralized structure of word processing
Dictation/recording equipment
The better-quality-of-work advantage of word processing
The integrated structure of word processing
Historical development of word processing
Word processing: A description
Copier equipment
The greater-productivity advantage of word processing
The special-purpose structure of word processing
The increased-efficiency advantage of word processing
The decentralized structure of word processing
Current developments in word processing

9. Use a tape recorder to record your dictation of the letter shown in Exhibit 4-12. As you dictate the letter, provide the necessary directions to the transcriber so that the letter, when transcribed, will be identical to the "dictated" version of the letter in Figure 4-12b.

5

Request Letters and Memos

After studying this chapter, you should be able to

1. Identify the letter plan used in writing each request letter in this chapter.
2. Identify the qualities of effective claim letters.
3. List situations for which the different types of credit-request letters are written.
4. Describe several ways to improve the effectiveness of letters requesting credit.
5. Prepare effective letters of the type discussed in this chapter.
6. Identify ways to improve the effectiveness of request-type memos.
7. Prepare effective memos of the type discussed in this chapter.

A variety of situations demand the preparation of request letters and memos. For example, if you are interested in obtaining information about a product from its manufacturer or information from the former employer of a job applicant, you will prepare a letter in which you request the desired information. This chapter describes the following types of request letters: inquiry, claims, orders, invitations, reservations, credit, and favors. Or perhaps you are interested in obtaining sales figures about a product your company manufactures. If you decide to make your request through a written document, you will probably prepare a request memo.

How do request letters differ from persuasive letters?

Request letters and memos are among the most common types of documents in the business world. Although these documents make requests of their recipients, they differ markedly from persuasive messages (sales letters, collection letters, and special request messages), which also make requests. The basic difference between request and persuasive messages is that request messages contain less motivationally oriented material. Recipients of request messages generally are more willing to comply with the asked-for action than are recipients of persuasive messages. Thus, motivationally oriented material designed to obtain compliance is simply not as important in a request message.

INQUIRY LETTERS

Letters of inquiry are a type of business message that asks the recipient for information or assistance. The two most common types of inquiry letters are those that request information about (1) products or services and (2) people.

Requesting Information about Products or Services

Organizations that receive letters of inquiry about their products or services consider their responses to these letters as effective public relations tools. Most organizations welcome letters of inquiry because of their impact on generating sales. Large organizations often employ individuals whose major job responsibility is preparing responses to inquiry letters.

What is your goal in preparing an inquiry letter?

Your goal in preparing inquiry letters is to make the recipient's response to your request as easy as possible. For the reasons previously identified, you need not be particularly concerned about motivating the recipient to respond. Rather, your main concern is to present your inquiry in the clearest possible manner so the recipient will be able to respond completely and accurately without your having to prepare additional correspondence.

The inquiry letter begins with the request rather than with explanatory material. Placing the request after the explanatory material makes for a slow-start opening, as in the first of the following examples. The revision corrects this problem.

Change: I am thinking of purchasing a new letter-quality printer for my ABC personal computer system. This printer would be used primarily when the computer is being operated as a word processor. I use the Electronic Word Processing software package. Will all of the F-10-80 printer functions be operational when using my computer system and word processing software?

To: Will all of the functions on the F-10-80 letter-quality printer be operational when using the Electronic Word Processing software on an ABC personal computer system?

Notice how much faster the revised version gets to the main purpose of the letter. The first version lacks conciseness and tells the reader something that can be easily inferred: the printer will be used primarily when the system is functioning as a word processor.

What question should be asked first in inquiry letters?

When requesting information about a product or service, you may have several specific questions to ask. The most important question is usually asked first, followed by less important questions. If you have a number of questions, you may want to put them in an enumerated list, as in the following example.

Could you please send information that answers the following questions about the S-R electronic typewriter:

1. Can the typewriter be used as a computer printer?
2. If so, does it require a serial or parallel interface?
3. What is the typewriter's memory capacity?
4. What is the printing speed of the typewriter?
5. Can a fabric ribbon be used on the device?

Where is explanatory material included in inquiry letters?

After opening with your request, add essential explanatory material. Explanatory material may include the reason for the request or information of use to the recipient in preparing a response. For example, assume you received the following letter.

> Will you please send me information about the activities available to families visiting the Jackson Hole area?
>
> I will appreciate your sending this information as soon as possible as we are planning a trip to Yellowstone Park this summer.

In responding to this letter, you will need to make several basic assumptions, which may or may not be correct, or send a letter seeking clarification. For example, if children are coming, what are their ages? Does the family prefer out-of-door or in-door activities? Does the family prefer strenuous or more sedentary-type activities? Is the family interested in nighttime as well as daytime activities? Including these details in the letter would have simplified the task of preparing a helpful response.

The following paragraph is a sample of an effective explanation section of an inquiry letter.

> The TAC computer system being considered comes with several software packages, including the Word Write word processing package. Currently, I need a word processing system but also need a typewriter for some of my work. Purchasing an electronic typewriter that can also be used as a computer printer will enable me to save several hundred dollars.

What type of closing should be used in inquiry letters?

The last section of the inquiry letter is an *action-oriented closing,* which suggests the action you wish the reader to take. This type of closing tends to produce better results than the familiar "I will appreciate your assistance" closing. When appropriate, enhancing the ease with which the recipient can respond is advised. You may also want to provide the date by which you wish to have the reply to your request. Notice the difference between the following two closings.

> Change: I will appreciate your sending me the requested information.
>
> To: Replying to these questions by June 15 will enable me to decide whether the S-R electronic typewriter will meet my needs. Your answers to my questions, which can be sent on the pre-addressed card I'm enclosing, will be appreciated.

What is the suggested plan for inquiry letters?

In sum, the suggested plan for an inquiry letter includes the following elements:

1. An opening that contains the primary request and secondary requests
2. An explanation that includes the reasons for the request or provides additional helpful background information
3. A closing that suggests the action you wish the recipient to take, that makes action easy to take (if appropriate), and that expresses appreciation for assistance

Exhibit 5-1 shows an ineffective letter requesting information about a database software program. Exhibit 5-2 is an improved version of the letter. Note how much more specific the request is in Exhibit 5-2.

Requesting Information about a Person

What type of opening is appropriate when requesting information about a person?

Beginning an inquiry letter with your request is a little abrupt when your request concerns information about a person. For example, a company considering a job applicant often requests information from at least one previous employer about the quality of the

I am interested in learning more about your database software program. Please send me any information you may have about this software program.	A slow-start opening.
I plan to use the database software to maintain a variety of different types of records.	A section containing a weak explanation about why the information is desired.
Thank you for sending this information to me.	A closing that "thanks in advance."

Exhibit 5-1 Ineffective letter requesting information about a product.

Will you please send me information that answers the following questions about your D-B database software program: 1. Will the program operate on a DECCA 8000 computer? 2. Is this software program interactive? 3. How many fields can be created for each record? 4. Does this software package come with a teach disk? 5. Do you provide a toll-free number for user support?	A fast-start opening that lists questions for which answers are desired.
This database program will be used to maintain the following types of employee records: name, Social Security number, present job title, years with the company, years in present position, number of years of formal education, and present salary.	A section that contains explanatory material.
A prompt response to this request will enable me to decide which database program is most suitable. Your answering these questions, in addition to your providing any other information that might be helpful, will be greatly appreciated.	A courteous, action-oriented closing.

Exhibit 5-2 Effective letter requesting information about a product.

applicant's work performance. Beginning the letter with the first of the following two paragraphs is abrupt, whereas the revised paragraph, by preparing the reader for the request, is more effective.

Change: Does William Duff work well with others? Is his work always well done? Does he get his work done on time? In his application for a job as assistant personnel manager, he provided your name as a reference.

To: Mr. William Duff, who has listed your name as a reference, is being considered for the position of assistant personnel manager. Will you please provide answers to the following questions:

1. How well does he work with others?
2. How effective are his oral and written communication skills?
3. How would you rate the quality of his work in comparison with your other employees?
4. How well does he meet deadlines?
5. How do you rate his enthusiasm and initiative?
6. Why did he leave your company?

The wording of the questions in an inquiry letter largely determines how much information you are likely to receive in an answer. If you desire more than a yes or no answer, you need to structure the questions to elicit a less succinct response. For example, a yes or no answer is probably all that would have been provided had the first question in the previous example been "Does he work well with others?"

When selecting questions for letters requesting information about the work performance of former employees, make certain the questions are bona fide. That is, restrict your questions to their work performance. Unless you can prove that your question relates to job performance, it should not be included. Asking questions about job applicants that are unrelated to their job performance may have legal repercussions.

The explanation section of a letter inquiring about a job applicant can also include a discussion of pertinent job requirements. With this information, the recipient will be in a better position to judge whether the applicant seems qualified. Note how the first of the following two paragraphs contains too little detail on job requirements, whereas the second paragraph is more effective.

What should be included in the explanatory section of letters that request information about a job applicant?

Change: A customer service representative performs a variety of duties that include the following: interacting with customers and other employees.

To: Among the duties performed by a customer service representative are the following: (1) answering questions asked by customers, (2) referring customers to others who can answer their questions, (3) keeping detailed records about the nature of the service provided, (4) keeping abreast of new developments likely to stimulate customers' questions, and (5) interacting with other employees.

The first of the following two paragraphs contains a weak, open-ended closing. The revision shows the benefits of using an action-oriented closing with a suggested reply date when requesting information about a person. You may also wish to affirm your intention to treat as confidential any information you receive.

What should be included in the closing of letters in which information about a person is requested?

Change: Your assistance will be greatly appreciated.

To: Your answers to the above questions will be helpful in assessing Ms. Rickardo's suitability for the position of customer service representative. Having this input by June 15 will enable us to maintain our schedule for filling this position. Information you provide about Ms. Rickardo, which we will keep confidential, will be greatly appreciated.

The suggested plan for a letter requesting information about a job applicant includes the following:

What is the suggested plan for letters that request information about a person?

1. An opening mentioning the name of the person who has given the reader's name as a reference
2. A list of the questions you would like to have answered
3. A brief discussion of the common duties of the job for which the applicant has applied
4. A courteous, action-oriented closing

Exhibit 5-3 illustrates a poorly prepared letter that inquires about a person's work performance; Exhibit 5-4 is an effective revision of the same letter. Specific answers are likely to be obtained for the specific questions asked in Exhibit 5-4.

We have a vacancy on our staff for a sales representative. John Jack, a former employee of yours, has applied for this position and has used your name as a reference.	An opening void of the request for information.
Would you please provide me with information that will be helpful in deciding whether or not to hire Mr. Jack?	A section that contains a delayed request for vague information.
I shall appreciate your assistance.	A closing that lacks action orientation.

Exhibit 5-3 Ineffective letter requesting information about a person.

Davidson Corp.
8993 Grant Avenue Royal Oak, MI 48723
(517) 442-9028

June 25, 199x

Ms. Janet Graham, Sales Manager
Anderson Manufacturing Corp.
1232 Main Street
Detroit, MI 48283

Dear Ms. Graham:

Mr. John Jack, a former employee of yours, listed your name as a reference on his application for a sales representative position in our company. Your providing answers to the following questions will enable me to better assess his suitability for employment:	An opening that contains background information and the primary request.
1. How well does Mr. Jack work with others? 2. How well developed are Mr. Jack's oral and written communication skills? 3. How well developed are Mr. Jack's leadership skills? 4. In comparison with other employees of yours, how would you rate Mr. Jack's performance? 5. Why did Mr. Jack leave your company? 6. If you had an opportunity to do so, would you re-employ Mr. Jack? Why?	A section that identifies the desired information.
Among the duties commonly performed by our sales representatives are the following: serving our present clients, acquiring new clients, and preparing a variety of reports.	A section that contains a discussion of the duties to be performed by the job holder.
The information you provide, which will be held in strict confidence, will enable us to better assess Mr. Jack's qualifications for a sales representative position. Because we hope to fill this position by August 1, receiving your input by July 10 will be appreciated.	An action-oriented closing that mentions the confidential handling of information.

Sincerely,

William F. Smith
Human Resources Manager
fg

Exhibit 5-4 Effective letter requesting information about a person.

Requesting Information about Credit Applicants

Inquiry letters can also request information about *credit applicants*—individuals who wish to be able to purchase goods or service in exchange for a promise to pay the seller at a specified future date. Credit reports by credit bureaus are often used to obtain pertinent information about credit applicants. Credit references also provide similar information.

A fast-start opening (1) requests answers to questions and (2) mentions the reader was listed as a reference on the applicant's credit application. Note how jumpy the first paragraph is compared to the second paragraph.

What should be included in the opening of letters that request information about a credit applicant?

Change: We have received Jack Chun's application for a charge account. He listed your name as a credit reference on his credit application. Will you please respond to the following questions?

To: Will you please respond to the following questions about Jack Chun, who listed your name as a credit reference on his application for credit?

When soliciting information from credit references, the questions are similar to those that follow. In some cases, the questions are printed on a separate form; in other cases, the questions are incorporated into the letter. A fill-in-the-blank format, such as the following, is easier for the respondent to prepare a faster response.

1. How long has this individual had a credit account with your company?
2. What is the credit limit this individual has been extended?
3. What is the largest amount of credit ever extended to this individual?
4. Has this individual ever been delinquent in paying his/her credit account? No______; Yes______. If you answered "yes," how many times?______ What is the average length of time this individual's credit account has been delinquent?
5. What is today's balance of this individual's account?

The statement that assures the confidential treatment of information can be incorporated into the closing as in the following.

Any information you can provide will be treated confidentially. Receiving the desired information by June 10, which will be greatly appreciated, will enable us to expedite Mr. Chun's application.

The suggested plan for an inquiry letter of this type includes the following elements:

What is the suggested plan for letters that request information about credit applicants?

1. An opening mentioning the applicant's name and that the recipient of the letter was listed as a credit reference on the applicant's application
2. A list of the questions you would like to have answered
3. A statement that assures the confidential treatment of the information
4. An action-oriented closing that expresses appreciation to the individual for providing the credit reference

Your answering the following questions about the creditworthiness of Sally Brown, who has listed your name as a reference, will help us assess her suitability for a Skinner's charge account.	An opening that mentions the credit applicant's name and that requests information about the applicant.
1. What is the credit limit you currently extend to Ms. Brown? 2. How long has Ms. Brown had a credit account with your company? 3. What is the maximum amount of credit you have ever extended to Ms. Brown? 4. How many times in the last three years has Ms. Brown been delinquent in paying her account? 5. What is the current amount of credit extended to Ms. Brown?	A section that presents questions designed to facilitate the reader's ease in responding.
You have our assurance that this information will be treated confidentially.	A section that assures the confidentiality of information.
Your sending answers to these questions within the next 10 days will be appreciated. If we can ever reciprocate, please let us know.	An action-oriented closing that offers to return the favor.

Exhibit 5-5 Effective letter in which credit information is requested.

Exhibit 5-5 shows a sample letter requesting credit information from a credit reference. Note that specific questions are asked.

General Inquiry Letters

Letters of general inquiry are messages in which the writer asks the reader for answers to general rather than specific questions or seeks general rather than specific information. Except for the way you state your request, the other sections of general inquiry letters are similar to the types of inquiry letters previously discussed.

Although the opening of a general inquiry letter can be less specific than the opening of more precise inquiry letters, try to avoid preparing an opening so general that the recipient will have difficulty responding. The first of the following two paragraphs illustrates this problem. The revised version is more helpful to the recipient in preparing a response.

Change:	Do you have packets available to individuals visiting your city? If so, please send me one.
To:	Please send me information about activities to do and historical sites to see while families visit in the Detroit area.

The first opening does not make clear that suggested activities should be family oriented, whereas the second opening directly mentions this fact. In addition, although the recipient of the first letter can probably surmise the desired information concerns things to see and do in the Detroit area, the revised version explicitly mentions Detroit. Both openings get to the point quickly; however, the revised opening, because of its greater specificity, is more helpful to the person preparing the response.

The next paragraph after the opening explains why the requested information is important. Note how the following paragraph includes several pertinent details.

Planning to accompany me to Detroit for a convention I am attending June 14–18 are my wife and two sons, ages 14 and 12. While I am attending daytime meetings, they plan to do as much sight-seeing in the Detroit area as possible. They will not have access to a car; therefore, they will have to depend on public transportation to get around.

Without the details in this paragraph, the writer of the request may receive in reply a quantity of useless information. With these details, the recipient has a better idea of the type of information that would be helpful to the person making the request.

The suggested plan for the general inquiry letter includes the following elements:

1. An opening that contains the request
2. An explanation that includes the reasons for the request or that provides additional background information helpful to the recipient in complying with the request
3. A courteous, action-oriented closing

The weaknesses in the general inquiry letter shown in Exhibit 5-6 have been eliminated in the improved version shown in Exhibit 5-7. Note the number of helpful details included in Exhbit 5-7.

Included in Checklist 5-1 is information that will help you prepare effective inquiry letters.

Exhibit 5-6 Ineffective general inquiry letter.

Letter	Comment
I am interested in obtaining information about the Delta office copier I recently saw advertised in an office publication.	An opening with a vaguely worded request for information about a product.
Until now, my office could not justify the purchase of a copier. Rental was more feasible. Now, it appears that we may be able to justify purchasing a copier.	A section that contains a weak explanation of the reason for the request.
I will appreciate your assistance.	A weak closing.

Exhibit 5-7 Effective general inquiry letter.

Letter	Comment
Please send me the illustrated promotional packet mentioned in your current Delta Max office copier ad.	An opening that requests specific information about a specific product.
The feasibility of purchasing a copier is being investigated for use in an office in which 350-500 copies are made per month. The copier will also need to be capable of reducing and enlarging material.	A section that presents a discussion of important background information.
Your sending the requested materials by August 15 will be appreciated as I plan to make a purchasing decision within the next few weeks.	An action-oriented closing.

OPENING

1. Is the inquiry stated in the opening sentence—or at least in the opening paragraph?
2. If multiple requests are made, are they listed in order of importance, with the primary request listed first, followed by the secondary requests?
3. If more than a yes or no answer is desired, will the wording of your request enable you to obtain what you desire?
4. Is the wording of the request stated clearly so that the reader will know exactly what is being asked of him or her?

MIDDLE

1. Is a sufficient amount of background information provided, enabling the reader to comply with your request?
2. If appropriate, does the information you include in the middle section provide sufficient justification for your inquiry?
3. Has information been included to help the reader realize the benefit of complying with the request?

CLOSING

1. Is the closing courteous?
2. Does the closing briefly mention the action desired of the reader?
3. If a deadline is a critical factor, has the deadline been stated?
4. Have any special measures been taken to enable the reader to respond more easily?

Checklist 5-1 Letters of inquiry.

CLAIM LETTERS

Customer claims and requests for adjustments can be expected in today's high-volume business operations. With business transactions, as with other human activities, errors occur. Regardless of how much effort employees put into error-free operations, some errors will occur. The manner in which an organization deals with the claims it receives will affect its reputation.

A *claim letter* is a message designed to inform its recipient about the writer's dissatisfaction with a product or service. Organizations especially welcome receiving claim letters when the nature of a problem situation is likely to produce legitimate complaints from other customers. Remedying the situation that causes a complaint before it becomes a monstrous problem for the organization is a highly desirable business practice.

Bases for Claims

Routine claims about small sums of money are easily adjusted. Claims arising because of defective products are actually small in number; a greater number of claims occur because merchandise fails to meet expected quality standards. Although the seller may not be at fault for the defective product, the disappointed buyer naturally directs the claim to the company from which the item was purchased. Responsible business firms usually take immediate steps to settle claims and to make adjustments.

What are the bases for claims about service?

Claims against service connected with purchases are far more common than claims against products. The following list summarizes the bases for service-oriented claims:

1. Merchandise not received
2. Part of the merchandise not received
3. Incorrect merchandise received
4. Substituted merchandise not wanted
5. Damaged merchandise received
6. Merchandise received too late
7. Merchandise sent to wrong address
8. Error made in price of merchandise

9. Error made in discount
10. Error made in statement
11. Charge included for goods returned
12. Statement received for bill already paid
13. Employees demonstrated incompetence or rudeness

Included in Communication Capsule 5-1 are suggestions for improving the effectiveness of claim letters.

Communication Capsule 5-1 Qualities of Effective Claim Letters

Before you begin the process of preparing a claim letter, you will want to be familiar with the following qualities of an effective claim letter:

1. An effective claim letter does not threaten. To threaten in a claim letter shows a lack of good judgment on the part of the writer.
2. An effective claim letter presents all the facts relevant to the situation. A complete discussion of the analysis and/or background of the situation will help the letter recipient when preparing a response.
3. The writer of an effective claim letter does not take his or her anger out on the recipient—who most likely had nothing to do with the writer's dissatisfaction with the product or service.
4. An effective claim letter, by containing you-attitude and reader-benefit material, will help its recipient realize the advantage of making an adjustment.
5. An effective claim letter makes a definite request, such as one of the following:
   a. Replacement of the product or service
   b. Partial or full refund of the purchase price of the product or service
   c. Replacement shipment containing the desired merchandise
   d. Repair of the defective product
   e. Cancellation of an order or a portion of the order
   f. Correction of an error in billing, such as overcharging for merchandise, tax, shipping, and so forth
   g. Clarification of a procedure
6. An effective claim letter conveys the assumption that the company/organization wants to comply with your requested adjustment.
7. An effective claim letter contains a realistic, honest, and fair adjustment request.

Structure of Effective Claim Letters

Carefully planned claim letters encourage the recipient to take a specific action designed to benefit the writer. To ensure such action, your first concern as a writer is to state clearly, specifically, and completely the nature of your claim. Refer to your order or invoice number, date of the order or invoice, missed delivery dates, and other specific reference material the reader needs to assess the validity of your claim. If possible, include photocopies of invoices or sale slips. The reader typically wants answers to one or more of the following questions: Exactly what happened? In what way was the company negligent in providing the desired goods or services? Precisely which merchandise was omitted from the order? How did the original order read?

What is your main concern in writing an effective claim letter?

Many claim letters are written by people angry at the mistake that has caused them to write. If you let anger seep into your letter, however, it will be counterproductive. Instead, remember that the primary purpose of a claim letter is to stimulate action that will rectify an error or compensate for a loss. The chances of your receiving a satisfactory adjustment will improve if you avoid antagonizing the reader. Thus, you should never make disparaging remarks about the quality of products or services you received.

What is the primary purpose of claim letters?

The opening paragraph in a claim letter should explain to the reader why you are writing and what you desire. Note the difference between the two opening paragraphs that follow. In the first paragraph, the inclusion of disparaging remarks about product quality delays the request. The revised version is more direct, which is a desirable characteristic for the opening of a claim letter.

What should be included in the opening of claim letters?

Change: Had I known on October 5 what I know now about the quality (or lack thereof) of your blank cassette tapes, I would not have purchased a box of 12 tapes. In fact, I would not have purchased even one tape.

To: On October 5, I purchased a box of 12 blank Ajax-brand cassette tapes that are being returned, along with a request for a cash refund of $45.48.

What are the characteristics of the explanatory materials included in claim letters?

After you identify your request in the opening paragraph, you should present your explanation in an impersonal and courteous manner and as precisely and directly as possible. Notice the tonal differences between the following two paragraphs.

Change: Tapes of the quality of those I purchased should never be allowed on the market. The subtle sounds in the music I want to record cannot be detected on playback. In addition, on playback, I noticed distracting interference that I do not get when using higher-quality tapes. Perhaps this tape would be suitable for use on a child's recorder—but never for a professional musician.

To: All of my professional appearances are recorded for use in the piano classes I teach at Oakdale College. Because my students learn much from these recorded tapes, recording clarity is essential. The three tapes I used did not produce the desired clarity, especially in the playback of the subtle sounds. The tape also contains distracting background noise that cannot be recorded over or erased.

Also useful is the inclusion of you-attitude material in a claim letter when such material is appropriate for the situation. Be careful, however; inappropriate you-attitude material often weakens a claim letter more than does the absence of you-attitude material. Including material similar to that in the first of the following two paragraphs obviously reduces the effectiveness of a claim letter. In contrast, the revision includes appropriate you-attitude material.

Change: I believe we all benefit by having the shortcomings of our products or services pointed out. By overcoming these shortcomings, we can improve our relationships with our customers or clients.

To: Perhaps you will want to test the remaining nine unopened tapes to determine whether they are like the three that were used. So you can also hear the distracting background noise, I did not erase the material recorded on the three tapes.

What type of closing is appropriate for claim letters?

The closing of effective claim letters should suggest how you want your claim met, leaving no doubt in the reader's mind about the action you desire. The first of the following two closings is ineffective because it is not action oriented and contains overused and worn-out terminology. The action-oriented nature of the revised closing is far more effective.

Change: Your prompt attention to this matter will be greatly appreciated.

To: Because I have replaced these tapes with others, I will appreciate your quickly refunding the purchase price of the 12 tapes being returned.

What is the suggested plan for claim letters?

The suggested plan for a claim letter includes the following elements:

1. A request that mentions the desired adjustment

2. An explanation that provides important information to justify the need for an adjustment
3. A section that contains you-attitude material (if appropriate)
4. A courteous, action-oriented closing that mentions the desired adjustment

The claim letter illustrated in Exhibit 5-8 is not likely to enhance the relationship between the writer and the recipient. The weaknesses inherent in Exhibit 5-8 are removed from the revised version found in Exhibit 5-9. Notice the appropriate you-attitude material in the third paragraph of Exhibit 5-9.

Checklist 5-2 can be used to improve the effectiveness of claim letters.

Exhibit 5-8 Ineffective claim letter.

Letter	Comment
Let's see if you can stand behind your service better than the quality of products you manufacture. The third time the Transparency Maker was used that we purchased from you last month, it malfunctioned and has malfunctioned four more times since then. Obviously, we received a lemon that I am returning to you—along with a request that it be exchanged for a new machine.	A curt opening that contains a delayed request for the adjustment.
A machine as undependable as this one does not have much going for it. We simply cannot afford to keep such an undependable machine. It seems as if the machine was typically inoperable at the times when it was most needed.	A section that contains a weak discussion about why the adjustment is desired; lacks you-attitude material.
I will appreciate your prompt attention to the replacement of the Transparency Maker that is being returned.	A weak closing.

Exhibit 5-9 Effective claim letter.

Letter	Comment
The Transparency Maker purchased from you on December 12 is being returned. We are requesting that it be replaced with a new Maker.	An opening that presents the desired adjustment.
On five occasions during the month that we have had the Maker, it was inoperable at critical times. Because we purchased the machine primarily to make transparencies on very short notice, several of our executives were severely inconvenienced when they were unable to make transparencies for use during their presentations. When the Maker is inoperable, we either must use an outside service or do without the desired transparencies.	A section that provides important details about the need for the adjustment.
The concern your company has for its customers convinces me that you will want us to own a Maker worthy of its excellent reputation.	A section that incorporates you-attitude material.
Your replacing the Maker soon will be appreciated so our executives have available a fast and efficient transparency-making service.	A courteous, action-oriented closing.

OPENING
1. Have you stated in the opening paragraph, preferably in the opening sentence, the nature of your claim?
2. Have you avoided in the opening paragraph any expression of anger or disgust with the product or service about which you are requesting an adjustment?
3. Have you been honest and fair in your statement regarding your request?

MIDDLE
1. Is your discussion of the problem with the product or service stated factually and nonemotionally?
2. Is your discussion of the problem without sarcasm, hostility, or threats?
3. Have you included a sufficient amount of background information to help the reader become familiar with the problem?
4. Have you conveyed the assumption that the company/organization to which you are writing will want to comply with your request?
5. Have you included copies of any documentation the reader may need during the review of your situation?

CLOSING
1. Is your closing courteous?
2. Have you briefly summarized the nature of your request?

Checklist 5-2 Claim letters.

LETTERS REQUESTING CREDIT

Requests for credit and requests for credit information about an individual are usually transmitted on forms specifically designed to obtain the needed information. *Letters requesting credit* are messages often prepared by businesses when they wish to obtain goods or services in exchange for their promise to pay for them at a specified future date. The letter requesting credit may be accompanied by an order for merchandise.

Among the types of letters pertaining to the request for credit covered in this section are the following:

1. Routine request for credit
2. Combined credit request and order
3. Routine request for additional information from a credit applicant

A fourth type of letter related to a request for credit—requesting information from credit references—was discussed earlier in this chapter. (Exhibit 5-5 shows an example of such a letter.)

Credit bureaus, which are found in all parts of the country, significantly decrease the investigative work the credit-granting company does prior to making a credit decision. The first time people apply for credit, information about their background will be collected and stored in the computer files of a credit bureau.

What types of information about individuals do credit bureaus collect?

The type of information collected by the credit bureau typically includes an individual's name, current address, age, marital status, bill-paying characteristics, bank references, employment history, divorces, number of dependents, bankruptcy activity, tax liens, and court actions. The information stored in the computer is periodically updated, which enables businesses to obtain up-to-date information when making credit decisions.

Routine Requests for Credit

When using a letter to request credit, you have two options: (1) to send a credit-request letter without placing an order or (2) to send a letter combining a request for credit with an order. In this section we discuss letters requesting credit without an order; in the next, we discuss letters combining the request for credit with an order.

What type of opening is appropriate for credit-request letters?

A fast-paced opening is desirable when preparing letters requesting credit without an order. Notice the difference between the pace of the two openings in the following two paragraphs. In the first paragraph, too many details get in the way of the request. In the second, the opening paragraph contains only the request.

> Change: My family and I recently moved to San Antonio from Miami, where we resided for the last 15 years. The reason for the move was to take advantage of a promotional opportunity within Drummond Corporation, which has been my employer for more than 20 years.
>
> To: Will you please open a charge account for my wife and me in the names of
> Mary B. Brown
> David S. Brown
> 1819 Darvin Avenue
> San Antonio, TX 58764

After the opening, you will want to include relevant information to help the recipient make a positive decision about your creditworthiness. Included in this section is information about the length of time in your present location, length of time in your former location, names and addresses of credit references, place of employment, job title, and annual income. In addition, you may want to provide the name of the bank where you have a checking account, as well as that of your former bank if you have lived in your new location only a short time. The following paragraph illustrates how to pull together specific information.

What type of information should be included in the middle sections of credit-request letters?

> Last month we moved here from our former residence at 2839 Virginia Street in Miami, Florida, where we had lived for 15 years. The move was made because of a promotional transfer by my employer of 20 years, the Drummond Corporation. As a branch manager, I earn $53,500 annually. Our checking account (No. 33-456-867) is at the San Antonio National Bank. We previously banked at the First National Bank of Miami. While living in Miami, we had charge accounts at the following stores:
>
> Dillinger's
> 12 Main Street
> Miami, FL 02912
>
> Deloy Department Store
> 22 Main Street
> Miami, FL 02912
>
> J. Markums,
> 18 Broadway Ave.,
> Miami, FL 02912

An appropriate closing should offer to provide additional information considered useful by the reader for making a decision about the credit applicant. Note how the following closing makes clear the writer's cooperative attitude:

What type of closing is appropriate for credit-request letters?

> Please let me know if I can provide you with additional information that might be helpful in making a credit decision.

The suggested plan for a credit-request letter includes the following elements:

What is the suggested plan for credit-request letters?

1. An opening requesting credit
2. A section providing relevant information for determining applicant's creditworthiness
3. A courteous, action-oriented closing

Exhibit 5-10 shows an ineffective routine request for credit. Exhibit 5-11 is an improved version of the letter.

Combined Request for Credit and Order Letter

When preparing a letter combining a request for credit with an order, you should include the essential elements of an order letter and a letter requesting credit. The sug-

My wife and I are interested in opening a charge account at Dillmans Department Store. Would you please open an account for us?	A slow-start opening.
We lived in San Diego from 1975 until just recently when we moved here. We had charge accounts at the following stores in San Diego: Drake Department Store, J. L. Jackson Department Store, and Knapps.	A section that presents a limited amount of background information.
Because we enjoy the convenience of charge-account shopping, will you please open an account for us as soon as possible?	An action-oriented closing.

Exhibit 5-10 Ineffective credit-request letter.

Please open a charge account for my wife, Ellen S. Brown, and me, John D. Brown.	A fast-start opening that presents the request.
Transferred here recently by my employer, the Dickson Manufacturing Company, I am the plant manager in the new Dickson facility that just opened. Before we moved, I worked at the Dickson Plant in San Diego for ten years. Our address for the last five years was 4539 Acron Avenue, San Diego, CA 87382.	A section that provides important details that will be helpful in making a credit decision.
The following information should be helpful in assessing our creditworthiness: Annual income: $72,000; Present bank: Austin National Bank (Account No. 334-3567); Former bank: San Diego National Bank (Account No. 43338-2398); Present monthly mortgage: $650; Average monthly revolving charge-account balance: $235. In addition, while living in San Diego, we had charge accounts at the following stores: Drake Department Store 1 Main Street San Diego, CA 87380 Knapps 520 South Main San Diego, CA 87380 J. L. Jackson Department Store Crossroads Mall San Diego, CA 87389	A section that provides additional important details.
Please let me know if you need additional information in making a credit decision.	A courteous, action-oriented closing.

Exhibit 5-11 Effective credit-request letter.

gested plan for a combined credit-request and order letter contains the following elements:

What is the suggested plan for combined credit-request and order letters?

1. A fast-start opening that refers to your order and your desire to have it filled on a credit basis
2. A clear identification of items being ordered
3. Information necessary to encourage the recipient to make a positive decision about your creditworthiness
4. A courteous, action-oriented closing

Exhibit 5-12 is an example of a combined credit-request and order letter. Note that all of the important elements are included.

Letters Requesting Additional Information from a Credit Applicant

Occasionally, companies require additional information about the applicant before making a credit decision. Because asking for this letter is not a routine request for additional information, it should be written in a low-key, nonoffensive manner. Requests for additional information are generally made after the applicant has returned a completed application to the company.

Opening this type of letter with the direct request is generally considered too blunt. A preferred beginning is to express gratitude or appreciation to the individual for submitting an application. Note in the two following openings the more positive tone of the revision.

What type of opening is appropriate for letters in which additional credit information is requested?

Change: Would you please send us an up-to-date list of your outstanding charge account balances? The data we received with your application were several months old.
To: Your interest in opening a charge account at Bullinger's of Oklahoma City is greatly appreciated.

The opening is followed with an identification of the desired information. In discussing this request, you should avoid hurting the recipient's feelings or making him or her feel guilty or threatened. The first of the following two paragraphs on the next page establishes an unnecessary negative tone, whereas the information in the revised version is presented much more tactfully.

Exhibit 5-12 Effective combined credit-request and order letter.

Please open a charge account for Bill's Hardware and Paint Store and then ship on credit the following items.

A fast-start opening that mentions the order and the desire to open a credit account.

QUANTITY	CAT. NO.	DESCRIPTION	UNIT PRICE	TOTAL
4	189873	Power Saws	$49.98	$199.92
3	278171	Power Sanders	51.89	155.67
				$355.59

A section that clearly identifies the items being ordered.

Because I anticipate placing an order several times each month, being able to purchase merchandise on credit would add to the convenience of my operations. Letters of credit and other information helpful in your making a credit decision are obtainable from my bank, The First National Bank, 3451 South Street, Oklahoma City, OK 76488. Should you need additional information for use in evaluating my credit background, please write me.

A section that provides essential information used in determining credit worthiness.

Receiving the power tools by September 27 will be appreciated as I am planning a "Fall-Fixit Sale" that begins on September 30.

A courteous, action-oriented closing.

Change: We restrict our accounts to those whose liabilities do not exceed a certain percentage of their assets. We are sure you can appreciate the restricting of our charge accounts to those who are worthy of credit. To do otherwise would obviously result in our having to increase the cost of our merchandise in order to cover the losses incurred by extending credit to individuals who are not worthy of credit.

To: Obtaining an up-to-date list of your liabilities will enable us to calculate accurately several important financial ratios. Granting credit to individuals whose ratios are within a specified range benefits all of our customers because we are able to maintain merchandise prices at a level lower than otherwise would be possible.

What is the purpose of resale material in letters in which additional credit information is requested?

The inclusion of *resale material*—wording designed to bolster the confidence of the applicant in the company—can be especially effective in letters requesting additional information about a credit applicant. You should always include it, if possible, in the letters you write. The following paragraph effectively uses resale material.

Bullinger's of Oklahoma City has just received word of its selection for the "Yorktowne Distributor of the Year Award." This prestigious award is given annually to the distributor of Yorktowne products that has the largest annual percentage increase in sales. The significant increase in sales experienced by our company is attributed to our customers' growing awareness of the quality of Yorktowne products.

What type of closing is appropriate for letters in which additional credit information is requested?

The appropriate closing for a letter requesting additional credit information is action oriented. It explains what will occur upon receipt of the requested information. In addition, suggesting a specific date for submitting the requested information may help you obtain the requested information more quickly. Note how the revision between these two closings tells the reader specifically what to do to help you make your decision immediately.

Change: We look forward to hearing from you.

To: If you send us the requested information by July 28, we should be able to make a credit decision by August 15. Please let me know if you would like us to delay shipping your recent order until after your credit application has been processed or whether you prefer to send a check for $198.43, which will enable us to send your order immediately.

What is the suggested plan for letters in which additional credit information is requested?

The suggested plan for a letter requesting additional credit information includes the following elements:

1. An opening expressing appreciation for the applicant's interest in a credit account, as well as appreciation, if relevant, for the order he or she placed
2. An identification, stated in an impersonal, courteous way, of the type of information you need to make the credit decision
3. Inclusion of resale material to bolster the applicant's confidence in the writer's company
4. A courteous, action-oriented closing

Exhibit 5-13 shows an effective letter requesting additional credit information.

Checklist 5-3 contains suggestions for improving the effectiveness of letters requesting credit.

Sampson Hardware
Supply Company

1887 Grant Avenue
Bethel, CT 06893

(413) 887-8943

April 10, 199x

Mr. Samuel Cornworth
Cornworth Hardware
P. O. Box 2483
Madison, CT 06734

Dear Mr. Cornworth:

Your interest in opening a charge account at Sampson Hardware Supply Company and your recent order are appreciated.

An opening that expresses appreciation.

For us to continue processing your credit application, a list of your present creditors and the amounts owed is needed. This same information is requested from all of our credit applicants.

A section that presents an impersonal request for additional information.

You will be pleased to learn that we were just selected as the exclusive national distributor of the popular Kearney power tool line. If you decide to stock these tools in your store, your customers will enjoy the convenience of shopping locally rather than having to order from Kearney. We will send you stock information on the Kearney line when it becomes available.

A section that presents resale material.

When we receive the requested information, we will continue processing your application. If you wish to receive your order before your charge account is opened, please send us a check for $355.59. Your order will then be sent within 24 hours.

A courteous, action-oriented closing.

Sincerely,

David Grant
Credit Manager

vt

Exhibit 5-13 Effective letter requesting additional credit information.

OPENING

1. Does the opening paragraph contain a request for credit?
2. Is the request presented courteously?
3. If the credit request is combined with an order, does the opening also mention the inclusion of an order?

MIDDLE

1. Has the necessary background information been provided to enable the company/organization to make a credit decision?
2. Is every detail of the background information correct?
3. If the request for credit is accompanied by an order, have all of the necessary details regarding the order been provided?

CLOSING

1. Is the closing courteous?
2. Is the closing action oriented?

Checklist 5-3 Letters requesting credit.

SPECIAL TYPES OF REQUEST LETTERS

Besides the basic request letters, several special types of request letters are commonly used, including order letters, letters of invitation, reservation letters, and favor-request letters.

Order Letters

Order blanks or purchase orders are typically used when ordering merchandise by mail. But when neither order blanks nor purchase orders are available, you can prepare an order letter, which is a completed order blank presented in letter format.

Of what content components are order letters comprised?

Order letters have three distinct content components: (1) pertinent information about the items being ordered; (2) directions for shipping the merchandise, including desired receipt date (if appropriate) and the desired shipping location (if different from your address); and (3) method of payment. Two common payment methods are sending payment with the order or charging the order to an existing charge account. Some individuals also request the opening of a charge account in their name at the time the order is placed.

Depending on the merchandise ordered, you made need to include the following information about each item:

quantity
catalog number
name of item
model number
color
size
pattern/finish/grade
weight
unit price
extension (unit price multiplied by quantity)

Omitting any of these details may cause recipients to try to provide this information on their own before they can fill the order or try to anticipate your preference, which may or may not meet with your approval.

What is the suggested plan for order letters?

The suggested plan for an order letter includes the following elements:

1. An opening mentioning your request: "Please ship by parcel post the following items:"
2. A section detailing the relevant information about the items being ordered
3. A section outlining the method of payment
4. A courteous, action-oriented closing

The order letter in Exhibit 5-14 omits several important details, the result of which is the need for clarification before the order can be filled. Exhibit 5-15 shows an effective order letter.

Letters of Invitation

A *letter of invitation* is a message that invites the reader to make a speech or to attend a formal or informal social event, such as a reception. Although these letters may not apply to business as often as other types of letters discussed in this chapter, businesspeople need to be knowledgeable about the various types of invitation letters.

```
I am ordering the following items from your
catalog, which I recently received: 1 crew
neck sweater, 2 pairs of argyle men's socks,
and 1 all-weather hat.

Please charge these items to my MasterCard
(Account No. 564-4444-554B) and send them to
the address shown at the top of this letter.
```

An opening without needed information about items being ordered.

A closing without needed action-oriented material.

Exhibit 5-14 Ineffective order letter.

```
4878 Greenvale Drive
Austin, KS 87437
June 12, 199x


L. Green and Sons
2874 Boston Road
Manchester, MA 04823

Ladies and Gentlemen:

Please ship by UPT the following items:
```

QUAN-TITY	CAT. NO.	DESCRIP-TION	SIZE	PRICE	UNIT TOTAL
1	55-89-3	Sweater	M	$28.99	$28.99
2 pr.	55-87-2	Socks	M	4.99	9.98
1	55-76-3	Hat	7	12.99	12.99
					$51.96

A fast-start opening that contains important information about items being ordered.

```
Please charge these items to my MasterCard
(account number 564-4444-554B, expiration date
of 9/9x).

The sweater is to be given as a gift;
therefore, your filling the order promptly so
that it will be received by July 10 will be
appreciated.

Sincerely,


Patricia A. Hamblin
```

A section that outlines details about merchandise payment.

An action-oriented, courteous closing.

Exhibit 5-15 Effective order letter.

Speaking Invitations

When writing a letter inviting someone to make a presentation, the inclusion of vital information about the event will help prevent inconvenience or misunderstanding. For example, failure to specify the exact time of the presentation may inconvenience the speaker. An even worse possibility is that the speaker will have to decline the invitation he or she previously accepted because of a misunderstanding about the presentation time.

What details should be included in letters of invitation?

Important details to include in the letter of invitation are the following: the name of the audience before which the presentation will be made; characteristics about the audience that will help the speaker tailor his or her remarks to it; desired length of the presentation; topic of the presentation; date; time; and the location of the presentation. Transportation and/or lodging arrangements that will be made for out-of-town speakers should also be mentioned in the letter as well as the amount of the honorarium if applicable.

What type of opening is appropriate for speaking-invitation letters?

As with other request letters, a fast-start opening extending the invitation is desirable. The first of the following two paragraphs delays the request; the revision, in contrast, has a fast-start opening.

Change: The annual meeting of the Administrative Management Society chapters in Pennsylvania, Ohio, and West Virginia is being held in Pittsburgh on October 8–10. This meeting will be held at the downtown Holiday Inn.

To: The committee planning the annual meeting of the Administrative Management Society chapters in Pennsylvania, Ohio, and West Virginia cordially invites you to be a guest speaker at one of the sessions on the afternoon of October 10. Because you were recommended as an outstanding speaker by several persons, we are especially hopeful that you will be able to accept this invitation.

After the opening, the next section contains details, as much as possible, about the presentation. This is especially needed when inviting busy people to make a presentation. Without the details, the speaker has to prepare a letter asking for additional information before he is able to determine his availability.

Note how much essential information is missing from the first of the following paragraphs. The revised version contains all the reader needs to know.

Change: The individuals who will be attending this meeting are typically involved with the administrative management function within their respective organizations. Although some are more involved with the office function, others are more involved with the financial function. Are you available to make an hour-long presentation during this meeting?

To: The individuals who typically attend this meeting have varied backgrounds, with the following job titles being the most common: office manager, comptroller, personnel manager, and executive vice-president. Although the decision about the topic of your presentation is yours to make, we suggest that it pertain to the functions performed by individuals with these job titles.

Sessions from 1 to 2 and from 3 to 4 are still available. Please choose the most convenient time. If you are unavailable at either of these times on October 10, we could schedule your presentation at another time during the afternoon of October 8 or any time during the day on the 9th. All sessions will be held in the downtown Holiday Inn in Pittsburgh.

To express appreciation for your taking time to make a presentation at this meeting, you will receive an honorarium of $150. We also invite you to be our guest at the closing banquet, which begins at 6:30 on the evening of October 10.

What type of closing is appropriate for speaking-invitation letters?

A speaking-invitation letter should have an action-oriented closing. Specifically, this means identifying the action you wish the recipient to take, which is to let you know of his decision. You may also wish to indicate the date by which you would like a response.

The first of the following two paragraphs, because it lacks action-oriented material, is vague and weak; the revised version, because it contains action-oriented material, is not.

Change: I look forward to hearing from you.

To: The program planning committee hopes you will be able to accept this invitation. Can you please inform me of your decision by July 16?

What is the suggested plan for speaking-invitation letters?

The suggested plan for a speaking-invitation letter includes the following elements:

1. An opening extending the speaking invitation while mentioning the date and location of the invitation
2. A description of the characteristics of the audience that will help the speaker direct the presentation to them
3. An invitation to the speaker to select the presentation time, if appropriate

4. A discussion of the accommodation arrangements to be made for the speaker, if appropriate
5. A courteous, action-oriented closing

The letter in Exhibit 5-16 omits several of the important elements of speaking-invitation letters. Exhibit 5-17 is a revised letter, containing the elements missing in Exhibit 5-16.

Exhibit 5-16 Ineffective speaking-invitation letter.

Are you available to speak to a group of credit managers on August 10? If so, please let me know as soon as possible.	An opening that lacks important details about the event.
I am responsible for finding two speakers for our annual credit managers' association meeting that will be held here in Omaha August 10 and 11. So far, I have contacted six people to speak—and only one has accepted my invitation. I hope you will also be able to accept this invitation.	A section that presents a discussion of the event, written with an I-viewpoint.
Because our organization operates on a shoestring budget, we are only able to pay you an honorarium of $200. We would like for you to be our guest at the luncheon on August 10.	A section that presents a discussion written with a negative tone.
Please let me know as soon as you can whether or not you will be able to accept this invitation.	A weak closing.

Exhibit 5-17 Effective speaking-invitation letter.

As program chairperson of the summer conference of the Credit Manager's Association of Nebraska, I cordially invite you to speak on time management at one of our morning sessions on August 10. The conference will be held at the Hilton Inn in Omaha.	An opening that contains the invitation and that presents important details about the event.
A time management presentation similar to the one you made at the Administrative Management Conference last year would be well received by many of our members. I have implemented a number of the time-saving suggestions you made during that presentation. Your suggestions have helped me eliminate many of the time-management concerns frequently discussed by our members.	A section that contains you-attitude material.
Persons who attend these conferences are typically credit managers in medium- to large-size companies. Most also supervise a staff of one to three employees.	A section that contains a discussion of the characteristics of the audience.
If you are able to make a presentation at our conference, please select one of the following session times that best fits into your schedule on the morning of August 10: 8:45-9:45, 10-11, or 11:15-12:15.	A section that invites the reader to select the time of the presentation.
As an expression of our appreciation for your making a presentation, we will pay you an honorarium of $200. We also cordially invite you to be our guest at the luncheon, which begins at 12:30 on the 10th.	A discussion of the reimbursement to be offered.
The conference planning committee wishes to have the program finalized fairly soon. Could you please let me know your decision by May 1?	An action-oriented closing.

Social-invitation Letters

Most social-invitation letters are considered informal. When more formality is required, a formal invitation, usually printed or engraved, is often used. Exhibit 5-18 shows a printed formal invitation.

When preparing social-invitation letters, important information about the event includes the following: the date, time, and location, and the directions for responding, if appropriate. In addition, include any other information applicable to the reader.

What is the suggested plan for social-invitation letters?

The suggested plan for a social-invitation letter includes the following elements:

1. A fast-start opening containing the invitation
2. A discussion of the important details applicable to the invitation
3. A discussion of any other information of interest
4. A courteous, action-oriented closing mentioning what you wish the recipient to do, including any deadline date.

Exhibit 5-19 shows an effective social-invitation letter.

Exhibit 5-18 Effective printed formal invitation.

```
                    Mr. Henry A. Albion

          requests the pleasure of your company
                       at a dinner
                       in honor of

                  Governor Harold Exxon

          on Friday, the twenty-first of April
                     at seven o'clock
                     in the Blue Room
                      Sheraton-Hilton
                          Dallas
R.S.V.P.                                       Black Tie
498-3857
```

Exhibit 5-19 Effective social-invitation letter.

Letter	Notes
Please join us at a luncheon on May 10 to celebrate Mr. John Brown's tenth year as president of Jundall Corporation. This important event, which begins at 12:30, will be held at the Cornwall Restaurant on Ridley Road in Des Moines.	A fast-start opening that presents the invitation and that contains important information about the event.
In addition to Jundall's executive staff, a few of the corporation's longtime clients are also being invited. If you wish, you will have an opportunity to join others in making a public tribute to recognize Mr. Brown's significant accomplishments during his career at Jundall.	A section that presents a discussion of other important information.
Please let me know by May 1 whether you will be able to attend the celebration and if you wish to deliver a tribute.	An action-oriented closing.

Reservation Letters

Reservations for hotel/motel accommodations are generally made either though travel agencies or the toll-free reservation number of the hotel/motel. Using toll-free numbers is especially common when making reservations at hotels and motels belonging to a chain.

When you are attending a convention, room reservations are generally made on a form provided by the hotel/motel. The same information on the reservation form should appear in a reservation letter, a message designed to request a room reservation. When you need to prepare such a letter, the following should be included:

Type of room desired (single, double, suite)
Number of persons occupying the room
Arrival and departure dates
Arrival and departure times
Mention of a deposit or late-arrival guarantee (if appropriate)
Request for a written confirmation

The suggested plan for a reservation letter includes the following elements:

What is the suggested plan for reservation letters?

1. A fast-start opening identifying the type of room desired and the days needed
2. A section mentioning arrival and departure times as well as information about deposit or late-arrival guarantee
3. A courteous, action-oriented closing referring to your desire for a confirmation, if appropriate

Exhibit 5-20 shows an appropriate reservation letter.

Letters Requesting Favors

Letters requesting favors are messages in which the recipient is asked, in a nonobligatory manner, to do something for the writer. Business executives frequently need to ask others for favors in both their business and nonbusiness areas of responsibility. When requesting a favor, the writer especially needs to express ideas tactfully and courteously as well as persuasively; because in responding positively, the reader usually receives less tangible benefits than in responding to an inquiry about products or services that may lead to a sale.

If you are requesting a favor, first ask yourself two questions: (1) Have I sufficient reason for making this request? (2) Am I asking a favor of a person reasonably expected to grant the favor?

Exhibit 5-20 Effective reservation letter.

Letter	Comment
Will you please reserve for my family a room with two double beds for the nights of September 20 and 21? The reservations are for my wife and me and our two sons (ages 6 and 4).	A fast-start opening that identifies the desired accommodation.
Arrival will be before 6 p.m. on the 20th and departure early on the 22nd.	A section that discusses the arrival and departure dates.
So that we can finalize our itinerary, would you please send me within 10 days a written confirmation of our reservation?	An action-oriented closing.

One of the best ways to obtain a special favor is to prepare a carefully worded letter. The letter should have a positive tone, be courteous, and show appreciation for the recipient's granting of the favor. However, the recipient should not be thanked in advance of the person's granting the favor.

What type of opening is appropriate for favor-request letters?

A letter requesting a favor should have a fast-start opening. The following two paragraphs illustrate the difference between a fast-start and a slow-start opening for this type of letter.

> Change: The students in the data processing class I teach at State University are always interested in seeing state-of-the-art computer installations. The article in last week's *Business Record* about your installation was very interesting to my class. Would you be able to provide my students with a tour of your new computer installation?
>
> To: Would you be able to provide a tour of your new computer installation to a group of 15 eager-to-learn students in my data processing class at State University? They became aware of your state-of-the-art installation through the article in last week's *Business Record.*

After stating the nature of your favor, provide additional pertinent information about it. This information helps the recipient become more aware of your desire to have the favor granted. Next, explain why the favor is important to you and others. The following paragraph shows an effective request for a favor:

> All students in this class are seniors in the data processing program at State University. Nearly half have work experience in data processing. These students would be especially appreciative of having an opportunity to see a state-of-the-art-installation. Viewing such an installation will contribute significantly to their understanding of the vital nature of the data processing function in an insurance company.

What type of closing is appropriate for favor-request letters?

The closing of a letter requesting a favor should be action oriented and express appreciation for the possibility of the favor being granted. The first of the following two paragraphs expresses appreciation, but it is not action oriented. The revision corrects this omission.

> Change: Any assistance you can provide will be greatly appreciated.
>
> To: To learn of your decision regarding a tour, I will call you next week. My students would be greatly appreciative of an opportunity such as this to enrich their educational backgrounds.

What is the suggested plan for favor-request letters?

The suggested plan for a favor-request letter includes the following elements:

1. A fast-start opening identifying the nature of the favor request
2. A presentation of additional information to help the recipient become aware of the writer's interest in having the favor granted
3. A courteous, action-oriented closing

The letter in Exhibit 5-21 is unlikely to motivate its recipient to grant the favor; the version in Exhibit 5-22 is more effective.

A friend of mine recently told me about the excellent presentation you made to a class of his several years ago. Would you be willing to make a similar presentation in my class?	An opening that presents the request but that is quite deficient in the information that is provided.
Having speakers come into high school classes is an excellent way to bridge the gap between the real and educational world. We often find that speakers are able to "tell it like it is" because of their vast, rich experiences.	A section that presents additional information.
Please let me know at your convenience whether you might be available to speak to my accounting class.	A section that lacks action-oriented material.

Exhibit 5-21 Ineffective favor-request letter.

Are you available within the next two months to make a presentation on the topic of accounting careers before my accounting class? Because the class meets from 1:00 to 1:50, a presentation lasting 30 minutes with a twenty-minute question-answer period would be ideal.	A fast-start opening that presents vital information about the request.
John Davidson recently told me about the excellent presentation you made on accounting careers before one of his classes several years ago. He indicated that several of his students chose an accounting career after hearing your presentation. Several of my students are considering an accounting career—and your presentation would be helpful as they make their decisions.	A section that provides additional information about the request.
Your helping enrich the educational experiences of my students would be greatly appreciated. I will call you February 10 for your decision.	A courteous, action-oriented closing.

Exhibit 5-22 Effective favor-request letter.

WRITING MEMOS

Chapters 3 and 4 contain a number of suggestions that should improve your ability to write memos as well as letters. Especially helpful suggestions deal with the courtesy, correctness, conciseness, concreteness, and completeness elements of your messages.

Although letters and memos share a number of common characteristics, a number of differences also exist, including the following:

What are the differences between letters and memos?

1. Letters are typically used to communicate with individuals outside the organization, whereas memos are typically employed to communicate with insiders. But letters can also be used internally and memos externally.
2. Letters and memos have their own distinctive formats. In fact, format is often a more distinguishing feature than is content or the writing style used in their preparation.
3. Although letters are an informal type of business document, business writers often use memos for more informal situations than they do letters. Writers of memos who are well acquainted with their readers tend to write more informally than they

would when they are preparing a letter or a memo for someone whom they do not know well. Jargon is also often more appropriate for use in memos than it is in letters.

4. Memos are more often sent to multiple readers than are letters.

Format

One of the distinguishing characteristics of memos is their distinctive format, especially the headings section, which includes the following items: date, to, from, and subject. Some organizations use a memo format that separates the date from the other three headings as the following illustrates.

July 15, 199x

TO: John Cornelius, Executive Vice President
FROM: Darlene Nelson, Accounting Department Supervisor
SUBJECT: Jim O'Riley's Promotion Recommendation

In other organizations, the date has the same status as other headings, as illustrated in the following example:

DATE: July 15, 199x
TO: John Cornelius, Executive Vice President
FROM: Darlene Nelson, Accounting Department Supervisor
SUBJECT: Jim O'Riley's Promotion Recommendation

In most cases, headings are presented in all caps. The initial letter of each word that appears after the heading is capitalized, as shown in the headings sample. The first word following the "Subject" heading appears two spaces after the colon, and the first word of each of the other items following a head aligns with it.

To save time, most organizations provide memo stationery with the headings preprinted. The stationery also probably contains the organization's name as well as the words "Interoffice Memorandum" or "Memorandum."

If you use a courtesy title (Mr., Mrs., Ms., Dr.) in the "To" line, then you should also use your courtesy title in the "From" line. Rather than employing courtesy titles, some memo writers prefer job titles (President, Assistant Vice President, etc.). Memo writers also generally sign their name or place their initials near their printed name in the "From" line, an action that makes the memo "official."

In writing the "Subject" line, take care to make it concise, meaningful, and clear. The reader should be able to determine the subject of the memo simply by reading the subject line.

When memos contain multiple pages, they need an appropriate heading at the top of each page after page 1. Either of the following two formats is appropriate (beginning 1 inch from the top of the page).

Mr. John Jones
Page 2
December 27, 199x

Mr. John Jones   Page 2   December 27, 199x

Appendix C presents additional memo-format guidelines.

Organization

What are the basic sections of memos?

Just as letters generally have three basic sections—opening, middle, and closing—so do memos. In most instances, the wording of a memo and a letter can be identical. In fact, the effectiveness of many memos would improve if their writers structured them just as they structure the letters they write for the same situations.

As you begin to write a memo, remember the following:

1. Analyze the situation about which you are writing in order to avoid omitting relevant information.
2. Assess your audience, especially if the memo is going to multiple readers. Every business message you write will be more effective if it is designed with your audience in mind, whether it is read by one reader or twenty readers.
3. Focus on the structure of your memo. Being aware of the nature of the situation about which you are writing and your audience allows you to maximize your memo's effectiveness. Make sure the opening, middle, and closing sections of the memo contain the content appropriate for the type of memo you are preparing.
4. After preparing the initial draft, revise it to conform with the suggestions presented in Chapters 3 and 4. Ask yourself the following questions:
   a. Is the content of the memo courteous?
   b. Is the memo without negative tone when such a tone is neither needed nor appropriate?
   c. Is the content clearly presented?
   d. Are the actions desired of the reader clearly outlined (when appropriate)?
   e. Does the message identify for the reader the benefit in complying with the writer's request (if appropriate)?
   f. Is the message concisely written, using the fewest words possible?
   g. Are the sentences and paragraphs of an appropriate length?
   h. Does the message contain sufficient detail, given the nature of the situation and the reader's background and understanding of the situation?
5. Check the final draft for appropriate format and correctness of content, grammar usage, punctuation, and spelling.

Because the structure appropriate for various types of memos tends to parallel the structure of letters, information about specific types of memos is presented in this chapter. (See also Chapters 6, 7, and 8.

REQUEST MEMOS

Request memos are messages, presented in a distinctive format, in which the reader who typically works for the same organization as the writer is asked to do something. Although the situations for which you might make a request of a co-worker are almost endless, the following are some of the most common ones:

1. Request for specific data/information
2. Request for specific materials
3. Request for assistance/input into a given situation
4. Request for attendance at a meeting

The tone and approach you use in request memos will probably be influenced by your reader. The tone you use in making a request of a superior will likely differ from the tone in a memo sent to a subordinate. Recognizing power differences between you and your reader will enable you to avoid making demands of or giving orders to superiors but to make requests of subordinates in a firm but polite way.

Within the three main sections of the body of the memo, you will provide the following information:

What information is presented in each section of the body of a request memo?

Opening	Presentation of primary request/secondary requests
Middle	Discussion of reasons for request and/or discussion of background information the recipient may find helpful in complying with your request
Closing	Presentation of action desired of recipient Expression of appreciation for assistance

Just as request-type letters use a direct approach in the opening, so should request memos. A direct approach will enable you to reach the main point of your memo immediately, which involves mentioning your primary request and any secondary requests. The alternative, the indirect approach, delays the request until the middle section of the memo.

Note how the opening section of a memo in which sales figures are requested makes a specific request immediately.

> Will you please send me a copy of June's sales figures for both the Eastern and Southern regions? This information will be incorporated into a report I am preparing for Vice President Greenlee.

Following is the opening section of a memo requesting a department head to provide the purchasing department with maintenance information about XYZ brand of copiers.

> Please provide me with detailed information about the maintenance required for XYZ copiers in your department since their purchase three years ago. We need this information to determine whether these copiers should be replaced with new XYZ copiers or a different brand.

The content of the middle section of the request memo is designed to help the reader respond more completely and easily with the request(s) being made. The complexity of the situation often determines the importance of the middle section of the request memo. The more complex the situation, the more important the middle section will be. The content of the middle section should focus on helping the reader comply with your request.

Depending on the situation you are writing about, the middle section of your request memo should consist of one or more paragraphs. As you write the middle section, try to maintain paragraph unity (the content of each paragraph is limited to one main topic and any related ideas) and appropriate paragraph length (average of four to six lines).

The following is the middle section of the memo requesting June sales figures, whose opening we previously presented. Note how the content of the material "rounds out" the request made in the opening section.

> President Collins asked Vice President Greenlee to make a comprehensive study of our monthly sales (for a year's time) in the Eastern and Southern regions. The outcome of the study will determine whether sales are currently at a sufficient level in these two regions to warrant our building a warehouse in each region.
>
> The data I have already compiled for the months of July of last year through May of this year are arranged by individual product. For each product, I have the dollar amount of sales, in addition to the number of units sold. Please provide me with the same data so that the information being presented is consistent from one month to the next.

The following paragraph is the middle section of the request memo concerning XYZ copiers, whose opening we previously presented. Note how the content helps the reader better understand the reason for the request.

> Several department heads have told me from time to time of their dissatisfaction with the XYZ copiers we installed in seven departments three years ago. Now that we have been given permission to begin replacing these copiers, I must decide whether to replace the existing XYZ copiers with new XYZ copiers or ones of a different brand. An examination of the maintenance records for each of our XYZ copiers will help me in making that decision.

What are two ways of closing a request memo?

In the closing section of the request memo, you have the opportunity to do either or both of the following: (1) summarize the action you desire the reader to take and (2) express appreciation for assistance. Because the desired action has been discussed in greater detail earlier in the memo, a brief summary statement should suffice. If you desire the reader's compliance with your request by a certain date or within a certain time, incorporate this information into the closing paragraph of the memo on June sales figures, as the following example illustrates.

> Your providing me with the sales figures and number of units of each product sold during June in the Eastern and Southern regions will be appreciated. Having this information by July 18 will enable me to get the report completed in time to comply with Vice President Greenlee's deadline.

In the second example of direct-request memos, note how the closing section summarizes the request, the deadline for complying with it, and expresses appreciation.

> Because of the need to make a purchasing recommendation by June 30, your providing me with the requested maintenance records on the XYZ copiers by June 15 will be appreciated.

Exhibit 5-23 shows a complete memo inviting the recipient to serve on a salary survey committee.

SUMMARY

Several types of request letters are used in the business world. Some specifically request information about products, services, or people, whereas others make a more general inquiry.

Claim letters, order letters, letters of invitation, reservation letters, letters requesting credit, and letters requesting favors are other types of request letters.

```
                         INTEROFFICE MEMORANDUM

   DATE: September 18, 19xx
     TO: William Green, Supervisor, Records Management
   FROM: Janet Graham, Director of Human Resources Management
SUBJECT: Invitation to Serve on Salary Survey Committee

Will you please consider serving on the salary survey committee for 19xx? Your
supervisor recommended you as a person who has the knowledge and background to
make an outstanding member of this important committee.

The twelve-member salary survey committee, which is one of the standing
committees of the human resources department, is responsible for determining
salary ranges for all nonsalaried positions in the company. Once the ranges are
determined, then unit supervisors make recommendations regarding annual salary
increases for their subordinates.

In the past, this committee has met on the average of four hours per month. You
will be given release time from your job as the committee meets during work
hours. Normally, meetings last approximately two hours two times a month.

If you have questions about the committee or its activities, please let me
know. I will appreciate having by October 2 your decision regarding committee
membership.
```

Exhibit 5-23 Effective memo requesting reader's participation on salary survey committee.

Whereas letters tend to be prepared for individuals outside the organization, memos are prepared for individuals inside the organization. The content of specific types of letters is similar, if not identical, to the content of identical messages presented in memo format.

Regardless of the type of message you are preparing, you should ensure that you include the essential elements for that type of document and make sure your writing techniques are appropriate to the audience and situation.

REVIEW QUESTIONS

1. What should be included in the opening of an inquiry letter?
2. What should be included in the closing of an inquiry letter?
3. How does the opening of an inquiry letter requesting information about a product or service differ from the opening of an inquiry letter requesting information about a person?
4. Identify several qualities of effective claim letters.
5. What is the main purpose of the claim letter?
6. In a claim letter, what material should follow the discussion of the nature of the claim?
7. What kind of you-attitude material is appropriate for a claim letter?
8. What are the content components of order letters?
9. What material should be included in the opening of a letter requesting credit?
10. What are the important details to include in social-invitation letters?
11. What is included in the effective closing of a letter requesting a favor?
12. What are the common differences between letters and memos?
13. What type of information is included in the three main sections of the body of a request memo?

APPLICATION PROBLEMS

1. Prepare a written critique of the following claim letter, evaluating grammar usage, punctuation, conformity with prescribed letter plan, and conformity with the writing essentials discussed in Chapters 3 and 4.

It was certainly embarrassing to give my niece an electric knife that I purchased in your store which did not run. I had your store deliver the knife to my niece (Ms. Mary Brown, 43 Maple Street, Lincoln) so I did not try it before I gave it to her. One has the right to assume that when you pay the prices that you folks charge that the merchandise should not have problems. I probably could have purchased an identical knife that worked from M-Mart—and for much less. Please deliver a new knife (Sunray, Model 23, $29.95) to my niece as soon as conveniently possible. She will give you the first one at that time. Let me tell you this—I will think twice before I shop in your store again.

2. Using the proofreader's marks shown in Exhibit 4-8, edit the following inquiry letter.

Will you please tell me more about the building cite I recently saw advertised in the April 10 issue of the *Dallas Herald.* I am looking for a facility has that around 2500 square ft. of wearhouse space and around 1000 square feet of office space. Right off hand it appears that this facility may meet me needs good. Could you please send to me a list of the specifcations it offeres.

If it appears that the facility may meet my needs I will want to inspect it soon. Due to the fact that our lease is about to expire on our present facility, please respond without a lengthy delay.

3. (Inquiry letter) You are the manager of purchasing for Southwest Business College, which is located at 1890 Main Street, Springfield, MO 64702. The president of the college recently authorized the purchase of new typing tables for one of the college's typing rooms. Although the tables to be replaced are only a few years old, they have proven for several reasons to be unsatisfactory. For example, the typewriter well is not adjustable, which makes the table uncomfortable for use by extremely short and extremely tall students. In addition, the table top is covered with a piece of wood-grain plastic film rather than plastic laminate. On several tables, the film has been cut and is now beginning to tear off. The leg braces, rather than being welded, are attached to the legs with small bolts that regularly need to be tightened. You are interested in obtaining information about the Model 10-70 typing table manufactured by Continental Table Company, which is located at 389 Monroe Street, Kansas City, MO 64390. Specifically, the information you desire is about those conditions that have caused the present tables to be less than satisfactory, in addition to the following: the length of warranty on the Model 10-70 tables, choice of finishes that are available (tops and legs), and the possibility of a discount on a 45-table order. Today is July 2, and you are interested in having the new tables in place by the beginning of the fall semester, which is August 23.
4. (Inquiry letter) Assume that you (vice president for sales in the Mellon Electronics Company, 2890 South Street, Omaha, NE 68408) are considering hiring Mary Carneigy as your secretary. On her application form, she listed John Smothers, director of personnel at Smithson Corporation, 2876 North Street, Des Moines, IA 56745, as a reference. Prepare a letter to send to Mr. Smothers, soliciting information about the following: the quality of Ms. Carneigy's work, ability to work under pressure, crisis-handling skills, level of initiative, and skills in oral and written communication. You expect your secretary to be able to function with a minimum of direction, have excellent secretarial skills, compose effective letters and reports, and cope with adverse situations effectively. The job has to be filled three weeks from today, which is September 21, when your present secretary leaves.
5. (Request letter) You are the chairperson of a search committee responsible for finding a new head of the Business Department at Northern College, located in

Miami, KS 45434. The deadline for receiving applications has now passed, and your committee plans to develop a form letter to solicit information from the references listed by the applicants. The following were listed as important criteria on the job vacancy notice: scholarly promise, leadership potential, effective administrative skills, effective teaching skills, and knowledge of the budgeting process. Prepare a draft of the form letter to be sent to each individual listed as a reference on the applications submitted by the top five candidates.

6. (Claim letter) You, the owner of the Parisian Gift Shoppe, 38 Main Mall Street, Atlanta, GA 23417, just took receipt of a shipment from the Hallwood Distributing Company, 5732 Baker Avenue, Charlotte, NC 21211. One reason you decided to place this order with Hallwood (your first) is because of its policy of shipping within 72 hours of the receipt of the order. Although the shipment date was within three days (you placed a phone order on September 21, and the postage on the package showed a September 23 mailing date), the shipment did not arrive until October 14. You were counting on having the merchandise available for your Fall-Fest, which ended on October 12. Obviously, Hallwood is not responsible for the slowness of the U.S. Postal Service, but it can be held accountable for the fact that you received someone else's order. None of the twenty-three wood carvings, which cost $423, that you ordered was received. Instead, you received an assortment of twenty-four pewter figurines that you cannot use because you no longer carry pewter items. Write a letter asking for a cancellation of your order for the wood carvings and for a full refund of the $423 that you charged to your Value-Line charge account, which you have already paid. Indicate that the shipment of pewter is being returned COD by UPS.
7. (Order letter) You were recently looking at the catalog of Builder's Supply Company, Towne Square, Salem, MA 01229. As the owner of Pete's Hardware, 13 Main Street, Pella, IA 58575, you are always interested in finding sources for some of the hardware that residents in your community use to remodel old farmhouses. Specifically, you are interested in expanding your line of brass hinges, doorknobs, and strike plates, in addition to period light fixtures. Builder's Supply Company carries a complete line of the brass hardware and period light fixtures for which you have so many requests. Because the catalog you were looking at did not have an order blank, you must prepare a letter ordering the following items:

   8 pair of brass hinges (No. 1343) at $7.49 for each pair
   6 pair of brass hinges (No. 1279) at $5.49 for each pair
   6 brass door assemblies (No. 1894) at $15.49 each
   4 brass door assemblies (No. 1984) at $21.49 each
   5 antique brass light fixtures (No. 2181) at $34.98 each

   Send along a check for the amount of your purchase. Shipping is free, and no sales tax is applicable.
8. (Invitation letter) You are the convention chairperson for the Tri-State Business Educators Association. One of your responsibilities is to find speakers for the twelve sessions to be held during the two-day convention beginning on May 14. The convention site is the Riverside Inn (12 Riverside Drive, Akron, OH 45765). A committee member has suggested you contact Ms. Mary Maxum (8758 Greenwood Street, Apt. 23, Columbus, OH 45874) as a possible speaker for the information systems session to be held from 10 to 11 A.M. on May 14. She heard Ms. Maxum speak at a conference last year and found her to be very informative—as well as entertaining. Although your association cannot pay its convention speakers an honorarium, it pays transportation (27 cents a mile) and provides lodging

and meals. Speakers are also invited as the association's guests for the closing banquet beginning at 6 P.M. on May 15. Because the convention is only five months away, you want to have a response from Ms. Maxum relatively soon.

9. (Reservation letter) You, your spouse, and two children (ages seven and five) plan to travel to the Colorado Rockies during the two weeks of your vacation (August 2–16). You want to spend four nights (August 6–9) at the Day's Rest Inn on Highway 16 in Estes Park, CO 78773. Your brother and his family stayed at the Inn last summer and gave it a good recommendation. Write a letter requesting a room at the rear of the motel, with two double beds. You decide to include in your letter a preaddressed postcard to be sent by the motel owner confirming your reservations and informing you of the nightly rate.
10. (Credit-request letter) You are interested in opening a charge account at the Jackson's Department Store that just opened in the Cedar View Mall in Laramie, Wyoming. When you called Jackson's Credit Department, the credit representative suggested you send a letter with the following information about you: number of years at present residence—six; job title/employer—-associate professor, University of Wyoming; annual income—$38,000; and the name of your bank—First National Bank of Laramie. Prepare a letter requesting the opening of a charge account.
11. (Credit-request letter) You are the credit representative for Jackson's Department Store in Laramie, Wyoming. You recently received a letter from William S. Brooks (2314 Harvard Avenue, Laramie, WY 78643) requesting that a charge account be opened in his name. Although he provided several pieces of information in his letter (number of years at present residence; job title/employer; annual income; and the name of his bank), Mr. Brooks did not enclose a list of his present charge accounts. Nor did he include the amount he presently owes (mortgage, loans, revolving charge accounts, etc.). Before you can open a charge account for him, you must have this additional information—which all credit applicants are required to provide.
12. (Favor-request letter) You have been invited to Boston for a home-office interview for an accounting position at Lemark, Selling, and Deman. You know nothing about Boston other than it has terrific seafood restaurants! Your father suggested you contact one of his college friends (William S. Drake, 3443 Grambling Boulevard, Newton, MA 23821) to see if he can show you around the Boston area. Mr. Drake retired from the military three years ago. Although you have never met personally, you feel you are somewhat acquainted from the Christmas messages his family has sent your family throughout the years. Write the letter to Mr. Drake, asking if he might have time to show you around Boston the morning of April 9 or the afternoon of April 10. You plan to arrive the evening of April 8, and you have hotel reservations at the Downtown Hospitality Inn. Your flight leaves Logan Airport at 5:30 P.M. on the tenth.
13. (Request memo) You are the president of a large computer manufacturer that sells personal computers throughout the United States. Because you don't have as much time as you would like to receive feedback about how the company might better satisfy its employees, you decide to seek input from each of the company's five vice presidents. In your memo to them requesting their input, you suggest that they talk with a sizable number of their subordinates. Then, after they have compiled their list of suggestions, they are to select the seven suggestions that would have the greatest impact on employee morale and then transmit this final list to you. You will then examine the various suggestions and determine which ones are possible to implement in terms of feasibility and finances. Prepare the memo to be sent to the vice presidents, seeking their input. You would like to have their responses one month from today.

14. (Request memo) You recently agreed, when asked by the president of your company, to serve as the company representative for the annual Community Drive. This means you chair the company's fund-raising efforts for the drive. The purpose of the drive is to make a coordinated effort to raise funds supporting local charitable organizations, including such groups as Boy Scouts, Girl Scouts, Gateway Hospice, Domestic Violence, Sheltered Workshop, Action, Literacy Council, and so forth. The financial donations received by the Community Drive are allocated among the various groups for which financial support was approved earlier by its board of directors. As with any fund-raising drive, success is often determined by the effort of the participants. In your company last year, only 120 of the 250 employees gave a total of $2,395. Your goal this year is to get 180 employees to contribute $4,200.

    Rather than try to do all the work yourself, you decide to ask each of the seven department heads in your company to name someone from his or her department to serve as its representative. Because the drive ends six weeks from today, you would like to have the names of the individuals a week from today. Prepare the memo to send to all your department heads, asking that they appoint a department representative to help you and then provide you with that person's name.

6

Good-News Letters and Memos

After studying this chapter, you should be able to

1. List the characteristics of effective good-news letters.
2. Identify the plan used for preparing letters replying to inquiries and responding to credit requests.
3. Discuss the factors considered in determining creditworthiness.
4. Identify ways to improve the effectiveness of adjustment letters and order-acknowledgment letters.
5. Identify ways that will improve the effectiveness of letters that grant favors.
6. Identify the plan for preparing letters of congratulations and letters accepting invitations.
7. Prepare effective letters of the type discussed in this chapter.
8. Prepare effective memos of the type discussed in this chapter.

Many business situations require the preparation of *good-news letters and memos*—written messages designed to communicate good news to receivers. When well written, these messages help companies/organizations improve relationships with their employees, customers, and clients. Writers of effective good-news messages take advantage of every opportunity to capitalize on the positive elements of the situations about which they write.

The types of good-news letters examined in this chapter include the following:

1. Letters replying to inquiries
2. Letters granting adjustments
3. Letters acknowledging orders
4. Letters granting favors
5. Letters of congratulations
6. Letters accepting an invitation

What characteristics do good-news letters possess?

Effective good-news letters have a number of unique characteristics, including those discussed in Communication Capsule 6-1. In this chapter, we also discuss preparing good-news and informative memos.

Communication Capsule 6-1 Improving the Effectiveness of Good-News Letters

Among the suggestions you will find helpful in preparing effective good-news letters are the following:

1. *Begin with the good news or main idea.* One of the best ways to put the reader in a positive frame of mind is to present the good news first. When you are replying to a letter you received, putting the good news or main idea in the opening paragraph is especially desirable.
2. *Use a fast-start opening.* The nature of each letter presented in this chapter enables you to use a fast-start opening, in which you will avoid presenting obvious information. For example, telling the reader that you have received the person's letter is not a fast-start beginning. You obviously have received the letter—or you would not be replying. Similarly, a fast start avoids telling the reader something she can easily infer.
3. *Provide explanatory details or information of primary and secondary importance.* In most letters presented in this chapter, you will have an opportunity to provide more information than just the good news. The letter will be incomplete if it is missing the details or information of primary importance. Although the message may be complete without including the material of secondary importance, consider its inclusion if it will be helpful or of interest to the reader. Types of material of secondary importance that fit nicely into several of the good-news letters covered in this chapter are resale, sales-promotion, and reader-benefit material.
4. *Incorporate a you-viewpoint.* Because the letters included in this chapter contain good news for the reader, the material must be written from a you-viewpoint. The letters will have a much stronger psychological impact when they focus on the reader rather than on the writer. Minimizing the use of *I, we,* and *our* will help you achieve a you-viewpoint.
5. *Incorporate an appropriate closing.* A variety of closings are appropriate for the letters discussed in this chapter. In each type of letter, a courteous, friendly closing is important. In some letters, this is accomplished by offering to provide additional help if and when desired. In other letters, the closing will express the desire to serve the customer in the future.

LETTERS REPLYING TO INQUIRIES

Letters of reply to inquiries are messages that provide the reader with information about products, services, and persons. Each of these letter types possesses the general characteristics presented in Communication Capsule 6-1 in addition to specific characteristics discussed in this section.

Letters Providing Information about Products or Services

What characteristics do favorable-reply letters possess?

A favorable reply to a letter of inquiry about a product or service must be accurate and comprehensive. You should be certain not only about the correctness of your response but also that you answer every question asked in the inquiry. In addition, you need to consider providing any additional information to help the reader become more familiar with the product or service mentioned in the original correspondence.

The response to a letter of inquiry should be timely, certainly within a few days. Delaying the response may signal that you consider the inquiry to be unimportant—or that you do not consider responding a top priority. If you cannot reply within a reasonable time, send a brief letter explaining the delay and the anticipated response date. The following is such an acknowledgment.

The information you requested about our new line of desktop computers will be sent next week. Our systems staff is preparing calculations on some technical data that will provide the answers to your questions.

Your interest in this new line of computers is appreciated.

A letter responding to an inquiry about a product or service should have a fast-start opening. Try to present the main idea—which probably will be the answer to the basic question asked in the inquiry letter—near the beginning. Note how the pace in the first of the following opening paragraphs is slower than the revision.

What type of opening is appropriate for favorable-reply letters?

Change: Thank you for your recent letter in which you inquired about our new desktop computer.

To: Yes, the memory of the H-D 3000 in our new desktop computer line can be expanded to 1.2MB by inserting two H-D 3987 boards. A service contract you also inquired about is available for an annual charge of $125.

The opening is followed by a section containing additional details or information of interest to the reader. The writer also answers questions of secondary importance here. The amount of information and its relevance to the inquiry will affect the reader's perception of the writer's helpfulness.

In the first of the following two paragraphs, the writer gives a minimum amount of information. The writer of the revised version provides more information and will be perceived as being much more helpful.

Change: The installation of the memory boards is an easy process. Any of our trained service technicians can install these boards in a few minutes.

To: The factory-trained service technicians who work for the H-D computer dealer in your area, the J. H. Johnson Computer Company, are able to install these memory boards in approximately 30 minutes. The cost of each board is $135. The memory of the H-D 3000 computer can be upgraded to 1.2MB for less than $300.

Letters responding to inquiries about a product or service are appropriate for the inclusion of resale or sales-promotion material. *Resale material* is used to convince the inquiry writer that he or she has made (or will make) a wise decision in purchasing the product or service of interest. *Sales-promotion material,* in contrast, is designed to promote a product or service in which the reader may be interested. The purpose of sales-promotion material is not to put pressure on the reader but rather to make the person aware of another product or service he or she might find useful.

What is the nature of the resale material in favorable-reply letters?

The following letter responding to an inquiry about the H-D 3000 desktop computer effectively uses resale material.

During the six months the H-D 3000 has been on the market, it has received rave reviews in several computer magazines. After you read the four reviews enclosed with this letter, you will likely agree that the well-designed keyboard, the high resolution of the screen, and the upgradable nature of its memory make the H-D 3000 a superior product. Adding to these features is its exclusive three-year warranty; you can, therefore, easily understand why the H-D 3000 is receiving such positive reviews.

The closing for a letter responding to an inquiry about a product or service should be friendly and courteous. Express appreciation for the inquiry or offer to answer other questions. When appropriate, suggest the action you would like the reader to take.

What type of closing is appropriate for favorable-reply letters?

The weaknesses inherent in the first of the following closing paragraphs is deleted from the revised version.

Change:	Thank you for your interest in the H-D 3000.
To:	Thanks for the opportunity to tell you about the H-D 3000. Should you have additional questions, please write me. Or, if you would like to see a demonstration of the H-D 3000, please visit our dealer in your area, the J. H. Johnson Computer Company.

The suggested plan for a letter responding to an inquiry about a product or service includes the following elements:

What is the suggested plan for favorable-reply letters?

1. A fast-start opening answering the primary question or mentioning that the requested information is being sent
2. The inclusion of answers to questions and/or a presentation of details or information of secondary importance
3. The inclusion of resale, sales-promotion, or reader-benefit material
4. A friendly, courteous closing, suggesting, when appropriate, the action you would like the reader to take

The letter illustrated in Exhibit 6-1 lacks a number of the elements of effective letters responding to inquiries about products or services. The letter in Exhibit 6-2 is a much-improved version of the same letter. The inclusion of resale material in Exhibit 6-2 has a desirable impact.

Letters Responding to an Inquiry about a Person

Two situations necessitate the preparation of letters responding to an inquiry about a person. These situations occur when you are asked to provide information about (1) a person for whom you serve as a reference (such as a former or current employee) and (2) a person's creditworthiness.

Besides the general characteristics they share with other letters, letters of response that answer an inquiry about a person possess a number of special characteristics. This section specifically discusses letters in response to an inquiry about a job applicant's work performance. The same material is easily adaptable for response to inquiries about the creditworthiness of an applicant.

What type of opening is appropriate for letters replying favorably about a person?

A fast-start opening in a letter responding to an inquiry about a person refers to the person's name and the nature of the relationship between the person and you. In addition, you can, if it is appropriate, express appreciation for being able to offer the requested information. Note the difference between the slow start of the first of the following two paragraphs and the fast start of the revision.

Exhibit 6-1 Ineffective response to inquiry.

Letter	Comment
We have received your recent letter in which you inquired about the Model 87 printing calculator. Thank you for your inquiry.	A slow-start opening that presents obvious information.
The Model 87 can be used either as a printing calculator or as a display calculator. You also asked about whether it will operate on batteries as well as on 120-volt current. The calculator can be operated on either batteries or on 120-volt current.	A section that contains brief, almost-incomplete answers.
Please let me know if you have any other questions about our calculator.	A closing that lacks friendliness.

Omni Electronics, Inc.
P.O. Box 38 *(231) 899-8334* *Eli, Nevada* 89494

December 16 199x

Mr. Harvey Blackmond
1991 Greenfield Court
Oklahoma City, OK 73701

Dear Mr. Blackmond:

Yes, the Model 87 Omni printing calculator about which you recently inquired can be used either as a printing calculator or as a display calculator. The calculator's dual power source will enable you to operate the machine either on batteries or on 120-volt current.

A fast-start opening that gives immediate answers to questions.

Another feature of the Model 87 you may find especially useful is its triple memory, which facilitates the simultaneous holding of three different amounts in memory. This triple-memory feature is especially attractive to engineers.

A section that contains additional information designed to help create reader's interest in the product.

The Model 87 calculator performs more functions than any other comparably priced calculator. A review of this machine, which recently appeared in the *Office Equipment News*, indicated that the Model 87 has the best repair record among competing calculators and that it is the easiest calculator to learn to operate. These two advantages are undoubtedly responsible for the increasing popularity of the Model 87.

A section that contains resale material designed to entice the customer to purchase the product.

Thanks for your inquiry about the Model 87. For a demonstration, please visit the Omaha Office Equipment Company, the Omni dealer in your area.

A courteous, action-oriented closing.

Sincerely,

Janice Cornwell
Customer Service

Exhibit 6-2 Effective response to inquiry.

Change: I have received your letter of June 22 in which you inquired about Ms. Mary Smith, who has applied for a secretarial position in your organization.
To: During the two years that Ms. Mary Smith was my secretary, her work performance was excellent.

The section following the opening answers the specific and general questions asked in the inquiry letter. You should also consider including additional information of use to the reader. The information, solicited and unsolicited, must be honest. Besides answering questions in the inquiry letter, including your impression of the person's ability to perform the duties of the job is highly desirable.

Your response will also be more helpful to the reader if you can provide evaluative statements about the person's performance. You can accomplish this effectively by comparing this person's performance with that of others who currently have or had similar duties. Specific information will be more useful to the reader than general information.

What are evaluative statements?

If you must present negative information, prepare remarks relevant to the situation. Unless this information relates to the person's ability to perform the job for which he has applied, you may want to consider omitting it. Some experienced writers, when preparing this type of letter, invite the reader to call. These negative aspects can then be mentioned.

The following examples show how the previous suggestions can be effectively incorporated into the response to an inquiry about a person's work performance:

> Here are the answers to your questions:
>
> 1. Yes, Ms. Smith is a self-starter. Rarely did I have to give her directions for carrying out her job duties.
> 2. Yes, Ms. Smith's work is meticulously done. I recall only one instance in which she had to retype work because of the manner in which the first typed draft was prepared.
>
> Other information you may find helpful in evaluating Ms. Smith's suitability for employment includes:
>
> 1. Of all the secretaries I've had, Ms. Smith is the most eager to learn and to develop professionally. These professional strengths are important attributes for the secretary to a vice president.
> 2. The level of Ms. Smith's secretarial skills, understanding of business operations, and personality will enable her to handle competently the work in a vice president's office.

What should be included in the closing of letters responding to inquiries about people?

The ending of the letter responding to an inquiry about a person should summarize your opinion about the applicant's suitability for the job for which she is applying. The statement should be sincere; otherwise, the reader may question your honesty.

Because it is too general, the first of the following two closings detracts from the letter writer's effectiveness. The revision, because it is specific, conveys a more positive impression of the applicant.

> Change: I am glad to have had this opportunity to convey to you my impression about Ms. Smith.
>
> To: Ms. Smith, whom I found to be an exceptional secretary, is referred to you with my top recommendation. If she is given the opportunity to work for you, I am sure you will readily concur with my evaluation of her work performance.

The suggested plan for a letter responding to an inquiry about a person includes the following elements:

What is the suggested plan for favorable-reply letters?

1. A fast-start opening mentioning (a) the person's name, (b) the nature of the relationship between you and the person, and (c) appreciation for being able to provide the requested information
2. A section answering specific and general questions asked in the inquiry letter, as well as any additional information of use to the reader
3. A closing providing your impression of the person's suitability for the position for which he or she has applied

The letter in Exhibit 6-3 does not follow several of the suggestions presented in this section. Note that Exhibit 6-4, which is a revision of the letter in Exhibit 6-3, corrects these problems. The reader should appreciate the additional details offered in the revised letter.

Your letter in which you inquired about the suitability of Mr. John Diaz for a financial analyst position arrived recently. Mr. Diaz worked here from 198x to 198x. His last position was assistant financial analyst.	A slow-start opening that presents obvious information.
Mr. Diaz is a bright, hard-working individual. He is cooperative, gets along well with others, and has a take-charge attitude. We were all very pleased with his performance.	A section that presents information about the applicant.
I am glad to have this opportunity to recommend Mr. Diaz to you.	A weak closing.

Exhibit 6-3 Ineffective letter responding to an inquiry about a job applicant.

Mr. John Diaz, about whom you recently inquired, was highly regarded when he worked for us from 1987 to 199x. I am pleased to recommend him as a financial analyst, a position for which he is well qualified.	A fast-start opening that contains the essential elements of the beginning for this type of letter.
Those of us who supervised Mr. Diaz found him to be a bright, hard-working individual. He was most cooperative, always got along well with others, and had a take-charge attitude. In addition, Mr. Diaz has an excellent aptitude for working with numbers. When compared with his coworkers, he consistently placed in the top 10 percent.	A section that provides a discussion which answers the questions that were asked by the person making the inquiry.
Mr. Diaz could always be counted on when needed, which was an especially fine attribute that was always appreciated. On several occasions, his performance was clearly beyond what was reasonably expected. Coupling this attribute with his philosophy that an employee never stops learning contributed to his considerable success while he worked here.	A section that provides a discussion of additional information of interest to the reader.
The respect I have for Mr. Diaz enables me to give him a top recommendation. If he is given the opportunity to work for you, I am confident that you, too, will soon feel the same way about him.	A closing that provides an overall evaluation of the applicant's suitability for employment.

Exhibit 6-4 Effective letter responding to an inquiry about a job applicant.

Checklist 6-1 suggests a number of points to use in assessing the effectiveness of your response to inquiry letters.

LETTERS ABOUT CREDIT

Today's businesses use a number of letters about credit. Before a company decides to grant credit, it must assess the applicant's creditworthiness.

Determining Creditworthiness

Deciding whether to extend credit to customers is often a complex process requiring an extensive investigation into the background of the applicants. The investigation focuses on the three C's of credit—capital, capacity, and character.

OPENING

1. Does the letter contain a fast-start opening in which you provide the information of greatest interest to the recipient?
2. Have you avoided telling the recipient what he or she can easily infer, such as the following: "I have received your letter of June 10 . . .," "This is in response to your letter of June 10 . . .," or "Thank you for your recent letter. . . ."
3. Is the opening without any material or wording that might be perceived as having a begrudging tone?
4. Is the opening "you-oriented" rather than "I-oriented"?

MIDDLE

1. Have you included additional desired information not appropriate for inclusion in the opening paragraph? (If the opening paragraph would be too long if you included all of the desired information there, then the middle section of the letter is the appropriate place to put the additional information.)
2. Does the wording/content of this section convey the impression that you have "gone out of your way" to assist the reader?
3. Does this section contain, if appropriate, resale material, sales-promotion material, or reader-benefit material?
4. Have you avoided negative wording by telling the reader what you can do rather than what you cannot do?

CLOSING

1. Is the closing courteous?
2. Is the closing action oriented, if appropriate?
3. Is the closing void of a doubtful tone ("I hope you will find the enclosed material helpful")?
4. Is the closing void of such negative, trite expressions as "Please feel free . . .," "Please do not hesitate to . . .," or "Enclosed you will find . . .?"

Checklist 6-1 Responses to letters of inquiry.

1. *Capital*, which refers to a person's assets, includes such items as cash, stocks, property, and real estate. This factor receives extensive consideration. To settle an unpaid account, legal action may be necessary to obtain the applicant's assets. Therefore, the creditor will want to make sure the debtor has sufficient assets.
2. *Capacity*, which refers to the ability to pay, includes the amount of the individual's income, the amount of other debts, the health of the individual, and the nature of the individual's livelihood.
3. *Character*, which refers to a person's honesty and integrity, is especially important. A trustworthy person usually has a sincere desire to meet financial obligations, thus avoiding either interest charges or a poor credit reputation.

Most businesses commonly extend credit to their eligible customers. Because charge customers are likely to purchase at a faster rate, companies often use selling on credit to increase sales volume. Businesses also use credit to increase their net profit by levying finance charges on their credit transactions.

Although advantageous in certain instances, the extension of credit is somewhat disadvantageous in other instances. For example, selling to customers on a credit basis requires that businesses install credit departments. The process of extending and refusing credit adds significantly to the amount of paperwork. Much of this paperwork involves the various types of credit letters we discuss.

The types of credit accounts commonly used by businesses include the following:

What types of credit accounts are commonly used in the business world?

1. *Regular credit account*: This type of credit account is also known as a thirty-day charge account. If the amount of the account is paid in full within the specified period (usually twenty-five to thirty days), no interest is charged. A variation of this

account is the revolving charge account, which requires partial payment within a certain period while interest accrues on the unpaid balance.

2. *Ninety-day-same-as-cash account*: This type of account requires three equal payments. If the account is paid in full within ninety days, no interest is charged. On accounts in which the balance is not paid in full by the due date, interest is generally charged from the date of purchase. This type of account is often used for the purchase of major home appliances or furniture.
3. *Long-term installment account*: This type of account usually is interest-bearing and may run as long as sixty months on major purchases. Long-term installment accounts are often employed for the purchase of automobiles.

Letters commonly associated with the extension of credit are used to

1. Solicit prospective credit customers.
2. Submit a request for credit.
3. Request information about credit applicants.
4. Request additional information from credit applicants.
5. Extend credit to credit applicants.
6. Deny credit to credit applicants.
7. Make a credit counteroffer.

The letters from this list that have an inquiry, disappointing-news, or persuasive nature are discussed in Chapters 5, 7, or 8. Chapter 7 provides information about letters used to deny the extension of credit to credit applicants and to make a credit counteroffer. This chapter describes credit letters communicating the good news of extending credit.

Letters Extending Credit to Applicants

What are the purposes of letters that extend credit to applicants?

Letters extending credit to applicants, which are among the easiest type of good-news letter to write, notify customers that you are opening a charge account in their name. Because you are able to grant the applicant's request, the need to incorporate persuasive material or to minimize the impact of negative information—two concerns of various other types of credit letters—are unimportant.

What should be included in the openings of letters that extend credit?

Letters extending credit have three purposes: (1) They inform the applicant that credit has been granted; (2) they outline the company's credit policies to help prevent future misunderstandings; and (3) they serve as a sales-promotion device. Another purpose, when a combined order and request for credit is received, is to explain that the customer's order has been (or is about to be) shipped.

A letter extending credit begins with the good news first. When a request for credit is unaccompanied by an order, the letter granting credit should open by notifying the applicant that credit has been granted.

In a letter extending credit, providing the good news first makes for a fast-start opening. Do not slow down your pace by beginning with obvious information. To illustrate, note how slow the first of the two following paragraphs is compared with the revision.

Change:	We have received your application for credit and have processed the information. We are glad to report that we can open a charge account in your name.
To:	Welcome to Smyths' as a new charge customer. Your credit card, which is enclosed with this letter, will enable you to charge your purchases at all twenty-nine Smyths' stores throughout the country. You may begin using the card just as soon as you place your signature on the backside of the card.

In addition, the first opening has a begrudging tone; the revised opening is more courteous, friendly, and helpful.

When a credit application accompanies an order, an appropriate opening referring to the status of the order can be followed by a statement mentioning the newly established credit account. This order is preferred because the customer is likely more interested in the status of the order than in the status of the credit application. The opening will also mention that the order has been charged to the customer's new account, as the following shows.

> Your order for six sets of the popular Linwood art prints was shipped via UPS this morning and should arrive within four days. The amount of the order ($397.43) was charged to your newly opened account.

What should be included in the middle section of letters that extend credit?

In the section after the opening, you may want to discuss your reasons for extending credit, especially if they reflect exceptionally favorably on the customer. For example, if the applicant's credit references gave her especially high ratings, you may want to mention this because of its positive psychological impact on her. Other favorable information you may want to include in this section are the customer's prompt bill-paying habits and the favorable ratio between assets and liabilities.

In addition, this section should outline the rules and terms governing the use of the charge account. Because the various types of accounts differ, take special care to inform fully the customer of the rules and terms. Include the closing date of the statement, finance charges, the date by which payment must be received if further finance charges are to be avoided, annual membership charge, and whom to contact if (1) a billing error occurs, (2) a card is lost or stolen, or (3) an address is changed. Besides discussing the important rules or terms of the account in the letter, an increasing number of companies enclose a separate document for this purpose.

What is the purpose of resale and sales-promotion material included in letters that extend credit?

The inclusion of resale and/or sales-promotion material in letters granting credit is recommended. If an order accompanies the credit application, resale material further convinces the customer of his wise choice in ordering this specific merchandise. Resale material also sells the customer on doing business with your company.

In contrast, sales-promotion material is used to inform the customer of an upcoming sale, new merchandise just received, a new line of merchandise the company is selling, or other merchandise related to the type just ordered by the customer. The following paragraphs of letters granting credit show the effective use of resale and sales-promotion material.

> The art prints you ordered have been among our best sellers this summer. The colors in the prints coordinate well with the new pastel colors currently popular and widely used in home and office interiors.
>
> You will be interested to learn that we just received permission from Clare Weymouth, another popular still-life artist, to prepare a portfolio of her work that will also coordinate well with today's popular pastel interior colors. This portfolio is sure to be just as popular as the sets of Linwood prints you recently ordered. As a credit customer, you will soon receive information about the Weymouth portfolio.

What type of closing is appropriate for letters that extend credit?

The closing of a letter extending credit should express anticipation of a future pleasant relationship. This can be accomplished by mentioning your ability to serve the customer in a courteous, prompt manner; inviting the customer to a sale available only to charge account customers; offering to be of personal assistance whenever desired; or stating a "satisfaction-guaranteed" policy.

Your application for credit has been received and processed. An account has been opened in your name.	A slow-start opening that presents obvious information before the good news.
The closing date of your account is the thirteenth day of each month. Shortly after that, you will receive a statement listing current charges. To avoid an interest charge of 1.5 percent on the unpaid balance, payment must be received by the fifth day of the following month.	A section that contains an overly brief explanation of the important rules governing the charge account.
Other important information about your account is summarized on the enclosed sheet.	A section that only makes reference to the rules sheet.
We appreciate your interest in opening a charge account at Drummonds.	A weak closing that does not look forward.

Exhibit 6-5 Ineffective letter granting credit.

Note the difference in the rather indifferent tone of the first example and the friendly and helpful future-oriented tone of the revision.

Change: We appreciate your business and your interest in opening a charge account.
To: You can always count on prompt, courteous service when ordering from us because we guarantee your satisfaction with our merchandise and service. We look forward to a long, pleasant relationship.

The suggested plan for a letter granting credit includes the following elements:

What is the suggested plan for letters that extend credit?

1. A fast-start opening quickly giving the customer the good news: that the order is being shipped and/or that credit is being extended
2. A section discussing the most important rules and terms governing the account and, perhaps, the basis for the extension of credit
3. A section including resale material or, when appropriate, sales-promotion material
4. A courteous closing focusing on the future

Exhibit 6-5 shows an ineffective letter granting credit. The letter in Exhibit 6-6 is an improved version of that letter. Note the helpful tone of the revised letter.

Checklist 6-2 has a number of items to use in judging the effectiveness of your letters granting credit.

ADJUSTMENT LETTERS

Defects, errors, and misunderstandings occur regardless of how much a company tries to prevent them. A courteous, conciliatory, persuasive adjustment letter explains circumstances that might impact negatively on the already strained goodwill between the writer and the reader. Therefore, *adjustment letters*, which provide excellent opportunities for building goodwill and repairing the past, are designed to notify the reader that you are granting his or her claim request. Thus, they help restore the reader's confidence.

The content of adjustment letters depends on several factors. Is the request to be granted? Is the company, the customer, or a third party at fault? In some cases, the cause of the difficulty may be unknown. The content of the adjustment letter will depend on these considerations and the company's policy toward adjustments.

■ *Drummonds* (204) 772-8241 2839 Main Street Fairfield, VA 09343	
February 18, 199x	
Mrs. Virginia Bivins 12809 Blasewell Fairfield, VA 09343	
Dear Mrs. Bivins:	
Your new Drummonds charge card is on its way. After you sign your name on the back, you may begin using this special card immediately.	An opening that presents the good news first, along with directions for using the card.
Being able to open charge accounts for customers like you who receive especially favorable ratings is always pleasurable. Each reference listed on your application mentioned your prompt bill-paying habits.	A section that explains the basis for the extension of credit.
The closing date of your account is the thirteenth day of each month. A few days later, you will receive a statement of current charges. No finance charges will be assessed if your payment is received by the fifth day of the following month. Should you wish to extend your payment period, all you need do is pay the amount of the minimum charge appearing on the monthly statement. A finance charge of 1.5 percent (18 percent APR) of the unpaid balance will be added to your statement the following month. Other information about your account is provided on the enclosed sheet entitled "Rules Governing a Retail Credit Agreement."	A section that outlines the important rules governing the use of the card and account.
Our new fall merchandise is arriving daily. Drummonds plans an "early-bird" sale on selected merchandise early next month. As a charge customer, you will receive advance notice of this sale before it is announced to the public.	A section the contains sales-promotion material designed to interest the customer in the merchandise.
Drummonds guarantees your satisfaction with its merchandise and service. You can always count on friendly, courteous service at each of our locations.	A courteous, forward-looking closing.
Sincerely,	
Jonathan Stone Credit Manager	

Exhibit 6-6 Effective credit-granting letter.

Astute businesspeople are continually reminded of the perishable nature of goodwill, especially because no asset is more important to company success. To build and maintain customer goodwill, companies encourage employees in adjustment departments to become skilled in handling every type of adjustment, with the greatest possible speed, courtesy, and tact.

Positive customer relations established through satisfactory products and services can evaporate instantly if a single adjustment letter is negative or offends the reader. Every adjustment letter should project a positive company image.

Well-planned adjustment correspondence based on the you-viewpoint can repair damage and reaffirm customer allegiance. The central idea in the you-approach is

OPENING

1. Does the letter contain a fast-start opening notifying the applicant that he or she has been extended credit?
2. If an order was placed at the time credit was requested, is the status of the order mentioned in the opening?
3. Is the opening void of wording that the reader can easily infer: "I have received your credit request . . .?"
4. Is the opening "you-oriented" rather than "I-oriented"?

MIDDLE

1. If appropriate, have you presented a discussion of the basis for the extension of credit (excellent assets-liabilities ratio, excellent credit references, excellent cash flow, etc.)?
2. Are the rules, policies, or terms of the credit account thoroughly and clearly discussed?
3. Are all items in this section presented accurately? (Please be aware that the inaccurate presentation of rules, policies, or terms can result in a lawsuit between the parties involved.)
4. If appropriate, have you included resale material, reader-benefit material, or sales-promotion material?

CLOSING

1. Is the closing courteous?
2. If appropriate, is the closing action oriented?
3. Is the action desired of the reader clearly and fully described?
4. Does the closing look to the future by mentioning the writer's assurance of a long, positive relationship?

Checklist 6-2 Letters involving the extension of credit.

courtesy, always a key aspect of developing a company's positive image. Review every adjustment letter to ensure you have fully considered the following points:

1. Have you reestablished goodwill between your company and the claimant?
2. Have you used carefully chosen words that will have a positive impact on goodwill?
3. Has the customer been encouraged to deal with the company again?

Why should letters that grant adjustments focus on the you-viewpoint?

By focusing on the you-viewpoint, the adjuster can soothe the irritant and retain or reestablish good relations. Frequently, your actual message matters less to the customer than the manner in which it is presented. Just what the claim actually is depends on the circumstances of the particular situation and the honesty of the individual. Even when the customer is in error, focusing on the you-viewpoint means that satisfying her comes first. Because she is probably annoyed, your letter needs to present a conciliatory tone. Also helpful is focusing on how you plan to handle the situation rather than a long discussion of the details of the problem situation.

Although most companies believe they can expand business by operating on the principle of absolute customer satisfaction, other companies adopt a modified point of view. In these companies, the following attitude prevails: "When the customer is right, give him or her full credit; when the company is right, sell the customer on the company's point of view."

Many companies do more than simply welcome claims—they invite them. Signs in stores, restaurants, hotels, motels, and other establishments invite comments on service or reports of any discourteous treatment by employees. Manufacturers enclose slips asking purchasers to report any defects in materials or production. Some companies send letters inviting at regular intervals frank reaction to their services.

In writing a letter granting an adjustment, avoid a begrudging tone. You never want to convey the impression that granting the adjustment is a questionable—perhaps even unwarranted—action. In addition, remember not to use words with negative connotations. Examples of such words are *complaint, problem,* and *claim,* all of which can be inflammatory. Instead, indicate that you appreciate knowing about the customer's situation.

What type of opening is appropriate for letters that grant adjustments?

A good-news adjustment letter should open with the good news about the adjustment. The first of the following two paragraphs is slow; the revision corrects the problem.

Change: We have received your letter of June 22 in which you requested a replacement of the inoperable electric mixer that was in an order shipped to you on June 15.

To: An electric mixer to replace the inoperable mixer you received in a recent order is on its way. Your request for a replacement mixer was certainly appropriate.

The next paragraph of a positive adjustment letter contains an explanation of the cause of the problem. When your company is at fault, a frank admission of error is appropriate. But avoid making excuses for the problem, and do not promise that it will never occur again. Such promises often require a future retraction! Although the explanation section is important, it need not be lengthy. An apology is also appropriate. Note the defensive tone of the first of the following paragraphs. The revision is forward-looking.

Change: It is hard for us to believe that our quality-control measures did not detect the problem with the mixer you received. Of one thing you can be sure: It will not happen again.

To: Although our quality-control program is 99.5 percent effective—the highest achievement record in the industry—a few defective products slip by undetected. Our goal is to achieve a 100 percent detection record.

What is included in the middle section of positive adjustment letters?

The next section of a positive adjustment letter can contain resale and/or sales-promotion material. If you believe the customer is discouraged with the product that prompted the claim letter or is upset with your company, resale material may be more appropriate than sales-promotion material. On the other hand, if the customer does not seem discouraged, then sales-promotion material may be preferable.

The first of the following two paragraphs uses resale material designed to rebuild the customer's confidence in an electric mixer. The second paragraph contains sales-promotion material about an upcoming sale.

The first time you try your new electric mixer, you will readily discover how easy it is to use. Its variable-speed control enables you to select the precise mixing speed for the ingredients you are mixing. The sure-grip handle comfortably fits hands of all sizes. And the powerful motor maintains a constant speed even with hard-to-mix ingredients. This mixer is destined to become an indispensable appliance the first time it is used.

The brochure enclosed with your replacement mixer lists the merchandise that will be on sale until July 15. The prices of our mid-summer sale merchandise are as much as 50 percent lower than their regular prices. To order any of these items, just use the convenient toll-free number listed above.

What type of closing is appropriate for adjustment letters?

The closing of the adjustment letter gives you another opportunity to rebuild any goodwill that may have been lost in the past. In addition, avoid material in the closing that will remind the reader of the problem. Because you have already apologized, another apology is unnecessary. Rather, focus on the positive by (1) referring to the satisfaction the reader will derive from the item you are replacing, (2) extending an invitation to an upcoming sale, (3) indicating your desire to serve the customer in the future, and so forth.

The tone of the following two closing paragraphs is distinctly different. The tone of the first lacks friendliness and cordiality, whereas the revision conveys the writer's concern about the reader.

Change:	We regret the first electric mixer you received was inoperable.
To:	Many excellent buys are available during our in-progress midsummer sale. An order can be conveniently placed by calling us on our toll-free number (1-800-234-2345) or by using the order blank attached to the sale brochure.

The suggested plan for an adjustment letter includes the following elements:

What is the suggested plan for adjustment letters?

1. An opening presenting the good news first
2. A section discussing the cause of the problem
3. A section containing resale and/or sales promotion material
4. A friendly, cordial closing

Exhibit 6-7 shows an ineffective good-news adjustment letter. Exhibit 6-8 presents an improved version of the same letter. The resale material in Exhibit 6-8 is designed to rebuild the customer's confidence in the product and company.

Sometimes companies make a favorable adjustment even when the customer, who uses a product improperly, is at fault. Perhaps the claimant is a customer of long standing; and as an accommodation, her claim is granted. Exhibit 6-9 is an example of a well-written adjustment letter, describing the proper use of a product.

Checklist 6-3 presents a list of questions to help you in evaluating the effectiveness of good-news adjustment letters.

Exhibit 6-7 Ineffective letter granting an adjustment.

Letter	Comment
Your letter of April 10 in which you requested a replacement of your GT clock-radio has been received. We are sorry you are having problems with this appliance.	A slow-start opening that presents obvious material.
You will be glad to learn that a new clock-radio is on its way to you. It should arrive within ten days.	A delayed presentation of the good news.
An examination of the radio you returned to us revealed several manufacturing defects that were not found by our quality-control inspectors. Although defects do not often go unnoticed by our inspectors, they were not found in the radio you purchased.	A section that contains an overly negative explanation of the cause of the defect.
We are sorry for any inconvenience you may have been caused by our carelessness.	A redundant apology that ends on a negative note.

A new GT clock-radio was sent to you by UPT this morning. The $5 certificate attached to this letter can be applied toward the purchase of your next GT appliance.	An opening that presents the good news first.
The goal of our quality-inspection program is to achieve a 100 percent error-detection record. Although that record has nearly been achieved, a few defective products slip by--and yours was one of those.	A section that explains the cause of the problem; a negative discussion handled in a positive way.
The GT clock-radio you purchased has become our top-selling appliance. Unique features, especially the programmable station selector, are responsible for its popularity. This feature will enable you to go to sleep at night listening to one radio station and wake up in the morning listening to another station–without your having to change the station selector.	A section that presents resale material designed to rebuild the customer's confidence in the product.
Your giving us an opportunity to live up to our motto, "Absolute Satisfaction Guaranteed," is appreciated.	A courteous closing.

Exhibit 6-8 Effective letter granting an adjustment.

Within the next few days, you will receive a new lamp globe to replace the damaged one you recently sent us.	An opening that presents the good news first.
An inspection of the globe revealed that the damage resulted from excessive heat build-up, which occurs when a bulb larger than 60 watts is used in the lamp. A label attached to the lamp socket indicates the maximum bulb size to be used in the lamp is 60 watts.	A section that contains "education" material designed to help the customer avoid the same situation in the future.
"Touch-n-glow" table lamps have just been added to our product line. To turn these attractive lamps on or off, you simply touch any part of the metal base. The shades for these lamps are available in a variety of fabrics and shapes. The brochure that is enclosed illustrates the available bases and shades.	A section that contains sales-promotion material designed to spark the reader's interest in other products.
Mrs. Jones, we are pleased to have you as a customer. Please let us know when we can be of service again.	A courteous closing.

Exhibit 6-9 Effective adjustment letter that contains directions on product use.

ORDER-ACKNOWLEDGMENT LETTERS

The *order-acknowledgment letter* informs the customer that his or her order was received and that it has been shipped (or will be shipped), expresses appreciation to the customer for the order, and builds goodwill.

Whereas some companies acknowledge first orders from new customers, other companies acknowledge all orders exceeding a certain dollar amount. The information in this section refers to the acknowledgment of the first order by a customer. It can easily be adapted to letters acknowledging an order other than the first one, such as a large order by a valued customer.

An order-acknowledgment letter should have a fast-start opening that presents the good news first. The reader is more interested in learning about the status of his or her

OPENING
1. Does the opening contain news about either the requested adjustment or a modified adjustment?
2. Do you avoid a slow start, indicating to the reader that his or her letter has been received?
3. Is the granting of the adjustment done courteously and in a way that avoids a begrudging tone?
4. Is the opening approached from a you-viewpoint?

MIDDLE
1. Is the nature of the situation that caused the need for an adjustment thoroughly, but concisely, discussed?
2. If appropriate, does the discussion of the situation indicate that legitimate requests for adjustment are appreciated as they help the company/organization improve the quality of its goods or services?
3. Does the middle section contain information designed to help rebuild the customer's confidence in the product or service?
4. If appropriate, have you attempted to sell the customer on using other products or services offered by your company/organization?
5. Is the apology sincere but brief?

CLOSING
1. Is the closing courteous and, if appropriate, action oriented?
2. Does the closing have the customer's interest as a primary consideration?
3. Does the closing indicate that you are interested in continuing to work with the customer in other business transactions?

Checklist 6-3 Good-news adjustment letters.

order than receiving a "thank-you." Although a thank-you opening is appropriate, it should follow the information about the status of the order. The first of the following two examples shows a slow-start opening; the revision is a fast-start opening.

What type of opening is appropriate for order-acknowledgment letters?

Change: Thank you for your recent order for three pairs of slacks.
To: The three pairs of slacks you recently ordered were sent by UPS this morning, and they should arrive in three days. Your order and the check for $139.45 are appreciated.

The inclusion of resale and/or sales-promotion material is also appropriate in order-acknowledgment letters. To decide whether to include resale material or sales-promotion material, apply the rule used in adjustment-granting letters. For frequently replaced merchandise, including sales-promotion material may be preferable. But for infrequently replaced merchandise, including resale material may be preferable.

What type of information is appropriate for inclusion in the middle section of order-acknowledgment letters?

Whenever possible, include material reflecting your desire to serve the customer in order-acknowledgment letters. This material can take many forms, such as a reference to your practice of shipping within twenty-four hours of order receipt, your satisfaction-guaranteed policy, your honoring major credit cards, and so on. Sometimes service-attitude material becomes a separate section. In other instances, it is incorporated into other sections, such as a sales-promotion paragraph. The choice is yours to make.

The closing of an order-acknowledgment letter should be forward-looking. Mention your interest in serving the reader or your willingness to answer any questions the reader may have about your products. The first of the following two closing paragraphs is weak because of its indifferent tone; the revision is much more effective because of the orientation to the future.

What type of closing is appropriate for the closing of order-acknowledgment letters?

Change: We appreciate your business.
To: Having you as a new customer is a pleasure. You can always count on fast, courteous service when ordering from the Emmery Company.

Your book order that was shipped this morning should arrive in three to five days. We appreciate having you as a customer.	A fast-start opening that presents good news first and that expresses appreciation.
Johnson's has just become a distributor of books published by Smith-Holly Publishers. As a new distributor, we are able to offer for a limited time a 10 percent discount on the wholesale price. A current list of Smith-Holly titles and their discounted prices is enclosed. You will notice that many of the year's best-selling books are Smith-Holly titles. An order blank is attached to the list.	A section that contains sales-promotion material designed to promote a new line of merchandise.
Recently expanded warehouse facilities enable us to process most orders within 24 hours of their receipt. We also provide a rush-delivery service, enabling you to receive a shipment the day following the receipt of the order.	A section that contains service-attitude material designed to enhance the customer's desire to purchase.
You can always count on efficient, courteous service when ordering from the Masters Book Distributing Company.	A forward-looking closing.

Exhibit 6-10 Effective order-acknowledgment letter.

What is the suggested plan for letters that acknowledge orders?

The suggested plan for an order-acknowledgment letter includes the following elements:

1. A fast-start opening referring to the status of the order and thanking the customer for his or her business
2. A section containing resale or sales-promotion material, whichever is appropriate, and also incorporating material with a service attitude
3. A forward-looking closing

The letter in Exhibit 6-10 shows a well-written order-acknowledgment letter. Note how sales-promotion material is incorporated into the letter.

Rather than writing an order-acknowledgment letter, some companies use a form message that can be printed on a postcard. The variable information is inserted either by hand or by printer device. The following example shows a message that announces the shipment of the order (or the pending shipment of the order).

> Your order was shipped this morning (or will be shipped on ______) by United Parcel Service. Normal delivery time for an order shipped this distance is ______ days. We sincerely appreciate your business.
> Very truly yours,
>
> ____________________________
>
> JOHNSON PLASTICS COMPANY
>
> Mary Brown, Order Correspondent

LETTERS GRANTING FAVORS

A *favor-granting letter* tells the reader that you are able to accommodate the request made of you. This type of letter would seem at first glance to be an extremely easy letter to write. But many favor-granting messages either omit the spirit of willingness to grant the favor or imply a grudging consent that dilutes the spirit of such letters.

The opening paragraph of a favor-granting letter should be cheerful and cordial. The granting of the request, about which the reader is most interested, should be mentioned first. The following is an effective beginning for such a letter.

What type of opening is appropriate for letters that grant favors?

> Yes, I will be pleased to show your students our beautiful new facility. A tour of our building will enable them to see the latest in interior office design.

If your favor has a limitation or a restriction, specify what this entails. For example, the following appropriately discusses a limitation.

> So that the tour can be completed before the employees leave at 4:30, it should begin no later than 3:00. Should you prefer to begin the tour earlier in the afternoon, that will be possible, as my schedule is clear all afternoon on May 23.

The granting of a favor with a limitation or a restriction often necessitates some action on the part of the reader. The following paragraph effectively outlines the requested action.

> Will you please call me at 453-3456 when you decide on the time you would like the tour to begin? We can finalize other details at that time.

The closing of a favor-granting letter should be cordial and courteous, as well as action-oriented, if appropriate. If you are asking the reader to do something, refer to that action in the closing.

What type of closing is appropriate for letters that grant favors?

> The opportunity to show your students our new facility is eagerly awaited. Please let me know when you would like the tour to take place.

The suggested letter plan for a letter that grants a favor includes the following elements:

What is the suggested plan for letters that grant favors?

1. A cordial, courteous opening that mentions the granting of the favor
2. A discussion of restrictions or limitations that pertain to the granting of the favor
3. A discussion, if appropriate, of any action the reader is to take in accepting the favor
4. A cordial, courteous closing that, when appropriate, is action oriented

An example of a well-written letter granting a favor appears in Exhibit 6-11.

In preparing a letter of thanks, include the following elements:

1. An opening expressing appreciation for or thanks to the person for granting you the favor
2. A discussion of how the favor will be beneficial
3. An offer to be of similar help, if appropriate
4. A friendly, courteous closing

Green Insurance Co.

Serving Des Moines Since 1927

102 Green Street (305) 443-6545
Des Moines, IA 54231 FAX (305) 443-9036

September 25, 199x

Mr. David Coultier
9843 Syracuse Rd.
Columbus, OH 34843

Dear David:

When your nephew arrives on October 10, please have him call me at 443-6545. We will be delighted to give him a tour of Des Moines.	A cordial opening that mentions the granting of the favor.
If Rob is available for either lunch or dinner, we would like to have him as our guest.	A section that contains a discussion of the desired action.
Thanks for giving us the opportunity to meet your nephew. We will do everything we can to make sure his visit to Des Moines is a pleasant experience and that he receives a proper introduction to our city.	A cordial, courteous closing.

Sincerely,

Harry Martin
Agent

Exhibit 6-11 Effective letter granting a favor.

Both Rob and I appreciate your being available to show him around Des Moines on October 10. He will call you when he arrives.	An opening that expresses appreciation to the reader for granting the favor.
Your showing him around Des Moines will help him decide whether he wants to accept his company's offer to relocate there. Because he does not know any one who lives in Des Moines, he will appreciate your assistance as he makes his decision.	A section that discusses how granting the favor will benefit the person receiving the favor.
If I may return the favor, please let me know. Rob is also eager to return the favor whenever he can.	A statement of an offer to reciprocate.
Both Rob and I appreciate your helping him.	A courteous closing.

Exhibit 6-12 Effective thank-you letter for the granting of a favor.

Exhibit 6-12 shows a letter of thanks for the granting of a favor. The sincerity of the message gives the letter a genuine tone.

LETTERS OF CONGRATULATIONS

A *letter of congratulations*, an excellent public relations tool, recognizes the achievement or accomplishment of a business acquaintance. Letters of congratulations probably would be the most common type of business letter written if they were prepared as frequently as they should be.

Congratulations on your being recognized as Austin's Young Business Leader of the Year. You are certainly a deserving first recipient of this award.	An opening that congratulates the reader on the accomplishment.
The countless hours you have devoted to improving the business climate of Austin finally "paid off" when it was recently recognized as one of the state's most desirable business communities. You can be proud of the fact that you gave your time and effort for the good of the community–and not for any personal gain.	A section that presents a discussion of your impression of the importance of the reader's accomplishment.
You have my best wishes for the continued success and happiness that you certainly deserve.	A courteous closing that extends best wishes.

Exhibit 6-13 Effective letter of congratulations.

Some companies maintain a regular newspaper-clipping service to identify the persons for whom congratulatory letters are appropriate. When a special event relating to a client or associate is reported in the paper, for example, the article is clipped and enclosed with the congratulatory message. Some occasions or events for which congratulatory letters are appropriate are job promotions, elections to office, achievements in a special interest or hobby, receipts of awards, birthdays, and retirements.

What qualities should letters of congratulation possess?

An indispensable quality of letters of congratulations is sincerity, often attained through the mention of specific details. Trite, stilted phrases signal insincerity, thereby damaging the goodwill that congratulatory letters should create. In addition, you should acknowledge the achievement or accomplishment with enthusiasm and friendliness. You will probably find that when you are writing a letter of congratulations to someone whom you do not know well or who ranks higher than you in your company, the use of a more formal tone is normal. Finally, avoid any hint of a patronizing attitude.

What is the suggested plan for letters of congratulation?

The suggested plan for a congratulatory letter includes the following elements:

1. An opening congratulating the reader for his or her accomplishment or achievement
2. A section expressing your understanding of the importance of the accomplishment or achievement
3. A courteous closing extending best wishes for continued success

Exhibit 6-13 shows an example of a well-written congratulatory letter.

LETTERS RESPONDING TO INVITATIONS

A *letter responding to an invitation* accepts a social-business invitation or an invitation to a business-related event. The letter should convey appreciation and enthusiasm and should be sent promptly following the receipt of an invitation. Although letters accepting an invitation may be fairly brief, you should include certain essential elements.

The opening should convey your acceptance. Also incorporate into the acceptance important details about the event: date, time, and place. These details should be present (1) to verify the accuracy of these details in case of error, and (2) to provide a record of the details if the invitation is misplaced. The letter ends with a courteous, positive, and forward-looking closing that expresses appreciation for the invitation.

The suggested plan for a letter of acceptance for a social-business invitation includes the following elements:

What is the suggested plan for letters in which social-business invitations are accepted?

1. An opening cordially and enthusiastically accepting the invitation
2. A review of the important details about the event
3. A courteous closing expressing appreciation for the invitation

Exhibit 6-14 shows a well-written letter accepting an invitation to a social-business event. Note how the important details about the event are incorporated into the letter.

After the event has taken place, proper etiquette may require your sending a thank-you message to the individual(s) who hosted the event. The beginning of such a message should include a cordial expression of thanks. Next discuss the importance of the event and follow with a cordial expression of appreciation in the closing.

What is the suggested plan for thank-you letters?

The suggested plan for a letter of thanks for an event includes the following elements:

1. An opening containing a cordial, sincere thanks
2. A discussion of the highlights of the event
3. A courteous, cordial closing

Exhibit 6-15 shows a well-written letter expressing appreciation for the invitation for a social business event.

Exhibit 6-14 Effective letter accepting a social-business invitation.

Letter	Comment
Mrs. Brown and I enthusiastically accept your invitation to the retirement dinner for Mr. Robinson. This event will be a fine tribute to Jack, whose accomplishments as executive vice president of Willoby Corporation are extensive.	An opening that mentions the enthusiastic acceptance of the invitation.
Because the retirement dinner is to be a surprise to Jack, we will say nothing to him about it before that evening.	A section that reviews details of the event.
Mrs. Brown and I appreciate your inviting us to this important event. We will see you at The Embers Restaurant at 6 p.m. on October 20.	A closing that expresses appreciation and reviews other important details.

Exhibit 6-15 Effective letter expressing appreciation for a social-business invitation.

Letter	Comment
Mrs. Brown and I sincerely thank you for inviting us to Mr. Robinson's retirement dinner. We were especially pleased to join others in paying tribute to such a hard-working, dedicated employee of the Willoby Corporation.	An opening that expresses cordial thanks for the event.
Jack's impromptu after-dinner remarks were quite impressive. The graciousness with which he delivered those remarks was noteworthy. As always, he gave others all the credit for his success.	A section that discusses the event's highlights.
Thanks for giving us the opportunity to help honor Jack.	A cordial closing.

Yes, I am available to speak at the May meeting of the Personnel Administrators Association—and I enthusiastically accept your invitation to talk about new legislation affecting personnel management.	An opening that enthusiastically conveys the acceptance.
Also, my schedule will enable me to join your group for the dinner that begins at six on the eighteenth. I will arrive at The Continental a few minutes before six.	A section that confirms important details about the event.
Thank you for inviting me to speak to your group.	A courteous closing.

Exhibit 6-16 Effective letter accepting a speaking invitation.

You may receive a letter inviting you to speak before a group. Your return letter should state your acceptance in the opening paragraph. Mention here also such important details as date, time, and place to confirm their accuracy. If you have been given the opportunity to select the subject and/or topic of your presentation, also state what you have chosen.

The suggested plan for a letter accepting a speaking invitation includes the following elements:

What is the suggested plan for letters that convey the acceptance of speaking invitations?

1. An enthusiastic opening mentioning the acceptance of the invitation
2. A confirmation of the important details, including the subject or topic of your presentation, if appropriate
3. A courteous closing

Exhibit 6-16 shows an effectively written letter accepting a speaking invitation.

GOOD-NEWS AND INFORMATIVE MEMOS

Memos that present their readers with good news or inform their readers about an event or a change in procedure use the direct organizational plan. Therefore, the opening contains your main point or purpose.

The following outlines the content appropriate for the three major sections of good-news and informative memos:

What content is appropriate for the three major sections of good-news and informative memos?

Opening section	Presentation of main point
Middle section	Elaboration of main point (significance to reader, benefit to reader, explanation of change, reasons for change, and so forth)
Closing section	Presentation of desired action or presentation of additional information about main point

As with any type of business document, the tone of your writing is critical to the success of your message. Unless you are careful when writing informative memos, you may find yourself using a tone that others perceive to be abrupt or dictatorial. If this occurs, your readers may become less likely to want to accept your message.

The following is the opening paragraph of a good-news memo from the president of the DEF Company to the Auditing Department. The purpose is to announce the appointment of a new manager of the department.

> Congratulations to Ms. Mary Johnston upon her appointment as manager of the Auditing Department. She will assume this position on July 1, the day that Bill Brown retires from that position.

What is contained in the middle section of a good-news and informative memo?

The middle section of a good-news or informative memo contains an elaboration of essential details or relevant additional information. Note in the following paragraph, which is the middle section of the good-news memo announcing a new head of the Auditing Department, how the company president discusses the significance of the appointment.

> Ms. Johnston, who is currently an auditing group supervisor in a Big Six accounting firm, is well suited for the position as head of the Auditing Department. She has had ten years of professional experience working for the same firm in Dallas, Austin, and Houston. Ms. Johnston recently decided it was time for a career change, so she applied for the position here (one of forty to do so). With a bachelor's and master's degree in accounting from the University of Texas at Austin, she is highly qualified.
>
> Those who visited with Ms. Johnston when she interviewed for the position were impressed by her professional attitude, her charming personality, and her breadth and depth of experience in the auditing field. All of the individuals with whom we visited where she currently works were unanimous in their high praise of her as a person and as a professional.

What is the purpose of the closing section of good-news and informative memos?

The closing section of good-news and informative memos is designed to "close out" or summarize the situation. Exhibit 6-17 shows the closing section of the good-news memo announcing the appointment of Ms. Johnston as the new head of the Auditing Department. Note how it requests some action.

> At 8 a.m. on July 1, I am hosting in Room 331 a coffee hour in Ms. Johnston's honor. Please join me in giving her a warm, cordial welcome as the new head of the Auditing Department.

Exhibit 6-17 shows a memo announcing an upcoming committee meeting.

Exhibit 6-17 Informative memo notifying readers of a meeting.

```
                    Interoffice Memorandum

   DATE: January 12, 199x
     TO: Members of Job Evaluation Committee
   FROM: Janet Brownlee, Chair; Job Evaluation Committee
SUBJECT: Meeting, January 27, 3:30 p.m., Room 201

The Job Evaluation Committee will meet on Thursday, January 27, at 3:30 p.m.
in Room 201. The meeting will likely last until 5.

The meeting will focus on examining several job evaluation methods, informa-
tion about which is enclosed with this memo. Please review this material
before the meeting so we can spend time discussing the pros and cons of each
method. By February 15, we will need to make a decision about which method
to use in evaluating our office support positions.

Please let me know whether you are able to attend the meeting or if you have
questions or concerns about the committee's upcoming work.

Enclosure
```

SUMMARY

Some of the good-news letters you will write in business are letters replying to inquiries about products, services, and people; letters responding to credit requests; letters granting adjustments and acknowledging orders; letters granting favors; letters offering congratulations; and letters accepting invitations.

Good-news letters offer a fast-start opening by beginning with the good news or main idea, provide explanatory details or information of primary and secondary importance, incorporate a you-viewpoint, and have an appropriate closing.

In deciding whether to grant credit, applicants consider the factors of capital, capacity, and character—the three C's of credit. The most common types of credit accounts are regular credit accounts, ninety-day-same-as-cash accounts, and long-term installment accounts.

Although the letter plans for preparing the various types of good-news letters have common elements, they also have differences of which you need to be aware.

Good-news and informative memos rely on a direct organizational plan. Present your main point in the opening section, provide additional relevant information in the middle section, and "close out" the memo in the last section.

REVIEW QUESTIONS

1. Identify the characteristics of good-news letters.
2. What type of opening should you use when writing a letter responding to an inquiry about a product?
3. When should you include resale material in a response to an inquiry about a product? When should you include sales-promotion material?
4. How does the opening of a response to an inquiry about a product differ from the opening of a response to an inquiry about a person?
5. What are the three C's of credit?
6. What types of credit accounts are typically used in business?
7. What are the purposes of a letter extending credit to customers?
8. In a letter extending credit, how does the use of resale material differ from the use of sales-promotion material?
9. What information should be included in the opening of a good-news adjustment letter?
10. What determines whether you should use resale or sales-promotion material in a good-news adjustment letter?
11. What information should be included in the opening of an order-acknowledgment letter?
12. What are the elements of the plan for a letter granting a favor?
13. What content is appropriate for each of the three main sections of a good-news memo?

APPLICATION PROBLEMS

1. Prepare a written critique of the following letter, evaluating grammar usage, punctuation, conformity with prescribed letter plan, and conformity with the writing essentials discussed in Chapters 3 and 4.

> It is with a great deal of pleasure that I notify you that you have been qualified for one of our prestigious charge accounts. Not everyone qualifies, but then I'm sure I don't have to tell you that.
>
> I hope you enjoy using the card often, just make sure your pay your account in a timely manner. We don't want to have to send the sheriff after you—but then we are sure you will pay as you don't want to have the sheriff coming after you any worse than we want to have to send him after you.
>
> You have our best wishes and congratulations on being the proud owner of a Ellington's charge account.

2. Rewrite the letter in application problem 1, correcting the weaknesses you identified in your critique. Make any assumptions you need to regarding the content of the letter, and supply any missing details.
3. (Response letter) You are the customer service representative for the Arco Products Company, located at 19 Pine Avenue, Chicago, IL 67544. Your company is one of the nation's largest manufacturers of electronic entertainment equipment, such as video cassette recorders, televisions, stereos, and tape recorders. Your company is widely recognized for the superior workmanship in the products it manufactures. Because of its reputation, Arco has many customers who wouldn't buy anything but Arco equipment. You recently received a letter from a potential customer (Charles Smith, 1212 Hornblower Avenue, Sacramento, CA 98944) who asked several questions about the Arco B-8910 video cassette recorder. Mr. Smith wanted to know the length of the programming period on the VCR and the number of programs that can be recorded during that period (four programs in fourteen days), how many heads the B-8910 has (four), and who is the closest Arco dealer to Sacramento (Walt's TV and Appliances, 1232 Jackson Boulevard, San Jose, CA 18235). In your reply, you also decided to mention that the B-8910 has stereo audio. Arco's nationwide Mid-Summer Sale begins in two weeks. During this time, all dealers will be reducing the price of their entire Arco line by 30 percent.
4. (Response letter) You and a friend, P. J. Clark, just began the Gourmet Catering Service, located at 984 Louisiana Street, Dayton, OH 48454. Both of you realized the void created when the most famous caterer in Dayton, the Catering Kitchen, recently went out of business. Although you haven't begun to advertise yet, you are getting some business through word of mouth. In fact, you just received a letter from Mrs. Barbara Chenowith, 9874 Riverside Drive, Columbus, OH 45854, who is planning her family's annual reunion. Mrs. Chenowith is interested in having a sit-down dinner catered for approximately fifty people on August 23. Mrs. Chenowith asked several questions to which you need to respond, including the following: Are you available at 6 p.m. on August 23? (Yes); What do you suggest for a menu that would appeal to people of every age? (A turkey dinner with all the trimmings); Can the meal be provided for less than $6 per person? (Yes, it can be catered for $5.45); Are all dishes and food servers provided? (Yes); Can you find a place to hold the event? (The Gardner State Bank Community Room is an excellent place and will easily accommodate 60-70 persons; it is next door to a park). Prepare a letter that responds to Mrs. Chenowith.
5. (Response letter) You are a public relations assistant for the Mass Central Insurance Company, located at 345 Beacon Street in Boston, MA 09821. Your company just developed a new term insurance policy that promises to become a leader in a short time. The Progressive Term Policy will be advertised in all the national weekly magazines in two weeks. Accompanying the ad is a coupon that interested parties can send back to Mass Central to request more information. Interested parties also receive a letter along with the packet of information. You are responsible for preparing the "form" letter that will be included with the packet of information. Because high-speed word processing equipment is available, the letters are to be personalized with the recipient's name. You decide to mention several of the policy highlights in the letter: provides a greater amount of coverage per dollar of premium than the three leading term policies; after twenty years, the term policy can be converted to a paid-up whole-life policy equal to 20 percent of the value of the initial term policy; insured has a choice of level premiums or level amount of coverage; and Mass Central has a well-trained, large field staff ready to serve insured's needs. Prepare the letter.
6. (Response letter) You are the executive vice president of the State Bank of Dillard, 1243 Michigan Avenue, Dillard, MI 48843. From January 1985 until January

1992, Ms. Linda Smith was your secretary. You found her to be an exceptionally fine employee. She and her family left Dillard when her husband was transferred to Indiana by his employer. Today, you received a letter from Mr. John Gentry, president of the Guardian National Bank, Box 1, Guardian, IN 54344. He indicated that he is considering hiring Ms. Smith as his secretary. His decision will probably be influenced by your input. He asked for information about her trustworthiness (absolutely no concern), the quality of her work (always done without error), her ability to work well with others (gains immediate respect of others), her attitude (very positive), and her initiative (puts a considerable amount of effort into everything she does). You also decide to mention that she frequently participates in self-development activities, that she passed the Certified Professional Secretary exam the first time she took it, and that she has a considerable amount of ability to offer as an employee. In all respects, you would probably judge her to be in the "top 1 or 2 percent of individuals in the secretarial field," and she certainly has your support for this position. Prepare the letter you plan to send to Mr. Gentry.

7. (Credit-granting letter) As credit manager for Handley's Department Store, you are responsible for preparing letters that extend credit to customers. In response to the letter you recently sent to solicit prospective credit customers, you received a signed application from Ms. Mary Jane O'Donnell, 345 University Drive, Ponca City, TX 54478. She is a senior at Ponca City College and will be graduating in three months. Experience has taught you that individuals who are about to be graduated or who have recently graduated from college are often excellent credit customers because they have higher-than-usual purchasing needs, they do not attempt to save as much as their counterparts, and their salaries enable them to pay their accounts on time. Prepare a letter extending credit to Ms. O'Donnell. Her credit limit is $300. Remind her that an enclosure entitled "Rules Governing the Use of Your Handley's Charge Account" accompanies the letter. Among the important rules you decide to mention in the letter are (1) the interest rate on unpaid balances is 1.5 percent per month (18 percent APR), (2) a minimum charge of 10 percent or $10, whichever is greater, is to be paid each month the account shows activity, (3) the closing date of the account is the twenty-eighth day of each month, and (4) to be credited properly, payments on account must be received within twenty-five days after the account's closing date. You may also want to mention that your Santa's Helper Sale will run from November 19-24, and the prices on many items in the store will be reduced by 20 to 25 percent.

8. (Good-news adjustment letter) You work in the adjustments department of the Arnold Manufacturing Company, located at 6876 Outer Belt Drive, St. Louis, MO 63723. The company manufactures a variety of lawn and garden power tools. Although Arnold's tools are sold in hardware and garden stores across the Midwest, the company has customers throughout the Continental United States who purchase by mail order. You recently received an electric hedge clipper returned by John Abrahamson (18 Lake Lane, Utica, NY 10189) who had purchased the clipper by mail order on June 2. The curt note attached to the clipper explained that the tool did not work when it was received. He is asking that you send him another clipper as a replacement. An examination of the clipper revealed that onc of the internal electrical wires was improperly soldered, preventing a suitable contact. Your company has quality-control measures to find such flaws, but this slipped by undetected. Grant Mr. Abrahamson's request that you replace the original clipper with another one that works properly. The replacement clipper was shipped this morning by UPS. Mention in the letter that Arnold is now carrying a rubber hose line. These hoses are guaranteed for seven years; they are available in a variety of colors, lengths, and diameters; and a new quick-coupler device is attached to each hose end that eliminates the threaded couplers. Quick-couplers with threaded ends are also available, facilitating attachment of hoses with conventional ends.

9. (Order-acknowledgment letter) You work in the order department of Grant's (19 State Lane, Concord, NH 12321), a large mail-order house specializing in a variety of kitchen accessories. Several years ago, Grant's began sending its first-time customers a letter acknowledging the order and thanking them for their patronage. You have been given the assignment of preparing a new form letter to be used to acknowledge an order. Because Grant's prefers to use a form letter (although it is printed on word processing equipment), the message you prepare will need to be suitable for all responses. This means you will have no opportunity to mention in the letter what merchandise was ordered or how beneficial the merchandise will be to its recipient. From time to time, you will change sales-promotion material in the letter to reflect current activities. Prepare a form letter suitable for use in acknowledging a first order. The sales-promotion material to be included in this letter should mention that a mid-winter sale will be in progress from January 15 to February 15—the time that the company's business is slowest. The sale items are presented in a special mailer to be sent with the acknowledgment. Mention that many of them have been reduced by 15 to 25 percent and you guarantee shipping an order within forty-eight hours of its receipt. Also mention that you honor major credit cards.
10. (Favor-granting letter) You are the head of the auditing unit at Jackson Electric Company, 1123 Industrial Drive, Omaha, NE 68443. You just received a letter from a college friend of yours (Nick Cormun, 18 Seaside Road, Boston, MA 18713) who asked if you would be able to spend a few hours with his younger brother Greg when he is in Omaha on June 18 and 19. Greg is an accounting major at Boston University and cannot decide in what area of accounting he wants to specialize. He has an interview at one of the banks in Omaha on June 18 and 19. Nick suggested the evening of June 19 might be good as Greg doesn't leave Omaha until the next morning. You are excited to meet Nick's brother, to tell him about a career in auditing, and to show him around Omaha just in case he gets the job in the bank. You would like for Greg to call you when he arrives (office phone: 484-0874; home phone: 854-4848) so you can make final arrangements. Suggest to Nick that Greg be a dinner guest in your home the evening of June 19.
11. (Congratulatory letter) You are the president of the Cincinnati Chapter of Administrative Management Society and just saw in the business section of the *Cincinnati Times* that Rebecca Smith, one of your newer members, has received a job promotion. She is currently office services supervisor of the Greater Cincinnati National Bank (10 Main Street, Cincinnati, OH 48443) and will become director of operations for the bank on September 15. This is a big promotion that Rebecca certainly deserves. Your next-door neighbor is Rebecca's boss who is always telling you about the excellent work that Rebecca does. And, of course, you are aware of Rebecca's abilities, as she was the chairperson of last year's Administrative Management Society's professional seminars. These seminars were the most profitable they have ever been, thanks in large part to Rebecca's hard work. They went off without a hitch—which is unusual. Write a letter congratulating Rebecca on her well-deserved promotion.
12. (Congratulatory letter) You are a student in Professor John Smith's written communications class at Eastern State College, Champion, IL 68543. You were just reading the school's paper, *The Advocate*, and noticed in an article summarizing the school's board of regents' actions that Professor Smith was just promoted from assistant to associate professor. You were especially glad to read this information because you have found his class to be one of the best—if not the best—you have ever taken. He makes learning about writing exciting, has helped you master writing fundamentals, motivates his students to be the best they can be, and shows a considerable amount of concern for their welfare. Write a letter congratulating Professor Smith on this well-deserved promotion.

13. (Invitation-acceptance letter) You are currently a director on the board of the North Platte Chamber of Commerce. One of your specific duties on the board is to represent the Chamber at a variety of social/business functions. You just received a letter from Ms. Sally Thomas, North Platte High School, North Platte, NE 58533, asking you to provide a short welcome at the banquet that follows a statewide teachers' meeting. Your spouse has also been invited to attend the banquet. As a former teacher, you especially appreciate the opportunity to deliver the welcome. The banquet will begin at 6:15 P.M. on April 12 in the White Horse Hotel. Both you and your spouse appreciate the dinner invitation. Prepare a letter accepting this invitation.
14. (Good-news memo) You are the assistant to the president of Dickson Electronics, Inc., in Sommerset, NJ. Although the company you work for manufactures a number of electronic components used in various types of equipment, its transistor line is its "bread and butter." Recently one of the country's premier manufacturers of systems boards for personal computers signed a multiyear $1.2 million contract with Dickson to supply it with a variety of transistors. This is very good news for the company, as it helps secure the jobs of Dickson employees. Also, because Dickson has an employee profit-sharing plan, employees will enjoy an increased level of financial reward. John Dickson, the president of the company, has asked you to prepare a memo to all employees announcing the signing of the contract. He has also requested that you include in the memo information about the significance of this lucrative contract to Dickson and to its employees. Prepare the memo that will be sent out under Mr. Dickson's name.
15. (Informative memo) As executive vice president of Arcula Shipping Co., a three-state trucking line (Arkansas, Louisiana, and Texas), you are responsible for informing employees of changes in the company's operating policies and procedures. The company recently implemented a new fringe benefit—life insurance—for all its full-time employees. Although the insurance is not mandatory, the company will pay half the premiums for any employee interested in enrolling in the program. The insurance is provided by The Rock Insurance Company of Boston. The amount of insurance provided each employee is determined by multiplying the employee's base salary by 2.5. The program will become effective next January 1. Enrollment information will be made available later. Prepare for the employees a memo announcing the new life insurance program.

7

Disappointing-News Letters and Memos

After studying this chapter, you should be able to

1. Discuss ways to improve the effectiveness of disappointing-news letters.
2. Discuss the "do-nature" suggestions for preparing disappointing-news letters.
3. Discuss the "don't-nature" suggestions for preparing disappointing-news letters.
4. Identify the elements of the letter plan used in preparing the various types of disappointing-news letters.
5. Prepare effective letters of the type discussed in this chapter.
6. Prepare effective memos of the type discussed in this chapter.

A variety of situations arise in the business world that require the preparation of letters and memos conveying disappointing news. Your goal in writing these messages is to deliver negative news in an unoffensive way, which will help avoid alienating your reader.

The potential for disappointing the recipients of negative-news letters and memos requires special effort when you plan and prepare these messages. Each word you choose has to be weighed carefully. So does the location of the negative information in each document; placing the refusal too early in the message may damage the goodwill that business writers work so hard to create.

The following types of disappointing-news letters are discussed in this chapter:

1. Negative responses to inquiries
2. Negative responses to adjustment requests
3. Negative responses to credit requests
4. Problem-order letters
5. Declines of invitations
6. Declines of favor requests

This chapter also discusses ways to improve the effectiveness of disappointing-news memos. The manner in which such memos are prepared often influences how they affect the reader.

ORGANIZING DISAPPOINTING-NEWS LETTERS

Where is the refusal statement presented in direct- and indirect-plan letters?

Disappointing-news letters convey negative news to the reader. Two options are available when organizing these messages: the indirect organizational plan and the direct organizational plan. The location of the statement of refusal in the letter determines which plan is used. The *indirect plan* delays the refusal statement until after the facts have been presented and the reasons for the refusal have been discussed. In contrast, the *direct plan* presents the statement of refusal at the beginning of the letter. Of the two options, business writers generally prefer the indirect plan because it softens the blow to the reader by discussing the reason(s) for the disappointing news before its delivery.

The following outlines show the difference between the indirect and direct options:

Indirect Option

1. Begin with a neutral or buffered beginning.
2. Review the facts and analyze the reasons for refusal.
3. State the refusal (and make counteroffer if appropriate).
4. Courteous closing.

Direct Option

1. State the refusal immediately.
2. Review the facts and analyze the reasons for the refusal.
3. Make counteroffer (if appropriate).
4. Courteous closing.

A review of the letter in Exhibit 7-1a, organized around the indirect plan, and the letter in Exhibit 7-1b, organized around the direct plan, reveals differences between the two plans. Although the letters contain essentially the same information, the order of the information varies considerably. The buffered opening of the indirect letter tends to maintain goodwill more effectively than does the opening of the direct letter. An opening with a direct approach may cause readers to perceive the message as abrupt and harsh.

Exhibit 7-1a Disappointing-news letter using indirect plan.

As a long-term financial contributor to organizations that help the community's less-fortunate children, we are very supportive of the activities of the Providence House Society. We were pleased to read the recently published newspaper article about the successful lives that several of your former dependent children are now enjoying as adults.

The property insurance carrier we use prohibits the use of our parking lot and adjacent lawn for noncompany events. When we called our agent about purchasing a one-day liability insurance policy so you could hold your annual spring outing on our premises, we found the special insurance had to be purchased for a minimum of thirty days. Because the cost of this special insurance is prohibitive, we are suggesting the use of the facilities at Palmer Park. You will be able to purchase through the city's Parks and Recreation Department one-day liability insurance coverage for special events held at this park.

Should you decide to have your outing at Palmer Park, we would like to donate to Providence House Society an amount equal to the cost of this one-day special insurance coverage. As soon as you discover how much the cost of the coverage will be, please let me know so a check can be sent.

Best wishes for a successful spring outing.

```
The cost of the special insurance that would be needed for Providence House
Society to hold its annual spring outing on our premises is prohibitive.
Because our property insurance prohibits the use of our parking lot and
adjacent lawn for noncompany events, we contacted our insurance agent about
purchasing a special liability policy. We learned the special insurance had to
be purchased for a minimum of thirty days.

As we are a longtime financial contributor to organizations that help the
community's less-fortunate children, we want to make sure your annual spring
outing is a success. Therefore, we suggest you use the facilities at Palmer
Park. The city's Parks and Recreation Department sells one-day liability
insurance coverage for special events held at the park.

Should you decide to have your outing at Palmer Park, we would like to donate
to Providence House Society an amount equal to the cost of this one-day special
insurance coverage. As soon as you know how much the cost of the coverage will
be, please contact me so we can send you a check.

The recently published article about the successful lives several of your
former dependent children are now enjoying as adults was heart-warming. Success
stories like these attest to the excellent work of Providence House. Best
wishes for continued success.
```

Exhibit 7-1b Disappointing-news letter using direct plan.

IMPROVING THE EFFECTIVENESS OF DISAPPOINTING-NEWS LETTERS

You can eliminate much of the negative tone in disappointing-news letters by carefully selecting appropriate words to use throughout your message. The following discussion outlines how to develop each of the sections of disappointing-news letters.

Neutral or Buffered Opening

The purpose of the neutral or buffered opening is to diffuse as much as possible the situation about which the letter is being written. The *buffered opening* is material at the beginning of the disappointing-news letter that softens the blow, thereby keeping the reader from becoming more annoyed or angry. Stating the refusal in the opening sentence, a characteristic of the direct plan, is likely to intensify the reader's anger.

Presented in Communications Capsule 7-1 are several suggestions for improving the effectiveness of neutral or buffered openings.

Communication Capsule 7-1 Improving the Effectiveness of the Buffered Opening

In developing the neutral or buffered opening, you will find these suggestions helpful:

1. Avoid the use of irrelevant material. Examples of material considered irrelevant in a neutral or buffered opening are the following.

> Brown's was just named as the exclusive Jackson-Barr Furniture dealer in San Antonio.
>
> Brown's greatly appreciates loyal customers like you.

2. Avoid the use of information that may cause the reader to assume a request is being granted. Examples of material that may have caused the reader to believe his/her request was being granted are the following.

Thank you for your recent request for a replacement of the Kitchen-Helper toaster you purchased from us last year.

Gordon Electronics, the exclusive dealer of Kitchen-Helper appliances in Tulsa, stands behind the products it sells.

3. Do not apologize unless you are at fault. The following statement is an example of a wrongful apology.

We are sorry your recently purchased Jackson electric drill, which was used in ways other than those recommended in the owner's manual, has resulted in your dissatisfaction with this product.

4. Keep the buffered opening an appropriate length. If it is too short, it may seem abrupt; if it is too long, it is likely to arouse the reader's suspicion. An example of a buffered opening that is too short, which causes it to seem abrupt is the following.

You are entitled to many years of excellent service from the Arbor hedge trimmer you recently purchased from Ames.

5. Avoid the use of a slow-start opening that contains obvious statements. Examples of obvious statements are the following.

We have received your letter of March 2 in which you requested an adjustment on your account.

This is to inform you that your letter of March 2, in which you requested an adjustment on your account, has been received.

6. Consider the buffer to be a transitional expression paving the way for outlining the reasons you cannot grant the request.

Among the types of material suitable for inclusion in the buffered opening of disappointing-news letters are

1. Material in a previous communication used as a basis for discussing points about which you and the reader agree.
2. Material expressing your desire to be cooperative.
3. Material assuring the reader that you have carefully considered the situation.
4. Material relaying any favorable information appropriate for the situation.
5. Material showing empathy for the reader's dilemma.
6. Material expressing appreciation to the reader.

Among the words you will want to avoid using in the buffered opening are the following: *loss, claim, forced, problem, difficult, unfortunate,* and *mistake.*

Review of the Facts and Analysis of the Reasons for the Refusal

Why should the facts be reviewed and the reasons for the refusal be analyzed?

This section of the letter reviews the facts and analyzes the situation, enabling the reader to understand your reasons for refusing the request. The more convinced the reader is that you made the correct decision under the circumstances, the more likely you will keep the reader's goodwill. In the indirect plan, the reasons for the refusal are stated before the actual refusal. If you outline the facts carefully, the reader may have already concluded that the refusal is warranted before actually reading the refusal.

You should summarize the facts of the situation in a clear-cut, straightforward manner. Present your reasons for saying no as convincingly as possible, emphasizing those that benefit the reader. If you can incorporate reader benefit into your reasons, the reader will probably better understand your decision than if you rely solely on reasons without reader benefit. In addition, you avoid making direct accusations or implying anything that seems to question the reader's motives or behavior.

In some cases, the reasons for the refusal may have both favorable and unfavorable elements. Psychologically, the preferred approach is to discuss the favorable elements before the unfavorable ones. To illustrate, suppose you are denying credit to someone because of an unfavorable assets-liabilities ratio, although all his credit references reported that he paid his bills on time. In this case, discuss the applicant's bill-paying habits before mentioning his unfavorable assets-liabilities ratio, which led to your refusal. Moreover, presenting general reasons before specific reasons may soften the blow.

In addition, present your ideas in a rank order, with the reason most important to the reader presented first. Tell your reader only what he or she needs to know. Saying more may cause the reader to believe that you are simply trying to justify a reason that may not be the true reason for saying no.

State the Refusal

The more clearly you discussed the facts in the previous section, the less likely the reader will have ill feelings toward you when reading the refusal statement. In fact, you may be able in some instances to use an *implied refusal*, a technique that prevents your having to explicitly state the refused request in a disappointing-news letter. However, if the chance exists for misunderstanding the implied refusal, you should write a more explicit statement.

Note how the discussion of reasons in the first of the following two paragraphs enables you to imply the refusal. Contrast it with the explicit refusal in the second example.

> *Implied:* The warranty accompanying your camera provided you with free parts and labor for one year following the date of its purchase. Our records show you purchased your camera nearly two years ago.
>
> *Explicit:* The warranty accompanying your camera provided you with free parts and labor for one year following the date of its purchase. Because you purchased your camera nearly two years ago, we are not obligated to provide you with free repairs to your camera.

How should the refusal be stated?

When appropriate, weave the statement of refusal with a positive counterproposal. This is where you can emphasize what you can do for the reader rather than what you cannot do. For example, suppose you are unable to extend credit in the amount requested but can extend it for a lesser amount. Focusing attention on what you can do will help maintain the reader's goodwill.

Integrating resale material with the statement of refusal can also help soften the statement of refusal. Some disappointing messages appropriately contain material designed to resell the reader on the services, products, or practices of the organization for which you work. If the situation is appropriate for the use of resale material, you should consider its inclusion.

What is the purpose of resale material in the refusal statement?

Place the actual statement of refusal in the least emphatic position in the paragraph. Because the beginning and ending of paragraphs tend to carry more emphasis than the middle of paragraphs, this means putting your refusal in the middle. Basically, in this section avoid negative words or phrases, such as *wrong, unqualified, reject, we must refuse . . .* and *we are unable to grant. . . .*

Where should the statement of refusal be placed?

The information found in the following Ethics Episode should help you assess the ethical nature of the organizational plan you use to deal with your refusal.

ETHICS EPISODE

In your disappointing-news messages, your intentions are important. In fact, your intentions will determine whether you are acting ethically or unethically. For example, if you unknowingly misstate yourself when writing a refused adjustment letter, your action is not as serious as if you purposely misstate yourself or if you intentionally wish to deceive the reader. Because we don't intentionally want to hurt someone, we sometimes forego honesty in the interest of being tactful. In these cases, if you "stretch" the truth, you may be acting unethically. But if you avoid telling the "whole story"—perhaps so you don't hurt the reader's feelings—your actions may not be as serious.

Consider the following two situations, both of which involved the preparation of disappointing-news messages:

1. Suppose you work in the customer service department of a tool manufacturing company. One of your responsibilities is to determine whether customers' claim requests are honored. Also suppose you recently received a request from a customer that his malfunctioning electric drill needs to be replaced. You found the customer's letter to be insulting, rude, and disrespectful. An examination of the registration card revealed the warranty had expired ten days before the receipt of his requested adjustment. Normally, the customer service department has a twenty-one-day grace period, meaning that the warranty will be honored for a period of up to three weeks after the warranty expires. Because of the tone of the letter you received from the customer, you decide to deny the request. You tell the customer that the company does not honor claims on products "out of warranty," when, in fact, it routinely does for up to three weeks after the warranty expires. Your intention in replying is to "get even" with the reader by denying his claim because he was rude to you. To make adjustment decisions on the basis of factors other than accepted or approved operating policies that result in treating people differently is not ethical.
2. Suppose you are a unit supervisor in a large company. Also suppose one of your subordinates asked to be considered for promotion as he considers himself to be on a "fast track." Others generally perceive him as being arrogant and abrasive, although fairly competent. When you discussed the subordinate's promotion with your superior (whose approval is necessary), his reply was as follows: "No way; John has much to learn before he is ready for a promotion. He has a serious attitude problem. Besides, he hasn't been here long enough to be promoted." When you write the memo to explain to John the reason why his promotion was refused, you are confronted with the following dilemma: Should you be tactful at the expense of being honest or be honest at the expense of being tactful? Being tactful, you can tell him that his promotion was declined because he hasn't worked for the company a sufficient length of time. Being honest, you can tell him that his current attitude makes him unsuitable for promotion at this time. If you decide to be tactful and tell him that he hasn't worked for the company a sufficient length of time to be promoted, you are probably not acting unethically simply because you are not telling the whole story.

Courteous Closing

A courteous closing helps to reduce any negative feelings the reader has after reading your refusal, thereby promoting a positive present and future business relationship. Thus, the closing should have a positive rather than a negative tone. Above all else, it must sound sincere because the reader will "pick up" on any insincerity and probably react negatively to it.

What characteristics should the closings of refusal letters possess?

You can develop a courteous closing that encourages goodwill in some of the following ways:

1. Explain what further action the reader is to take (such as providing additional documentation, completing a form, and so forth) and the date by which the action is to be taken.
2. Review why the reader's continued business or potential business will be appreciated.
3. Offer to be of help in the future (if appropriate).
4. Express good wishes (if appropriate).

DO'S AND DON'TS TO FOLLOW IN PREPARING DISAPPOINTING-NEWS MESSAGES

What suggestions do you have for improving the effectiveness of disappointing-news letters?

Suggestions for enhancing the effectiveness of disappointing-news messages follow. The sentence(s) following each suggestion illustrates its use.

Do Suggestions

1. Use a neutral or buffered opening that produces agreement rather than disagreement.

> When you purchase a Garden Wise lawn mower, you have every right to expect that it will be of the quality commonly associated with the Garden Wise name.

2. Discuss the facts and analyze the situation in sufficient detail, which will help convince the reader of your honesty and sincerity.

> We consider a number of factors when reviewing applications for credit. Included are such factors as length of time at one residence, length of time of current employment, income, assets, bill-paying record, and amount of current financial obligations.

3. Consider using an implicit rather than an explicit refusal.

> The warranty that came with your Mix-Rite electric mixer is in effect for the first year of ownership, beginning with the date of purchase. Our records show your mixer was purchased more than two years ago.

4. Capitalize on what you can do for the reader rather than on what you cannot do.

> We are offering you a 2 percent discount on all cash purchases for the next six months.

5. Use resale material whenever appropriate.

> Of the various hardware lines we sell, our Brown & Dickson line is by far our best selling.

6. Use sales-promotion material whenever appropriate.

> You will be pleased to know that we just received authorization to distribute the Stockton Sportswear line. To help introduce this new line to our customers, we are offering a 3 percent introductory discount on all Stockton merchandise ordered on or before July 1.

7. Offer suggestions to prevent a recurrence of the problem situation.

> To keep your Trim-Lite lawn and garden trimmer operating at peak performance, we recommend that you use only Trim-Lite oil in the oil-gas mixture.

8. Make a counteroffer or counterproposal, if appropriate.

> For your immediate best interest, we believe a credit limit of $500 rather than the $700 you requested is appropriate.

9. Make reader action easy, if appropriate.

> If you would like us to substitute Ace nails in the same quantity and size for the out-of-stock Beckett nails that you ordered, please call me on our toll-free line (1-800-123-4567). The Ace nails can be shipped immediately after we hear from you.

Don't Suggestions

What should you avoid doing in preparing disappointing-news letters?

1. Don't use negative words or phrases.

> We regret that we cannot exchange your recently purchased X-213 radio for the R-174 radio, as you requested.

2. Don't use an accusatory tone.

> Your new power rake malfunctioned because you failed to assemble it properly.

3. Don't place the statement of refusal in a position of emphasis.

> The following outlines our reasons for declining your request: Notices were placed throughout the store indicating that all reduced merchandise was being offered on a final-sale basis. Furthermore, your sales slip was stamped with a "Final Sale" note. Adherence to this policy allows us to offer a greater number of sales throughout the year.

4. Don't use company policy to justify your refusal. Hiding behind company policy is normally perceived as a shallow excuse.

> Our company has a policy that prohibits the use of our facilities for anything other than official company business.

5. Don't make predictions that are unlikely to occur.

> Now that you have heard our side of the story, we are certain you will agree with our decision.

6. Don't apologize for the action you are taking.

> We are sorry we cannot grant your request.

7. Don't use a slow-start opening.

> We have received your letter of January 2.

8. Don't use a meaningless closing.

> Thanks for getting in touch with us.

9. Don't suggest that problems may arise again in the future.

> Should you feel, after we repair and return your Recordex VCR, that it is not giving you the quality of service to which you are entitled, please contact me.

10. Don't use phony or insincere empathy.

> We know just how upset you were when the heating coil in your coffee maker burned out in the middle of your dinner party.

TYPES OF DISAPPOINTING-NEWS LETTERS

Different types of disappointing-news letters are used in the business world. Although businesses mostly use the indirect organizational plan in preparing these letters, they may use the direct plan in situations in which the writer has already sent several disappointing-news letters to the reader. The writer now believes the time has arrived to use the more forceful, blunt opening in the direct-plan letter, hoping this approach will finally convince the reader of the impossibility of granting the request.

Negative Response to Inquiries

The most common disappointing-news letters in the business world are *negative answers to inquiry letters*, messages in which you communicate disappointing news to the reader as a response to his or her earlier-received inquiry. Because the situations in this category rarely generate more than one letter, the indirect plan is applicable in the overwhelming majority of cases.

Even in a direct approach, a neutral or buffered opening is appropriate because it helps neutralize the situation. Note that in the first part of the following two opening paragraphs nothing blunts the negative news; but in the revision, the blow is softened.

What type of opening is appropriate for negative responses to inquiry letters?

Change: We have received your letter of January 13 in which you inquired about the availability of the city's swimming pool for private use. It simply is unavailable for your use.

To: The gymnastics summer sports clinic you are planning is certain to be as well attended and received as the clinics you coordinated in the past.

The section that follows the opening reviews the facts and analyzes the reasons for the refusal. The writing in this section should be straightforward and convincing. Once you have presented the facts, you can state your refusal. Again, to soften its impact, try to interweave the refusal into a counterproposal when the inclusion of a counterproposal is appropriate. Note how effectively the following revised paragraph reviews the facts presented in the first paragraph and then interweaves the refusal into a counterproposal.

What should be included in the middle section of letters conveying negative responses to inquiry letters?

Change: We regret that the city swimming pool can no longer be rented for private use. A policy prohibiting the rental of the city swimming pool for private use has now been in effect for six months.

To: When the city commissioners negotiated a new liability insurance contract for various city functions/facilities last year, a provision was included that prohibited the renting of several city facilities, including the swimming pool, for private use. By taking this action, the city commission was able to save nearly $15,000 on its annual insurance premiums. Although the city pool is no longer available for private use, the swimming pool at the YMCA can be rented for private use. You can contact the YMCA executive director, Jim Bellows, to discuss the rental of the Y pool.

The closing paragraph of a negative response to an inquiry can include several types of material, including an expression of good wishes and a focus on continuing, if possible, a good business relationship. Note the difference in the revision of the following two paragraphs.

What type of closing is appropriate for negative responses to inquiry letters?

Change: We were glad to learn of your interest in renting the city pool. We regret that we cannot accommodate your request.

To: Your interest in helping our youth develop their gymnastics skills is commendable. Best wishes for another successful summer clinic.

What is the suggested plan for negative responses to inquiry letters?

The suggested letter plan for preparing a negative response to an inquiry, using the indirect plan, includes the following elements:

1. A neutral or buffered opening
2. A review of the facts and an analysis of the reasons necessitating the refusal
3. A statement of refusal (and counteroffer if appropriate)
4. A courteous closing with, if appropriate, action orientation

The letter in Exhibit 7-2 fails to follow a number of the suggestions in this chapter for improving the effectiveness of disappointing-news messages. Furthermore, it does not comply with the suggested plan. Letters like it have a negative impact on the reader's goodwill.

Letter	Comment
As of January 1, 199x, our company has had a policy that prohibits the touring of our facilities by the public.	An opening that contains negative news and that uses "policy" as an excuse.
We regret we had to implement such a policy. However, the disruptive and sometimes destructive nature of the public forced us to implement this policy that prevents our conducting tours, including those requested on a special basis, throughout our premises.	A section that presents a "harsh" explanation of the reason for the negative news.
We hope you understand our decision to implement this new policy.	A closing that lacks you-attitude.

Exhibit 7-2 Ineffective negative response to an inquiry.

Letter	Comment
The automobile industry project your high school business class is undertaking sounds interesting. The various project activities the class has decided on will add considerably to students' understanding of this vital industry.	An opening designed to help buffer the negative news presented later.
Since the first of the year, our plant has been closed to public tours. Because our tour guides have been reassigned to other positions in the company, even special requests for tours must be declined.	A section that reviews the reasons necessitating the refusal, in addition to presenting a counteroffer.
As an alternative to plant tours, our Public Relations Department recently put together a VCR tape that illustrates the various steps involved in manufacturing an automobile. The use of this tape is free. The Public Relations Department also has a variety of brochures and pamphlets that you may wish to share with your students.	
If you are interested in showing our tape to your class, please contact Ms. Brown at 624-5200 to arrange a showing time that will conveniently fit into your schedule. If you wish, Ms. Brown can send you multiple copies of the brochures and pamphlets.	A section that outlines the action to be taken if the counteroffer is accepted.
Those of us in the automobile industry are especially appreciative of teachers who help increase student awareness about this important sector of the economy.	A courteous closing that contains you-attitude material.

Exhibit 7-3 Effective negative response to an inquiry.

OPENING
1. Does the opening paragraph contain buffered or neutral material, the content with which the reader will agree?
2. Is the content of the opening relevant?
3. Have you avoided wording that might convey a false hope that you are able to comply with the reader's earlier request/inquiry?
4. Does the opening provide a smooth transition into the next section of the letter?

MIDDLE
1. Have you reviewed the facts completely, factually, and impersonally, taking care not to belittle or hurt the reader's feelings?
2. Have you been as positive as possible in reviewing the situation?
3. Has the refusal been implied rather than explicitly stated?
4. Is the refusal located in an unemphatic position within the paragraph?
5. Have you been able to convey how others besides yourself may ultimately benefit by refusing the reader's request/inquiry?
6. Have you captured the essence of you-attitude in the wording of this section of the letter?
7. Have you avoided apologizing if you or your company is not at fault?
8. Have you avoided "hiding behind company policy" as the reason for your refusing to comply with the reader's request/inquiry?

CLOSING
1. Is the closing courteous and friendly?
2. Is the closing as positive as it would have been had you been able to comply with the reader's request/inquiry?
3. Is the closing void of negative information?
4. If you wish for the reader to take other action, does the closing mention that action?

Checklist 7-1 Negative response to inquiry letter.

Exhibit 7-3 illustrates a rewritten version of the letter in Exhibit 7-2. Note how much more effectively the buffered opening in Exhibit 7-3 maintains the reader's goodwill. By the time the reader has read through the material in the second paragraph, only a subtle refusal—implied rather than stated explicitly—is necessary. In addition, the writer's counteroffer helps soften the disappointing material in the letter. Informing the reader how to take advantage of the counteroffer is even more helpful, as is the courteous closing, expressing appreciation to the reader.

Checklist 7-1 contains questions to help you evaluate the effectiveness of your refused request or refused inquiry letters.

Negative Response to Adjustment Requests

Adjustment-refusal letters, messages in which you refuse customers' claim requests, are some of the more challenging of the disappointing-news letters to compose. Customers who write these claims often do so in anger. So even though you need to respond negatively, you need to be sensitive to the reader's feelings if you hope to maintain or rescue your customer/client relationship. The reader probably has a financial investment in the goods or services for which he is requesting an adjustment. For these reasons, the writing of such letters is especially challenging.

Why do adjustment-refusal letters need to be prepared?

Two common situations that elicit negative adjustment messages are (1) the reader's failure to use a product according to the directions and (2) the reader's misuse of the product. Customer complaints about account balances and services also generate this type of correspondence. Companies vary widely in how they respond to these claims or complaints. Some always give customers the benefit of the doubt whereas others never give customers the benefit of the doubt when they are clearly at fault. The disappointing-news messages in this section pertain to situations in which the reader is at fault.

What type of opening is appropriate for adjustment-refusal letters?

The opening of a negative response to an adjustment request should contain neutral, buffered material. Avoid an opening that delivers the bad news first, which the first of the following two paragraphs does but the revision corrects.

> Change: Because of negligence on your part, we cannot replace the Deloit chain saw you recently purchased from us.
>
> To: The Deloit chain saw, because of superior workmanship, is designed to give you many years of satisfactory service when used according to the manufacturer's instructions.

Note how the revised version also incorporates resale material as it presents information with which the reader will agree.

What material should be included in the middle section of adjustment-refusal letters?

Before the refusal itself is either stated or implied, the next section should discuss the reasons and an analysis of facts behind the refusal. The more effectively you present your reasons, the more convinced the reader will be that your decision is correct. In addition, the reader will probably guess that the request is being turned down even before you actually state your refusal. Note how much more effectively the following revised version, which avoids the accusatory tone of the first paragraph, presents this important section of the refusal letter. The implied rather than explicitly stated refusal softens the blow of the disappointing news.

> Change: The instruction manual that accompanied your chain saw clearly states on page 4 that "An oil-gas mixture (one 8 oz. can of Deloit two-cycle oil to two gallons of gasoline) must be used." Failure to operate the engine on a proper oil-gas mixture will ruin the engine because no other lubricant is used. The fact that your negligence ruined the engine and that the warranty is made void by operator misuse, we are not obligated to replace your saw as you requested in your recent letter.
>
> To: One of the advantages of the Deloit chain saw, when compared with other chain saws, is its two-cycle engine that operates on an oil-gas mixture. The lubricating oil is mixed with the gas (one 8 oz. can of Deloit two-cycle oil to two gallons of gasoline), which eliminates your having to check the oil each time you use the saw or your periodically having to drain and replace the oil. The inspection of your saw engine revealed it has been operated on gasoline that contained an insufficient amount of the two-cycle engine oil. This voids the manufacturer's warranty that came with your saw.

The next section of the adjustment-refusal letter can include resale material, sales-promotion material, or, if appropriate, constructive suggestions. The following is an example of resale material—designed to rebuild the reader's confidence—that may be included in an adjustment-refusal letter.

> If you wish, your engine can be rebuilt at the Deloit Service Center. The normal charge for rebuilding our saw engines is $68.50, which includes parts and labor. Our rebuilt engines have a six-month warranty. Repair time typically takes three weeks. For your convenience, we are enclosing with the saw—which is being returned to you by UPS—a mailing label imprinted with the address of the Deloit Service Center.

An appropriate closing for the adjustment-refusal letter thanks the reader for his or her business. Your closing should avoid describing the nature of the problem. The first of the following two paragraphs refers to the problem, whereas the revision focuses on business promotion.

Change:	We regret that you have experienced problems with your Deloit chain saw.
To:	The opportunity to help you with your future lawn-care equipment needs will be appreciated.

The suggested plan for a letter refusing the adjustment request includes the following elements:

What is the suggested plan for adjustment-refusal letters?

1. A neutral or buffered beginning
2. A discussion of reasons and analysis of facts necessitating the refusal
3. A statement of refusal
4. Resale material, sales-promotion material, or constructive suggestions (if appropriate)
5. A courteous closing with, if appropriate, action orientation

Exhibit 7-4 shows an adjustment-refusal letter that will offend the reader. Not only does the letter fail to follow the plan, but also it is harsh and accusatory.

Exhibit 7-5 is an improved version of Exhibit 7-4. In Exhibit 7-5, the writer has followed the suggested letter plan, and the tone of the letter is also more appropriate.

When is partial adjustment to an adjustment request appropriate?

Partial adjustments are sometimes appropriate for certain situations. For example, perhaps the customer requesting the adjustment is an excellent customer with whom the company has enjoyed a longtime relationship. In this situation, continuing the relationship is more important than the cost the company will incur in making a partial adjustment. Or, in some instances, a shared responsibility for the problem makes it desirable for you to offer a partial adjustment.

A *partial-adjustment letter* can be organized according to the same plan as an adjustment-refusal letter but with a slight modification. Instead of stating the refusal (either implicitly or explicitly), the partial adjustment is clearly, thoroughly, and nongrudgingly explained. Because the partial adjustment is less than what the reader requested, you need to present your offer in a convincing manner. The most appropriate closing for such letters is a discussion of the action you wish the reader to take if she accepts the partial adjustment.

What is the suggested plan for partial-adjustment letters?

This suggested plan for the partial-adjustment letter includes the following elements:

Exhibit 7-4 Ineffective adjustment-refusal letter.

You are incorrect in assuming that we are obligated to repair your camera at no cost to you because it is still under warranty. You will see, if you read your warranty, that "Camex is not responsible for repair work on cameras resulting from misuse or damage." Your camera has obviously been dropped, which damaged the automatic winding mechanism.	A rude opening that contains the refusal as well as several "put downs" in the explanation.
We will be happy to repair your camera for an estimated cost of $85.23 for parts and labor. While the actual repair cost could be less, it will not exceed the estimated cost.	A section that contains weak resale material designed to rebuild the customer's confidence in the product.
Let us know of your decision.	A discourteous closing.

CAMEX CAMERA COMPANY

(342) 443-2883 442 Stevens Boulevard Flint, MI 48871

March 15, 199x

Ms. Jennifer Holiday
123 Flint Hills Road
Wichita, KS 69831

Dear Ms. Holiday:

In your recent letter, the statement that you believe you are entitled to many years of service from the Camex camera you recently purchased from us is one with which we agree. The quality of your Camex is unrivaled in today's market.

An opening that contains buffered material on which the reader and writer will agree.

When we received your camera, a service technician examined it to determine why the film is catching in the automatic advancing mechanism. His examination revealed a broken pin and several bent or sprung parts in the mechanism that prevent the film from automatically feeding through the camera. The technician also found several scratches on the camera case that appear to have been caused when your camera was dropped on a hard, rough surface, such as a concrete floor.

A section that contains a thorough explanation of the reasons necessitating the refusal.

The limited warranty that came with your camera covers for a three-year period the cost of repair (parts and labor) resulting from defective materials or poor quality workmanship. The warranty also mentions several exclusions that make it void, one of which is damage resulting from the camera's being dropped. The warranty exclusions enabled you and thousands of our other customers to purchase the highest-quality camera equipment on the market today.

A section that continues an explanation of the reasons why the request cannot be granted, followed by an implied refusal.

The service technician who examined your camera estimated the repair cost to be $85.23 for parts and labor. Although the actual cost could be less, it will not exceed the estimate. Our skilled service technicians can repair your camera so it will again provide you with the photography quality you appreciate and the satisfaction to which you have become accustomed. The repair work should be completed in less than two weeks after we receive your authorization. Camex, the only camera manufacturer to do so, will guarantee the repair work with a two-year warranty that covers parts and labor.

A section that contains resale material to help rebuild the customer's confidence in the product and in the writer's company.

Please use the enclosed card to let me know if you want us to repair your camera or to return it to you in its present condition.

A courteous closing that mentions the action the reader is to take if she accepts the offer.

Sincerely,

Janelle A. Daniels
Customer Service
Representative

Enc.

Exhibit 7-5 Effective adjustment-refusal letter.

1. A neutral or buffered opening
2. A review of reasons or analysis of facts
3. A discussion of the partial adjustment being offered
4. Resale or sales-promotion material or, if appropriate, helpful suggestions
5. A courteous closing with, if appropriate, action orientation

Exhibit 7-6 shows a letter using this organizational plan.

The other organizational plan for partial-adjustment letters is to discuss the adjustment in the opening. This alternative works better in some situations than the first alternative. Because the customer is receiving good news immediately, although the adjustment is less than what was originally requested, the second alternative may restore goodwill more quickly than if the writer delayed mentioning the partial adjustment.

Exhibit 7-6 Effective partial-adjustment letter with buffered opening.

Letter	Commentary
When you purchased the five silver-leaf maple trees from Green Thumb Nursery last spring, you had every right to assume that in a few years they would provide ample shade as well as enhance the attractiveness of your yard. Your continued patronage the last five years indicates you have been pleased with our stock and service.	A neutral opening that contains information with which the reader will agree.
The soil samples we analyzed from the area of your yard where the trees were planted revealed high levels of salt. Although some trees can tolerate excessive levels of salt in the soil, silver-leaf maples cannot. The guarantee we offer on our trees expired three months before you reported to us the condition of your trees. By that time, they had suffered irreparable damage. Had we known about this soil condition before planting these trees, we would have recommended either another variety of tree or another location in your yard more suitable for these trees.	A section that reviews the analysis of the situation, along with the implied refusal.
Silver-leaf maples of the size you purchased from us last year are now on sale for $49.99 each (regular price is $64.99). We will be happy to plant free as many as five of these maples (a $75 value) if you purchase replacement trees from us.	A section that presents a discussion of the partial adjustment being offered.
Perhaps you will want to take advantage of our offer to do a free analysis of the soil in the various areas of your yard where you would consider having the replacement trees planted. Because other salt-sensitive trees you have purchased from us have done well, we assume the salt content in the soil is lower in some areas of your yard than in other areas.	A section that contains resale material designed to rebuild the customer's confidence in the company.
You are encouraged to make your decision about our offer soon while large supplies of stock are still available. Now is also a good time to think about purchasing your bedding plants while our "Spring Dreams Sale" is in progress.	A section that contains sales-promotion material.
To accept our offer, please contact me. I will be pleased to help you personally select top-quality replacement trees.	A courteous, action-oriented closing.

The coupon that accompanies this letter entitles you to free planting of five silver-leaf maple trees (a coupon verifying this $75 value is attached) if you purchase your replacement trees from Green Thumb Nursery. Silver-leaf maples of the size you purchased from us last year are now on sale for $49.99 each (regular price is $64.99). Your continued purchasing from us the last five years indicates you have been pleased with our stock and service.	An opening that discusses the partial adjustment; the refusal is implied.
The soil samples we analyzed from the area of your yard where the trees were planted revealed a high concentration of salt. Although some trees can tolerate excessive levels of salt, silver-leaf maples cannot. The guarantee we offer on our trees expired three months before you reported their condition to us. By that time, they had suffered irreparable damage. Had we known about this condition before planting these trees, we would have recommended either another variety or another location in your yard more suitable for silver-leaf maples.	A section that contains a review of the analysis of the situation.
So we can plant your replacement trees in a suitable location, we are offering to do a free analysis of the soil in the various areas where you would consider having the new trees planted. We know your yard has areas suitable for silver-leaf maples because a variety of other salt-sensitive trees you have purchased from us have thrived.	A section that contains resale material designed to rebuild the customer's confidence in the company.
You are encouraged to make your decision about our offer soon while large supplies of stock are still available. Now is also a good time to think about purchasing your bedding plants while our "Spring Dreams Sale" is in progress.	A section that contains sales-promotion material.
If you decide to accept our offer, please contact me. I will be pleased to help you personally select top-quality replacement trees.	A courteous, action-oriented closing.

Exhibit 7-7 Effective partial-adjustment letter with adjustment discussed in opening.

The suggested plan for partial-adjustment letters that open with a discussion of the offer includes the following elements:

1. A discussion of the partial adjustment being offered
2. A review of reasons or analysis of facts
3. Resale, sales-promotion material, or, if appropriate, helpful suggestions
4. A courteous closing with, if appropriate, action orientation

Exhibit 7-7 shows a letter organized according to this plan.

Checklist 7-2 identifies several elements of adjustment-refusal letters that will help you evaluate the effectiveness of these messages.

Negative Response to Credit Requests

When a business receives a credit application from a customer with a substandard credit background and/or financial status, a credit-refusal letter must be prepared. The *credit-refusal letter* informs the reader that the request for credit is being denied. The

OPENING

1. Does the opening contain buffered, neutral material that the reader will not be able to take issue with or find offensive?
2. Have you been able to avoid giving the idea that you are granting the reader's adjustment request?
3. Is the material in the opening concise?
4. Does the opening contain relevant material?

MIDDLE

1. Have you discussed completely and factually your view of the situation?
2. Have you discussed the reasons you are unable to comply with the reader's request?
3. Have you presented your reasons in a logical order, perhaps beginning with the strongest and ending with the weakest?
4. Have you been able to imply the refusal rather than explicitly state it?
5. Is the refusal located in an unemphatic position within the paragraph?
6. Have you included one or more of the following—whichever is/are appropriate for the situation?
   a. Resale material—designed to help resell the reader on the worth of the product/service for which he or she is seeking an adjustment
   b. Sales promotion—designed to inform the reader about another of your company's product/service in which he or she may be interested
   c. Constructive suggestions—designed to help the reader avoid the same situation again in the future
7. If appropriate, have you discussed the alternative action you are taking or that you would like for the reader to take?

CLOSING

1. Is the closing positive, friendly, and courteous?
2. Have you avoided including negative information in the closing?
3. If appropriate, have you briefly mentioned the action you wish the reader to take?

Checklist 7-2 Negative response to adjustment request.

goal is to present the information about the refusal tactfully so that the applicant will continue to be a cash customer.

What is the desired goal in preparing credit-refusal letters?

In some instances, the customer submits the credit application along with a merchandise order. In other instances, he requests an application for credit before submitting an order. When the credit application and order are submitted simultaneously, the credit-refusal letter can serve another purpose, which is to acknowledge receipt of the order.

In preparing credit-refusal letters, you should be aware that a total refusal is not always warranted. For example, suppose that the applicant's current income is insufficient for you to extend credit in the amount of the accompanying order but is sufficient enough for you to extend a lesser amount of credit. Letters granting partial credit are clearly easier to prepare than those totally refusing credit.

When you believe the applicant has the potential for eventually becoming a credit customer, then you should consider explaining to her what she must do in order to qualify for credit in the future. For example, when refusing credit because of an unacceptable ratio between the applicant's assets and liabilities, you may want to inform the customer that another application will be welcomed when her assets-liabilities ratio meets the required standard.

Another element to consider for inclusion in credit-refusal letters is resale material, which often helps persuade the reader that the merchandise she ordered is superior to that offered by your competitors; therefore, it will be in her best interest to pay you cash for the merchandise. Moreover, readers often interpret the inclusion of resale material as evidence of the writer's desire to be helpful. In addition, some writers effectively use resale material to compliment the reader on the good judgment she displayed in selecting the merchandise and for her business.

What type of opening is appropriate for credit-refusal letters?

Use a neutral or buffered opening for a credit-refusal letter. Avoid a slow-start opening that acknowledges receipt of the reader's credit application. The first of the following two paragraphs makes this mistake, whereas the revision corrects the problem.

> Change: We have received your application for a Brown's charge account.
> To: Your expressing confidence in us by applying for a Brown's charge account is sincerely appreciated.

The next section of your letter should first explain the situation and then state the refusal. If you explain your reasons well and show sensitivity to the reader, you may be able to imply the refusal rather than explicitly state it. The harshness of the first of the following two paragraphs is bound to alienate the reader. The revision, by implicitly refusing credit, shows more sensitivity toward the applicant's feelings.

> Change: We are unable to open a charge account for you because you have too many debts in relation to your income. We have found that our charge customers whose monthly revolving charge account payments exceed 15 percent of their take-home pay often experience financial difficulties. Because your revolving charge account payments currently consume 22 percent of your take-home pay, we believe it unwise for you to assume any more debt at this time.
> To: Brown's has been able to sell merchandise at competitive prices for the last fifty years because its operating costs are among the lowest of the country's major department stores. One way we've been able to reduce operating costs is to open charge accounts for applicants whose monthly revolving charge account payments are less than 15 percent of their take-home pay. An analysis of the financial data you provided reveals that your current monthly revolving charge account payments are 22 percent of your take-home pay. To assume additional debt at this time may result in your financially overextending yourself, a situation you surely will want to avoid.

You may want to make a counteroffer, such as extending a reduced line of credit, offering a temporary cash discount on merchandise purchases, or suggesting the applicant purchase on a cash basis until the person may qualify for the opening of a charge account.

Resale or sales-promotion material also can be effectively included in credit-refusal letters, as the following paragraph shows.

> During our annual summer sale, which begins July 5, you will find numerous items reduced from 25 to 50 percent. Because this sale will not be announced to the general public until July 7, you will have first pick of many items on which you can save with the use of your cash discount coupon up to 60 percent on the marked price.

What type of closing is appropriate for credit-refusal letters?

Finally, a courteous closing can remind the applicant that you will appreciate receiving another credit application in the future. The reader may find hopeful your mentioning the conditions necessary to qualify for an application. The first of the following closings does not end on an optimistic note, but the revision corrects the problem.

Change:	Thank you for your interest in opening a Brown's charge account.
To:	When your monthly charge account payments are reduced to approximately 15 percent of your take-home pay, we encourage you to submit another credit application. In the meantime, please take advantage of the many excellent values for which Brown's is well known.

The suggested plan for a credit-refusal letter includes the following elements:

What is the suggested plan for credit-refusal letters?

1. A neutral or buffered opening
2. An explanation and tactful refusal to grant credit
3. A counteroffer, if appropriate
4. Resale or sales-promotion material, if appropriate
5. A courteous closing with, if appropriate, action orientation

Because it ignores a number of suggestions for writing effective credit refusals, the letter in Exhibit 7-8 is certain to cause the credit applicant to take her business elsewhere.

Exhibit 7-9 shows a much-improved revision of the letter in Exhibit 7-8. The revision incorporates the effective letter writing principles presented in this chapter and the suggested letter plan. The sales-promotion and reader-benefit material will be helpful in convincing the reader to maintain a relationship with the writer's company—even on a cash basis.

Included in Checklist 7-3 is a list of questions to guide you in preparing effective credit-refusal letters.

Exhibit 7-8 Ineffective credit-refusal letter.

Letter	Comment
Your order dated October 10 along with your application for credit have been received. In addition, we have received references from those individuals you listed on your application.	A slow-start opening that contains obvious information.
Granting you credit at this time is not possible. An examination of your assets to liabilities ratio reveals a substandard level. We require a 2:1 ratio; yours is 1.5:1. Therefore, we believe it would be unwise for us to grant you credit. We have to be extremely careful in these days of declining profit to avoid the risk of incurring bad debts.	A section in which the refusal is stated at the beginning of the paragraph, with negative wording used throughout.
We hope you will understand our decision and send to us a check for $598.32, the amount of your order, in the enclosed envelope. That will enable us to send you your order without additional delay. We encourage you to continue purchasing on a cash basis until your assets-liabilities ratio reaches the 2:1 level.	A section that presents a discussion of the desired action but lacks you-viewpoint.
We hope to hear from you as soon as possible.	A closing that lacks you-viewpoint.

Golden Goose Clothing

(412) 377-8834 652 Main Street

(412) 377-8829 (FAX) East Lansing, MI 48837

September 12, 199x

Mrs. Janet Smith
Smith's Clothing Store
2884 Pioneer Ct.
Hammond, IN 34571

Dear Mrs. Smith:

The children's clothing you ordered from us recently indicates you have excellent taste in selecting spring merchandise for your store. Several items you chose are among our best sellers this season.

An opening that compliments the reader.

You can take pride in the fact that the references you listed on your credit application gave you excellent marks in each of the areas about which we requested information. This speaks favorably for a children's clothing store that has been in business for a relatively short time. It also speaks favorably about your management practices.

A section that presents additional compliments.

For us to be able to offer our merchandise at competitive prices, our credit customers are expected to have a 2:1 assets-liabilities ratio. We calculated your assets-liabilities ratio to be 1.5:1. Experience shows that when we maintain the 2:1 ratio requirement, we are able to minimize our risks and subsequently to offer our merchandise at the lowest possible price. As a result, our customers are able to increase their profit margin because they are able to purchase their merchandise at a lower price.

A section that explains the situation and makes an implied refusal.

Because of your assets-liabilities ratio, we encourage you to continue purchasing on a cash basis. To help you improve your ratio as quickly as possible, we extend you a 5 percent discount on all cash orders for the next six months, including the order we recently received.

A section in which the desired action and a counteroffer are discussed.

The Smart-Look line of children's clothing has just been added to our product line. Sales indicate this line promises to be one of our most popular. You can see by examining the enclosed brochure that this line provides excellent values because of moderate prices.

A section that contains sale-promotion material.

When your assets-liabilities ratio becomes 2:1, please complete another credit application. In the meantime, your present order can be filled if you send a check for $568.40 ($598.32 less the 5 percent discount) in the enclosed envelope. We are eager to help supply your stock needs.

A courteous, action-oriented closing.

Sincerely,

Nancy Brown
Credit Manager
Enclosure

Exhibit 7-9 Effective credit-refusal letter with a counteroffer.

OPENING

1. Does your opening contain buffered or neutral material?
2. Have you avoided including material implying you are granting the reader's credit request?
3. Is the opening concise?
4. Is the opening void of irrelevant material?

MIDDLE

1. Have you presented information providing the basis on which your company extends credit?
2. Have you avoided "hiding behind company policy" regarding the extension of credit?
3. Have you used an impersonal approach in your discussion of the reasons, to help the reader avoid taking the refusal personally?
4. Have you implied the credit refusal rather than explicitly stating the refusal?
5. Is the refusal located in an unemphatic position within the paragraph?
6. Have you mentioned that the reader may actually benefit from your not granting credit because without it he or she need not be concerned about becoming overextended?
7. Have you encouraged the reader to apply for credit in the future when the reader's situation becomes consistent with the company's credit extension guidelines?
8. If appropriate, have you discussed with the reader the action you would like for the reader to take?

CLOSING

1. Is the closing courteous?
2. Is the closing positive?
3. If appropriate, have you briefly mentioned the action you wish the reader to take?

Checklist 7-3 Negative response to a credit request.

Problem-Order Letters

A variety of situations periodically make it impossible for merchandisers to fill customers' orders. *Problem-order letters* inform readers about a dilemma in the filling of an order. The situation creating the problem may be the customer's fault, or the problem may stem from the merchandiser. Regardless of who causes it, the situation can be at least partly defused if the merchandiser sends a letter to the customer acknowledging the delay. You can also use these letters to request additional information from the customer. For example, perhaps the customer did not state on the order form her choice of fabric color. Therefore, before you can fill the order, you need to ask her to select the color.

Specific situations requiring the preparation of problem-order letters include the following:

What type of situations require the preparation of problem-order letters?

1. Incomplete orders
2. Orders requesting out-of-stock items that can be backordered (an order the company promises at a later date)
3. Orders requesting out-of-stock items that cannot be backordered
4. Orders requesting out-of-stock items that cannot be backordered; however, the writer has substitute items to suggest

Some merchandisers prefer forms to convey the news about the problem order. Using forms is much faster than preparing letters, but recipients tend to view forms as being cold and impersonal. Merchandisers who value their customers' business should take the time and effort to prepare a personal letter.

What is the goal of the opening of problem-order letters?

The opening of a problem-order response can either improve or worsen the situation. Conveying positive rather than negative information is crucial to focusing on a positive approach. Note the negative impact that the first of the following two sentences is likely to have and how the revision corrects the problem.

Change:	We regret we cannot ship your order in its entirety at this time.
To:	The printer ribbons you recently ordered were shipped this morning by UPS and should reach you by the end of the week. These ribbons are guaranteed to print 40 percent longer than original Beta printer ribbons.

Note how the revision paragraph shows more concern for the customer. In addition, although it conveys disappointing news (the company shipped the ribbons late), the opening contains positive information (they have been shipped) that should help defuse the reader's irritation at the delay.

What is included in the middle section of problem-order letters?

The next section of the problem-order letter should explain the reasons for the delay. The reader will appreciate an honest, sincere explanation. The following paragraph is an effective example of this section. Note now the reader stresses the popularity of the disks before informing the reader of the problem.

> The popularity of our R-10 floppy disks that you ordered has occasionally resulted in their selling faster than our supply can be replenished. The manufacturer of these disks plans to open a new plant, which will result in the doubling of our monthly allotment. When the plant reaches full production, we anticipate having a continuous supply of these disks.

Sometimes you will be in a position to suggest a course of action that may be helpful to the customer. For example, if a viable substitute (one with features like those in the ordered item and that is also comparatively priced) is available for a backordered item, you may want to suggest it as an alternative. Or, if the customer needs to tell you whether she wishes to have the out-of-stock item placed on backorder, this is an appropriate section in which to discuss a substitution. The first of the following two paragraphs lacks concern for the customer, whereas the revision suggests a positive resolution of the problem.

Change:	Please let me know as soon as possible whether you want us to send the out-of-stock floppy disks you ordered when they become available—or if you want us to cancel this portion of your order.
To:	As a substitute for the R-10 disks currently out of stock, I suggest you try our R-8 disks that we can ship immediately. Although the R-8 disks cost $1.79 less per box than the R-10 disks ($11.97 rather than $13.76), the quality of both types of disks is comparable. If you decide to order the R-8 disks, we will refund $17.90, the difference between the cost of 100 R-8 and R-10 disks. Please call me on our toll-free line (1-800-567-1897) if you wish to order the R-8 disks. If we do not hear from you, we will send the R-10 disks once they become available.

Note how in the revision the writer gives the customer the option of disagreeing with the suggested alternative and responding by phone.

What type of closing is appropriate for problem-order letters?

The closing of a problem-order letter must be sincere, positive, and courteous. The first of the following is too trite to be sincere, but the revision ends on a positive future-business note.

Change:	We look forward to having the pleasure of your business in the future.
To:	To express our appreciation for your confidence in our products and service, a coupon is enclosed entitling you to a $5 discount on your next order.

Unfortunately, we cannot at the present time ship all of the items you recently ordered from us.	An opening that immediately presents the rejection.
The twenty R-78 rakes you requested are on backorder. At this time, we do not know exactly when they will be shipped. As soon as they come in, we will send all of your merchandise to you.	A section that presents a weak discussion of the facts and that lacks resale material.
Please give us an opportunity to serve you again.	A weak closing.

Exhibit 7-10 Ineffective problem-order letter.

The suggested plan for problem-order letters includes the following elements:

What is the suggested plan for problem-order letters?

1. A buffered beginning expressing thanks for the order and mentioning which items are being shipped now or one containing resale material
2. An explanation of the reasons for the delayed shipment
3. Suggested course of action containing reader-benefit material (action you wish the reader to take, such as selecting a substitute item or accepting or rejecting the new shipping date for backordered items)
4. A courteous closing with action orientation

The letter in Exhibit 7-10 is unlikely to convince the reader that the backordered items are worth the wait. The absence of resale material adds to the letter's cold, impersonal tone. Another problem is the negative emphasis.

The letter in Exhibit 7-11 conforms to the organizational plan presented for problem-order letters, emphasizing what the writer can rather than cannot do.

Declining Invitations

Invitations are a routine part of business. From time to time, you will have to prepare a *declining-invitation letter*, which informs the reader of your inability to accept his or her invitation.

The need to emphasize the positive rather than the negative is just as important in refusal letters as in other types of disappointing-news messages. If you would welcome a future invitation—for example, to speak at a convention—mention this in the letter. But be careful to avoid begging or an insincere tone in expressing your interest.

Depending on the circumstances, you may be able to suggest an acceptable alternative. If suggesting an alternative time or date seems appropriate, consider doing so.

What type of opening is appropriate for letters in which an invitation is declined?

The tone of the opening in your letter should convey the extent of your interest in the invitation. Tact is extremely important. The following two paragraphs produce quite different results in the impression they create. The tone of the first paragraph is curt; the revision establishes goodwill.

Change: I am unable to accept your invitation to speak at the May meeting of the Claremore Civic Club.

To: The Claremore Civic Club is doing many things to make our community a better place in which to live—thanks to you and its other dedicated, interested members. My son thoroughly enjoys playing on the new equipment your group recently purchased and installed at Johnson Park.

The hoes and shovels you recently ordered from us are on their way and should reach you by the end of the week. We appreciate having the opportunity to once again supply you with these top-quality gardening tools.	A buffered opening that expresses appreciation for the order.
The employees of the manufacturer of the R-78 rakes you ordered have been on strike for a month. Because the manufacturer's inventory of these rakes is depleted, wholesalers like us around the country have also experienced a depletion of their stock of these rakes. The popularity of the R-78 rakes will keep them in short supply for a time after the manufacturer's employees go back to work.	A section that explains the reasons for the delayed shipment.
Because the spring planting season is just around the corner, having an adequate supply of rakes on hand in your hardware store is critical. Until the R-78 rake again becomes readily available, you may be interested in stocking the Garden-Rite 2304 rake, which is even of higher quality than the R-78. Garden-Rite uses a steel alloy in its rakes that is twice as strong as the steel used in the R-78. This new alloy makes the teeth on the Garden-Rite rake much less susceptible to breakage. Mud is also much less likely to cling to this new alloy.	A section that contains resale material.
If you would like us to send twenty Garden-Rite 2304 rakes, please let me know. They will be shipped the same day we hear from you. Otherwise, we will backorder the R-78 rakes and send them to you just as soon as they arrive.	A section that discusses the suggested course of action, along with reader-benefit material.
According to our sales representative, your new store in Peoria is doing well. We wish you continued success.	A courteous closing.

Exhibit 7-11 Effective problem-order letter.

An honest explanation of the reasons for your decline indicates the sincerity of your refusal. Whereas the first of the following two paragraphs seems insincere, the revision of the refusal, by being specific, appears genuine.

> Change: I will be out of town on the day of your May meeting.
>
> To: On the day of your May meeting, my family and I will be in Florida enjoying a long-awaited ten-day vacation. If I were going to be in town on that day, I would have been honored to speak to your group.

The sincerity of your interest in accepting the invitation (although not at this time) can be enhanced by suggesting an alternative course of action, as the following paragraph illustrates.

> At the moment, my schedule is open on the days of your June, July, and August meetings, should you be looking for a speaker at these times.

The tone of the closing should indicate the sincerity of your interest. The trite expression of goodwill in the first of the following two paragraphs indicates the writer's insincerity, whereas the more personal tone of the revision suggests the writer's sincerity.

Change: Best wishes for finding another speaker for your May meeting.
To: The impact of the Claremore Civic Club on our community has been admired. Please convey my appreciation to the club members for all of their hard work.

The suggested plan for refusing an invitation includes the following elements:

What is the suggested plan for letters in which invitations are declined?

1. An expression of appreciation for the invitation
2. An explanation of facts
3. A suggestion of alternative course(s) of action, if appropriate
4. A courteous closing with, if appropriate, action orientation

Because the tone of the letter in Exhibit 7-12 is insincere, it may cause the recipient to conclude that the reasons for the decline are also not genuine. The reader will then believe that the writer simply was not interested in accepting the invitation.

In contrast, the genuine sincerity of the letter in Exhibit 7-13 should convince the recipient that the writer, if given another opportunity, will be pleased to accept the invitation. This letter is much more likely to produce a better relationship between the writer and the reader than is the letter in Exhibit 7-12.

Refusing Requests for Favors

From time to time, people in the business world need to prepare *favor-refusal letters*, which inform the reader of the inability to accommodate an earlier request. Refusals may be in response to requests to use company facilities, borrow company equipment, delay a credit payment, obtain information, and contract requirements. Requests of a nonbusiness nature may also need to be refused from time to time, such as when declining a request for a favor. Regardless of how absurd you believe the favor is, a courteous opening is essential.

Note the lack of courtesy in the first of the following two openings on the next page and how the revision corrects the problem.

Exhibit 7-12 Ineffective letter declining an invitation.

I have another commitment during the time that you recently asked me to speak at your convention. Unfortunately, I will be unable to speak at your convention because I shall not be able to get out of the other commitment.	A discourteous opening that contains the refusal.
Thank you for thinking of me in your search for convention speakers who have expertise in microcomputer applications.	A discourteous closing that lacks you-viewpoint.

Computer Management Consultants

(407) 345-1234
1231 North Avenue
Chicago, IL 60093

July 1, 199x

Dr. Edward J. Green
Executive Director
Computer Management Association
1384 Drake Avenue
Boston, MA 07953

Dear Dr. Green:

Thank you for inviting me to speak at the upcoming convention of the Computer Management Association. I've always found Boston to be an excellent site for conventions.

A courteous opening in which appreciation for the invitation is expressed.

The consulting firm for which I work recently began offering public seminars in various cities throughout the country. I am scheduled to offer a three-day seminar in Los Angeles during the same three days of your convention. Otherwise, I would be pleased to speak at your convention.

A section that contains an explanation of the facts that necessitate the decline of the invitation.

One of my colleagues who also has expertise in microcomputer applications is available during the time that you asked me to speak. Her presentation skills are excellent, and I am certain she could contribute significantly to the success of your convention.

A section that presents an alternative course of action.

If you are interested in contacting my colleague about the possibility of her speaking at your convention, please send me a note or call me at (407) 345-1234.

A courteous counteroffer.

Best wishes for a successful convention.

A cordial expression of good wishes.

Sincerely,

Daniel J. O'Tool
Consultant

Exhibit 7-13 Effective letter declining an invitation.

Change: Your request to use our facilities for the organizational meeting of a personnel management association has to be denied.

To: Thank you for spearheading an event that several businesspeople have visualized for some time: the founding of a local chapter of Personnel Administrators Association. The potential for such a chapter here is tremendous.

The next section of a letter denying a favor should explain the reasons for the refusal and present an implied refusal. The following paragraph illustrates how this section can be effectively presented.

Our community room is normally available for such uses as you requested. However, because of the extensive remodeling project under way at Smith-Jackson, our new community room will not be available until September 15.

In some instances, you may find it appropriate to include reader-benefit material or to suggest a counterproposal. Note how effectively the following paragraph introduces the counterproposal.

> The new community room will be available to nonprofit groups, such as the Personnel Administrators Association, on an ongoing basis. The facility will be furnished with tables and chairs and is designed to accommodate up to one hundred persons. This room can be reserved up to a year in advance of the event being scheduled.

The closing of the letter refusing a favor must also be courteous and, if appropriate, action oriented, as shown in the following paragraph.

> Please call me before May 10 if the PAA executive board decides to hold its meetings in the new community room.

The principles of disappointing-news letters identified throughout this chapter are also relevant to letters refusing favors. The suggested plan for a letter declining a favor includes the following elements:

What is the suggested plan for letters in which requests for favors are declined?

1. A buffered opening
2. An explanation of reasons the favor is being refused
3. An implied refusal
4. Reader-benefit material and/or counterproposal, if appropriate
5. A courteous closing with, if appropriate, action orientation

Exhibit 7-14 shows a letter refusing a financial contribution to a charitable organization. The cold and impersonal tone of the letter will surely impress on the recipient that she erred in requesting a donation.

Exhibit 7-15, in contrast, is a warm, personal letter that shows support for the charitable organization's activities, even while declining the request for a donation.

Exhibit 7-14 Ineffective letter declining a favor request.

If we made a financial contribution to each charitable organization that solicited us, we would soon become financially burdened. As you can appreciate during these economically tough times, we are fortunate some months when we just break even. What little we have left over after our expenses are paid is now being used to retire early some of our debt.	A discourteous opening that lacks tact in discussing the reasons necessitating the refusal.
When conditions improve and our company becomes more profitable, we will consider requests such as yours.	A closing that lacks you-viewpoint.

The residents of Merrimac appreciate the fine work of the Christmas Connection on behalf of the community's less-fortunate residents. The Christmas Connection has a long tradition of making Christmas available to those who would not otherwise be able to enjoy the Christmas Season.	A courteous opening that expresses appreciation.
For each of the last ten years, the Arjay Corporation, by making a significant contribution to Worthy Cause, has provided financial support to a number of the community's charitable and nonprofit organizations. The Board of Directors of Arjay decided that because the company may not always be able to make a financial contribution each time it receives a request from a charitable or nonprofit group, the fairest way to help such groups is to make contributions to Worthy Cause. Because Christmas Connection receives funds from Worthy Cause, a portion of our recent contribution will be coming your way.	A section that explains the reasons why the favor request must be refused.
Because we want to do everything we can to assure the success of your flea market on November 15, each of our employees has been asked to donate items that can be sold at this event. We will collect these items here and deliver them to you in time for the flea market. The proceeds from the sale of the items our employees donate can certainly be put to good use during the Christmas Season. If you need volunteers to help with the flea market, please let me know; I will "spread the word" throughout our company.	A section that outlines a counterproposal designed to help rebuild loss of goodwill resulting from declining the favor requested.
You can take great pride in the accomplishments of the Christmas Connection during the years you have served as its executive director. Our community is indeed fortunate to have you among its residents.	A courteous closing that contains you-viewpoint.

Exhibit 7-15 Effective letter declining a favor request.

DISAPPOINTING-NEWS MEMOS

What is the difference between the direct and indirect organizational options when preparing a disappointing-news memo?

A variety of business situations may result in the need to deliver disappointing news to employees. Disappointing-news messages can be delivered by either a memo or a letter. In preparing a *bad-news* or *disappointing-news memo*, which communicates negative information to employees, you have two organizational options: direct and indirect. The primary difference between them is the location within the document where the disappointing news is delivered. The direct option delivers the disappointing news immediately. The indirect option delivers the disappointing news later in the document.

Although the indirect option is generally advised for use in preparing disappointing-news memos, you might decide to use the direct option under the following circumstances.

Under what circumstances would you use the direct option when preparing a disappointing-news memo?

1. When the reader(s) won't take the disappointing news personally
2. When the disappointing news involves a significant portion of the organization's employees rather than just one or a few employees
3. When the employees may be anticipating the disappointing news

4. When the reader won't view the news as being an "attack" on his or her character, performance, or worth to the organization
5. When the reader expects you to use the indirect plan

Assume, for example that in each of the last ten years, Hanson Corporation has given each employee a year-end bonus. This year, however, the company is unable to do so because of a substantial investment in new equipment that will have a significant impact on its ability to remain competitive over the long run. In this situation, the direct plan can be used to notify the employees that an end-of-year bonus will not be forthcoming. Nothing in the message should be taken personally by the employees, and the situation affects each employee equally.

But, on the other hand, assume that the positions of several employees are being eliminated because the implementation of new technology has made them obsolete. Using the direct plan in a memo notifying these employees that their positions are being eliminated is not recommended. Rather than opening the memo with the disappointing news, a neutral or buffered opening, followed by a discussion of the reasons why the action is necessary, is recommended.

The following identifies the content appropriate for each of the three main sections of a disappointing-news memo using the indirect plan. The content appropriate for each section using the direct plan follows this list.

Indirect

Opening section	Inclusion of neutral or buffered material
Middle section	Discussion of the reasons why the action is necessary, followed by the presentation of the disappointing news, presenting the disappointing news through implication as much as possible
Closing section	Presentation of neutral or positive information (offer to be of assistance, expression of gratitude, etc.)

Direct

Opening section	Presentation of the disappointing news
Middle section	Discussion of the disappointing news and/or reasons for the action
Closing section	Presentation of neutral or positive information (offer to be of assistance, expression of gratitude, etc.)

What content is appropriate to include in each section of a disappointing-news memo, using the direct plan?

The following paragraph is the opening section of a memo (using the indirect plan) sent by a supervisor to a subordinate. The memo is intended to notify the subordinate that his recent actions (failure to attend a mandatory training session) were unacceptable.

> Delmar Corporation has utmost concern for the safety of its employees. This concern is likely responsible in part for the 100 percent injury-free record the company has now had for the last five years.

The middle section of the memo prepared for the subordinate follows. In this section, the reasons for the need to participate in a training program are discussed, along with the implication of the disappointing news.

> The manufacturer of the new press on which you work strongly urges that all operators of the press participate in a training program. Because of our concern for your safety and the safety of those with whom you work, John Brown, our director of production, has decided that all press operators are required to be trained properly. Therefore, when you have completed the required half-day training, you will be able to return to your present position. However, in the meantime, you are being assigned—effective today—to work with the turbine set-up crew in Building C.
>
> You are scheduled to participate in the mandatory training program next Tuesday, January 15, from 8 A.M. to noon. The program will be held at 3458 Beltline Highway in the Contross Building.

The closing section of the memo follows. Notice that it avoids further discussion of the negative aspects of the situation. Its focus will be viewed positively by the reader.

> A car in the motor pool has been reserved for you to drive to the training program. Please check with Janet Brown in the motor pool regarding the necessary procedures for obtaining the vehicle.

Following is the opening section of a memo that uses the direct plan to "make official" a rumor that has been frequently heard the last few weeks regarding a reduction in the amount of the annual salary increase in Hardwick Company. Notice that employees are unlikely to take the situation personally, which makes appropriate the use of the direct option.

> Several months ago, we anticipated the awarding of a 5 percent general salary increase for all full-time employees. With the 7 percent decline in sales since the beginning of the third quarter, the general salary increase has been reduced to 2 percent, with the possibility of a 3 percent merit increase awarded to deserving employees.

In the middle section of the memo for Hardwick's employees, the reasons for the action are discussed. The purpose of the discussion is to convince the employees of the need for the action.

> Although we can only speculate at this point why sales have decreased as much as they have, we need to be concerned that the trend may continue. The strongest reason offered for the decline in sales is because our current technology no longer allows us to be as cost competitive as we were as recently as two years ago. Accordingly, we will soon begin looking at the feasibility of installing new technology so we can maintain the cost competitiveness we have enjoyed over the years.
>
> To proceed with the salary increase program we anticipated earlier, other sacrifices would need to be made, most likely resulting in a reduction of the number of full-time employees. We believe you will agree that a reduction in the amount of the general salary increase is a better short-range alternative to laying off employees.

The closing section of the memo focuses on the future rather than on the negative aspects of the present situation. Notice how it attempts to maintain the employees' faith in their employer.

If our sales make a significant turnaround in the near future, the possibility of a midyear salary adjustment remains available. You will be kept apprised of new developments.

SUMMARY

The types of disappointing-news letters presented in this chapter are negative responses to inquiries, negative responses to adjustment requests, negative responses to credit requests, problem-order letters, declining of invitations, and declining of requests for favors.

Two options are available for organizing disappointing-news letters: the indirect plan and the direct plan. When the indirect plan is used, the refusal is delayed until after the facts have been presented and the reasons for the refusal have been discussed. The direct plan presents the refusal at the beginning of the letter.

To improve the effectiveness of disappointing-news letters, you should use a neutral or buffered opening and then review the facts completely and properly. In addition, you need to be concerned about analyzing the reasons for the refusal as well as your statement of the refusal. The closing can also impact the effectiveness of your letter.

Suggestions of a "do nature" that will help you write more effective letters are the following: Consider an implicit rather than an explicit refusal, focus on what you can do rather than on what you cannot do, use resale material, and make reader action easy, if appropriate. Some "don't nature" suggestions are these: don't use an accusatory tone, don't place the statement of refusal in a position of emphasis, or don't apologize for the action you are taking.

The suggestions you learned for writing a disappointing-news letter will generally serve you well in writing a disappointing-news memo. Unless a good reason to do otherwise exists, you will generally want to use an indirect structure.

REVIEW QUESTIONS

1. What two options are available to you when organizing disappointing-news messages?
2. How do you develop an effective neutral or buffered opening in a disappointing-news letter?
3. Where should the statement of refusal be placed in a disappointing-news letter?
4. How do you develop an effective closing in a disappointing-news letter?
5. Identify several suggestions of a "do-nature" to follow when preparing disappointing-news messages.
6. Identify several suggestions of a "don't-nature" to follow when preparing disappointing-news messages.
7. What type of opening is appropriate for a negative response to an inquiry letter?
8. What situations typically cause an adjustment refusal?
9. What type of material can you include in an adjustment-refusal letter aimed at rebuilding the customer's confidence?
10. What circumstances might cause you to make a partial adjustment?
11. What types of counteroffers are typically presented in credit-refusal letters?
12. Where in a letter refusing a favor request is the refusal included?
13. In a disappointing-news memo, what is the major difference between an opening that uses the indirect plan and one that uses the direct plan?
14. What content is found in the middle section of a disappointing-news memo that uses the indirect plan?

APPLICATION PROBLEMS

1. Prepare a written critique of the following letter, evaluating grammar usage, punctuation, conformity with suggested letter plan, and conformity with the writing essentials described in Chapters 3 and 4.

> It is with great disappointment that I inform you that we are unable to open a charge account in your name, as you requested. The reason being that you simply have too many outstanding bills at this point in time.
>
> If at some point in time in the future you are able to reduce your debt-load, we encourage you to apply again for a charge account. Those of our customers who have these accounts tell us how great it is.
>
> As I mentioned before, I am truly sorry that I cannot accommodate your request—but perhaps we can in the future. You have my personnel best wishes for success.

2. Rewrite the letter in application problem 1, making sure the weaknesses you identified in your critique have been eliminated. Make any assumptions you need to supply any missing details.
3. (Request refusal) You work in the customer service department of Halley Publishing Company, which is located at 349 Smithfield Road, Lyme, CT 10922. One of the books your company recently published, *Writing Powerful Letters and Reports,* is receiving a considerable amount of attention—which pleases you very much. Early reports from the sales staff indicate the book is tentatively being adopted for use this fall in business writing classes at nearly one hundred colleges and universities. Halley's policy is to provide free of cost the teacher's manuals accompanying a textbook only after the company has received a firm commitment that a specific college/university will use it. Without a firm commitment, the company charges $5 for each teacher's manual. You just received a letter from Dr. Donna Jacobson, Professor of Business Communications, Ridley College, Ridley, NJ 07845, requesting a copy of the manual. An examination of your records indicates that Ridley College has not made a firm commitment yet; therefore, you will need the payment in hand before you can send the manual. Indicate that should Ridley adopt this text, you will be pleased to refund the $5 charge for the teacher's manual. Write a letter denying her request. Keep in mind that the tone of your letter may determine whether *Writing Powerful Letters and Reports* is adopted at Ridley College in the future.
4. (Request refusal) You are the executive vice president of the Dade Clothing Company, a manufacturer of children's clothing, at 9874 Southside Drive, Muncie, IN 58474. For several consecutive years, Dade has generously contributed to the Muncie Home for Children, located at 9832 Pine Oak Drive, Muncie, IN 58474. You have just received a letter from Ms. Darla Krinen, president of MHC, inviting Dade to again make a generous contribution. For several months now, Dade's profitability has diminished, largely because of the competition of foreign markets. At a meeting last month, the executive committee approved a list of cost-cutting measures to be implemented immediately. Among these measures that will help save employees' jobs are the following: temporary freeze on replacing employees in noncritical jobs, delay in all equipment/furniture purchases, reduced maintenance, and a temporary freeze on providing financial support to community agencies/groups. Write a letter to Ms. Krinen, explaining that you will be unable to make the usual contribution. You have been authorized to tell her that if the financial picture turns around in the near future, you will be pleased to submit her request to the committee making these contribution decisions.
5. (Adjustment refusal) You are the manager of the Fashion Palace, one of the most popular ladies' clothing stores in Springfield, MO 58575. The store, located at 12 Main Street, just celebrated its fiftieth anniversary with a storewide sale. The sale items were offered on a final-sale basis. The no-returns policy enabled you to reduce the price of sale merchandise an additional 10 percent over its usual sale price. To make sure that all customers who purchased final-sale merchandise were aware of the no-return policy, a large notice mentioning the final-sales condition

was attached to the sale rack. The sales slip was also stamped "Final Sale—No Returns." In this morning's mail, you received a package from Mrs. Gladys Day, 387 Freeman Road, Joplin, MO 58986. The package contained a "final-sale" dress she bought during the anniversary sale and a note asking that you take the dress back and refund the $94.95 plus sales tax that she paid for it. In the note, Mrs. Day said that after she got home, she didn't like the dress as well as she thought she did. She hopes "you understand." Although Mrs. Day shops in your store frequently, she is considered by the sales staff to be "rude, demanding, and nasty." In fact, several of the experienced salespeople refuse to wait on her. Write her a letter explaining that the dress is being returned to her by UPS and a refund will not be forthcoming because she bought the dress on a final-sale basis. Consider suggesting that if the fit of the dress is what bothers her, your alterations department can make alterations. (Her large size does make her difficult to fit.) The store values her business enough that you do not want to alienate her.

6. (Adjustment refusal) You are the claims manager of the Gateway Furniture Company, located at 34 Valley View, White Water, MN 58543. Mr. and Mrs. Kenneth Johnson, 4543 South Street, Highland Park, IL 60074, recently purchased a wooden serving tray with a picture laminated on it. A sticker attached to the tray clearly stated the following: "Do not put hot pans or dishes on tray. Do not submerse tray in water." You just received the tray Mr. and Mrs. Johnson purchased and their note requesting a full refund of $39.95 plus sales tax because the picture "has not been mounted properly, which causes bubbles to appear under the picture." You know that each tray was carefully inspected before it was put on the floor. Therefore, you also know the tray was not in its present condition when the Johnsons purchased it. A close examination of the picture reveals that a hot dish or pan has been placed on the tray, no doubt causing the bubbles under the picture. Because you cannot afford to replace the tray, suggest that they contact the tray manufacturer (Superior Products Company, 384 Dell Road, Raleigh, NC 23484) to see whether the tray can be repaired. Indicate in your letter that you are returning the tray by parcel post.
7. (Credit refusal) You are the credit manager for Jameson's Auto Supply Company, located at 454 Western Avenue, Little Rock, AK 68754. You recently received a credit application from Mr. John Atterly, the owner of John's Auto Parts at 5686 Dukat Road, Memphis, TN 58543. On his application, he indicated that he has been in business for seven years. He listed The First National Bank of Memphis as his bank reference. In checking with the bank, you learn that Mr. Atterly has been in business for three years, is often slow in making payments on his loans, and has a loan with an outstanding balance of $10,898. The bank also mentioned that the store's sales have almost tripled in each of the three years it has been open. What really bothers you as credit manager is Mr. Atterly's dishonest response about the number of years he has been in business. In completing the form, he signed his name, certifying that the information he provided was accurate, when, in fact, it was not. Write a letter denying Mr. Atterly's request for credit. You do want his business—but on a cash basis. Offer Mr. Atterly a 5 percent cash discount on his next order of $700 or less.
8. (Credit refusal) You are the credit manager for John Hart Company (9865 Wilson Avenue, Detroit, MI 48856), a distributor of exercise equipment. You recently received a credit application from the Be-Strong Exercise Room (6574 Grant Avenue, Mt. Pleasant, MI 48865) owned by Jack and Bill Smith, who are brothers. Their application indicated that the business opened two months ago. You received favorable reports about the two owners from their credit references—but quite a different story appeared in the Mt. Pleasant Credit Bureau report you received. From the report, you learned that Jack declared bankruptcy last year after his home construction company began experiencing financial problems. His liabilities were

$103,453.24; assets were valued at $9,045. You also learned that Bill Smith served three years in a Michigan prison (from January 1975 to December 1977) after he was convicted of an armed robbery of a convenience store. Your analysis of the data supplied by the Smiths on their application for credit reveals an unbalanced assets-liabilities ratio. Increasing their assets by $10,000 or decreasing their liabilities by the same amount would result in a ratio that comes closer to meeting your expectations. Although you would welcome filling orders on a cash basis from the Be-Strong Exercise Room, you cannot open a credit account for the Smith brothers. To entice them to order from you on a cash basis, send along two $20 cash discount coupons that can be applied toward the cost of two different orders that exceed $150. Write an appropriate letter.

9. (Credit refusal) You are the credit manager of Blue Ridge Valley Paint Distributing Company, located at 4543 Petersburg Drive, Petersburg, VA 12234. One of your customers, Mr. Paul Brown, owner of Brown's Paint Store, 4543 Salem Drive, Richmond, VA 12298, recently sent you a $589 order for paint and painting supplies. He asked that the order be charged to his credit account. In looking at his account, you discover that he is already $58.87 over his $600 credit limit and that he has not responded to your three requests for payment on his account. Write a letter to Mr. Brown, explaining that before you are able to send this order on credit, you will need to receive full payment of his account ($658.87). Of course, you will be pleased to send the order immediately if he sends you a check for $589. You are glad to see that he has ordered 48 tubes of Scrape-No-More, a new product that is put on glass before painting the surface next to the glass. After the paint has dried, a sharp knife or blade is used to make a cut that separates the Scrape-No-More compound on the glass from the compound on the painted surface. Then the Scrape-No-More compound is easily peeled (usually in one piece) from the window. Customers who have used this product claim that they will never be without it again.
10. (Order refusal) You are the manager of the order department at Metalcraft Lawn Furniture Company, 4564 Greenwood Avenue, Deerfield, IL 60015. Until recently your company was strictly a mail-order operation. Four months ago you began selling through dealers. Now, if a dealer is located in an area from which a mail order was received, your policy is to decline the order and to refer the customer to your local dealer. You recently received an order for a wrought-iron patio set (glass-top table and four chairs) from Mr. Grant Parker, 12 Summit Circle, Branson, MO 54484. Your dealer in Branson is Ozark Lawn and Garden Center, 2834 Main Street. Write a letter refusing Mr. Parker's order but send along a manufacturer's rebate coupon worth $20, explaining that the patio set he ordered has become your best-selling item. Remind him also that the set now comes in two additional colors: slate gray and midnight blue.
11. (Order refusal) You work in the order department of Townley Tool Company, located at 4543 Connecticut Street, Albany, NY 14430. You have just received an order from A-B-C Hardware, Main Street, Adoka, IA 78685 for five socket sets (Stock No. 58574). You dropped this particular item several months ago when you began carrying another socket set (Stock No. 58665) that contained ten more sockets (for a total of forty-four sockets). The wholesale cost of the No. 58665 set is only $2.14 more (total of $14.12) than the cost of the No. 58574 set. Write a letter to A-B-C's manager, Mr. Jack Price, explaining that you no longer sell the set he ordered. Ask if he wants you to send him ten No. 58665 sets. If so, you will bill him for the $21.40 cost difference.
12. (Speaking invitation) You are well known as a speaker on a variety of management topics. In addition to your full-time job as executive assistant to the president of A-1 Insurance Company (900 East Street, Decatur, IL 61005), you give,

on the average, three or four of these presentations a month. Most requests come from professional associations that have evening dinner meetings. You have just received an invitation to talk on time management—the topic you receive the most requests to speak about—from the vice president (Mr. Tom Bennett, 1893 Niles Road, Bloomington, IL 64334) of the Bloomington (IL) Chapter of Professional Engineers. The letter of invitation indicated that this group meets the first and third Tuesdays of each month—and you were invited to speak the first Tuesday in May. In looking at your calendar, you notice that your son's high school graduation ceremony is that evening. Your schedule, however, is clear for the evening of the third Tuesday should a speaker be needed for that meeting. Write Mr. Bennett a letter declining his invitation.

13. (Favor request) You, the president of Allied Building Materials, Inc., 7868 Rand Road, Wheeling, IL 60984, just received a letter from Mr. Mark Lee, 1873 Greenbelt Drive, Des Plains, IL 60985, asking permission to use your parklike grounds for a picnic the Wheeling Rotary Club hosts each year for the children in the Wheeling Children's Home. The grounds your building is located on attracts considerable attention, which means that you get many requests similar to this one. Allied decided several years ago that it would not make these grounds available for public use. The lake on the grounds could provide a liability situation for which the company does not have insurance protection. Write Mr. Lee a letter declining his request. Suggest the use of the Wheeling City Park for the picnic.
14. (Disappointing-news memo) Several years ago, the university (Southeast State University, Pittsfield, KS) where you are the assistant to the president gave its staff employees the opportunity to take one tuition-free class per semester. Only one restriction was placed on the time of the day that employees could attend the class: If they chose to enroll in a class during normal working hours, then they would forego the daily 30 minutes of break time to which they were entitled. The 150 minutes of break time basically offset the 150 minutes per week an employee spent attending the class. A new labor contract with the union representing the office employees on campus requires that employees take their breaks. Therefore, the university can no longer afford to give employees time off to participate in classes and also provide them with their break time. The staff advisory council recently recommended to the university's president that employees now be restricted as to the time of day they can enroll in a class. Three options are now available: Enroll in a 7 A.M. class, a 12 P.M. class, or a class beginning at 5 P.M. or later. The president has accepted the recommendation of the staff advisory council and has asked you to prepare for her the memo communicating change in procedure to be sent to all staff employees.
15. (Disappointing-news memo) For some employees in Detrick Company (Great Falls, MT), where you are vice president for human resources, an unrestricted smoking policy has been a source of much frustration. But the employees who smoke have been grateful for the unrestricted policy. Because of the ever-increasing concern other employees have about the dangers of secondhand smoke, the executive committee recently decided to ban all smoking within the building. For smokers, this ban will be the source of considerable consternation. You are to write the memo announcing to all employees the in-premises smoking ban that will begin the first working day of next month. Because of the company's commitment to helping employees maintain a healthy lifestyle, you have decided to pay for a smoking-cessation consultant to provide classes for all employees who want to quit smoking. This announcement of these classes is also part of the memo. Prepare the memo informing employees of the smoking ban and offering the smoking-cessation program.

8

Persuasive Letters and Memos

After studying this chapter, you should be able to

1. Describe the elements of the persuasion strategy.
2. Outline the suggestions for preparing effective sales letters.
3. Outline the suggestions for preparing letters that solicit potential credit customers.
4. Identify the characteristics of collection letters.
5. Identify and describe the types of appeals in the collection series.
6. Explain the differences between stages of the collection series.
7. Prepare effective letters of the type discussed in this chapter.
8. Prepare effective memos of the type discussed in this chapter.

Why is persuasion incorporated into persuasive letters?

In many of the letters discussed in Chapters 5 to 7, writers may ask for information or respond to requests with some assurance that their message will elicit appropriate results. But preparing persuasive letters demands a different approach because the situation, by itself, may not create sufficient desire in the reader to comply with your request. Successful persuasion hinges on recognition of the reasons or goals that drive the persuasive process. Questions that will assist you in determining the goals before you draft the persuasive message are as follows:

1. Why is persuasion needed in this particular situation? For instance, are we trying to convince the reader to do something, to believe something, or to not take action?
2. What am I trying to persuade the reader to do?
3. Where is the recommended action to take place?
4. How should the reader proceed? A persuasive message will outline the steps required for accomplishing what is described in the persuasive message—Do it Now, Send no Money, Six Simple Steps, and so on.

Persuasion is a technique used to gain compliance from the recipient of the message. *Persuasive letters,* or letters with the goal of changing the receiver's beliefs, actions, feelings, attitudes, or values must include information that will entice the reader to take the action you are requesting.

Writers of persuasive messages must remain aware of potential communication barriers that may prevent the reader from complying with their request. Although many potential barriers exist, the major ones the writer must consider are the following:

1. Reader's lack of interest
2. Reader's lack of need
3. Reader's dissatisfaction with products or services

Persuading the reader to comply with your request will be increasingly difficult if one or more of these barriers exist; but by anticipating them, you can adjust your communication style to reduce their impact. The persuasive letters described in this chapter are sales letters, letters soliciting potential credit customers, and collection letters. Although these types of persuasive letters play different roles in business communication, they share a common objective—to appeal to readers so they will comply with the request.

THE PERSUASION STRATEGY

Persuasive business letters primarily use the indirect approach because the direct approach may not work. The assumption is that stating the request too directly at the beginning of the letter may represent unwanted or bad news. Rather, presenting facts and information that make your message appear beneficial prepares the reader for the message that follows. The four steps discussed in the next sections should help you organize effective persuasive messages.

Attracting Favorable Attention

How is favorable attention attracted in persuasive letters?

Because many persuasive messages are unsolicited, attracting favorable attention is especially important. A carefully designed theme containing reader or listener benefit is the base approach to use for this goal; therefore, your first sentence should gain attention.

Note how the first of the following two paragraphs does little to attract the reader's attention. The revision, by using a famous quote, immediately gains the reader's attention.

Change: A small monthly donation to "Cleaning up the American Highways" is needed, and I know you agree that this is an important and worthy project, and I am pleased to welcome you aboard.

To: "America the Beautiful" describes a situation that you and I can enjoy and preserve for our children and grandchildren. The diversity, the unspoiled beauty, and the freedom—yes, the freedom to enjoy all this beauty—is a basic American right and privilege.

The American highway is rapidly becoming a convenience junkyard for America's mobile society. I need your help to preserve the beauty of our highways for our children and grandchildren. "Cleaning up the American Highway" is a nonprofit volunteer organization dedicated to maintaining the beauty of America's highways. For a small donation of $15 a month, you can do your part in maintaining "America the Beautiful."

You can gain attention by beginning your message with a question or statement that encourages continued reading because the reader wants to know "What's in this for me?" Therefore, you should highlight an idea close to the reader's needs, interests, curiosity, or excitement. Unlike other business letters, the first paragraph of the persuasive message should represent a personal concept rather than simply expressing information about your organization or yourself. Some successful attention-gaining techniques are the following:

1. Using a famous quote
2. Outlining a bargain
3. Asking a question
4. Describing an outstanding feature
5. Making a shocking statement
6. Announcing a gift
7. Asking a question and outlining an outstanding feature
8. Using a famous proverb
9. Using a news announcement

Examples of attention-gaining openings appear in the following sentences.

1. *Famous quote:* Home is where the heart is, and coming home is the best part of the day.
2. *Bargain:* Earn while you learn on your own personal computer!
3. *Question:* Could you use an extra hour a day?
4. *Outstanding feature:* The 12-volt "Lift-O-Jack" will raise and lower your car in less than two minutes!
5. *Shocking statement:* Twenty-five percent of America's high school age students drop out before finishing.
6. *Gift:* Here's a gift for the new mother.
7. *Question/feature:* Would you like to own your own business and have employees who pay you for the privilege of working?
8. *Proverb:* A stitch in time saves nine.
9. *News announcement:* According to recent governmental reports, the financial protection of Americans is 36 percent below the family-need level.

Creating Interest

How can interest be created in persuasive messages?

After capturing the reader's attention, the writer of persuasive messages should follow with a lead-in that captures the reader's interest. Creation of interest is normally accomplished by being positive, by giving clear definitions of the product or service, and by identifying special features. For example, you should sell the sizzle—not just the steak; homecoming, not just the mum; and a technique, not just a product.

Product information and facts are important to persuasive messages, but the actual sales appeal must be psychological. This is accomplished by explaining or describing the product or service in terms of an emotional benefit to the reader. Chinaware, for example, may be basically plates and cups; but to a host or hostess, it has other meanings. Described in terms of the emotional benefits it offers, chinaware

1. provides memorable meals.
2. has beautiful patterns that tell guests they are important.
3. provides for total color coordination.
4. has unique shaping for eloquent aesthetic appearance.
5. gives your table a new look.
6. sets the mood for relaxed dining.

Creating interest, then, is often accomplished not only by clear and precise descriptions of all the tangible or physical characteristics but also of all the intangible or value aspects of the product or service.

Physical descriptions include such points as construction, beauty, performance, and functions. *Value descriptions* include emotional aspects, such as comfort, entertainment, recognition, health, and security. To increase reader interest, you should stress one or more of the following advantages:

Appreciation and approval by others	Comfort	Enjoyment
Beauty	Distinction	Entertainment
	Efficiency	Health

Money	Pride	Savings
Peace of mind	Profit	Self-preservation
Pleasure	Recognition	Solution to a problem
Popularity	Respect	Success
Prestige	Safety and security	

Note how the first of the following two paragraphs fails to create reader interest because it stresses only one advantage, whereas the revision is more successful because it stresses several.

> Change: A year's subscription to *The Modern Home* costs just a few cents each day. Yet, you will find it difficult to put a price on much of the information you find in each issue.
>
> To: You can almost smell the aroma of the food pictured in the foods section of each issue of *The Modern Home*. The fragrance of the flowers shown in the gardening section of each issue almost becomes reality. And the descriptions of the vacation spots presented in the traveling section of each issue are so vivid that you will have to pinch yourself to realize you are not really there. For only pennies a day, you can receive a magazine containing much information that you will consider essential.

Establishing Reader Desire and Conviction

Through careful planning, successful sales letters employ obvious and sometimes not-so-obvious elements of motivation. Many hidden feelings, such as fear, frustration, and desire, can be used effectively to convince people to purchase a product or service.

How are reader desire and conviction established in persuasive messages?

Psychological emphasis is more successful when it attracts the true desire of the reader. What people say they want may not be what they actually desire. For instance, most people will appear conservative, rational, and open-minded about products and services, but experienced writers of sales letters understand they can reach prospective customers by selling

1. style, attractiveness, and neat appearance rather than just clothing.
2. feelings, ideals, respect, and comfort rather than items or products.
3. knowledge rather than books.
4. holes rather than drill bits.
5. economy and pleasure of making personal items rather than tools.
6. comfort rather than air conditioning.
7. cleanliness rather than soap products.
8. beauty and hope rather than cosmetics.

Facts and information provide a basis for such objective qualifiers as height, weight, width, shape, size, watts, texture, and other product qualities and specifications. These facts provide an opportunity for the reader to make a comparison.

Ideas stress the more important intangible psychological appeals, such as sensation, satisfaction, and pleasure. Ideas, unlike facts and information, are rarely quantifiable.

A successful persuasive message provides adequate facts and information to ensure quality comparisons and also ideas that will help the reader decide on your product or service.

To attract attention, develop interest, and establish desire and conviction, you may use many different combinations and approaches, including (1) facts, figures, and information; (2) details about construction, design, or quality control; (3) product quality and reliability as tested and verified by independent laboratories or specific manufacturers; (4) testimonials; and (5) samples, trials, and free demonstrations.

The first of the following two paragraphs is weak in arousing reader motivation for conviction; the revised version is much more effective.

Change:	Your personal integrity and self-preservation need not be challenged by other people. With just a few low-cost lessons, you can be the successful, confident person you have always dreamed of being.
To:	Remember: No one can intimidate you without your permission. You can develop and control a new self-concept simply and easily with the Delta Home Study Course.

Explaining Desired Action

Effective persuasive letters should not make readers work at determining what action they must take. Rather, the writer must state the action clearly and concisely. An action closing should ask for the desired action in a confident, unassuming manner while reminding readers of the benefits they may expect and the anticipated timing of the action.

Not only should you emphasize the action, but also you should make it easy to understand and accomplish. Encourage readers to act now or within a stated time frame. You should close with a reader-benefit statement. Usually, this statement should incorporate the same information as that in the opening paragraph.

You can make the appropriate action easy for readers to accomplish in several ways, such as by including fax numbers, electronic mail orders, and reply envelopes. The action-gaining methods in the following sentences are from successful persuasive messages from major corporations:

Stimulating Action through Persuasive Offers

1. Send no money.
2. Examine for ten days on approval.
3. This offer is good until November 26.
4. The price will be increased by $20 after July 4.
5. Enjoy a special 15-percent discount if full payment accompanies your order.
6. We will refund your money if you are not completely satisfied.

Eliciting action is, as indicated, the overall goal of persuasive letters. Emphasis on *simple* action is more important than *simply* emphasizing action.

Emphasizing Simple Action

1. Send your order on the enclosed easy-order blank.
2. A postage-free envelope is enclosed for your convenience.
3. You may pay by check, money order, or through our deferred-payment plan.
4. Our toll-free number is . . .

Action orientation is also accomplished by suggesting an immediate response.

Suggesting Immediate Response

1. Mail the enclosed card today.
2. Mark the easy-order blank and send it today.
3. You can receive your free copy by returning the enclosed card today.

The first of the following sentences makes it more difficult for the reader to act than does the revision.

Change:	The whole process of adequate hospitalization protection can be yours by filling out and returning the enclosed medical questionnaire.
To:	Call our toll-free number today to receive at no additional cost three months of free hospitalization and medical coverage.

THE SALES LETTER

In actual volume, many organizations prepare more sales letters than any other type of business letter. *Sales letters* distributed by an organization promote a product or service. These letters are usually mass produced and compete directly with those of other organizations. The persuasion strategies presented in the previous section also work in preparing successful sales letters.

What is the suggested plan for sales letters?

The suggested plan for a sales letter includes the following elements:

1. An opening attracting the reader's attention
2. A section capturing the reader's interest in the product or service you are selling
3. A section fueling the reader's desire and conviction
4. A courteous, action-oriented closing

The letter in Exhibit 8-1 shows an ineffective sales letter. Notice that the four essential elements of effective persuasive letters (attracting favorable attention, creating interest, establishing desire, and explaining the action you want the reader to take) are either weakly presented or lacking. Exhibit 8-2 contains the same information but corrects the obvious weaknesses of Exhibit 8-1.

Sales letters, as you might expect, are much easier to write when you are promoting a top-quality product or service. Avoid an overconfident tone, which may have a negative impact. You should also try not to use statements suggesting a basic lack of confidence in the product or service, such as "I hope you will agree . . ."; or "If you agree . . ."; or "I am quite sure you will agree . . ."; or "Many of our customers agree. . . ." Such statements lead the reader to believe that the writer has doubts about the product, service, or overall quality, which in turn generates doubt in the minds of the readers.

Included in the following Ethics Episode is a discussion of ethics and the development of a sales letter.

ETHICS EPISODE

Sales promotion through enticing advertising is essential for an organization to remain competitive in a worldwide marketplace. Most sales letters are prepared by highly skilled professionals who are employed by the company or by an outside firm whose services are contracted when the need arises. Regardless of the type, size, or format, sales letters have a common purpose—to convince people to spend money on a particular product or service.

Obviously, employees possess a clearer understanding of the nature, purpose, and overall possibilities of the company's products and services. Nevertheless, at first glance sales letters that are prepared by company insiders often appear too general, too conservative, and too legalistic. In contrast, outside firms often possess more experience and greater ability with sales letters, but they often have only limited knowledge about the company's strengths and weaknesses. Therefore, sales letters from outside service organizations may be inaccurate in their descriptions of or claims about the product or service capabilities.

Local, state, and district courts are literally bombarded with litigation stemming from product ineffectiveness or product failure to fulfill the standards claimed in sales. For example, many states consider sales letters as contracts; therefore, an organization involved in interstate commerce must carefully edit sales messages that imply or promise anything that cannot be delivered. Fraudulent statements concerning price, quality, quantity, or capability greatly increase the possibility of litigation. In addition, the use of a person's name or photograph without written permission may constitute unauthorized invasion of privacy.

Simply avoiding what is illegal is not a license for people who specialize in the preparation of sales letters. Ethics, when preparing sales letters, means that one should persuade but not exploit or maneuver readers of the message. Naturally, an effective sales letter accentuates the positive and de-emphasizes negative aspects of the product or service. Sales letters must be carefully edited so they do not distort the truth.

Sales letters should serve the customers and prospective customers of an organization with an accurate and truthful description of products or services. Perhaps a good rule to follow when preparing or reviewing company sales letters is to tell the truth, the whole truth, and nothing but the truth.

Exhibit 8-3 illustrates a letter attempting to persuade its recipients to buy HOW TO SAY IT, a book designed to help its readers become more effective communicators. Notice how the writer gets the reader's attention with the two statements above the salutation, as well as with the content of the opening paragraph. The writer then creates interest by offering a "FREE 15-day trial . . ." Desire and conviction are established through the statement, ". . . you'll be able to get others to feel what you feel, think what you think." Action is simple: "Just print your name below and return this entire letter in the enclosed postpaid envelope."

The sales letter in Exhibit 8-4 contains "seasonal" persuasion and incorporates the previously discussed elements of a successful persuasive letter.

Exhibit 8-5 illustrates a persuasive letter designed to create action through emphasis on health and self-preservation.

Persuasive letters are important if a business is to remain competitive. Although organizations must adhere to the belief that the customer is always right, the writers of persuasive letters, nevertheless, try to influence their readers' attitude, choice and action.

An important point to remember is that sales letters always use persuasion; but persuasive sentences, paragraphs, and messages do not always involve sales promotion. Use Checklist 8-1 as a guide for developing persuasive sales messages.

Soliciting Prospective Credit Customers

Letters designed to solicit prospective credit customers are basically promotional in nature. These letters must also be persuasive because their purpose is to entice prospective customers to open a charge account.

What four things does the opening of a letter designed to solicit prospective credit customers accomplish?

The opening of a letter designed to solicit credit customers probably determines whether the letter is read. The opening has four tasks to accomplish: (1) attract the recipient's attention; (2) entice the recipient to read the entire letter; (3) stimulate the recipient to want to complete an application blank; and (4) ensure the reader's completion of the blank. The opening—more than any other section of this type of letter—is likely to determine whether the letter fulfills its purpose.

Exhibit 8-1 Ineffective sales letter.

Please allow me a few minutes of your most valuable time to explain the deal of a lifetime.	A weak opening.
Wouldn't you like to borrow without having to fill out all those complex financial forms normally required by a bank? Our quick-credit personal application card will provide you with $3,000, and your payments will be delayed for six months.	A section that fails to create interest.
If you are interested in our offer, please call us using the following toll-free number: 1-800-243-6781. For additional information, just return the enclosed card.	A closing that lacks emphasis or action.

XYZ Corporation
1828 King Boulevard Omaha, NE 68543
(414) 874-1121

September 12, 199x

Mr. Edward Johnson
1223 Davidson Boulevard
Lincoln, NE 68588

Dear Mr. Johnson:

Congratulations, Mr. Johnson; you are preapproved for a special credit opportunity at XYZ Corporation.

An effective opening that creates interest.

Only a small percentage of Americans possess the degree of financial responsibility required to satisfy our stringent selection criteria for a preapproved XYZ Electronics credit card. You are one of the few with exceptional creditworthiness.

A section that uses an effective interest-building approach.

Your preapproved credit authorization certificate is enclosed. Simply take the certificate to your local authorized Electronics dealer, and you can take your new Electronics equipment home the same day. A charge-account agreement form is also enclosed for your review.

A section that stimulates.

As an Electronics charge customer, you will enjoy the ease of charging your purchases, and you will also receive advance notice of special sales. During two of our yearly sales, our charge account customers are invited to take advantage of special sale prices one day before the sale is announced to the public.

A section that outlines the advantages of being a charge customer, which also helps create interest.

Your special Electronics charge privileges include a credit limit of $5,000. The special card will arrive at your home just a few days after you sign and return the enclosed agreement form. This offer expires on December 31, so act today. You will be pleased that you took advantage of this special, limited offer for an exclusive XYZ Electronics credit card.

A closing that outlines the action to be taken.

Sincerely,

Mary Hartlee
Credit Manager

Exhibit 8-2 Effective sales letter.

After the opening has attracted the reader's attention, he or she should be invited to open a charge account. To begin directly with the invitation may discourage some individuals from continuing to read. In the two paragraphs that follow, note the more inviting tone of the revision.

Change: We want to take this opportunity to extend to you an invitation to open a charge account at Sniders.

To: Sniders has had a long-standing tradition of serving its customers. In fact, concern for customers has helped Sniders become one of the leading furniture stores in the Greater Houston area. To help us serve you—one of our preferred customers—even better, you are invited to complete the attached application for credit.

PRENTICE HALL
Career & Personal Development
Englewood Cliffs, NJ 07682

Master them at our expense for 15 days . . . .

Potent new techniques of "force communications" that help you get your own way in any business or social situation!

Dear Customer:

Imagine being able to write letters that are immediately and politely acknowledged . . . give instructions that are promptly (and correctly!) carried out . . . prepare speeches that motivate and inspire your audience.

Imagine, too, never being at a loss for just the right words to clearly express the way you feel—whether your purpose is to congratulate or complain, express sympathy or anger, raise funds, confirm an appointment, or turn down a request.

You don't have to imagine any longer. Just print your name below and return this letter in the enclosed postpaid emvelope and I'll send you a FREE 15-day trial copy of Prentice Hall's instant reference book called HOW TO SAY IT.

This one-of-a-kind resource lets you custom-tailor everything you say or write with scores of interchangeable key words, phrases, sentences, and paragraphs to create the power, personality, and style that gets people to respond to you the way you want them to.

HOW TO SAY IT puts all the power and persuasiveness of the English language at your command. With the help of this resource you'll be able to get others to feel what you feel, think what you think. You'll create an aura of command that people will immediately recognize when you speak to them!

Try HOW TO SAY IT for 15 days—without risk or obligation!

Just print your name below and return this entire letter in the enclosed postpaid envelope. We'll rush HOW TO SAY IT to you for a FREE 15-day examination. Then, if you're 100% delighted, honor our invoice for just $29.95, plus state sales tax where applicable, and postage and handling. Otherwise return it and owe nothing at all!

Sincerely,

Richard B. Hopkins

Richard B. Hopkins

YES! Send me HOW TO SAY IT for a FREE 15-day examination!

Please print your name clearly and return this letter in the enclosed postpaid envelope.

MPGoo8 42436-6 CBR-83118-A4(1)

Exhibit 8-3 Commercial sales letter.

Source: *How To Say It*, Rosalie Maggio, © 1990. Reprinted by permission of Prentice Hall/A Division of Simon & Schuster.

A discussion of the advantages of using credit follows the opening. The reader-benefit material included in this section must be convincing. To cite unconvincing advantages will not entice the reader to complete the application blank. The first of the following two paragraphs is weak; the reader-benefit material in the revision is more convincing.

Change: By charging a purchase, you will have an opportunity to enjoy the use of the merchandise without having to delay purchase until you can pay for it with cash.

To: You as a charge customer of Snider's will enjoy the following special benefits:

1. You will receive notices of special sales before the general public is notified. Thus, you will have first pick of the sale merchandise.
2. You are able to shop by telephone simply by charging your purchases to your charge account.
3. You are able to defer the full payment of your account balance if you so choose. This can be done simply by paying the minimum amount on the unpaid balance plus a small interest charge.

Who really thinks much about furnaces in the summertime?	An opening that gains attention by asking a precise question.
National Heat-Pump, Inc. does, and we recommend you give some thought to your heating system while the weather is still warm—and before the first freezing temperatures arrive.	A section that contains information designed to create interst.
Furnaces are built to last; but even the most efficient systems require regular preseason check-ups for the most economical operation. Pipes, pressure gauges, combustion chambers, controls, switches, thermostats, and gas or oil lines need to be checked to ensure safe, economical heating.	A section that creates desire and conviction.
Our preseason heating system service is more economical and efficient when we are not on the run with emergency service requests during the season's first cold snap. Knowing your heating system is ready for the winter months will also provide peace of mind because you will be confident your furnace is in proper operating condition. Even more important, you will avoid the inconvenience and cost of emergency repair service.	A section that continues with the development of desire and conviction.
Give yourself peace of mind by having your furnace checked before winter arrives. Call us today at 661-6666 for an appointment to have your entire system checked. We will schedule one of our qualified heating system specialists to come to your home at your convenience.	A closing that explains the action to be taken.

Exhibit 8-4 Effective sales letter based on time persuasion.

If you decide to use sales-promotion material in the letter designed to solicit credit customers, this material can appear in the next section. *Sales-promotion material* is designed to inform the customer about additional products in which he or she may be interested—a new line of merchandise the company has added, a distinctive award the company has just received, or an upcoming sale.

Conversely, *resale material* is designed to convince the customer that he or she has made a wise choice. Resale material can also be included after the discussion of the advantages of having a charge account.

The following paragraph effectively uses sales-promotion material.

> Sniders' was just selected as the exclusive dealer of Markline furniture in the Greater Houston area. The dealers of this top-quality furniture line are carefully selected by Markline Corporation. The loyalty of such long-term customers as you has enabled us to be chosen as the Markline dealer in the Greater Houston area—an honor for which we are indeed proud.

The persuasive sales material presented up to this point has been aimed at convincing the customer of two things: that the person will wisely continue to do business with your company and that opening a charge account is in the customer's best interest. Now is the time to review the action you wish the prospective customer to take—to complete the attached application blank. The following paragraph illustrates how to present this material.

Health Care

(403) 782-8821 1298 Smithfield Blvd. Eli, NV 87343

January 12, 199x

Mr. Jonathan Fields
1287 Liberty Lane
Oklahoma City, OK 73981

Dear Mr. Fields:

Of the top ten risk factors leading to cardiovascular disease, seven are directly related to diet.

An opening designed to attract favorable attention.

Consider these startling statistics: Recent estimates suggest that 29 million Americans suffer from cardiovascular disease. The United States Department of Agriculture estimates that proper diet might reduce cardiovascular disease mortality by 25 percent. An average American male has a 33 percent chance of developing some form of heart disease before age 60.

A section that creates interest

An optimum health program involves five essentials:

A section that creates desire and interest.

1. Building superior cells.
2. Improving body chemistry.
3. Improving body immunity.
4. Aiding digestion and assimilation.
5. Reducing toxins in the body.

Considering today's typical American diet, these five essentials are absolutely necessary for an optimum health program. Health Care will outline for you a complete health restoration and maintenance program. We guarantee that our program will enable you to look and feel better and healthier—or we will refund your money.

A section that continues with the development of desire and conviction.

Take action now! Return the enclosed card; an experienced Health Care representative will come to your home to explain our complete program on a no-risk, no-obligation basis.

A closing that outlines the desired action.

Sincerely,

David Cromwell
Medical Specialist

Enclosure

Exhibit 8-5 Effective sales letter about health care.

Within a few days after we receive your completed application blank, a Sniders' charge account will be opened in your name. Because you have been prequalified for a charge account, only a minimum amount of information is necessary to complete the form. Once you have entered the requested information, simply sign your name on the appropriate line and drop your application in the mail.

OPENING

1. Have you used an effective opening in the first paragraph that attracts the attention of the intended audience?
2. Have you outlined a specific benefit that can serve as a building block or selling point for the remainder of the letter?
3. Have you stated your message in such a manner that the intended audience will focus on the item to be sold rather than on the attention-getting approach?
4. Is your opening positive so the intended audience will not become irritated with a persuasive process that has little to do with the actual product?

MIDDLE

1. Do you include important physical descriptions of the product?
2. Does your message explain how the reader will benefit from the use of this product? Does your persuasion show how this product will fulfill specific needs?
3. Have you included copies of documentation to assist the reader in evaluating the true value of the product?
4. Have you included or evaluated the sales potential associated with local dealers or stores carrying your product?

CLOSING

1. Is your closing brief and businesslike?
2. Is your closing courteous?
3. Will your closing effectively motivate the reader to take action? Have you made the action easy for the reader to take?
4. Have you listed the specific action you wish the reader to take?
5. Have you included any unintentional guaranty or warranty that you cannot actually provide?
6. Have you considered whether a special inducement for action would be effective? (Time limits, coupons, special limited discounts, credit purchases, free gifts, etc.)

Checklist 8-1 Sales letters.

The closing of a letter soliciting credit customers should make the prospective customer feel appreciated. Note the more assertive future-oriented closing in the following revision.

Change: We are here to serve you. Please help us serve you better by opening a charge account.

To: Although we have had many opportunities to serve you well in the past, we anticipate being able to serve you even better in the future.

The suggested plan for a letter designed to solicit prospective credit customers includes the following elements:

1. A goodwill opening enticing the individual to read the letter
2. A section identifying the advantages of using credit
3. A section containing sales-promotion and/or resale material
4. A discussion of the action you wish the prospective customer to take
5. A courteous, friendly closing to make the prospective customer feel appreciated so that he or she will plan to use the charge account soon

Exhibit 8-6 shows an ineffective letter soliciting prospective credit customers. Exhibit 8-7 is a revision of the same letter, which is sure to entice more people to complete the application.

If you are like most of our customers who have a Continental charge card, you soon learn that it is one of your most valued possessions.	An opening that implies the reader is like many other people.
We are inviting you to complete the attached charge-card application so you also can discover how valuable a Continental card is.	A delayed invitation to complete the application blank.
In addition to having all the advantages of being able to charge your purchases at Continental, you will also receive notices of our special sales before they are announced to the general public. Thus, you will have first pick of sale items.	A section containing a weak discussion of the benefits of having a charge account.
We suggest that you enhance the convenience of your shopping at Continental by opening a charge account. We look forward to receiving your application.	A weak closing that lacks you-attitude.

Exhibit 8-6 Ineffective letter soliciting prospective credit customers.

Since the time that the Continental Department Store was founded nearly fifty years ago, serving our customers has been paramount. So we can serve you even better, we invite you to complete the attached application for credit.	An upbeat opening that will entice the recipient to read the entire letter and an invitation to complete the application blank.
As a Continental credit customer, you will enjoy several benefits, including the following: 1. You will be able to shop over the telephone—and your purchases can be simply charged to your account. Purchases exceeding $25 are delivered free. 2. You will be able to take advantage of our sale prices two days before the spring and fall semiannual sales are announced to the public. 3. You can defer paying in full your monthly account balance by paying a minimum amount of $10 or 10 percent of the balance, whichever is greater. Unpaid balances are subject to a 1.5 percent monthly (18 percent APR) interest charge.	A thorough discussion of the advantages of using credit.
Continental just joined a buying group to which several other large department stores belong. Our customers benefit in two primary ways: a wider selection of merchandise from which to choose and savings resulting from volume buying.	A section that contains sales-promotion material designed to help convince the customer to complete the application.
You are among a select group of our customers who have been prequalified for a Continental charge account. A few days after we receive your application, a Continental credit card will be sent to you. Simply put the signed application in the mail.	A section that contains a discussion of the action desired of the reader.
Continuing to serve you in the future as we have in the past is very important to Continental.	A courteous, forward-looking closing.

Exhibit 8-7 Effective letter soliciting prospective credit customers.

COLLECTION LETTERS

Collection letters are used by an organization to entice its charge customers to pay an outstanding charge-account balance. They are classified as persuasive messages because they include motivationally oriented material that is designed to get the reader to comply with your request. The intended reader may be unwilling to comply with your request; therefore, you may need to include extra measures to ensure compliance. Request letters that simply ask for payment result in limited success because they do not contain the motivationally oriented material characteristic of persuasive letters.

What items are included in the suggested plan for letters designed to solicit prospective credit customers?

When drafting a collection letter, you must attract the reader's attention. Then you need to get the reader interested in complying with your request. Finally, you must explain what action you wish the individual to take. Note how this pattern parallels the one used in preparing sales letters.

Communication Capsule 8-1 contains a discussion of the concerns businesses have for collecting accounts receivables.

Communication Capsule 8-1 Business Credit and Collection Problems

A major concern of business organizations is the collection of overdue accounts receivable. Numerous factors complicate the seriousness of the overdue account problem. First, business organizations obviously must provide for credit purchases by their customers. Certainly this is not a legal requirement, but it is a survival "requirement" for conducting business in a highly competitive domestic and international market.

Consumers are encouraged to "buy now" and "pay later." Prospective customers are literally bombarded with advertisements persuading them to "Just Do It" or "If It Feels Good—Do It!" However, the overexpenditure of available funds gives rise to a major business problem: the collection of overdue accounts!

Naturally, companies attempt to screen credit applicants to avoid the seriousness of future collection procedures. However, payment of amounts owed when all available cash has been expended is a "lose-lose" scenario for business organizations. If they do not collect the overdue amounts, they may eventually face bankruptcy. If they raise the price of their products to cover the lost revenues from uncollectible accounts, they become less competitive in the marketplace. If they attempt to collect the overdue amounts, and in so doing, irritate the people who owe the money, badwill, not goodwill, is the final result.

The percentage of credit customers who do not pay on time may not be very large when compared with the company's total number of customers, but even 5 percent of a company's accounts that are uncollectible may place it in serious financial difficulty. Uncollected money means the company will need to borrow from a financial institution, such as a bank, to restore operating funds required for maintaining inventory and paying salaries. The interest that the company is charged for this loan is a direct loss to the company.

Some businesses employ exacting and even harsh collection practices with near-perfect success. But these organizations, in turn, suffer when their collection methods become common knowledge. People like to purchase more than they like to make payments. This is similar to people who like to fish but do not like to clean the fish. When the enjoyment is gone, the product broken or depreciated, and the sounds and enjoyment of that eloquent dining experience at that expensive restaurant faded, the necessity of firm, concise, definite, and courteous collection letters remains a necessary action from well-meaning companies sent to well-meaning previous customers. Businesses must extend credit to survive in a highly competitive market, but they also must suffer the problems that collecting past-due accounts represent.

Collection letters are prepared after a creditor fails to meet one or more payment deadlines. The collection process usually does not start when the creditor misses the first payment deadline—most companies send a collection letter after the second or third payment deadline is missed.

Credit-granting procedures involve careful screening of applicants, but screening applicants too closely can cause a company to lose a portion of its sales. Potential customers who are denied credit will take their business elsewhere. Most companies extend credit to good-risk customers who have proven they will always pay, although not necessarily on time. Credit policies in a majority of companies prohibit the extension of credit to customers known to be poor risks. Because the majority of customers subjected to collection procedures eventually pay their past-due amounts, most collection correspondence is written with this knowledge.

Requiring customers to pay promptly is necessary for two reasons. First, working capital in the form of accounts receivable is not available for the company's use until it is converted into cash. Excessive levels of uncollected accounts receivable will create cash-flow problems for the company. Second, customers who have past-due accounts with a company are likely to take their business elsewhere. When this occurs, the company is missing out on potential sales. Therefore, positive attempts to persuade customers to pay before their accounts become past due benefit the company by providing a steady cash flow.

What is the goal of collection letters?

The ultimate goal of a collection letter is to maintain goodwill while securing the money owed to the company. Lack of concern about the customers' goodwill will probably cause them to trade elsewhere, which, in turn, makes the collection process much more difficult.

Collection letters should rely extensively on psychology to persuade customers to pay their past-due account. For example, an approach that does not use psychology might insinuate that the slow-paying nature of the customer makes the person a poor credit risk. A more psychological approach might be to imply the company is certain the customer intends to pay but just hasn't yet.

Characteristics of Collection Letters

What characteristics should collection letters possess?

Well-designed collection letters possess several characteristics. For example, the first letters in the collection series are low-key, usually without any direct request for money. Instead, they simply suggest that perhaps the customer has forgotten to pay. If the first letters are not successful, progressively stronger approaches are used, ultimately threatening the customer with legal action. An untimely threat of such action will typically cause the customer to take his or her business elsewhere.

An essential characteristic of collection letters is sensitivity to the specific circumstances of the situation. For example, a collection letter sent to a customer of good standing for several years is usually worded quite differently than a collection letter sent to a customer who is continually late in paying.

Another characteristic of the collection letter series is timing. Prompt-paying customers are generally sent letters less frequently than slow-paying customers. In addition, the time span between letters in the collection series is longer during the first letters in the series and shorter during the last letters in the series.

Wording that attempts to avoid alienating the customer is another characteristic of collection letters. Convincing the delinquent customer to send payment is a primary goal, but an equally important secondary goal is maintaining the person as a customer after the account has been paid.

Collection letters should contain resale material designed to convince customers they made the proper choice in dealing with the company. Effectively used resale material will help persuade the customer to pay and continue doing business with the company.

Use of Appeals in the Collection Series

Another characteristic of the collection series is the use of one or more appeals in writing the message. Some of the most common are appeals to fair play, good credit reputation, pride, and fear of legal action.

Appeal to Fair Play

What message is contained in the fair-play appeal?

The fair-play appeal essentially says to the customer: "We've been fair with you by providing the quality of product and service that you have the right to receive, and now you need to be fair with us by paying your account in full." The wording in this type of appeal should remind the customer of the following: The charge account or contract states that in return for providing goods and services, the company has the right to expect the customer to pay promptly. This appeal also relays the message that you are confident the reader wants to play fair.

The following is an example of a fair-play appeal in a collection letter.

> The special instructions in your order indicated the glassware was needed by March 31, so we shipped the order by air express—at our expense.
>
> We believe we have been fair with you, and we are certain you intend to be equally fair with us. Will you, therefore, please send us your check for the amount due?

Appeal to Good Credit Reputation

What message is contained in the appeal to good credit reputation?

A collection letter appealing to the reader's good credit reputation concentrates on the company's desire for the reader to maintain a good credit rating. This appeal is most effective early in the collection letter series. Most credit customers do not wish to be classified as poor credit risks; therefore, they will feel compelled to pay their accounts. The few credit customers who care very little about their credit ratings will not consider this appeal any more effective than other appeals. The following appeal to a customer illustrates the method for emphasizing the maintenance of a good credit reputation.

> The favorable comments made by several of your credit references when you applied for credit are well remembered. You have enjoyed a fine credit reputation that we do not want to see you lose. Is the past-due status of your account an oversight? Being able to provide equally favorable recommendations for you as a credit customer in years to come is something we want to be able to do. Please protect your credit reputation by sending us your check for $389.04.

Appeal to Pride

What message is contained in the pride appeal?

Another appeal commonly used in collection letters is reference to pride. This appeal asks the reader to act in ways that he or she can be proud of—specifically to pay the past-due account. The message explains that the company has always been proud of the customer because of his or her prompt handling of credit transactions with the company. The goal is that the customer will decide to pay so others can continue to be proud of his or her bill-paying practices. The following is an example of pride appeal.

> During the six years you have had a charge account with us, we have been very proud of the way in which you have met your financial obligations. We are certain that you, too, take pride in keeping your account balance up-to-date.
>
> Your paying the balance of your past-due account by June 10 will enable you to continue to take pride in your good credit reputation.

Appeal to Fear of Legal Action

What message is contained in the legal-action appeal?

When all other appeals have failed to convince the customer to pay, the company may include a statement threatening more intense action in the final collection letter. Usually, the realization that the company will take such action if payment is not received by a specific date causes the customer to pay. To use the appeal early in the collection process will undoubtedly cause irreparable damage to the reader-writer relationship. The following example shows an appeal to a fear of legal action.

You have been provided, we believe, adequate time to pay your account, or at least to explain why you have not paid your account. Now we are forced to take more drastic action.

Unless we receive full payment on or before August 1, we will turn your account over to our collection agency. At the same time, we will inform the Allied Credit Bureau of your unwillingness to pay your account.

To avoid the inconvenience of a poor credit reputation, please pay your account in full by August 1. Doing so will enable you to protect your credit reputation.

Types of Letters in the Collection Series

The previous information outlined approaches for use in collection series letters. Most collection series consist of several distinct stages. In each successive stage of the collection series, the message becomes more insistent.

Sometimes the stages in the collection series are modified to meet the needs of the specific situation. You may, for example, mail two letters in the same stage to a customer. Or, if evidence warrants the elimination of one or more stages, you may compress the series. The various stages in the collection series include the following:

What stages are found in the collection series?

1. Duplicate statement
2. Reminder letter
3. Inquiry letter
4. Request letter
5. Ultimatum letter

Duplicate Statement

Circumstances normally warrant the sending of a duplicate statement to the customer whose account is delinquent. In many cases, a rubber stamp is used to imprint the duplicate statement with one of the following: "Please remit today," "Second request," "Past due," or "Just to remind you." You may also attach gummed stickers imprinted with these phrases to remind the customer of the past-due status of the account.

If a company has experienced previous difficulty in collecting money from a customer, you may bypass sending a duplicate statement.

Reminder Letter

If the duplicate-statement stage of the collection series is not successful, a reminder letter is then sent. At this point, the assumption is that the customer has forgotten to pay. Many companies use reminder letters to promote sales, in addition to reminding the customer of the past-due account.

What should the opening of reminder letters do?

The opening of a reminder letter either courteously asks for payment of the past-due balance or presents neutral material. If several reminder letters are sent to a customer before an inquiry letter is sent, the first of the reminder letters is likely to open with neutral material; the later ones are likely to open with a suggestion that the customer pay.

Note the curt opening of the first of the following reminder letters. The revision is more effective because of its positive tone.

Change: Don't you think the past-due status of your charge account has existed long enough? We do. Therefore, we will appreciate your paying us as soon as possible.

To: As the owner of a profitable business, you are well aware of the benefit of a good credit reputation. We are certain you have simply overlooked paying the $187.54 balance on your charge account that currently is two months past due.

You may include the reminder statement either in a separate paragraph following the opening or incorporate it into the opening paragraph. In the preceding revision of a reminder letter, the reminder appears in the opening paragraph.

Regardless of the location of the reminder section, you will need to guard against its alienating the reader. If this occurs, collection will likely become even more difficult. The first of the following two paragraphs is an ineffective reminder. Note the improved tone of the revision.

Change: I am sure you are aware that your account has a past-due balance of $238.83. The duplicate statement that we sent you last month should have been a sufficient reminder to settle your account.

To: Will you please take a minute to write a check for $238.83, the past-due balance of your account? We are certain you have simply overlooked sending us your check.

The next section of the reminder letter can include sales-promotion material and/or resale material, depending on which is more appropriate. The first of the following two paragraphs contains sales-promotion material; the second, resale material.

What should be included in the middle section of reminder letters?

Our two-week Summer Breezes Sale begins June 4 when many items will be reduced as much as 10 to 30 percent. You will find many excellent values during this sale.

The Browning food processor you charged on your account two months ago has likely become an indispensable appliance in your kitchen by now. The manufacturer just introduced several new attachments that will make your processor even more versatile. Stop by our housewares section to see a demonstration of these new items.

The appropriate closing for a reminder letter is courteous and action oriented. The first of the following two closings lacks an action orientation, whereas the revision specifies when, where, and what action the reader should take.

What type of closing is appropriate for reminder letters?

Change: We appreciate your business.

To: A preaddressed post-paid envelope is enclosed for your convenience in mailing us your check today. If you plan to be in Ballards within the next few days, just bring your check to our credit department. We will be pleased to stamp your statement "Paid in Full."

The suggested plan for a reminder letter includes the following elements:

What is the suggested plan for reminder letters?

1. A courteous opening
2. A reminder that the customer's account is past due
3. A section that includes resale and/or sales-promotion material
4. A courteous, action-oriented closing

Exhibit 8-8 shows an ineffective reminder letter. Note how the letter in Exhibit 8-9 more effectively meets the requirements of reminder letters.

Inquiry Letter

When the duplicate statement and the reminder letter fail, an inquiry letter is the next step. At this point, you can no longer suggest that the customer has forgotten to pay.

If you were like the majority of our other customers, you would never have allowed your Grayson's charge account to become past-due.

An opening that lacks courtesy.

You have now owed us $342.87 since June 10, the day on which payment was to have been received for the merchandise we sold you on account on May 2. In case you have forgotten, the past-due status of your account is costing you money because 1.5 percent interest per month is being charged on the unpaid balance. As of July 11, the interest charge is $5.14, making the current balance of the account $348.01.

A discourteous section that explains the facts.

Get a check to us as soon as possible so that you can avoid further interest charges.

A discourteous, action-oriented closing.

Exhibit 8-8 Ineffective reminder letter.

Grayson's
Since 1928

(712) 343-2871 987 Fifth Street Spokane, WA 89004

July 3, 199x

Mr. Sam Nelson
Artists' Haven
8443 Tulsa Road
Bellingham, WA 89432

Dear Mr. Nelson:

You understand, I'm sure, the benefits of a good credit record; therefore, the past-due status of your Grayson's charge account must simply be an oversight on your part.

A courteous opening.

Please take a minute to prepare a check for $348.01, the current balance of your account. Since June 10, the day by which payment of $342.87 was to have been received, your account has accumulated $5.14 in interest charges. To avoid additional charges, please send us a check for the current balance of the account.

A section that reminds the customer that the account is past due.

The Collingwood metal art frames you purchased are sure to be popular among your customers. The corner clamp patented by Collingwood makes these metal frames very easy to assemble.

A section that contains resale material.

Please send us your check today in the stamped, preaddressed envelope that is enclosed.

A courteous, action-oriented closing.

Sincerely,

Betty Brandt
Credit Manager

Enc.

Exhibit 8-9 Effective reminder letter.

Instead, you must assume the customer has become dissatisfied with the products or service and is unwilling to pay or has experienced a personal catastrophe and is unable to pay.

The goal of the inquiry letter is to entice the customer to pay. However, you may have to settle for an intermediate goal of just obtaining a response explaining the reasons for nonpayment. If the customer explains, for example, that he or she has been fired, you may suggest that the person phone you to arrange a deferred-payment schedule.

Begin the inquiry letter with a buffered opening containing material with which the reader will agree. Note the harsh tone of the first of the following two openings.

> Change: Why haven't you paid the $129.58 that you have now owed us for three months? We are running out of patience.
>
> To: As the owner of a business, you are aware of the need for customers to pay their accounts on time. You appreciate your customers who pay their accounts on time, just as we appreciate our customers who pay on time.

What type of opening is appropriate for inquiry letters?

After the opening, present a review of the facts. In this section, you should specify the length of time the account is past due and its balance. You may also inquire about why the customer is late in making payment. Note the abruptness of the first of the following two paragraphs and the more friendly, personal tone of the revision.

> Change: On June 10, we credited your account for $124.34, the amount of the fishing gear you ordered from us. Interest charges of $5.24 have now accrued. We are sure all of this gear has sold, so what seems to be the problem?
>
> To: On June 10, we shipped your order of fishing gear and credited your account for $124.34. Since that time, interest charges of $5.24 have accrued, which makes the amount you currently owe total $129.58. You have always paid your account on time and have seldom had interest charges accrue. Therefore, we are concerned that some unforeseen circumstances may have arisen, preventing your usual prompt payment. If this is the situation, please contact me immediately so an alternative payment plan can be arranged.

You can also include resale and/or sales-promotion material in the inquiry letter. An example of resale material is shown in the following paragraph.

> Many of our customers have been telling us this summer that they are unable to stock a sufficient supply of our fishing gear. We are sure that you also found our fishing gear to be popular among your customers.

What should be included in the middle section of inquiry letters?

After this section of the inquiry letter, you should discuss the action you wish the reader to take. Although you may have requested payment or an explanation earlier in the letter, this section should reinforce your desire to receive payment. The following paragraph shows an example of this important section.

> Your sending us a check for $129.58 today will be appreciated. If you are not able to remit the entire overdue amount, please provide me with an explanation. A deferred-payment schedule could possibly be arranged.

The closing of the inquiry letter is both courteous and action oriented. When appropriate, you may also appeal to the reader, as the following example shows.

> Your account can be maintained with a "preferred-status customer" if you will send us your check today or explain the reason for the past-due balance of the account.

What is the suggested plan for inquiry letters?

The suggested plan for an inquiry letter includes the following elements:

1. An opening containing buffered material
2. A review of the facts of the situation and an inquiry about the reasons for the past-due status of the account (An appeal should be incorporated, if appropriate.)
3. A section containing resale and/or sales-promotion material
4. A discussion of the action desired by the company
5. A courteous, action-oriented closing incorporating an appeal, if appropriate

A sample of an ineffective inquiry letter is shown in Exhibit 8-10. The sample letter in Exhibit 8-11 shows an effective revision.

Request Letter

When previous collection attempts have not been successful, sending a request letter is the next step. A request letter presents a strong request for the creditor to pay the balance of his or her account. The request-letter step of the collection series is warranted when a company no longer assumes the reader is not paying the account because of an oversight or because of dissatisfaction with the company. Instead, the assumption is that the customer is being somewhat troublesome, which mandates exertion of a little more force. Previous appeals can be used to good advantage in this stage of the collection process. The appeal used in the request letter must be appropriate for the individual and also for the circumstances surrounding the situation.

What type of opening is appropriate for request letters?

The request letter opens with a presentation of the facts. Although the letter should not be discourteous, some of the courtesy expressed in the opening of the earlier letters in the series is omitted from the opening of the request letter. But, although the opening is to the point, it should not be rude. The first of the following two paragraphs is discourteous, but the revision corrects this problem.

Exhibit 8-10 Ineffective inquiry letter.

Letter	Comment
Your inattention to our previous correspondence about your past-due account is particularly annoying.	A discourteous opening.
The deadline for paying for the merchandise you purchased from us on May 2 was three months ago. Each month that you allow this account to remain unpaid, you are being charged 1.5 percent interest. The original charge of $342.87 has now accumulated $10.36 in interest charges. Your account today has an outstanding balance of $353.23. We are unable to allow this inattention to go on much longer.	A section that explains the facts.
You are given until August 20 to send us a check for $353.23.	A threatening closing.

You value prompt-paying customers as much as we do. If you are like us, you become concerned when a longtime, valued customer allows an account to remain unpaid. This is a serious concern of ours, also.	A buffered opening.
Our concern, Mr. Johnson, is that a purchase of $342.87 credited to your account on May 2 has not yet been paid. Interest charges of $10.36 have now accumulated, which makes your current account balance $353.23. Because you have always taken pride in paying your account on time, we wonder whether some extenuating circumstance has prevented your paying this account. If this is the situation, please let us know immediately so we can arrange an appropriate payment plan. Otherwise, we will appreciate your paying us as soon as possible.	A section that reviews the facts and inquires about the reason for the past-due status of the account.
Have you yet had an opportunity to examine our sale catalog recently mailed to you? This sale, which lasts until Labor Day, includes a wide range of items that are reduced 50 percent or more.	A section that contains sales-promotion material.
Protect your credit record by sending us a check for $353.23 today. If this payment is not possible, please provide an explanation about why you are unable to pay at this time.	A section that discusses the action desired by the company.
Receipt of your payment or explanation will allow us to protect the "preferred-customer" status that you currently enjoy. You will want to have available your credit account privileges when our big spring sale begins in a few days.	A courteous closing that contains a credit-reputation appeal.

Exhibit 8-11 Effective inquiry letter.

Change: Customers like you are difficult to understand. We have given you every opportunity to protect your credit rating by paying the $459.94 you owe us, but apparently you really don't care much about your rating. We insist on your immediate payment.

To: If you pay the $459.94 you have owed us now for three months, you can avoid losing the good credit reputation you have enjoyed for so long. As the owner of a business, you are well aware of the necessity of maintaining a good credit record.

After the opening, the next section should include an appropriate appeal. The following paragraph uses the pride appeal.

For the four years that you have been a credit customer of ours, we have been very pleased with your payment record. I am sure you are just as proud of your preferred-customer status—and that you put a high priority on keeping that status.

What should be included in the middle section of request letters?

After the appeal, discuss the action you wish the reader to take. Sometimes, two alternatives are available: either payment of the past-due account or an explanation for lack of payment. Ideally, the reader will choose the first alternative. If not, the reader may offer an explanation, thereby enabling you to make other payment arrangements. Note how in the first of the following two paragraphs, the writer threatens the reader, but the revision, despite its firmness, contains no threats.

Change: You decide which of the following two alternatives you want to choose: paying your account in full or explaining why you haven't made a payment in three months. If you fail to do either, our last-resort alternative will be exercised the next time we have to write to you requesting payment.

To: Your lack of response to our previous correspondence leaves us with two alternatives: to request immediate payment of your entire account balance or to require an explanation of why you have not paid your account in full. If unforeseen circumstances are responsible, please contact me so arrangements for an alternative plan of payment can be considered. This will enable you to reduce your financial obligation while protecting your credit reputation.

Including resale material and/or sales-promotion material in a request collection letter is appropriate, as in the following paragraph, which contains a sales-promotion pitch.

We are now the Midwest's distributor for Grant's paints that are well known throughout the country for their durability and application ease. Why not plan to add this excellent line of top-quality paints? Your customers will be pleased with the product, and you will be equally happy with the profits.

What type of closing is appropriate for request letters?

The closing of the request letter should be courteous, strong, and action oriented. The following paragraph shows these elements.

Please take advantage of this opportunity to protect your good credit rating. We must have your check or an explanation by June 10.

The suggested plan for a request collection letter includes the following elements:

What is the suggested plan for request letters?

1. An opening presenting the facts
2. A section including the appropriate appeal
3. A request for action (either payment or an explanation)
4. A section containing resale or sales-promotion material
5. A courteous, action-oriented closing

An ineffective request letter is shown in Exhibit 8-12. An effective version appears in Exhibit 8-13.

Ultimatum Letter

The final letter in the collection series is the ultimatum letter, which is sent when the other letters do not produce satisfactory results. The basic characteristic of this letter is a statement that legal action will be initiated unless prompt payment is received. Once the threat of legal action is made, it should be carried out immediately if the customer again fails to meet the payment deadline. Although the ultimatum letter should be polite, it must stress the urgency of the situation.

The content of the ultimatum letter should convey that the reader must pay now or be prepared to face the consequences, which the letter should clearly outline. Among the consequences most companies use are the courts, a collection agency, or an attorney.

The opening of the ultimatum letter once again reviews the facts for the reader. Because the reader is by now well aware of the situation, the opening can be quite brief. The following is an example of an appropriate opening.

What type of opening is appropriate for ultimatum letters?

> Five months ago when you asked us to charge to your account an order amounting to $434.23, we readily agreed to do so because you had always paid us on time. We are giving you one more opportunity to pay the amount you owe.

Exhibit 8-12 Ineffective request letter.

We simply cannot figure out why you would allow your credit reputation to almost dissolve right before your eyes. When the reputation is gone, it is very difficult to get back.	**A discourteous opening.**
You now have two alternatives: to continue to allow your account to remain past due, which will virtually destroy your credit reputation with us; or to pay us $358.52, the amount you owe us, immediately. Should the latter not be possible, the least you can do is to explain this situation to us.	**A section that discourteously presents the facts.**
You simply cannot afford to continue to ignore our requests for payment. Let us hear from you by the end of the week.	**A discourteous closing.**

Exhibit 8-13 Effective request letter.

Paying the $358.52 you currently owe will enable you to avoid losing your good credit reputation. As a merchandiser, you certainly are aware of the benefits enjoyed by those who have a good credit reputation.	**An opening that presents the facts.**
You value, I'm sure, your preferred-customer status because you have always paid your account on time. Please take the necessary steps so you can continue to maintain the preferred status of your account.	**A section that presents the credit-reputation appeal.**
To avoid losing your preferred-customer status, we will need your payment of $358.52 by August 20. If you are unable to pay your account in full by that date, please send a partial payment now; and we will make arrangements with you to pay the remainder on a deferred basis. Either of the payment alternatives will enable you to maintain your account status.	**A section that presents a request for action.**
Collingwood Art Frames just expanded its metal product line to include bronze-finish frames. Because you have been so successful selling Collingwood frames in other finishes, I am sure you will want to carry this new line as well. The bronze frames are illustrated in the enclosed brochure.	**A section that contains sales-promotion material.**
Your account status will be maintained if we receive your payment or partial payment and explanation on or before August 20.	**A courteous, action-oriented closing.**

What should be included in the middle section of ultimatum letters?

After the opening, you should introduce the legal-action appeal. Note how the following paragraph incorporates this appeal.

> To avoid the inconvenience of a damaged credit reputation and the inconvenience of appearing in court, please send us a check for $434.23 by July 1.

To remove doubt in the reader's mind about your intended action, include a statement of ultimatum after the legal-action appeal. The ultimatum shown in the first of the following two paragraphs is not clear, whereas the revision corrects the problem.

> Change: Your continued lack of response to our request for payment will cause us to take drastic action. Please help us avoid having to do so.
>
> To: If we do not have your check for full payment of your account by July 1, we will immediately instruct our attorney to initiate required legal action for collecting the past-due amount. A report classifying you as a nonpaying customer will also be filed with your local credit bureau. Both of these actions will have a serious impact on your credit reputation.

What type of closing is appropriate for ultimatum letters?

The closing of the ultimatum letter should be courteous as well as firm and action oriented. Note how in the following two closings the revision ends politely and with a helpful enclosure.

> Change: Let us hear from you immediately.
>
> To: Please be assured that we do not wish to take steps that will damage your credit record. However, your continued failure to respond to our requests for payment leaves us with no other viable alternative. A preaddressed envelope is enclosed for your convenience in sending us your check today.

The suggested plan for an ultimatum letter includes the following elements:

1. A review of the facts
2. A section including the legal-action appeal
3. A statement of ultimatum
4. A courteous close

An ineffective ultimatum letter is shown in Exhibit 8-14. Exhibit 8-15 shows an effective revision of the same letter.

You will find Checklist 8-2 helpful when preparing collection letters.

The Use of Form Letters in the Collection Series

Many companies use form letters in the collection letter series. Letters that have been particularly successful make up the bulk of a company's standard form letter collection series.

Sophisticated text-editing software simplifies the personalizing of form messages. From experience, companies have learned that personalized letters not only create a better impression but also are more effective than mass-produced letters.

National and international organizations use a number of standard paragraphs when constructing collection letters. For example, ten different opening paragraphs may

You have now backed us against a wall. If we do not have your check for $363.89 by September 10, we will turn your account over to our collection agency and also notify the Metropolitan Credit Bureau of your defaulting on this account.	A threatening, discourteous opening.
We have been very reasonable with you. We can wait no longer.	A section that mentions an ultimatum but that fails to mention what it is.
This is the last time you will hear from us requesting payment on this account. Should you fail to pay by September 10, our collection agency will be in touch.	A discourteous closing.

Exhibit 8-14 Ineffective ultimatum letter.

On May 2 we shipped your credit order totaling $342.87. A few days later, we mailed your monthly statement that stated the balance of your order was due on or before June 10. Following that original statement, we have sent you four additional letters requesting a payment or an explanation. None of our letters have brought a response from you.	An opening that reviews the facts.
Brown's cannot afford for customers to carry past-due balances on their accounts; therefore, we request payment of your account balance of $368.89 before September 15. Failure to pay in full by that time will force us to turn your account over to our collection agency. The Metropolitan Credit Bureau will also be notified of this situation.	A section that presents the legal-action appeal.
Please send us your check for $368.89 by September 10 so we can avoid undertaking legal action to collect the amount you owe.	A section that presents the ultimatum.
You understand why we can no longer allow this payment failure to continue. You likely cannot allow your customers to carry outstanding balances on their accounts either. A stamped, preaddressed envelope is enclosed for your convenience in sending us your check.	A courteous closing.

Exhibit 8-15 Effective ultimatum letter.

exist for the request letter. Perhaps fifteen different paragraphs are available for the various appeals. Each paragraph has an identification number; therefore, the collection manager gives the keyboarder the desired paragraph numbers for each collection letter. Paragraphs stored on text-editing equipment permit instantaneous recall of the selected paragraphs, which are then printed automatically.

PERSUASIVE MEMOS

Of the various types of business memos, persuasive memos are among the most important and perhaps the most difficult to write. Your goal is to entice the reader to do something he or she may not initially want to do. The most successful persuasive memos follow the general persuasion strategy. The steps of this strategy, as previously indicated, include the following:

OPENING
1. Is your message designed for a person rather than an accounts receivable number?
2. Does your message portray a "you benefit" rather than an "I versus you" tone?
3. Is your message firm but tolerant?
4. Have you balanced the two major characteristics of a collection letter: collection and goodwill?
5. Have you considered the situation in a historical perspective rather than an isolated event perspective? (The type of message should be matched with the history of each particular situation.)

MIDDLE
1. Have you clarified the amount due, the account number, and your previous attempts to collect?
2. Have you employed a positive tone and a sincere willingness to help?
3. Have you made it easy for the person to respond?
4. Have you considered the appropriate level of action and designed the wording of the message to reflect the proper amount of urgency?
5. Have you implied to the reader that you do not prefer to take any drastic action but may be required to do so if payment is not received?
6. Have you set a definite date when you must receive the payment?
7. As the situation becomes more serious, have you conveyed the urgency of the matter?
8. Have you properly protected your company and yourself from legal problems that may result from carelessly written collection messages?

CLOSING
1. Is your closing courteous but firm?
2. Did you make your action request definite in terms of the actual amount to be paid, the place where it should be sent, and the deadline for receiving the payment?
3. Have you considered the use of a final persuasive message to encourage the reader to take the requested action?
4. Did you clearly show how the reader will benefit by sending the requested payment?

Checklist 8-2 Collection letters.

What are the steps in the persuasion strategy?

1. Attract favorable attention
2. Create interest
3. Establish reader desire and conviction
4. Explain desired action

The content you will include in each of the three sections of persuasive memos comprise the following:

Opening section	Attract favorable attention
Middle section	Create interest and establish reader desire and conviction
Closing section	Explain desired action

Suppose you have been assigned the responsibility of chairing your organization's annual Community Drive campaign. Your goal in writing a persuasive memo is to convince as many of your colleagues as possible to contribute as much as they can to ensure the success of the drive. Note how the following opening section is designed to attract the readers' attention.

> The price of a cup of coffee or a soft drink a day. A quarter (the cost of coffee and soft drinks in the snack bar) is not much to ask. But that is all it would take from each employee for Armitron Corp. to meet its goal of contributing $7,000 to this year's Community Drive efforts.

In the middle section of the memo, your goal is to create reader interest, desire, and conviction. The absence of one or more of these attributes greatly reduces the memo's effectiveness. Note how the writer of this middle section creates interest, desire, and conviction by explaining how the funds raised by the Community Drive have helped residents in the community.

What is the goal of the middle section of a persuasive memo?

> Consider the Brownell family, a local family with three small children that has had more than its share of bad luck this past year. Mr. Brownell lost his job several months ago. Because of a congenital eye condition, Mrs. Brownell is unable to work. They were making ends meet with unemployment compensation and savings until fire destroyed their house in June. Although they escaped unharmed, the Brownells lost virtually everything—including their car. The local Action office, a Community Drive agency, supplied them with clothing, minimal furniture and temporary housing. The Brownells are certain they would have become homeless had it not been for Action.
>
> Or consider Mrs. Dunham and her two preschoolers. During the seven years Mrs. Dunham and her husband were married, she was often the victim of his physical abuse, usually following a "night out on the town." After several of these assaults, she had to seek medical attention for her injuries. But because she had no independent income, Mrs. Dunham decided to stay with her husband until August when he also began to abuse the children. Without family to turn to for help, she sought assistance from the local Domestic Violence office, another agency supported by the Community Drive. Domestic Violence helped her obtain necessary legal action against her husband, a place to live, and counseling she and her two children badly needed. Mrs. Dunham no longer has to fear for her safety or the safety of her two children. Recently she was able to begin a job training program that will enable her to become self-supporting.
>
> Or consider Cub Scout Pack 23 at Glenwood Elementary School, a school with a large number of children from lower socioeconomic families. Twenty-three of these lower-income boys attending the school were attracted to the Cub Scout program. However, they became discouraged when their families could not afford the Cub Scout uniforms. One phone call is all it took to obtain for them the uniforms and other scouting materials they need. This would have been impossible had the Boy Scouts not been a Community Drive supported agency.
>
> In our community, such situations occur many times each day. Without successful fund raising, the Community Drive would simply have to turn its back on at least some of the people it helps, and a horrible tragedy would probably result.

The closing of the persuasive memo is designed to elicit reader action. The easier you make the desired action, the more likely you will get the response you desire.

What is the goal of the closing in a persuasive memo?

> As you decide whether to contribute to this year's Community Drive campaign or how much you should contribute, please remember the Brownell family, Mrs. Dunham and her two children, and the 23 Cub Scouts. Also remember the other hundreds of individuals in the community whose stories I've not related to you but who are the benefactors of the Community Drive. When you contribute, you can smile with satisfaction as you say, "I did my part in helping make the lives of these individuals a little more pleasant."
>
> When you return (November 10 deadline) the enclosed card either with a check for the amount of your donation or the required signature for payroll deduction, I will give you a coupon that you can exchange for a free cup of coffee or a soft drink in the snack bar. This is my way of saying THANK YOU!

SUMMARY

Persuasive letters include sales letters, letters that solicit prospective credit customers, and collection letters. Each type of letter uses persuasion strategy.

Effective collection letters contain several characteristics, including the use of appeals. The collection series employs the following appeals: appeal to fair play, appeal to good credit reputation, appeal to pride, and appeal to fear of legal action.

The collection series has the following stages: duplicate statement, reminder letter, inquiry letter, request letter, and ultimatum letter. The content of the letter depends on the stage. Every collection letter, regardless of its stage, should be written with the assumption that the customer will eventually pay.

Persuasive memos are designed with four goals: attract favorable attention, create interest, establish reader desire and conviction, and explain desired action.

REVIEW QUESTIONS

1. What steps are necessary to develop an effective persuasive letter?
2. What techniques are available to capture the reader's attention in the opening of an effective persuasive message?
3. What type of material should the last section of the persuasive message include?
4. What should the opening of a letter that solicits prospective credit customers accomplish?
5. What are the characteristics of collection letters?
6. What types of appeals are used in preparing collection letters?
7. What are the stages in the typical collection series?
8. What appeal is most appropriate for use in the ultimatum letter?
9. Explain the use of word processing in preparing collection letters.
10. Using a persuasive approach, describe a "home microcomputer" psychologically.
11. What are some of the legal considerations to consider in preparing a sales letter?
12. What elements should appear in each of the three sections of a persuasive memo?

APPLICATION PROBLEMS

1. (Persuasive message) As a recent graduate from Grant College, you have just accepted a position in the Grant College High School and College Relations Department. Your major responsibility is recruitment of current high school seniors as prospective freshman students at Grant College. The college is primarily an undergraduate institution with strong programs in business, liberal arts, and science. Last year 8,600 students attended Grant College, which is located in East Prairie, Montana. Grant College uses the trimester rather than the semester plan. A major advantage of a trimester plan is that students can complete more credits each year than in a college operating on the semester system. As a result, a bachelor's degree is completed in less than the traditional four years. First trimester begins the last week in August and ends the Friday before Christmas each year. Second trimester begins the first available school day after January 1. Third trimester begins on the Monday following the fifteen-week second trimester and continues for fifteen weeks. The trimester system involves one-hour classes rather than the usual fifty minutes in the semester system. Actual total time in class is the same for both systems, but the semester system requires sixteen weeks of classes.

   Prepare a persuasive message that will encourage high school seniors to attend Grant College next fall. Some of the points you should try to weave into your persuasive message are the following:

   a. A trimester system allows graduation in two and two-thirds years if students take fifteen credit hours per trimester.
   b. A trimester system allows those who prefer attending two terms a year to get into the job market earlier in the summer than those who attend a semester-system college.
   c. Completion of an undergraduate degree in less time will permit students who depend on financial aid to accrue less debt and also to begin paying back loans a full year and a third earlier than if they were on a semester system.
   d. Having more time to work during the summer helps students earn more money for their college expenses.
   e. Summer school is available for students wishing to take two trimesters and a summer session.

f. Students on a three-term trimester plan can take six hours for the full term and another nine hours during the nine-week summer session, which totals fifteen credits for the trimester.

As you prepare your message, remember that many other colleges are recruiting these same students. Present the most important information in the most persuasive manner.

2. (Sales letter) Select an advertisement from a magazine or newspaper that includes a picture of the product being promoted. Draft a sales letter to sell this product to a cross section of the U.S. population. Use the basic principles for effective persuasive messages. Attach the original advertisement and the picture of the product when you submit your assignment to your instructor.
3. (Sales letter) Write a sales letter about a new product, the "Night Byte Light." The letter is to be sent to regional discount stores in your area. This invention operates with a battery (not included) and attaches to the end of a fishing pole. The line passes through the gadget. When a fish bites, the light blinks. Suggested retail price is $9.95, and wholesale price to the stores is $4.50. This is a new, untested product. However, your company, "The Fish Fad Farm," boasts several new big sellers during the past eight years, including the easy hook hanger and the scrappy sea bait, each of which had million-dollar sales. These two products were also highly profitable items for the stores that contracted to sell them.
4. Compose four attention-getting and interest-building first paragraphs for persuasive messages and use one of the following in each: outline a bargain; apply a famous quote; ask a question; and outline an outstanding feature. Your purpose is to gain attention and build interest in a special vacation offer to sunny Bermuda. The cost is $1,900 per person for ten days, including transportation, meals, tips, and admission to a minimum number of events of interest.
5. (Credit-customer solicitation letter) You are the credit manager for Handley's Department Store, in the East Mall, Ponca City, TX 54478. One of your responsibilities is to prepare letters soliciting credit customers. Several months have passed since you sent the last letter, so you decide to prepare another letter to mail around September 15—just before customers begin to think about the Christmas season. You know from experience that a number of the customers who responded to your letters in the past have been unaware of the advantages of purchasing on credit. Therefore, you have found it useful to include this material in your letters. Among the specific advantages to promote are advanced notice of sales before they are announced to the public, the ability to buy merchandise without paying cash at time of the purchase, occasional special discounts for credit customers, and convenience of shopping without checks or large amounts of cash. You also know that charge customers, on the average, spend about 10 percent more per purchase than do cash customers, which is certainly financially advantageous to the store. Because the people on the list to receive your letter have already been prequalified, all they need to do is sign the credit application form you are enclosing. You believe the potential customer may also be pleased to learn that Handley's just joined an exclusive buying group, which will not only double the number of merchandise lines the store sells but will also cause lower prices because of the volume buying. Prepare the letter.
6. You are the collection manager for Balley Office Supply Company, 4984 Leadville Road, Memphis, TN 58744. Balley, a large office-supply wholesaler, sells primarily to office supply stores in the south and southwest. Eight years ago, Green's Office Supply, 398 Main Street, Jackson, MS 32823, opened a charge account. The average yearly credit purchases of Green's Office Supply is $6,200. Since opening an account with Balley, Green's Office Supply has never been late with its payments on account. For this reason, its credit limit is $1,000. Your policy is to re-

quire a minimum payment of 10 percent of the account balance within thirty days of the closing date. One percent interest per month is charged on any unpaid balances after thirty days of the closing date. Green's closing date is on the tenth of the month.

On March 1, Balley shipped Green's the following items: 10 boxes of 20-lb. copier paper ($310); 3 boxes of Model 17 staplers ($127); and 1 box of assorted ballpoint pen refills ($18). The order amounted to $455, and the tax was $18.20. The total amount charged to Green's account was $473.20.

a. (Duplicate notice) Today is April 20, and Balley has received neither an explanation nor a payment on the statement you sent Green's on March 10 for the March 1 order. Prepare the appropriate written action.
b. (Reminder letter) Today is May 1, and Balley still has not received payment for the March 1 order—nor has Balley received an explanation from Green's. You decide to write a letter reminding Green's of the past-due status of its account. You also decide to tell Green's about the new line of desk accessories in which it may be interested. The accessories are contemporary in style and are constructed of acrylic plastic. They are available in smoke, clear, avocado green, sky blue, and seal brown. The line is also available in a natural-look simulated leather. The line includes a desk pad, notepad holder, pen-pencil holder, file tray, desk organizer, and a wastebasket can. Offer to send a descriptive brochure to Green's.
c. (Inquiry letter) On May 10, you received a request from Green's for the descriptive brochure on the new line of desk accessories that Balley has just added. No mention is made of their past-due account. Write a letter to accompany the descriptive brochure.
d. (Request letter) Today is May 20, and Balley receives from Green's an order (to be charged) for ten more boxes of copier paper. Because of the past-due status of Green's account, the sales department has put its account on "hold." You receive from the sales department a copy of the order. Balley's policy is to require cash on orders from companies that have a past-due balance of more than sixty days. Write a letter to Green's explaining this policy; ask for immediate payment of the March 10 statement.
e. (Request letter) Today is June 1, and Green's account has reached the "problem state." You decide to send Green's a tactful but urgent request for payment on the account that has been due since April 10.
f. (Ultimatum letter) Today is June 25, and Green's still has not responded to any of Balley's requests for payment. Time has arrived to prepare an ultimatum letter in which the next step of legal action is stated. Prepare that letter.

7. (Reminder letter) You are the collection manager for Allgren's, a department store in Denver, Colorado. One of the store's preferred charge customers, Ms. Mary Greenlee, 123 United Street, Denver, CO 87434, purchased an on-sale 19-inch color television set four months ago. Until she made this purchase, Ms. Greenlee regularly used her charge account and always paid her account on time. The last time she used the account was to charge the television set. You know that she had to have the television set worked on twice the first month of its use; however, you do not know why her account has had a past-due balance of $478.48 since June 4 (today is September 1). Ms. Greenlee purchased the television set on a 120-days-same-as cash plan. Therefore, no interest is charged on the purchase until October 4, after which the account will be charged 1.5 percent per month (beginning with the first month) if the account is still past due. Write her a letter (this will be the third one) asking that she pay immediately. Explain that if she fails to pay the balance by October 4, an interest charge of $29.64 will be added to the account, plus an additional 1.5 percent per month for each month thereafter.

8. (Collection letter) You are the collection manager for Grant's Drug Store, located in Southside Mall, Ft. Collins, CO 28748. You decide to change your collections procedures. Only two letters will be sent after an account becomes past due: The first letter is to remind the customer of the past-due status of his or her account, and the second letter is to be used to indicate that unless payment is received by a certain date, the account will be turned over to the Ft. Collins Collection Agency. Both of these letters will be form letters in which specific information about each situation will be added to the letter. Prepare the two form letters, leaving blanks for the variable information you will insert once you begin to use the letters. The company has a word processing center; therefore, the letters will be processed on computer equipment.
9. (Persuasive memo) You were recently appointed to serve as chair of this year's four blood drives (done quarterly) in the organization in which you work. Previously, an informative-type memo was sent to each employee that simply announced the date, time, and place of the blood drive. In the past, only a few employees have ever given blood during these drives. Accordingly, you have decided to begin this year's drive with a persuasive memo. Although you can announce in the memo the time and date of the first drive (four weeks from today, 9 A.M. to 3 P.M.), your primary goal in preparing the memo is to increase by at least four times the number of donors who want to give blood. Prepare the persuasive memo to send to all employees.

9

The Résumé

After studying this chapter, you should be able to

1. Describe the activities to be completed before writing the résumé.
2. Describe the different styles of résumés.
3. Identify the typical content of résumés.
4. Discuss what factors determine an appropriate order for the various sections of résumés.
5. Discuss the guidelines for preparing effective résumés.
6. Prepare an effective résumé.

The résumé and the letter of application, which typically accompany each other, determine whether a job applicant creates a favorable impression on a potential employer. During the preliminary screening process, many applicants are eliminated from further consideration because their résumés and letters of application do not create as favorable an impression as do the application materials submitted by other applicants.

The résumé, which is discussed in detail in this chapter, and the letter of application, which is discussed in Chapter 10, are two of the final activities in the job-seeking process. Before the applicant can prepare the résumé and the letter of application, several preliminary activities need to be completed.

PRELIMINARY ACTIVITIES

The applicant should consider undertaking the following preliminary activities: a self-analysis, an analysis of the job market, and an analysis of the company or companies to which he or she is sending applications.

What preliminary job-application activities should be undertaken?

Analyzing Yourself

Before you can determine whether you meet the requirements of the job(s) for which you are applying, you may need to analyze yourself. Self-analysis is the process of identifying your skills, interests, personal characteristics, and achievements to prepare more effective job application materials.

In the process of analyzing yourself, you should answer three questions: (1) Who am I? (2) What are my aspirations and interests? (3) What are my qualifications?

What questions should you ask yourself when undertaking a self-analysis?

Who Am I?

To help you fully understand yourself, begin with an analysis of your family background. Consider the extent to which your parents or guardians influenced your aspirations, beliefs, ideals, and values.

Next examine your relationships with others. In many instances, we better understand ourselves by assessing how others view or react to us and to our beliefs. In addition, assess your leadership potential and your ability to work with others. You may also wish to evaluate your personal and professional accomplishments.

Assess your philosophy of life and your attitude toward work. Try to determine the amount of satisfaction you will derive from the kinds of tasks that compose the jobs for which you are applying.

What Are My Aspirations and Interests?

Most individuals, when applying for a job, have fairly definite ideas about their career goals. Although college graduates usually apply for the types of jobs for which their college studies have prepared them, some seek jobs totally unrelated to their college major. You may also need to determine which of the following types of work may be more satisfying: general or specific work, physical or mental work, structured or unstructured work, or creative or routine work. In determining your aspirations and interests, you will undoubtedly want to consider the challenges inherent in the jobs for which you are applying as well as their potential in terms of career progression. Some individuals undertake this step by listing the things they would like to do and the things they would prefer not to do. After all, being aware of the things they would rather not do is probably just as important as being aware of the things they would like to do.

What Are My Qualifications?

An especially important aspect of your self-analysis is determining whether your qualifications match the job requirements. Several experiences in your background, such as education, work experience, and leadership potential, will probably help qualify you for the position you desire.

Why do you need to analyze your qualifications?

You probably should omit information pertaining to high school experiences unless you definitely know that the individual to whom you are sending your résumé desires such information. An exception perhaps would be an individual who has won a prestigious state, regional, or national award, in which case this information might be listed on the résumé. Your college experiences are probably specifically related to the position for which you are applying and therefore should be thoroughly detailed on the résumé.

Another aspect of your life that may be an important job qualification is your work experience. Although some work experience may not be related to the jobs for which you are applying, most potential employers appreciate being apprised of the nature of your work experience. For example, working as a cafeteria bus person during your first two years of college may have nothing to do with the job you are seeking. However, it does indicate to employers evaluating your background that you have initiative and are willing to work.

Leadership potential may also be a qualification for the job for which you are applying. For example, if you held leadership positions in various college organizations, some employers may interpret this as evidence of your leadership potential. Extracurricular activities may also demonstrate your ability to assume responsibility.

In sharing the information about your background with employers, remember that results attract their attention. Results can be reflected in a number of ways: academic accomplishments, job-related experiences, extracurricular activities, community service, and leadership experiences.

Analyzing the Job Market

Some job applicants, especially those unfamiliar with the job market or the requirements of certain jobs, thoroughly analyze the job market before applying for a particular job. Several resources are available to help you in your assessment.

Assessing the Job Market

A wealth of information awaits you in your analysis of the job market. The following sources may be useful in assessing job opportunities in general or specific areas:

Accountants Index
Guide to American Business Directories
Insurance Year Book
Kelley's Directory of Merchants, Manufacturers, and Shippers of the World
Oil and Petroleum Yearbook
Polk's Bank Directory
Poor's Register of Directors and Executives
McKittrick Directory of Advertisers
Moody's Manual of Investments, American and Foreign
Standard and Poor's Facts and Forecasts
Standard Corporation Records
Survey of Current Business
Thomas' Register of American Manufacturers
Rand McNally's Banker's Directory
Reader's Guide to Periodical Literature
Reference Book to Dun & Bradstreet
U.S. Census of Manufacturers
U.S. Government Organization Manual
The Wall Street Journal

In some instances, these references may describe job opportunities. In other instances, the references will provide you with listings of other sources to which you may refer. Among the information that might be included is demand for positions in the near future and distant future, regions of the country where demand is greatest, and so forth. Classified advertisements in local and regional newspapers may also be of use.

You might also want to use an electronic résumé database service. Job seekers and employers are increasingly turning to such services. Usually costing up to $50 for a twelve-month membership, these services store their clients' résumés in an electronic database. When using an electronic résumé database service, you may want to consider preparing an electronic résumé that is scanned for input into the database rather than using a traditional résumé. Information about preparing electronic résumés is presented later in this chapter.

When an employer is looking for an employee with certain specific qualifications, the database service can quickly scan all the résumés it has to identify qualified individuals. Some popular electronic résumé database services and their toll-free numbers are Job Bank USA (800-296-1872); KiNexus (800-828-9422); Peterson's Connexion (800-338-3282); and SkillSearch (800-258-6641).

In addition to electronic résumé database services that use electronic résumés, you might also find helpful another electronic means of locating jobs. The Internet, which is discussed more fully in Appendix E, is a super computer network that operates worldwide. Several different job banks are maintained on the Internet. If you have access to the World-Wide Web on the Internet (and you likely will if you have access to the Internet), you will find the following resources helpful in your job-searching efforts. They are accessed using the following Internet (URL) addresses:

http://www.careermosaic.com/cm/
http://rescomp.stanford.edu/jobs.html
http://galaxy.einet.net/GJ/employment.html
http://helpwanted.com/
http://www.espan.com

Various electronic "help wanted" bulletin boards on America Online and Compuserve may also help you locate open positions.

Determining Job Requirements

After you have assessed the job market and identified the types of jobs that most interest you, the next step is to determine requirements for these positions. In some instances, you may be familiar with these requirements. In other instances, you may need to study or analyze what they require.

What sources are helpful in determining job requirements?

One of the best sources to use when determining job requirements is the *Dictionary of Occupational Titles*, a publication of the U.S. Employment Service that contains descriptions of more than twenty thousand job titles and alternate titles. After reading the types of duties that normally comprise the jobs in which you are interested, you can easily determine the specific requirements of these jobs. Two other helpful sources are the *Occupational Outlook Handbook* and the *College Placement Annual.*

Exhibit 9-1 Questions to use for undertaking an occupational analysis.

1. What is the history of the occupation?
2. How does the occupation fit into society in general?
3. How many workers are employed in the occupation, and what are the growth trends?
4. What common duties comprise the job?
5. What qualifications are job holders expected to have?
6. What is the nature of the education and experience requirements?
7. Is the position generally considered to be at job-entry level?
8. How much time is required for someone without previous experience at a similar job to become fully qualified?
9. What is the nature of the career path?
10. What occupations are related to the occupation that interests you?
11. What is the average beginning salary? Anticipated salary trends?
12. What fringe benefits are common?
13. What are the employment conditions?
14. What section of the United States has the greatest number of positions available at this time?
15. What are the advantages and disadvantages of this occupation?
16. Is the occupation likely to become obsolete during your lifetime?
17. Does technology affect this occupation now? Is it likely to in the future?

Analyzing job requirements enables you to clarify the physical, social, and cultural aspects of the environment in which you are seeking employment. Having a good grasp of these factors will help you locate a job you will enjoy and avoid those you would likely find unenjoyable. When analyzing an occupational field, being able to answer the questions in Exhibit 9-1 will be helpful.

After assessing the job market and determining job requirements, the next step is to analyze the company or companies to which you are applying.

Analyzing the Company to Which You Are Applying

Why should you analyze the companies to which you are applying?

An analysis of each company is important because it will (1) help you decide whether you want to work for the company; (2) help you determine whether you are qualified for the job; and (3) provide you with information to use during an interview.

Many sources of information about companies are readily available. The following are some of the most common.

Annual Reports

Much information about companies appears in their annual reports. Besides financial information, annual reports contain information about company officers; local, branch, or regional offices; products manufactured (or services provided); and perhaps an organizational chart. By examining the organizational chart in such reports, you may be able to identify possible career progression tracks. You can obtain annual reports in a variety of ways. Most college and university libraries have the annual reports of the nation's larger companies. In addition, the placement offices of many colleges and universities keep up-to-date annual reports of the companies that interview on their campuses. You can also obtain an annual report by writing directly to the companies themselves.

Local Offices or Companies That Sell the Company's Products

In many instances, companies have local offices in cities throughout the country. Employees of these local offices or companies are generally quite willing to discuss the company in which you are interested as well as its products or services.

Individuals Who Are Familiar with the Selected Company

In some instances, you may also be able to visit with someone in your area who is familiar with the company in which you are interested. For example, the person may have done business with the company or have a relative who is an employee. Even if you are unable to learn much from this person about the company itself, you may still be able to gain a wealth of valuable information about your chosen field.

Individuals Affiliated with College and University Placement Offices

Individuals affiliated with college and university placement offices can often provide information about the company. For example, alumni whom they have helped place with the company may informally report back to them about job satisfaction.

Financial Manuals

Moody's Manual and *Poor's Register* are two financial manuals you can use to obtain detailed information about a company. These manuals contain the names of company officers, locations of home and branch offices, product lists, and financial information. A number of industries (especially technologically oriented ones) also have specialized manuals from which useful background information about a company can be obtained.

```
1. Position Requirements
   a. Ability to prepare sales forecasts
   b. Ability to supervise field salespeople
   c. Ability to prepare budgets
   d. Ability to conduct market research projects
   e. Ability to analyze information about competitors
2. Education
   a. Completed courses in sales management, marketing, and marketing research
   b. Completed courses in human relations, management, and accounting
3. Work Experience
   a. Have worked for marketing research firm for two summers
   b. Have worked as a sales representative for three years during vacations
   c. Have worked as a bookkeeper for one summer
4. Other Factors
   a. Have held leadership positions (president, vice president, and treasurer)
      in three different organizations
   b. Was selected as the Marketing Student of the Year at Community College
   c. Like to work with people
   d. Can relocate anywhere in the country
```

Exhibit 9-2 Personal-position analysis.

Journal and Newspaper Articles

Journals of various professional associations and industry groups and newspaper articles sometimes contain information about a company. *The Wall Street Journal* is probably the most useful newspaper source available if you are seeking corporate information. *The Wall Street Journal Index* can help you locate articles of specific interest in the *Journal*. You can also use the *Business Periodicals Index*, which is updated several times each year, to locate journal articles about specific companies.

Once you have analyzed yourself, the job market, and the company or companies to which you are applying, your next activity is to consolidate your information and prepare a personal-position analysis. A sample personal-position analysis is shown in Exhibit 9-2. In your own analysis, include the following information: (1) the requirements of the position, (2) your educational preparation for the position, and (3) the relevant work experiences that have prepared you for the position. Your personal-position analysis may also contain a section identifying other experiences, such as having lived abroad, that qualify you for the position.

THE RÉSUMÉ

What is the function of the résumé?

The *résumé*, also known as a data sheet, a vita, or a personal qualifications profile, presents information about your background as it relates to the needs of prospective employers. Supporting the letter of application, the résumé is prepared before the letter. Essentially, the résumé is your autobiography. Because it presents your entire background, you can then condense information in the letter of application accompanying your résumé.

Increasingly, employers are viewing résumés as tangible evidence of applicants' qualifications for a position, as well as evidence of their ability to communicate effectively. Employers may also use résumés to try to assess how applicants feel about themselves.

Types of Résumés

What two types of résumés are used?

Two types of résumés exist: general and specific. *General résumés* are appropriate for any number of different jobs for which you are applying. *Specific résumés* are appropriate for only one job in a particular company.

The type of résumé you are preparing will influence your wording of certain parts of the document, including the heading, the career goals section, and the experience section. The following example illustrates the differences between the headings of the two types of résumés:

General

Résumé
MARY ANDERSON

Specific

Mary Anderson
Applicant for Sales Representative Position
with
ARNOLD-PIERCY CORPORATION
January 10, 199x

Some employers believe a specific résumé is more advantageous in securing a particular job than is a general résumé. The personalization of the résumé, with the title of the position for which you are applying as well as the company name, indicates that the résumé was prepared specifically for a particular job in a particular company.

Job seekers with easy access to text-editing or word processing equipment may find the specific résumé preferable. Using computers, they can easily change information that varies from résumé to résumé (heading and career goals sections, primarily) and include the pertinent information for each company to which they are applying. Job applicants without ready access to such equipment may have to use a printed (offset or xeroxography) general résumé that is appropriate for a number of jobs in a number of companies.

Besides their different headings, specific and general résumés differ in the career goals and work experience sections as indicated in the discussion that follows.

Content of the Résumé

Although the content sections of résumés are fairly standard, some flexibility does exist in selecting which sections to include. Perhaps the best guide in determining appropriate content is to weigh the potential impact on the reader of including certain information. If some specific information will, in your estimation, help you better sell your qualifications to the reader, include that information. An example is a proficiency in French for a person who may eventually be considered for an international assignment.

The following sections are typically included in a résumé:

1. Heading
2. Career goals or objectives
3. Education
4. Work experience
5. Summary of job skills/key qualifications
6. Activities, honors, and achievements
7. Special interests
8. References

Heading

Headings on a résumé can range from information that includes only the applicant's name to information that includes the applicant's name, temporary address, permanent address, telephone number, the title of the position for which the applicant is applying, and the name of the company to which the résumé is being sent. After deciding on the type of résumé (general or specific) to prepare, use your own judgment in selecting what information to include in the heading. Several examples of effective headings follow:

a. Anthony B. Roberts

Address (until May 15, 199x)	*Address (after May 15, 199x)*
135 Liberty Court	1987 Deerfield Road
Omaha, NE 67501	Wahoo, NE 67234
(204) 377-8673	(204) 675-9812

b. Susan Henry's Qualifications
as a buyer for
JOHNSON'S DEPARTMENT STORE

c. QUALIFICATIONS OF SUSAN HENRY AS
BUYER FOR JOHNSON'S DEPARTMENT STORE
Address: 4567 Dryden Street, Ely, NV 89111 Phone: (309) 367-2304

d. MARY D. BROWN
145 Franklin Drive
Bowling Green, KY 45890
Phone (214) 564-3356

Career Goals or Objectives

What are the characteristics of an effective career goals section on a résumé?

The type of résumé you are preparing largely determines the specificity of your goals section. In a general résumé, this section will obviously be more wide-ranging than if you are preparing a specific résumé. In a résumé for a specific job with a specific company, you must state your goals to reflect clearly the requirements of the job for which you are applying. In preparing a specific résumé, you can mention the name of the company in your goals statement (See example No. 4 below).

The *career goals* section of the résumé informs the reader about your career aspirations. Therefore, prepare this section with as much clarity of thought and specificity as possible. For example, avoid general statements portraying yourself as a jack-of-all-trades.

If you believe you can improve your chances of being offered a job by providing both short-range and long-range goals, then do so. If you are willing to relocate or travel, you may also place this information in the goals section. Looking at the examples that follow, you will notice that you may write in either complete or incomplete sentences. If your career goals section contains two or more sentences, then be consistent and make every sentence complete or every sentence incomplete.

The following are examples of career goals:

1. My short-range goal is to sell small business computers. My long-range goal is to become a marketing executive in a company that manufactures computer equipment.
2. Responsible position as a computer programmer. Willing to travel.
3. A staff accounting position in a leading public accounting firm. Long-term goal is to become a partner in a leading public accounting firm.
4. A women's fashion buyer for a progressive department store, such as Bullock's. Long-term goal is to become the manager of the marketing department in such a store.
5. To obtain a responsible entry-level job as a word processing operator and eventually to become the manager of a word processing center.

Education

Why do most college students present their education information before their work experience information?

For most college graduates seeking their first job, their education better qualifies them for employment than does their work experience. If this is true for you, present information on the résumé about your education before information about your work experience. But if your work experience is more important—and it is likely to be after you have five to ten years of experience in your field—then present that section first.

The information in the education section generally appears in reverse chronological order, which means you list your most recent education experience first. Include the following information in the education section:

What type of information about education is presented on the résumé?

1. Colleges/universities/technical schools attended, including location and inclusive dates of attendance
2. Major area studied
3. Degree(s) awarded or to be awarded
4. Actual or anticipated graduation date
5. Grade-point average, if it will help
6. Titles of courses completed relevant to the position for which you are applying (optional)

Several examples showing the presentation of educational information on the résumé follow. Note three specific formats: (a) by date, (b) by skills attained, and (c) by college/university.

a. 199x–199x: University of Michigan, Ann Arbor. Accounting major. Bachelor of Science degree in Accounting to be awarded on May 10, 199x.
Grade-point average: In major, 3.78/4.00; overall, 3.75

199x–199x: McComb County Community College, Dearborn, MI. General business major.
Grade-point average: Overall, 3.80/4.00

b. *University of Michigan, Ann Arbor—199x–199x*

Major: Accounting
Degree: Bachelor of Science degree in Accounting
GPA in Major: 3.78/4.00

Accounting Skills	Principles of Accounting, Intermediate Accounting, Cost Accounting, Tax Accounting, Advanced Accounting, Accounting Systems, Auditing
Business Skills	Management, Marketing, Business Law, Business Policy, Personnel Management
Communication Skills	Written Communication, Technical Writing, Speech and Oral Communication
Quantitative Skills	Calculus, Quantitative Methods, Statistics, Finance, Production and Operations Management

McComb County Community College, Dearborn, Michigan, 199x–199x

Major: General Business
GPA: 3.78/4.00

c. University of Michigan, Ann Arbor, 199x–199x
Major: Accounting
Degree: Bachelor of Science degree in Accounting
GPA in Major: 3.78/4.00
McComb Community College, Dearborn, Michigan, 199x-199x
Major: General Business
GPA: 3.80/4.00

Increasingly, companies are verifying the educational claims made by job applicants. In some cases, the checking is done before employment; in other cases, after employment. In many companies, individuals who misstate their educational background, the discovery of which is made after they begin working, are immediately discharged. Therefore, you will want to avoid misstating your educational background, either intentionally or unintentionally.

Work Experience

The order in which you present information about your educational background and work experience is determined by which one of the two areas best qualifies you for the position for which you are applying. Although your educational background will probably be more important for your first full-time job as a college graduate, experience is apt to be more important after you have worked for a few years.

Do not underestimate the value of part-time and summer jobs, especially those related to the job you are seeking. Although most part-time and summer jobs may have little or no relevance to the type of job you are seeking upon graduation, they can still teach valuable lessons, such as how to become a responsible employee, deal with the public, show the proper attitude toward work, and learn to work with others. The majority of employers like to be made aware of your part-time or summer jobs, regardless of how remotely related or even unrelated they are to the type of job you presently seek.

Some employers give preference to applicants who have used their part-time jobs to pay for substantial portions of their college education. Listing your part-time work experience enables prospective employers to evaluate you better than when using another criterion.

The information you present about each of your work experiences should include the following:

What information about work experience is presented on résumés?

1. The title of the job, including its major responsibilities
2. The inclusive dates of employment for the job
3. The name of the employer and its location
4. The significant accomplishments of the job
5. The reason you left the job (optional)

The information in the work experience section and the education section of the résumé should be arranged in the same order; that is, list your present or most recent job first and the least recent position last.

Using action verbs in presenting the material in the work experience section is recommended. Examples of action verbs are *worked, performed, handled, maintained, developed, processed*, and *calculated.*

Several formats exist for presenting work experience information on the résumé. You may list it by (a) date, (b) job title, (c) functional skills attained, and (d) employer name. Using the functional-skills format is especially appropriate when you have had several years of work experience after college.

If you choose the date format for presenting educational information, you may also want to use the same format for presenting work experience information. Or, if you use the skills-attained format in presenting the educational information section, you may want to use it in your work experience section. Similarly, using the college/university name format in the education section means that you might also use the employer name format in the work experience section. Examples of the four formats for presenting work experience information follow.

What formats are available for presenting information on résumés?

a. September 199x: to present	Davidson's Furniture Store, Darby, Michigan Worked part time during school year as a bookkeeper and full time during the summers. Per-

formed computerized bookkeeping operations. Developed several of the computer bookkeeping programs that are used. Occasionally served as store manager during absence of store owner.

June 199x to September 199x	Fuller Construction Company, Dunlap, Michigan Worked full time as a construction laborer on a road construction project. Frequently drove a dump truck and occasionally operated an asphalt roller.
September 199x to June 199x	Men's Dormitory, Algoma College, Darby, Michigan. Worked part time as a front-desk receptionist and as a cashier in the snack bar. Took messages, answered questions, gave directions, counted snack bar cash receipts, and prepared deposit slips.

b. *Bookkeeper*: Davidson's Furniture Store, Darby, Michigan, September 199x to present (part time during school year and full time during summers). Performed computerized bookkeeping operations. Developed several computer bookkeeping programs that are used. Occasionally served as store manager during absence of store owner.

Construction Laborer: Fuller Construction Company, Dunlap, Michigan, June 199x to September 199x. Worked full time as a construction laborer on a road construction project. Frequently drove a dump truck and occasionally operated an asphalt roller. Quit job to return to college.

Receptionist and Snack Bar Cashier: Men's Dormitory, Algoma College, Darby, Michigan, September 199x to June 199x. Worked part time as front-desk receptionist and as cashier in the snack bar. Took messages, answered questions, gave directions, counted snack bar cash receipts, and prepared deposit slips. Quit job to take full-time summer job.

c. *Have developed effective management skills*

As production manager (198x-198x) and later as vice president (198x to present) of Arjay Corporation, Cincinnati, I have had many varied management experiences. As vice president, I am responsible for five operating units. During my vice presidency, these five units have reduced their operating costs by 43 percent and have increased their productivity by 15 percent.

Have excellent record in program implementation

During my vice presidency, I have developed several programs designed to increase employee job satisfaction that have been very well received. Several companies have patterned their programs after the ones I developed. Programs include quality circles, team building, MBO, and job enrichment.

Have excellent communication skills	In college, I was a communications major. Since that time, I have won several public speaking awards in Toastmasters. Have also had several articles published in professional management journals.
Have excellent analytical skills	A significant part of my job as vice president involves analyzing data and making decisions on the basis of my analysis. Am frequently consulted by president for analysis and interpretation of data with which he works.

d. *R-K Engineers, Inc., Cleveland, Ohio*
Draftsperson, June 199x to present
Duties: Work part time preparing engineering drawings to show location of utilities in new residential subdivisions, as well as preparing drawings for street construction in new areas

Engineering Aide, September 199x to June 199x
Duties: Worked part time performing a variety of tasks, including data calculations, some basic drafting, and lettering on engineering drawings

Intern, September 199x to September 199x
Duties: Worked part time during senior year of high school performing a variety of tasks, including running errands, maintaining library, filing materials, and duplicating engineering drawings

Parisian Restaurant, Cleveland, Ohio
Bus person, September 199x to September 199x
Duties: Worked part time clearing tables, setting tables, preparing table setup for banquets, and cleaning floors in eating area

Summary of Job Skills/Key Qualifications

What is the purpose of the summary of job skills/key qualifications section of the résumé?

This section outlines the important job skills you have attained and your key qualifications for the position for which you are applying. When this section is complete, it should "set you apart" from other applicants, thus putting you in a more competitive position. If you have easy access to text-editing or word processing equipment, you may decide to tailor this section to meet the needs of each organization to which you apply.

The following shows several ways to present this section:

a. Among my job skills that would be helpful in this position are the following: excellent oral and written communication skills, ability to motivate others, ability to work well with others, and fluency in French and German.
The key qualifications I have for this position are the bachelor's degree, accounting major, three years' experience as a summer intern in a CPA firm, and excellent communication skills.

b. *Job skills*: Proficient in using the following computer software packages: Lotus 1-2-3, DBase IV, WordPerfect; effective communication skills; quick learner; and leadership potential.
Key qualifications: Bachelor's degree, accounting major, 3.75 overall grade-point average, work experience as a junior accountant, and experience with a number of computer software packages.

Activities, Honors, and Achievements

Several types of information belong in this section. If you are about to be graduated from college or are a recent college graduate, you may want to present information about your college activities, including honors, awards, club/organization memberships, and positions held in these clubs/organizations. The reader will be interested in this information as a way of assessing your leadership potential, your ability to work well with others, and possibly your ability to communicate effectively.

If you were graduated from college several years ago, you may want to include information about your present organizational memberships and leadership positions you hold rather than about your college activities. Also, even if you received honors and awards a number of years ago, you may include information about them in your résumé.

The two most common formats for presenting information about your activities, honors, and achievements information are by date and by title. The following shows each format:

a. *College Activities*

199x–199x	Member, Accounting Club. Held the following positions: Treasurer, 199x–199x; President, 199x–199x.
199x–199x	Member, Phi Beta Lambda, National Business Fraternity. Vice President, 199x–199x; President, 199x–199x.
199x–199x	Residence Hall Council, Undergraduate Dormitory. Floor Representative, 199x–199x; Secretary, 199x–199x.

Honors

199x–199x	Dean's List, Algoma College
199x	Chosen as the Accounting Student of the Year, Algoma College
199x	Elected to Beta Gamma Sigma, National Business Society

b. *College Activities*

Accounting Club, Algoma College, 199x–199x
  Treasurer, 199x–199x
  President, 199x–199x
Phi Beta Lambda (National Business Fraternity), Algoma College, 199x–199x
  Vice President, 199x–199x
  President, 199x–199x
Residence Hall Council, Undergraduate Dormitory, Algoma College, 199x–199x
  Floor Representative, 199x–199x
  Secretary, 199x–199x

Honors

Dean's List, Algoma College, 199x–199x
Chosen as the Accounting Student of the Year, Algoma College, 199x
Elected to Beta Gamma Sigma (National Business Scholastic Honorary), Algoma College, 199x

Special Interests

If you have space on your résumé to list your special interests, some employers appreciate this information. They will likely use it to determine what interests you and basically what type of person you are. Each item you list should be a legitimate special interest because during the interview, interviewers frequently ask questions about these special interests.

The following shows how you might list the special interests on the résumé:

Special interests: photography, listening to classical music, playing racquetball, reading, and watching all competitive sports.

References

How much emphasis is put on information supplied by references?

More and more, employers are not emphasizing references on résumés as they did in the past. The prime reason is their awareness that you will probably use only those people who will give you a favorable recommendation, which tends to diminish their validity. But, even though some employers may not attach much significance to references, such letters can be helpful in some cases.

In identifying the references on your résumé, list the full name, title, address, telephone number, and the nature of the relationship between you and each reference. Before you use any individuals as references, you need to obtain their permission. References may include your professors, previous employers, influential friends, community leaders, and other businesspeople.

A growing number of applicants, rather than listing their references on the résumé, indicate that credentials are available upon request. Most college students put their credentials on file in the placement office at their college or university. If you have done this, you might then put a statement similar to this in your references' section: "Credentials are on file in the Placement Office of Algoma University and are available upon request." Making credentials available only to interested employers is more economical than sending them to every employer for whom you are writing a résumé and letter of application.

Some applicants, rather than putting their credentials on file in a placement office, ask their references to prepare individual letters of recommendation. Making these letters available only to the interested employers is especially appreciated by these individuals.

If you decide to list your references on the résumé, the following is an acceptable format:

*Dr. James Smith	Telephone:	(212) 879-7892
Professor	FAX:	(212) 879-7800
Algoma College		
Darby, MI 48875		
#Mr. Hall Dickens	Telephone:	(212) 879-7575
Attorney at Law	FAX:	(212) 879-7551
123 Main Street		
Darby, MI 48875		
@Dr. David Jones	Telephone:	(212) 879-7832
Professor	FAX:	(212) 879-7841
Algoma College		
Darby, MI 48875		

---

*College Advisor
#Former Employer
@Accounting Professor

Included in the following Ethics Episode is information that will help you avoid an ethics dilemma when you prepare your résumé.

ETHICS EPISODE In compiling the data/information to include in your résumé, one of the more significant challenges will be to decide how to best present the data/information you include. You need to guard against purposely distorting data/information or unknowingly including false information. Committing either offense is unethical and perhaps even illegal. Distorting certain items on the résumé is more serious than distorting other items. For example, if you indicate on your résumé that you are a college graduate when, in fact, you are not, you are being more unethical than if you indicate you are a member of a civic group when you are not.

Employers view very seriously the misrepresentation of the content on one's résumé. Serious misrepresentation, when discovered, commonly leads to immediate termination of employment.

Another action, although less common, is the charging of the employee with a fraudulent act, perhaps resulting in criminal prosecution.

Consider the seriousness of the following unethical actions committed by job applicants:

1. Assume a job applicant who is currently completing the requirements for a bachelor's degree indicates on his résumé that he has an overall grade point average of 3.47 when, in fact, he has a 2.52 average. The situation will be even more serious if the job applicant's stated grade point average was the factor that resulted in his being offered the job rather than another applicant with a 3.33 average. When the employer examines this person's transcript to verify his grade point average following the receipt of an official college transcript, he will likely be severely reprimanded or perhaps even discharged. Even if he is allowed to continue working for the employer, he will have difficulty rebuilding a reputation that he is trustworthy.
2. Assume another job applicant applied for a position that mentioned in the vacancy notice the need for applicants to possess excellent written and oral communication skills. Because the applicant possessed most of the other requirements, she decided to apply for the position, mentioning in the summary of key skills section of the résumé that she possessed "excellent communication skills." An examination of her record shows she earned grades of C and D in English composition and a D in written business communication. Furthermore, she received an F the first time she enrolled in speech communications and a D when she repeated it. The unethical action of overstating an important job requirement by this job applicant will undoubtedly be obvious if she is hired and her job tasks depend on the use of effective oral and written communication skills. Once this individual is on the job—should she be offered the position—she will have to live with her conscience, knowing that she obtained a position by false pretenses, as well as deal with the continual frustration of not being able to perform communication-related tasks effectively.

To avoid creating an ethical dilemma for yourself as you prepare your résumé, remember the following:

1. Be honest in terms of the information you include.
2. Avoid "stretching" certain elements or sections as a means of making you seem better qualified for a position than you actually are.
3. Avoid assuming that you can probably "get by" with including on your résumé information that is not easily verified.

New Developments in Résumé Preparation

What new developments are affecting the preparation of résumés?

Recently, résumé writing has undergone some changes. The following is a brief discussion of some of the more important shifts.

1. *Omission of certain personal information.* Some of the information that applicants formerly included in the personal section of their résumés is now information that an employer cannot legally ask. Several relatively new laws make it illegal for an employer to ask questions or to solicit information that can be used in a discriminatory way against you. Because the employer can no longer solicit this information (unless it is a bona fide occupational qualification—and rarely is it), most do not expect you to provide this information. Included are such items as age, gender, religious preference, nationality, place of birth, national origin, race, and so forth.

2. *Exclusion of a photograph.* Employers can determine a number of things about you by looking at a photograph, including several things they cannot legally ask about such things as your age, gender, and race. Therefore, they do not expect you to provide a photograph unless your appearance is a bona fide occupational qualification, such as if you are applying for a job as a model.

3. *Inclusion of information about your job skills and key qualifications.* As employers increasingly expect this information on the résumé, you may be diminishing your opportunity for employment in some companies should it be omitted.

Included in Communication Capsule 9-1 are a number of guidelines for preparing your résumé.

Communications Capsule 9-1 Guidelines for Preparing a Résumé

When preparing your résumé, the following guidelines are helpful:

1. If you are preparing a quantity of résumés, select a duplicating process that produces excellent copies. Use good-quality bond paper, either white or off-white, beige, or gray. Do not use carbons in preparing résumés, nor a spirit or mimeograph duplication process. Preparing copies by offset, copier, or laser printing is recommended.
2. If your résumé requires additional pages, you should put an appropriate heading at the top of each page after page 1, as in the following:
   Résumé for Mary Smith, Page 2
   This way, if multiple pages become separated from one another, the recipient can easily determine which pages go together.
3. Your résumé must be free of errors. A résumé that contains errors reflects adversely on the applicant. In some companies, applicants who submit résumés with errors are automatically eliminated from further consideration—even if it's one minor error.
4. Use capitalization, underlining, boldface, and indentation to emphasize certain words or phrases.
5. Avoid special design techniques, such as borders or other types of graphic features.
6. Prepare your résumé and letter of application on the same type of paper.
7. Your résumé should be typeset or prepared using desktop publishing, if possible, as it will tend to have a more attractive appearance than a résumé prepared by a conventional typewritten process. The use of typesetting permits more information in less space.
8. Use a format with eye appeal. This involves a sufficient amount of white space on a page. Otherwise, with too much information on one page, the document seems cluttered. The lack of eye appeal may ultimately have a negative impact on the reader's impression of you as a job prospect.

Sample résumés are shown in Exhibits 9-3 and 9-4.

The information in Checklist 9-1 will help you prepare an effective résumé.

ELECTRONIC RÉSUMÉS

The use of electronic résumés is increasing dramatically as greater numbers of individuals are using electronic résumé database service companies in their job searching efforts. An electronic résumé differs from a traditional résumé in several distinguishable ways, including the following:

1. Whereas traditional résumés use action verbs, electronic résumés use nouns.
2. Because electronic résumés are scanned for input into a database, important physical appearance characteristics exist. A sans serif font (such as Helvetica or Univers) scans more effectively than a serif font, and the font size should range between 10 and 14 points. To be avoided are italics, shadow lettering, underlining, horizontal or vertical rules, and bullets.
3. The electronic résumé is dependent on key words, primarily nouns and adjectives. They are frequently located in a separate section immediately following the individual's name and address. The primary reason for putting the keywords in a separate section is that some résumé scanning software quits reading after identifying a maximum number of keywords, perhaps 50. If the keywords are spread throughout rather than in a separate section at the top, any keywords—regardless of how critical they are—following the maximum number will not be identified. Thus, the job applicant may appear to be less competitive than other job applicants, when, in fact, he or she is better qualified than any other.

JOHN D. SMITH
123 Grover Street
Batting, OH 31312
(212) 387-8844

Career Goal	My career goal is to work as an accountant; and after three years of accounting experience, I plan to sit for the CPA Examination. Eventually, I would like to become a partner in a large CPA firm.
Education	
199x-199x	*STATE UNIVERSITY, BATTING, OH.* Major: Accounting. Was awarded a Bachelor of Science degree in Business Administration (with high honors) on June 1, 199x. Have completed 36 hours of accounting courses and 24 additional hours of business/economics courses. Major grade point average: 3.80/4.00. Overall grade point average: 3.76/4.00.
Work Experience	
June 199x to June 199x	*KEN'S AUTO SALES, BATTING, OH.* Worked part time during school year, full time during summers as a bookkeeper and cashier. Maintained accounts receivable and accounts payable ledgers, operated cash register. During the last year, I supervised another part-time bookkeeper.
June 199x to June 199x	*STATE UNIVERSITY HEALTH CENTER, BATTING, OH.* Worked part time as an orderly. Duties included helping patients in and out of bed, walking patients, transporting patients to and from the laboratory.
June 199x to June 199x	*PORT ARTHUR HOSPITAL, PORT ARTHUR, OH.* Worked full time as an orderly, performing typical orderly duties.
Summary of Job Skills	Proficient in use of Lotus 1-2-3, Windows, Ensemble; speak fluent Japanese; have excellent oral and written skills
Summary of Key Qualifications	Bachelor's degree, accounting major, accounting/bookkeeping experience, and self-motivated
Activities	Beta Gamma Sigma, 199x-199x; Delta Sigma Pi, 199x-199x, Vice President, 199x-199x, President, 199x-199x; Phi Kappa Phi, 199x-199x

Résumé for John D. Smith, page 2

Achievements	Dean's Honor List, 199x, President's Honor List, 199x
Special Interests	Jogging, skiing, swimming, reading, and photography

References

Dr. Ken Adams, Head Accounting Department State University Batting, OH 31312 (581) 497-2362 (Academic Advisor)	Dr. Judith Smith Accounting Department State University Batting, OH 31312 (581) 497-2362 (Accounting Professor)
Mr. Kenneth Johnson Ken's Auto Sales 14 Otto Street Batting, OH 31312 (581) 497-3975 (Proprietor)	Dr. John Quincy University Health Center State University Batting, OH 31312 (581) 497-9841 (Administrator)

Exhibit 9-3 Résumé.

MARY HALL'S

Qualifications for Marketing Researcher

in Poncey's Corporation
123 Main Street
Johnson, TX 64231
(408) 477-1212

Career Objective

To work as a marketing researcher for Poncey's Corporation. Long-term goal is to become director of marketing research.

Education

DAVENPORT UNIVERSITY, SMITHFIELD, MICHIGAN
Major: Marketing
Minor: Psychology
Degree: Bachelor of Science degree in Marketing (May 10, 199x)
Grade point average: 3.78/4.00

Research Skills	Statistics, Marketing Research, Quantitative Analysis, Business Calculus, Consumer Behavior, Advanced Marketing Research, Operations Management
Business Skills	Management, Personnel Management, Logistics, Accounting, Marketing Management, Promotional Strategy, Sales Management, International Marketing, Distribution
Communication Skills	Written Communication, Report Writing, Technical Writing, Speech and Oral Communication, Sales Promotions

SMITHFIELD COMMUNITY COLLEGE, SMITHFIELD, MICHIGAN
Major: Business
Degree: Associate of Arts degree (June 1, 199x)
Grade point average: 3.90/4.00

Work Experience

Have developed effective marketing research skills	As a part-time employee of Thomas Marketing Research Corporation (September 199x to present), I have been involved in many research projects. During the last year, I have been the manager of several of these projects, including responsibility for all phases of marketing research. I have received special commendations from clients for the quality of three of these projects.
Have developed effective managerial skills	As manager of a number of marketing research projects for Thomas during the last year, I have been totally responsible for all phases of several of these projects, which has provided an opportunity to work closely with others. I have received high ratings from those with whom I've worked on these projects.
Have developed effective communication skills	As a marketing researcher, I have had considerable experience in writing reports and orally presenting research results. I received the 199x marketing research project award for a course project I developed.
Have developed effective analytical skills	Much of my time spent during the last year has been helping others analyze the data collected for other research projects. This experience has broadened my analytical skills considerably.

Summary of Job Skills

Proficient with microcomputer usage and a number of business software packages, well-developed oral and written communication skills, and excellent presentation skills.

Summary of Key Qualifications

Bachelor's degree in marketing, market research experience, team player, and willing to learn.

Exhibit 9-4 Résumé presented in a functional format.

Résumé for Mary Hall, Page 2.

College Activities

Marketing Club, Member 199x-199x. Was vice president in 199x and president in 199x.
Beta Gamma Sigma, Member 199x-199x. Membership limited to top 10 percent of graduating class.
Alpha Kappa Psi, Member, 199x-199x. Was elected vice president for 199x-199x.

Honors

Alpha Kappa Psi Silver Key Award, 199x; Marketing Club Outstanding Member Award, 199x.
Graduating Magna Cum Laude.

Special Interests

Boating, water skiing, stamp collecting, reading, traveling, swimming, playing chess.

References

Credentials, which are on file at Placement Office at Davenport University, are available upon request.

Exhibit 9-4 *continued*

OPENING

1. Have you included the vital heading information, including name, address (school and, if appropriate, home), and phone number(s)?
2. Have you included a career objective, including the type of work you currently seek?

EDUCATION

1. Have you (in reverse chronological order) listed for each college/university you've attended its name and location, inclusive dates attended, degree(s) earned/anticipated, anticipated graduation date, college major (and perhaps minor), and, if helpful, grade-point average and scale?
2. Have you listed the titles of courses you've completed that are relevant to the job for which you are applying (assuming you have space)?

EXPERIENCE

1. Have you (in reverse chronological order) listed for each part-time, summer, or full-time job you've held, the name and location of the employer, inclusive dates of employment, current job title, current job duties, and any significant achievements?

SUMMARY OF JOB SKILLS/KEY QUALIFICATIONS

1. Have you listed (in descending order of importance) the job skills/key qualifications you have acquired either through your educational or work experience that qualify you for the position for which you are applying?

ACTIVITIES, HONORS, ACHIEVEMENTS

1. Have you listed the activities in which you have participated in college, such as professional, civic, social, or academic groups, including the inclusive dates of membership?
2. Have you listed your leadership responsibilities in each of the activities listed above?
3. Have you listed your honors, awards (including scholarships), and/or achievements (both academic and nonacademic) during the time you've been a member of these groups?

SPECIAL INTERESTS

1. Have you listed your special interests (if sufficient space is available)?

REFERENCES

1. Have you listed the names, addresses, and telephone numbers of those serving as a reference (if sufficient space is available)? Otherwise, you can indicate that "references are available upon request," or you can list the name of the placement office from which letters of reference can be obtained.

Checklist 9-1 Résumé.

Among the items included in the keyword list are the following:

a. Job titles held by the applicant
b. Names of job-related tasks performed by the applicant
c. Special skills or knowledge possessed by the applicant
d. Degree(s)
e. College major
f. Certification or designations
g. Degree-granting institution
h. Class rank
i. Special awards or honors
j. Interpersonal skills or traits possessed by the applicant

4. Several other important considerations should be followed in preparing an electronic résumé, including the following:
   a. Do not fold the résumé; if a line of print is on the fold, the scanning process may be less effective.
   b. Some employers are now scanning the résumés they receive, especiallly larger employers. Consequently, consideration should be given to submitting an electronic résumé along with the traditional résumé if the applicant believes the opportunity exists for his or her résumé to be scanned.
   c. The electronic résumé can be more easily prepared if a traditional résumé is prepared first. The traditional résumé provides a base of keywords that are listed in the electronic résumé.
   d. Individuals preparing their first electronic résumé may want to examine job vacancy notices for the type of postion for which they are applying to help identify keywords that should be incorporated.

Shown in Figure 9-5 is an electronic version of the résumé shown in Figure 9-3.

JOHN D. SMITH
123 Grover Street
Batting, OH 61312
(212) 387-8844

Keywords: Accountant. Bookkeeper. Cashier. Accounts receivable ledger. Accounts payable ledger. Bachelor's degree. Business Administration. Lotus 1-2-3. Windows. Ensemble. Japanese. CPA examination. Ohio. Beta Gamma Sigma. Leadership. Phi Kappa Phi. Dean's Honor List. President's Honor List. Excellent oral communication skills. Excellent written communication skills. Self-motivated. Quick learner. Detail minded. Top 10 percent of class. IBM-compatable computers. State University, Batting, OH.

Goal: To work as an accountant and to pass the CPA Examination. Want to become a partner in a large CPA firm.

Education	State University, Batting, OH. 199x to 199x Accounting major. Bachelor of Science degree in Business Administration awarded June 1, 199x. High honors.
Experience	Ken's Auto Sales, Batting, OH. June 199x to June 199x Part time during school year; full time during summers. Performed bookkeeper and cashier duties. Maintained accounts receivable and accounts payable ledgers. Supervised another bookkeeper.
	State University Health Center, Batting, OH. June 199x to June 199x Worked part time as an orderly.
	Port Arthur Hospital, Port Arthur, OH. June 199x to June 199x Worked part time as an orderly.
College Activities and Honors	Beta Gamma Sigma, 199x–199x; Delta Sigma Pi, 199x to 199x, Vice President, 199x to 199x, President, 199x to 199x; Phi Kappa Phi, 199x to 199x; Dean's Honor List, 199x; President's Honor List, 199x.

Exhibit 9-5 Electronic Résumé.

SUMMARY

Before you prepare a résumé, you need to complete several activities, including a self-analysis, an analysis of the job market, and an analysis of the company or companies to which you are applying. The more thoroughly you complete these preliminary activities, the easier will be the actual résumé preparation process.

Two types of résumés are found: general and specific. General résumés are appropriate for any job you are applying for; specific résumés are appropriate for only one particular job.

The various sections in most résumés are the following: heading; career goals or objectives section; education section; work experience section; job skills/key qualifications section; activities, honors, and achievements section; special interests section; and references. The order of the sections may vary, depending on the length of your work experience.

REVIEW QUESTIONS

1. In getting ready to apply for a job, why should you make a self-analysis? How do you analyze yourself?
2. How do you analyze the job market when getting ready to apply for a job?
3. Why should you analyze the organization to which you are applying for a job? How do you analyze the organization?
4. What is the purpose of a personal-position analysis?
5. What are the two types of résumés, and how do they differ?
6. What are the basic content sections of résumés?
7. What are the elements of an effective career goals section of a résumé?
8. What types of information about your educational background should appear in your résumé?
9. When should your educational background appear before your work experience background in a résumé?
10. What is unique about the functional format of the work experience section of the résumé?
11. What types of information are commonly included in the activities, honors, and achievements section of the résumé?
12. What suggestions can you offer to improve the effectiveness of résumés?

APPLICATION PROBLEMS

1. Using the information in this chapter, undertake a thorough self-analysis in preparation for writing a résumé. Be honest with yourself as you make the self-analysis. What did you learn about yourself that you did not already know?
2. Using the information in this chapter, thoroughly analyze the job market of interest to you. What did you learn about the job market that you did not already know?
3. Using the information in this chapter, thoroughly analyze the company (or one of the companies) you would like to work for after college. Did this analysis change your level of excitement about working for the company? If so, how?
4. Using the guidelines in this chapter, prepare a personal-position analysis.
5. Using the sample résumé headings illustrated in this chapter, prepare three different headings for your own résumé. Which one do you like best?
6. Prepare a career goals section for your résumé.
7. Assume you have now been out of college for ten years and that the career goals section of your old résumé parallels exactly what you have accomplished so far in your career. You now decide to seek a higher-level job than your present position. Prepare the career goals section for the résumé you plan to use in seeking a job in another company.
8. Using two of the following three formats—date, skills attained, and college/university—prepare the education section of your résumé.

9. Using two of the following three formats—date, job title, and employer name—prepare the work experience section of your résumé.
10. For the career goals section of the résumé that you prepared in application problem 6, use the functional format to create the work experience section of your new résumé. Assume that you have had a number of good work experiences during the ten years following your graduation from college and that you have developed a number of important job skills.
11. Prepare a résumé using the format you prefer. Make sure your résumé follows the guidelines described in this chapter.

10

Letters about Employment

After studying this chapter, you should be able to

1. Describe the qualities of well-written letters of application.
2. Discuss the items that appear in the opening, middle, and closing sections of the letter of application.
3. Identify the letter plan for preparing interview follow-up letters, letters accepting a job offer, letters refusing a job offer, and letters of resignation.
4. Prepare effective letters of the type discussed in this chapter.

During the job-search process, you will probably need to write several letters to prospective employers. The various letters are a letter of application (also known by some as a cover letter), an interview follow-up letter, a letter accepting a job offer, and a letter refusing a job offer. This chapter describes in detail the nature of these letters and explains how best to prepare each type. In addition, we discuss one other type of letter relating to employment—the letter of resignation.

LETTER OF APPLICATION

Once you have identified the position for which you plan to apply and then prepared your résumé, the next step is to write a *letter of application*, which is a message designed to inform the reader of your desire for a position in his or her organization and to request an interview for that position.

What is the purpose of letters of application?

The letter of application functions as a personal advertisement in that you use it to sell the reader on your qualifications for the position you are seeking. To sell yourself, focus on what you can do for your prospective employer and why you believe you are well qualified for the position. Because your résumé and letter of application will compete with the résumés and letters from other applicants, obviously, the better you sell the prospective employer on your qualifications, the better your chances are of being granted an interview. Furthermore, the more effectively you consider the employer's perspective, the more attention your letter will likely receive. Tailor the letter to the unique requirements of the position for which you are applying, the company to which you are applying, and the industry to which the job belongs.

Depending on your situation, you can use three different kinds of application letters. When you send a letter not knowing whether an opening actually exists in a company, the letter is called an *unsolicited application.* When you send a letter to a post office box number or to a newspaper box number, not knowing the identity of the company in which the opening exists, it is called a *blind-ad letter.* And when you send a letter knowing that an opening exists in a company, this is called a *solicited letter of application.*

What types of letters of application are used?

If a résumé accompanies the letter of application, then the letter does not need to be as thorough as when the letter is sent by itself. A letter accompanying a résumé, therefore, becomes a supplement to, rather than a substitute for, the résumé.

Qualities of Well-Written Letters of Application

One of the most important qualities of any effective business letter, and especially the letter of application, is the use of you-attitude. The first of the following examples shows how selfish-sounding the I-attitude seems in an application letter. The revision, written in the you-attitude, is more effective because it gives the reader a reason to hire the applicant.

What qualities should letters of application possess?

Change: I wish to be considered an applicant for the position of sales representative.
To: A degree in marketing and my personal qualities would enable me to be the "enthusiastic, hard-working sales representative" you advertised for in Monday's *State News.*

Another illustration of the difference between you-attitude and I-attitude appears in the following two sentences:

Change: In June, I was graduated from Marshall College, where I was an accounting major.
To: A close match exists between my qualifications and the requirements for the auditing position you listed in your letter recently sent to State College's Placement Office. Therefore, I am confident of my ability to perform well as an auditor in your company.

The length of letters of application is another important quality. Although a two-page résumé is permissible, the letter of application should be limited to one page. If your first draft is longer than a single page, revise to make it shorter. The letters prepared by most people are four to five paragraphs long.

How long should letters of application be?

Another important quality of a successful letter of application is that it is addressed to a person rather than to a title when possible. Clearly, to address a letter to the "Human Resources Manager" does not create as favorable an impression as addressing the letter to "Mr. John Chalaupe." Take the time and effort to learn the name of the person to whom you are sending the letter.

You can obtain through several means the name of the person to whom you are sending the letter of application. The *College Placement Annual*, which you can probably find in your college's placement office, identifies the name and title of the person responsible in many companies for college-level recruiting. *Moody's Manual* may also contain the name of the person to whom the letter should be sent. In some cases, you may have to call the company to obtain the name of the person.

Another quality of well-written letters of application is that they are neat and error free. Your letter should be error free because many companies view such carelessness quite negatively; indeed, some companies, upon discovering an error, automatically eliminate an applicant from further consideration. Examples of errors are misspelled words, incorrect job titles, typographical errors, and grammatical and punctuation errors.

Although you may send a photocopied or a printed version of your résumé, the letter of application should always be an original. The employer also receives a better impression when your letter is produced on the same kind of paper as is the résumé.

Another important quality of successful application letters is that they convey the impression of confidence. Positioning yourself somewhere between being overconfident and underconfident seems a happy medium—a reality-based confidence you must transmit to the reader. Letters that suggest overconfidence may put off readers who see you as a braggart or an egotist. Such letters also may leave the reader afraid that you may not be able to perform the job.

What is the nature of reader-benefit material included in letters of application?

Well-written letters also contain reader-benefit material, explaining what you can do for the reader. Your education and training and/or personal traits usually constitute the main reasons the employer will hire you for the job you want. A major weakness of many letters of application is the writer's failure to convert factual information of this nature into reader-benefit material.

In letters of application, present the most important information first. This principle, you may recall, also applies to the résumé. For example, if you believe that your education better qualifies you for a position than your work experience does, present information about your educational preparation before information about your work experience.

Finally, do not pattern your letter of application too closely after the sample letters you study. If you and other readers pattern your letters after the same sample, a prospective employer may receive several similar letters. If this happens, your chances of obtaining an interview may diminish.

Letter Plan

What is the suggested plan for letters of application?

A letter of application, like most other types of letters, follows a suggested plan. Being persuasive in nature, the letter includes the following elements:

1. An opening containing reader-benefit material that will make the reader want to read the letter and the résumé
2. A middle section outlining your qualifications for the job
3. A closing section requesting an interview

Opening Section

The opening of your letter of application will probably "make or break" the letter. Your goal is to entice the reader to want to read the entire letter—and then to respond favorably to the request for an interview.

What information is included in the opening section of letters of application?

The kind of opening varies from one application letter to another, depending on the circumstances. For example, you may wish to include the name of the person who told you about the opening and/or provide information about how your qualifications for the job fit the requirements of the position. Another type of opening includes a discussion of newsworthy information about the company (e.g., having its best year profitwise, starting a new product line). You can also provide information about one of the company's significant accomplishments (e.g., recently named employer of the year in the community, recently joined *Fortune* 500 list). Whatever type of opening you choose, make sure to include the title of the position for which you are applying in your first paragraph.

When preparing solicited applications, you should also try to mention how you found out about the vacancy: Either provide the name of your informant or the publication listing the vacancy. Being specific will create more interest in the letter, especially if the reader and the person you name in the opening are acquainted. Some readers will assume you are a well-qualified applicant if a credible person suggested you apply for the position.

What information should be included in the opening section of solicited letters of application?

The first of the following three examples of application-letter openings is weak because it lacks specificity and seems to be written without care. The second and third examples are much better. The second example refers to the specific person making the referral, whereas the third example mentions the name of the publication in which the writer found the employer's ad. Note also that the effective examples are written from a you-viewpoint and mention the positions for which the writers are applying.

Change: Please consider me an applicant for the position that I recently learned was available in your company.

To: Ms. Lea Dunham, Director of Placement Services at State University, informed me about an opening for an auditor in your accounting department. Because my college training and work experience qualify me for such a position, please consider me as an applicant.

To: Your ad in the June 21 issue of *Community News* for an ambitious, hard-working sales representative lists requirements similar to my qualifications. A degree in marketing and four years of sales experience make me confident of my ability to be the type of employee you wish to hire. Please consider my application for this opening.

Another kind of opening is to mention several of your most important qualifications for the position. In using this approach, write with a you-viewpoint rather than an "I-viewpoint," a principle violated by the first of the following three paragraphs but corrected in the other two openings.

Change: I would like to have the opportunity to put my educational and work experience qualifications to use as an employee in your company. Please consider my application for an open position in your company.

To: Several years of retail work experience in a women's clothing shop, a degree in fashion merchandising, and an appreciation for hard work would enable me to perform well as the sportswear buyer you are seeking. I would like to be considered for this position.

To: An ability to communicate well both orally and in writing, a degree in business administration with a concentration in information processing, and a summer internship in the data processing department of a petroleum company are the qualifications I have that closely match the requirements of the systems analyst position open in your company. I would like to be considered for this opening.

You may also attract the reader's attention by opening with a reference to a significant accomplishment of the company or a newsworthy event. Note how weak the first of the following three paragraphs is compared with the two revisions. Part of the problem with the first paragraph is its vagueness, which both revisions correct, each in its own way.

Change: The article about your company I recently read certainly convinced me that your company would be an excellent place for me to begin my career. Please consider me an applicant for an opening in your company.

To: The recent article about Baylor Steel Company, which appeared in the *Houston Gazette*, convinces me that the foresight of your managers will allow the company's expansion plans to succeed at a time when other steel companies are scaling back their operations. Please consider me an applicant for a transportation coordinator position should your expansion plans create such an opening.

To: When you begin hiring the accounting staff for your new plant that will open in Dallas early next year, I would like to be considered for an auditor's position if an opening exists for a person with my educational and work background. An article I recently read about the state-of-the-art equipment that will be installed in your new plant was fascinating. This equipment should enable Johnson Corporation to continue as the leading manufacturer of small kitchen appliances.

What information should be included in the opening section of unsolicited letters?

When preparing an unsolicited letter of application, opening with a list of your qualifications is especially effective because you need to capture the reader's attention immediately. The following opening of an unsolicited letter outlines the writer's qualifications for a particular job.

If you have an opening for a sportswear buyer who has several years of retail work experience, a degree in fashion merchandising, and an appreciation for hard work, I would like to be considered as an applicant.

Middle Section

The middle section of your application letter will be the longest section as this is where you discuss your qualifications for the job. Your goal in writing this section is to convince the reader that you are indeed qualified. In developing the middle section, you have flexibility in deciding which of the following elements to include, according to which elements are appropriate to you, your experience, and the job for which you are applying:

What information is included in the middle section of letters of application?

1. Your understanding of the requirements of the position (if this is a solicited letter)
2. Your educational preparation that helps qualify you for the position (solicited and unsolicited letter)
3. Your work experience that helps qualify you for the position (solicited and unsolicited letter)
4. Any special qualifications you may have that others may not have (solicited and unsolicited letter)
5. Personal information, such as your grade-point average, the percentage of college expenses you have paid for, the college activities in which you have participated, honors and awards you have received, evidence of your ability to work with others, and so forth (solicited and unsolicited letter)

Because of the one-page limitation on letters of application, focus on what you consider to be the most significant information the reader should know about you. Emphasize the key points, those that show what you can do for the potential employer.

Should you provide in your letter of application a lengthy discussion of requirements of the job for which you are applying? Why?

When reviewing the requirements for the position, you should avoid a lengthy discussion simply because the reader is aware of the job requirements. Your primary goal is to convince the reader that you have studied the position sufficiently to know that your qualifications match its requirements.

In the following example, note how the revision is more specific than the original.

Change:	I understand you are looking for a hard-working, ambitious employee.
To:	A background in statistics qualifies me as the research coordinator you are seeking who is required to have an analytical background and to be familiar with statistical applications.

Among the requirements often listed in vacancy notices for which you will need to discuss your qualifications are the following: educational and experience requirements or other requirements, such as the ability to work well with people, a positive attitude toward travel, effective communication skills, and so forth. When preparing an unsolicited letter, use your own judgment in deciding which of your qualifications to highlight.

What determines whether you present educational or experience qualifications first in letters of application?

If you are about to be graduated from college or have been recently graduated, your educational preparation is most likely your most important qualification for the job. On the other hand, if you have several years of relevant work experience, then experience may be the more important qualification. The more important of these qualifications should be discussed first.

The first of the following three paragraphs is too vague in presenting the writer's educational qualifications for the job for which he is applying. Note how much more thoroughly the revised paragraphs detail these qualifications.

Change:	The training I received as a business major in college will enable me to perform well as an employee in your company.
To:	As a marketing major at the University of Colorado, I studied the broad functional areas of business as well as completed twelve marketing courses and a number of elective courses that will be helpful as a sales representative. In the advanced selling course, my sales presentation enabled me to win the R. D. Bell Outstanding Sales Presentation Award. Courses in marketing research, technical writing, and business communication were beneficial in my learning how to write effective marketing reports.
To:	The accounting and data processing courses I studied at the University of Houston enabled me to become familiar with accounting theory, procedures, and practices, as well as with computerized accounting processes. An understanding of the role of data processing in accounting would enable me to work effectively with your clients who have installed computerized accounting systems. Elective courses in written and oral communication will also enable me to communicate effectively with these clients.

Should you call attention to a lack of work experience in a letter of application? Why?

In the section on work experience, avoid calling undue attention to your inexperience. Employers realize that college students may not have had an opportunity to work in a job closely related to the jobs for which they are applying. The jobs you have held, regardless of whether they are full time or part time or whether they are related to the job you are seeking, have strengthened your qualifications. Each of your jobs has probably given you something positive that you can take with you to the job you are seeking.

As you present information about your work experience background, show how your previous experience (1) will be useful in the job for which you are applying; (2) has helped you learn to be a responsible, hard-working employee; and (3) has given you an opportunity to work with others.

Note how vague the first of the following paragraphs is about the writer's work experience compared with the information about the writer's work experience in the revision.

Change: Many aspects of my previous work experience would be useful should I be given an opportunity to work in your company.

To: For each of the last three summers, I have worked as an intern in a Big 8 CPA firm. This experience has given me an opportunity to apply much of my acquired textbook knowledge. A job this past summer in the accounting systems unit enabled me to have experience with computerized accounting. For the last half of the summer, I was allowed the privilege of making client visitations by myself. The ability to handle responsibilities and to work well with others—two important attributes learned from my work experience—would be valuable as a junior accountant in your firm.

If you believe you have special qualities for the position, discussing them may be to your advantage. The following paragraph illustrates how you can effectively describe a special quality of yours.

An article about your company appearing recently in *Today's News* indicated that a branch is about to be opened in Paris. Having lived in France for two years, I am able to speak French fluently and have a strong desire to live in France once again.

In the final part of the middle section of your letter of application, you may also outline personal information that will enable the reader to better assess your qualifications for the position. In writing this part, use a you-viewpoint rather than an I-viewpoint. The following paragraphs illustrate how to present a variety of different types of personal information in the letter of application.

The ability I have to work well with others has been developed in a variety of ways, including the following: working as a student volunteer in a local senior citizens' home, serving as vice president and president of my sorority, and having a part-time cashier's job in a local department store.

Part- and full-time jobs enabled me to earn approximately 80 percent of my educational expenses. Scholarship money covered the remainder of the expenses. Although the need to work prevented me from becoming as involved in college activities as I would have liked, I did hold leadership positions in Alpha Kappa Psi, a national professional business organization, and in the Management Club. My experiences in these organizations would be invaluable as a management trainee.

Of the eight semesters I've attended State University, I was on the Dean's list for six. A grade-point average of 3.45 (4.00 scale) will enable me to graduate with honors. During my sophomore and junior years, I was presented with certificates for the highest grade-point average among management majors.

Be sure to provide all information requested in the vacancy notice when developing the middle section. If the notice asks you to identify the salary you expect to receive, provide the requested information. Some experts believe you should state the specific dollar amount; others suggest you include a statement similar to, "I would expect to receive a salary commensurate with the requirements of the position and with my qualifications." The decision about including a specific dollar amount is yours to make. If you identify a specific dollar amount, try to avoid over- or underpricing yourself. Following is an example of how you can provide a specific dollar amount.

> Given my background, training, going rates for this position, and the cost of living in the Boston area, a beginning salary of $32,000 is competitive.

The middle section, as you have seen, generally comprises two to four paragraphs. In developing this section, keep an eye out for paragraph unity. At the same time, try to guard against too many short paragraphs as they will detract from the appearance of your letter.

How many paragraphs does the middle section of letters of application normally comprise?

Somewhere in the letter—perhaps in the middle section—you should refer to the enclosed résumé, if you are enclosing one. Because the reader will be aware that a résumé is being enclosed, the statement "A résumé is enclosed" is unnecessary. A more appropriate reference to the enclosed résumé may be as follows: "My work experience, outlined on the enclosed résumé, has taught me many valuable lessons about working with others."

Closing Section

Asking for an interview in the last paragraph of your letter makes the closing action oriented. Do not make your request by simply asking for an interview—it's too abrupt. It will seem less so if you include other material, such as an offer to provide additional desired information or the dates you might be available for an interview.

What information should be included in the closing section of letters of application?

Generally, you will indicate in the closing of your letter that you will appreciate the prospective employer's contacting you regarding an interview time. An alternative approach is to indicate in the closing paragraph that you will contact the prospective employer regarding the possibility of establishing an interview time.

Note how in the following paragraphs, the two revisions use this approach to correct the problem. The first two revisions indicate that you will appreciate the prospective employer's contacting you; the third revision indicates that you will contact the prospective employer.

> Change: May I have an interview at your convenience?
>
> To: Additional information about my qualifications for this position can be discussed during an interview, although this letter and the attached résumé do outline several. You can reach me at 764-1234 between 10 A.M. and 1 P.M. each day of the week to let me know a time that is convenient for you to talk with me about the auditing position.
>
> To: After you have studied my résumé, please call or write to let me know a time that is convenient for you to discuss the sales representative position with me. Should you need additional information, please let me know.
>
> To: During the morning of July 2, I will call you to determine if you need additional information to assess my qualifications as well as to discuss the possibility of setting a time for an interview.

A well-written solicited letter of application is shown in Exhibit 10-1. An effective unsolicited letter of application is shown in Exhibit 10-2. Note the difference in the openings of the two letters.

1893 Smith Avenue
Dallas, TX 75431
September 10, 199x

Mr. Harry Johnston
Director of Human Resources
Adamson Corporation
P. O. Box 4432
Houston, TX 76721

Dear Mr. Johnston:

Your company's accounting vacancy notice that recently appeared in the *Denver Gazette* listed two primary job requirements that match my qualifications: a bachelor's degree in accounting and one year of successful accounting experience. Please consider me as an applicant for this accounting position.

An opening containing reader-benefit material that mentions how the writer learned of the vacancy and what are the job requirements.

The nature of my educational preparation and work experience has enabled me to acquire several other important qualifications, including the following: the ability to communicate effectively in writing as well as orally, to work well with others, and to accept responsibility. In addition, I have learned how to manage my time well.

A section that presents the writer's job qualifications.

As an accounting major at the University of Texas - Arlington, I completed 36 hours of accounting, in addition to related courses in computer systems, computerized accounting systems, systems analysis, and management information systems. The accounting courses completed are listed on the enclosed résumé. I was selected by the accounting faculty at the University of Texas - Arlington to receive the John Cole Distinguished Senior Accounting Student award. My 3.89 overall grade-point average enabled me to be graduated with high honors.

A section that presents a discussion of the writer's educational preparation, including honors and grade-point average.

Since graduating last spring, I have been employed as a junior accountant at the Cromwell Accounting Group where I have received two promotions since beginning work. Other experience includes working as an intern in a Big 8 accounting firm during my junior and senior years. My work experience and educational preparation recently enabled me to pass all five parts of the Texas CPA exam.

A section that presents a discussion of the writer's work experience.

During this past year, I have been actively involved in several professional and civic organizations. Leadership positions currently held include serving as vice president of the Mesquite CPA Association and secretary-treasurer of the Boulder Optimists Club.

A section that presents a discussion of the writer's leadership activities.

After you have reviewed my résumé, please notify me of a time that would be convenient for you to discuss this accounting position. If you need additional information, please let me know.

A closing that presents a request for an interview and an offer to provide additional desired information.

Sincerely,

Jonathan B. McNeeley

Exhibit 10-1 Effective solicited letter of application.

1984 Chicago Blvd.
Deerfield, IL 60012
March 15, 199x

Mr. David Harms
Personnel Director
Tomilson Electronics Corp.
1238 Michigan Avenue
Chicago, IL 60909

Dear Mr. Harms:

An article recently appearing in the *Chicago Post* convinces me your company will be one of the leaders in the electronics industry during this decade. If your company will need additional sales representatives to accommodate expanded business operations, please consider me an applicant for such a position.

An opening containing reader-benefit material that mentions the basis for the writer's desire to work for the company.

For the last three years, I have worked as a sales representative for the Harmson Company here in Chicago. In each of the last two years, I have received the company's award for having the highest annual dollar sales volume. In addition, I have received several letters of commendation from Mr. Jack Raymer, Harmson's president, in recognition of my sales performance.

A section that presents a discussion of the writer's work experience and job-related awards received.

Illinois State College awarded me the bachelor's degree in marketing in 199x. I completed thirty-two hours of coursework in marketing and eighteen hours in a communications minor. As a senior, I won the Sales and Marketing Student Association's Sales Presentation of the Year award. Other details about my educational preparation are outlined on the enclosed résumé.

A section that presents a discussion of the writer's educational preparation.

Integrating the knowledge from both the marketing and communications areas of study with my work experience gives me the following important job qualifications: how to make effective sales presentations, how to prepare effective oral and written reports, and how to conduct market analyses.

A section that presents a discussion of the writer's job qualifications.

Having the opportunity to discuss my qualifications for a sales representative position in your company will be appreciated. Please let me know a time that is convenient for you to talk with me.

A closing that presents a request for an interview.

Sincerely,

Hamilton B. Smith

Exhibit 10-2 Effective unsolicited letter of application.

A number of the questions in Checklist 10-1 will guide you in preparing an effective letter of application.

If you have not received a response to your letter of application within three to four weeks, consider sending an inquiry about its status. In this type of letter, you should

What is the suggested content of application-inquiry letters?

1. Question whether the letter of application and résumé sent earlier has been received. (If several weeks again pass without your hearing from the letter's recipient, you can likely conclude that you are not being considered for the position and, therefore, should focus your attention on other possibilities.)

OPENING

1. Has the you-attitude been captured in the opening paragraph?
2. Have you explained how your qualifications fit the requirements of the position for which you are applying?
3. Have you mentioned the title of the position for which you are applying?
4. Have you revealed how you learned about the opening (if you are preparing a solicited letter)?

MIDDLE

1. Have you discussed the requirements of the position for which you are applying (if you are preparing a solicited letter)?
2. Have you discussed the match between your qualifications and the requirements of the position?
3. Have you mentioned any special qualifications you have that might set you apart from other applicants?
4. Does the discussion of your qualifications capitalize on your strengths?
5. Have you adequately addressed any weaknesses in your background?

CLOSING

1. Is your closing courteous?
2. Have you requested an interview?
3. Have you offered to provide additional information that may aid the reader in assessing your qualifications?
4. Have you provided information about how, when, or where the reader will be able to contact you?

Checklist 10-1 Letter of application.

2. Identify the title of the job that interests you.
3. Reaffirm your interest in the job.
4. Identify new qualifications you have acquired since sending the letter of application.
5. Offer to send any additional information the employer may desire.

Exhibit 10-3 is a sample ineffective inquiry letter. An effective revision is shown in Exhibit 10-4.

Communication Capsule 10-1 discusses a number of general skills employers like to have their employees possess.

Exhibit 10-3 Ineffective letter that inquires about the status of an application.

Three months should be ample time for you to decide whether or not my qualifications match the requirements of the auditing position I applied for.	A curt opening that puts down the reader.
As I explained to you in the application, I am very much interested in working as an auditor in your company.	A weak reaffirmation of why the writer wishes to work for the company.
Please let me hear from you as soon as possible about the status of my application.	A weak closing that lacks the you-viewpoint.

On March 1 I sent you a letter of application and a résumé for the auditor's vacancy that was advertised in the February 25 issue of the *Daily Moines Chronicle*. Have you received these materials?	An opening that provides a discussion of the background details and inquires whether the application materials were received.
Because my qualifications match the requirements listed for the auditor's position, I am confident of my ability to perform well as an auditor. I was recently notified of my passing the Iowa CPA exam, which should enhance my qualifications for an auditing position.	A section that reaffirms the writer's interest in the job and mentions recent additional job qualifications.
Please let me know whether you would like additional information for use in assessing my qualifications for the auditing position.	A closing that offers to provide additional material the reader may need.

Exhibit 10-4 Effective letter that inquires about the status of an application.

Communication Capsule 10-1 Do You Possess These Skills?

Potential employers often examine the letter of application for evidence that you possess certain skills. Of special interest are those skills affecting your on-the-job success. Among the skills frequently desired of job applicants are the following:

1. *Ability to work with others:* Positions in the business world are becoming more and more interrelated. Therefore, employees have to work cooperatively with one another. As evidence, you can cite situations where you have had to work closely with others in carrying out projects, you can cite leadership positions you've held in professional/community/civic organizations, and so forth.
2. *Ability to write well:* For positions that especially require good writing skills, potential employers can use both the résumé and the letter of application to assess your writing skills. For these reasons, among others, make sure that both are well written.
3. *Ability to speak well and to make effective presentations:* Oral communication and presentation skills are becoming more important components in an ever-increasing number of positions. Cite evidence that you have had an opportunity to polish these skills through course work, job tasks, or leadership positions in professional, community, or service organizations.
4. *Ability to cope with pressure:* As job holders are being subjected to increased job pressures, potential employers look for evidence of your ability to cope with the ever-increasing pressure. As such evidence, you might mention that, as an undergraduate, you had a part-time job, maintained a high grade-point average while taking a normal class load, and participated in numerous campus or community activities.
5. *Ability to lead others:* Most college graduates will eventually be responsible for leading others. Therefore, your application materials will be examined to determine how much experience you've had in this area, as well as to determine how effectively you've led others. Two areas stand out: your supervising subordinates in the jobs you've had and your holding key leadership positions in campus organizations, including sports teams.
6. *Ability to manage your time well:* As a college student who perhaps works part time, who is involved in campus activities, and who enjoys academic success, you've had to manage your time well. As an employee, you will have to manage your time equally well. As evidence that you have learned to manage your time well, you might relate the extent to which you have been involved in the three areas just mentioned.
7. *Ability to work well with the public:* Most business employees have to interact with the public. Your ability to relate to others is often a critical factor in how potential employers evaluate you. As evidence, you may want to provide information about your other part-time or full-time positions that required you to work well with the public.

OTHER TYPES OF EMPLOYMENT-RELATED LETTERS

In addition to the letter of application, several other employment-related letters are common. Among these letters are interview follow-up letters, letters of acceptance, letters of refusal, and letters of resignation.

Interview Follow-up Letter

What is the purpose of interview follow-up letters?

The job *interview follow-up letter* is a message designed to thank the interviewer for spending time with you during the interview and to confirm your continuing interest in the position. The letter should be sent within a week's time after the interview—and in less time, if possible. Additional purposes are to restate why you believe you are qualified for the position and how you can put your qualifications to use for the prospective employer.

What should be included in the opening section of interview follow-up letters?

An effective way to begin the letter is with a fast-start opening that thanks the reader for spending time with you. In some cases, you will have been asked to return a completed application form. Mentioning its inclusion in the opening of the letter is recommended. Avoid providing obvious information as in the first of the following paragraphs (the revision corrects the problem).

Change: I interviewed with you earlier this week for the position of systems analyst.
To: Thank you for talking with me earlier this week about the systems analyst opening. Following the interview, I am even more convinced that the job closely matches my interests.

You can present several types of information in the section following the opening. These include

What information should be included in the middle section of interview follow-up letters?

1. New material that may be helpful to the interviewer assessing your qualifications.
2. A clarification of any mistaken notion you believe the interviewer may have received during the interview.
3. A discussion of how you feel about the company now that you have had the interview.
4. An expression of gratitude to the interviewer for any special insight you may have gained from him or her.

The following are examples of middle sections. In each pair, the first example is weak; the second example corrects the problem.

Change: I was favorably impressed with everything I learned during the interview.
To: During the interview, you stressed the need for all employees in your company to have well-developed writing skills. Upon returning from the interview, I was pleased to learn that a paper written last semester for a marketing class has been selected for publication in the *Marketing Review*, the official journal of the student division of the American Marketing Association. One of the factors that determines the suitability of an article for publication in this journal is quality of writing. I am confident my writing skills, which have been developed through work and educational experiences, would meet the requirements of the job.

Change:	The information you gave me during the interview was helpful.
To:	The additional insight gained during the interview further convinced me of the wisdom of my decision to begin my professional career as a sales representative. If given the opportunity to work for Dixon Corporation, I am confident my educational and work experience background would enable me to be the enthusiastic, progressive, and innovative sales representative you want to hire.
Change:	Although I may not have all the qualifications of the job, I am confident of my ability to be an excellent employee.
To:	You indicated during the interview that you are seeking a financial analyst who has had some work experience. I am confident that maturity and the experience gained from several part-time jobs would be a suitable trade-off for a lack of experience in financial analysis. As my résumé shows, I had an internship last summer in one of the large brokerage houses in Chicago. Approximately 60 percent of my time was spent doing financial analysis work.

What information should be included in the closing of interview follow-up letters?

You can include several types of material in the closing of your interview follow-up letter, such as an offer to send needed additional information, a statement of thanks for the interview (if not already expressed earlier in the letter), a statement expressing confidence that your qualifications meet the job requirements, or a statement mentioning that you are looking forward to hearing from the reader. Note how little is said in the first example that follows, whereas the revisions are action-oriented.

Change:	I appreciate your spending time with me.
To:	Should you need additional information to help in the assessment of my qualifications for the accounting position, please let me know. You can depend on me to be a hard-working, dedicated employee.
To:	Because my educational background and work experience meet the requirements of the job, I am confident of an ability to be the caliber of employee you are seeking. Please let me know your decision.

What is the suggested plan for interview follow-up letters?

The suggested plan for an interview follow-up letter includes these elements:

1. A fast-start opening in which the interviewer is thanked
2. A section in which one or more of the following is presented: new material that may be helpful to the interviewer, material that clarifies any mistaken notion the interviewer received from your answers during the interview, material that discusses your present feelings about the firm and/or the job, or material that thanks the interviewer for his or her assistance
3. A courteous closing in which one or more of the following is presented: an offer to send additional material, a statement of appreciation (or thanks if not included in the opening), a statement expressing confidence in your ability to perform well, or a statement expressing your desire to hear from the interviewer

I am one of the students at Northeast College who interviewed you last week while you were on our campus. I hope your visit here was enjoyable.	An opening that contains obvious information.
You certainly gave me an excellent insight into the career opportunities at Dartmouth Company. Now, more than ever, I would like to have the opportunity to work for your company.	A section that presents a weak presentation of how the interview was helpful.
I do appreciate your spending the extra few minutes with me.	A closing that fails to convey the writer's interest in the job.

Exhibit 10-5 Ineffective interview follow-up letter.

Exhibit 10-5 is an ineffective interview follow-up letter. A revision of the same letter is shown in Exhibit 10-6.

Checklist 10-2 contains a list of questions to use in preparing interview follow-up letters.

Exhibit 10-6 Effective interview follow-up letter.

9845 Grant Road
Boston, MA 09874
October 17, 199x

Ms. Tammy O'Doole
Manager of Human Resources
Smithson Corporation
29883 Beltline Highway
Boston, MA 09754

Dear Ms. O'Doole:

Thank you for telling me about your company's management training program last week when you visited Northeast College. I am convinced it is exactly the type of program in which I would like to begin my professional career.	An opening that thanks the reader for the interview and reaffirms the writer's interest in the job.
Especially appreciated was your explaining in detail the types of experiences management trainees have during their participation in the training program. Because I want to explore several managerial areas before making a final career choice, this feature of your program is quite appealing.	A section that presents a discussion of the part of the interview the writer found especially helpful.
If you would find additional information helpful in assessing my qualifications, please let me know. I am confident of my ability to perform well as a management trainee.	A closing that offers to provide additional information and mentions the writer's confidence in his ability to perform well.

Sincerely,

David Greenfield

OPENING

1. Have you thanked the reader for the time he or she spent with you during the interview?
2. Have you mentioned your ability to comply with any special requests the interviewer made of you during the interview, such as providing a transcript?

MIDDLE

1. Have you discussed how you feel about the position for which you interviewed now that you have learned more about it?
2. Have you discussed how certain of your qualifications closely parallel the requirements of the position?
3. Have you expressed your confidence in performing the job tasks well should you have the opportunity?

CLOSING

1. Is your closing courteous?
2. Have you offered to provide the reader with additional information needed in assessing your suitability for the position?
3. Have you expressed a desire to hear from the reader about his or her decision as soon as possible after it has been made?
4. Is the opening you-oriented?

Checklist 10-2 Interview follow-up letter.

Letter of Acceptance

How soon should a letter of acceptance be sent?

You will know your diligent efforts in finding a position have paid off when you receive a job offer (perhaps as early as a few days to perhaps as long as six weeks after your interview). The *letter of employment acceptance* notifies the reader of your interest in the position that he or she has offered you. The letter should be sent fairly soon after the receipt of the offer—perhaps within a week, although don't feel pressured to respond that quickly if you believe you should wait. In such an instance, you should probably inform the prospective employer that you appreciate the offer but that you want to think about it for a short time before making a decision.

The opening of the letter should mention that you appreciate the offer and that you are accepting it. In the following examples, note the more enthusiastic tone of the revision.

Change: I accept your offer to join your staff as a production assistant.
To: Thank you for offering me the position of production assistant. I am pleased to accept the position for a salary of $1.800 a month.

In the next paragraph, you should enthusiastically outline why you believe you will enjoy working for this company. The first of the following paragraphs fails to convey sincere enthusiasm, whereas the revision shows excitement.

Change: I was very impressed by the quality of the working life your company provides its employees.
To: Ever since I made an in-depth study of your company for an assignment in a finance class two years ago, I have wanted to work for Armco. Undertaking this project convinced me that Armco is at the leading edge of the electronics industry. The information I heard during my recent interviews further convinces me of the bright future this company has.

You should also include a statement confirming your starting time and date, as illustrated in the following example.

> Of the two alternative dates you gave me for beginning work, the first date, July 1, is entirely acceptable to me. I will report to Mr. Johnson's office at 8 A.M.

The ending of your letter of acceptance should communicate your enthusiasm and appreciation for the opportunity to work for the company. The first of these lacks enthusiasm or excitement about beginning the job.

> Change: My plans are to report for work at 8 A.M. on July 1.
> To: The opportunity to work for Armco Corporation excites me very much. I am appreciative for having the opportunity to join its staff.

The suggested plan for a letter of acceptance should include these elements:

What is the suggested plan for letters of acceptance?

1. An expression of appreciation for the offer and your acceptance of the offer (Mentioning the job title and the monthly salary is recommended.)
2. A statement suggesting why you believe you will enjoy working for the company
3. A statement specifying your starting time and date
4. A courteous closing, conveying your enthusiasm

A sample letter of acceptance is shown in Exhibit 10-7.

Exhibit 10-7 Effective letter conveying the acceptance of a job offer.

The offer you made me for the position of production assistant in your Toledo plant, paying $2,000 per month, is gratefully accepted.	An opening in which the enthusiastic acceptance of the job offer is conveyed.
The management style used at Jimanez Corporation is especially attractive to me. I sincerely believe that most employees want to be able to provide more input into their jobs and also that their input can be a significant contributor to organizational success. The extensive use of participative management throughout Jimanez Corporation undoubtedly contributes considerably to its success.	A section that presents a discussion about why the writer is pleased to be able to work for the company.
The starting date of May 12 is acceptable to me. I will report to Mr. Thompson's office at 8 A.M.	A section that discusses the writer's plans for beginning work.
The opportunity to work for Jimanez Corporation is appreciated. I am enthusiastic about beginning my career as a production assistant.	A closing that conveys enthusiasm.

Letter of Refusal

Although the *letter of employment refusal*, which notifies the reader that you are not accepting the position he or she offered you, is basically a negative letter, you should avoid including material in the letter that may cause the reader to develop anything but a positive reaction toward you. You may not be interested in working for this particular company at the present time, but you may be in the future. As a general rule, make the reasons for declining the job as impersonal as possible. Furthermore, you will want to avoid hurting the reader's feelings.

The opening of the letter of refusal should express appreciation for having been offered a job. In the first of the following examples, the writer is too blunt; the revised version is more courteous.

What information should be included in the opening of letters of refusal?

Change: Because I have accepted a job in another company, I am not interested in your offer.
To: Thank you for offering me an auditor's position in your Accounting Department.

After the opening, you should provide an impersonal, brief explanation of your main reasons for declining the offer. Note the insulting tone of the explanation in the first sample and the tactful tone of the explanation in the revision.

What information should be included in the middle section of letters of refusal?

Change: The company in which I accepted a job offer has more to offer its new, young employees than any other company I interviewed.
To: At the time of the interview, I explained why a staff accounting position was my first job choice. Dartwell Corporation of Memphis has offered me a staff accounting position that I have accepted.

The closing of a letter of refusal should provide a courteous expression of appreciation, incorporating a you-attitude tone.

What information should be included in the closing of letters of refusal?

Change: I am glad I had the opportunity to talk with you about this position.
To: Your taking time to discuss career opportunities in your company is greatly appreciated.

The suggested plan for a letter in which a job offer is declined includes the following elements:

What is the suggested plan for letters of refusal?

1. A courteous opening in which you express appreciation for having been offered a job
2. An impersonal—but brief—explanation of the reasons for your declining the offer
3. A courteous closing

Exhibit 10-8 shows a sample letter of refusal.

Thanks for offering me a position in your Public Relations Department.	An opening in which the writer expresses appreciation for the offer.
During one of my interviews, I indicated my preference, if given the opportunity, would be to work in Atlanta. I will have that opportunity as Reston Paper Company has offered me a position that I've accepted.	A section that presents an impersonal discussion of why the writer is not accepting the offer.
Your interest in and concern for me as an applicant for a job in your company was especially gratifying.	A cordial closing.

Exhibit 10-8 Effective letter of refusal.

Letter of Resignation

Although you may have negative feelings about a job, expressing them in a *letter of resignation*, which officially notifies the reader that you are terminating employment, is inappropriate. The writer gains nothing from revealing such feelings—and perhaps has much to lose. For example, the person accepting the resignation is likely to remember the negative comments when asked to recommend the former employee for another job. This, in turn, may result in a less-than-enthusiastic recommendation. Most businesspeople believe the *exit interview* is the appropriate time for an employee to express the negative feelings about the job.

What information is included in the opening of letters of resignation?

The opening of the letter of resignation should begin with a courteous statement of your intent to resign and the reason for your resignation. The first example offers no explanation, whereas the revision corrects the omission.

Change: I hereby resign from my present position, effective July 31.
To: Having accepted another job that will enable me to take advantage of new job skills recently acquired through the completion of the master's degree course work, I have decided to resign from my present job effective July 31.

What information is included in the middle section of letters of resignation?

In the middle section of the letter of resignation, discuss the elements of your present job that have been especially enjoyable. Here is an example of this message.

The five years that I have worked for Bagnell Company have been most enjoyable. Especially rewarding were the opportunities I had to orient and train new employees. In fact, working with new employees is so enjoyable that I chose training and development as the major thrust of my master's degree.

What information is included in the closing section of letters of resignation?

The closing of the letter of resignation should contain a sincere statement of appreciation. The first of the following paragraphs lacks sincerity, whereas the revision strikes a sincere note.

Change: Thanks for all that you have done for me.
To: Mr. Jones, you are largely responsible for the satisfying and fulfilling experience I have had here. I will always be grateful to you for encouraging me to be creative and innovative in my job.

The suggested plan for a letter of resignation contains the following elements:

What is the suggested plan for letters of resignation?

1. A courteous opening stating your intent to resign from your present position and the reason for the resignation
2. An identification of the aspects of your position you have enjoyed or found beneficial
3. A courteous closing

Exhibit 10-9 is an effective letter of resignation.

The following Ethics Episode discusses the importance of providing accurate information in your employment-related messages.

ETHICS EPISODE

A growing number of employers are discovering an increasing percentage of job applicants are embellishing their application materials to the extent that applicants' qualifications are mildly to grossly overstated. Among the reasons qualifications are overstated are the following:

1. A desire among applicants to make themselves more competitive
2. A desire on the part of job placement services—companies that prepare the résumé and letter of application—for their clients to be successful in obtaining a permanent position for a high percentage of their clients
3. A natural tendency for some applicants to overrate or overassess the worth of some of their qualifications for a position

Whether the embellishment of one's qualifications is knowingly or unknowingly done, the outcome is the same: The person who does it or permits it is being unethical. When the embellishment of one's qualifications results in an unfair employment advantage, the seriousness of one's actions increases.

Consider the following situations that result in unethical behavior on the part of a job applicant:

1. Suppose you have been a member of a number of campus organizations during the time you've been in college, including several organizations related to your major and several campus-service organizations. However, except for one of these organizations, you are only a dues-paying member. With the others, you attend none of their meetings nor do you participate in any of their activities. You list all of these organizations on your résumé and indicate in your letter of application that you have been "extensively involved in campus activities," hoping the reader believes you have well-developed leadership skills. This is a deceitful embellishment of one of your qualifications. Being a dues-paying member and being an active, involved member are two different things.
2. Suppose you were asked, as part of the process of applying for a position in the human resources department of a large company, to provide a sample of your writing. The purpose for submitting the writing sample is to judge how well you write, which is an important requirement for the position inasmuch as writing is a frequent job duty. Your writing skills are generally considered as being "quite average"—neither excellent nor poor. Accordingly, you decided to have a senior English major write the sample you submit. During your interview, several employees mentioned to you how well written your sample was. Just as your having someone write a paper for you that you submit as a requirement in a college course represents academic dishonesty, your having someone write the sample you submit for your application represents unethical behavior.

During the application process, some employers attempt to determine whether applicants cheated during their college experiences. Thus, they may talk to applicants' professors and/or advisers, or college/university student conduct officers, or the applicants during the interview if they cheated during college. Increasingly, employers believe that engaging in unethical behavior in college is a prelude to engaging in unethical behavior in the workplace.

Because I have accepted another job that will enable me to become extensively involved in computer systems, I wish to resign from my present job, effective June 30.	An opening that mentions the writer's intention to resign.
On several occasions I have mentioned to you a desire to become more involved with computer systems because that is the area of greatest personal interest. The various positions I've held here have given me the necessary background to become more involved in computer systems. Your letting me expand my job duties was also beneficial as I was able to become more knowledgeable about this area.	A section that presents an impersonal discussion of the reasons for the resignation.
Ms. Brown, I will always be appreciative for all that you've done for me while I've worked here.	A closing that expresses appreciation for having had the opportunity to work for the present employer.

Exhibit 10-9 Effective letter of resignation.

SUMMARY

In preparing an effective letter of application, you need to be aware of the qualities of well-written application letters and the content typically included in the opening, middle, and closing sections.

Other types of letters used in the employment process are interview follow-up letters, letters of acceptance, letters of refusal, and letters of resignation. Each type of letter has a standard plan, which will be useful to follow in writing such letters.

Your ability to prepare effective employment-related letters is a skill you will use throughout your career.

REVIEW QUESTIONS

1. How do the three different types of letters of application differ from one another?
2. Identify the qualities of effective letters of application.
3. What is the purpose of the opening section of a letter of application?
4. What different types of content can be in the opening of a letter of application?
5. What elements can be in the middle section of a letter of application?
6. In writing the work experience section of a letter of application, what should you try to show?
7. What is the purpose of the closing section of a letter of application?
8. What constitutes an effective opening in an interview follow-up letter?
9. What types of material can be in the closing of an interview follow-up letter?
10. What are the elements of an effective job acceptance letter?
11. What are the elements of an effective job resignation letter?

APPLICATION PROBLEMS

1. Critique the following letter of application for its grammar usage, punctuation, conformity with essential elements of a letter of application, and conformity with the writing essentials presented in Chapters 3 and 4.

> I may be just the hard working, dedicated sales representative you recently advertised for. If being judged the marketing major most likely to succeed—which I was—means anything, then I am certain I could the successful employee you are looking for, please give me a chance to prove my worth you.

During the three years I have attended State College, I have always made the deans list. In fact, because of my above average intelligence, I have been able to handle an accelerated academic load which will enable me to graduate in three and one-half years.

Because I was so busy with various campus activities and studying, I did not have time for a part-time job. But then I really didn't need to work as my parents are financially able to put me through college. In the summers, I chose to travel rather than work, and got to spend three summers in Europe.

Heres hoping you will give me the opportunity to prove my worth to you by inviting me to come for an interview.

2. Critique the following letter for its grammar usage, punctuation, conformity with essential elements of an interview follow-up letter, and conformity with the writing essentials in Chapters 3 and 4.

I sure did enjoy the time I spend with you last Tuesday when you chatted with me about the opening in your company. I must say that of all the interviews I have had so far, you done a better job of explaining to me the requirements of the job you are looking to fill. So many times interviewers are not all that familiar with the job duties and that leaves me with lots of questions.

If only I can have an opportunity to work for your company, I can prove to the higher-ups that I am a worthy employee. If I didn't believe that I wouldn't be applying for a job.

I told you that I would let you know what kind of perfume I was wearing at the interview. As I told you, I borrowed it from my roommate and didn't pay any attention to what it was. It was "Scandia". I am sure your wife would greatly apprecaite a bottle.

Please let me hear from you soon as I have to make a decision before to much longer.

3. (Solicited letter of application) You will be graduating from college at the end of this semester and are now beginning to look for full-time employment. Prepare a letter of application for a job opening you learned about from your major adviser, who believes you are especially well qualified for the job. By the way, your adviser knows Mr. Jack Harmeson, the individual to whom you are to send your letter of application.
4. (Unsolicited letter of application) You will be graduating from college at the end of this semester. Because you want to live in Denver after graduating (the college you attend is on the West Coast), you do not have many leads on actual openings. You decide to send several letters inquiring into the possibility of openings in several companies for which you would like to work. Prepare a letter in which you present your qualifications, in addition to inquiring about the possibility of an opening.
5. (Interview follow-up letter) You have applied for several jobs in a variety of companies. So far your efforts have resulted in your being interviewed for positions in two companies. One of the jobs for which you have interviewed really appeals to you. Write the interviewer a follow-up letter in which you mention that you were especially intrigued by management-by-objectives philosophy of the company as well as intrigued by its flexible benefits package. Convey your impression that you are well qualified for the position.
6. (Job acceptance letter) You have just received a job offer from the company that you were so impressed with in application problem 5. You received an attractive offer for the job you really want. Write a letter of acceptance and confirm your intention of beginning work at 8 A.M. on May 10, two days after your college graduation. Convey your enthusiasm for having the opportunity to work for this company.

7. (Job refusal letter) You have just received a job offer from the company that you thought you were so impressed with in application problem 5. Now that you have had an opportunity to learn more about the job and the company during the home-office interview, you have decided to accept another offer—one from a company that you believe better meets your needs. Specifically, you want to work for an international company, with the expectation that you may eventually have a job abroad. The company that you were originally so impressed with is not an international company—and the more you learned about international companies, the greater was your desire to work in one.
8. (Job resignation letter) You have now worked for three years in the company whose job offer you accepted after graduating from college. You had hoped during that time to get an overseas assignment. So far, this hope has not materialized, and the prospects of it materializing in the near future seem rather bleak. You recently had a job offer from another international firm, and this job will immediately take you to the company's Paris office. You have decided to accept the job offer. Write a letter, stating your intention to resign from your present job sixty days from today. Explain your reasons for accepting the new job. During the time you have worked for your present employer, you have been especially pleased with the assistance you received from several people, including your immediate supervisor—the person to whom you are sending your letter of resignation. You appreciate your supervisor's continual encouragement, her giving you a chance to try new things (some of which worked and others that didn't), and her letting you assume new tasks only when she was certain that you were ready.

11

Communicating through Interviews

After studying this chapter, you should be able to

1. Identify the most common types of business interviews.
2. Describe the purpose of the different types of business interviews.
3. Discuss the differences among the types of questions used in business interviews.
4. Identify several ways of increasing the effectiveness of employment interviews.
5. Participate in an effective employment interview.

Business personnel spend a large part of their time interviewing and being interviewed. Interviewing is a skill essential to professional success and one that most interviewers need to develop. Interviewing skills, like so many other types of communication, are developed through practice. This chapter provides interviewing tips and information. But it is the practice in interviewing that will help you become an effective participant in the interview process. Therefore, we discuss the various types of interviews as well as common interview questions. Because you will be involved with employment interviews as part of the job-hunting process, the major focus of this chapter is employment interviews.

An interview, regardless of its type, includes two or more people who assume different communication roles. The *interviewer* is responsible for arranging the interview, including such items as time, location, and purpose of the interview. In addition, the interviewer often assumes the responsibility for determining the format for the interview. The format is usually informal, but some interviewers prepare a checklist or outline of the specific points or questions they want to cover. Although this procedure aids memory, it should be a guide rather than an inflexible plan. Interviews that become too structured lose spontaneity, flexibility, and realism. The best interviews allow the participants to adjust to each other.

The *interviewee* must also prepare carefully for the interview. Important points for the interviewee to consider include the intended purpose of the interview and the expectation of the interviewer. One of the best ways for an interviewee to plan for an interview is to anticipate the kinds of questions the interviewer might ask. If you are the interviewee, you might even consider drawing up a list of possible questions. Communication Capsule 11-1 is an interview preparation checklist.

Communication Capsule 11-1 Interview Preparation Checklist—Employment

```
I.   Investigate the employment market   ______
     Study the job market to determine exactly which types of organizations are of interest
     to you. Contact industry personnel:
     A. People who do what you would like to do
     B. Successful people from this field
     C. Individuals who possess important information that you need
II.  Prepare for specific information   ______
     A. Major journals or magazines
     B. Career specific jargon
     C. Problems in the profession
III. Plan for a good impression   ______
     A. Dress appropriately.
     B. Arrive on time.
     C. Maintain effective eye contact.
     D. Utilize an enthusiastic voice.
IV.  Responding to questions   ______
     A. Anticipate all types of questions.
        1. Personal information
        2. Educational background
        3. General abilities
        4. Work experience
     B. Guidelines for answering
        1. Be clear.
        2. Be concise.
        3. Be positive.
        4. Be courteous.
V.   Closing stage of the interview   ______
     A. Watch for indications of the end of the interview.
     B. Anticipate an opportunity to ask questions that you may have.
     C. Do not be shocked if a position is offered on the spot.
     D. Close with courtesy and sincerity.
```

Obviously, potential interview areas are nearly limitless; therefore, constructing a document similar to the checklist shown in the communication capsule is useful as a preparation tool. However, you should not take this document with you to the actual interview because it will tend to structure your responses and make you appear less spontaneous.

BASIC ORGANIZATION OF INTERVIEWS

What phases are found in the basic organization of interviews?

Whatever the basic type and goal of the interview, its organization includes three phases: the opening phase, the question-response phase, and the closing phase. An effective opening establishes rapport between the communicators. An effective question-response phase is truly the heart of the interview, in which both communicators ask questions, respond to statements, and provide feedback. An effective closing summarizes the major points covered and conclusions reached.

The Opening Phase

The *opening phase* of an interview is essential for making the interviewee feel at ease. An effective opening includes three basic elements: rapport, orientation, and motivation. Rapport is the establishment of a comfortable, relaxed feeling that allows the communicators to become and remain receptive to the interview. Established in the first few minutes of the interview, rapport has a great impact on its ultimate outcome.

Creating an environment that encourages rapport rests more heavily on the interviewer because he or she is in control of the interview setting. The interviewer can take steps to ensure an environment that is free from distractions. In addition, the interviewer can move to a position that is near the interviewee, rather than remain sitting behind a desk. When the interviewee arrives, the interviewer should rise, shake hands, and make the person feel welcome. Conversation should remain relaxed and, when possible, center around common interests, current events, mutual acquaintances, and even the weather if it is unusual. The interviewee can help establish rapport by creating a good first impression through arriving on time, dressing appropriately, being prepared, and appearing confident and relaxed.

The *orientation aspect* refers to establishing a mutually clear overall view of the purpose for the interview. An effective orientation includes the following:

What aspects are included in the orientation aspect?

1. Verification of the interviewee's name.
2. The interviewer's name and the reason for the interview. This is especially important in the exit, grievance, and performance-appraisal interviews.
3. Purpose or desired outcome of the interview. Even when the purpose seems obvious, never assume mutual understanding. The purpose should always be summarized by the interviewer.
4. Identification of desired information and how it will be used.
5. Estimated length of the interview as a common courtesy to the interviewee.

The final aspect of the opening phase of an interview is motivation. Experienced interviewers realize that having a person show up for an interview does not mean that the individual will provide honest, candid responses. Motivation techniques vary depending on the person being interviewed and the reasons for the interview. Appeals may be made to the interviewee's honesty, pride, ambition, leadership, or desire to assist others. The interviewer may provide motivation by including information about the importance of the application process to the overall continued success of the organization.

An exit interview is most successful when interviewees can be motivated to answer candidly and accurately. Interviewees are informed that their comments will not become part of a permanent file but rather will help open management's eyes to areas that need greater attention. In addition, friends and fellow workers may ultimately benefit from candid, truthful, and carefully considered responses. During an information-seeking interview, interviewees can be motivated by direct or indirect appeals to their sense of honesty and integrity.

Question-Response Phase

Regardless of the type of interview, participants should carefully prepare for the question-response phase. Effective questions are seldom composed on the spur of the moment nor do interviewees possess the ability to prepare answers to questions when taken completely by surprise.

Before the interview, the interviewer should plan for the question-response phase by deciding what information needs to be sought, verified, or provided. Only then can the interviewer design questions to collect desired facts and information. Anticipating probable interviewee responses will also help the interviewer appropriately adjust the nature or organization of the questions.

Meanwhile, before the interview, the interviewee should anticipate possible questions and then carefully outline the information he or she wishes to communicate to the interviewer. For example, grievance interviews require the interviewee to anticipate questions about the exact nature of the grievance. The grievance interview requires the interviewee to bring appropriate documentation. In contrast, appraisal interviews require the interviewee to anticipate questions about facts and information on his or her strengths, weaknesses, accomplishments, and future performance objectives. Thus, the employment interview requires the interviewee to come to the interview with a list of strengths, areas of knowledge, and past accomplishments (typically in résumé form).

Closing Phase

The closing of an interview should be mutually agreed upon by communicators. The *closing phase*, as indicated, includes a summary of the major points covered during the interview and any possible conclusions. Besides the summary and conclusions, the closing phase should also contain agreement on what steps both parties should take in the future, including arranging, if necessary, another meeting.

A final element aspect of the closing phase is the ending. Here, both the interviewer and the interviewee express appreciation for time spent and cooperation shown.

TYPES OF INTERVIEWS

Among the various types of interviews common to the business world are employment interviews, performance-appraisal interviews, disciplinary interviews, persuasive interviews, and exit interviews. Each has specific uses.

Employment Interviews

What types of interviews are found in the business world?

An employment interview is the most important aspect of the job-seeking process. Your letter of application and résumé initiate a process that finally leads to an actual interview. The *employment interview* is the employment procedure that determines who will actually be hired.

What two types of employment interviews are used?

Two types of employment interviews are used in the employment process: the initial interview, which is a screening interview, and the office interview reserved for the finalists of the initial interview. The purpose of the initial interview is to determine whether the applicant possesses the minimum qualifications for the job. An office interview is designed to assess the applicant's poise, enthusiasm, interests, and communication skill. The two types of employment interviews are covered in detail in the last section of this chapter.

Appraisal Interviews

What is the purpose of the performance-appraisal interview?

Performance-appraisal interviews provide feedback to employees about the quality of their work performances. Companies usually schedule interviews on a regular basis—perhaps every six months during the employee's probationary period and once a year thereafter. An appraisal interview should capitalize on the strengths of the interviewee and minimizes the weaknesses. Employees are usually aware of their own weaknesses, so an extensive discussion of them is considered counterproductive. Disciplinary action should not occur during a performance-appraisal interview. Action against an employee whose performance is substandard is an appropriate activity of the disciplinary interview.

The performance-appraisal interview has grown in popularity to the extent that more than 80 percent of various organizations in business, government, education, industry, and service use it.

Included in the following Ethics Episode are suggestions for improving the ethical nature of the performance-appraisal process.

ETHICS EPISODE

Sometimes people are promoted to managerial-type positions because they possess highly regarded technical knowledge, and little consideration is given to their communication ability. The situation often becomes even more problematic because of the lack of training on effective interviewing techniques that these new managers receive.

Performance-appraisal interviews require interviewers to identify positive behavior that interviewees should exhibit. In addition, neither supervisors nor interviewees should dominate the proceedings. Experience provides a person with interviewing techniques that may have proven to be effective and efficient in the past. However, both the interviewer and the interviewee may believe that his or her knowledge about performance appraisal is the best and perhaps is even the only way to accomplish the task. This lack of objectivity on the part of both the interviewer and the interviewee is more often than not the major reason for ineffective performance-appraisal interviews.

Suggestions for conducting effective and ethical performance-appraisal interviews are as follows:

1. Determine the objective criteria by which to judge the performance.
2. Prepare a balanced exchange of information and ideas, ranging from ideal performance to actual results.
3. Carefully differentiate between an employee who *will not* work and an employee who *cannot* work.
4. Guard against becoming defensive, and plan your remarks to minimize the chance of the interviewee also becoming defensive.
5. Make an open, honest, and informal appraisal.
6. Provide complete, factual, and detailed information.

Interviewers should set the parameters about what is and is not negotiable during the interview. They also should allow interviewees to question authority without fear of penalty.

A performance-appraisal interview should be designed to improve performance. Therefore, the more effective performance-appraisal interviews result in a specific plan for performance improvement. The plan typically specifies who will do what, when it will be done, and how it will be evaluated and adjusted.

Interviewing techniques often appear to be straightforward and easy to arrange. But managers with or without experience in performance-appraisal interviews should understand that possession of power and authority and protecting the worth and dignity of the person being evaluated always require exacting, ethical procedures.

A key part of performance-appraisal interviews is the joint determination of ways or strategies for the person being rated to overcome his or her weaknesses. Discussing this is far more useful than a lengthy discussion of weaknesses. A person being rated is usually quite concerned about the performance-appraisal interview because he or she fears that a poor-quality interview will make salary increases and promotions more difficult.

Disciplinary Interviews

What is the purpose of the disciplinary interview?

When an employee needs a reprimand for actions that are inconsistent with policy, procedure, or expectation, or the employee's actions need some correction, companies turn to the *disciplinary interview.* The disciplinary interview occurs on an as-needed basis. Typically conducted by the employee's supervisor, it is supposed to help the interviewee eliminate the behavior or actions that necessitate the disciplinary action.

The disciplinary interview begins with the identification of the problem that needs correction. If possible, the interviewee should introduce a desirable solution for the problem. This technique is designed to lead the interviewee to disclose why the problem persists and, when feasible, how he or she thinks the difficulty might be resolved.

Depending on the nature of the problem, the interviewer should consider obtaining legal counsel before conducting a disciplinary interview, especially if the situation may result in the interviewee's taking legal action against the interviewer or the company. The National Labor Relations Board and the U.S. Supreme Court concur that an employee has the right to request third-party representation at any disciplinary interview. Therefore, supervisors are encouraged to design the disciplinary interview format around the following questions that the employee would want answered:

1. What was done wrong?
2. Why was it wrong?
3. What is the penalty?
4. Is the penalty fair?
5. What will happen if the problem persists?
6. What can be done to improve performance or behavior?

The disciplinary interview is a procedure of last resort. Only when all else has failed should the company take such a drastic step. The major disadvantage of disciplinary interviews is the continuing defensiveness of the interviewee if the procedure is not handled skillfully.

Persuasive Interviews

What is the purpose of the persuasive interview?

The purpose of the *persuasive interview* is—as you might expect—to persuade someone to take a specific action. The strategy generally followed is for the interviewer to outline the desired action and to provide a rationale for that action. The employee should then have an opportunity to react, after which the interviewer may offer additional persuasive information. The types of situations eliciting persuasive interviews range from the simple (asking the interviewee to represent you at a meeting) to the complex (convincing the interviewee to take on expanded job duties).

Many superior-subordinate situations are actually persuasive interviews. Convincing your boss you deserve a raise or persuading your coworkers to accept your suggestions for reorganization of position responsibilities are examples of persuasive interviews. During these interviews, the persuasive techniques should be neither coercive nor dishonest. This means avoiding trickery of all kinds. Instead, persuasive interviews must appeal to the values and needs of the interviewee. The facts and evidence the interviewer uses should relate to the interests and opinions of the interviewee, rather than making comparisons with other employees, or to the well-being of the entire organization.

Exit Interviews

What is the purpose of the exit interview?

An *exit interview* takes place when an employee terminates his or her association with an organization. The interview should occur on one of the last days the employee is on the job. Someone other than the employee's immediate supervisor typically conducts the interview. In many cases, the interviewer is from the personnel department.

The exit interview is designed to obtain feedback to enable the organization to implement changes that improve its operating effectiveness. For example, suppose a number of employees are leaving because of low pay. Unless this information is made available to the appropriate individuals, the high attrition rate will probably continue with the most-valued employees at special risk. Therefore, if the organization has the financial resources to increase employees' salaries, it must seriously consider this possibility.

In exit interviews, interviewers must be skilled in "reading between the lines." In some cases, employees will try to disguise their true feelings, especially if they are negative. For example, an employee who is leaving for another job in the same industry may want to keep open the possibility of working for the company once again several years from now. When a discrepancy occurs between what employees verbalize and what their nonverbal cues communicate, the nonverbal communications are generally more accurate.

TYPES OF QUESTIONS USED IN INTERVIEWS

Among the types of interview questions are open questions, closed questions, loaded questions, neutral questions, probing questions, leading questions, and mirror questions. Each type is used to accomplish a specific purpose.

Open Questions

What are open questions?

Open questions give the interviewee leeway in responding, because they are quite broad and so generally require a fairly lengthy answer. When asking open questions, the interviewer introduces the topic or subject on which he or she wishes the interviewee to expound.

Among the advantages of open questions are the following: Their general nature encourages the interviewee to view them as nonthreatening; they are typically easy to answer; and they give the interviewee an opportunity to do more of the talking and the interviewer an opportunity to observe.

Disadvantages of open questions are their time-consuming nature and the difficulty in quantifying answers, which may create problems when trying to compare applicants' answers. The following are examples of open questions:

1. Can you tell me about your childhood?
2. Why do you want to work for our company?
3. What is your philosophy of life?
4. What is your educational background?
5. What is your evaluation of this company?

Closed Questions

What are closed questions?

Closed questions, which are much more restrictive than open questions, are used to solicit responses that are typically brief and, at times, require only a few words.

The advantages of closed questions in contrast to open questions include the following: Answers consume less time, answers are less difficult to quantify, and inexperienced interviewers find them easier to use. The disadvantages of closed questions are these: Answers tend to provide limited information, and, because of this, the interviewer's ability to evaluate certain elements of the interviewee's communication skill is more limited.

Examples of closed questions include the following;

1. Which course in your major did you like best?
2. Do you feel you have well-developed leadership skills?
3. How many brothers and sisters do you have?
4. Do you feel communication skill is important to a salesperson?
5. Did you make the reservations for this trip?

Loaded Questions

What are loaded questions?

Loaded questions are designed to direct the interviewee's response. Their nature makes them unsuitable for certain types of interviews because they place the person being interviewed under pressure and create a stressful situation. As you will see from the following examples, a loaded question often requires the interviewee to justify his or her attitudes, beliefs, or actions:

1. Why is your grade point average so low?
2. Why haven't you participated in more extracurricular activities?
3. What do you like least about your present job?
4. You perform effectively under pressure, don't you?
5. Explain why you would be in favor of labor unions?

Leading Questions

What are leading questions?

Leading questions guide the interviewee in a specific direction—but not to the degree that loaded questions do. Many interviewers use leading questions to verify the accuracy of information offered by the interviewee. When improperly used, leading questions may bias the interviewee's responses because they often appear to request action that may appear unnecessary, unimportant, or at times even illegal. Examples of leading questions include the following:

1. You do have a car, don't you?
2. You have enjoyed college, haven't you?
3. You do have a good relationship with your present supervisor, don't you?
4. Don't you think our president is a super guy?
5. You wouldn't mind some extensive travel, would you?

Neutral Questions

What are neutral questions?

Neutral questions differ from leading or loaded questions in that they do not attempt to direct or guide the interviewee's responses. The main advantage of neutral questions is that they are pressure-free and so do not create as stressful a situation for the interviewee as some loaded or leading questions often do. Examples of neutral questions are:

1. How do you feel about management by objectives?
2. How do you feel about participating in a six-month training program?
3. Why did you choose to minor in _______?
4. How do you like your new position?
5. How well do you get along with Mary?

Probing Questions

What are probing questions?

Probing questions are unplanned and result from the interviewee's remarks. Interviewers ask questions to clarify or to gain additional information about an earlier response. Some examples of probing questions are the following:

1. Why do you feel that your education has not been put to good use in your present job?
2. Why do you think the future is bright for accountants?
3. Why would you want to leave a job that you really like?
4. How does your work experience add to your overall ability?
5. Explain why your GPA is so high.

Mirror Questions

What are mirror questions?

Interviewers use *mirror questions* to solicit additional information from the person being interviewed. These questions mirror the interviewee's previous response. A portion of the interviewee's previous answer is incorporated into the next question to elicit greater depth and quality of information. When an interviewee's response needs amplification, the interviewer can ask for clarification by simply repeating the response either verbatim or by a paraphrase.

> Interviewee's response: I really like my present supervisor because he continually challenges me.
> Interviewer's question: Challenges you?

Interviews need not be a stressful experience that is dominated by the interviewer. Through research, planning, and self-assurance, the interviewee can transform the interview process into meaningful dialogue for both participants.

Preparing for the Employment Interview

What should you do to prepare for the employment interview?

An employment interview is actually a discovery process in which the interviewer and the interviewee attempt to gain additional information from each other. The interviewee wants to learn more about the company and the job, whereas the interviewer wants to learn more about the interviewee's background and capabilities.

Communication Capsule 11-2 identifies a number of things you, the interviewee, should avoid during a job interview.

Communication Capsule 11-2 Things Not to Do during a Job Interview

The main purpose of an employment interview is to encourage communication between the interviewer and the interviewee. The interviewer is trained to appraise what you say, how you say it, how you walk, how you sit, your eye contact, and your listening and concentration ability. The following is a listing of what an interviewee should not do during an interview:

1. Do not be late for your interview. In fact, you should plan to arrive a few minutes early in case one of the previous interviews did not consume the allotted time.
2. Do not play with your watch, with money in your pocket, with your ring, with your hair, or with any items that may be placed on the interviewer's desk close to your chair.
3. Do not mumble or say "you know" or "OK."
4. Do not use slang, swear, crack jokes, chew gum, smoke, or lie.
5. Do not lean on the interviewer's desk, interrupt, glance at your watch, or constantly adjust your tie or other clothing.
6. Do not wear excessive jewelry, sunglasses, winter coats, gloves, hats, caps, or scarves.
7. Do not hide any aspect of your previous record, overstate qualifications, brag, become angry, call the interviewer by his/her first name, or become involved in any negative aspect of your current employer, classes, or university.
8. Do not talk nonstop, too fast, too softly, or without emotion.
9. Do not ask about your chances for the position.
10. Do not bring up the topic of salary. When the time is right, salary will be discussed.

A firm handshake is important during the initial contact. Offer your hand to an interviewer first and maintain firm, even pressure during the handshake. The length of a handshake will vary, but a minimum of three seconds and a maximum of five seconds is a common length of time for a handshake. Do not worry if your hands are always cold or if your hands appear a bit damp from nervousness. You can do nothing about these minor physical problems, so simply prepare yourself for a statement about cold or damp hands. Refusing to shake hands is not an appropriate solution to cold or damp hands. Wait to sit until requested by the interviewer, and be certain to sit erect but not so stiff that it appears abnormal.

Even though you may have already provided the interviewer with information about your background, he or she will be interested in learning more about you. The interviewer will be evaluating your character, your motivation, your intelligence, your ethics, and your personal values. Do not become too concerned about questions the interviewer utilizes to assess your employment potential. However, you should be able to identify an illegal question if it is asked either intentionally or unintentionally.

What kinds of questions cannot be asked during the employment interview?

Federal and state laws outline the kinds of questions interviewers cannot ask of applicants. These detailed laws are based on the belief that all persons, regardless of race, sex, national origin, religion, age, or marital status should be able to compete for jobs and advance in the job market according to their occupational qualifications such as: experience, education, and specific skills. An employer is not required to hire anyone who is not qualified; but race, sex, national origin, religion, age, or marital status cannot be used to judge an applicant's qualifications. Skills, experiences, and education are the factors that determine an individual's qualifications for the job. Communication Capsule 11-3 provides additional information about legal/illegal questions.

Communication Capsule 11-3 Discriminatory Questions Forbidden by Law[1]

Prospective employers are legally required to offer equal opportunity; therefore, the law forbids certain discriminatory questions. The Equal Employment Opportunity Commission (EEOC) provides specific regulations about the types of questions and information employers may request. These regulations not only protect women and members of minority groups but also identify discriminatory questions against both sexes based on race and age. According to these regulations, interviewers may not ask about the following during job interviews:

1. An applicant's race or color of skin.
2. An applicant's religious denomination or affiliation.
3. An applicant's lineage.
4. An applicant's citizenship.
5. An applicant's military discharge record.
6. An applicant's membership in clubs, organizations, or lodges.
7. An applicant's marital status, or former name.
8. An applicant's personal family situation such as: names and relationships of people with whom he/she lives; questions concerning spouse's employment, salary, dependents, children, or child care arrangements.
9. Questions about height, weight, gender, pregnancy, or disability unless they are linked to actual job requirements.
10. An applicant's health, unless it is related to job performance ability.
11. A photograph of the applicant or questions about his or her color of skin, hair, or eyes.
12. An applicant's arrests or prior criminal convictions that are not reasonably related to fitness to perform the job.
13. Questions about convictions that are more than seven years old.

[1]*EEOC Laws, Regulations and Orders, Part III* (Washington, D.C.: U.S. Printing Office, 1978), pp. 1–11.

You may decide to answer an illegal interview question that presents no real harm to you. For example, your health may be excellent and so a question about it may not seem to pose any problem. However, after responding to the question, you should consider informing the interviewer that you are aware of the law and wish to learn how the question directly applies to job requirements. When the illegal question is such that a reply can damage your employment potential, you should decline to answer. However, be aware that this may cost you the job.

Moreover, if you believe that the interviewer's questions are venturing into illegal or discriminatory areas, you may have a cause for legal action. Formal complaints can be filed with the EEOC or a state agency responsible for the monitoring of fair employment practices. When discriminatory questions cross over into the area of physical disability, you may contact the U.S. Department of Labor or the corporation's equal opportunity officer. Always consider the overall impact of your action (or inaction), because your recollection of the actual questions and events will be judged against those of the interviewer. You may jeopardize money, time, and good will; and even jobs may be in jeopardy if you decide to file formal charges.

Tips for a Successful Interview

Before the interview, you may have conducted an informal investigation into the company but still desire more information about its inner workings and detailed specifics about the job for which you are being interviewed.

As an interviewee, anticipate being asked to complete an application form. The various forms companies use are similar in form and style, although some may include specific questions common to a particular field or specialty. A few examples of important items of information on application forms are the following:

1. The names, addresses, titles, and phone numbers of individuals who can attest to your ability and accomplishments. These are the persons you list as references.
2. Your social security number.
3. Your employment experience, including the names and addresses of your current and previous supervisors.
4. Your educational preparation, including college/university attended, dates attended, major, and degree awarded.
5. A list of your special skills and qualifications.

Once the interview date has been set, you should begin preparing for the interview. Your preparation should include undertaking appropriate research that will help you strengthen your personal credibility plus enhancing your personal self-assurance. Learning more about the company will stop you from asking elementary and irritating questions as well as demonstrate personal interest in and enthusiasm for the organization and the job.

Many excellent sources are available for gaining facts and information about the company. The following sources are particularly helpful: the company's annual report, *Dun and Bradstreet's Million Dollar Directory*, *Moody's Manual*, and *Poor's Register*.

As you conduct your research, become familiar with the following types of information that should be useful during the actual interview:

1. Name of major company officers
2. The products the company manufactures or sells (or its chief type of business)
3. Annual gross revenues
4. Recent and/or significant accomplishments of the company
5. Significant problems experienced by the company
6. Projected future outlook for the company

Becoming familiar with this information and incorporating it into your answers and/or questions, you will distinguish yourself as a well-prepared applicant. For example, asking "What is the company's gross revenue?" is less impressive than asking, "Considering last year's gross revenue of $850 million, what are the company's plans to expand into other areas or products?"

Handling Interview Details

The following personal organization suggestions will help you prepare for the logistics of the interview:

1. Record the date, time, and place of the interview. Obtain the interviewer's name and become familiar with his or her position. Many interviews are arranged over the telephone; this suggestion will help you avoid forgetting this vital information.
2. Review your résumé. Try to determine areas that may require additional clarification or areas on your data sheet that are likely to generate questions. Determine the types of additional information the interviewer may ask you to provide.
3. Compose answers to questions the interviewer is likely to ask you about, such as your goals, achievements, and activities.
4. Become familiar with both the company and the position. Be prepared to ask pertinent questions to obtain additional information that will help you assess the position and/or the company.

5. Attempt to gain additional information about the interviewer's background, job title, and the level of authority he or she has for the actual hiring process.
6. Become familiar with nonverbal cues that can enhance your interviewing performance. Included are such cues as proper eye contact, a poised appearance, and a relaxed (but not too relaxed) image.

During the Interview

The interviewer will begin to evaluate you the moment you meet face-to-face. Obviously, proper eye contact is essential, but also important are a firm handshake, self-assurance, and appropriate assertiveness. Interviewers are trained to evaluate both what you say and how well you say it; the interviewer often forms an initial impression of your employment acceptability within the first few minutes of the interview.

During the interview, you must be a good listener. Like writing and speaking, listening—which is an important communication skill—can be improved with practice. The following suggestions will be helpful in developing better listening skills:

1. Concentrate on listening. Increase your listening awareness by becoming alert to all the sounds around you. Do not tune people out, but practice on voices and sounds to increase your awareness.
2. Listen eagerly and with an open mind.
3. Pay attention. Concentrate on what the interviewer is saying. Do not let your mind wander. Failure to pay attention may result in your asking a question that the interviewer has already answered.
4. Listen for the most important ideas. Be sure you comprehend the information provided by the interviewer. Ask questions for clarification.
5. Look at the interviewer. Maintaining eye contact with the interviewer conveys the impression that you are interested and confident.

The interview truly begins when the interviewer starts to discuss the company and the position. During this phase you may expect questions about your background and experience. Although you may be invited to ask questions whenever they arise, try not to interrupt the flow of the interview. Therefore, you may need to delay your own questions until near the end of the interview.

What questions should you ask during the interview?

Questions that you may wish to ask—unless, of course, the interviewer volunteers the information—are the following:

1. What does the job actually entail? (This is aimed at becoming familiar with job duties, the immediate supervisor, etc.)
2. Where does the job fit into the organizational structure? (This will help you become familiar with normal promotional channels.)
3. Does the position require extensive travel?
4. Does the company have an in-house training program?
5. What is the nature of performance reviews?
6. How often are transfers likely to be made? Does the employee usually have input into the relocation decision?
7. What is the normal time between promotions?

If your qualifications are somewhat less than those listed on the job vacancy notice, you should consider trying to convince the interviewer—if you have an opportunity to do so—that these limiting qualifications will not be all that detrimental. Examples of limiting qualifications are a low grade-point average, limited participation in outside activities, and limited work experience. Accentuating the positive while responding to, but not hiding, the negative is a wise course of action.

You will often be asked a series of opened-ended questions, such as why you chose the major you did or additional detail about your career goals. These questions are designed to determine how well your qualifications match the stated requirements of the position for which you are applying. Even though correctly anticipating every potential question is impossible, you will find it advantageous to prepare answers to questions that have become rather standard. Among these questions are the following:

1. Tell me about yourself.
2. Explain how you handled a major problem or crisis during your college years.
3. What are your long-term goals? Where do you hope to be in ten years?
4. Why do you feel that you will be successful in this job?
5. What leadership positions or roles have you held?
6. How do you spend your spare time?
7. What have been your most satisfying and least satisfying personal experiences?
8. What do you consider to be your greatest strength?
9. Give me some examples that support your stated interest in ________.
10. What do you know about our company?
11. Which were your favorite college courses? Which course did you like the least? Why?
12. What did you learn or gain from your part-time and summer job experiences?
13. Which geographic location do you prefer? Why?
14. Would you prefer on-the-job training or a formal training program?
15. What can you do for us now? What can we do for you?
16. Why did you choose your major?
17. Are you an aggressive person?
18. Tell me about your extracurricular activities and interests.
19. Why did you leave your last job?
20. What type of person rubs you the wrong way?

Naturally, a list of possible questions the interviewer might ask is virtually limitless. However, preparing mental answers to questions you consider as highly probable is strongly recommended. Communication Capsule 11-4 provides suggestions for answering the most difficult interview questions—those about your greatest weakness.

Communication Capsule 11-4 What is your Greatest Weakness?

A frequent and very difficult interview question to answer asks the interviewee to expose his or her greatest weakness. The question may be asked in several different ways such as (1) "What are your shortcomings?" (2) "What do you consider to be an area where you need the most development?" (3) "If I were to contact several people who are familiar with your abilities, what would you think they would say is your greatest Defect? Fault? Flaw?" (4) "Explain your greatest weakness."

Regardless of how the question is asked, never respond by indicating that you have no weaknesses or shortcomings or by saying "I don't know." These answers reflect a lack of self-knowledge. But you also do not want to provide information that might hurt your chances of obtaining the job. Therefore, your answer must fall into the category of a truthful but nondamaging response. Study the "truthful but nondamaging" weaknesses shown in the following list; then select two or three that you can use when the question about your greatest weakness is asked.

1. Sometimes I am not very assertive.
2. I am too conservative. (Do not be too liberal.)
3. My friends have more fun than I do because I am too much of a perfectionist.
4. Sometimes my speech is too rapid, and I have to remember to slow down.

5. At times I am too serious about tasks assigned to me.
6. I become impatient with people who are always late or do not complete tasks assigned to them.
7. My friends say I am too idealistic.
8. My vocabulary is not as extensive as I would like it to be.
9. My handwriting is not always as neat and clear as I would like.
10. I am self-conscious when meeting new people.
11. Sometimes I worry about tasks and deadlines unnecessarily.
12. Up to this point I have been too dependent on my parents for financial, psychological, and mental support.
13. Perhaps I am too practical and meticulous for my own good.
14. Grades are important to me, but my friends are more involved in campus activities.
15. Sometimes I suffer from a lack of self-confidence.

Interviewing is a two-way process. The interviewer will be evaluating your suitability for employment in his or her company, and you will be trying to determine whether you want to work for the company. A well-planned, effective interview will allow both parties to accomplish their interview objectives.

Making a Good Impression during the Interview

What can you do to make a good impression during the interview?

Throughout your lifetime, you will have many opportunities to create or reestablish a positive impression. During an employment interview, your goal is the creation of a good impression by presenting yourself as the most desirable person for the job. The interviewer, on the other hand, is looking for the applicant who possesses specific attributes or capabilities that are considered important for job success. Unfortunately, no formula exists that guarantees success, but attention to the following will help you avoid common pitfalls encountered during interviews.

1. Appropriate dress is important for a good first impression. Be sure you are neat and clean. You need not worry about the cost of the outfit you are wearing. Rather, concentrate on simple, tasteful, and comfortable business attire. Do not wear gaudy clothing or flashy jewelry. The image you project can greatly influence your career destiny. Because first impressions are usually formed within three minutes, you should have a professional appearance.

Changing from casual attire to business attire can be uncomfortable. Before the actual interview, you should give a new wardrobe a test run. Finding out before the day of the interview that a shirt collar is too tight or that a belt is the wrong color decreases preinterview stress. Interviewers are keenly aware of two rather visible characteristics of potential success, a commanding presence and an instinctive ability to act and react in an appropriate manner. These two characteristics are reflected in how you see yourself, which, in turn, affects how others perceive you. Remember that interviewers are more favorably inclined toward the well-qualified candidate who looks the part.

2. Be on time. Arriving a few minutes early is far better than arriving just on time or even a few minutes late. Interviewers know that lateness is a habit that can be quite costly in terms of achievement and job-related success.

3. Be confident and courteous. Sit when asked, shake hands when prompted, avoid smoking (even if offered a cigarette), and concentrate on the interview process. Make sure you pronounce the interviewer's name correctly during the interview. Sit in a relaxed position, but do not sprawl out or place your feet on another chair or table. Demonstrate a reasonable sense of humor, but do not participate in jokes or funny stories.

4. Keep eye contact with the interviewer. Concentrate on the question you are being asked. Listen carefully, and wait until the interviewer has finished asking the question before you begin answering.

5. Provide thoughtful, direct, and honest answers. Think—really think—before answering any of the questions.

6. Avoid asking questions about salary. When you are considered to be a serious candidate for the position, the interviewer will bring up the subject of salary. If you are asked the salary you would expect to receive, providing a salary range in three or four thousand dollar intervals is appropriate.

The Office Interview

What is the purpose of the office/plant interview?

Following the initial interview that probably occurred on campus, you may be invited to visit the company's office or its plant. This represents a second opportunity for you to sell your skills and qualifications.

During the office visit, anticipation is important, but mental, emotional, and professional flexibility are even more critical. For example, you may or may not be met at the airport. Representatives of the company may take you out for evening meals, or they may provide you flexibility to arrange evening activities for yourself. Positions that will demand a strong will and intellectual ingenuity may result in a stress interview for determining how well you adjust to situations that are not what you expect.

The company visitation usually consumes at least one whole day and may even include some employment testing. Be prepared for a variety of tests that assess your aptitude and your decision-making ability. Some companies use paper-and-pencil tests; others assess your ability through simulated on-the-job situations.

Company interviews may also be used to assess your poise, stamina, enthusiasm, and knowledge. During the day, you can expect to have interviews with a variety of people in many different positions, such as supervisors, managers, and prospective departmental peer-group members. You may also have to participate in informal conversations during lunch and breaks.

During the office interview, the interviewer will be observing and evaluating you. The following are some specific evaluations the interviewer may make:

What do interviewers evaluate during office/plant interviews?

1. How mentally alert and responsive are you? Competition for top jobs is very keen. Factors such as eye-contact, real or manufactured interest, and responsiveness to questions in the correct and expected manner will be some of the ways the interviewer will evaluate answers.
2. Is the applicant able to draw proper inferences and conclusions? The interviewer will often use open-ended questions and even elusive political inquiries to determine the applicant's judgmental ability.
3. Does the applicant demonstrate a degree of intellectual depth when communicating, or is his or her thinking ability shallow and lacking in depth?
4. Has the candidate used, up to this point, common sense regarding career/life planning? Although common sense is difficult to identify, the following factors might prove relevant: physical energy, reaction to pressure, resistance to or acceptance of change, sense of humor, appearance and grooming, breadth of interests, creativity, and financial stability.
5. What is the applicant's capacity for problem solving? The interviewer will assess an applicant's ability to see the big picture and apply textbook learning to actual business situations.
6. How well does the applicant respond to stress and pressure? Application of ability and skill in difficult and pressure-filled situations is a common denominator of success. Many interviewers place applicants in controlled stress situations to view their ability to handle stress.
7. Can the applicant succeed in the position for which he or she is being interviewed? The interviewer is looking to see whether the applicant possesses the technical skill, personal traits, and the ability to succeed.

8. Will the applicant succeed in this position? Does the applicant have the personal and intrinsic motivation to succeed? Are interests and objectives consistent with organizational goals?
9. Can the applicant be trusted? In other words, does he or she have personal integrity, honesty in dealing with people, and moral and ethical standards? The interviewer evaluates trustworthiness by assessing the applicant's candor in answering questions, spontaneity and consistency of responses, and willingness to discuss his or her shortcomings.
10. Is the applicant professionally and socially mature? Self-confidence is important to job success. Applicants will be evaluated in relation to their willingness to take risks and make decisions. In addition, an interviewer is interested in an applicant's ability to discuss shortcomings, their leadership ability, and their overall professional promise.

Negative Factors

A large percentage of applicants are rejected during the initial interview. The more obvious reasons are weak credentials, refusal to relocate, poor personal appearance, ineffective communication skills, obvious lack of interest in the company, and failure to meet minimum requirements. However, interviewers also are skeptical of applicants who are defensive about their shortcomings, evasive in their responses, possess strong prejudices, lack social understanding, or demonstrate a negative disposition.

Other factors recruiters consider negative are arrogance, lack of a sense of humor, difficulty in making decisions, extreme aggressiveness, laziness, lack of career goals, unwillingness to start at the bottom and move up, and overemphasis on money.

But the major negative characteristic attributed to the interviewee who loses out during the initial interview is lack of courtesy. An applicant may easily avoid this fate with a simple expression of appreciation for the interviewer's time.

Following Up

One of the simplest, yet commonly ignored, rules of successful interviewing is acknowledging that the company has taken time and interest in the applicant. Successful people make it their business to thank others for favors, whether big or small. From the beginning of a job search, you should always acknowledge and thank the people who assisted in the interview process.

A timely and well-written interview follow-up letter can enhance the overall success of the interview process. Even if your interest in a company wanes after the interview, common courtesy requires a letter of thanks.

For what is the personal job search progress record used?

During the interview process, a personal job search progress record will help you remember the people and the companies that have extended interview courtesies to you. A sample job search progress record is shown in Exhibit 11-1.

After you accept a job offer, you will also distinguish yourself as a courteous person if you notify those companies in which your application is still viable that you are no longer available. See Chapter 10 for a description of such a refusal letter.

SUMMARY

Modern businesses depend on a variety of different types of interviews. Among these are employment interviews, performance-appraisal interviews, disciplinary interviews, persuasive interviews, and exit interviews. Each has a specific purpose and function. Interviewers ask a number of different types of questions during the questioning phase of an interview. Common types of questions include open, closed, loaded, leading, neutral, probing, and mirror. Because some question types are particularly helpful in obtaining specific kinds of information from the interviewee, the interviewer should know the intended uses of the various types of questions.

JOB SEARCH RECORD

	CONTACT METHOD					EMPLOYER RESPONSE				FOLLLOW-UP METHOD			EMPLOYMENT OFFER		COMMENTS
Employer Contacted Person, Title Address, Phone	Date	Campus Interview	Letter	Resume	Phone Call	Date	Letter	Phone Call	Date of Interview	Date	Letter	Phone Call	Starting Date	Salary	

Exhibit 11-1: Job Search Progress Record.

Before you participate in an employment interview, prepare adequately for the event. Becoming aware of the items that interviewers consider important during the employment interview will enable you to present the best possible picture of your preparation and ability.

REVIEW QUESTIONS

1. Explain the purpose of the performance appraisal interview.
2. What are the important planning and execution aspects of an exit interview?
3. Prepare a list of suggestions that should be followed when preparing for an interview.
4. Of what value are such publications as *Dun and Bradstreet's Million Dollar Directory*, *Moody's Manual*, and *Poor's Register* in preparing for an interview?
5. How can a person become a better listener during an interview?
6. What can be done to ensure a good initial impression during an interview?
7. What is the purpose of the office visit?
8. What are some of the points an interviewer will evaluate during an employment interview?
9. What two types of letters are commonly associated with the interview follow-up process?

APPLICATION PROBLEMS

1. Assume you are preparing for an on-campus interview. Prepare a list of your goals, strengths, and experience. Include evidence of specifics demonstrating your character and ability.
2. In preparing for the on-campus interview (application problem number 1), list the questions you would like to ask the interviewer.
3. Select three companies for which you would like to work. Using the variety of information sources at your disposal, compile information about each company that will be helpful in an interview.
4. Assume you have scheduled an on-campus interview. Study your résumé and prepare a list of ten questions you think the interviewer is likely to ask.
5. Obtain a copy of a friend's résumé and then conduct a mock interview with your friend. Afterward, discuss ways each of you could improve your interview performance.
6. Prepare a three-page report on "Improving Interviewing Effectiveness" from the perspective of an interviewer.
7. Prepare a three-page report on "Improving Interviewing Effectiveness" from the perspective of a job applicant.
8. Interview a person responsible for conducting employment interviews for a corporation in your city or region. Prepare a report for presentation to your classmates on the essentials of employment interviewing from the perspective of an interviewer.
9. Prepare a two-page report on "Interviewer Assessment of the Job Applicant's Ability." Include in your report techniques that might be used in the assessment process.
10. Contact two major employers from your community and request application forms. Analyze each form in terms of the kind of information requested and list which, if any, unlawful questions are included.

12

Preparing Informal Reports

After studying this chapter, you should be able to

1. Describe the differences among the classifications of business reports.
2. Describe the differences among the types of informal reports.
3. Discuss the purpose of each type of informal report.
4. Discuss the uses of each type of informal report.
5. Prepare effective informal reports.

The purpose of a business report is to present information on a particular subject in an organized and objective format for individuals to use as they work toward the achievement of a business goal. In today's business world, managers often rely on reports to help them make decisions and solve problems. To a large extent, how effective their decisions are depends on the sufficiency and accuracy of the information contained in such reports.

Informal business reports are used both inside and outside the organization. For example, outsiders, such as consultants, often use reports in an attempt to make an organization's operations more effective. One of the common inside uses of reports is to facilitate changes in organizational operations.

This chapter includes a discussion of the importance of business reports, classifications of business reports, formats of informal reports, and the following types of informal reports: justification, periodic, progress, staff, feasibility, and audit.

THE IMPORTANCE OF BUSINESS REPORTS

The pace of today's business operations seldom allows managers sufficient time to gather by themselves all the information they need to make important decisions or to solve problems. In many instances, a subordinate gathers or collects the information managers need and then presents this information in a report.

Besides being a source of information for managerial decision makers, reports provide a permanent record of information, something that is often impossible when in-

What is the most important function of reports?

formation is conveyed orally. Written reports are becoming more significant in an ever-increasing number of organizations because of the growing need for information permanency.

What are the secondary purposes of reports?

Reports serve other valuable business functions. They often outline processes or procedures that individuals are expected to follow. Furthermore, reports create goodwill both inside and outside the organization. For example, reports used to present information to stockholders and other interested parties can create goodwill for the organization.

Organizations also use reports in many other ways. A manager may sometimes assign a report to a subordinate to evaluate the individual's competency in certain areas. Or a manager may use the information contained in a report as a springboard to create or generate additional ideas for solving problems. In addition, some managers find that reports are a way of filling technological or information voids in their backgrounds.

Communication Capsule 12-1 contains a number of suggestions designed to improve the effectiveness of informal reports.

Communication Capsule 12-1 Writing Effective Informal Reports

As the writer of informal reports, you can follow several steps to ensure the effectiveness of your work. Among these are the following:

1. Consider the reader as you prepare the report. The more effectively you can tailor the report to your reader, the more useful the report will be. When you consider the reader, you will provide the background information he or she needs to understand the report, use terminology he or she understands, write at a level appropriate for him or her, and so forth.
2. Use the appropriate organization plan, direct or indirect, for the type of report you are preparing. Although some reports follow a direct plan, which means they get to the main idea immediately, others follow an indirect plan, which delays the main idea.
3. Make sure the information/data you are presenting is accurate. One of the surest ways to destroy the effectiveness of a report is to present inaccurate information/data. The presentation of such information/data often totally destroys the usefulness of the report and calls into question the capability of the writer.
4. Make sure the conclusions are based on facts. Most of the informal reports in this chapter contain conclusions. When you offer a conclusion in an informal report, you need to make sure it is based on one or more facts presented in the report and is indeed a conclusion, not simply a restatement of a finding.
5. Make sure the recommendations are realistic and supportable. Just as informal reports often contain conclusions, they also often contain recommendations. The recommendations must be relevant for the situation.
6. Make sure the information you present is objective. One situation that weakens many informal reports is the presence of subjective information/data. When subjective information/data are included, you will have difficulty verifying the accuracy of the material you are presenting. Therefore, the reader will be unable to determine whether he or she should consider the content of the report as a basis for a decision.

CLASSIFICATIONS OF BUSINESS REPORTS

We can classify business reports in several different ways. The most popular scheme is to distinguish them by their level of formality. Therefore, reports are often classified as either *informal* or *formal.*

How are reports classified?

Informal reports typically are shorter and are written and presented in a less-structured manner than are formal reports. Furthermore, they are prepared using a more-personalized writing style. Informal reports have three formats: memorandum, letter, and manuscript, each of which is described in this chapter. Among the various types of informal reports we discuss are justification reports, periodic reports, progress reports, staff reports, feasibility reports, and audit reports.

How do informal reports differ from formal reports?

Formal reports (see Chapters 13 and 14 for a discussion of formal reports) tend to be more analytical than informal reports, although some informal reports—especially manuscript reports—may also be analytical. When compared with informal reports, formal reports generally have a more "dressed-up" appearance, contain standard parts, are often longer, and are typically written in a more formal style.

Whereas businesses are relying less on formal business reports, they are increasingly turning to informal reports. A growing number of managers believe formal reports, when compared with informal reports, take too long to prepare and contain too much information. The types of informal reports organizations issue vary considerably, with some organizations distributing most or all of the various types of informal reports, and others circulating only one or two of the types discussed in this chapter.

FORMATS OF INFORMAL REPORTS

Three formats of informal reports—memorandum, letter, and manuscript—are used to present informal reports. Each type of report is illustrated to enhance the reader's understanding of its similarities and differences.

Memorandum Reports

What are the categories of informal reports?

Although the memorandum report is primarily an internal report, it may also be distributed externally. Memorandum reports are considered to be informal especially because of their format. The memorandum format can present information contained in justification, periodic, progress, and staff reports, each of which is discussed in this chapter.

For what are memorandum reports commonly used?

Memorandum reports are commonly used for routine matters; thus, they often have multiple readers. They can be useful for initiating action, responding to a request, or following up telephone conversation, as well as for numerous other reasons. They may be sent upward, downward, or laterally within the organization. As a memorandum report writer, you need not be as concerned about eliminating jargon as when you are writing letter reports that may be sent outside the organization. Within the same organization, most employees will have a fairly good grasp of the common jargon found within reports.

The format of memorandum reports is fairly standard. If printed memorandum forms are unavailable, you can type the following headings on a sheet of paper:

DATE:
TO:
FROM:
SUBJECT:

If the writer's signature is important, the memorandum can be either signed or initialed beside the writer's name in the heading or below the message. The typist should include his or her initials on the left margin below the message. A report in the memorandum format is shown in Exhibit 12-1.

Letter Reports

How do letter and memorandum reports differ from one another?

One of the basic differences between memorandum reports and letter reports is their destination. Memorandum reports are generally distributed internally, whereas letter reports are often sent to someone outside the organization. Letter reports are useful for presenting limited amounts of information. Usually one to four pages in length, they have a regular letter format.

The structure of letter reports varies widely, with the circumstances determining which parts to include. The opening sentence may refer to the authorization, the date of the authorization, and the name of the individual who made the authorization. Such an opening sentence follows.

INTEROFFICE MEMORANDUM

August 14, 199x

TO: Jack Hatchell, President
FROM: John Doe, Office Manager
SUBJECT: Records Management Conference

A summary of the Records Management Conference I attended in Detroit on August 10 is included in this report.

Summary of Sessions Attended

The following summarizes each of the sessions I attended:

1. Filing Equipment: This session was designed to acquaint participants with the latest filing equipment. Much of the equipment on display was automatic.
2. Computer Output Microfilm: This session was designed to familiarize participants with the computer output microfilm concept and its various applications.
3. Records Retrieval: The purpose of this session was to acquaint participants with the various factors that need to be considered in developing a records retention schedule.
4. Records Transfer: In this session, participants learned about new developments in transferring records from active status to inactive status.

Recommendations

On the basis of my attending the conference, I recommend the following:

1. That we investigate the possibility of purchasing lateral filing equipment.
2. That we evaluate the validity of our records retention schedule and revise as needed.

Thank you for giving me the opportunity to attend this most informative conference. If you have any questions about the sessions I attended, I will be pleased to answer them.

sd

Exhibit 12-1 Memorandum report.

> As you requested on December 14, I am submitting the following report on the 199x capital expenditures of the Rockland branch office.

Letter reports frequently have a single reader, unlike memorandum reports. The report is often sent to the reader in response to a request he or she made. In such cases, the following opening sentence may be appropriate.

> The information you requested July 17 about the health care facilities of General Hospital is contained in the attached report.

Some letter reports are unsolicited. The following opening sentence is appropriate for an unsolicited report.

> Because you are vitally concerned with hospital facilities, you might be interested in the enclosed report about the feasibility of expanding the health care facilities of General Hospital.

The second section of the letter report is the report body, which may include (1) a presentation of findings by the report writer about the situation under study; (2) an analysis of the situation; or (3) information of general interest to the report reader.

What is included in the second section of letter reports?

To add credibility to the report, some writers include in this section information relating to the depth of the study, the individuals consulted, the nature of the materials read in preparing the report, and so forth.

Many reports present only information because the situation does not require analysis or recommendations. But if recommendations and suggestions based on the findings or data are appropriate, they should be included. If the report reader is likely to consider the recommendations section as the key part of the report, place it before the findings section. The organizational structure should, then, immediately give the reader the information of greatest concern or interest.

The last section of the letter report—the closing—often contains an offer to be of additional assistance should or when the need arises. The offer indicates a willingness to be cooperative or helpful, which is desirable in building goodwill. Following is such an example.

> Should you wish to discuss any of the content of this report, please contact me at 444-1233.

The writer-reader relationship often determines the appropriate writing style for informal letter reports. Although an informal writing style is typical, the relationship may make the formal writing style more appropriate. For example, personal pronouns *(I, you, we)* are appropriate for an informally written report but are inappropriate in the more formally written reports.

If the report writer is preparing a letter report for his or her superior, depending on the relationship with the superior, a writer may choose to use a somewhat more formal writing style (although still considered informal) than when writing to a subordinate or a coworker. Jargon is not appropriate if the reader is in a field other than the writer's and will not understand the terms used.

You may use any acceptable letter style to present the report to the reader. If the report is lengthy, side and paragraph headings are appropriate, as is the enumeration of material. Both design elements make the report easy to read. To further aid the reader, you may include graphic illustrations and tabular information. Details about graphic aids appear in Chapter 14.

A sample letter report is shown in Exhibit 12-2.

Manuscript Reports

A report that is too long for either the memorandum- or letter-report format but not long enough for formal-report format can be presented as a manuscript report. The characteristics of manuscript reports are the following: They are not as long as formal reports; they do not contain a synopsis, letter of transmittal, table of contents, letter of authorization, appendix, or bibliography; and they are usually written in a less formal style. The format of a manuscript report, however, does resemble the format of a formal report—perhaps most closely resembling the term papers you have prepared in your college courses.

How do manuscript reports and formal reports differ from one another?

The manuscript report is appropriate for a variety of research, investigative, or survey problems. Manuscript reports tend to deal with only one topic, which limits the scope of most of these reports. Formal reports, in contrast, sometimes contain information about more than one topic.

Richardson's, Inc.
1200 Main Street (301) 456-5845 Grant, NY 01232

November 12, 199x

Mr. Henry Jackson
General Manager
Richardson's, Inc.
1200 Main Street
Grant, NY 01232

Dear Mr. Jackson:

Here is the report you requested on June 15 about the nature of the physical improvements made at the branch office.

Physical Improvements to General Office Area

The general office area has been completely renovated. New tile has been installed in the general office area, and the carpet in the managers' and supervisors' offices is new. A new fluorescent lighting system has been installed, which adds greatly to the overall appearance of the office area. Heating and cooling ducts have been integrated into the lighting fixtures. New furniture was purchased for some employees and some of the work areas. Because the new furniture is streamlined and the old furniture has traditional styling, the two styles are not well coordinated.

Suggestions for Additional Improvements

As a response to your request for suggestions to improve the branch office facilities, the following recommendations are being made:

1. Purchase more of the new streamlined furniture.
2. Renovate the restroom facilities.

Substantial progress has been made in improving the appearance of the branch office. If you need additional information, please let me know.

Sincerely,

Darlene James
Administrative Assistant

op

Exhibit 12-2 Letter report.

How does the direct plan differ from the indirect plan?

Writers of manuscript reports can choose between two organizational plans: the *direct,* or deductive, plan or the *indirect,* or inductive, plan. When using the direct plan, immediately present a short summary, your conclusions, and recommendations. Then add your facts, ideas, or findings. When using the indirect plan, present the facts, ideas, and findings before the conclusions and recommendations. In business, the direct plan is more common, often attracting the reader's immediate interest. Because the most important information appears at the beginning of the report, busy executives generally prefer the direct organization plan. The indirect organization plan is more common for reports prepared for general nonbusiness readership because it provides information before conclusions and recommendations.

In many formal reports, supporting data, including diagrams, illustrations, and tables, appear as appendices; in manuscript reports, such supporting data usually appear in the body. Whatever supporting data (such as numerical data or financial data) you include, be prepared to discuss it.

What suggestions will help you write more effective manuscript reports?

The following guidelines should help you in writing an informal manuscript report:

1. State at the beginning of the report its purpose or objectives.
2. Avoid broad generalizations that your data cannot substantiate.

SUBCOMMITTEE REPORT ON CURRICULUM REVIEW

The Subcommittee on Curriculum Review was organized on August 10, 199x, by Dean Jon Fritchie and was given a three-part assignment: (1) to review the required business core in the College of Business Administration, (2) to report the findings of the faculty, and (3) to make recommendations.

Summary of Findings

The members of the Subcommittee on Curriculum Review believe the business core required of all majors in the College of Business Administration is generally realistic. Several recommendations are being included in this report.

Conclusions

The Subcommittee arrived at the following conclusions about the required business core in the College of Business Administration:

1. Although the business core is realistic for the most part, certain modifications are appropriate.
2. The suggested revisions can be made without affecting the integrity of the business core.
3. The suggested revisions will be received favorably by the majority of the faculty in the college.
4. The revisions can be made without affecting the accreditation of the various programs in the college.

Recommendations

The Subcommittee was asked for appropriate recommendations. On the basis of its investigation, the Subcommittee submits the following:

1. Accounting III (the first course in a two-course sequence of Intermediate Accounting) should be an elective, except when required for a specific degree program, such as accounting.
2. Business Writing should be a required course of all majors.
3. An additional three-credit economics course should be required in addition to the eight credits of economics already required.
4. The content of Business Law I, II, and III should be condensed into two business law courses to be identified as Business Law I and II.
5. A new course on international business should be developed.
6. Business Statistics I, II, and III should be reduced to a two-course sequence to be identified as Business Statistics I and II.

Findings of the Investigation

The findings of this study were obtained through extensive investigation procedures. The sources of information used in the investigation process were as follows:

1. Reports from various accreditation agencies.
2. Catalogs from colleges and universities generally recognized as having reputable programs.
3. Information and opinions from various faculty members.
4. Published journal articles.

The findings of the investigation are presented in the same order as the recommendations are presented. Only the significant findings pertaining to specific recommendations are included in this report.

Accounting. The majority of colleges and universities whose programs were examined now require a two-course sequence in accounting principles.

Exhibit 12-3 Manuscript report.

3. Write the report in a style appropriate for the reader-writer relationship.
4. Make sure the conclusions and recommendations are based on the data or findings.
5. Write the report in a concise, direct style.
6. Use side headings and enumerations when and where appropriate as a means of aiding the reader.

Exhibit 12-3 is a sample of a manuscript report.

TYPES OF INFORMAL REPORTS

Informal business reports fall into several categories. The six major types are justification, periodic, progress, staff, feasibility, and audit reports. Some reports will have overlapping content, such as findings, conclusions, and recommendations.

Justification Reports

For what are justification reports used?

The *justification report* is a type of business document that justifies a recommendation, a course of action, or a decision. An example of such a report is one that recommends implementation of a new employee orientation program designed to help acquaint new hires with various company policies, procedures, and operations. The justification report is neither authorized nor commissioned. Instead, the writer initiates the writing of the report. The justification report follows a direct or deductive plan; that is, the recommendation and conclusions are presented before the facts and findings. The writer chooses this plan because, typically, the most important section is the recommendation.

The suggested plan for a justification report includes the following sections:

What is the suggested plan for presenting justification reports?

1. *Statement of purpose and recommendation:* Present the purpose for writing the report and ensuing recommendation as concisely as possible. The following is an example.

> Because of the increasing difficulties with our Brand X copiers, I recommend their replacement with Brand Y copiers.

2. *Outcome of the recommendation, if adopted:* Create a brief statement outlining the expected outcomes of adopting the recommendation. Expected outcomes may be in the form of cash savings, increased productivity, better service, and so forth. The following is an example of such a statement.

> The company will save an estimated $320 a year on repair bills and maintenance charges. Additional savings will result because employees will not experience as much down time.

3. *Suggested plan for implementing the recommendation:* Although this section is optional, its inclusion is essential in some justification reports. For example, in deciding whether to go along with the recommendation, the reader should be aware of suggested implementation procedures.

4. *Discussion of recommendation and/or advantages and disadvantages:* For readers to make an objective decision, they may need more information. For example, readers may be unfamiliar with the situation and thus need background details. But if the recommendation concerns an easily understood situation or a situation with which readers are familiar, a list of advantages and disadvantages of implementing the recommendation may be sufficient. A thorough discussion of the recommendation as well as its advantages and disadvantages is especially appropriate when the report is likely to have multiple readers.

5. *Statement of conclusions:* The last section outlines the writer's conclusions about implementing the recommendation. To be useful, the conclusions must be valid, supportable, and concisely written.

You can present the justification report to the reader in one of three formats: the memorandum report, the letter report, or the manuscript report. Because this report is generally an internal document transmitted from one employee to another, companies tend to prefer the memorandum format.

```
Interoffice Memorandum

   DATE: July 15, 199x
     TO: William Buck, Office Manager
   FROM: Sally Brown, Office Services Supervisor
SUBJECT: Need for Automatic Collator
```

The following information outlines the need for the purchase of an automatic collator:

Statement of Purpose and Recommendation

Because of the increasing employee time consumed by manually collating documents, the possibility of purchasing an automatic collator should be investigated.

Outcome of Recommendation

By using an automatic collator, considerable employee time could be saved. The result would be higher employee productivity and greater efficiency because employees could use their time to perform more important tasks.

Suggested Plan for Implementing Recommendation

An examination of the automatic collators manufactured by several companies is recommended. Because of the different features on the various devices, some collators would be more suitable than others.

Advantages and Disadvantages

The use of an automatic collator would result in the following advantages: (1) employees would not have to perform the rather menial task of collating; (2) employee time could be better used by performing other tasks; (3) employee morale would improve if employees do not have to collate manually; and (4) greater accuracy of collated documents could be expected.

The only disadvantage seen in purchasing an automatic collator is the purchase cost, which is estimated to be approximately $800.

Conclusions

Among the conclusions are the following:

1. An automatic collator can be justified on the basis of the number of sheets of paper that have to be collated.
2. When employees are relieved of the task of collating sheets of paper, they have more time to perform more important tasks.

Exhibit 12-4 Justification report.

The justification report is easier to read if headings are used to identify each section. If you choose the memorandum or letter, the subject line should accurately identify the nature of the report's recommendation. Similarly, if you select the manuscript report format, place the title of the report on both the title page and the first page. A sample justification report is shown in Exhibit 12-4.

Checklist 12-1 should help you improve the effectiveness of your justification reports.

Periodic Reports

For what are periodic reports used?

A *periodic report* presents information on a regular basis—perhaps weekly, monthly, quarterly, semiannually, or annually—to provide a written record of past or present situations or events. Some of the more familiar periodic reports are annual reports, stockholder reports, bank statements, financial statements, and budgets.

Subordinates frequently prepare periodic reports for their superiors. For example, a department manager may ask each supervisor who reports to him to prepare a monthly cost breakdown of anticipated expenditures. The department manager may then synthesize the information in each of the reports into one departmental report, and this final report is transmitted to a higher managerial level.

OPENING
1. Have you used the direct (deductive) plan?
2. Is the opening concise?
3. Is the purpose of your report clearly stated?

MIDDLE
1. Have you been able to quantify the outcome of the recommendation should it be adopted?
2. Are the outcomes feasible and plausible?
3. Have you explained in detail your ideas for implementing the recommendation?
4. Are your ideas for implementing the recommendation realistic and feasible?
5. Have you discussed the recommendation in sufficient detail to give the reader an accurate picture of your ideas?
6. Have you presented the advantages in a decreasing order of importance?
7. Have you avoided overstating the advantages?
8. Have you avoided understating the disadvantages?

CLOSING
1. Are your conclusions realistic?
2. Have you avoided simply restating your recommendation as a conclusion?
3. Do you have a factual basis for the conclusion(s) you are presenting?

Checklist 12-1 Justification report.

Periodic reports can have a narrative format or a tabular format, or the company may issue a standardized form. Presenting quantitative information in a table or on a form often makes it easier for the reader to comprehend the material.

The memorandum, letter, and manuscript report formats are also appropriate for presenting periodic reports to the reader. When you choose any of these formats, a subject line (memorandum or letter) or title (manuscript) that accurately reflects the report's content should be used.

Although most periodic reports do not include suggestions or recommendations for a particular course of action, some report writers like including such information. The writer-reader relationship should guide the writer's decision here. A sample periodic report is shown in Exhibit 12-5.

Exhibit 12-5 Periodic report.

Interoffice Memorandum

August 10, 199x

TO: Richard Dawson, Executive Vice President
FROM: Mark Sanchez; Manager, Credit Department
SUBJECT: Expenditures for the Credit Department During July, 199x

The expenditures of the Credit Department for July that you asked me to calculate are as follows:

	Beginning Balance	*Ending Balance*	*Expense*
Salaries	$96,000	$87,000	$9,000
Supplies	9,000	8,200	800
Telephone (Long Distance)	300	230	70
Printing	250	220	30
Equipment Rental	480	440	40

dm

Progress Reports

Progress reports present information about the current status of a project, plan, or situation. They are prepared occasionally, usually when substantial progress occurs on a project. Although progress reports are prepared on an irregular basis, in contrast to periodic reports, the distinction between them is becoming less clear because an increasing number of organizations are interchanging the two types of reports. Nevertheless, progress reports keep top-level decision makers informed about recent developments, especially when they must make crucial decisions about a certain phase or aspect of a project.

For what are progress reports used?

The reader's familiarity with the project determines the content of the progress report. If the reader is fairly well informed, he or she will probably need fewer details. But a reader with limited or no knowledge will want more background information. Although a progress report that is one in a series should briefly review the progress of the project up to the point of the last report, it should focus on updating the subsequent progress.

The suggested plan for preparing a progress report includes the following elements:

What is the suggested plan for progress reports?

1. *Introduction:* This section discusses the purpose of the project, the individuals involved (if necessary), and the projected completion dates.
2. *Summary of progress already reported:* The detail required in this section depends, to a large extent, on the reader's familiarity with the project. Essentially this section offers a synopsis of the preceding progress reports.
3. *Detailed summary of progress since last reporting:* The information here should accurately update any progress since the last report. For a reader familiar with the project, this section is often the most important.
4. *Nature of exceptional progress:* This optional part can report any work that is ahead of or behind schedule. Depending on the circumstances, the reader may find this section quite useful. For example, suppose that the reader is the manager who has overall responsibility for the construction of a new addition onto the existing building. This part of the report informs her that the subcontractor who is responsible for one of the major subprojects is running three weeks behind schedule, which, at least initially, is going to delay the completion of the project by three weeks. Decision makers find such exceptional progress information helpful.
5. *Summary of work yet to be completed:* The summary should give the reader a clear picture of what remains to be done on the project.

Individual progress reports that are part of a series should each have the same format. The writer-reader relationship and the degree of formality should determine which format—memorandum, letter, or manuscript report—to choose. For consistency, also use the same headings and categories each time you add a new report in the series. Exhibit 12-6 is a sample progress report.

The information in Checklist 12-2 should help you improve the effectiveness of your progress reports.

Staff Reports

The staff report, which generally uses the memorandum format, is often prepared because of a request. *Staff reports* are frequently prepared after the solution of a particular problem. Therefore, their format generally follows a problem-solving sequence.

You do not have to follow a rigid organizational plan in preparing staff reports. But the following sections are appropriate for inclusion:

What is the suggested plan for preparing staff reports?

1. *Overview:* The opening provides a brief view of what is to follow. For some readers, this is essential for putting the problem in perspective.
2. *Purpose:* In this section, you outline the nature of the problem you are studying and identify the primary objectives of the study. To assist the reader, identify the scope of the study. This will also help you more clearly delineate the problem.

```
                    Interoffice Memorandum

July 17, 199x

     TO: David Smith, Vice President
   FROM: Dick Johnson, Assistant Vice President
SUBJECT: Status Report on the Development of a Training Program

The following outlines the status of the development of the training program I
have been working on for several months.

Introduction

The purpose of this research project is to determine the need for a training
program at XYZ Corporation. The project, which is being undertaken by Beth Smith
and me, is to be completed by January 1, 199x.

Summary of Progress Already Completed

The progress that has been reported up to this point includes the following:
1. Determination of objectives of the project.
2. Definition of parameters of the project.
3. Development of an appropriate research instrument (questionnaires and
   interviews).

Detailed Summary of Progress

Since the last progress report was prepared, the following have been completed:
1. Obtained approval of the questionnaire and interview record.
2. Pilot tested the questionnaire and interview record.
3. Determined method for selecting the respondents.
4. Selected the respondents.

Nature of Exceptional Progress

The project is six days behind schedule because of a strike at Johnson Printing,
the company with which we have contracted to print the questionnaires. The
strike ended July 14, and we expect printed questionnaires this week.

Summary of Work Yet to be Completed

The following work remains to be done: distribution of questionnaires,
completion of interviews, analysis of data, and preparation of the final report.

rt
```

Exhibit 12-6 Progress report.

OPENING
1. Have you considered the reader's familiarity with the project as you prepare the report?
2. Have you given the reader enough background information?

MIDDLE
1. Have you accurately summarized the progress that has already been completed?
2. Have you provided enough detail in summarizing the work already completed in order for the reader to have a good grasp about how well the project is proceeding?
3. Have you discussed in detail the work completed since the last progress report was prepared?
4. If appropriate, have you included a discussion of work that is running ahead of schedule or behind schedule?

CLOSING
1. Have you identified all of the work that remains to be completed?

Checklist 12-2 Progress report.

3. *Discussion of facts:* This section identifies and discusses the key facts. In a statistical study, the section consists mainly of a discussion of the data and their significance or meaning. In an informational report, this section deals with the important facts relevant to the problem.

4. *Conclusions:* This section provides a list of conclusions based on your analysis of data or facts. Available data or facts must support these conclusions.

5. *Recommendations:* The closing lists recommended courses of action. The recommendations must be realistic and consistent with the analysis of facts and data. Because the competence of report writers is often judged by this section, be especially careful in making your recommendations.

The staff report can be made more effective if the writer targets the reader's background and need for the report. In many cases, a manager will assign a subordinate the task of writing the report. A subordinate who is familiar with the reader is generally aware of the type of information the reader will need or want to assess the problem being studied or to make a decision concerning the problem. An example of the staff report appears in Exhibit 12-7.

Checklist 12-3 contains suggestions for improving the effectiveness of staff reports.

Feasibility Reports

What is the purpose of feasibility reports?

Feasibility reports provide information about the practicability of taking a particular course of action. A feasibility report has a twofold function: to provide information about whether the course of action is feasible; and if so, to present information about various alternatives to the course of action. Feasibility reports often contain a recommendation regarding which alternative seems most feasible. In some instances, the recommendation is designed to solve a problem; in other instances, the course of action is designed to improve a situation that is not necessarily problematic at the moment.

The credibility of the writers of feasibility reports is critical, especially when outsiders, such as consultants, prepare the reports. Obviously, determining the credibility of employees who write these reports tends to be less difficult than judging the credibility of outside writers.

Feasibility studies may include the following sections:

What is the suggested plan for presenting feasibility reports?

1. *Identification of the nature of the situation (and a statement of the problem, if appropriate).* This section must be written with objectivity and clarity of thought. If the writer allows biases to contaminate the information in this section, the report's usefulness is greatly diminished. Following is an example of an objective statement:

> The study on which this report is based determined the feasibility of XYZ Company's installing a flexible benefits program for its employees.

2. *Identification of the important characteristics the writer believes should be met to improve the situation (or solve the problem).* In this section, the writer identifies and discusses the important characteristics that must be met. This enables the reader to assess more easily the appropriateness of the various characteristics under consideration for improving the situation or solving the problem. In addition, the reader can determine whether the suggested alternatives are feasible in relation to these characteristics.

3. *Identification and comparison of the various alternatives for improving the situation (or solving the problem).* This section discusses the various alternative solutions in the context of the characteristics presented in the second section. In addition, the various alternatives are compared with one another according to their relative advantages and disadvantages.

4. *Identification of the recommended alternative.* This section recommends the alternative that seems most advantageous. The recommended alternative usually has the greatest number of relative advantages and fewest number of relative disadvantages.

Interoffice Memorandum

October 17, 199x

TO: David Jones, President
FROM: Dan Brown, Vice President
SUBJECT: Investigation of the Word Processing Center

Overview

A report on my investigation of the word processing center, which you requested on May 16, follows. This report includes a discussion of the facts of the investigation, conclusions, and recommendations.

Purpose

This study was undertaken because of apparent inefficient procedures being used in the word processing center. The result is skyrocketing costs for producing work, as well as poor production rates.

The primary objectives of this study were
1. To identify the reasons for increasing costs.
2. To determine why the production rates in the word processing center have been decreasing.
3. To determine why the employees in the word processing center are not satisfied with their jobs.

The scope of this study was limited to the word processing center. Other office areas or procedures were not included in the investigation.

Discussion of Facts

One objective of this investigation was to determine why costs of producing work are increasing so rapidly. The investigation revealed that the cost of supplies has increased by 32 percent during the last two years. Although we have no control over the increase, the employees in the word processing center might become more waste-conscious as a means of reducing the costs of supplies.

The cost of equipment maintenance has also increased because of rising costs as well as increased equipment malfunctions. One automatic typewriter in the word processing center that is only two years old has had a much higher breakdown record than any of the other typewriters.

We have also had an increase in employee salaries, which, of course, adds to the cost of the center's operations.

Another objective of this investigation was to determine why the production rates of the word processing center have been decreasing. The investigation revealed that an increasing number of the managers are using the word processing center for preparing more technical and statistical information than has been prepared in the center in the past. Because of frequent changes in this material, which results in the rekeyboarding of much of it, the production rate of the center, understandably, has decreased.

Production rates have also decreased because the word processing center has had difficulty hiring trained employees. The production rate cannot be optimized while new employees are being trained.

Conclusions

The following conclusions are based on the results of the investigation:
1. Definite problems exist within the word processing center. Some of these problems can be easily remedied but others are quite complex.
2. The word processing center concept is worthwhile; but as it exists in our organization, the center should be modified to become more efficient.
3. Because of the complexity of some of the problems in the word processing center, outside professional help is needed to solve the problems.

Recommendations

The following recommendations are offered:
1. That the structure of the word processing center be modified as quickly as possible.
2. That because of the magnitude of the job and the expertise needed, outside consultants be hired.

dp

Exhibit 12-7 Staff report.

OPENING
1. Have you considered the reader and his or her needs in writing the report?
2. Have you clearly identified the nature of the situation that resulted in the need to prepare a staff report?
3. Have you identified the nature of the problem being studied?
4. Have you identified the primary objectives of the study?
5. Have you identified the scope of the study?

MIDDLE
1. Have you discussed in sufficient detail the important facts, which will help the reader grasp the ideas you are presenting?
2. Have you verified the accuracy of the facts you are presenting?
3. Have you presented all relevant facts, regardless of whether you agree with them?
4. Have you eliminated all irrelevant facts?

CLOSING
1. Are your conclusions verifiable and supportable?
2. Are the conclusions in fact conclusions?
3. Are the recommendations realistic and in line with the facts and conclusions you have presented?

Checklist 12-3 Staff report.

You can select any of the informal report formats discussed earlier in this chapter to present the feasibility report. Use the formal report format discussed in Chapter 13 if a higher degree of formality seems necessary. In other words, the writer should choose whichever format is most appropriate for the situation. Exhibit 12-8 is a sample feasibility report.

Audit Reports

For what are audit reports used?

Audit reports provide information about the results of an investigation into some phase of organizational operations. Perhaps the most familiar type of audit report is the one an accountant prepares annually to transmit information about an organization's financial condition. In addition to financial audit reports, other areas that may be investigated and reported upon are affirmative action, complex or extensive projects, quality of newly hired personnel, salary plans, fringe benefits, and so forth.

In some cases, employees may prepare audit reports. In other cases, such as financial audits, outsiders must be the preparers. The two factors that determine whether insiders or outsiders prepare the reports are (1) legal requirements governing the preparer and (2) level of expertise the preparer needs. If none of the company's employees have the expertise to undertake the audit or to prepare the report, the organization will most likely hire an outsider.

What is the suggested plan for presenting audit reports?

An audit report should include the following sections:

1. *Introductory section.* This section contains various information, including the need for the study, relevant background factors related to the area under study, and an overview of the review process.
2. *Body section.* This section presents data that have been collected and then evaluates them.
3. *Closing section.* This section presents the conclusions based on the data that have been collected and makes recommendations.

A sample audit report is shown in Exhibit 12-9.

The Ethics Episode raises some ethical concerns that need to be considered in preparing informal reports.

ETHICS EPISODE Generally, business employees have a greater opportunity to be unethical in writing business reports than they do in writing business letters. Why? The situation about which the letter is being written often makes it quite difficult to deceive the reader because of the level of familiarity he or she has about the information in the letter, often unlike the reader's familiarity with the content of a business report. In fact, readers of some business reports may know nothing about the situation being discussed; therefore, deceiving them is easier, at least initially. Deceiving the reader of a business letter or a report, either intentionally or unintentionally, is not an ethical practice. Intentional deceit is viewed more negatively, however, because of the immoral nature of the action.

Because you will probably be unable to include in a report all of the information about the situation, you will need to determine—judiciously—which information to include and which to exclude. To help you make this decision, consider the impact on the reader of the inclusion of the information in the report. If you perceive that the information will help the reader, then you should probably include it; on the other hand, if the information will not help the reader in his or her decision-making efforts, then perhaps you should exclude it. Knowing as much as you can about the person you are writing the report for will help you in deciding what information to include.

Consider the unethical nature of the following situations regarding the selection of report content:

1. Suppose you work in the human resources department of a company, and you have been assigned the responsibility of preparing a report regarding employee interest in a new dental insurance program. The account executive of your current dental insurance provider has offered you an under-the-table payment of $5,000 if your company signs a new three-year contract. You survey a percentage of the employees and find that, overall, their preference is to change to a new provider because of general dissatisfaction with the current provider. Now you have a dilemma. Do you distort the data you collected (you know that it cannot be easily verified) to show an employee preference for keeping the current provider, or do you indicate in your report that employees prefer to change providers? If you indicate in your report that employees indicated a preference for keeping the current dental insurance provider, you are acting unethically. Furthermore, you are acting illegally if you accept the $5,000 bribe. Because more employees indicated a preference for changing to another provider rather than keeping the current provider, you have only one legitimate recommendation to include in your report—and that is to indicate an overall employee preference for changing to a new provider.
2. Suppose you are preparing a report for your superior regarding the company's establishment of a flextime program whereby most employees will be able to determine their work starting times. For example, employees would be able to begin work anytime between 6 A.M. and 10 A.M. and end their workday eight hours later. Because you favor this program, you decide in your report to embellish several advantages and avoid mentioning several of its significant disadvantages: coordination of work among employees who work together but who choose to begin their workdays at different times, supervision of employees, and increased utility costs because the offices are occupied between 6 A.M. and 7 P.M. The only disadvantage you mention in the report is the added security concern for employees who choose to begin their workday early or end it late. Allowing your biases to contaminate the content of your report is an unethical practice.

In choosing which information to present in a report and which to disregard, you will be acting unethically if you purposely select the information consistent with your viewpoint and disregard the information that is not consistent with your viewpoint. This unethical action biases the report content and is a serious report-writing flaw.

Interoffice Memorandum

DATE: October 12, 199x
TO: Jack Adamson, Executive Vice President
FROM: Darlene Jensen, Office Services Supervisor
SUBJECT: Installation of a New Word Processing System

On several occasions, we have discussed the desirability of installing a new word processing system to replace the six-year-old stand-alone word processing system we currently use. At the time the stand-alone system was installed, the equipment was state of the art.

In installing a new word processing system, the following identify the important characteristics that should be used in judging its desirability:

a. The system should be expandable. One of the concerns I have had for several years is that we can no longer obtain equipment identical to our present stand-alone equipment. Because we have the need for additional work stations, a different brand of equipment will have to be purchased, which will destroy system compatibility if we continue to use the present stand-alone system.
b. The system should be integrated. An efficient word processing system is integrated, which means various pieces of office equipment—such as desktop computers, microcomputers, and terminals—are capable of being electronically attached to one another. Thus, each word processing station can also function in other ways—to prepare graphics, to maintain spreadsheets, and so forth.
c. The system should be capable of performing all current word processing functions. To purchase a system that cannot perform all functions is tantamount to purchasing a system that is several years old.

Among the alternatives available for installing a new word processing system are the following:

a. Replace the old stand-alone system with a new stand-alone system. Although stand-alone systems can be expandable, they cannot be integrated. Stand-alone systems are capable of performing all word processing functions.
b. Replace the old stand-alone system with a new integrated system. These systems are expandable; they can be integrated with other devices; and they are capable of performing all word processing functions.

The recommended alternative is the installation of an integrated system because it possesses the essential characteristics that a new system should possess. Furthermore, an integrated system is less apt to become obsolete as quickly as is a new stand-alone system. The primary disadvantages of integrated systems are their cost and the installation time. Training time on both systems should be approximately equal.

Exhibit 12-8 Feasibility report.

Interoffice Memorandum

January 12, 199x

TO: Mr. David Wellman, Vice President for Corporate Relations
FROM: Mr. Sam Snead, Director of Personnel
SUBJECT: Fringe Benefits Program at Americo Company

Several weeks ago you asked that I provide you with information about our fringe benefits program. Specifically, you wanted to know what percentage of our total payroll is allocated for fringe benefits so you can determine the relative cost of our fringe benefits program.

After undertaking a fairly laborious search of the information related to this topic, I discovered that last year (the most recent year for which data are presently available), companies on the average spent 37.6 percent of their total payroll costs for the company-provided fringe benefits. This percentage is expected to increase by approximately 8 percent for this year. Last year, we spent 37.2 percent of our payroll costs on fringe benefits. The following statistics are available for the years 198x-199x:

Year	National Average	Our Average
199x	37.2	37.1
199x	37.1	37.0
199x	36.8	36.9
198x	36.3	36.5
198x	36.0	36.1
198x	35.8	35.7

I was unable to find separate statistics for the various categories (banking, wholesale, manufacturing, etc.). The composite information presented above was made available by the Colorado Clearing House. I have complete faith in the accuracy of this information.

The information presented above provides rather conclusive evidence that our expenditures for fringe benefits are neither too high nor too low. Therefore, I recommend that we make no changes. In some years, we are somewhat above the national average, but in other years we are a little below the national average. As long as we continue to pay out in fringe benefits an amount that approximates the national average over the long run, I recommend we make no changes. On the other hand, should we ever fall considerably behind or significantly ahead of the national average, then I would recommend we implement the necessary changes to ensure the consistency of our fringe benefit-expenditures with the national average.

Exhibit 12-9 Audit report.

SUMMARY

Business employees use business reports extensively in carrying out their assigned duties. Managers often depend on these reports to support their decision-making and problem-solving efforts and to outline processes or procedures that they expect employees to follow. Reports also create goodwill for the organization.

Business reports are classified as either informal or formal. Both classifications are distinctly different. Businesses now use informal reports more frequently than formal reports.

The most common formats of informal reports are memorandum, letter, and manuscript reports. Some types of the three formats are justification, periodic, progress, staff, feasibility, and audit. Each type has specific purposes and uses.

REVIEW QUESTIONS

1. Identify the important functions of business reports.
2. What types of informal reports are common in the business world?
3. Why are memorandum reports considered to be informal?
4. What is the typical destination of a memorandum report? A letter report?
5. How do manuscript reports and formal reports differ?

6. How does the direct plan differ from the indirect plan in presenting information in a manuscript report?
7. What is the primary purpose of justification reports?
8. What is the typical purpose of a periodic report?
9. What is the typical purpose of a progress report?
10. What content sections are often found in staff reports?
11. What is the typical purpose of a feasibility report?
12. What is the typical purpose of an audit report?

APPLICATION PROBLEMS

1. (Memo report) You work in the office services department of Browning Corporation, a manufacturer of fishing gear. Each month you are responsible for preparing a memo for your supervisor (Mr. Jack Green, manager of office services) in which you show the number of copies run through each of the company's copy machines. The following is that information: Copy machine No. 1 (Executive Suite), 4,890 copies; Copy machine No. 2 (Computer Room), 5,987; Copy machine No. 3 (Word Processing Center), 8,804; Copy machine No. 4 (Duplicating Room), 12,874; Copy machine No. 5 (Mail Room), 2,876. Prepare the memo report, presenting this information to Mr. Green.
2. (Letter report) You are the president of the college chapter of the American Marketing Society. You recently received a letter from the national president, Wade Thurston, 4543 Midville Road, Midville, OH 48455, requesting information about various aspects of last year's chapter activities. He wanted to know the topics of the monthly meetings, the speaker's name, and the number of members and nonmembers who attended. He also wanted to know what kinds of fund-raising projects your chapter sponsored as well as the amount of money each netted. Finally, he wanted to know what types of member recruitment activities the chapter held. The following summarizes the information he requested: September—The Proctor-Smith Story, John Bennett, 48 members/5 nonmembers; October—Successful Marketing Surveys, Theresa Blackstown, 50/10; November—Creative Selling, Tim Riley, 45/7; December—A Marketing Career in Federal Department Stores, 45/3; January—How to Sell Yourself in the Employment Interview, Don Smith, 56/12; February—Field trip through Brown Advertising Agency, 31/14; March—A Career in Marketing Research, Janet Cole, 51/5; April—Spring Banquet, 54/20; May—Success: How Is It Measured? Jack Green, 56/5. Three fund-raising projects were held: used-book sale, netted $367.44; college calendars, $183.23; stadium cushions, $311.22. To recruit new members, the following activities were held: a get-acquainted social and a picnic. Prepare a letter report in which you provide the information Mr. Wade Thurston requested.
3. (Manuscript report) You have been asked by the director of the Cultural Arts Program of Midwest College to collect a variety of data that she and her advisory committee can use as input in planning next year's cultural activities. Ms. Laura Smith, the director of the CAP, desires this information because she noticed that the number of students attending these programs has diminished over the last few years. Therefore, she is concerned that perhaps events programmed in the last few years may not have met their student needs. The following summarizes the information you collected from 100 students whom you interviewed about their CAP experiences last year:
   a. Year in School: Senior—22; Junior—25; Sophomore—28; Freshman—25
   b. Major: Undeclared—15; Business—18; Arts and Letters—22; Physical Science—18; Education—17; Agriculture—10
   c. Of the Cultural Arts Programs held last year, how many did you attend? None—27; 1—28; 2—15; 3—11; 4—10; 5—9

d. Did you have a CAP season ticket last year? Yes—34; No—66
   If you answered "yes," what caused you to want to purchase a season ticket? Breadth of programs—10; Quality of programs—8; Interest in any cultural event—8; Interest in becoming more "worldly" through attending cultural events—8
   If you answered "no," what caused you to not want to purchase a season ticket? CAP events conflicted with work/class schedule—27; Not interested in majority of CAP events—23; Cannot afford price of CAP season ticket—10; Have other extenuating commitments—6
e. What would you like to see included in CAP programming that was not included during the last year? Scheduling of more pop-music groups—29; Scheduling of more rock-music groups—25; Scheduling of more operatic groups/individuals—21; Scheduling of more ballet groups—18; Have no complaints about programming—7
f. How do you feel about the pricing of the CAP events? Too costly—43; Moderately costly—23; Priced fairly—18; The CAP is a bargain—16
g. Would you be willing to pay more for CAP if the quality of programming improved as a result? Yes—34; No—66

Prepare a manuscript report for Ms. Laura Smith that contains the preceding data.

4. (Justification report) You work for the Zee-Mart Corporation. With several of your coworkers, you belong to the local Administrative Management Club. At a recent meeting, you heard the guest speaker, Mr. John Grantham, explain in detail the quality-circle concept. You and those you work with who attended the meeting believe that the quality-circle concept has enough merit to suggest the development of such a program at Zee-Mart. Accordingly, you decide to prepare a report to send to Mr. Adam Whiteburg, the company's president, recommending the development of the program. The quality-circle concept, which has enjoyed enormous success in Japanese companies, functions through the voluntary participation of employees in various work units. The members of the various quality-circle groups meet on a regular basis to devise ways to overcome problems they experience in their jobs. In some cases, outsiders are brought in to help solve the problem. The supervisor normally serves as the leader of the quality-circle group. This is how the program begins functioning—by training supervisors to become leaders of their groups. Next, the groups are formed and start operating. Meetings are held during the work day. One hour per week may be allocated for the quality-circle group meetings. Because the suggestions for overcoming or solving the problems brought before the various groups come from the employees themselves, the suggestions are often very workable and, typically, are readily accepted by the employees. In companies that initiate such programs, Mr. Grantham suggested that one employee assume the responsibility for organizing and developing the concept. He also recommended the appointment of a committee responsible for advising the person organizing and developing the concept. In addition, he also mentioned that the typical quality-circle program is very cost effective because the savings from solving work-related problems exceed the expense incurred by giving employees company time for their meetings. Present the justification report in memo format.
5. (Periodic report) You are the assistant to Ms. Janet Miller, vice president for production at Grant Computer Company, a manufacturer of components of desktop computers. Ms. Miller is quite involved in a number of professional associations. As treasurer of the local chapter of Administrative Marketing Society, one of her responsibilities is to present an updated budget at each of the monthly meetings of the executive board. She has asked you to prepare an updated budget for the June board meeting. The following figures were prepared for May's budget presentation:

	Monthly Expenditure	*Year to Date*	*Balance*
Membership	63.54	129.69	298.88
Publicity	14.98	87.87	112.89
New-Member Orientation	23.85	00.00	76.75
Newsletter	9.88	45.87	87.12
Postage	4.88	18.82	64.10
Supplies	00.00	54.12	94.32
Board Meeting Expenses	43.89	129.09	420.80
Speaker Recognition	8.98	35.92	103.32
Spring Banquet	00.00	00.00	150.00

Prepare a report, using the memo format, in which Ms. Miller presents the current budget that incorporates the changes resulting from the following expenditures during this month: Membership, $34.23; Publicity, $12.87; New-Member Orientation, 00.00; Newsletter, $10.83; Postage, $1.87; Supplies, 00.00; Board Meeting Expenses, $39.43; Speaker Recognition, $8.98; Spring Banquet, $34.40. By the way, remember the "Year-to-Date" column does not include expenses for the current month; rather, it summarizes data from January through the last month.

6. (Progress report) You are an assistant to the executive vice president of Greenfield Corporation, Mr. Jack Ellingson. Among Mr. Ellingson's responsibilities is overseeing various remodeling projects undertaken from time to time, such as the current remodeling of the mailroom. The purpose of the remodeling is to accommodate the installation of new equipment that will improve the operating efficiency of the company's mailroom operation. Richard Key, the president of the corporation, has asked Mr. Ellingson to prepare for him each month a report detailing the progress of any construction projects. Because of your competence in report writing, Mr. Ellingson has given you the responsibility of preparing these reports. The following summarizes information that you were able to obtain from the supervisor of the mailroom relating to the completion of this project: As of today, May 28, the following work has been completed: The partition between the mailroom and the storeroom has been torn out, the new sound-absorbing ceiling panels have been installed, the new sound-absorbing wall panels have been installed, and the new floor tile has been installed. The new light fixtures that were to have been installed two weeks ago have not yet been delivered because the manufacturer is on strike. If the new lights are not received within two weeks, the anticipated completion date of the project (June 20) will probably not be met. The walls and ceiling cannot be painted until the new fixtures are installed. The new mailing equipment was shipped from the manufacturer two days ago and should arrive within ten days of its shipment. As soon as it is delivered, a representative of the manufacturer will install the equipment. Normal installation time takes five days, including the equipment testing. Prepare the June report, using memo format, to update Mr. Key on the status of the project.
7. (Progress report) You are now ready to prepare the July report to present to Mr. Key (see application problem 6). Since the last report, the following has occurred: The equipment arrived and has been installed. The inserter did not work because of a broken switch. The switch has been ordered but has not yet been delivered. Just as soon as it is, the manufacturing representative who installed the new equipment will return to install the switch. The lighting manufacturer is still on strike. The contractor who is remodeling the mailroom telephoned the manufacturer yesterday (June 27) to see if the contract for the lighting fixtures could be terminated. If so, fixtures could be obtained immediately from another source, enabling the project to be completed within a week of the receipt of the fixtures (one day for installing the fixtures, four days for painting). You have not yet heard whether or not the lighting contract

can be terminated; but if it can be, expected project completion date of the project is now July 10. Prepare the report, using memo format, for Mr. Key.

8. (Staff report) You are director of personnel for the Rambo Insurance Company, which is located in Detroit. You have noticed that during the summer months—especially during July and August—many employees begin to slow down on their jobs around 3:30 to 4 each afternoon. Part of the slowdown can be attributed to having less work to do during these two months—and part, you surmise, to the fact that employees are tired and are eager to leave. You have also noticed that employee socializing has increased during the slack period. You have observed that the slow-down phenomenon has had a negative impact on the employees' attitudes. You are willing to present to the executive committee a plan in which one-fifth of the employees would get to leave at 4 P.M. each day. During a week's time, all employees would get off an hour early. You estimate the cost of this would be a total of $498.87 per week, a figure based on the average hourly salary for all employees in the company. Actually, the cost would be considerably less because most employees are apt to be less productive that last hour, regardless of the amount of work they have to do. When you mentioned your desire to investigate the leave-early plan to Mr. Grant Becker, executive vice president of Rambo, he suggested you prepare a staff report presenting ideas. He will take the report to the executive committee. Present the report in memo format.
9. (Feasibility report) You are the administrative assistant to Ms. Joan Davidson, executive vice president of Smith-Harold Corporation, located in Memphis, Tennessee. Several employees have suggested to Ms. Davidson that the company install an in-house travel agency because of the number of employees who travel and because of the frequency of their travel. Accordingly, Ms. Davidson asked you to undertake the project. You have contacted several other companies that have an in-house travel agency. In each case, you were told that in-house agencies are cost effective when the company spends $50,000 or more per year on travel. Last year's travel expenditures for Smith-Harold were $37,874. The expenses seem to be running about the same for this year. You were repeatedly informed by the companies with in-house agencies that cost effectiveness is critical. You were also told that unless the agency can be a full-service agency, employees will not use the services enough to justify its installation. The reason is that they appreciate the convenience of comprehensive one-stop service. In addition, you were told the agency must be capable of doing more for the employees than the community's agencies presently do. Unless these conditions can be met, the installation of an in-house agency probably is not feasible financially. As you see it, the company has several alternatives: Do nothing, deal exclusively with one of the full-service agencies, install a very limited in-house agency primarily for making plane reservations and use exclusively an outside agency for all other services, or install a full-service agency. Of the alternatives, the one that seems to be most feasible at this point is to deal exclusively with one outside agency. Prepare an appropriate feasibility report, using the memo format.
10. (Feasibility report) You are the office services supervisor for Hubbell Manufacturing Company. The company presently allows smoking throughout the headquarters building, except in unusually dangerous areas. Excessive cigarette smoke in the office services area has caused a number of your excellent employees to either transfer to another office or to quit to work for another company. Although you personally have nothing against employees smoking at their desks, you decided to make an informal survey of employees throughout Hubbell to assess their feelings about implementing a no-smoking policy. You found approximately half of the employees favor such a policy, but the other half oppose it. You also found that those who oppose the policy would be less opposed if certain areas would be designated smoking areas whereas other areas would be desig-

nated nonsmoking areas. When you mentioned these findings to Ms. Betty Hudson, executive vice president, she asked that you prepare a feasibility report, recommending a no-smoking policy. In preparing the report, you believe the following should be considered in making a decision: the effect of a no-smoking policy on employees, the feasibility of designating certain areas as smoking areas, and the long-term impact of breathing smoke. As you see it, you have several alternatives to present: Do nothing, implement a total no-smoking policy through the building, designate certain areas as smoking areas and other areas as nonsmoking areas, or designate some offices as smoking offices and others as nonsmoking offices. Prepare the feasibility report, using memo format. You are responsible for deciding which alternative to recommend.

11. (Audit report) You are the personnel manager of Abbott Corporation. At several recent executive committee meetings, several vice presidents have expressed concern about the apparent decline in the quality of employees the company has been hiring. This disturbs them very much as the company has always prided itself on the quality of its employees. Among the complaints heard about the newly hired employees are the following: Employee skill levels are not as good as they used to be, employees' attitudes are not as positive as they used to be, employees' tardiness and absenteeism rates are on the rise, and employee turnover is up. The vice presidents have asked you to prepare for them an audit report they will use in making decisions about this situation. You decided to collect a variety of information before you began writing the report. Among your findings are the following: Employee skill levels are decreasing throughout the nation (article that appeared in the August 12 issue of *The Wall Street News*); employees nationwide are not as loyal as they used to be, and this is reflected in their attitudes (article that appeared in July issue of *Psychology News*); across the country, employee absenteeism, tardiness, and turnover rates are higher now than they were as recently as three years ago (article that appeared in the *Houston Post*). After collecting this information, you conclude the problem is not unique to your company—that it exists nationwide. This evidence makes you feel a little better about the situation. Obviously, you would like to be the exception rather than the rule. You also conclude the problem began about three years ago when your company first started feeling a financial pinch, and it could no longer afford to pay the top-level salaries that it had in the past. You believe the company is getting the type of employee for which it is paying. Prepare the audit report, and present it in memo format.

13

Preparing Formal Reports: Prewriting Phase

After studying this chapter, you should be able to

1. Explain how to define the report problem, identify the reader, and limit the report topic.
2. Develop effective preliminary outlines for a formal report.
3. Explain how to determine outlines for a formal report.
4. Discuss the various primary and secondary research methods for preparing a formal report.
5. Explain how to categorize, tabulate, and interpret data for a formal report.
6. Discuss why objectivity is necessary in report writing.

Before actually starting to write a formal report, you must complete a number of activities. Carefully performing each activity of the prewriting phase makes the writing phase easier.

Most of the activities or steps in the prewriting phase must be completed in sequence. For example, before beginning to collect data or gather information for the report, you must define or identify the report problem and the report purpose. The nature of the report you are writing will likely determine the amount of time the following steps take to complete.

What steps does the report writer usually complete when writing formal reports?

To prepare a formal report, the report writer normally must

1. Determine the report problem (and purpose, if appropriate).
2. Identify the reader(s).
3. Limit the topic of the report.
4. Develop a preliminary outline of the report.
5. Determine the appropriate method—primary or secondary—of collecting data/information.

6. Collect data/information.
7. Classify and tabulate data/information (if appropriate).
8. Interpret the data/information.
9. Write the report.

The prewriting phase is especially important because misinterpreting data can invalidate the research results the report discusses. In addition, incorrectly identifying the intended readership of the report may result in a writing style inappropriate for the report reader or the absence of appropriate background information to ensure reader understanding.

DETERMINING THE REPORT PROBLEM

The first step in the prewriting phase is to identify and analyze the report problem. Often, if you are asked to prepare a report, the person who authorizes it identifies the problem. The *report problem* section specifies the reason or reasons for the preparation of the report. Whatever the problem is, you should state it as specifically, clearly, and succinctly as possible.

What is the difference between the report problem and its purpose?

In some cases, you may choose to let the report problem stand by itself, whereas in other cases, you may combine the problem with the *report purpose,* the section that identifies the benefits of solving the problem. Thus, the report problem is the basis of the purpose. Whether the problem stands by itself or is combined with the purpose is your decision.

What three formats are useful in formulating the report problem?

You can identify the problem and purpose of the report in three different ways: a statement, a question, or an infinitive phrase. In each of the following examples, the problem appears in italics, and the purpose is presented in boldface:

Statement

1. The *causes of low employee productivity will be examined* as a means of **increasing the profitability of ABC Corporation.**
2. The *feasibility of installing a word processing system will be investigated* as a means of **reducing operating costs of XYZ Corporation.**

Question

1. Will examining the *causes of low employee productivity* help ABC Corporation **increase its profitability?**
2. Will the *installation of a word processing system* help **reduce the operating costs of XYZ Corporation?**

Infinitive Phrase

1. To identify the *causes of low employee productivity* **to increase the profitability of ABC Corporation.**
2. To investigate the *feasibility of installing a word processing system* **to reduce the operating costs of XYZ Corporation.**

In the first example of each of the three forms, as you can see, the problem and the purpose have been identified. Low employee productivity (reason for preparing the report) is the problem, and determining ways to increase the firm's profitability (benefits to be realized by solving the problem) is the purpose. In the second example, investigating the feasibility of installing a word processing system is the problem (reason for preparing the report), and the purpose involves reducing operating costs (benefit to be realized).

Some formal reports are prepared for reasons other than to provide information for solving a problem. For example, you may simply present information. In such reports, you still should state the problem, but you do not have to give the purpose because no benefit will be realized. For example, suppose you are preparing a report to offer information about a new product. Therefore, you may state the problem as follows: "The reason for preparing this report is to present information about Product A."

You should guard against working with report problems that are not specifically or clearly worded. You will most likely have considerable difficulty offering recommendations for solving problems when their precise nature is unclear. Then ask the person who originally authorized the report to approve the revised wording.

The following are some suggestions to help you formulate the report problem:

What suggestions are useful in formulating the report problem?

1. *Review and analyze all available information.* If the authorization is in writing, review and analyze it. If you have received an oral authorization, you may have to clarify the problem by discussing it thoroughly with the person who made the authorization.

2. *Conduct a preliminary investigation.* When a review and analysis of available information are insufficient, you may need to conduct a preliminary investigation before formulating the report problem. The preliminary investigation may consist of one or more of the following: research of secondary sources or library materials, investigation of relevant organizational records, and/or discussion with people closely associated with the problem.

3. *Obtain approval of the statement of problem.* If you are responsible for formulating the report problem, you can save a considerable amount of time, effort, and money by asking the person who authorized the report to examine your statement. In this way, you should be able to correct any ambiguities and omissions before starting your actual research. If the authorizing document clearly and specifically states the report problem, this step is unnecessary.

What are the factors of the report problem?

Once you have the report problem clearly worded, identify the *factors* that have a significant impact on the problem. In reports that are mainly problem solving in nature, the factors are the causes of the problem. If the report is basically informational, the factors are the areas you must investigate.

To identify the factors of a problem-solving report, consider again the following statement:

> The reason for preparing this report is to identify the causes of low employee productivity to increase the profitability of ABC Corporation.

The factors are the causes of the problem, which may include poorly trained employees, low employee morale, inefficient work procedures, lack of adequate equipment or materials, and so forth.

To identify the factors of an informational report, consider the following statement:

> The feasibility of installing a word processing system will be investigated as a means of reducing operating costs of XYZ Corporation.

Here, the factors are the areas to investigate, which include actual per-unit cost of document preparation, using present procedures; anticipated per-unit cost of document preparation, using word processing; acceptability of word processing to employees; impact of word processing on reducing turnaround-time of document preparation; and impact of word processing on the quality and efficiency of the document-preparation process.

In an informational type of report prepared to "present information about Product A," the following factors may be identified and investigated about the product: its specifications, characteristics, and processes used in its manufacturing, its uses, and its servicing requirements.

IDENTIFYING THE READER(S)

To prepare an effective formal report, you must identify its reader or readers. Failure to target the report to the reader can significantly reduce its effectiveness. Although most frequently the reader is the person who authorized the preparation of the report, others may read it later.

Why should you identify report readership during the prewriting phase?

During the prewriting phase, the reasons for identifying the readership are the following:

1. By knowing who will read the report, you can present sufficient background information. Without knowing the reader, you risk presenting either too much or too little background information.
2. For the report to have its greatest impact, you should write in a style and at a level that considers the readers' capabilities. Writing at too high a level prevents the reader from fully understanding the content of the report and too low a level results in uninteresting reading. Using jargon, technical language, or terms that the reader will not understand also may significantly reduce the report's effectiveness.
3. By knowing your reader, you are likely to be familiar with how he or she plans to use the information presented in the report. You should then be able to give the reader the specific information he or she needs to make full use of the report.

LIMITING THE TOPIC OF THE REPORT

Another step in the prewriting phase is establishing *topic limits* (also known as *scope* or *boundaries*), which identifies what the report covers and what it does not. The factors of the problem discussed earlier in this chapter will be helpful in identifying the boundaries of the report.

How can you limit the report topics?

You can limit report topics in several ways:

1. By functional area (marketing, sales, production)
2. By time (1950–1960, 1960–1970, 1970–1980, 1980–1990, 1990–2000)
3. By geographical region or area (South, Northwest, Central)
4. By product (chemicals, rubber, wood)
5. By problem (lack of communication, decreased production, increased costs)
6. By characteristics (size, specifications, uses)

In most cases, when the scope of the report is wide, your coverage should also be wide-ranging. Similarly, in most cases, when the topic is more narrow, your coverage should be more detailed.

DEVELOPING A PRELIMINARY OUTLINE OF THE REPORT

The next activity in the prewriting phase of report preparation is to develop a preliminary outline. Without an outline, you may have the tendency to develop the report illogically, to "wander" in discussing the important facts, and to exclude important information while including irrelevant or unimportant information. You can considerably simplify this process by considering each activity you have completed up to this point: (1) defining the report problem and purpose; (2) identifying the readership; and (3) setting the topic limits. Your preliminary outline will enable you to identify topics that need to be investigated separately.

For what is the preliminary outline used?

The preliminary outline, by identifying the topics you plan to investigate, can guide you through the process of gathering data/information. Preliminary outlines are often developed using the topic format shown later in this section. After collecting the information/data, you may decide to make another outline, called the final outline. The final outline, by identifying the sequence of topics for the final report, is like a "map" for you to follow to reach your destination. Many writers prefer the discussion format, also presented later in this section, for the final outline. Sometimes the sentences you create in developing the outline can become the topic sentences of the paragraphs in your report.

Organizational Arrangements

What three organizational arrangements are used in preparing formal reports?

The three organizational arrangements for preparing reports are inductive, deductive, and chronological. Each arrangement is appropriate under certain circumstances. To decide which is most appropriate, you must consider the nature of the situation. If you believe your reader may be reluctant to accept some of your recommendations, the inductive arrangement is likely a wise choice. On the other hand, if you believe the reader will favor all of your recommendations, then the deductive arrangement can be used. The chronological arrangement is used sometimes when investigating a series of events.

The *inductive arrangement* is a structure that moves the report contents from the known to the unknown or from the specific to the general. Introductory information appears first, followed by facts obtained through the research. An analysis of the facts follows. The unknown, which consists of the summary, conclusions, and recommendations, is then presented. By custom, most formal reports use the inductive arrangement, regardless of the extent to which writers believe the reader will approve of their recommendations.

The *deductive arrangement* is a structure that moves the report contents from the unknown to the known or from the general to the specific. Thus, you present the summary, conclusions, and recommendations first, followed by facts, then by an analysis of the facts. The deductive arrangement is useful for readers whose main concerns are the summary, conclusions, and recommendations. Such readers may look at the facts and the analysis that follows only if they need more information than what is in the summary, conclusions, and recommendations.

The *chronological arrangement* is a structure that organizes the report contents according to several different chronological sequences: past to present, present to past, and present to future.

Both the inductive and the deductive arrangements are possible within the chronological organizational plan. Summary, conclusions, and recommendations are at the beginning or end of the report, depending on whether the inductive or deductive plan is used, with findings arranged chronologically. The chronological arrangement is best suited for reports having historical or time significance.

Outline Notation

What are the common types of notation used in outlining?

Outline development requires the use of some form of symbolic notation. The most common type of notation uses Roman and Arabic numerals as well as letters of the alphabet.

```
I. XXXXXXXXXX
   A. XXXXXXXXXX
   B. XXXXXXXXXX
      1. XXXXXXXXXXX
         a. XXXXXXXXXX
         b. XXXXXXXXXX
            (1) XXXXXXXXXX
                (a) XXXXXXXXXX
II. XXXXXXXXXXX
```

The second type of symbolic notation, which is increasingly popular, replaces Roman and Arabic numerals with numbers and decimals. Various sections of the report are identified as shown below.

1. First degree
    1.1 Second degree
    1.2 Second degree
        1.21. Third degree
        1.22. Third degree
            1.221. Fourth degree
            1.222. Fourth degree
                1.2221. Fifth degree
2. First degree (second major division)

The preliminary outline, after you have made necessary adjustments based on your data/information findings, should greatly assist you in devising the report's headings and subheadings. The information contained in the updated preliminary outline can also be useful when preparing the table of contents because it contains a listing of the main topics covered in the report. (See Chapter 14 for suggestions for preparing headings and a table of contents.)

Report writers must determine an appropriate organizational division of the information in the body of the report; which division is selected depends on the nature and intended use of the information. Types of divisions you can choose to break down the information are chronological or time element, geographical, important factors, characteristics, cause and effect, and quantity elements.

To illustrate, consider a formal report designed to present information on potential purchasers of a new typewriter. The most appropriate division is characteristics of potential consumers—for example, buying habits, income levels, and educational attainment. Faulty divisions are geographical location of potential consumers or chronological. Neither of these two divisions seems relevant to the report's purpose.

If you chose characteristics of the potential consumer to break down the information, your preliminary outline might have the following subdivisions:

Buying Habits

1. Use of comparative shopping techniques
2. Use of performance ratings of comparable products
3. Use of store sales, etcetera

Income Levels:

1. $10,000 or less per year
2. $10,001 to $15,000 per year
3. $15,001 to $20,000 per year, etcetera

Educational Attainment:

1. 11 years of schooling
2. 12 years of schooling
3. 13 years of schooling, etcetera

This example also shows how to use parallelism in constructing an outline. That is, the wording of all subdivisions under each major division are parallel. An example of faulty parallelism would be to place "Taking advantage of store sales" as a subdivision under "Buying habits."

Wording

How do the two outline wording options differ from one another?

You have two options in selecting the wording of the divisions and subdivisions on the preliminary outline: the topic format and the discussion format. Topic format consists of one or two words to identify a division or subdivision. The discussion format consists of a longer phrase containing information about the division or subdivision. Although business writers often prefer the topic format in preparing the preliminary outline because they have not collected information/data, they prefer the discussion format in preparing the final outline because by then they have gathered the information/data. The following are examples of both formats.

Topic:

I. Introduction
   A. Background
   B. Purpose
   C. Scope
   D etc.
II. Characteristics of the Potential Consumer
   A. Buying habits
   B. Income level
   C. Educational attainment
   D. etc.

Discussion

I. Introduction to the Report
   A. Report authorized by Jack Adams in September 199x
   B. Purpose of report to study potential purchasers of Acron microcomputer
   C. Scope of report limited to study of potential consumers of Acron microcomputer
II. Characteristics of Potential Purchaser Varied
   A. Buying habits of potential purchaser different from habits of purchasers of competing products
   B. Income levels of households of potential purchasers above national average of $15,267
   C. Educational attainment of heads of households of potential purchaser less than 13 years

Although the discussion format tells a more complete story about the report than does the topic format, its use will require your rewording of the headings and subheadings in the text of the report and in the table of contents. This is because headings and subheadings and the table of contents are composed of a minimum of words rather than clauses. Many readers, nevertheless, prefer the discussion format because it is a good preview of the report text.

DETERMINING APPROPRIATE METHOD OF COLLECTING INFORMATION

What factors should be considered in determining the appropriate method for collecting information?

The ultimate value of a formal report depends greatly on the appropriateness of the information in it. The various methods of collecting information are not equally well suited for all situations. To determine the appropriate method for collecting information, the report writer should consider the following:

1. Intended use of the report
2. Nature of the report topic
3. Availability of information
4. Financial and time constraints for completing the report
5. Ability of the report reader to understand the research methodology
6. Ability of the report writer to employ the various methods of collecting information

Information-collection methods can be categorized as either primary or secondary research methods. *Primary research methods* involve collecting data or information, using questionnaires, personal interviews, surveys, observation, and certain types of company records. Therefore, primary data/information are collected specifically for use in the report. *Secondary research methods* involve using printed sources of information, including books, periodicals, private company publications, government publications, and certain company records.

How do primary and secondary research methods differ from one another?

Primary Research Methods

In most instances, primary research requires the categorization, tabulation, and interpretation of data you have collected before the actual writing process begins. Each of these steps is discussed later in this chapter.

Use of Company Records

Company records are especially suited for collecting information for use in formal reports dealing with the various operations of an organization. In fact, you would probably be unable to obtain the needed information from any other source. Examples of such company records are sales data, information from consultants' reports, audit reports, market data, performance appraisals, accounting records, and so forth.

Company records frequently contain financial and statistical information, which can be misinterpreted easily unless extreme care is exercised. Work closely with employees familiar with financial and statistical information. If you are unfamiliar with the information but try to interpret and analyze it, misinterpretation may result.

When company records are the major source of primary information for formal reports, the information in them will need to be adapted to fit the needs of the situation. For example, with company financial information, you may have to make additional calculations before the data are appropriate for the situation.

Observation

Another method used to collect information involves observing a certain occurrence or occurrences and subsequently recording what is observed. The observation method is especially suited for situations in which the number of occurrences of a certain phenomenon is important for the report problem. In some instances, the only way to determine the number of occurrences is to observe and record them as they take place.

For what situations is the observation technique especially suited?

For example, suppose that a clothing manufacturer wishes to determine the popularity of six new spring colors. One way to assess this is to determine the number of times each of the six colors is seen in clothes worn within a given time period. An assumption is made that the more frequently the color is seen, the more popular the color is. The researcher has to devise a method, perhaps a log, for recording the observed data.

Questioning People

Another method for collecting information is to question people. Because some research projects involve a large number of people, the inclusion of each person in the project is not always feasible. In an election year, for example, media personnel frequently conduct surveys to determine which candidates are most likely to win the election. Because questioning all voters is not feasible, researchers select a representative group, often called a sample, of the voting population.

The theory of sampling is formulated on the assumption that if a sufficiently large number of items (people, for example) are randomly selected from the whole or total, the sample will possess the same characteristics as those that constitute the whole. Sampling theory is based on the use of a *random sample,* which means that each person in the relevant population has an equal chance of being selected.

What is a random sample?

Several techniques exist for randomly selecting the individuals to include in the survey. One of the most efficient, precise methods is to use a table of random numbers. Such tables and the directions for their use are included in statistics books.

Questionnaire Method

This data-collection method requires the use of a *questionnaire,* which is an instrument especially designed to collect desired data from the respondents. Considerable care must be taken in developing the questionnnaire. Although the wording of the items may appear to be clear and precise to the individual who developed the questionnaire, respondents may have difficulty determining the intent of some of the questions.

The following suggestions will be helpful when the questionnaire method is being used:

What suggestions will help in developing effective questionnaires?

1. *Construct an easy-to-complete questionnaire.* The easier the instrument is to complete, the greater is the chance that the respondents will complete it. In addition, easy-to-complete questionnaires usually improve the accuracy of responses. To make the questionnaire easy to complete, provide checklists rather than require that respondents provide a written response, such as a listing.

2. *Include instructions for completing the questionnaire, if instructions are needed.* When using instructions, place them as closely as possible to the items to which they relate. If you doubt that respondents will know what you are asking them to do with the questionnaire or a portion of it, you must include instructions.

3. *Construct the questionnaire so that the respondents' answers are easy to tabulate.* If you have essay-type questions in the questionnaire, decide how to tabulate information in the answers. Without sufficient preplanning, you may be unable to tabulate the answers, a situation that renders such questions useless. The arrangement of checklists in a vertical rather than a horizontal pattern makes tabulating easier. Before you finalize your questionnaire, try tabulating answers.

4. *Give the respondents a deadline for returning the completed questionnaire.* Because of human nature, many people will delay responding to a questionnaire. If you include a deadline for returning the questionnaire, people are more likely to respond. If your return rate is too low to achieve statistical reliability, then you most likely will have to administer a follow-up mailing.

5. *Consider eye appeal and the format of the questionnaire.* Respondents are more likely to complete a questionnaire with an appealing design and format. For example, a questionnaire with much type and little white space is less appealing (and harder to read) than is a questionnaire with a good amount of white space. Similarly, a questionnaire in a small type size is less appealing and more difficult to read than is a questionnaire in a larger type size.

6. *Limit the use of the questionnaire to topics for which information from other sources is unavailable.* If you can collect the needed information from sources other than questionnaires, do so. Whenever possible, use accurate information from other readily available sources.

Included in Communication Capsule 13-1 are a number of suggestions to follow in writing specific questionnaire items.

Communication Capsule 13-1 Ways to Improve the Effectiveness of Questionnaires

The following suggestions should help you improve the effectiveness of the items included in the questionnaires you prepare:

1. *Avoid using questions that prejudice the respondents' answers.* An example of this kind of question is, "Is red your favorite color?" Some respondents may respond that red is their favorite color because it was mentioned in the question. The accuracy of responses to the question can be improved by listing the color possibilities on the questionnaire and by asking respondents to place a check mark beside their favorite color.

2. *Avoid the use of words that mean different things to different people.* In a question that asks respondents if they frequently shop in the downtown area of a particular city, different people will interpret the meaning of the word "frequently" differently. One respondent may consider twice a month to be frequent, whereas another interprets frequent to mean at least twelve times a month. You can improve this question by asking the respondents how often within a given period they shop downtown.
3. *Arrange the questions in a sequential pattern.* Place related questions in close proximity to each other rather than interspersed throughout the questionnaire. When possible, arranging the questions in a general-to-specific sequence is psychologically advantageous because the respondent will not need to respond immediately to the more challenging questions. Also desirable is the placement of the easy-to-answer questions at the beginning of the questionnaire and the more difficult-to-answer questions at the end of the questionnaire.
4. *Avoid questions the respondents consider to be personal.* Questionnaires frequently contain items inquiring about respondents' yearly incomes or ages. Some people are sensitive about reporting this personal information, and asking them to provide it will probably adversely affect their willingness to respond. Respondents are less apt to find as being offensive the use of ranges for reporting answers to personal items. To illustrate, the following technique can help you ask respondents to identify their age: 18–24____; 25–31____; 32–38____; etc.
5. *Keep the number of questions to a minimum.* One of the most common reasons that individuals do not respond to a questionnaire is its length. If the questionnaire becomes too long, the researcher should consider omitting or consolidating questions.
6. *Avoid asking compound questions in a single questionnaire item.* Compound questions, which can result in two answers, are difficult for individuals to answer. Such an example is the following: Do you prefer a two-color or a four-color book? _______ Yes; ______ No.

How do structured and unstructured questions differ from one another?

Two basic categories of items are on questionnaires: unstructured or open-ended items and structured or closed-ended items. The nature of the questions asked will determine which category to use.

Unstructured questions allow respondents to make detailed responses. For example, asking respondents to "identify the three most common causes of employee job dissatisfaction" is likely to elicit a more-detailed response than giving respondents a list of causes and then having them rank the causes. Responses to unstructured questions, though, are more difficult to categorize in the data-tabulation process than are responses to structured questions.

Structured questions restrict respondents to at least one answer from a list of possible responses. Types of structured questions include the following: multiple-choice, ranking, either-or, checklist, fill-in, and scaling. These questions are easy to tabulate because they elicit standardized responses. But the limited choices do not allow for depth of response.

What types of structured questions are found on questionnaires?

Multiple-choice questions usually give the respondent three or more possibilities from which to choose one or more responses. Because you cannot always identify all possible choices, an "other" choice is often provided. The following is a multiple-choice item.

Which one of the following best describes your present position?
____ A. Division manager
____ B. Department manager
____ C. Area supervisor
____ D. Supervisor
____ E. Other (please specify) ________________________________

The *ranking* technique gives the respondent an opportunity to rank order a list of items. This type of item is well suited to determining preferences.

Please identify in the following list of fringe benefits your order of preference by placing a "1" beside the benefit most preferred by you, a "2" beside your second preference, etc.:
_____ Retirement program
_____ Medical insurance
_____ Life insurance
_____ Paid vacations
_____ Dental insurance
_____ Disability insurance

Either-or questions give the respondent an opportunity to choose between two alternatives. In some instances, the adding of a third choice, such as "Don't know," "Am not sure," or "Undecided," may be inappropriate.

Do you believe that all managers need a college degree?
Yes; __________ No; __________ Undecided

Checklists give the respondent an opportunity to check more than one alternative choice. To make the categorizing and tabulating process as easy as possible, all potential alternatives should be listed among the checklist items. In addition, an "other" alternative is often included.

In the list that follows, please place a check mark beside each of the major household appliances you presently own.
_____ Washer
_____ Dryer
_____ Range
_____ Refrigerator
_____ Trash compactor
_____ Dishwasher
_____ Freezer
_____ Television set
_____ Stereo
_____ Video cassette recorder
_____ Home computer
_____ Other (please specify) ______________________________

Fill-in questions require short answers. These questions are useful when you cannot predetermine all possible alternative items to list for a specific question. You can also use fill-ins when the list of alternatives that you must provide is too long.

Please list the foreign countries in which you have traveled.

____

Scaling questions are used to obtain information about the intensity of the respondents' feelings about a particular topic or issue. Also called the Likert scale, a scaling question gives respondents several choices, perhaps as many as five or seven, and they select the choice that most clearly reflects their feelings. Basically, scaling questions allow the respondent to scale their responses along a continuum.

All business majors should have a speaking fluency in a foreign language.
1. Strongly agree
2. Agree
3. Neutral
4. Disagree
5. Strongly disagree

Interview Method

The *interview* is a data-collection technique in which the researcher or someone designated by him or her asks interviewees a series of questions pertinent to the research topic. The interview method is well suited for collecting detailed information and for asking unstructured or open-ended questions.

When the population contains a large number of individuals, a random sample may be required. Depending on the situation, you may need more than one interviewer. Large research studies are especially likely to use multiple interviewers. Because a lack of consistency among interviewers may affect the data, each interviewer must use the same interrogative procedures. To ensure consistency in interrogation procedures, interviewers may need to participate in a training program before conducting the interviews. Field testing the interview questions for clarity and understandability before the actual interview process is also advisable.

What is an interview guide?

Most interviewers use an interview guide listing the questions to be asked and providing space for the interviewee's answers. If the interviewee does not fully understand a question after it is read, the interviewer is able to clarify the intent of the question, something that is not possible with the questionnaire method, for example.

The interview method is often made more effective when the interviewer tells the interviewee what he or she hopes to accomplish during the interview. This helps set an appropriate stage of what is to follow. The questions asked need to focus on the more important points. At the end of the interview, reviewing the questions to ensure that all have been asked is wise.

Among the types of interview questions used are close-ended, open-ended, leading, and so forth. These types of questions are discussed in detail in Chapter 11.

Experimentation

Today businesses are turning increasingly to experimental research because, if well designed, such studies produce extremely accurate results.

What is involved in using the experimental method?

In simple terms, the *experimental research method* involves measuring one or more *variables* (topics or areas of research interest) that the researcher is studying. By measuring the variables, then subjecting the participants to the *treatment* (the research strategy), and again measuring the variables after the treatment, the researcher can determine the effect of the treatment on the variables.

The experimentation method typically uses either one group or two groups. In the one-group alternative, the researcher first measures the variable of interest by a pretest, then administers the treatment to the group, and next measures the variable of interest a second time by a posttest. Assuming that the research has tightly controlled the experimentation process, any differences between the first and second measurements of the variable of interest can most likely be attributed to the treatment. However, we should point out that the measurement differences can also possibly be attributed to a variety of extraneous factors, which, if present, will weaken the research results.

For example, suppose that a researcher wishes to determine the impact of a ten-hour training program on workers' skill in operating a new piece of equipment. First the researcher pretests the level of skill (the variable) demonstrated by each worker in operating the equipment. Then the workers participate in the training program (treatment). At the conclusion of the training program, the researcher remeasures the level of skill possessed by each worker—this time by means of the posttest. If the workers' skill levels increased and if the researcher can be sure that the increase is attributable solely to the training program, the amount that the workers increased their skill in operating the equipment can be used to assess the impact of the training program.

The two-group alternative is often used by the researcher to provide more credible research results than the one-group alternative may provide. The researcher uses two groups: the *control group* (the group that does not receive the treatment) and the experimental group (the group that receives the treatment). The individuals in both groups must be essentially alike in relevant background factors (gender, age, intelligence, years of employment, etc.). Even greater research outcome credibility is possible if the individuals are randomly assigned to the respective groups.

In the two-group process, the researcher begins by pretesting the variable of interest among both groups. If the pretest scores of both groups are similar, the researcher can be reasonably sure that the two groups are essentially the same. The experimental group is then subjected to the treatment, whereas the control group is not. Next the researcher posttests both groups on the variable of interest. Assuming that both groups had the same experiences during the entire research process—except in terms of treatment—any differences between the posttest measurements of both groups can be attributed to the treatment.

For example, suppose that the researcher wants to determine the impact of a new training program on the efficiency of employees' use of word processing equipment. After each employee is randomly assigned to either the control and experimental group, the researcher administers to both groups a pretest measurement of employee efficiency in operating the equipment. Then the experimental group is subjected to the new training program (treatment). After the treatment, the researcher reevaluates both groups according to their efficiency of equipment operation. Any differences in the posttest scores of the two groups can most likely be attributed to the training program, especially if the pre and posttest scores of the control group did not change significantly.

Secondary Research Methods

The use of secondary information in formal reports should not be overlooked. If someone else has already prepared material related to your area or topic of interest, the use of secondary information is often quite expedient.

What sources of secondary information are used?

Sources of secondary information include the following:

Abstracts	Books
Almanacs	Brochures
Annual reports	Bulletins
Articles (periodicals)	Company correspondence
Biographies	Company reports

Dictionaries
Directories
Documents
Encyclopedias
Government publications
Handbooks
Manuals
Newsletters
Pamphlets
Yearbooks

Depending on the situation, you should be cautious about using material prepared by someone else without assessing its technical accuracy. In addition, you must credit that source. If an abundance of secondary information is available, you will need to determine which information to use and which to eliminate.

You may easily locate information about specific topics in most public libraries and in in-house libraries when they exist. In a public library, the card catalog (most likely computerized today) contains listings of books, manuals, handbooks, and government publications about specific categorical topics. Several guides or indexes to listings of periodical articles are also available. The contents of these indexes are typically arranged alphabetically by topics. The listings of articles pertaining to each topic appear below each topic heading. The *Readers' Guide to Periodical Literature* is one such guide.

Most of the academic disciplines now have guides or indexes that list articles on specific topics within specialized disciplines. For example, the *Business Periodicals Index* lists titles of articles in business-related periodicals. Because the various guides and indexes commonly list articles by topic, you must turn to the topic of interest. For example, if you wish to obtain a list of periodical articles on quality circles, simply look for the topic of "Quality circles." Under this heading, you will find a list of the articles on this that have been published during a specific time period in the various periodicals indexed in the *Business Periodicals Index.* In addition, some of the more widely circulated newspapers, such as the *Wall Street Journal* and the *New York Times,* also have their own topical indexes of articles printed in their respective papers.

The following is a list of guides and indexes that report writers may find helpful:

Guides to Periodicals

Magazines for Libraries, R. R. Bowker, Co., New York

Standard Periodical Directory, Oxbridge, New York

Ulrich's International Periodicals Directory, R. R. Bowker, Co., New York

Union List of Serials in Libraries of the United States and Canada, H. W. Wilson Co., New York

New Serial Titles, Library of Congress, Washington

Guides to Periodical Indexes

Accountants' Index and Supplements, American Institute of Certified Public Accountants, New York

Accounting Articles, Commerce Clearing House, Chicago

AMA 10 Year Index of AMA Publications, American Management Association, New York

Applied Science and Technology Index, H. W. Wilson Co., New York

Bibliographical Index, H. W. Wilson Co., New York

Business Education Index, Delta Pi Epsilon, Little Rock, Arkansas

Business Periodicals Index, H. W. Wilson Co., New York

Cumulative Index of the National Industrial Conference Board Publications, National Industrial Conference Board, New York

Engineering Index, Engineering Index Service, New York
Engineering Index Annual, American Society of Mechanical Engineers, New York
Funk and Scott Index of Corporations and Industries, Funk and Scott Publishing Co., Detroit
Index of Economic Journals, Richard D. Irwin, Inc., Homewood, Illinois
Management Index, Keith Business Library, Ottawa, Canada
Poole's Index to Periodical Literature, Houghton Mifflin Co., Boston
Readers' Guide to Periodical Literature, H. W. Wilson Co., New York
Social Science and Humanities Index, H. W. Wilson Co., New York

Guides to Periodical Abstracts

Journal of Economic Literature, American Economic Association, Menasha, Wisconsin
Personnel Management Abstracts, Bureau of Industrial Relations, Ann Arbor, Michigan
Psychological Abstracts, American Psychological Association, Washington
Sociological Abstracts, Sociological Abstracts, Inc., New York

Guides to Newspaper Indexes

Index of the Christian Science Monitor, H. M. Cropsey, Corvallis, Oregon
National Observer Index, Dow Jones and Company, New York
New York Times Index, New York Times Co., New York
The Wall Street Journal Index, Dow Jones and Co., New York

Guides to Books

Books in Print, R. R. Bowker, New York
Cumulative Book Index: A World List of Books in the English Language, H. W. Wilson Co., New York
National Union Catalog, Library of Congress, Washington
Paperbound Books in Print, R. R. Bowker Co., New York
Publisher's Weekly, R. R. Bowker Co., New York
Subject Guide to Books in Print, R. R. Bowker Co., New York

Vertical files containing brochures, pamphlets, handouts, and reports on selected topics are in many libraries. These files are also useful as secondary sources of information.

What is a computerized database?

An increasing number of libraries have computerized databases available. Sources of information on an enormous number of topics are made available in a matter of minutes—perhaps even seconds. Instead of having to search manually for a needed source, the computer does the searching.

In using a computerized database, you enter keywords or phrases into the computer. Before beginning the actual search, examine the database directory to determine the keyword(s) or phrase(s) necessary to obtain the desired information. Only keywords or phrases in the directory will be operable in carrying out the search. After the search is completed, you may use a computer to prepare a printout of the citations (journal name; author name; issue date, number, volume; page numbers) contained in the database.

Among the databases of interest to business report writers are the following:

ABI/INFORM
DIALOG

ACCOUNTANTS
DOW JONES NEWS RETRIEVAL
PREDICAST F & S INDEX
LABORDOC
MANAGEMENT CONTENTS
TRADE AND INDUSTRY INDEX

Note Taking

How do bibliography and data set cards differ from one another?

When collecting secondary information, you will need to use a systematic means of note taking. One efficient method for taking notes involves preparing two sets of cards: the bibliography set (contains all the relevant bibliographic information about the source that you will need to use in a citation) and the data set. The bibliography set, which is prepared first, contains the bibliographic information for each source the researcher plans to use. After the bibliography set is prepared, the cards are then alphabetized and numbered sequentially. As shown in Exhibit 13-1, the number in the upper-right corner is the sequential number and indicates that this particular card is the fifth card in the bibliography set.

A second set of index cards, the data cards, record the notes you take while reading the various sources. In the upper-right corner, enter the sequential number from the appropriate bibliography card. The number 5 in the upper-right corner of a data card means the notes on that card came from the fifth card in the bibliography set. When organizing the information before writing the report, you will find that recording only one category of information on each data card is helpful. For example, instead of entering two categories of information—such as characteristics and advantages of LIFO—on the same card, you can prepare two cards: one on the characteristics of LIFO and another that contains the advantages of LIFO. Also enter the page number(s) where the information on each data card was found. Page numbers are typically recorded immediately following the material entered on the card. This process is shown in Exhibit 13-2.

Exhibit 13-1 Cards in bibliography set used in note taking.

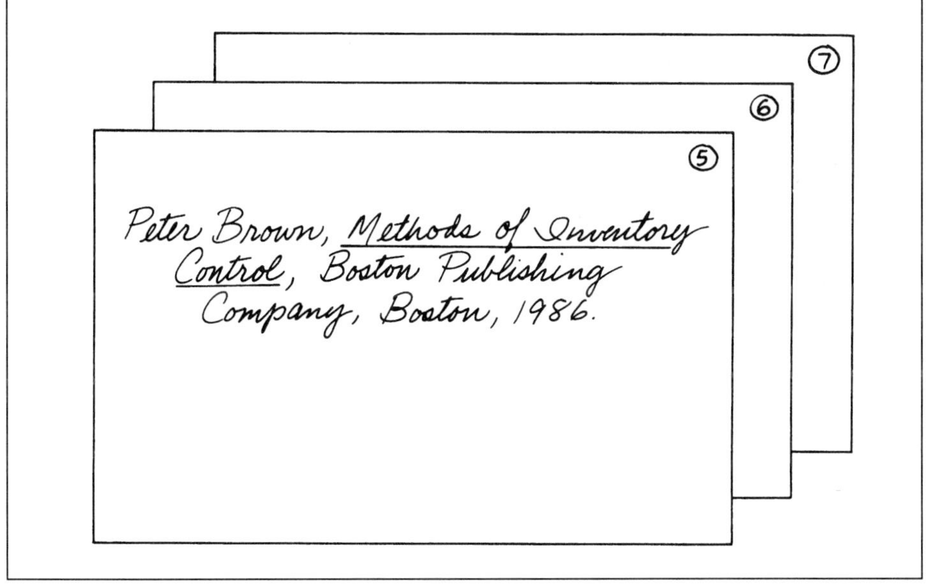

7
6
5
Peter Brown, Methods of Inventory Control, Boston Publishing Company, Boston, 1986.

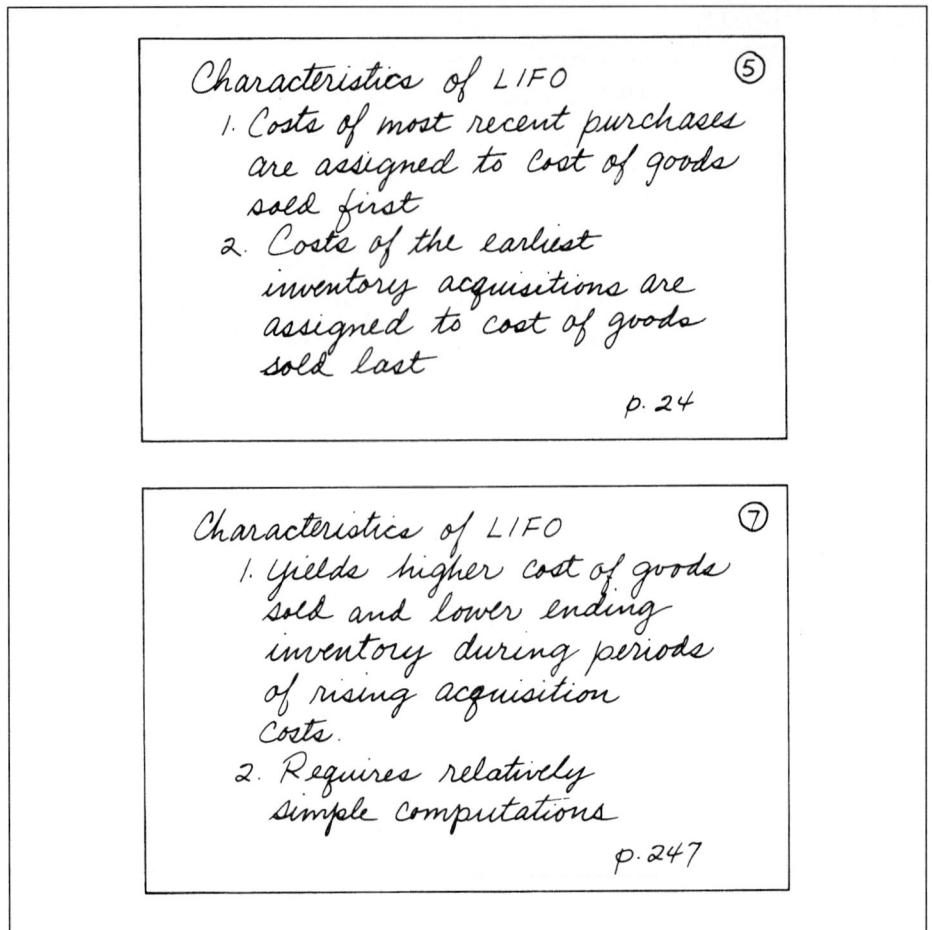

Characteristics of LIFO ⑤
1. Costs of most recent purchases are assigned to cost of goods sold first
2. Costs of the earliest inventory acquisitions are assigned to cost of goods sold last
p. 24

Characteristics of LIFO ⑦
1. Yields higher cost of goods sold and lower ending inventory during periods of rising acquisition costs.
2. Requires relatively simple computations
p. 247

Exhibit 13-2 Cards in data set used in note taking.

Next, enter each subdivision of the preliminary outline on separate sheets of paper. If you find information on a data card relating to a specific subdivision in the report, enter that information on the appropriate sheet, along with the sequence number and the page references for each piece of information. A system frequently used places the sequence number before a colon, followed by the page number after, as the following shows: (5:239). As a shortcut, attach the cards (by tape or staples) to the appropriate sheets. Exhibit 13-3 illustrates this process.

As an alternative to preparing handwritten notes, increasing numbers of business writers are photocopying the material they want to include in their reports. After the material is collected and photocopied, they arrange the copied material in an alphabetical sequence (by author's name); then they number each photocopied set sequentially. For example, the fifth article in the sequence would be identified as Article No. 5. As they read the material, they write beside the information they desire to incorporate in their report the outline identification number (note V.1.A. beside the headings of the "photocopied" information in Exhibit 13-4). "V.1.A." means that this information pertains to that section of their outline. The marked information is then cut out and attached (stapled, glued, or taped) to the appropriate outline page. The handwritten numbers to the left of the cut-out material indicate the article number (3 and 7, respectively) and the page number of the article on which the material appears (24 and 67, respectively).

V. Characteristics of LIFO

1. Costs of most recent purchases are assigned to cost of goods sold first

2. Costs of the earliest inventory acquisitions are assigned to cost of goods sold last

(5:24)

3. Yields higher cost of goods sold and lower ending inventory during periods of rising acquisition costs

4. Requires relatively simple computation

(7:247)

Exhibit 13-3 Subdivision of report outline with notes.

```
V. Courtesy
   1. Positive Tone
      A. Advantages of Using
```

Positive Tone **V.1.A.**

One of the characteristics of business writing crucial to message success is tone. In fact, tone often determines—more than any other factor—how successful the message is. The use of positive tone throughout the message will enable you to make the reader feel better about himself or herself, thus helping assure the success of your message. Regardless of the nature of the situation you are writing about, avoid using a negative tone the reader may take personally.

Tone: **V.1.A.**

Make it Positive

The use of a positive tone in business writing makes sense for several reasons. Among these are the following: the reader will be more likely to want to comply with your request; it will help enhance the relationship between the writer and the reader; and it results in more concise writing than is generally found with negatively worded messages.

Exhibit 13-4 Annotation of photocopied materials.

CATEGORIZING THE DATA

What is involved in categorizing data?

If the formal report contains primary data that you must tabulate before they are usable, you need to determine appropriate categories for them. For example, suppose that your questionnaire contains an item asking respondents to list the number of books they have read during the past year. To make the responses more meaningful, consider organizing your data into categories that will enable you to see trends, themes, and/or relationships. The categories in this example might be 0–3 books;

4–6 books; 7–9 books; 10–12 books, and so on. If you decide not to present the data in a category format, then you will have to list the number of respondents who have read no books, 1 book, 2 books, 3 books, and so forth.

Unless you develop some systematic categorization, questionnaire items with more than eight to ten possible responses may become cumbersome when presented in the report. Often report writers determine categories at the same time they develop their questionnaire. They then use the same categories in tabulating the data.

Unstructured items tend to be more difficult to categorize than structured items. You will need to verify the accuracy of the categories into which you place individual responses. Otherwise much of your work may be diminished in its usefulness. In some cases, you may find "reading between the lines" is needed to select the appropriate category for an individual's response.

When determining the categories, be careful to use those that give significant meaning to the data. Extremely broad or narrow categories are likely to obscure the true meaning of the data presented in the report. An extremely broad category would be salaries ranging from $0 to $50,000, $50,001 to $100,000, and so forth. An example of an extremely narrow category would be salaries ranging from $0 to $4,000, $4,001 to $8,000, $8001 to $12,000, and so forth.

TABULATING THE DATA

Once you have determined the appropriate categories, the next step is to tabulate the data. When a fairly small number of questionnaires are included in the study, you may complete the tabulating process manually by recording on a tally sheet the responses to each item in the questionnaire.

But when you must tabulate a large number of questionnaires, a mechanical process may be especially desirable. One of the more common mechanical means involves coding each possible response for each item on the questionnaire. The coded response to each item is then entered on a medium (such as optical scanning sheets) that can be mechanically processed. The machine tabulates the number of responses to each category.

Once you have tabulated numerical data, the mean, median, and mode can be calculated. The *mean,* which is the average of all the numbers in a series or group, is found by adding each number and dividing the total by the number of items in the series. For example, consider the following series of numbers: 10, 9, 7, 6, 6, 5, 4. The mean is 6.71 (47/7). The *median* is the number at the midpoint in a series (6, in this instance) arranged in either ascending or descending order. The *mode* is the number in the series that occurs most frequently (6, in this instance). The mean, median, and mode are used in the statistical analysis of the data you present in a report.

INTERPRETING INFORMATION

The last step in the prewriting phase of the preparation of a formal report is the *interpretation of the information,* a process that involves assigning meaning to data. The mere presentation of facts and data does nothing to help the reader benefit from the report. But once the facts and data have meaning, you are likely to benefit substantially from their inclusion. For example, suppose you state that the sales volume of a certain product increased $10,759 over last year's sales. This statement lacks meaning. Unless you know the percentage amount of increase or the base sales figure, it is virtually useless.

Why does information have to be interpreted?

You can also misinterpret information, causing the reader to draw inappropriate conclusions. Some of the more common types of interpretation errors include the following:

What types of interpretation errors are made?

1. *Supporting the contrary because of lack of evidence.* An interpretation error occurs when the report writer believes a lack of evidence can be used to support a contrary conclusion. For example, suppose that you want to prove that employee absenteeism tends to be higher on clear days than on cloudy days. But the evidence did not support this claim. You would then be making an interpretation error if you state that

because insufficient evidence existed to support the original claim (absenteeism is higher on clear days), the opposite must be true (absenteeism is lower on clear days).

2. *Drawing conclusions based on insufficient information.* Many inexperienced report writers make interpretation errors because they draw conclusions from inadequate information. The greater the amount of evidence available to the report writer, the more certain the writer can be that his or her conclusions are the logical result of the evidence. This error in interpretation occurs because report writers forget that conclusions cannot always be logically drawn from the evidence. To draw such conclusions reflects adversely on the work of the report writer.

3. *Exaggerating information.* The report writer can render information virtually useless by exaggerating its quantitative value. Another way information can be distorted is to downplay its significance.

4. *Using unreliable data or information.* A report that includes unreliable data or information is also useless. If you collect primary data and if your statistical procedures are valid, the chances are fairly good that your data are reliable. When you use secondary data or information, you should, as previously indicated, make certain that they are reliable. This means assessing the appropriateness of the statistical procedures. In some instances, you can validate secondary information by comparing it with data from other sources.

5. *Using faulty cause-effect relationships.* Another interpretation error of some significance is a faulty cause-effect relationship, which means that the effect of a certain cause is not what it is claimed to be. An example of a faulty cause-effect relationship is that cloudy skies cause rain. This is faulty because, though a relationship between clouds and rain exists, the presence of certain atmospheric conditions on cloudy days can cause rain—not the cloudy skies themselves.

What situations inject bias or prejudice into the report-writing process?

6. *Allowing personal feelings to influence the interpretation process.* An objective report contains material that is free of the report writer's prejudices and biases. Some writers have difficulty keeping their personal feelings from surfacing in written reports. Especially inappropriate is letting personal feelings influence the interpretation of data. Not only is the interpretation of data distorted, but also the influence of personal feelings could result in an incorrect conclusion or an inappropriate recommendation. The best way to prevent this type of interpretation error is to base your interpretation solely on supportable information. In addition, a lack of objectivity in report preparation often results in a lack of content believability.

7. *Comparing data that are not comparable.* Report writers who compare noncomparable data are likely to make serious errors in interpretation. For example, to compare the purchasing power of the average family today with the purchasing power of the average family twenty years ago is worthless because the value of today's dollar is considerably less than it was twenty years ago. Therefore, a valid comparison is impossible unless today's dollar and the dollar of twenty years ago have been put on a comparable base.

Once you have interpreted the data, you need to point out the relationships, consistencies, inconsistencies, similarities, and differences in these data. This process is what gives meaning to your information.

At this point, you may draw conclusions and make recommendations. Remember that evidence in the report must support your conclusions. The recommendations outline the writer's suggestions for action, based on the evidence in the report. Conclusions are the logical outcome of the information presented in your report. Recommendations are specific actions you suggest be taken on the basis of your findings and subsequent conclusions.

SUMMARY

Before beginning to write a formal report, you must complete several preliminary steps, including defining the report problem. In addition, you must identify the reader(s) of the report as well as the scope of the topic. The next step involves developing a preliminary outline of the report.

Another important aspect of report preparation is deciding on the appropriate method of collecting information. You can collect primary information through company records, observation, questioning people, questionnaires, interviews, and experimentation. An alternative is using secondary research.

Once the data are collected, categorizing, tabulating, and interpreting them are important. When writing, be aware of the ways you can improve your objectivity, a characteristic critical to the success of your report.

REVIEW QUESTIONS

1. How does the report problem differ from the report purpose?
2. In what formats can you present the report problem and purpose?
3. What suggestions can you offer to help the writer of a report problem?
4. Why should the writer of the report identify the reader before the writing process begins?
5. In what ways can report topics be limited?
6. How does the inductive arrangement differ from the deductive arrangement in a formal report?
7. How does the topic format differ from the discussion format in the wording of report outlines?
8. What factors help determine the most appropriate method for collecting information for a formal report?
9. What types of primary research methods are available to the report writer?
10. What suggestions can you offer to help in developing a questionnaire?
11. How is a computerized database useful to report writers?
12. Why does primary data have to be categorized?
13. What is the purpose of data interpretation?
14. What are the interpretation errors a report writer should avoid?

APPLICATION PROBLEMS

1. Prepare a report problem and purpose for each of the following situations:
   a. A study that compares the effectiveness of merit salary increases versus across-the-board salary increases. The individual who authorized the study was interested in determining the impact that each had on employee motivation.
   b. A study that determines the nature of employees' communication strengths and weaknesses. The information will be used to design a training program to help employees overcome their weaknesses.
   c. A study that determines the impact of work standards on increasing employee productivity. Information will be helpful in determining need for implementing a work measurement/work standards program.
2. Critique the following report problems and purposes, and then rewrite each:
   a. The purpose of this report is to compare the relative effectiveness of an in-house letter-writing seminar in helping employees overcome their writing problems.
   b. The purpose of this report is to assess the impact of MBO on employees' attitudes to improve the motivation of employees in ABC Corporation.
   c. The purpose of this report is to evaluate the desirability of installing a profit-sharing plan as a means of motivating employees to increase their efficiency.
3. For each of the situations in application problem 1, identify the factors of the problem.
4. For each of the situations in application problem 1, identify the report limits.
5. Select one of the situations in application problem 1 and prepare a tentative outline, using the inductive arrangement. Then revise the outline, using the deductive arrangement.

6. Using the topic captions, prepare an outline for application problem 1 in Chapter 14.
7. Using discussion captions, prepare an outline for application problem 2 in Chapter 14.
8. Develop a questionnaire designed to collect data about students' attitudes toward a required English proficiency exam they must pass before they can graduate from Northern College. Include at least one question in each of the following formats: multiple-choice, ranking, either-or, checklist, fill-in, and scaling.
9. Prepare an interview form to be used when interviewing students to learn their preferences for the "ideal" spring-break vacation. This information is desired by a travel agent who will use your findings to develop a variety of spring-break packages.
10. You have been hired by a representative of a fast-food franchise chain to develop an interview form to assess the eating-out habits of the students at your college. The information will ultimately be used to assess the need for another fast-food restaurant near the campus. Develop the interview form.
11. You have been hired by a local grocery store to develop a questionnaire that will be sent to a selected sample of community residents. The purpose of the questionnaire is to determine which television programs broadcast on the local television station (Channel 6, KSTV) are viewed on a regular basis by the questionnaire recipients. The store plans to have its commercials run during the most widely viewed programs between 7 P.M. and 10 P.M. on Tuesday and Thursday evenings. (Make up the titles of the programs.)
12. Using the data presented in application problem 2 of Chapter 14, prepare the questionnaire that might have been used to collect those data.
13. Using the data presented in application problem 3 of Chapter 14, prepare the questionnaire that might have been used to collect those data.
14. Using the information presented in application problem 4 of Chapter 14, prepare the form on which the data might have been tabulated.

14

Preparing Formal Reports: Writing Phase

After studying this chapter, you should be able to

1. Discuss the purpose of each preliminary part in a formal report.
2. Describe the appropriate content for a letter of authorization and a letter of transmittal.
3. Explain the purpose of the introduction section in a formal report.
4. List the differences among the summary, conclusions, and recommendations sections in a formal report.
5. Prepare an effective formal report.

Formal reports have an important function of disseminating information for use by managers and executives in their decision-making efforts. For example, a formal report may be used to disseminate the findings of a comprehensive study of the marketing potential of a new product, of an organizational or departmental restructuring, or of a study of competing products or services. Although one or more of the types of informal reports discussed in Chapter 12 may also distribute these findings, a formal report will be more appropriate and effective. Perhaps the complexity of the report's topic requires a greater in-depth analysis than informal reports permit.

How are formal and informal reports different from one another?

Formal reports differ from informal reports in the following ways:

1. Formal reports are generally longer.
2. Formal reports follow a rather conventional, standardized format.
3. Formal reports are likely to make significantly greater use of graphic illustrations.
4. The material in formal reports tends to be written in a more formal style.

The information in formal reports may be primary information, secondary information, or a combination of both. Primary information refers to data or information most often collected through questionnaires or interviews. Secondary information is collected from books, periodicals, reports, and other types of documents. When using secondary information in a report, its source(s) must be identified and perhaps its credibility established.

PARTS OF THE FORMAL REPORT

What parts are included in formal reports?

Most of the following parts are required in a formal report; however, some are optional, with inclusion only if a specific situation demands their use. Typically report writers insert optional parts when their report is quite long or is extremely formal. In the following list of the parts of a formal report, an asterisk appears after each optional element:

A. Preliminary parts
   1. Title fly*
   2. Title page
   3. Letter of authorization*
   4. Letter of transmittal*
   5. Table of contents
   6. List of illustrations*
   7. Abstract/synopsis
B. Body parts
   1. Introduction
      a. Background of the report
      b. Statement of problem and purpose
      c. Scope
      d. Methodology
      e. Definitions
      f. Limitations
      g. Historical background of the report topic
      h. Report organization
   2. Text
C. Ending parts
   1. Summary*
   2. Conclusions
   3. Recommendations
D. Appended parts
   1. Bibliography
   2. Appendices*

A formal report appears at the end of this chapter. The report shows each of the required and optional parts as well as the proper mechanics of presentation.

Preliminary Parts

Of the four main sections of formal reports—preliminary, body, ending, and appended parts—you have greater flexibility in deciding which of the parts in the preliminary section to include than what to include in the other three sections. These preliminary parts give the reader an overview of the information found in the report. Essentially, they provide a road map.

Title Fly

What information is included on the title fly?

The title fly page contains only the title of the report. Because the title page, which is discussed next, also contains the title of the report, some perceive the title fly to be virtually useless. Nevertheless, if you open with a title fly, type the title in capital letters and place it approximately one to one and one-half inches above the vertical center of the page.

If the title requires two or more lines, making the top line of the title the longest, with each successive line shorter than the previous line, improves the appearance of the title fly page. The title, therefore, appears in a "V" arrangement. Although the title fly page is counted in numbering pages, the page number is usually not typed on the page.

Title Page

Most report writers choose to omit the title fly page. Therefore, the title page is typically the first page of a formal report. Most title pages contain the following:

What information is included on the title page?

1. Title of the report
2. Name and title of the person for whom the report is prepared
3. Name and title of the person who prepared the report
4. Company, city, and state of the report writer
5. Date of presentation

The title on the title page should be typed in capital letters and underscored. A "V" arrangement of the title is also recommended.

When a title fly page exists, the title page is numbered. The title page is considered as page i when the title fly page is not used. But if a title fly page is used and you choose to number the title page, it becomes page ii, with the number centered at the bottom of the page.

Letter of Authorization

Although the report writer does not prepare the letter (or memorandum) of authorization, it is discussed in this chapter to assist writers who need to prepare such documents. The *letter of authorization* is the document that gives the writer the necessary permission, direction, or charge to prepare the report.

Many report assignments are made orally. Although oral authorizations are as legitimate as written authorizations, be careful about undertaking reports with oral authorization, especially if the report assignment is controversial. Obtain a written authorization in case any aspect of the report assignment eventually needs verification. Written assignments are less open to dispute at a later date. Moreover, a written authorization clearly and concisely records the report assignment. The written authorization, which may be in either letter or memorandum format, typically includes the following sections:

What information is included in the letter of authorization?

1. An authorization for you to begin preparation of the report
2. The statement of problem (and purpose, if appropriate), the scope, and the limitations of the report
3. A discussion of relevant background information
4. A discussion of conditions for preparing the report, including the due date, budgetary allowances, and, if appropriate, the amount of compensation you are to receive
5. A courteous closing with an offer to be of assistance if needed

Use lowercase Roman numerals for page numbers on the letter of authorization. The first page, with the number centered at the bottom, is page ii (assuming a title fly page is not used).

Many organizations now prefer eliminating the letter of authorization from all but the most formal of formal reports. This is because no formal report is ever prepared without proper authorization.

What is the purpose of the letter of transmittal?

Letter of Transmittal

Your last task in preparing a formal report involves composing the *letter of transmittal* (sometimes known as a cover letter), a document that formally sends the report to the reader. When reports are internal, the transmittal message can be sent via a memo. For reports distributed outside the organization, a letter more appropriately conveys the transmittal message.

The letter of transmittal should refer to the date the report was authorized and the topic. You should also summarize the limitations, report contents or findings, conclusions, and recommendations. Most writers express appreciation for the opportunity of writing the report and offer to answer any of the reader's questions about the contents.

If the letter of transmittal is only one page, the page number is typed in lowercase Roman numerals and centered at the bottom of the page. If the letter is two pages, a Roman numeral page number is also centered at the bottom of the second page. In some cases, you may prefer to attach the transmittal to the cover of the report. Then, no page numbers are necessary on the transmittal document.

Table of Contents

The table of contents allows the reader to scan the contents of the report without reading the entire document. The table is composed of the major headings and subheadings in the report. The page number on which each heading is found is also included on the table of contents. Leaders (alternating periods and spaces) are used to fill the space between each heading and its page number.

The preliminary parts of the report that appear before the table of contents are typically not listed in the table. Because the reader has probably already seen these parts, you need not list these pages on the table. The first preliminary part listed in the table of contents is the page immediately following it.

For some reports, you must decide whether to include the third-level headings. Moreover, just as the headings in the report follow parallel construction, so should the material in the table follow parallel form.

Some guidelines to help you design a table of contents are the following:

What format guidelines will help you prepare an effective table of contents?

1. Align Roman numerals and page numbers on the right.
2. Place the second line of a heading immediately beneath the first line. Single space the second line.
3. Use double spacing before and after second-level headings, but single space third-level headings, with double spacing before and after.
4. Fill the space between the headings and the page numbers with leaders. The leaders should align vertically.
5. Align the preliminary parts and the appended parts, which are not part of the report body, flush with the left margin.

List of Illustrations

What information is included in the list of illustrations?

To help the reader rapidly locate the graphic aids included in the report, a list of illustrations is useful. The illustrations list identifies the number of each graphic aid, the title of the graphic aid, and the page number on which it appears. Leaders fill the space between the titles of the graphic aids and the pages on which they appear.

If the table of contents and the list of illustrations are both quite short, you have the option of presenting on the same page both the table and the list. Otherwise, the list of illustrations appears on the next page.

Some writers prefer to separate the tables from all other graphic aids. The appropriate heading for the page listing the tables only is "List of Tables." The other graphic aids are then presented on a separate page identified as "List of Illustrations." If you list both tables and figures on the same page, the appropriate heading is "List of Illustrations." Regardless of whether you use the categorical or the combined approach, the number of the graphic aid, its title, and the page number on which it appears must be included.

Abstract

What is the purpose of the abstract?

Prepared after the report is completed, the *abstract* (also known as an executive summary or a synopsis) presents in condensed form either the contents of the report (*informative abstract*) or a description of the contents of the report (*descriptive abstract*).

The reader uses an informative abstract to learn about what you did and what you learned. It presents your conclusions and recommendations, as well as a discussion of your problem, purpose, and methodology. A descriptive abstract, on the other hand, basically provides for the reader an elaboration of the table of contents, using complete sentences. Unless instructions are otherwise, prepare an informative abstract. For many readers, an informative abstract provides most or all of the needed information. Therefore, readers may not have to read through the entire report, especially if the abstract is sufficiently accurate and thorough.

The abstract may use either the deductive or the inductive organizational arrangement. When using the deductive arrangement, present the conclusions and recommendations first, followed by the other sections. When using the inductive arrangement, present the material in the same order as it appears in the report.

If the letter of transmittal includes a short summary of the report, make your abstract less detailed than when you do not have a letter of transmittal. Although the length of the report to some extent dictates the length of the abstract (the summary is about one-tenth the length of the report), you are generally advised to try to keep the abstract to one single-spaced page. If your abstract is this brief, bulleted and numbered lists make the material easier to read.

The first page of an abstract is numbered with a lowercase Roman numeral centered at the bottom of the page. The page numbers of successive preliminary pages also appear at the bottoms of pages. The abstract makes no reference to graphic aids nor should it contain footnotes.

Parts of the Report Body

The body parts of the formal report consist of the introductory sections and the text of the report. At the beginning of each of the major sections, you should consider providing the reader with an overview of the content that will be found in that section, to aid reader understanding.

Introduction

An introduction, the first part of the body, provides a considerable amount of background information that puts the report in its proper perspective. Some readers see it as a preamble to the report, allowing them to assess the quality of the writer's research methods and procedures.

The formality and the perceived readership of the report determine the items included in the introduction. If the readership will benefit from a greater number of introductory items and if the report is quite formal, consider including most or all of the following introductory parts:

What information is included in the introduction?

1. *Background of the report.* Although some repetition may exist between the letter of transmittal and the background section, you may want to include both, particularly if your report is extremely formal. The background of the report section identifies the details of the authorization, including who authorized the report, how the authorization was made, and the date of authorization. This section may also include your name, with you identifying yourself as the person who carried out the research and who wrote the report.

2. *Statement of problem and purpose.* Because some reports do not include a background section, the first section in the body of many reports is the statement of problem section. The statement identifies the reasons the report was prepared. In some cases, the purpose and the statement of problem appear in the same section and even in the same sentence. You can also present each in a separate section.

Sometimes your report may contain more than one purpose. If so, also identify any secondary purposes in this section. The statement of primary and secondary purposes of the report will help the reader evaluate the benefits of such a report.

What is the function of the scope?

3. *Scope.* Another important section in some formal reports is the scope. Unless you state the report's scope—what the report includes and excludes—the reader has no way of knowing what you consider appropriate topics or areas for investigation. If you do not include the scope, some readers may think you inadvertently forgot to cover some topics, which may raise questions about your report-writing ability.

4. *Methodology.* A discussion of the research methodology assists the reader to assess the quality of the writer's research methods. Therefore, you should describe your research methodology in sufficient detail for the reader to make this judgment.

When the report contains a considerable amount of primary information, explain how you obtained your data. If you used a statistical test on the data, identify the test and the reasons for selecting it. If you used a questionnaire to collect the data, explain how it was developed and validated. You should also describe how the interview questions were developed as well as the interviewee selection process.

With secondary information, identify for the reader the location of the periodicals, reports, and other documents in the report. List the publications in the report in the bibliography at the end of the report. If you consulted only a few publications, you may list them in the methodology section.

5. *Definitions.* Some reports contain words or terms unfamiliar to the reader or that are used in an unfamiliar context. The definitions section defines these words or terms. Their inclusion will provide the reader and writer with a common frame of reference.

What are limitations?

6. *Limitations.* Limitations are conditions over which the report writer has no control that may hamper the report. Your introduction section is a good place to identify them. Because of your discussion of the report's limitations, the reader has greater assurance that you are not trying to cover up any weaknesses in it. Your credibility is, in fact, not jeopardized but enhanced because any conditions that may impact negatively on the report have been identified for the reader.

Some situations that may limit the report are inadequate time, monetary allocation, and amount of available information, as well as lack of cooperation by some people.

7. *Historical background of the report topic.* Your report may be one in a continuing series of reports on a specific topic. Obviously, the historical background of prior research about the topic is useful to the report reader. If the reader is fully aware of previous work on the topic, he or she is then aware of any continuing

problems relating to the topic. In addition, the reader has a better understanding of prior decisions.

8. *Report organization.* Formal reports, especially longer ones, often contain a discussion of their own organization. The function of such a discussion is to familiarize the reader with the parts in the body of the report, in order to make understanding the report's content easier.

Text of the Report

The text of the report immediately follows the introductory sections and is the major portion of the report. In this section, you present your findings, together with an interpretation and analysis.

How do deductively and inductively arranged paragraphs differ from one another?

In writing the report, focus on all the previously discussed qualities that characterize good writing. Select either deductive or inductive development of paragraphs. In deductive development, which most report writers prefer to use, the topic sentence appears at the beginning of each paragraph. Therefore, the topic sentence essentially provides an overview of the paragraph content. When paragraphs are organized in the inductive arrangement, the summary sentence appears at the end of the paragraph.

The present verb tense is the preferred tense in business reports, except when the writer refers to situations that have clearly already occurred or will occur. In such cases, choose whichever tense—past or future—that is appropriate for the situation. Also, avoid continual shifts in tense, as they make the text more difficult to follow.

In your report, headings act like road signs: They tell readers what is ahead in the report. Headings should be descriptive, yet concise. The three main levels of headings are first, second, and third. The following illustrates each of the three levels.

How do first-, second-, and third-level headings differ from one another?

> First level: Centered and in capital letters.
>
> THE CHARACTERISTICS OF PARTICIPATIVE MANAGEMENT
>
> Second level: On the left margin; initial letter of each word capitalized, with the entire heading underlined.
>
> <u>Employee Advantages</u>
>
> Third level: Indented same number of spaces as paragraphs, underlined, and followed with a period. Only the first word of the heading is capitalized.
>
> <u>Improved relations</u>. The use of participative management for improving relations among workers . . .

The proper spacing before and after headings is illustrated in the sample report at the end of this chapter.

The use of graphic aids in the body of the report also helps the reader interpret and understand the report. Because graphic illustrations are not complete in themselves, they need some explanation. Be careful to interpret completely the data in the illustrations. The preparation of graphic illustrations is discussed in detail later in this chapter.

What guidelines should be considered to help determine what material should be documented?

If the report contains secondary information, or material quoted from texts, periodicals, reports, and other documents, identify and credit the various sources. The following guidelines may help you determine which material to document and which material not to document:

1. Sentences, ideas, and thoughts solely those of the report writer do not need to be documented.

2. All material quoted verbatim needs documentation.
3. Paraphrased material needs documentation.
4. Material commonly considered to be general knowledge in a particular field does not need documentation, especially when you cannot attribute it to a particular person. However, if you quote such material verbatim, you must document it.

References are placed either (1) as footnotes at the bottom of the page on which the quoted material to which they relate appears or (2) as endnotes. A number of popular reference formats are used, including the traditional superscript system, the key number system, the author-date system, the MLA (*The MLA Style Manual*) simplified style, the APA (*Publication Manual of the American Psychological Association*) style and *The Chicago Manual of Style* endnote style.

Traditional superscript: The citation can either appear as a footnote or as an endnote. The citation is complete in itself and thus not dependent upon the bibliography reference.

[1]Dennis Johnson, *Effective Interviewing*, King Publishing, Inc., New York, 199x, p. 10.

Key number system: The citation lists only the number of the reference in the bibliography and the page number. This system is essentially combined with the bibliography to determine the author or title of the citation. In the following citation, the material was quoted from page 10 of the third bibliography entry. Note the parentheses around the citation.

(3:10)

Author-date system: The citation lists only the name of the author and the date of publication. A bibliography is required. When material is quoted verbatim, the citation will also include the page reference. Note the parentheses around the citation.

(Johnson 199x, p. 10)

MLA simplified style: The style advocated by the Modern Language Association also requires a bibliography. Only the author and the page number are listed. Should the paper contain citations of authors with identical names, then the year of publication differentiates between the citations. Note the parentheses around the citation.

(Johnson 10)

APA style: The style of the American Psychological Association also requires a bibliography. It cites the author's name and the year of publication but does not identify the page number in the original document being referenced. Note that parentheses surround the citation.

What information is included in an APA-style footnote?

(Johnson, 199x)

Chicago endnote style: The Chicago endnote style involves the placement of a superscript number at the location of the reference in the report text. The complete citation is presented in the endnote section of the report. The following illustrates this system:

What is an endnote?

. . . , as reported by Johnson.[1]

The following paragraphs provide a more detailed description of various aspects of the traditional superscript system. This system employs both footnote or endnote citations.

Texts:

[1]John D. Brown, *New Perspectives in Interviewing*, Business Publishers, Inc., New York, 199x, p. 10.

Periodical and newspaper articles:

[1]Samuel White, "The Art of Interviewing," *Personnel Functions*, Vol. 14, No. 9, p. 287, September 199x.

[2]John Mayden, "Interviewing: A Critical Skill," *Detroit Times*, January 16, 199x, Sec. C, p. 3, col. 2.

When using footnotes, you have the choice of beginning anew with the number "1" on each page or continuing the numbers sequentially from one page to the next. With endnotes, you use the sequential numbering system throughout.

Although the use of *ibid.*, *op. cit.*, and *loc. cit.* is losing popularity, report writers still need to be familiar with their use. *Ibid.* is employed when material from two different pages of the same source is consecutively cited.

[1]John D. Brown, *New Perspectives in Interviewing*, Business Publishers, Inc., New York, 199x, p. 10.

[2]*Ibid.*, p. 12.

The second footnote refers to page 12 of Brown's book.

When at least one intervening footnote from a different source separates two footnotes from the same source, *op. cit.* tells the reader that the source has already been cited but the page number is different from the original footnote.

[1]Jack Jones, "The Art of Persuasive Interviewing," *Journal of Practical Communication*, Vol. 10, No. 1, p. 27, January 199x.

[2]Mary Coswell, *Practical Personnel Management*, Readers Publishing Co., Denver, 199x, p. 72.

[3]Jones, *op. cit.*, p. 19.

Footnote 3 thus refers to page 19 of the document referred to in footnote 1.

A *loc. cit.* footnote is used when material is quoted from the same page of a source two or more times, regardless of whether intervening footnotes exist. Therefore, page numbers are not required in *loc. cit.* footnotes.

[10]David Samuels, "The Advantages of Functional Interviews," *Personnel Magazine*, Vol. 29, No. 5, p. 32, May 199x.

[11]Johnson, *op. cit.*, p. 23.

[12]Samuels, *loc. cit.*

[13]*Ibid.*, p. 14.

Footnote 12 refers to page 32 of the Samuels article previously quoted in footnote 10. Footnote 13 also refers to Samuels' article but the quote is from page 14.

You may sometimes decide to include discussion footnotes in your formal report. Rather than referring to a document from which you quote, you can rely on discussion footnotes to discuss a point you desire to make. For example, instead of including a discussion of the derivation of a certain word in the body of your report, you may decide to deal with the derivation in a footnote at the bottom of the page on which the word is first used.

Regardless of which documentation system you select, material that is quoted verbatim and that consumes three or more lines in a report is single spaced and indented five spaces from either margin. Such material does not require quotation marks, although a citation appears at the end of the quote. In contrast, material of two or fewer lines quoted verbatim requires quote marks because it is not set off physically from the text. Here, the citation appears immediately after the final quotation mark.

Because, by definition, paraphrased material is not a direct quotation, never use quotation marks with it. For a similar reason, paraphrased material does not have to be set off in any way from the regular text. The citation, however, appears at the end of the paraphrased material.

Ending of the Report

The ending of a formal report typically consists of conclusions and recommendations. Depending on the circumstances, a summary of the report findings may also be included. If you do not have an abstract in the report, you may want to summarize the report findings. But even if you include an abstract, a summary of findings at the end of the report may still be desired.

Summary

What is the purpose of the summary?

The *summary* recaps the major findings of the report. Usually the organizational approach is to recap the findings of each of the report's major divisions in order of appearance. Such organization enables the reader to locate more easily the material in the report to which the summary findings pertain. If you need to refer to the original discussion about a specific summary finding, this approach is especially useful. In most instances, the findings are enumerated, to make them more readable and, hence, understandable.

Conclusions

What are conclusions?

Remember to base your conclusions on the facts and details discussed in the report. That is, you cannot introduce new information in the conclusions section. *Conclusions*, which are essentially answers to the report problem, must be objective, uncontaminated from any preconceived ideas or notions.

Some inexperienced report writers provide conclusions that are essentially summary findings. Whereas findings do relate to the data or information presented in the report, conclusions go one step further and answer the report problem. The following examples from a report prepared to identify causes of poor employee productivity in XYZ Corporation with the primary goal of increasing profitability illustrate the difference between a summary of a finding and a conclusion.

> Finding: The employees in XYZ Corporation were found to be producing at 80 percent of their capacity.
>
> Conclusion: Subjecting the employees of XYZ Corporation to a training program will help them become more productive.

The following sentence is an example of a finding incorrectly labeled as a conclusion.

> Employees of XYZ Corporation are not as productive as they should be.

A possible conclusion derived from the finding is as follows.

> The development of a training program will enable the employees of XYZ Corporation to become more productive.

To make your report easier to read, number the conclusions and present them in the same order as the findings from which they were derived.

Recommendations

What are recommendations?

The *recommendations* in a formal report, based on your opinions and thoughts, identify the actions you suggest as a result of your research findings. Remember that recommendations are advisory in nature, because the decision makers for whom the report was prepared make final decisions.

Generally, where appropriate, you will make a recommendation for each of the conclusions. For example, in the report problem cited in the conclusions section, an appropriate recommendation might be as follows.

> XYZ Corporation should investigate the feasibility of installing an employee training program designed to help employees improve their productivity.

As you did with the conclusions, number your recommendations and present them in the same order as you presented your conclusions.

Some studies are inconclusive; thus, you are unable to derive conclusions from your findings or make recommendations. When that happens, frankly tell your reader so. If you firmly believe that the problem requires further study, let that be a recommendation.

Appended Parts

The appended parts of the formal report, typically the bibliography and the appendices, are the two final parts of the formal report.

Bibliography

For all but the shortest of formal reports, include a bibliography. In short formal reports, a bibliography is sometimes omitted if only a few secondary sources of information are used because the reader is able to "grasp" these sources without having them listed in the bibliography. Bibliographies list all works consulted, regardless of whether they are specifically cited. A references page, on the other hand, includes a list of only the cited works. In most formal reports, a bibliography is preferred over a references page.

What categories are used in presenting a bibliography?

You may categorize the sources in the bibliography according to the following breakdown:

1. Books
2. Periodicals

3. Newspapers
4. Reports
5. Unpublished materials
6. Miscellaneous

The bibliography entries are alphabetized under each of the categories. If you have consulted only a few sources in preparing the report, categorizing them in the bibliography may be unnecessary.

A specific format exists for each bibliography category. The following are the appropriate styles for each of the categories when you are using the traditional superscript footnote-endnote system:

1. Books

Brown, John D. *New Perspectives in Interviewing*. Business Publishers, Inc., New York, 199x.

2. Periodicals

Samuels, David. "The Advantages of Functional Interviews," *Personnel Magazine*, Vol. 26, No. 5, May 199x.

3. Newspapers

Mayden, John. "Interviewing: A Critical Skill," *Detroit Times*, January 16, 199x, Sec. C, col. 2.

4. Reports

Brown, David. "How to Prepare Reports." East Lansing, Mich.: Michigan State University, 199x.

5. Unpublished Materials

Johnson, Mary. Personal Interview. January 10, 199x.

6. Miscellaneous

Administration Club, Michigan State University. *Constitution and By-Laws*. 199x.

If you prefer, use either the key number system or the author-date system. The references are then alphabetized by author name if given or by title of publication, without reference to categories. When you use the key system, number the bibliography entries sequentially. The following shows a bibliographical entry when the key system is used and when the author-date system is used.

Key system
3. Johnson, Dennis. *Effective Interviewing*. New York: King Publishing, Inc., 199x.
Author-date system
Johnson, Dennis. *Effective Interviewing*. New York: King Publishing, Inc., 199x.

If you use the MLA, APA, and the Chicago styles, you have the option of replacing the word BIBLIOGRAPHY on the first page of the bibliography with the term WORKS CITED. The following illustrates the various formats for each of these styles.

MLA style
Johnson, Dennis. *Effective Interviewing*. New York: King Publishing, Inc., 199x.

APA style
Johnson, Dennis. (199x). *Effective interviewing*. New York: King Publishing, Inc.

Chicago style
Johnson, Dennis. *Effective Interviewing*. New York: King Publishing, Inc., 199x.

In numbering the pages of the bibliography, use Arabic numbers. Center the page number at the bottom of the first page of the bibliography but then position the page number in the upper-right corner for succeeding pages. You can find alternate methods of presenting bibliographic entries in style and theses manuals and handbooks.

Appendices

Materials appended to the report are usually supplementary or supportive in nature and, therefore, do not appropriately belong in the text of the report. Generally, material that is remotely related to the text material or material that is too long for the body of the report is placed in an appendix.

Examples of items frequently included as appendices are data-gathering instruments—such as questionnaires, data tables, diagrams, and illustrations—unnecessary for understanding and interpreting the material contained in the text. When in doubt about whether to place certain materials in the text or as an appended item, you should probably place them in the appendices.

If only one is used, the appropriate terminology is *appendix* rather than *appendices*. For multiple appendices, identify them as Appendix A, Appendix B, and so forth.

GRAPHIC PRESENTATION

If properly developed, graphic presentation of material in a formal report helps the reader more quickly grasp its significance. The main function of graphic aids is not to present the information but rather to support or further explain the data already presented in the written sections. A common practice among report writers is to present a portion of the material to the reader in text format, with the remainder presented in a graphic aid. Two categories of graphic aids appear in reports: tables and charts, including diagrams. Some people refer to charts as graphs.

A trend in graphics preparation is the use of computer technology. With the exception of the following tables, by using a computer software program and a laser printer, or a color printer, each of the aids in this chapter can be prepared almost effortlessly. Most plotters now available are also capable of producing multiple-color work. Some plotters can even produce color transparencies for use on overhead projectors. The more-sophisticated graphics preparation software programs are capable of importing data from spreadsheets and databases, further simplifying the creation process.

What steps compose the computerized graphics preparation process?

When relying on a computer to prepare graphics, you may have to perform the following steps:

1. Enter into the computer the type of chart desired (pie, multiple bar, etc.).
2. Enter the title and subtitle of the chart.
3. Enter the identity of the various components.
4. Enter the type of design desired for each component (hatching, cross-hatching, solid, open, etc.).
5. Enter the quantitative data for each of the components (or import it from a spreadsheet or database).
6. Enter the total magnitude of each of the components.
7. Enter the source notation.

Except for Exhibits 14-8 and 14-11, the master for each of the figures in this chapter was prepared using a graphics preparation software package and a laser printer.

Whether creating graphic aids by hand or by computer, the reader should never be responsible for interpreting the material presented in the aids. This means the text accompanying a graphic aid should provide the reader a full interpretation of the content of the graphic aid.

What suggestions will help improve the use of graphic aids in formal reports?

Included in Communication Capsule 14-1 are suggestions to help you work successfully with graphic aids in a formal report.

Communication Capsule 14-1 Suggestions for Using Graphic Aids

The following list summarizes the guidelines for using graphic aids in a formal report:

1. Introduce the material to which the graphic aid relates.
2. Refer, by figure number, the reader to the graphic aid. For example, "As Figure 12 illustrates, . . ." or "Figure 12 shows . . ."
3. Provide additional discussion and/or interpretation of the material presented in the graphic aid.
4. Place the graphic aid as closely as possible to its discussion in the report.
5. In discussing the graphic aid, make specific reference to it. For example, "The demographic characteristics of the consumers included in this study are summarized in Table 2."
6. If possible, the discussion of the material contained in a graphic aid should appear before and after the presentation of the aid.
7. If the aid and its discussion appear on different pages, tell the reader where the aid can be found. For example, "The cost breakdowns are illustrated in Exhibit 4, which appears on page 23."
8. Tables are identified as tables (for example, Table 3); all other graphic aids are identified as figures or illustrations (for example, Figure 4 or Illustration 7).
9. If the graphic aid is not your creation but is obtained from another source, the source of the aid should be fully identified; for example, *The Working Man*, p. 74. The source notation appears directly under the graphic aid.
10. Color, shading, cross-hatching, and variation in lines (solid, broken, etc.) are useful in preparing certain graphic aids. These design alternatives also improve the visual appearance of the graphic aid.
11. Exercise extreme care in determining the appropriate wording of the title as well as the various other components of the graphic aid.
12. The size of the graphic aid should be determined by its importance and amount of data it presents. Graphic aids that consume more than a third of a page generally appear out of proportion with the other material on the page.

The following sections will assist you in preparing the various types of graphic aids. Because the material illustrated in graphic aids easily lends itself to distortion, you need to be especially careful about the accuracy of the material being presented.

Tables

For what are tables typically used?

A *table* is a vertical (columnar) and horizontal (row) presentation of information. Tables typically present numerical information, although they also can very effectively present alphabetic information. The arrangement of the information in tables readily aids in the comparison and analysis of the presented information.

The complexity of tables varies considerably. Whereas some tables contain only a small amount of information and are quite simple, others contain much more extensive amounts of information. The components of a rather simple table are identified in Exhibit 14-1. Only the simplest of information can be presented in this illustration. The information in each of the columns must be comparable or related. For example, the table is appropriate for presenting the population of the various states during two different decades. Each of the years should be listed in the left-hand column, with the population of Texas and Oklahoma listed in the middle and right-hand columns, respectively.

More complex information may require the use of stubs and braced headings, as shown in Exhibit 14-2. The stub heading (year) relates to the information contained in each of the rows beneath the various columnar heads (personnel, accounting, finance), and the braced heading (departments) identifies the nature of the material contained in the various columnar headings.

If you are including numerous rows in a table, use either of the following two techniques: double-space after every third row, or insert a horizontal line between every third row. Each of these techniques provides visual guidance for the reader.

In some instances, you may desire to transform a questionnaire item into a table. Carefully designed questionnaire items facilitate the preparation of a table as Item No. 10 of the following questionnaire and the table based on it illustrate:

Exhibit 14-1 Simple table.

Table 1

POPULATION OF TEXAS AND OKLAHOMA, 1992-94

Year	Texas	Oklahoma
1992	14,894,434	3,789,484
1993	14,967,542	3,810,442
1994	14,997,445	3,994,231

Exhibit 14-2 Table with stub and braced headings

Table 1

ANNUAL NUMBER OF EMPLOYEES, BY DEPARTMENT

	Departments		
Year	Personnel	Accounting	Finance
1992	18	37	24
1993	20	35	26
1994	22	39	28

10. Please identify the importance to you of each of the following job attributes: (Check only one category for each attribute)

	Critical	*Very Important*	*Somewhat Important*	*Not Very Important*	*Unimportant*
a. Salary	_____	_____	_____	_____	_____
b. Mobility	_____	_____	_____	_____	_____
c. Independence	_____	_____	_____	_____	_____
d. Recognition	_____	_____	_____	_____	_____
e. Rewards	_____	_____	_____	_____	_____
f. Centrality	_____	_____	_____	_____	_____

Table 2

IMPORTANCE OF VARIOUS JOB ATTRIBUTES

(in percentages)

	Importance Rating				
Attributes	*Critical*	*Very Important*	*Somewhat Important*	*Not Very Important*	*Unimportant*
Salary	60.0	20.1	8.2	7.1	4.6
Mobility	30.2	48.6	10.3	8.9	2.0
Independence	10.3	39.2	8.3	17.9	24.3
Recognition	18.7	43.2	9.8	23.7	4.6
Rewards	42.9	27.4	10.8	10.7	8.2
Centrality	8.9	15.6	22.9	39.4	13.2

Pie Charts

Pie charts present data as wedge-shaped sections of a circle. They are especially useful for comparing the various parts that compose a whole. For example, pie charts are frequently used to show the percentages of the components of a whole. Because readers sometimes have difficulty visualizing the size of each part, the magnitude of each component is printed on the chart, as shown in Exhibit 14-3.

For what are pie charts especially suited?

Exhibit 14-3 Pie chart.

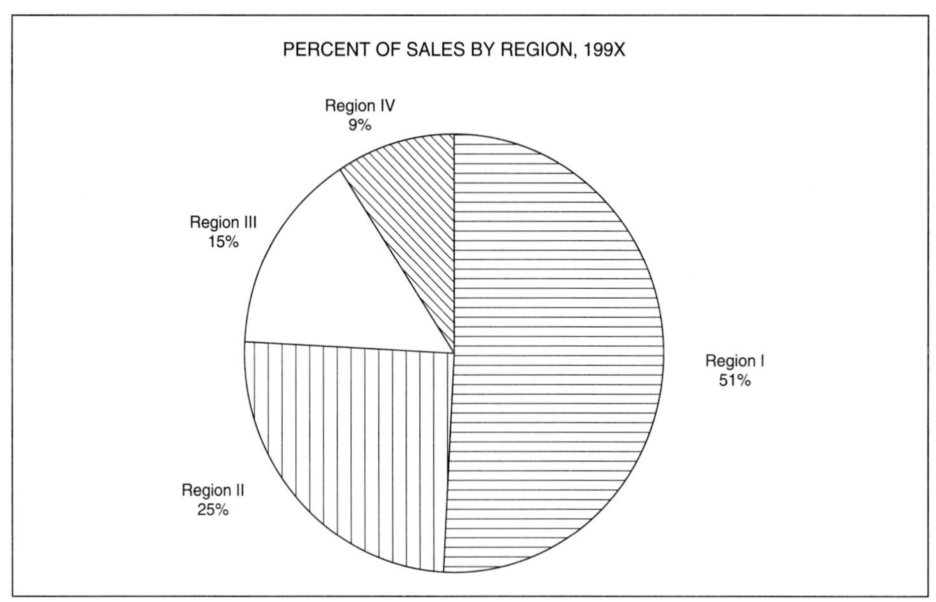

In constructing a pie chart, begin at the twelve o'clock position with the largest unit. Working in a clockwise direction, place the remaining units in a descending order of size. Consequently, the smallest wedge appears to the left of the twelve o'clock position.

The use of shading or cross-hatching helps the reader grasp the material being presented. In most cases, the identity of the smaller units will need to be presented outside the wedge. The nature of the unit should also be identified, such as percent, dollars, and so forth.

Bar Charts

For what are bar charts especially suited?

Another graphic aid for comparing the magnitude of numerical data are *bar charts,* which use bars, placed in either a vertical or horizontal arrangement, to represent each variable. Be careful to provide sufficient space for labeling the identity of each bar. Grid lines should appear at 90-degree angles to the bars. Therefore, if the bars are horizontal, the grid lines are vertical. In addition, the quantitative value of each grid line should also appear on the chart. The primary purpose of grid lines is to help the reader visually determine the length of each bar. Although the reader may be able to approximate the magnitude of each bar by comparing its length with the grid lines, you need to identify precisely the magnitude of each bar on the chart. A bar chart is shown in Exhibit 14-4.

Several categories of bar charts exist, each with a specialized value.

Multiple Bar Charts

For what are multiple bar charts especially suited?

The *multiple bar chart* is useful for comparing two or three variables in a series. For example, to illustrate the sales volume of hardware, painting supplies, and floor coverings in the five stores of a particular chain, you might use a multiple bar chart. Rather than prepare a separate chart for each of the variables, you can use a multiple bar chart to illustrate all three variables for the five stores.

To help the reader visually grasp the material contained in the multiple bar chart, give each variable its own design. Possibilities include open or blank design, cross-

Exhibit 14-4 Bar chart.

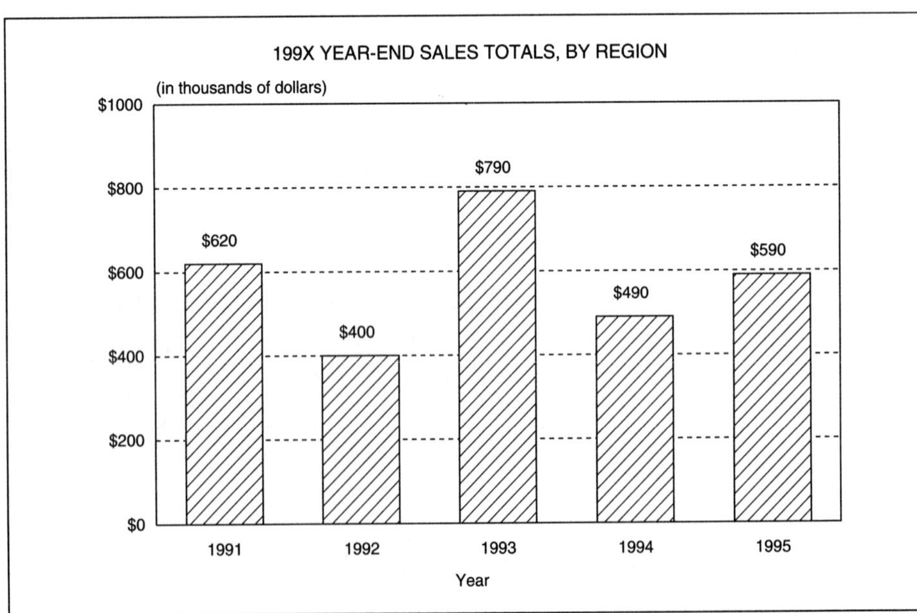

hatching, angled lines, and the like. The legend for each variable should appear on the chart. Other suggestions for preparing multiple bar charts are (1) limit the number of variables to a maximum of three (2) use grid lines and (3) identify the magnitude of each variable. Exhibit 14-5 is a multiple bar chart.

Bilateral Bar Charts

A *bilateral bar chart* shows the positive or negative deviation from a central point for a variable. For example, the bilateral bar chart is useful for showing the positive or negative percentage changes in the population of five selected U.S. cities for the years 1985–199x.

For what are bilateral bar charts especially suited?

The bilateral bar chart is used when the report writer wants to illustrate the percentage of change from zero. It has two sections—positive and negative. In creating a bilateral bar chart, the use, if possible, of grid lines is recommended. The exact amount of change for each item should also appear on the chart. A bilateral bar chart is shown in Exhibit 14-6.

Divided Bar Charts

The *divided bar chart* divides each bar into components of the same variable. Divided bar charts are used to show the magnitude of each of these components. For example, you might choose the divided bar chart to illustrate the number of books acquired each year by a university's library in each of five academic disciplines. From such a chart, the reader can determine the total number of books acquired in each of five years as well as the number acquired in each discipline.

For what are divided bar charts especially suited?

As in the multiple bar chart, each component in the divided bar chart will have a different design legend. Using grid lines is also recommended, as is identifying the magnitude of each bar. A divided bar chart is shown in Exhibit 14-7.

Symbol Bar Charts

The *symbol bar chart* is a type of graphic aid that uses appropriate symbols to show the magnitude of each variable. For example, to illustrate the population of certain

Exhibit 14-5 Multiple bar chart.

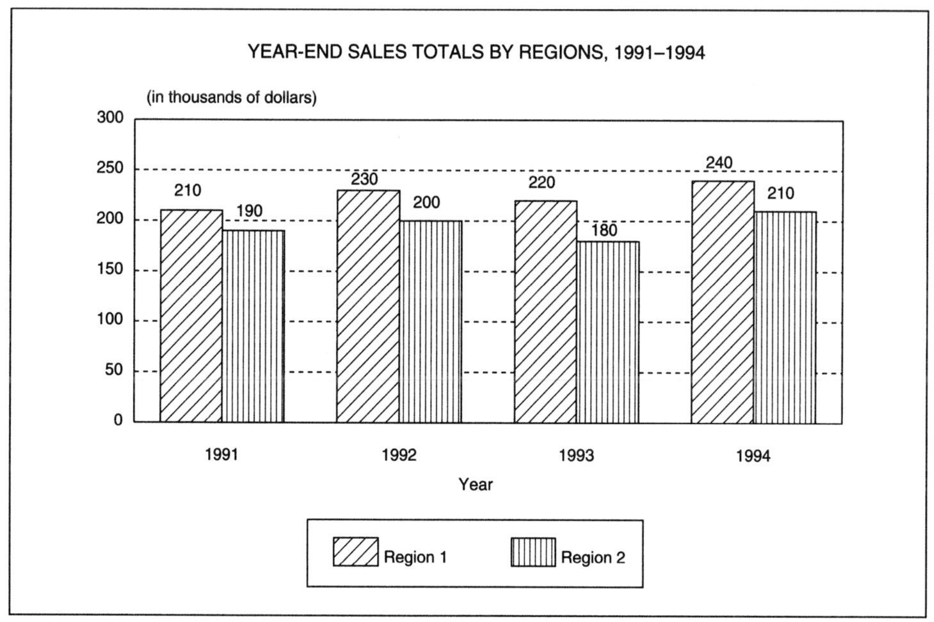

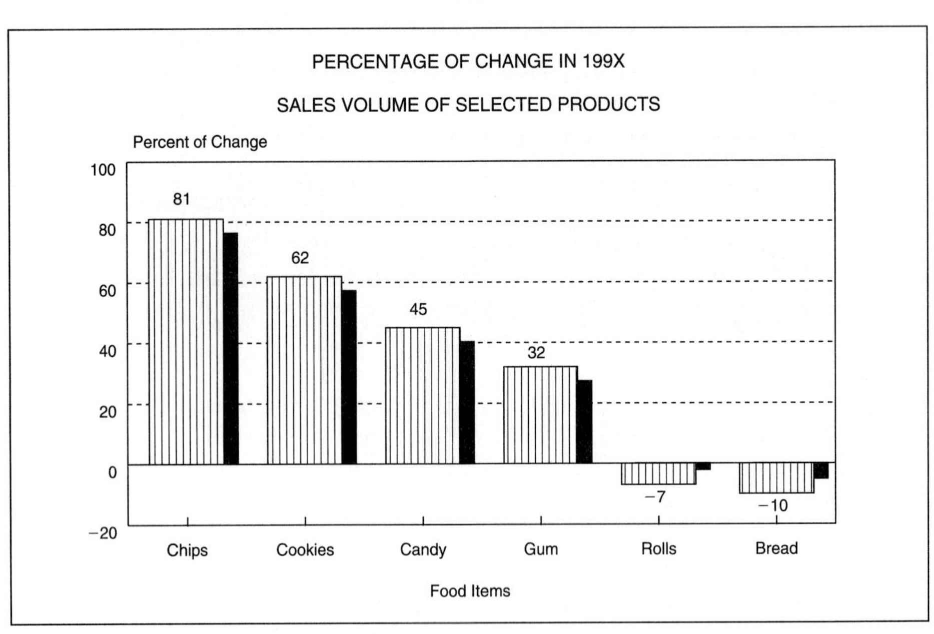

Exhibit 14-6 Bilateral bar chart.

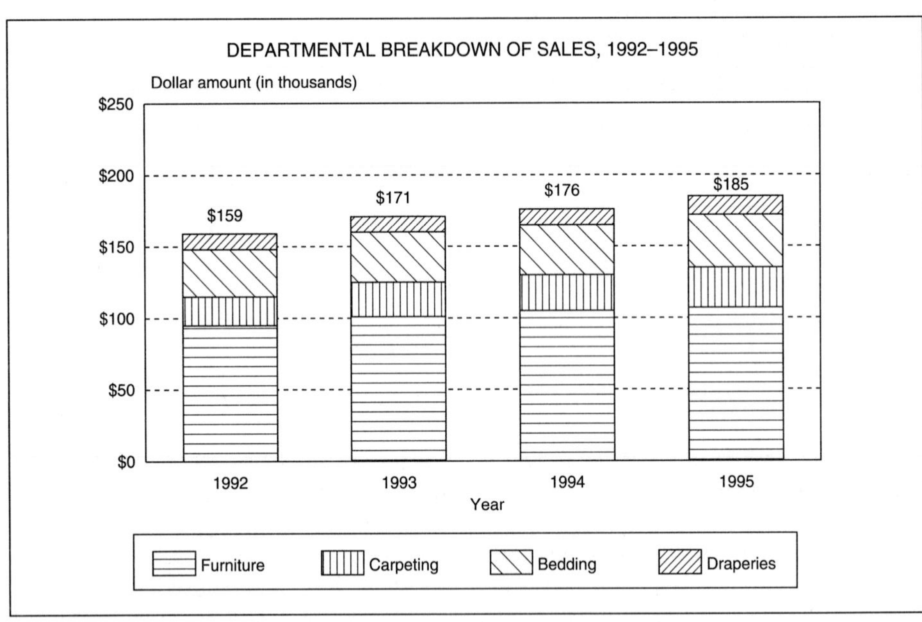

Exhibit 14-7 Divided bar chart.

cities, the bars may be composed of drawings depicting humans. For symbol bar charts, also use, if possible, grid lines and express the magnitude of each bar. An example of a symbol bar chart is shown in Exhibit 14-8.

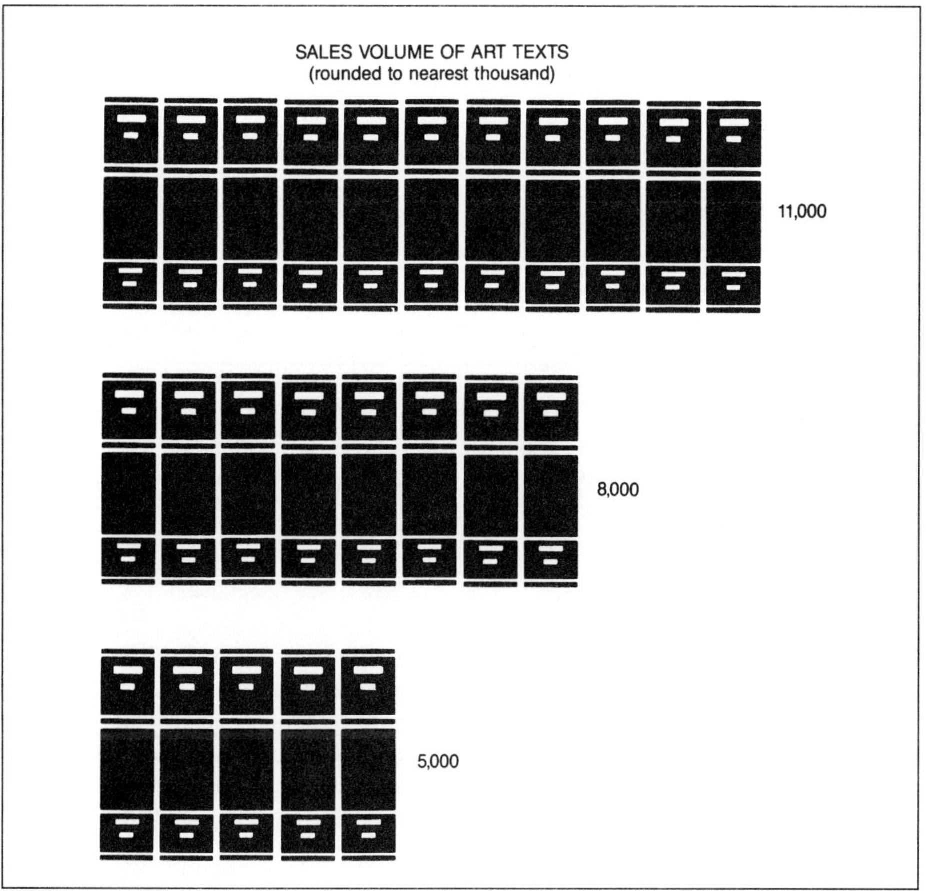

Exhibit 14-8 Symbol bar chart.

Line Charts

For what are line charts especially suited?

Line charts show changes in a continuous series of data during a given period. Such charts, for example, are used to depict changes in the stock market, sales volume, absenteeism, and production totals.

When line charts illustrate more than one variable, different line patterns or colors are employed for each variable. For example, a solid line may be used for one variable, a broken line for another, and a pattern of dots and dashes for a third. The legend for each variable must be clearly identified on the chart.

The following guidelines should be useful in preparing line charts:

1. Plot time on the horizontal axis.
2. Plot quantity on the vertical axis.
3. Make units of measurement on the vertical and horizontal scale reasonably proportionate to one another. Although not required to be precisely equal, they should be comparable to eliminate distortion.
4. Begin the vertical axis at zero, no matter how high the quantity values extend. If the values are quite high, the vertical axis can be broken, as the following chart illustrates:

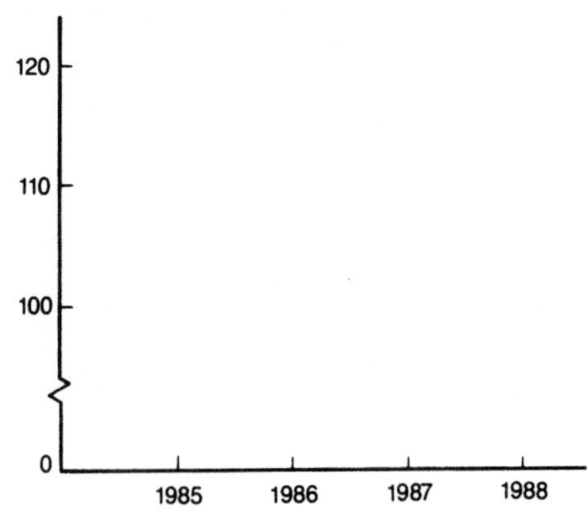

5. Use both vertical and horizontal grids to make the plotting of lines and the interpretation of the chart easier.

A line chart is shown in Exhibit 14-9.

Belt Charts

A variation of line charts, *belt charts*, are used to illustrate the total values of a series as well as the various component values that compose the total.

Belt charts are constructed by placing the largest component against the horizontal axis. The remaining components are then placed on the chart, with the second largest component placed immediately above (with no space between) the largest component, and the smallest component placed last. A belt chart is shown in Exhibit 14-10.

Maps

Report writers, of course, use other graphic aids, in addition to tables and charts. Of these, maps are among the most useful. *Maps* illustrate certain data characteristics of

Exhibit 14-9 Line chart.

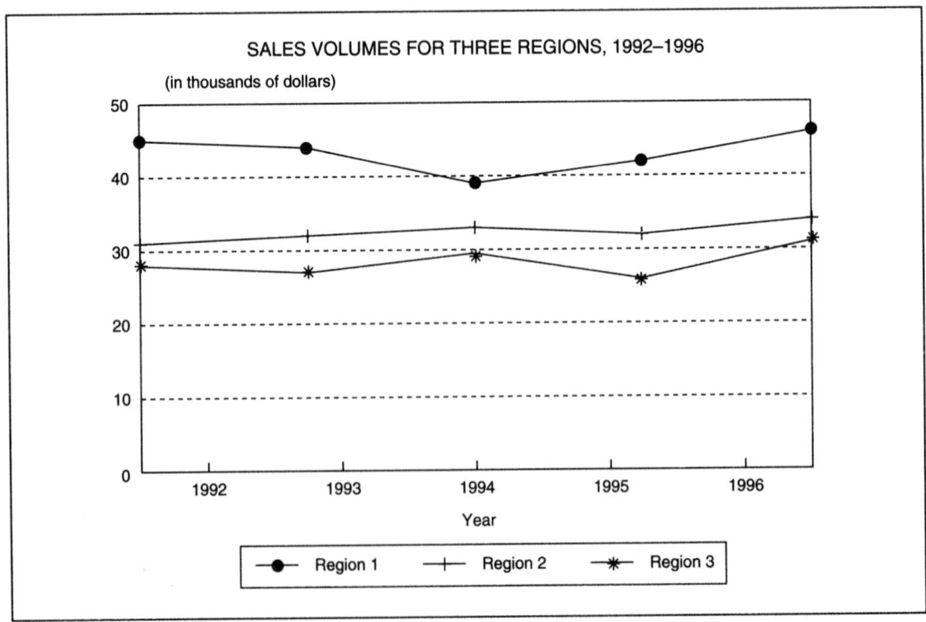

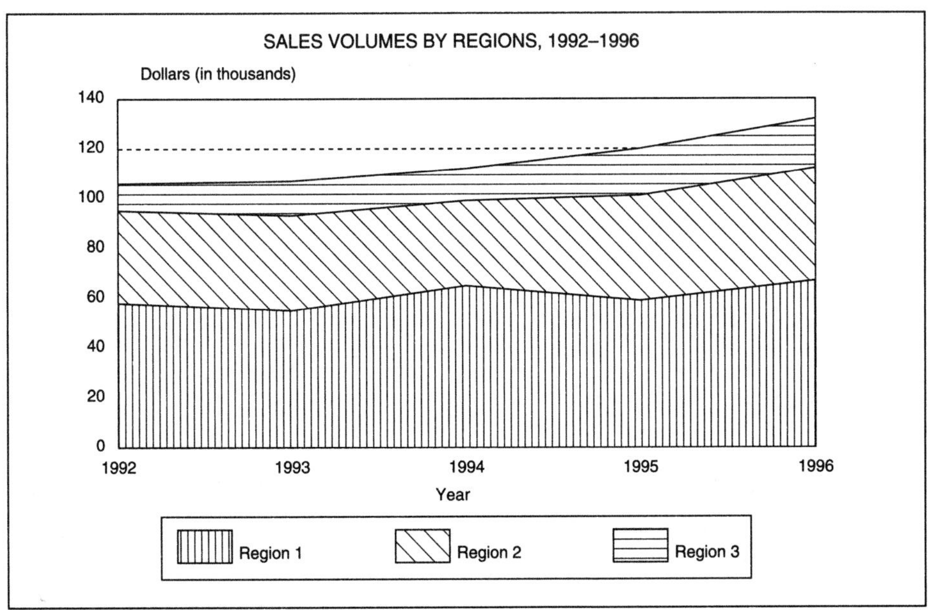

Exhibit 14-10 Belt chart.

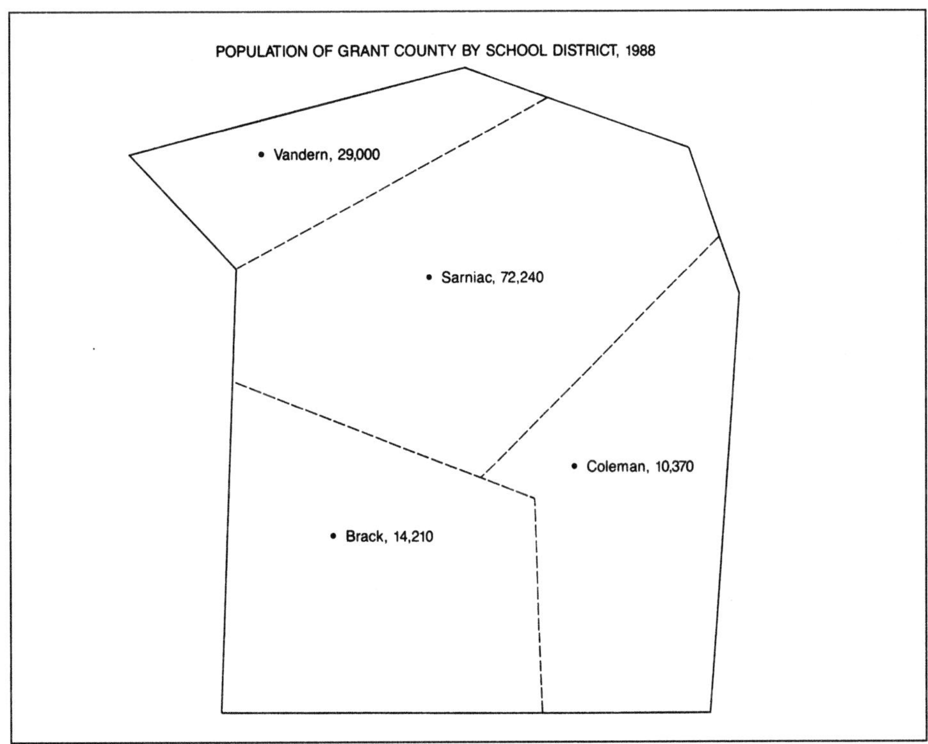

Exhibit 14-11 Map.

various areas or regions. Although maps frequently show quantitative data, they can also show nonquantitative data.

If needed, use different designs for each of the areas illustrated. Depending on the data being presented, a legend may be necessary. A map is shown in Exhibit 14-11.

The Ethics Episode contains a number of suggestions about preparing formal reports and the graphic aids in them. Abiding by the suggestions will help you avoid an ethics dilemma.

ETHICS EPISODE

Several areas of ethical concern arise when preparing formal reports. Among the areas are how the writer organizes and presents the material and the graphic aids the writer uses in the report.

ORGANIZATION AND PRESENTATION OF MATERIAL

The manner in which the writer organizes and presents the material in a formal report is an important concern. The organization and presentation of material may create an ethics dilemma when the writer's actions manipulate the reader—regardless of intention. An even more serious situation arises when the reader makes a seriously flawed decision based on the content of a report, especially if he or she were manipulated to make a decision.

Suppose, for example, the company for which you work has outgrown its current building. Therefore, a decision must be made soon regarding a new facility. You have been given the responsibility of surveying employees and preparing the report that summarizes your findings. Two choices were considered: relocating in Suburb A or finding a new facility in the downtown area near the current building. Because you live in the suburb being considered, your preference is for the company to move to the suburb. Accordingly, you indicated in a report that "A large majority of surveyed employees indicated they favored the company's relocating its building to Suburb A rather than trying to find a new facility in the downtown area." In reality, a "large majority" is only 58 percent rather than the 75 to 80 percent that the word "large" implies. The desire to manipulate your reader in this manner is unethical.

GRAPHIC AIDS

Writers who use graphic aids to distort information/data create an ethics dilemma for themselves. When a graphic aid appears on a page, many readers will examine the graphic aid before reading the text material that discusses the aid's content. If the aid's content has been purposely distorted, then the reader will likely have been manipulated even before he or she reads the text material about the graphic aid.

Consider the following situations regarding the preparation of graphic aids:

1. Suppose, for example, on a line chart, you intentionally distorted the aid by using x-axis and y-axis units of measurement that are quite dissimilar. Suppose the x-axis unit of measurement is one-fourth inch, but the y-axis unit of measurement is one-half inch. The slope line will have a considerably different angle on this line chart than it will when an identical unit of measurement is used on both axes. When you intentionally distort a graphic aid in this manner, you are acting unethically. When you unintentionally distort the aid in this manner, you are committing an error in judgment, either of which can have serious ramifications.
2. Suppose you use two symbol bar charts to present information about two points of information. However, you decide to use two different sizes of symbols on the charts to distort an accurate visual comparison. Knowingly deceiving the reader in this manner is an unethical action.

One of the quickest ways for a writer to lose credibility as a report writer is to act unethically in organizing or presenting information or preparing graphic aids for inclusion in the report. The more seriously flawed the decision on which the distorted information is, the more unethical your actions are.

FORMAT DIRECTIONS

Specific format directions for presenting left-bound formal reports follow:

Title fly: Title begins on line 30
- 1½-inch left margin
- 1-inch right margin
- Page number not needed

Title page: 2-inch top margin
- 1-inch bottom margin
- 1½-inch left margin

1-inch right margin
Page number not needed

Letter of authorization: 2-inch top margin
Minimum 2-inch bottom margin
1½-inch left margin
1½-inch right margin
Single-space body
Roman numeral for page number and centered 1/2 inch from bottom

Letter of transmittal: 2-inch top margin
Minimum 2-inch bottom margin
1½-inch left margin
1½-inch right margin
Single-space body
Roman numeral for page number and centered 1/2 inch from bottom

Table of contents: 2-inch top margin
1-inch bottom margin
1½-inch left margin
1-inch right margin
Double-space body but single space any carry-over lines
Roman numeral for page number and centered 1/2 inch from bottom

Abstract: 2-inch top margin
1-inch bottom margin
1½-inch left margin
1-inch right margin
Single-space body
Roman numeral for page number and centered 1/2 inch from bottom

First page of body: 2-inch top margin
1-inch bottom margin
1½-inch left margin
1-inch right margin
Double-space body
Page number not needed
Center first-level headings; triple space before and after
Second-level headings on left margin; triple space before and double space after

Remaining pages of body: 1-inch top margin
1-inch bottom margin
1½-inch left margin
1-inch right margin
Arabic number for page number, placed in upper-right corner, 1/2 inch from top and 1 inch from right margin; triple space after
Center first-level headings; triple space before and after

Bibliography: 2-inch top margin
1-inch bottom margin
1½-inch left margin
1-inch right margin
Arabic number for page number and centered at bottom of page, 1/2 inch from bottom

SAMPLE REPORT

Exhibit 14-12 identifies the proper mechanics for presenting the various report parts.

A STUDY OF THE CULTURAL EVENTS
PROGRAM AT STATE UNIVERSITY

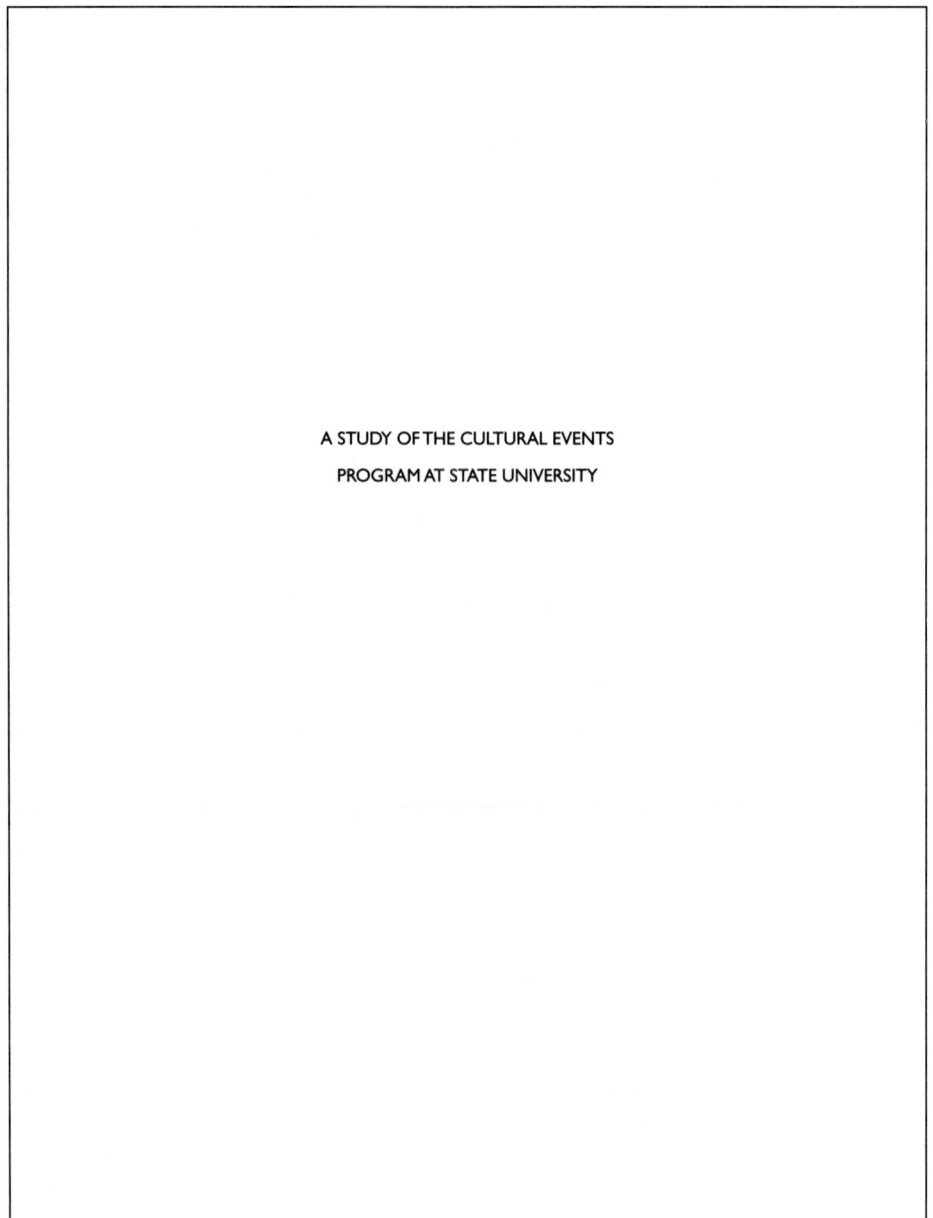

Exhibit 14-12 Sample formal report, title fly.

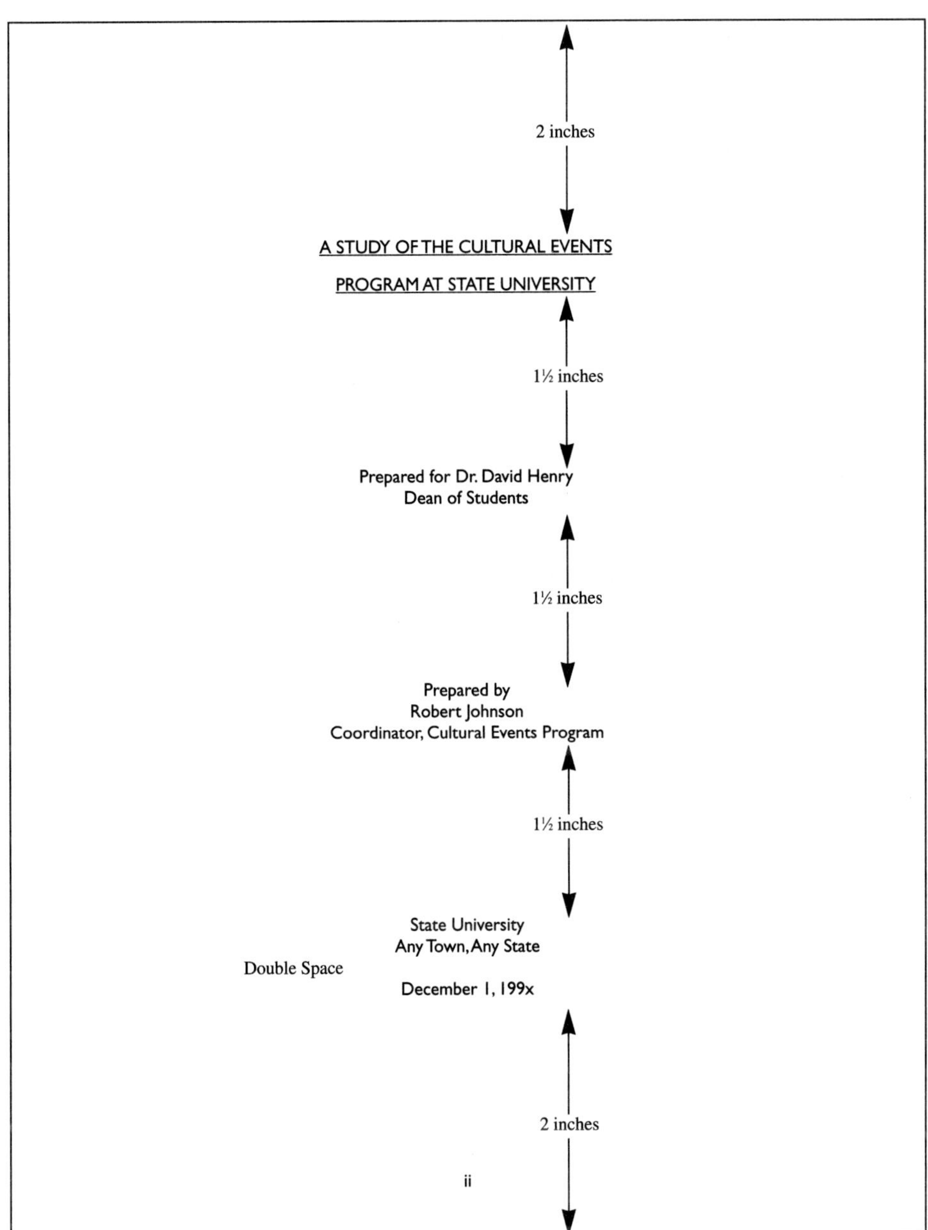

2 inches
A STUDY OF THE CULTURAL EVENTS
PROGRAM AT STATE UNIVERSITY
1½ inches
Prepared for Dr. David Henry
Dean of Students
1½ inches
Prepared by
Robert Johnson
Coordinator, Cultural Events Program
1½ inches
State University
Any Town, Any State
Double Space
December 1, 199x
2 inches
ii

Exhibit 14-12 Title page

State University

Any Town, Any State 12345 *444 444-4444*

September 19, 199x

Mr. Robert Johnson, Coordinator
Cultural Events Program
State University
Any Town, Any State 12345

Dear Bob:

At your earliest convenience, will you please undertake a study of the Cultural Events Program at State University? Because of your position as coordinator of the Cultural Events Program, you are well qualified to undertake this study.

In your study, please determine the students' needs and interests that should be considered in assessing the adequacy of the Cultural Events Program. Any residual benefits you can obtain from your study will also be greatly appreciated.

As you are well aware, a rather vocal student element has frequently criticized the Cultural Events Program at State University. I have been assured by President Wilson that if we have a good solid basis for further adapting the program, he will do all he can to support its strengthening. Of course, the Board of Trustees has final approval of any recommendations we may propose.

Please have the report to me by December 1 if at all possible. I know you are busy; but before we can make any changes, we do need facts. My budget will cover the cost of any expenses incurred in the preparation of this report.

Please call on me if I can be of assistance.

Sincerely,

David Henry

David Henry
Dean of Students

jm

iii

Exhibit 14-12 Letter of authorization.

State University

Any Town, Any State 12345 *444 444-4444*

December 1, 199x

Dr. David Henry
Dean of Students
State University
Any Town, Any State 12345

Dear Dr. Henry:

The study of the Cultural Events Program at State University you authorized me to undertake in your letter of September 18 is attached.

As you will note, several instances are mentioned in the report which indicate that our random sample is truly a representative sample of the total student population of State University. Therefore, I am confident of the validity of this study.

Three other colleges in the area have contacted me, asking about the possibility of their using the questionnaire developed for this study. Similar studies are being undertaken in these colleges. Each of the colleges seeking permission to use the questionnaire has been accommodated.

If you have any questions after you read the report, please call me.

Sincerely,

Robert Johnson

Robert Johnson, Coordinator
Cultural Events Program

ts

Attachment

iv

Exhibit 14-12 Letter of transmittal.

TABLE OF CONTENTS

Triple space Page

v

Exhibit 14-12 Table of contents.

LIST OF ILLUSTRATIONS

Triple space Page

vi

Exhibit 14-12 List of Illustrations.

ABSTRACT

Triple space

The problem of this study was to determine the cultural needs and interests of the students enrolled at State University, Fall Term, 199x. The purpose for doing this was to provide a basis for assessing the adequacy of the Cultural Events Program at State University.

A questionnaire determined the needs and interests of the students at State University. A randomly selected sample of 550 students received the questionnaire, and a 90 percent return rate (450 questionnaires) was achieved.

Of the respondents, 42.8 percent were male and 57.2 percent were female. Freshmen constituted 31 percent of the sample; sophomores, 26 percent; juniors, 23 percent; and seniors, 20 percent. The respondents' majors were as follows: liberal arts majors, 27 percent; social science majors, 24 percent; business majors, 18 percent; education majors, 16 percent; and science majors, 15 percent.

Fifty-three percent of the respondents work 20 or fewer hours per week, and 8 percent work over 40 hours per week. Sixty percent of the hours are worked between 5 p.m. and 10 p.m., Monday through Thursday.

Forty percent of the respondents indicated the ability to attend all events they cared to attend. Another 40 percent were unable to attend the events because of work or study.

vii

Exhibit 14-12 Abstract.

INTRODUCTION

Triple space

This report contains the results of a survey completed at State University during Fall Term, 199x.

Triple space

Background of the Report

Double space

Dr. David Henry, Dean of Students at State University, authorized the preparation of this study on September 18, 199x. Dr. Henry's letter of authorization instructed Mr. Robert Johnson, Coordinator of Cultural Events at State University, to begin work on the study at the earliest possible time.

Statement of Problem

The problem of this study, as identified by Dr. David Henry, was to determine the cultural needs and interests of the students attending State University, Fall Term, 199x.

Among the secondary problems were the following:

1. To determine the popularity of the current cultural activities provided by State University.

2. To identify the factors that discourage students from taking greater advantage of the Cultural Events Program.

3. To determine which categories of cultural activities the students would like to have offered in greater abundance.

Statement of Purpose

The purpose of this study, which involved collecting data from students regarding their cultural needs and interests, was to provide a basis for assessing the adequacy of the Cultural Events Program at State University.

Methodology

The methodology of this report consisted of developing a questionnaire (See Appendix for a copy of the questionnaire) designed to obtain the necessary information. An article entitled, "The Necessity of Cultural Activities," in the September, 199x, issue of the College Student Journal provided some background information (Jacobs, 199x).

After the questionnaire was developed, a randomly selected group of students at State University was used to val-

Exhibit 14-12 Body.

3

Limitations

The quality of the information in this report is limited by the accuracy with which the students responded to the questionnaire. If they responded honestly, the content of the report is considered to be accurate.

Triple space

DISCUSSION OF FINDINGS

Triple space

Included in this section is a discussion of the various findings resulting from the processing of the data collected by the questionnaire.

Grade Classification of Respondents

As shown in Figure 1, the greatest percentage of the respondents are currently in their freshman year (31 percent). Those in their senior year were least likely to respond (20 percent). Those in their sophomore and junior years comprised 26 percent and 23 percent, respectively.

Figure 1

PERCENTAGE OF RESPONDENTS BY GRADE CLASSIFICATION

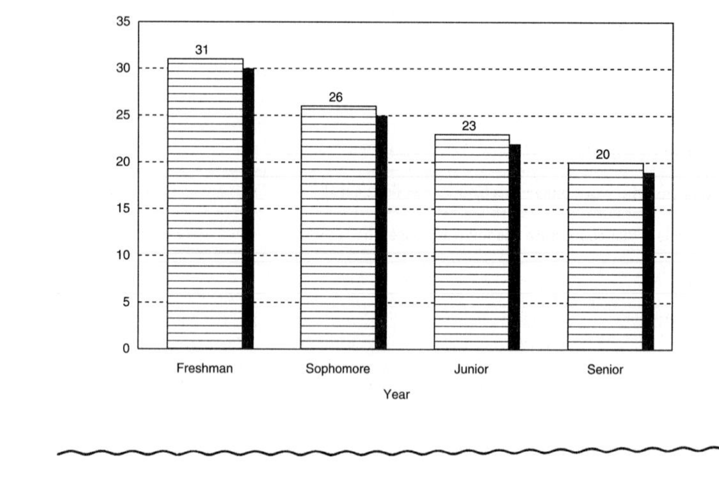

Exhibit 14-12 Body (*continued*).

4

Major in School

As illustrated in Figure 2, the greatest percentage of the respondents (27 percent) are liberal arts majors. Social science majors follow closely with 24 percent. Business (18 percent), education (16 percent), and science (15 percent) majors comprise the remainder of the students' areas of concentration.

Figure 2

MAJORS OF RESPONDENTS

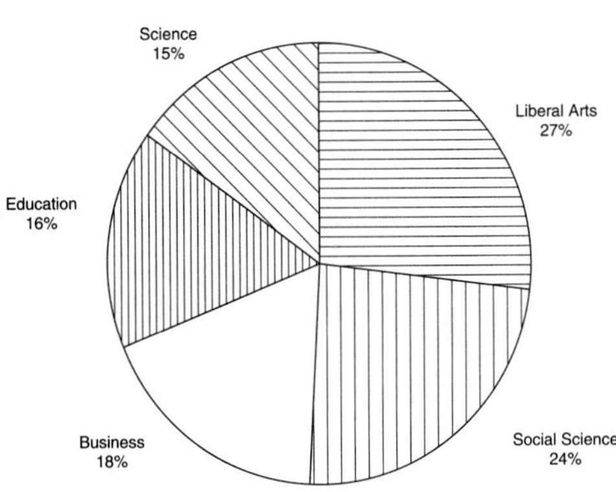

Number of Work Hours per Week

Of the respondents who work either part time or full time, a majority of 53 percent work 20 or fewer hours per week, as shown in Table 1 that appears on the following page. The largest percentage of those who work do so 16 to 20 hours per week. Eight percent of the respondents work over 40 hours per week.

Hours Worked after 5 P.M.

Because the majority of cultural events take place after 5 p.m., the report writer believed that determining the

Exhibit 14-12 Body (*continued*).

Table 1

PERCENTAGE OF RESPONDENTS WHO WORK PART TIME OR FULL TIME

Number of Hours Worked	Percentage
Fewer than 6	4
6–10	10
11–15	17
16–20	22
21–25	17
26–30	12
31–35	3
36–40	7
More than 40	8

questionnaire indicate that 60 percent of the hours are worked between 5 p.m. and 10 p.m., Monday through Thursday, 20 percent are worked between 5 p.m. and 10 p.m. on Friday, and 5 percent of the hours are worked between 5 p.m. and after 10 p.m. on any of these days.

Reasons for Not Attending More Cultural Events

The last item on the questionnaire was included to determine the respondents' reasons for not attending more cultural events. Forty percent of the respondents indicated they attended all the events they cared to attend, 25 percent indicated their work schedules prevented them from attending more cultural events, and 15 percent indicated the cultural events conflicted with their study schedules. Nineteen percent of the respondents indicated a lack of interest in the cultural events sponsored by the university. One percent identified "other" reasons for not attending more cultural events. The reason most frequently given was conflict with religious activities.

Triple space

SUMMARY, CONCLUSIONS, RECOMMENDATIONS

Triple space

This section provides a summary designed to recap the findings of the research efforts, conclusions based on the findings, and recommendations for improving the Cultural Events Program at State University.

Summary of Findings

Fifty-three percent of the respondents who work do so 20 or fewer hours per week, whereas 18 percent work more than 30 hours per week.

Although 15 percent of the hours worked by students are before 5 p.m. and after 10 p.m., Monday through Satur-

Exhibit 14-12 Body (*continued*).

Conclusions

The following conclusions are based on the findings of the research efforts:

1. A need for a new Cultural Events Program does not exist at the present time. Overall student satisfaction with the program is evidenced in part by (a) the number of favorable responses about certain aspects of the present program, and (b) the fact that the current program seems to meet the needs of most students. Only 19 percent of the respondents indicated a lack of interest in the present system.

2. The present Cultural Events Program is popular among the students. The number of students who attend at least one cultural event each week is the basis for this conclusion. Reasons cited for students' failure to take greater advantage of cultural activities included their work (25 percent) and study (15 percent).

Recommendations

1. The present Cultural Events Program should be retained as it now exists.
2. The feasibility of offering more weekend cultural events should be investigated.

Exhibit 14-12 Body (*continued*).

BIBLIOGRAPHY

Triple space

Jacobs, Ellory. "The Necessity of Cultural Activities," College Student Journal, 17:24–26, September, 199x.

(Author's Note: Although a bibliography is not normally prepared for one reference, this one is included for illustration purposes.)

11

Exhibit 14-12 Bibliography.

APPENDIX

12

Exhibit 14-12 Appendix.

CULTURAL EVENTS PROGRAM QUESTIONNAIRE

1. Gender: Male __________ ; Female __________

2. Year in School: Freshman __________ ; Sophomore __________ ; Junior __________ ; Senior __________

3. Major in School: Science __________ ; Social Science __________ ; Business __________ ;
   Liberal Arts __________ ; Education __________

4. Age: Less than 18 __________ ; 18 __________ ; 19 __________ ; 20 __________ ; 21 __________ ;
   22 __________ ; 23 __________ ; 24 __________ ; 25 __________ ; 26 __________ ;
   Over 26 __________

5. What percent of your educational expenses (board, room, tuition, books, supplies) do you personally pay for as opposed to someone else's paying for these expenses:

   I pay for __________ percent of my educational expenses.

6. Do you work either part time or full time during the school year?

   Part time __________ ; Full time __________ ; Don't work __________

7. If you work during the school year, what is the average number of hours you work each week?

   Fewer than 6 __________ ; 6–10 __________ ; 11–15 __________ ; 16–20 __________ ; 21–25 __________ ;
   26–30 __________ ; 32–35 __________ ; 36–40 __________ ; More than 40 __________

8. What percent of your work hours are between

   5 p.m.–10:00 p.m., Mon.–Thurs.: 0–5 ______ ; 26–50 ______ ; 51–75 ______ ; 76–100 ______
   5 p.m.–10:00 p.m., Fri.: 0–5 ______ ; 26–50 ______ ; 51–75 ______ ; 76–100 ______
   5 p.m.–10:00 p.m., Sat.: 0–5 ______ ; 26–50 ______ ; 51–75 ______ ; 76–100 ______

9. On the average, how many hours do you spend each week attending university-sponsored cultural events?

   0 ______ ; 1–2 ______ ; 3–4 ______ ; 5–6 ______ ; 7–8 ______ ; 9–10 ______ ; More than 10 ______

10. Rank the following in terms of the amount of time you spend each week attending the following university-sponsored cultural events. (1 = greatest amount of time; 8 = least amount of time).

    Movies __________ ; Recitals __________ ; Plays __________ ; Operas __________ ; Ballet __________ ;
    Concerts (instrumental) __________ ; Concerts (instrumental and vocal) __________

11. Rank the following in terms of the amount of time you would like to spend each week attending, assuming that each is offered as many hours each week as you desire (1 = greatest amount of time; 8 = least amount of time).

    Movies __________ ; Recitals __________ ; Plays __________ ; Operas __________ ; Ballet __________ ;
    Concerts (instrumental) __________ ; Concerts (instrumental and vocal) __________

Exhibit 14-12 Appendix (*continued*).

12. With which of the following statements do you most agree?

_________ A portion of student tuition should be allocated for financing the cost of university-sponsored cultural events.

_________ Students who attend the cultural events should bear the costs incurred in sponsoring the events.

13. Would you like to have an opportunity to determine which groups and/or cultural events appear at State University?

Yes _________ ; No _________

14. For what reason do you not attend more cultural events?

_________ I attend all that I wish to attend.

_________ I have a work conflict.

_________ I have a study conflict.

_________ The programs do not interest me.

_________ Other (please specify) ____

Exhibit 14-12 Appendix (*continued*).

SUMMARY

One of the distinguishing characteristics of formal reports is the number of parts or sections they contain, contrasted with the number that informal reports contain. Although some of the parts are optional, others are required.

The preliminary parts, some of them optional, are the title fly, title page, letter of authorization, letter of transmittal, table of contents, list of illustrations, and abstract. Each part has a specific format.

The actual body of the report consists of the introduction; the text of the report; and the report ending, composed of the summary, conclusions, and recommendations. The appended parts are the bibliography and the appendices.

Several additional features, such as the proper use of headings, documentation, and graphic aids will enhance the effectiveness of your report.

REVIEW QUESTIONS

1. In what ways are formal and informal reports distinguished from one another?
2. What parts of the formal report are required? What parts are optional?
3. What is the purpose of the letter of transmittal?
4. What is included in the introduction of a formal report?
5. Which verb tense is generally recommended for writing business reports?
6. Explain the differences in the format of each of the different levels of headings used in formal reports.
7. What material found in a business report needs to be footnoted?
8. When is an *ibid.* footnote used? An *op. cit.* footnote? A *loc. cit.* footnote?
9. What characterizes effective report conclusions?
10. What is the content of recommendations found in a formal report?
11. What are some of the important guidelines for preparing graphics to include in a formal report?
12. For what types of data/information are pie charts especially suited?
13. For what types of data/information are bar charts especially suited?
14. For what types of data/information are multiple bar charts especially suited?
15. For what types of data/information are belt charts especially suited?

APPLICATION PROBLEMS

1. Prepare a formal report based on the following data/information. The data/information were collected by means of a questionnaire completed by 240 of the 300 people who received it. First City Bank initiated the study to assess customer satisfaction with its automatic tellers. The bank will use the results of the study to assess the effectiveness of its teller-machine operations. Incorporate graphic aids in your report. Your instructor will specify which parts to include.
   a. What is your age? 16–25: 31; 26–35: 47; 36–45: 51; 46–55: 71; 56–65: 30; over 65: 10
   b. What is your gender? Male: 145; Female: 95
   c. On the average, how often do you use an automatic teller machine each week? 0 times: 34; 1 time: 45; 2 times: 56; 3 times: 58; 4 times: 33; 5 times: 10; 6 times: 4; more than 6 times: 0
   d. Which teller machine do you use most often? 9th Street: 74; Bob's Grocery Store: 60; Drive-in Bank: 106
   e. Which one of the following best explains the reason you use the teller machine most often at the location you identified in item d above? Convenient location: 156; Near where I work: 40; Near where I live: 20; Speed: 24
   f. How would you rate your satisfaction with the use of teller machines? Very satisfied: 48; Quite satisfied: 74; Neither satisfied nor dissatisfied: 78; Quite dissatisfied: 30; Very dissatisfied: 10

g. If you marked "Quite dissatisfied" or "Very dissatisfied" in item f above, which of the following most accurately reflects the reason for your dissatisfaction? Machine sometimes malfunctions: 13; Machine is sometimes out of order when I have made a special trip to use it: 20; I miss having a person assist me: 4; Machine is not always able to take care of my banking needs: 3
h. How would you rate the ease with which the machines are operated? Very easy to use: 110; Quite easy to use: 91: Neither easy nor difficult to use: 20; Quite difficult to use: 14; Very difficult to use: 5
i. For what type of transaction do you most often use the teller? Withdrawing cash: 154; Depositing money to account: 45; Transferring money from one account to another: 31; Making an inquiry about bank balance: 10
j. Are you satisfied with the maximum daily amount of cash you can withdraw from the machine? Yes: 198; No: 42
k. If you answered "No" in item j above, do you believe the maximum should be increased or decreased? For increasing: 34; For decreasing: 8
l. What percentage of your total banking needs is the teller able to accommodate? 75 to 100 percent: 78; 50 to 75: 124; 25 to 50 percent: 32; 0 to 25 percent: 6
m. In addition to the services the teller is capable of performing, list one additional service you would like for the automatic teller to be able to perform: Use to make loan payments: 184; Use to make inquiry about current money-market rates: 20; Use to inquire whether a check with a specified number has cleared the bank: 10; Use to inquire about amount of direct deposits to account: 26
n. Do you think First City Bank should install more tellers throughout the city? Yes: 210; No: 30

2. You are the assistant to the manager of the Food Place, the cafeteria in the Student Union at Westmont University. From time to time, the students who eat their meals in the cafeteria are asked to complete a questionnaire that solicits their answers to a variety of questions. The information is used as input for making decisions about various aspects of the cafeteria's operations. The data below are from the responses received from 100 of the 150 students who were randomly asked to complete the questionnaire. In preparing the formal report for the manager, incorporate graphic aids. Your instructor will tell you which report parts to include.
   a. Year in school: senior: 38; junior: 33; sophomore: 17; freshman: 12
   b. Gender: male: 57; female: 43
   c. Major: Arts and Letters: 23; Business: 31; Engineering: 31; Physical Science: 15
   d. On the average, how many meals do you eat each week in the Food Place? 0: 0; 1–3: 25; 4–6: 30; 7–9: 12; 10–12: 8; 13–15: 5; 16–18: 10; More than 18: 10
   e. Which meal do you eat most often in the Food Place? breakfast: 21; lunch: 59; dinner: 20
   f. Overall, how satisfied are you with the Food Place? very satisfied: 25; quite satisfied: 43; neither satisfied nor dissatisfied: 20; quite dissatisfied: 10; very dissatisfied: 2
   g. How satisfied are you with the taste of the food served in the Food Place? very satisfied: 35; quite satisfied: 38; neither satisfied nor dissatisfied: 20; quite dissatisfied: 7; very dissatisfied: 0
   h. How satisfied are you with the appearance of the food served in the Food Place? very satisfied: 32; quite satisfied: 35; neither satisfied nor dissatisfied: 17; quite dissatisfied: 13; very dissatisfied: 3

i. How satisfied are you with the variety in the food served in the Food Place? very satisfied: 29; quite satisfied: 32; neither satisfied nor dissatisfied: 14; quite dissatisfied: 17; very dissatisfied: 8
j. How satisfied are you with the service you receive in the Food Place? very satisfied: 36; quite satisfied: 34; neither satisfied nor dissatisfied: 20; quite dissatisfied: 8; very dissatisfied: 2
k. How satisfied are you with the atmosphere in the Food Place? very satisfied: 18; quite satisfied: 32; neither satisfied nor dissatisfied: 30; quite dissatisfied: 12; very dissatisfied: 8
l. How satisfied are you with the cleanliness of the Food Place? very satisfied: 52; quite satisfied: 30; neither satisfied nor dissatisfied: 10; quite dissatisfied: 6; very dissatisfied: 2
m. How do you feel about the price of the food available in the Food Place? very expensive: 10; moderately priced: 34; neither expensive nor inexpensive: 40; quite inexpensive: 8; very inexpensive: 8
n. Which one of the following most clearly reflects your reason for eating meals at the Food Place? convenience: 46; quality of food: 34; price of food: 10; atmosphere: 2; my friends eat at the Food Place: 8

Prepare the formal report.

3. You, the executive vice president of Willoby Corporation, have had several requests from department heads, supervisors, and employees to investigate the need for establishing a companywide training program. To help you determine the need for such a program, you decided to call a meeting of interested individuals to discuss the situation. At the end of the meeting, you distributed a questionnaire the participants were to complete. The tabulated results are presented below. You received a completed questionnaire from each of the fifty participants. You decide to prepare a formal report that summarizes the questionnaire responses. The report is to be prepared for Mr. Grant Skinner, Willoby's president.
   a. Gender: Male: 34; Female: 16
   b. Department affiliation: Accounting: 5; Word Processing: 8; Production: 7; Executive Area: 12; Marketing: 3; Data Processing: 10; Maintenance: 5
   c. Years with the company: 0–3 years: 18; 4–7 years: 12; 8–11 years: 4; 12 or more: 16
   d. Which of the following best reflects your job? Administrative: 8; Manager: 6; Secretary: 10; Clerk: 12; Specialist: 2; Supervisor: 12
   e. Which of the following best reflects how you became trained for your present position? Came into position trained: 22; Supervisor trained: 18; Self-trained: 10
   f. What is your level of agreement with the following statement? "A training program is badly needed at Willoby Corporation." Strongly agree: 28; Agree: 14; Neutral: 5; Disagree: 3; Strongly disagree: 0
   g. Which of the following best describes your reasons for wanting a training program at this time? Help me do better work in my present job: 20; Help my subordinates become better qualified: 20; Help me qualify for a job to which I would like to be promoted: 7; No clear-cut motive for wanting a training program: 3
   h. Would you be interested in attending training sessions held after work hours? Yes: 24; Perhaps: 10; No: 16
   i. Of the following areas, which one is the area in which you would most like to have a training session offered? Time management: 10; Effective communications: 13; Specific job skills: 15; Interpersonal relations: 5; Conflict resolution: 4; Organization of work: 3

j. If you believe you are qualified to provide a training session on a topic that others are interested in, would you be willing to volunteer your time to provide the session? Yes: 37; No: 13

Prepare the report.

4. You are assistant to the director of the Des Moines Parks and Recreation Program, Mr. LeMoyne Johnson. He asked you several weeks ago to prepare a questionnaire to assess parents' satisfaction with the youth sport programs offered by the Parks and Recreation Department. The results will be used to provide direction in revamping the operation of the youth sport programs. The questionnaire will be given to parents when they enroll their children in the upcoming soccer, flag football, and basketball youth sport programs. The following represent the tabulated results of the 78 questionnaires distributed and completed on September 24. You decided to prepare your report on the basis of the data provided on the 78 questionnaires.
   a. Number of children ages 0–14 in your family: 1–2: 45; 3–4: 35; 5–6: 10; 7 or more: 10
   b. Number of children in the various age groups: 0–2 years: 23; 3–5 years: 27; 6–8 years: 23; 9–11 years: 14; 12–14 years: 13
   c. Number of boys in the various age groups: 0–2 years: 11; 3–5 years: 14; 6–8 years: 12; 9–11 years: 7; 12–14 years: 6
   d. Number of girls in various age groups: 0–2 years: 12; 3–5 years: 13; 6–8 years: 11; 9–11 years: 7; 12–14 years: 7
   e. Identify the number of children in your family who participated in a Parks and Recreation Department youth sport program during the following time periods: Spring 93: 45; Summer 93: 32; Fall 93: 23; Spring 94: 38; Summer 94: 42; Fall 94: 35; Spring 95: 48; Summer 95: 48; Fall 95: 52
   f. Identify the number of your children who participated in each of the following youth sport programs during the Spring, Summer, and Fall 1995 time periods:

	Spring 95	Summer 95	Fall 95
Soccer	24		18
T-Ball		22	
Baseball		28	22
Wrestling	10		
Basketball	19		
Swimming		6	

   g. Overall, how would you rate your experience(s) with the Parks and Recreation Department? All experiences have been satisfactory: 32; Most experiences have been satisfactory: 28; About half of the experiences have been satisfactory: 10; Most experiences have been unsatisfactory: 8; All experiences have been unsatisfactory: 0
   h. Have you or your spouse ever participated as a referee or as a coach in a Parks and Recreation Department's youth sport program? Yes: 24; No: 54
   i. How satisfied are you with the time of the youth sport program practice sessions? Very satisfied: 21; Quite satisfied: 32; Neither satisfied nor dissatisfied: 20; Quite dissatisfied: 5; Very dissatisfied: 0.
   j. How satisfied are you with the time of the youth sport program games? Very satisfied: 25; Quite satisfied: 34; Neither satisfied nor dissatisfied: 13; Quite dissatisfied: 6; Very dissatisfied: 0
   k. How satisfied are you with the philosophy of the Parks and Recreation Department's youth sport program: Very satisfied: 30; Quite satisfied: 23; Neither satisfied nor dissatisfied: 10; Quite dissatisfied: 10; Very dissatisfied: 5;

Prepare the report.

5. Write a report on one of the following topics. Each topic is one for which a variety of secondary-source information is available, including textbooks and journal articles that are in the library. You may wish to interview appropriate persons to add primary information to your report. To help you determine the appropriate content to include in your report, a variety of subtopics (identified as A, B, C, D, E, etc.) is listed for each topic. Your instructor may ask that you include others as well. Because the subtopics may not be listed in a logical sequence, make sure you determine an appropriate order before beginning to prepare your report. After you have completed the library research, your instructor may ask you to present a tentative outline of the report's content.

1. Office automation—A, D, E, G, H, I, J
2. Employee motivation—B, C, H, I, Q
3. Flextime—D, E, G, H, I, J
4. Team building—C, D, E, G, H, I, J
5. Quality circles—D, E, F, G, H, I, J
6. Employee selection procedures—A, F, K, L, Q
7. Word processing—A, D, E, G, H, I
8. Evolution of management theory—M, N, C, T
9. Computer security—A, F, H, J, Q
10. Evolution of computers—M, N, S, T
11. Financial ratios—B, C, H, J, Q
12. Nonverbal communication—A, C, D, E
13. Product promotion—A, B, R, Q
14. Advertising channels—B, O, R, Q
15. Employee performance-appraisal techniques—B, C, D, E, H, I, L
16. Controlling office costs—B, C, D, E, H
17. Employee training techniques—A, B, K, Q, R
18. Oral communication—C, P, Q, R
19. Health maintenance organizations (HMO)—D, E, G, J, O
20. Effective employer-employee relations—A, B, C, H, J, Q
21. White-collar unions—D, E, H, I, O, P
22. Quality of work life (QWL)—A, C, D, E, H, I, R
23. Job enrichment—B, C, D, E, G, I, J
24. MBO—A, C, D, E, F, G, H, I, J
25. Salary incentive plans—A, C, D, E, H, I, J
26. Participative management—B, C, D, E, G, H, I, J
27. Employee compensation—A, B, F, J, L
28. New electronic office equipment—A, C, P, Q, R
29. Electronic mail—C, D, E, F, G, H, J
30. Telecommunications—A, C, D, E, G, H, J

A—Components of ______
B—Techniques of ______
C—Why ______ is important
D—Advantages of ______
E—Disadvantages of ______

F—Steps involved in ______
G—What ______ is
H—What ______ do/does for the organization
I—What ______ do/does for the employee
J—How ______ works
K—Building quality into ______
L—Forms used in ______
M—Stages of development ______
N—Significant individuals affecting development
O—Characteristics of ______
P—Functions performed by ______
Q—Benefits of ______
R—Measuring effectiveness of ______
S—New developments on the horizon
T—Lasting contributions of each stage of development

9. Using secondary-source information, write a report about the career field you plan to enter upon graduating from college. Include in your report information about such topics as the following: qualifications needed, opportunities available, salary, promotional opportunities, and future outlook. Your instructor may also suggest other topics for you to include in your report as well as identify the report parts to be included. Incorporate appropriate statistics and graphic aids in your report.

15

Administrative Communications

After studying this chapter, you should be able to

1. Discuss the differences among the types of proposals commonly used in the business world.
2. Discuss the recommended content for business plans.
3. Discuss the purpose of performance evaluation.
4. Describe the essential elements of preparing news releases.
5. Describe the essential elements of preparing agendas and minutes of meetings.

Administrative communications vitally affect the organization, both internally and externally. Although several other categories of administrative communications exist, this chapter deals with writing proposals, business plans, performance evaluations, news releases, agendas, and minutes of meetings. Several other chapters in this text provide coverage of other types of written administrative communication, including letters and reports.

Proposals are prepared for unique situations, such as responding to a request for a proposal, soliciting funds, describing the benefits of a product or service, or outlining a proposed research project.

When an individual supervises another individual, he or she is responsible for evaluating the performance of his or her subordinates. The evaluation form that most organizations use requires the preparation of a written statement about the subordinate's performance. The section on performance evaluation is designed to help you learn how to write more effective evaluation statements.

News releases, agendas, and minutes of meetings follow a structured format regarding the content they contain. Little variance should be found in how they are structured from one situation to another.

PROPOSALS

What is a proposal?

A *proposal* is a document that provides a plan for undertaking a proposed activity or that suggests a specific course of action. The most common types of proposals are those that

1. Respond to a request for a proposal (RFP).
2. Solicit funds to undertake a project.
3. Outline for a prospective customer how to use a manufacturer's product or an organization's services and what are the benefits of such use.
4. Outline a proposed research project.

Because proposals are created for unique situations, no universal organizational plan exists. A proposal prepared in response to an RFP will likely be quite different from a proposal soliciting funds from a foundation to support a research project. The proposal outlining the use and benefits of a manufacturer's products will be quite different from a proposal seeking authorization to undertake a research project.

All proposals must be persuasive to convince readers that what is suggested will benefit them. Your proposals will be more persuasive if you present the material in a logical sequence that considers various psychological dimensions. To illustrate, you will want to place strategically any negative information that you are including in the proposal. Furthermore, your proposals will be more persuasive if you provide concrete evidence rather than generalities to support your assertions. Concrete evidence provides readers with concepts, terms, or information with which they can readily identify, visualize, or comprehend, such as figures, schedules, and deadlines. Note the difference in the following examples.

General reference: "significant increase," "majority favor," "moderate growth"
Concrete reference: "increase of 30 percent," "60 percent favor," "growth of 10 percent"

What criteria are used in making evaluative comparisons of proposals?

Because your proposal will often compete with other proposals, you may find it helpful to see what you write through the eyes of prospective readers. The following are some questions they will probably have as they compare your proposal with competing proposals:

1. What is the nature of the project presented in the proposal?
2. What benefits are likely to accrue from undertaking the project discussed in the proposal?
3. What steps/procedures does the writer propose for carrying out the project, and are these steps/procedures feasible?
4. How well qualified is the writer to carry out the project presented in the proposal?
5. What potential problems are apt to surface in carrying out the proposed project?
6. How long will the project take to complete?
7. How much will the project cost to complete?

Requests for proposals (RFPs) are common in various state and federal government agencies. Government agencies that want to start a research project or develop a specific program frequently prepare an RFP that contains a description of the project an agency or company desires to undertake or the goods or services it needs. In addition, the RFP frequently provides an outline of the specific work to be done and lists detailed instructions on how to prepare the proposal. The more closely a proposal's content matches the information sought in the RFP, the more likely the proposal will be chosen. The writer should include any additional information in the proposal that might enhance its success.

Proposals That Solicit Funds

Proposals prepared to solicit funds that enable a person to carry out a project or to conduct research differ from proposals that respond to RFPs. Proposals that respond to RFPs are initiated by someone other than the proposal writer, whereas the worker initiates proposals that solicit funds.

What is the suggested plan for proposals that solicit funds?

The suggested plan for a proposal soliciting funds for a project includes the following elements:

1. Cover letter briefly outlining the nature of the proposal
2. Statement of the problem of the project and a discussion of the situation to be remedied
3. Objectives of the project
4. Procedures for carrying out the project
5. Dissemination of the findings of the project (if appropriate)
6. Evaluation of the project (if appropriate)
7. Facilities and equipment needed to carry out the project
8. Personnel involved in the project
9. Budget requirements for carrying out the project

Proposals That Outline Uses and Benefits of Products and Services

Manufacturing and service organizations often turn to proposals to identify the uses and benefits of their products or services for prospective customers. For example, a small company that wants to install its first data processing system may solicit proposals from several computer vendors, requesting each vendor to outline a proposed system. After comparing the various systems, as depicted in the outlines, the company then selects the one that best meets its needs.

What is the suggested content for proposals that outline uses of products/services?

When preparing a proposal for a prospective client, the following topical outline may work best:

1. Cover letter, with brief outline of the nature of the proposal
2. Background information about organization whose products and/or services you are proposing
3. Summary of analysis of client's need for proposed products and/or services
4. Information about products and/or services you are proposing, including specifications, configurations, costs, and so forth
5. Support services the vendor provides (if appropriate)
6. Outline of vendor and customer responsibilities
7. Implementation schedule (if appropriate)
8. Additional information or material to strengthen the proposal

Proposals That Seek Authorization to Undertake a Research Project

The content of research-oriented proposals is quite different from other types of proposals. Researchers frequently prepare research-oriented proposals to obtain approval for a specific research project, such as the research project required by those working on a new design for electronic equipment.

The following outline is useful in preparing such proposals:

What is the suggested content for proposals that seek authorization to undertake research projects?

1. Statement of problem
2. Objectives
3. Hypotheses (if appropriate)
4. Work schedule, including dates for completing various phases (if appropriate)
5. Outline of proposed research procedures, methodology, and design
6. Procedures for disseminating research findings (if appropriate)
7. Procedures used for evaluating the research project (if appropriate)
8. Additional information supporting worthiness of the project

Exhibit 15-1 shows a proposal prepared for a prospective customer on the installation of a new word processing system. This edited version eliminates much of the technical material that was included in the original proposal.

What suggestions can you offer that will be helpful in the writing of proposals?

Communication Capsule 15-1 contains suggestions to help you in writing proposals.

Communication Capsule 15-1 Suggestions for Writing Effective Proposals

A number of factors may determine whether your proposal is accepted or rejected. To help improve your chances of acceptance, follow these suggestions:

1. *Explain in your own terms the problem you intend to study or the project you intend to undertake.* When you explain in your own terms what you plan to do, you are more able to remain focused during the writing of the proposal. Although the proposal you are preparing may be solicited—for example a response to an RFP or to a potential client outlining how your company's equipment can solve the reader's problem—you still have the opportunity and right to state in your own terms what you plan to do.
2. *Clearly describe the work you expect to do.* This is a critical part of the proposal, as is the description. The kind of work you expect to do will probably determine to a great extent whether the reader selects your proposal rather than other proposals.
3. *Provide explicit details about the procedures, methods, equipment, materials, and personnel you plan to use.* The reader will probably intensively review these details to estimate whether your work will produce the desired outcome.
4. *Focus on the reader's needs and concerns as you develop the proposal.* The more effectively you address the reader's needs and concerns, the more likely your proposal will be chosen from among those submitted.
5. *Include all the parts necessary for the type of proposal you are preparing.* Some RFPs specify the content to be included in a proposal. When such information is available, you must include each identified part. Because the selection process will probably compare all submitted proposals, not including one or more parts will undoubtedly be a strong mark against you.
6. *Provide a cost-benefit analysis.* In many cases, the final decision is based primarily on one factor: What are we receiving for our investment? The more effective the cost-benefit ratio, the more success the proposal will likely enjoy.
7. *Show how your proposed solution is superior to that of others.* When you are convinced that your proposed solution is highly competitive, your proposal will probably be more successful. The reason is that confidence tends to show throughout an entire document.
8. *Make sure the proposal is well written.* The reader of the proposal may believe a strong correlation exists between your ability to write well and your ability to do what you say you can. Therefore, you need to make sure your proposal is well written.

BUSINESS PLANS

A *business plan* is a document commonly sent to individuals or institutions to obtain financial backing for a new business or for expanding an existing business. Because the reader will either accept or reject your plan, you will want to do everything you can to ensure its success. Increasingly, this means following a company-prescribed format and content. For this reason, contact the individual or the institution that will be receiving your business plan before you start preparation to obtain guidelines the company has set.

Arcot Corporation

Rapid City, SD 57908 **1231 Brownell Street** **(405) 343-8743**

August 10, 199x

Mr. David Woloski, Vice President
Decco Company
117 East Main Street
Port Huron, SD 57901

Dear Mr. Woloski:

The attached proposal outlines Decco Company's use of Concept 5 text-editing equipment. Your giving us an opportunity to explain how our equipment will meet your needs is appreciated.

The proposal contains information about the nature of your text-editing equipment needs as well as information about the equipment we are proposing. This proposal also contains information about the support services we provide our customers.

Concept 5 has just become the top-selling text-editing equipment in the country. Our quality products and unmatched service record have enabled us to achieve this distinction.

If you have questions after reading the proposal, please write or call me.

Sincerely,

Mary Linowitcz

Mary Linowitcz
Customer Support Representative

jd
Attachment

Exhibit 15-1 Proposal outlining the installation of a word processing system.

Proposal for Decco Company

This proposal, which is prepared specifically for Decco Company, recommends the installation of a word processing system that uses Concept 5 text-editing equipment.

Background Information

Arcot Corporation, the manufacturer of Concept 5 equipment, was founded in 1957. The company, which is located in London, New Jersey, has grown steadily since it was started. Arcot made the *Fortune* 500 list for the first time in 1972. Text-editing equipment now accounts for 74 percent of Arcot's sales. The corporation, which first started selling word processing equipment in 1970, also manufacturers copiers and mail-processing equipment.

Ninety-two percent of Arcot's customers are "repeaters," the highest repeat-customer percentage for any company in the industry.

Analysis of Need

Various types of work-load data were collected in Decco Company from July 18 to July 29. These data enabled Arcot to determine the types and quantities of typing/transcription tasks performed in Decco. This analysis resulted in the following conclusions:

1. That the installation of a word processing system in Decco is justifiable and cost worthy.
2. That on the basis of the work-load data, four Model 210 Concept 5 word processing units are needed.
3. That typing/transcription tasks can be performed more efficiently, at a lower cost, and with better quality than is possible with the present equipment.

Proposed Equipment

Arcot Corporation recommends that Decco Company install four Concept 5 (Model 210 text-editing typewriters). These devices have a one-page video display unit. The printer, which uses laser technology, is capable of printing eight pages per minute. The Model 210 uses floppy disks with a 260-page storage capacity.

The Model 210 sells for $8743, which includes the installation charge, a training manual, and a three-month free service warranty. This same device currently rents for $289 per month for a 12-month period.

Support Services Provided by Vendor

Thorough training manuals accompany each Concept 5 text-editing typewriter. These self-paced manuals take the average reader 24-28 hours to complete.

Arcot has developed a program to train operators on the use of the equipment. This 24-hour program costs $100 per trainee.

Arcot has a no-charge consulting service for its customers. Its purpose is to help customers get the most from their Concept 5 equipment. This service is especially useful for customers who from time to time change their systems.

Proposal for Decco Company, Page 2

Vendor and Customer Responsibilities

Concept 5 equipment carries a customer-satisfaction guarantee. If a customer is not totally satisfied with the equipment after three months of use, Arcot will remove the equipment, with no financial obligation to the customer.

This proposal only covers text-editing equipment. The customer is responsible for obtaining dictation/recording equipment and for providing the furniture on which the equipment is placed. The customer is also responsible for orienting and training the word originators to use the word processing system.

Implementation Schedule

At present, a three-week backlog in filling orders exists. Arcot guarantees a three-week delivery date, excluding any extenuating circumstances. Operators

Exhibit 15-1 *Continued*

The high failure rate of new businesses and the increasing number of business plans that financial institutions receive mean that the reader will carefully scrutinize your plan. This kind of attention, in fact, has caused many more business plans to be rejected than accepted.

When you do not have a prescribed outline to follow in preparing a business plan, you should consider including the steps outlined in the following sections:

1. *Discussion of your idea.* Your goal in writing this section is to justify your idea. The more effectively you justify your idea, the better your chances of having the business plan accepted for funding. This section includes a detailed description of the product(s) or service(s) you plan to offer. You will also need to insert information about how your product(s) or service(s) compare with the competition as well as show how/why yours is better than the competition. This portion of the business plan is basically conceptual.

2. *Discussion of the promotion of the product(s) or service(s).* In this section, include information about your ideas for delivery of the product(s) or service(s) to the customers. Explain your ideas for marketing. You should include detailed information about consumer need or desire for your product(s) or service(s). In addition, demographic data will aid the reader in determining whether the locality—considering the consumer base—can provide sufficient demand for the product(s) or service(s). This portion of the business plan basically involves the marketing aspect of your idea.

3. *Discussion of the company structure.* If your business plan concerns the founding of a new company, the reader will need evidence that the structure you are proposing is sound, legitimate, and effective. If your plan involves expansion of an existing company, the reader will also need evidence that your existing structure is effective and that any proposed changes in the structure resulting from your idea will be effective. This portion of the business plan is basically the management aspect of your idea. Other factors of concern are the size of the company, the skills/abilities of each principal, and future plans.

4. *Discussion of the financing of the idea.* This portion of the plan most directly involves the reader, for here is where you make your financial request. You will need to offer detailed information about how much money is needed and how it will be used. This portion of the business plan contains the financial aspect of your idea. If your plan is not for a start-up organization but for one already in existence, your reader will probably expect you to provide the company's statements and records.

In general, the more you can show you have completely thought through your idea, the more likely the reader will seriously consider it. Similarly, the more specific evidence you can offer to support your idea, the greater the likelihood of success.

PERFORMANCE EVALUATION

Managers, by evaluating the performance of subordinates, are able to identify employee strengths, weaknesses, and growth potential. *Performance evaluations* are used to provide input for decisions about promotions, salary increases, training programs, employee transfers, and reduction in workforce.

Although most evaluation methods require minimal writing, the majority do require some written statement evaluating the employee's performance. Modern evaluation methods rarely use only a checklist. Because the evaluation process is designed partly to help employees improve their performances, the inclusion of effectively written statements on the evaluation form can function as a guide. Depending on the type of evaluation, the amount of writing may vary from a sentence or two—typical of the rating-form technique—to many sentences—typical of the narrative evaluation technique.

What uses are made of the information obtained from performance appraisals?

Performance evaluation documentation has many applications. Besides providing input on decisions about promotions and salary increases, the documentation may also be used to effect a just-cause termination of an employee. When employees legally challenge their termination, the performance evaluation documentation often provides evidence that they were forewarned about the need to perform more effectively. This is important because organizations are no longer able to terminate employees "at will" as they did several years ago. Therefore, management relies, at least partly, on performance evaluation documentation to build a case against the employee. The documentation also is used to settle employee grievances against management. When preparing written statements about employees' performance, follow these guidelines:

What guidelines can you offer that will help you write more effective appraisal statements?

1. Be as specific as possible. Generalities will not help much if a legal problem arises.
2. Be honest. Should the performance evaluation documentation become evidence in a court of law but the employee has received several undeserved favorable ratings, he or she has a good chance of winning.
3. Document the write-up of unfavorable performance with the date(s) of the unsatisfactory performance.
4. Use concrete rather than abstract language.
5. Point out strengths as well as weaknesses.
6. Make sure the written comments are consistent with any checklist rating that you may include on the evaluation form.
7. Avoid words that may mean different things to different people. Examples are *somewhat, nearly, sometimes,* and *almost always.* Quantify statements or assertions wherever possible. For example, state that the employee has been absent twenty times during the past work year rather than that the employee has a high absentee rate.

Should you ever give an unsatisfactory rating of an employee's work performance that leads to his or her eventual dismissal, the use of legal counsel is advised. Abiding by the legal advice you receive will prevent you from violating the employee's due process.

Exhibit 15-2 is an evaluation form that contains written comments about the employee's strengths, areas in need of improvement, and growth potential.

NEWS RELEASES

Most large newspapers have a business editor who handles all business assignments. If this is not the case, the city editor or metropolitan editor generally assigns all stories and, with key staffers, determines what material appears in the paper. A visit to the appropriate editor, therefore, may help you establish a friendly relationship, with the possible benefit of favorable news coverage.

Even if you do not have a personal contact with a newspaper editor, a *news release* is information designed to reach a general audience through a published medium. The release is likely to create even more attention when an appropriate photograph accompanies it.

Subjects

For what are news releases used?

The subject of the news release will probably be a new product, a new employee, a new company service, or a company activity or organization the writer believes deserves publicity. News releases are sent to the appropriate editor. Because editors are flooded with such material, newspapers publish only a small percentage of material from these releases. If the information in a release is to have a chance of being published, it must be newsworthy in the editor's eyes and contain news of interest to readers of the publication.

Editors judge news releases by the following criteria:

What criteria are used to judge the worthiness of news releases?

- Timeliness—is the event happening now?
- Proximity—is the event close to the reader's location, frame of reference, or field of activity?

SUMMARY OF APPRAISAL

Staff Member Becky Brown Date of Review July 1, 199x

Position Title Coordinator Department Editorial

A. Narrative Evaluation
Write a summary of the employee's performance, highlighting those areas which best characterize him/her as an individual. Include key accomplishments, strengths, areas for improvement, and plans for development, improvements expected, and growth potential. If more space is needed, a separate sheet may be attached.

Becky has a great hunger to learn, to understand, and to apply her knowledge and insights to improving herself, her job, the journal, and the department. She is a self-starter with the creative and organizational skills to develop and recommend improvements and the initiative and poise to see that they are implemented. Becky makes mistakes, but these most often occur when she has been willing to take a chance—an important aspect of development—and she rarely makes the same mistake twice. She has never shied away from taking responsibility for her actions and decisions. Becky reacts positively to my instructions and suggestions and is always careful to query me as appropriate and to inform me of her progress. She has excellent communication skills and is able to develop and maintain rapport with editors, authors, advertisers and vendors. I have received very positive feedback from Editorial Board members, the ad representative, and the printer and typesetter that Becky responds to their questions and requests with confidence and competencies, thereby instilling in them confidence in our organization.

Becky has worked hard to learn to manage her time and resources more effectively and to set priorities. She must continue to develop her time-management skills and must overcome her feelings of guilt about recruiting others to help with projects—guilt that stems from her concern that she is not able to accomplish everything singlehandedly. Becky tends to become impatient with others when they disagree with her, when they don't follow procedures, and when they don't meet deadlines/expectations; she is a perfectionist who expects perfection from others. She must learn to curb her impatience; to be assertive—but not aggressive—when dealing with coworkers; to give feedback in a positive, courteous, and timely way; and to accept the reality that change, even when badly needed, often (of necessity) takes time. I hope that Becky will make time in the coming year to get to know her coworkers outside of the department and in this way come to understand their responsibilities, motivations, actions, and perspectives.

Becky is a professional of whom I may expect the highest quality of work in terms of accuracy, quantity, timeliness, and comprehensiveness. I am pleased to work with and to supervise her.

PLEASE COMPLETE THE REVERSE SIDE
The Summary of Appraisal (parts A & B) must be reviewed by those individuals indicated on the signature spaces before it is discussed with the employee.

Exhibit 15-2 Performance appraisal form. Courtesy: American College of Emergency Physicians.

- Importance—is the event significant to the reader?
- Policy—is the event consistent with the publication's editorial policy?

Ideally, every news item should answer the following questions:

1. Who did it?
2. What did he/she/they do?
3. Why did he/she/they do it?
4. When did he/she/they do it?
5. Where did he/she/they do it?
6. How did he/she/they do it?

Many business news releases describe the activity of an individual or a group of individuals, as Exhibit 15-3 illustrates. As you study this figure, please note the following:

1. The document is clearly identified as a news release.
2. The name and address of the organization in which the release originated appear on the release.
3. The name and phone number of the contact person are provided.
4. The release date is identified (either "IMMEDIATELY" or on a specific date).
5. The release is double-spaced.
6. The content of the release answers the journalistic five W's and one H (who, what, where, when, why, and how).
7. The release contains short sentences and paragraphs.
8. The most important information appears at the beginning, and the least important information appears at the end.
9. Either of the following is used to communicate the end of the release: -30- or ###.
10. Had the release continued to a second page, the following would have been typed at the bottom of the first page: -MORE-.

In contrast to a news release, a *personal business release* is usually a short item printed in a house organ. The release may contain some interesting news about an employee, such as that he or she has received some in-house award. A longer column in a daily newspaper may include a photograph that publicizes the appointment or promotion of a business executive to a high-level position. Businesses often submit information from house organs to newspapers, which, in turn, include grouped items under a general heading that appears in one section of the newspaper, as shown in Exhibit 15-4.

A personal information item should probably consist of a single paragraph. The most important news, either the person's name or what has happened to the person, should appear first.

Another type of release may be termed the *human-interest story*, which, like the personal story, emphasizes the activities of an individual but does not, however, deal directly with the business affairs of that individual. In a plant newspaper or house

Exhibit 15-3 News release about an employee.

Iowa Nursery Association
1236 High Street - Des Moines, IA 55273

News Release

For Release: Immediately

Contact: John Smith
(603) 298-8374

Dr. John Grantham, chief horticulturist for Johnson Seed Company, is the 199x recipient of the Outstanding Iowa Horticulture Award.

The award was presented at the fortieth annual convention of the Iowa Nursery Association, held recently in Ames.

Grantham has been on Johnson's staff since 1971. He began his career at Johnson as a junior horticulturist. Besides his duties at Johnson, he is an adjunct professor of horticulture at Iowa State.

Grantham, a native of St. Louis, has a B.S. degree from the University of Missouri and M.S. and Ph.D. degrees from Iowa State.

-###-

ILLINOIS NATIONAL BANK—Grant Barnes, formerly vice president of Continental State Bank, Chicago, was named president of Illinois National Bank.

ABC TRANSPORTATION COMPANY—Sally Gray was named vice president for planning and analysis at ABC Transportation Company, a Chicago-based subsidiary of Frontier Corporation, New York City.

CONTINENTAL BAKING CORP.—Ronald Jackson was named chief financial officer of this company's Home Products, Inc. subsidiary. He succeeds Marjorie Thayer, who retired earlier this year. Jackson was previously controller of Smith-Grant Corporation.

Exhibit 15-4 News release about business people.

To the Residents of Greenwood: This year's United Way Drive raised more money than ever before—thanks to all of the concerned residents of Greenwood. Not only did we meet our goal of raising $131,000, but also we surpassed the goal by $10,872, for a total contribution of $141,872!

The Greenwood United Way Board of Directors will be meeting shortly to determine how to distribute the monies. Never before has United Way received so many worthy requests for funds.

Several individuals are largely responsible for the success of this year's drive. The following division chairpersons challenged one another to see whose division could achieve the largest percentage increase over last year's contributions: Sadie Parcher, Division I; John Smith, Division II; Barbara Howell, Division III; and Mike Kendall, Division IV. Whereas each division surpassed last year's contributions by at least 10 percent, Division III had the largest percentage increase of 29 percent.

Please help us make next year's drive even more successful than this year's drive was! Thanks to all of you, it works!

Delores Brown, Chairperson
1986 Greenwood
United Way Drive

Exhibit 15-5 Letter to the editor.

organ, stories of unusual experiences of employees such as a vacation on an exotic island, unusual hobbies, and many other topics are subjects that appeal to fellow employees' interests.

For what are letters-to-the-editor releases used?

A *letter-to-the-editor release* addressed, as the name suggests, to the editor of a publication enables the business executive to explain his or her viewpoint. Brief, concise letters have the best chance of being printed. A favorable article about your industry or organization may prompt a letter-to-the editor release. Or the letter may be in response to an article that fails to explain adequately both sides of an issue. Exhibit 15-5 shows a sample letter-to-the-editor release.

When considering targets for news releases of different types, do not overlook the small weekly or biweekly newspapers. Although their readership is not as large as that of metropolitan newspapers, the editors of these publications will often print news releases because they have to fill space.

In general, a company's news release attempts to create an attitude toward certain products, the company itself or the industry the company is part of, a contemplated legislative action affecting the industry or organization, or some social pressure affecting the industry or organization.

Mechanics

The typical business news release written by an employee of a company consists of three parts: the *headline*, which the editor (if the paper is small) or a copy editor ordinarily supplies; the *lead*; and the *body*.

What are the three typical parts of news items?

The lead or opening paragraph should immediately tell the editor why your story is important. The general journalistic rule, "who, what, when, where, why, and how," applies also to the news release. Therefore, include the answers to these six questions at or near the beginning of the first paragraph. Succeeding paragraphs should elaborate on the lead by explaining statements and supplying further details. A news release not on current events may present the material in another format, depending on the nature of the information, amount of material, or the writer's purpose.

The best way to learn how to write business news releases is to study the journalistic style of the publication or publications to which you expect to submit your work. Observe especially the type of the material included as well as the average length of an item.

Skill in writing news releases, like other business writing skills, develops only with practice. The best way to learn is to start by writing brief and relatively unimportant items and then advancing, as your skill develops, to more important material.

Communication Capsule 15-2 contains a list of suggestions to help you prepare business news releases for submission to newspaper editors.

What suggestions can you offer to help improve the effectiveness of the news items you write?

Communication Capsule 15-2 Suggestions for Getting Copy into the Paper

The following list of suggestions, although not all-inclusive, will assist you in getting your copy into a newspaper:

1. Double- or triple-space the copy. Most newspapers use computers in the printing process and want first copy double- or triple-spaced.
2. Leave blank at least a third of the top of the first page (unless you are using a news release form). This provides space for the copy editor to write the heading and to make the necessary notations for the typesetters.
3. Set your left-hand margin at 1½ inches and other margins at 1 inch. If the item is short, allot a full page for it and use wider margins. This should make the material more attractive to the reader's eye.
4. Write short sentences. Twenty words are maximum; no sentence should be longer without good reason.
5. Write short paragraphs. The narrowness of the newspaper column and the difficulty of reading type in unbroken masses make following this suggestion mandatory.
6. Use adjectives sparingly. The best rule is: "When in doubt about an adjective, leave it out."
7. Double-check to be sure all names, particularly names of persons and of business organizations, are spelled correctly.
8. Make certain all titles of persons are correct—both professional titles and business positions.
9. Recheck any numbers included in the release. In business writing, an error in reporting an amount or a number may be disastrous.
10. If you wish to quote a person, obtain his or her permission; and be sure that what you quote is an accurate representation of the original.
11. Submit clean, legible copy on a good grade of paper. Copy coming from outside the newspaper office competes for space with other copy of the same kind; other things being equal, copy that is easiest to handle and easiest to read will be accepted.

Most newspapers follow the AP/UPI (Associated Press/United Press International) stylebook; therefore, it should be a part of every professional writer's library. Strunk and White's *The Elements of Style* is also excellent.

Some releases are based on interviews. Effective interviews are skillfully conducted conversations, although only excerpts will probably ever find their way into print. Not only should the interviewer be familiar with the topic of the interview, but also he or she should understand the specific meanings of the business terms the interviewee uses.

Before an interview, prepare a written list of questions to ask the interviewee. Such a list is handy for organizing your thoughts and for helping you remember to include all points that you need to cover.

In writing about the interview, the typical approach is to begin with the most significant or interesting point. This is the information that will most likely attract readers' attention, causing them to want to read the message.

When you transcribe words or phrases from an interview, be careful to retain the correct meaning. In the following example, note the incorrect "twist" put on the interviewee's words after the tape of the interview was transcribed into written form. Note that the question asked about "one key." The interviewee responded by identifying this "one key" and went on to identify another key. In transcribing the interview, the writer now identifies two keys, giving them equal status. Thus, the interviewer subtly distorts the original response.

> Question asked interviewee: What do you believe to be the one key to the success of your company?
>
> Interviewee's verbal response: I believe the one key to the success of this company is the well-trained workforce it employs. Of course, we must recognize the success of our product line, too.
>
> What was written: When Jamison Kelly was asked what he believed to be the key to the success of his company, he mentioned a well-trained workforce and the success of his company's product line.

News Releases and Crisis Management

One special use of news releases is during a crisis. Although no organization can ever predict when a crisis will occur or what it will be, the organization needs to be prepared to deal quickly and decisively with any crisis. Examples of crises that organizations have recently experienced include an over-the-counter headache remedy laced with a poison, a soft drink with a foreign object, a fast-food franchise that used tainted hamburger meat, and a flawed computer chip.

Most modern large organizations have policies to enable them to deal with crises as they arise. One common procedure is to make one person responsible for handling all communication with the public. This decreases the possibility that two or more employees may provide conflicting information about the crisis. Another common procedure is to issue immediate news releases explaining the crisis and what the organization is doing about it.

Because a news release provides more control over the crisis than does a news conference or interviews with organizational personnel, the news release is generally the first-used communication medium. Indeed, many organizations have later regretted the responses of employees during a news conference or interviews immediately after the crisis surfaces. Relying on a news release as the first source of communication provides the firm with an opportunity to better control crisis communications. A number of organizations have, in fact, found that well-managed crises do not always have a long-term adverse effect on their operations. Some have even discovered that in time they actually increase their share of the market.

AGENDA

What uses are made of agendas?

An *agenda*, which is a written document that lists the topics to be discussed during a meeting, should be available to the participants before the meeting. The agenda helps them prepare specifically for the topics to be discussed. Also, it will help the person presiding over the meeting keep the discussions "on track." Sometimes meetings are not as productive as participants expect because of an ineffective agenda or because of the leader's failure to follow the agenda.

Before a meeting is called, the leader should determine whether a meeting is, in fact, necessary. Perhaps an alternative to the meeting could take place, such as making a few phone calls or visiting with others on a face-to-face basis.

Order

The order of the items on the agenda is typically determined by parliamentary procedures, especially in formal meetings. *Robert's Rules of Order* is useful in determining an appropriate order of the agenda items.

What determines the order of items on agendas?

The items outlined next are often included on the agenda of formal meetings of organizations or associations. A number of the items are omitted in informal committee meetings.

1. Call the meeting to order
2. Roll call
3. Read and approve the minutes of the previous meeting
4. Treasurer's report (if appropriate)
5. Officer reports (if appropriate)
6. Committee reports (if appropriate)
   a. Standing committee reports
   b. Special committees' reports
7. Unfinished business
8. New business
9. Appointments of committees (if appropriate)
10. Nominations of officers (if appropriate)
11. Elections (if appropriate)
12. Announcements
13. Adjournment

The agenda is often included in the meeting announcement, which is likely to be sent in a memo or letter. In some instances, the leader may also solicit in the announcement other items participants may want to include in the agenda. The final version of the agenda can be distributed either in advance of the meeting or at its beginning.

For formal meetings of professional organizations/associations or corporations, the bylaws often stipulate how the meeting will be called, how the agenda will be prepared and presented, and how the agenda is to be amended to include additional items.

In presenting the agenda to the participants, follow the same order of items and format each time. To change the format each time a new agenda is prepared will likely create unnecessary confusion.

Preparation of Minutes

Minutes are a written record of important discussions and actions taken at a meeting. Because of the importance of an accurate record of meetings, the person who assumes responsibility for taking minutes should prepare thoroughly for the assignment. The recorder should carefully review the minutes for content, format, and detail. Taking verbatim notes is usually unnecessary, except for motions. Making a tape recording may be advisable, even though the minutes are later written in summary form.

What should be included in written minutes of meetings?

Written minutes should contain the following:

1. Date, time, and place of the meeting
2. Type of meeting
3. Presiding officer
4. Officers and members present
5. Approval or correction of the minutes of the previous meeting
6. Reports of officers and committees
7. Action on unfinished business from a previous meeting
8. Transaction of new business, including motions and resolutions
9. Appointment of committees
10. Election of officers
11. Adjournment

Although minutes of informal meetings may include important discussions, minutes of formal meetings, in accordance with *Robert's Rules of Order*, should contain only the action taken on any matter.

Motions

What should be included in the write-up of motions?

A record of all motions must include the following:

1. The name of the person making the motion
2. The exact wording of the motion
3. The name of the person seconding the motion, or, in informal minutes, the fact that the motion was seconded
4. The results of the voting

Reports of Officers and Committees

The treasurer's report is included in, or attached, to the minutes. Other reports may be summarized, with written copies of various reports usually being attached to the minutes.

Rough Draft of Minutes

The first step in the preparation of minutes is to prepare a rough draft. The recorder should write the minutes immediately after the meeting while events and actions taken are still fresh in his or her mind. Including on the left margin captions that identify various sections of the minutes is useful. Next the recorder should submit a draft of the minutes for approval to the presiding officer as well as to the people who made reports. If the minutes are unusually long or complicated, the recorder should prepare copies of the motions for each participant.

Minutes in Final Form

After the rough draft of the meeting minutes has been approved or corrected by the member(s) whose approval is needed, the recorder prepares a final draft. A special type of paper for formal meeting minutes' books can be obtained from stationery stores specializing in corporate supplies. For informal meeting minutes, any kind of durable paper may be used. Some of the larger corporations have strict regulations about the format of minutes, to which the recorder should closely adhere.

The final form of the minutes must, of course, be correct. Details of typing, arrangement, spacing, and general appearance of the minutes' book require special attention. The recorder should verify the spelling of names.

Communication Capsule 15-3 Guidelines for Use in Preparing Minutes

The following guidelines will assist you in preparing the final form of minutes:

1. Capitalize and center the heading.
2. Include the type of meeting, day, date, hour, place, and the name of the presiding officer.
3. List the names of members present and those absent. (In the minutes of stockholders' meetings, the names of those represented by proxies, and the amount of stock represented by each member or proxy are shown.)
4. Indent paragraphs five spaces.
5. Double-space between each paragraph, and triple-space between headings.
6. Indent resolutions fifteen spaces and type single-spaced. The word *whereas* is typed in capital letters, followed by a comma; the first word after *whereas* begins with a capital letter.
7. Capitalize the words "Board of Directors" and the word "Corporation" when reference is made to the group for which the minutes are written. References to specific officers of the corporation may be in capital or lowercase letters, but the capitalization should be consistent.
8. If captions are used, type them in capital letters in the margin.
9. Amounts of money mentioned in resolutions are written in legal form—in words followed by numbers. Amounts should be checked in the rough draft by both the person quoted and the presiding officer.
10. Leave a 1½ inch outside margin.
11. Use the past tense.
12. Record motions (except the motion to adjourn) exactly as stated, giving the name of the person who made the motion. For formal minutes, underscore motions or type them in capital letters.
13. In formal minutes, state that the meeting was properly called. The notice of the meeting can be included.
14. Number each page at the bottom, placing the number in the center of page.

What suggestions can you offer that will help you improve the effectiveness of the minutes you prepare?

Communication Capsule 15-3 contains a number of suggestions for preparing meetings' minutes.

Correction of Errors in Minutes

How are errors in minutes corrected?

The minutes of a meeting are approved at the next meeting. Any corrections are inserted prior to the meeting that follows. If the error is easily correctable, a line may be drawn through the error and the correction written; if correcting the error means an actual revision, the recorder includes the report of the corrections in the minutes of the current meeting.

Minutes' Book

Because minutes are important documents, organizations often preserve them indefinitely in a minutes' book. Although members may receive copies, the original copy of the minutes stays in the minutes' book. Corporation minutes are arranged in the book in the following order: (1) either the minutes of the organizational meeting or minutes of the meeting of incorporation; (2) minutes of the stockholders' meetings; and (3) minutes of the directors' meetings.

Indexing of Minutes

A card index can make it easier to find material in minutes' books. Minutes' index cards list the topics and the page reference in the minutes' book on which specific topics appear. The marginal captions used in preparing minutes will be helpful in preparing the index.

Exhibit 15-6 includes communications about an executive board meeting, including a notice to the members, the agenda, and the minutes of the previous meeting.

MEMORANDUM

May 20, 199x

TO: NMS Executive Board Members
FROM: John Beckett, Executive Director
SUBJECT: NMS Executive Board Meeting
Conrad-Halton Hotel, Chicago
June 19-20, 199x

The agenda is attached for the June 19-20 NMS Executive Board meeting in Chicago. The board meeting has been scheduled to begin in the Blue Room at 9 a.m. Thursday morning.

If you have suggested additions to the agenda, please notify J. L. Brown, president, NMS. If you plan to present a report, will you please prepare a written report for the executive secretary, making duplicate copies for all members of the board. Please bring your copy of the February, 199x, Executive Board minutes that are attached.

As usual, we anticipate a productive meeting. If you are unable to attend, please appoint a proxy and notify him/her of the time and place of the board meeting. Please return your postal reply card to the executive secretary.

Enclosures: Agenda—NMS Executive Board Meeting, June 19-20, 199x
Minutes—NMS Executive Board Meeting, February 18, 199x
Postal Reply Card

* * *

NATIONAL MANAGEMENT SOCIETY EXECUTIVE BOARD MEETING

Agenda
June 19-20, 199x

Blue Room
Conrad-Halton Hotel
Chicago

1. Call to Order	J. L. Brown
2. Roll Call	John Beckett
3. Approval of Minutes of February, 199x, Meeting	John Beckett
4. Report of the Executive Secretary	John Beckett
5. Report of the Treasurer	Dennis Hall
6. Report of the NMS President	J. L. Brown
7. Report of the NMS President-elect	Marcia Owens
8. Membership Report	Marsha Lenn
9. NMS Journal Editor's Report	A. C. Albert
10. 199x Convention Reports	J. O'Brien
11. Unfinished Business	Jack Proctor
12. New Business	Greg Bumpers
13. Adjournment	

NATIONAL MANAGEMENT SOCIETY MINUTES OF THE EXECUTIVE BOARD MEETING
February 18, 199x

Call to Order

The regular meeting of the National Management Society Executive Board was held in the Blue Room, Conrad-Halton Hotel, Chicago, Illinois, February 18, 199x. President J. L. Brown called the meeting to order at 9 a.m.

Roll Call

Roll was called by the executive secretary, John Beckett, with the following officers and board members present:

Officers: J. L. Brown, president; Marcia Owens, president-elect; Elmo E. Sanksar, treasurer; John Beckett, executive secretary; and William Watson, immediate past president.

Regional Representatives:

C. J. Bomberger, Southern Region; B. B. Watley, Eastern Region; Gary Finch, North Central Region; H. B. Jackson, Midwest Region; and Jack Proctor, Western Region.

Exhibit 15-6 Executive board notice to members, agenda, and minutes.

Ex-officio Members:

A. K. Curley, representative to the ALA Executive Board; Victor Beckham, ALA president; Bill Hackley, NMS Journal editor; and Marsha Lenn, membership chairperson.

Minutes

William Watson moved acceptance of the minutes of the June 18-19, 199x, meeting of the board be approved as distributed; C. J. Bomberger seconded the motion; motion passed.

Report of the Treasurer

Treasurer Dennis Hall presented the income and expense statement, cash recapitulation, and balance sheet, showing an excess of income over expenses of $2,429.15 for the period of June 17, 199x, to February 17, 199x; cash on hand, $5,764.98 (checkbook balance); and net worth, $10,525.75.

Report of the NMS President

J. L. Brown, president, represented National Management Society at Southern Region Management Society Association convention, New Orleans, in November. North-Central Region Management Society, Cleveland, in December, and Western Region Management Society, Honolulu, in April.

Report of NMS President-elect

Marcia Owens reported that NMS Service Bulletin, the *NMS Aid* will be distributed in October.

Membership Report

Marcia Lenn distributed copies of the membership report, which listed numbers as of February 10, 199x.

NNS Journal Editor's Report

A. C. Albertson, NMS journal editor, reported that 36,022 copies of the journal were distributed at a cost of $3,962 for postage and $751.44 for supplies.

Report of 199x Convention Committee

J. O. O'Brien, program co-chairperson, distributed copies of the 199x NMS convention program. He reported 5,120 preregistrations, 1488 for the opening banquet, 206 for the North-Central Region luncheon, 919 for the tours, and 386 for the closing brunch.

Unfinished Business

Because the NMS convention will be held in the Western Region in 199x, Jack Proctor moved that the Western Region Management Society convention not be held in 199x. Marcia Owens seconded; motion carried.

New Business

President Brown appointed A. K. Curley as chair of the Revision of the Constitution and Bylaws Committee. John Beckett and Gary Finch were appointed to the committee.

Meeting adjourned.

Respectfully submitted,

______________	______________
President	Executive Secretary

2

Exhibit 15-6 *Continued*

SUMMARY

Administrative communication comprises of a number of different types of written materials, such as proposals, performance evaluations, news releases, meeting agendas, and meeting minutes.

Although some proposals solicit funds, others outline the uses and benefits of products and services. Some proposals seek authorization to undertake a research project.

Exercise special care in writing performance evaluations and product information. Lack of good judgment may result in serious legal consequences.

News releases are a common communication tool that individuals and organizations use to provide mass print media with information thought to be of interest to the media's readership. The success of news releases depends on a number of important criteria.

Administrators often are responsible for preparing agendas for meetings they call as well as the minutes prepared following the meeting. Common formats for both types of documents should be followed.

REVIEW QUESTIONS

1. Identify common types of proposals.
2. What criteria do readers generally use to evaluate proposals?
3. What content should you include in proposals soliciting funds for a proposed project?
4. What content should you include in research-oriented proposals?
5. For what is a business plan used?
6. What are the uses of performance evaluations?
7. What criteria do editors use in judging business news?
8. Compare the business human-interest story with the personal business release.
9. For what reasons might a business executive write a letter to the editor?
10. List several suggestions that will assist you in getting business-related copy into a newspaper.
11. What are the benefits of meeting agendas?
12. What content is likely to be included in the agenda?
13. What information should motions contain?
14. Explain the procedures followed in correcting errors in minutes.

APPLICATION PROBLEMS

1. (Proposal) You are a professor of business communication at a Midwestern university. You coordinate sixteen sections of business communication classes with a limited enrollment of twenty-five students in each class. You have conducted a study of twenty chief executives in a major metropolitan area to obtain their opinions about the need for skills in business writing at the college level. You found the major need is for a strong background in the basics—grammar, mechanics, punctuation, spelling, effective sentences and paragraphs, and organization. Now you wish to conduct a second study, in which eight classes devote half the semester learning these basics through traditional teaching methodology. Your other eight classes will devote half the semester learning the basics through computerized instructions, using a software program, "Business Writing Basics." To conduct the study, you need twenty-five microcomputers for the classroom. Develop a proposal to send to a manufacturer of computer equipment requesting the twenty-five microcomputers for use in your study.
2. (Proposal) You are director of personnel in an organization that has forty thousand part-time representatives who sell cosmetics. Plans are under way for a computerized database in your firm. You wish to include personnel records in the database program. Write a memorandum to the vice president in charge of organizational planning and development that details your needs, outlines your operational pro-

cedures, and includes anticipated benefits of including personnel records in the program.

3. (News release) C. A. Swanson was just promoted to president of Financial Associates, Inc., a huge corporation (assets of $3.5 billion), which operates the nation's largest consumer finance business. At age 35, Mr. Swanson is much younger than most chief executives, and he has less than five years' experience with the company. He studied economics at Stanford and earned a law degree from Harvard. He plans to bring out a credit card, lower rates, and build up the executive-loan business. Some of the firm's best customers are bankers who want to borrow anonymously, he says. As director of communications, prepare a news release to appear in a column, "Business People in the News," in a leading business publication.
4. (Minutes) You are the secretary of the International Management Systems Association. The executive board of that organization met Friday, August 10; and you took the following notes at that meeting.

   Prepare the minutes in final form.

Called to order—10:00 a.m.
Buckley, President—presided
No. present—15. Minutes of February meeting approved as presented.
Treas. report—present bal.—$12,642.81. (You have copy of report.)
Budget Com.—Anderson, Chairperson. Acceptance moved and seconded.
Discussion. Motion carried.
Membership Com.—Crain, Chr., presented proposal for limiting membership.
(You have copy of proposal.) Acceptance moved and seconded.
Discussion. Motion carried.
Nominating Com.—Frazier, Chr.
Pres.—Joliet, Charles
V. P.—Hansen, T. J.
Secretary—White, Edward
Treasurer—Stout, Elbert
Acceptance of report moved, seconded, and carried. Nominations closed by motion. Buckley announced election of officers to be held at next regular meeting in conformance with the constitution.
Holder, Chr. of World Representation Committee, announced next IMSA meeting is scheduled in Tokyo.
Buckley announced next executive board meeting, February 6.
Motion for adjournment carried—12:45 p.m.

16

Oral Communication

After studying this chapter, you should be able to

1. Identify the essential characteristics of oral communication.
2. Discuss the advantages and disadvantages of speaking from a manuscript, from memorization, impromptu, and extemporaneously.
3. Discuss the voice characteristics.
4. Explain how to prepare for a stand-up speech.
5. Discuss the importance of listening.
6. Describe the levels of listening.
7. Identify the ways you can improve your listening skills.

Oral communication is an essential element in business communication. Effective oral communication is as important as a well-developed skill in written communication. Although written communication skills often take more time to perfect, oral communication consumes much more of your professional life.

Speaking before a large audience is an opportunity that many people may never experience, but speaking before smaller groups is a common professional experience. You may be required to present a report at a business meeting or to express your views at a local, regional, or national meeting.

ESSENTIALS OF ORAL COMMUNICATION

Oral communication involves making your wants, needs, ideas, and feelings known verbally to other people. Successful oral communication involves a simultaneous combination of several mental and physical processes. The most obvious element of oral communication is the physical process—in other words, the actual presentation. However, the mental and psychological elements of oral communication are as important as the actual presentation.

What are the uses of oral communication?

Oral communication is used to inform, persuade, and entertain. An *informative speech* presents facts, information, or general knowledge to an audience. A *persuasive speech* tries to change attitudes or thinking about a certain event, idea, or campaign. An entertaining speech attempts to provide fun and pleasure for the intended audience. Presenters of entertaining speeches often rely on humor to emphasize a point to the audience.

PREPARING TO COMMUNICATE ORALLY

Whenever you talk, you are involved in both a unique event and a unique moment. Your voice, choice of words, ideas, and feelings are either openly exposed or cleverly disguised. An important first step toward improved oral communication is taking personal inventory of your likes, dislikes, attitudes, and habits. Each time you talk, you reflect your true feelings, biases, and value systems.

What elements does effective oral communication comprise?

Effective oral communication requires control over several key elements, regardless of whether the message is designed for formal, informal, or social conversations. For each of these communications, you must do the following:

1. *Define the purpose.* Oral communication is most successful when its purpose is predetermined. Before you speak, determine the primary purpose for the oral communication. For instance, is the intended conversation needed to gather or present information? To make the other person more aware of a certain situation or event? To create an environment for appropriate feedback? To change or acknowledge actions or attitudes? Only after identifying your purpose, ideas, and viewpoints can you transmit them clearly to your intended receiver through a sequence of words.

2. *Assess the audience.* Evaluate the nature and background of the intended audience before designing your message. For example, a formal style is imperative for success in a formal presentation, although an informal style is most desirable for person-to-person and small, intimate group conversation. You should carefully assess your audience to prepare a presentation that relates to its occupational, educational, and experience characteristics. The information in Exhibit 16-1 will help you assess your audience.

Exhibit 16-1 Checklist for audience analysis.

I. Audience Size and Demographics
   A. How many will be in attendance? ________
   B. Common characteristics
      1. Profession ________
      2. Politics ________
      3. Religion ________
      4. Men/Women ________
      5. Age ________
      6. Ethnic groups ________
      7. Geographic regions represented ________
II. Audience/Speaker Relationship
   A. Expectation of the audience ________
   B. Biases toward your organization/your qualifications/or your topic ________
   C. Does this audience have a tendency toward acceptance of speakers or general hostility?
   D. What facts, ideas, or background information will enhance speaker credibility? ________
   E. General audience understanding
      1. Current information possessed by the audience fairly uniform? Varied? ________
      2. Semantics/vocabulary understanding/ routine information ________
      3. Specific details that will need to be explained ________
III. Anticipated Audience Reaction
   A. Potential mood of the audience ________
      Tired? Angry? Hungry? Restless? ________
   B. How can the audience benefit from your message? ________
   C. What kinds of information or data can be used to impress ________
   D. What is the best possible result? ________

3. *Arrange the data.* Successful oral communication is similar to a game plan for a sports team. Data must be accurate, organized, and meaningful. Your message should attract and hold attention, build interest, and set the stage for appropriate and intended action. Presentations are enhanced and improved through a variety of audio-visual aids, demonstrations, comparisons, statistics, and testimonials.

4. *Prepare the message.* The actual message is, of course, the single most important aspect of oral communication. Your message should be timely, to the point, and consistent with the overall intent of the communication. Attention and interest-holding devices should be integrated into the context of the presentation.

5. *Design the format.* A speech contains three parts: the introduction, the body, and the conclusion. You should prepare the outline for your speech around these three major parts. The outline thus becomes a guide to ensure clarity, completeness, focus, and conciseness. Shorter speeches are often more difficult to plan than longer speeches because very little time is available for emphasis and expansion of points and ideas.

What delivery styles are used in speech making?

6. *Make the delivery.* The actual delivery of the speech is as important as the content. You may select your delivery style from four basic procedures or formats: (a) manuscript reading; (b) memorization; (c) impromptu speaking; and (d) extemporaneous speaking. As you might expect, each of these formats has its own advantages and disadvantages. Each speaking opportunity requires a decision about a delivery method that is comfortable for you, fits your topic, and suits your audience.

Speaking from a Manuscript

Speakers sometimes read aloud to the audience from a manuscript. You may have witnessed this type of delivery most often in campaign speeches, official governmental reports, and radio or television reports.

Advantages

What are the advantages and disadvantages of the manuscript delivery method?

The main advantage of the manuscript delivery method is that in communicating technical material or "politically sensitive" material, the speaker has little fear of forgetting important points. In addition, speakers know in advance how long the presentation will take to deliver, which allows them to reserve time at the end to answer questions from the audience. The possibility of being misquoted is also minimized because copies of the manuscript are available to people in the audience.

An additional advantage of the manuscript method is greater ease in coordinating visual aids during the presentation. Appropriate notes or marks placed on special copies of the manuscript will provide important coordinating information for those assisting with the visual part of your presentation.

Disadvantages

Transmission skill is important for all communication procedures. A major disadvantage of manuscript reading is that many people do not read aloud very well. Therefore, reading from a prepared manuscript becomes boring, stilted, and basically unnatural. Although manuscript reading is the safest way to give a speech, most people consider it to be one of the most difficult to use.

Specific problems related to the manuscript delivery method include the tendency to lose your place, the development of a monotone presentation voice, difficulty in maintaining eye contact with the audience, or in changing tone and language to better meet the needs of the audience, and becoming so involved in reading that maintaining interest in the audience becomes secondary.

Speaking from Memorization

Memorization requires writing the entire speech and then learning it word by word. You deliver the speech from memory without looking at a manuscript, an outline, or notes.

Advantages

The significant advantage of the memorization method of delivery is its impact on the audience. Speakers who appear to have complete control of information, process, and application generate a feeling of trust and admiration from their audiences.

What advantages and disadvantages result from the memorization method?

Disadvantages

Speech memorization has more disadvantages than advantages. You might leave out an important part of the speech, or even worse, forget where you are and what comes next. You might experience some stagefright that causes memory to lapse, which may result in your being in front of an audience with nothing to say. Because you are concentrating on remembering, you may display a way of speaking that is unnatural or uncomfortable for the audience to perceive.

Major disadvantages of the memorization method are the difficulty of adding content and the difficulty of adjusting the speech to various audiences. Responding to questions about content without a manuscript or notes to refer to is an additional disadvantage.

Impromptu Method

The most common type of oral communication is the *impromptu speech* that is presented without extensive preparation—sometimes without *any* advance preparation. Individuals are comfortable with impromptu speaking when they feel knowledgeable or well informed about the subject matter. Examples of impromptu speaking include providing information or remarks about a business meeting you attended, speaking at a city council meeting, or other expressions of information and opinion based on fact and experience.

Advantages

A major advantage of the impromptu method of oral communication is not being tied to an outline or to a manuscript. This allows for easy and rapid adjustment to audience needs and wants.

What advantages and disadvantages result from the impromptu method?

Disadvantages

Because an impromptu speech is not carefully planned and organized ahead of time, it can often appear disorganized and difficult to follow. Also, in impromptu presentations, the speaker can sometimes talk extensively about an issue without ever getting to the point. The disadvantages appear to outweigh the advantages; few people select the impromptu method when asked to speak before a business or community meeting. Rather, when you accept such an invitation to speak, you should have in mind in some form or another information or other ideas you wish to share. You will find it helpful to have ideas, pertinent facts, and figures for review or reference during your talk.

Extemporaneous Method

Where impromptu presentations are the most common type of oral presentation, the extemporaneous business presentation is the most common method of delivery. An *extemporaneous speech* involves the gathering of pertinent facts, information, and ideas followed by organizing them in outline form. The actual presentation uses the outline as a guide. In extemporaneous speaking, the speaker knows what ideas to include and the order of their presentation but has not prepared the exact words and sentences to be spoken.

Advantages

What advantages and disadvantages result from the extemporaneous method?

Extemporaneous presentations have several distinct advantages for the speaker. First, delivery is spontaneous. Second, you can easily add or delete material and ideas from the outline without distorting the sequence or changing the entire manuscript. Sometimes your changes, in response to the reactions of your audience, will occur almost immediately. Another advantage is being able to maintain contact with the audience because you will not have to look to a manuscript for exact wording.

Preparation for the extemporaneous speech must be as careful as that for a written or memorized presentation. Your preparation should include establishing a purpose, gathering information, conducting research, and preparing the outline. For most speaking opportunities, the extemporaneous method is preferable to the other three methods of presentations.

Disadvantages

A major disadvantage of the extemporaneous speaking method, like the manuscript method, is the speaker's tendency to stick too closely to the outline while disregarding the reactions of the audience. Practice and rehearsal should eliminate this disadvantage.

Selection of the most appropriate presentation method includes consideration of the following: what best illuminates the topic, what best suits the intended audience, what most effectively presents the material, and what style best suits you.

Delivery Techniques

Once you have prepared your speech, your next task is to improve the actual delivery technique. Keep the following three suggestions in mind as you deliver your speech:

1. Observe your audience before you begin speaking.
2. Use an appropriate ice-breaker to ease the tension and capture the attention of the audience.
3. Deliver your speech in a natural manner. Do not use slang or incomplete sentences.

Delivery techniques include personal and interpersonal communication, because your voice, actions, dress, and overall appearance add to or detract from the intended impact of the message.

Voice Characteristics

With what voice characteristics do speakers have to be concerned?

A speaker's voice is important to the overall presentation of a message. The voice carries information and ideas to the intended audience; therefore, your audience will at least partly judge the quality of your presentation by your voice characteristics, including volume, pitch, speed of delivery, enthusiasm level, and pronunciation.

Volume

You can, of course, emphasize essential information and important ideas simply by speaking more loudly. Different speaking environments require adjustments, and a speaker must always speak loudly enough for the audience to hear without undue effort. If you speak too softly, the audience has to listen too intently, which can create hostility toward the topic and the speaker.

Pitch

What is pitch?

Pitch refers to the highness or lowness of the sound or tones that your voice transmits. When you speak, the pitch often automatically varies according to the topic or issue. When excited, people tend to speak at a higher pitch than when they discuss more somber and serious topics. For maximum results, a speaker's voice should sound natural and relaxed. During most speeches, your pitch will vary more than it does in an ordinary conversation; however, for maximum results, plan and control changes in pitch to avoid a monotone or overly dramatic voice.

Speed

Some people may talk too fast and others may talk too slowly. Talking more slowly when delivering a speech is helpful for bringing out important ideas. When presenting ideas that are not quite as important, you may use a faster speed. Never, however, speak so rapidly that the audience cannot follow your presentation. When you have a time limit for your speech, design it to fit the time allowed. Do not simply talk faster as you near the end of the allotted time in an attempt to present all the material. Covering too much material in a limited time will have a significant negative impact on the audience.

Enthusiasm

The speaker's voice will reveal his or her interest in the subject of the speech. A speaker with a dry, uninteresting, or flat voice will deplete the audience's interest and enthusiasm for the topic and probably also for the speaker. Your inability to speak with enthusiasm will diminish the impact of your message. A boring voice will make the most interesting material seem uninteresting; a voice full of excitement can make even complex subject matter appealing to an audience.

Quality

Voice quality is the general tone of a speaker's voice. This characteristic is what makes your voice distinct from other voices. Voice quality may be harsh, nasal, pleasant, neutral, or unpleasant. Voice quality is not a natural physical trait. A speaker can record his or her own speech to determine predominant qualities and then practice to overcome problems. Make every effort to train your voice to be as pleasant as possible. You will discover that audiences are more receptive to ideas if presented in a pleasant voice.

Pronunciation

Clear pronunciation is essential for successful oral communication. If you mispronounce words, your audience will doubt your ability and knowledge. The ability to separate content from such delivery techniques as pronunciation is outside the capabilities of an audience. An audience evaluates a speaker's refinement and learning on the basis of his or her pronunciation.

Emphasis

Clear speech consists of sounds that blend smoothly into words that combine to form phrases. A speaker uses *emphasis* to stress some words while deemphasizing others. For example, consider the following sentence: "I was going to attend the meeting; but because guests arrived at the cabin, I couldn't leave to get there on time." The words *was*, *to*, *but*, *at*, *the*, *I*, *to*, *get*, and *on* are somewhat unimportant to the speaker's intent. Therefore, the experienced speaker will not emphasize them. Experienced speakers will, however, place additional emphasis on *attend*, *meeting*, *because*, *guests*, *arrived*, *couldn't*, and *time*. They will also say a group of words in the same manner as a word with several syllables. When saying the word *individuality*, for example, you should place strong emphasis on *in*, *vid*, and *al* and less on *di*, *u*, *i*, and *ty*.

Placing correct emphasis will change a vowel from its full sound to a slight "uh" sound. This sound will be similar to the ending sound in the word *quota*, the beginning sound in the word *amount*, or the middle sound in *usable*. Speech and phonetics researchers refer to this as the *schwa* vowel, which is frequently used in speaking. By using the *schwa* sound, a speaker can establish a speaking style that has rhythm and that enhances the probability of communicating successfully.

But the *schwa* sound is not a substitute for consonants. Some commonly heard examples of failure to pronunciate correctly include the following: *git* (get); *spose* (suppose); *finely* (finally); *probly* (probably); *count of* (on account of); *intrest* (interest); and *cuz* (because).

Pronunciation errors affect clarity, although perhaps not seriously. But, if such errors are frequent, the result is often blurred inarticulate, and distractive speaking.

Nonverbal Emphasis

Experienced speakers use *nonverbal emphasis* such as facial expressions, arm movements, posture, and body movements to increase emphasis. Personal traits have an effect on the message because they are portrayed by the speaker. A speaker's personality traits and habits can partially or completely block messages.

The Importance of Word Choice

The difference between selecting a word and selecting the most precise or exacting word is often the distinction between blurred and sharp vision. The best choice of words for the situation brings what you are saying into sharp focus for the audience.

What factors should you consider in selecting words for use in a speech?

More specifically, proper word selection will decrease the possibility of misunderstanding and in the process will increase the possibility of successful communication. Select your words to match the situation, background, and knowledge of the listener. The following list shows some common difficult words and their easier-to-understand substitutes.

Difficult	*Simple*
abandon	leave
antagonist	foe
abhor	dislike
benevolence	kindness
brilliant	bright
commodity	goods
conjecture	guess
dexterous	skillful
dilatory	late
ecstasy	joy
fascinate	charm
grotesque	odd
hesitate	delay
intrinsic	real
jubilant	happy
knack	skill
laborious	hard
magnitude	size
navigate	guide
palpable	plain
ruminate	think
tolerate	allow
ultimate	final

vanquish	defeat
writhe	twist
zealous	intent

Use of difficult words presents the risk of losing your audience. For example, assume that you are a freshman in college listening to the following short talk by the president of the college.

> Welcome to your university. During your tenure here, you will discover many vital and fortuitous occasions for enhancing your academic provocation and accomplishment. The efficacy of valid intellectual pursuit is certainly indisputable. However, personal integrity will prove to be the culminating constituent relative to ultimate professional fulfillment. Past accomplishments may substantiate intellectual inclination, but the past is virtually incompatible with permanence at the upper division level. We are gratified with your propinquity and anticipate with exhilaration an exquisite and propitious semester.

Clearly the speaker is talking over the heads of the audience. This example illustrates the importance of choosing words that your intended audience is more likely to accept and understand. The following revision corrects the problems of the original speech.

> Welcome to State University. During the next four years, you will learn and grow through many social and academic experiences. A college degree will prove to be of great value in the years to come. However, you will succeed in direct proportion to the time and effort you are willing to expend. Your ability, as shown in your previous academic success, is obvious. However, you will now be competing with students who, like you, were also top students; and the competition will challenge your academic ability and test your ability to endure. We are pleased you are here, and we wish you our best for an exciting and successful semester.

Communication Capsule 16-1 suggests strategies for different audience types.

Communication Capsule 16-1 Audience Types and Strategies

Successful speakers plan their speeches and prepare their remarks to capture and maintain the audience's interest. But a speech that is appropriate for one group may be inappropriate for another group. The following information should assist you in planning for successful presentations through audience analysis and speaking strategies.

The Good Audience.

A good audience is one that accepts you, your expertise, and your content comfortably, warmly, and, at times, even lovingly. An example of an audience that would more than likely be accepting of the speaker's message is a company or departmental meeting where the manager announces a new salary and benefits package that will prove beneficial to nearly everyone in attendance. Obviously this audience is a delightful group to address and in most cases is very easy to identify. The speaking strategy for the warm, accepting, loving audience is a personal approach. Because you have little worry or concern about building or losing credibility, you may experiment with humor, some new procedures, or greater audience participation.

The Bad Audience.

The bad audience is one that, for whatever reason, is unreceptive of your message and suspicious of you as a speaker. Many groups may fit these descriptions, but a primary example would be presenting a message to a competing school, business, or political party. The speaking strategy for addressing a hostile group is to plan your remarks so that your facts are so noncontroversial that they cannot be logically challenged. Your speaking voice should be calm, and you should be prepared for a question-and-answer period.

The Ugly Audience.
An audience that is not at all interested in the subject matter and unreceptive to you as a speaker is one that speakers must dread. An example of an audience that may be viewed as "ugly" would be a state official presenting to a group of citizens the state's plans to use an area around their town for a toxic waste dump. A good or a bad audience provides an opportunity to organize your message around readily established strategies. In contrast, the ugly audience is one for which the speaker has limited knowledge about the proper approach. The speaking strategy for this audience is to be dynamic. Use material that moves fast and that will create some interest. Short exercises, humor, and items of current local, regional, or national interest are the types of material that will help energize at least a portion of this audience.

Nonverbal Language

Always be aware of your message and the overall makeup of your audience. A message that is misunderstood not only fails to communicate but also may actually create problems because both you and your audience must then spend additional time and effort to correct misconceptions and faulty information.

One aspect of nonverbal language is *personal appearance*, which is considered as important to successful oral communication as is the speaker's voice. A general rule for appropriate dress is to dress for the occasion; wear something that is neat, unassuming, and comfortable. Your clothing style should never distract the audience. For example, too much jewelry may be distracting as also would be an extremely tight suit.

What mannerisms do you have to be concerned about in making speeches?

Mannerisms also affect a speaker's relationship with an audience. Mannerisms include how the speaker consciously and unconsciously uses his or her body. Some mannerisms, such as jingling money in your pocket, clicking a pen, taking your glasses on and off too often, and pacing or laughing nervously, can distract and annoy the audience. However, a particular mannerism may add a great deal to the overall presentation. For example, a speaker can learn to develop a personal style for control and effective use of eye contact, facial expressions, posture, movement, and gestures. A speaker may use his or her eyes to capture and hold the eyes of various audience members during moments of silence. Facial expressions and body movements may also be used for effective contact with the audience. Experienced speakers may skip across the stage, stamp a foot, or blow into the microphone to create a sudden and loud sound throughout the auditorium. Personal style, professional experience, and visual poise will determine how a speaker uses nonverbal language.

Eye contact is the most direct way a speaker connects with an audience. You should establish eye contact with as many people in the audience as possible. Effective eye contact provides constant feedback and portrays interest, which is the first step toward gaining the interest and respect of the audience.

Facial expressions and posture help make your message more interesting and believable to your audience. Change your expressions according to the seriousness of the information you are presenting. You should carefully consider the manner in which you stand. You should not stand too stiffly, but you should also avoid the opposite extreme of slouching or slumping. Your facial expressions and your posture should convey the image of a speaker who is alert, confident, and energetic.

Movement and gestures—the way you move your head, hands, or arms to emphasize feelings or ideas also—affects your relationship with your audience. For maximum effectiveness, a gesture must be properly timed. A movement that is too early or too late is often worse than none at all. Also the use of too many or too noticeable gestures can become annoying to the audience.

PREPARATION FOR A STAND-UP SPEECH

Nearly everyone has heard a speaker who was so dynamic that the audience was almost under a spell. The ultimate purpose of effective oral communication, however, should not be simply to elicit powerful audience emotion. An effective presentation will create an intended response in terms of comprehension, perception, attitudes, beliefs, and future actions. Public speaking requires the speaker to determine the response or combination of responses that best accomplish his or her overall purpose.

If a speech is supposed to inform or to entertain, this does not mean the speaker should ignore other purposes. You may, as previously suggested, need to inform to persuade or to entertain to inform. Your primary purpose may create a need for additional approaches.

Supporting Material

After determining the purpose of your speech and finalizing the topic, you should do the following:

What categories of supporting materials are used in speeches?

1. Collect material to explain your topic and ideas.
2. Collect material to compare and contrast trends.
3. Illustrate information in easy-to-understand charts, graphs, and other visual aids.
4. Find or create examples that add meaning to your information.
5. Collect statistics that add to the intended message.
6. Gather opinions and conclusions of others.
7. State similar ideas in different words.

Preparing Your Outline

Because your outline is a road map to successful speaking, you should develop it gradually and systematically. After you select your topic, use the following steps as a guide for outline development:

What steps should be followed in preparing an outline of a speech?

1. State your specific purpose (a formulation of what you wish to accomplish in your speech).
2. State the major ideas in order.
   a. Number the ideas consecutively.
   b. Use complete, simple sentences to express yourself accurately and logically.
   c. Use one sentence or phrase for each idea.
3. State subordinate ideas.
   a. Indent subordinating ideas and number them consecutively.
   b. Use one sentence for each idea.
   c. Use similar sentence structure for stating each subordinate idea.
4. Recheck the entire outline.
   a. Does it represent proper outline form?
   b. Does it adequately cover the subject?
   c. Does it accomplish what you intended?

Outlining not only ensures organization but also enables you to make time and idea adjustments as the need arises. Without a solid outline, the audience may believe you do not have anything to say.

Controlling Speaker Stress

Uncontrolled anxiety will create increased tension for a speaker. Obviously, excessive tension and stress are conditions to be avoided or at least reduced to a manageable level. Some degree of speaker tension and stress is quite normal, but excessive stress prior to the presentation usually manifests itself in perceived negativism by the audience and, as such, is a major contributor to unsuccessful oral presentations. Practicing the following will help you maintain a proper level of speaker-induced stress for your oral presentations.

Stress Tip 1—Concentrate on relaxing your fingers and hands by placing them flat on the table with the palms down.

Stress Tip 2—Concentrate on relaxing the muscles in your legs.

Stress Tip 3—Slowly canvas the room without allowing your eyes to focus on any one object.

Stress Tip 4—Inhale and retain air in your lungs for several seconds.

Stress Tip 5—Slowly exhale the air from your lungs before you begin to feel pressure or increased discomfort.

Stress Tip 6—Concentrate on maintaining a limp torso for several seconds.

Stress Tip 7—Repeat steps 1 to 6 several times, but maintain a relaxed frame of mind.

Initially the tips for stress reduction may appear a bit cumbersome and may not even seem effective. However, keep practicing because the result will be reduced stress, and the payoff will be more effective speaking.

Gaining Attention

An audience is often willing to listen but not very excited about having to listen. From the outset, you must grasp the audience's attention or, in other words, pull the members of the audience away from their thoughts. You may use a variety of attention-getting approaches; the following are suggestions for effective introductory openings.

Direct Reference to the Subject

Introduce the audience to the topic by emphasizing something the audience should already know. For example, a speech about learning and perseverance could begin with a reference to Abraham Lincoln and some of the successes and failures that Mr. Lincoln experienced during his lifetime.

Reference to the Occasion

Verbally pat the audience on the back for being in attendance. The skill of the speaker and a little luck can get the audience to feel good about itself, if only subconsciously.

Rhetorical Question

A rhetorical question is one that the speaker asks but for which he or she does not expect an answer. For example, a speaker may relate an example of a person who was walking along the street and came in contact with a dog that proceeded to take a hunk out of his leg. The rhetorical question could be stated as follows: "Should dangerous animals be allowed to run at large, threatening anyone who crosses their path?" This rhetorical question could be followed by, "Should you and I be forced to carry weapons to protect us from attacks by uncontrolled animals?" The rhetorical question is a form of reference to the topic because it provides an audience the strong sense of what the speaker's message will emphasize.

Quotations

A quotation appropriate to the subject matter is a common method for gaining attention. For example, one might quote a famous president, a local political leader, or a person who is recognized and held in high esteem. Examples might include the following: John F. Kennedy, Will Rogers, Thomas Jefferson, and Winston Churchill.

Startling Statement

Experienced speakers use startling statements to gain an immediate response from the audience. A startling statement may refer to a feared depletion of physical resources, or it may pinpoint common fears of humans. Examples of topics that may be considered for use as a startling statement are as follows: inflation, money and retirement, death, taxes, cancer, killings, wars, and strength or erosion of moral conduct. Of the various ways to gain attention, the startling statement may be the most risky because it has instant potential to further your speech or stop your speech before it even gets started.

Humorous Anecdote

Humor, as an attention device, should be carefully related to your topic, should be designed for maximum speaker benefit concerning the topic that it depicts, describes, or scorns. Humor or even some jokes, when used tastefully, will gain attention; but off-color humor will almost always offend a portion of the audience, which is to the speaker's disadvantage.

Illustration

Experienced speakers often use illustrations to gain attention because a well-planned illustration consistently works better than most other approaches. Effective illustrations highlight a story about something that happened to you or people you know. The following are areas that you might remember for drafting your illustration: most embarrassing moment, traffic penalties, educational successes or failures, family situations, or sports achievements.

An effective attention-gaining opening prepares the audience for the body of your speech that will follow shortly. One last point about openings—keep their length to a maximum of three minutes.

Body of Your Speech

What factors do you have to be concerned with in developing the body of a speech?

Naturally, the main part of a speech is the body. Your introduction should lead into the speech, and the conclusions should take you out. In developing your speech, you need to focus on unity, coherence, and emphasis.

An effective guideline for developing the body of your speech is to include three or four major points with some explanation or elaboration of each.

Coherence refers to continuity of ideas and information. The various points for your presentation must be tied together. Coherence makes your speech easier to deliver and easier for the audience to follow.

In the body of your speech, expand on your most important, most complicated, and most pertinent ideas or points. As a speaker, you help your listeners by emphasizing your key points.

Concluding Your Speech

The conclusions should tie together important points, state resolutions, crystallize thoughts, and summarize the main ideas. Conclusions should proceed logically from the ideas presented. A conclusion may be in the form of summarizing a final point or referencing the introduction.

The Ethics Episode contains suggestions to help you avoid an ethics dilemma.

ETHICS EPISODE

Ethical communication is essential for organizational harmony and employee peace of mind. The following is a guide for designing your oral messages to ensure clarity and to protect yourself from accusations about being unethical.

First, determine what effect the message might have on the intended audience. If the intent of the message is for the benefit of the audience, could it possibly be perceived as abrupt, unfair, or harmful? For example, assume that the purpose of your message is to have workers accept a new fringe benefits package that will ultimately prove beneficial—but it could also be perceived as less desirable than the one currently available. Benefits must outweigh disadvantages, but the speaker must carefully prepare comments to lead the group gently in the intended direction. This is best accomplished through facts and projections rather than promises or emotions.

Second, you must determine whether the message is true. Have the data been distorted to accentuate the positive or to minimize the negative? Have you changed the facts? Have you deliberately not included information that would provide greater understanding?

Third, presentation style also involves ethical dimensions. How will your message be interpreted? Will your words seem to be kind? Inconsiderate? Peaceful? Rude?

Fourth, tact is essential for building and maintaining personal relationships, but respect earned through a record of integrity and honesty is essential for developing and maintaining business relationships.

Oral communication is complex and dynamic. If you couple this with possible job security on the part of the intended audience, the result is a very sensitive communication environment. Although no absolute rule for oral communication success exists, the communicator should simply try to take positive action and always try to do what is right.

The information shown in Exhibit 16-2 should help in preparing an oral presentation.

Exhibit 16-2 Checklist for oral presentations.

	Covered?
I. Planning the Presentation	
A. Analyze the audience.	________
B. Determine the main points.	________
C. Plan your attention getter.	________
D. Ask the 5 W's and 1 H question. (who, what, when, where, why, and how)	________
E. Design a memorable closing.	________
II. Visual Aids and Materials	
A. Selection of most effective visuals	
1. Flip chart	________
2. Transparencies	________
3. Slides	________
4. Films	________
5. Felt boards	________
B. Ordering Equipment	
1. Overhead Projector	________
2. 35 MM Slide Projector	________
3. 16 MM Film Projector	________
4. VCR and Television	________
5. Computer	________
C. Supporting Materials	
1. Take-up reel(s) for 16 mm	________
2. Extension cord(s)	________
3. Felt-tip markers	________
4. Transparency pens	________
5. Tape, tacks, stapler, staples	________
6. Handout material	________
7. Microphone	________
III. Oral Presentation Points	
A. Interest-getting opening	________
B. Full-range eye contact	________
C. Delivery speed and voice volume	________
D. Posture	________
E. Gestures	________
F. Questions/Response	________
G. Action Closing	________

THE IMPORTANCE OF LISTENING

Listening, so essential to oral communication, is estimated to consume more time than any other aspect of the communication process. In modern business, each day provides many opportunities for people to practice their listening skill. Lectures, oral assignments, committee meetings, conferences, discussions, radio and television programs, telephone calls, announcements, and sermons—all require attentive listening.

Why are hearing and listening not synonymous?

Listening is not, as you may believe, synonymous with hearing. Listening involves perception, association, and appropriate reaction. *Hearing* is the mental recognition of sound. *Listening* refers to perceiving sounds from the speaker, attaching meaning to the words, and designing an appropriate response, which, in turn, involves remembering what the speaker has said long enough to interpret what was meant. Listening also includes grasping what the speaker means by "seeing" the ideas and information from his or her point of view.

Listening for Total Meaning

Every message usually has two components: the content and the overall feeling, or attitude, that underlies the content. Both these components are equally important to the total meaning of the message.

For example, consider the following conversation between a boss and a secretary after the boss returned from a long and hectic meeting.

Boss:	Did I have any calls?
Assistant:	Yes, Mr. Brown called and said he was not planning to come to the office but asked me to have you call him at home.
Boss:	If Mr. Brown really needs to talk to me that badly, why doesn't he come into the office as he should?

What is the baseline meaning of the boss's message? The content of the message appears straightforward, but what about the underlying attitude? An assistant must learn to listen for information, emotion, and expected action. If the assistant in the previous example related the attitude of the boss to Mr. Brown, he or she would have breached a professional confidence. A boss must be able to confide in and expect professional judgment from an assistant. This confidence will, in turn, create a more relaxed office environment and will also promote an atmosphere that enhances more effective communication. An effective office team requires the various parties to listen between the lines for meaning and urgency and warranted action.

Levels of Listening

What are the levels of listening?

The different levels of listening are active listening, protective listening, partial listening, and preferential listening.

Active listening is listening from the speaker's viewpoint. The active listener tunes in to the speaker's total message, both verbal and nonverbal. In addition, active listeners interpret the speaker's meaning and mentally check the interpreted meaning for accuracy by rephrasing it for the speaker. Developing a sincere active interest in the speaker is not an easy task. At times you may listen with a personal agenda rather than an open mind. You may become more interested in gathering information for a response, a rebuttal, or to determine a convenient time for inserting your own viewpoint. Because active listening requires listening from the perspective of the speaker rather than being guided by personal aspirations and motives, it involves personal risk. The risk is the possibility of undergoing mental, emotional, or psychological change.

Protective listening prevents a listener from listening to a speaker because the listener has learned to tune out certain kinds of stimuli. Words like *control*, *taxes*, and *evaluation* may set off a whole sequence of negative thoughts in the mind of the listener. Although no one really likes to be subjected to hostile remarks, you need to control protective listening so that verbal attacks are perceived without your having to defend or retaliate.

Partial listening occurs when the listener responds to some stimuli while ignoring others. This will cause the listener to miss facts and points necessary for clarity and understanding. Effective listening must always be a complete process in which all the communicative stimuli the speaker transmits are acknowledged and evaluated.

A speaker's voice, mannerisms, grammar, and pitch will increase or decrease the listener's tendency toward partial listening. As a listener and a prospective speaker, you should consciously control the urge for partial listening. This will help create an environment that produces greater understanding and, in turn, more effective oral communication.

Preferential listening is directly affected by a person's beliefs, interests, or emotions. Just as people may see what they expect to see, listeners may listen for what they want to hear. Personal background, experiences, habits, and family tradition will many times change or distort the speaker's intended meaning into what the listener really wants to hear. Miscommunication is often the result of preferential listening.

To help you improve your listening skills, read the suggestions in Communication Capsule 16-2.

What suggestions can you offer that will be helpful in improving listening skills?

Communication Capsule 16-2 Improving Your Listening Skills

Effective listening requires concentration on what a speaker is saying or implying. Poor listening can many times be traced to a listener having too much time to think. An average rate for speaking is 125 words per minute, but a person normally thinks about four times that fast, which gives a listener about 400 words of thinking time a minute to spare. Untrained or careless listeners allow their minds to wander. During these "spare" moments, they tend to become impatient even when the speech is objectively important and interesting.

To improve listening, you must be ready to listen. Suggestions for improved listening are these:

1. Do not talk to or respond to people around you when the speaker is talking.
2. Have the necessary material to record important points, facts, figures, or ideas.
3. Do not write everything down, as this may keep you from listening to important points or ideas.
4. Listen for a speaker's main ideas and concentrate on their meaning.
5. Listen for ideas and try to interpret them as the speaker intended. Consciously control prejudices or biases about the speaker, the topic, or the organization.
6. Be fair and objective as you consider facts and ideas.
7. Listen for all the facts before you begin to form your opinions.
8. Avoid forming an opinion or evaluation too quickly, which will hinder your ability to be logical or objective.
9. Take the time to listen, weigh, and consider.
10. Keep an open and positive mind as a means of welcoming new viewpoints rather than resisting them.
11. Improve understanding by increasing your available vocabulary.

SUMMARY

An important skill for business employees is effectiveness in oral communication. Business employees spend a major portion of each working day communicating orally. The majority of such business communication is designed to inform or persuade.

Oral business communication includes speaking from a manuscript, speaking from memorization, impromptu speaking, and extemporaneous speaking. As you speak, your listeners will evaluate voice characteristics, such as volume, pitch, speed, enthusiasm, quality, and clarity of pronunciation.

Preparing for business presentations begins with an outline. The body of the presentation follows and expands the outline that was prepared. The speaker designs an effective opening for the particular presentation plus a closing that will leave the audience with the information and meaning that were intended.

The ability to listen effectively is an important attribute of managerial success. Types of listening include active listening, protective listening, partial listening, and preferential listening.

REVIEW QUESTIONS

1. List and explain the various uses of oral communication.
2. Explain the procedure and reasons for assessing your audience prior to your oral presentation.
3. What are the advantages and disadvantages of speaking from a manuscript? Of an extemporaneous speech?
4. Explain how voice characteristics have an impact on oral presentations.
5. List suggestions for preparing a stand-up speech.
6. Explain the impact of active listening on both the speaker and the listener.
7. How does protective listening differ from partial listening?
8. List six suggestions to help someone trying to improve listening skills.

APPLICATION PROBLEMS

1. Select a news story from the front page of your city newspaper and convert it into a talk to be presented to a local civic group. Explain the process you used in developing your talk for the intended group. Show your outline, complete with line-item detail needed for a twenty- to twenty-five-minute talk.
2. Observe, record, and analyze listening habits of students in one of your classes. Explain the types of listening you observed and prepare an outline for a speech about listening effectiveness. The information is to be presented at a national meeting of business communication professionals.
3. Develop an outline and appropriate plan for presenting a solution to one of the major issues for the study body at your college/university. Some suggested problem topics are the following: registration, parking, library, cafeteria, athletics, curricula, traffic on campus, and drop policy.
4. Assume you are the chairperson of the convention site selection committee for the American Federal of Communication Concepts. This national organization of people from business and education have research, process, and application interests in the improvement and enhancement of business communication.

   Your committee visited several cities, including Las Vegas, Los Angeles, San Diego, Denver, Houston, and New Orleans. Las Vegas was selected as the site for the next convention, and your task is to prepare a report to present at the next meeting of the FCC Executive Board meeting in Washington, D. C.

   Using your college/university library or other available sources, prepare an outline for an extemporaneous presentation. Your outline should include points that you and your committee members considered important to the selection of Las Vegas. Some of its assets are excellent room rates, reasonable food costs, easy access by all major airlines, complete accommodations for large and small groups, and the quality of shows and entertainment. Keep in mind that each of the other cities had some advantages but that Las Vegas was the one site that appeared to have the least number of disadvantages.

   Your oral report must address some of the major concerns expressed by strong and influential members of the FCC, such as the following: Selecting Las Vegas demonstrates to the general membership that the organization is more committed to play than to work; 65 percent of the membership comes from east of the Mississippi River, and, therefore, an east-coast site should be given higher priority. In addition, gambling may both distract and disrupt the concentration and overall worthiness of the entire convention.

Besides preparing your outline, you plan to use at least three sketches or drawings depicting information. These sketches or drawings should emphasize the more important or significant points.

5. Prepare an appropriate script for a speaking-from-memorization oral presentation about the importance of voice characteristics in oral presentations.
6. Prepare an outline for a fifteen-minute extemporaneous speech about text material of this chapter. Select the points that best present the overall picture of effective oral communication because the entire chapter cannot be summarized orally in fifteen minutes.
7. Prepare a speaking-from-a-manuscript report on the advantages and disadvantages of leasing versus buying electronic equipment for today's modern business world. Gather the facts you consider to be most important, and prepare your manuscript for a maximum five-minute presentation. You may be called upon to read your report in front of the class.
8. Listening is an extremely important component of the speech-making process. Prepare a five- to seven-minute speech to be read from a manuscript on the topic of "The Elements and Process of Improved Listening."
9. Prepare an outline for an extemporaneous speech to the personnel manager and his or her assistants about your training and experience for a position in the company communications division of the personnel division of Acme Company. The position involves both writing and editing company correspondence in the areas of persuasion, sales, credit, and collections. Please include line-item detail that will provide the necessary information. You may wish to review the chapters covering these topics as you determine which points to include. Remember, you are selling both your ability and your suitability for this prestigious position.

17

International Business Communication

After studying this chapter, you should be able to

1. Explain cultural differences that affect international business communication.
2. Identify the values important to Americans and contrast these values to those important to peoples of other cultures.
3. Describe language barriers that affect international business communication.
4. List nonverbal communication characteristics that affect international communication.
5. Identify important differences between business letters prepared by people in the United States and individuals from other cultures.
6. Outline procedures to follow when preparing for an international assignment.

The internationalization of American business and the rapidly increasing number of foreign companies with plants on American soil have made the United States a key player in the global business community. Of the recent developments affecting American businesses, the trend toward internationalization is among the most significant. As more American businesses become multinational, the ability of U.S. firms and American workers to communicate in a global marketplace becomes increasingly important.

The passage by the U.S. Congress in 1993 of the North American Free Trade Agreement (NAFTA) is certain to increase interactions among American, Canadian, and Mexican businesses. Although these interactions will occur in all three countries, more extensive language-oriented challenges for American companies exist when they transact business with Mexicans on Mexican soil or with French-speaking Canadians on Canadian soil. In these instances, language and cultural differences appear.

Obviously, companies and their employees engaged in international business must view their functional responsibilities from an international perspective. For example, involvement with the marketing of products in foreign countries requires an understanding of international marketing. Conversely, responsibilities for the financial aspect of international trade will necessitate an understanding of international finance and economics. Employees working in the international arena must be familiar with any special nuances of the business operations and procedures with which they are concerned.

International business communication cuts across all functional areas of international business. Therefore, regardless of the specific nature of your international business responsibilities, you will need to understand and be skilled in international business communication. A clear understanding of international business communication provides for people involved with it an important tool that helps them successfully complete their various job functions.

Businesses and individual businesspeople communicating with their counterparts in other cultures need a broad understanding of the significant differences in the meaning of nonverbal cues within cultures. In addition, if they communicate by written messages, they also need understanding of the various approaches to writing such communications by people of other cultures.

This chapter discusses four important components of international business communication: cultural differences affecting international business communication, nonverbal differences affecting international business communication, differences affecting written business communication within various cultures, and preparation for an international assignment.

CULTURAL DIFFERENCES AFFECTING INTERNATIONAL BUSINESS COMMUNICATION

Culture has been defined in many ways by a wide range of people from diverse backgrounds. *Culture* generally refers to the knowledge, beliefs, art, law, morals, customs, habits, and capabilities acquired by individuals who interact in a specific area of society.

What is ethnocentrism?

Every person is a product of his or her cultural environment. Though this provides stability and psychological comfort, it inherently limits one's understanding and acceptance of foreign cultures. *Ethnocentrism* is the belief that one's own culture is superior. From a multicultural perspective, members must recognize diversity. In ethnocentric organizations, employees believe their way is the best way to organize and complete work. Therefore, they insist on using their own values and procedures, with little or no tolerance of the differences between them and people of other cultures. The result is often a barrier to successful multicultural communication.

Most people, unconsciously, use their personal cultural background as a guide for judging the actions, views, customs, or manners of others. We may condemn someone because his or her views do not coincide with ours and lose sight of the fact that our words and actions may also be misunderstood. In this manner, ethnocentrism is quite similar to stereotyped reaction. Indeed, the greater the differences in education, experience, customs, intellect, and so forth, the more likely a miscommunication will occur.

Communication involves the exchange of both ideas and meaning. Obviously, communication includes sending both verbal and nonverbal messages, but it also includes messages of which the sender is totally unaware. A message that is transmitted includes words, behavior, and customs that the receiver must interpret before effective communication can occur. The translation of meaning from words and behavior is based on a person's background.

If, for example, a Japanese company adopts the stereotyped view of Americans as being greedy, materialistic, imperialistic, capitalistic, and brash, this belief will increase the potential of an unsatisfactory business relationship between it and any American company. Conversely, if the American company stereotypes Japanese as procrastinators in decision making, the chances of miscommunication between the two companies is also increased. In both cases, cross-cultural miscommunication may occur when the audience from one culture fails to interpret accurately a message sent by another culture. For effective cross-cultural communication, you need, therefore, to assume that differences exist and to then acknowledge, identify, understand, and accept these differences. For example, you may be more easily able to work with the slowness of the Japanese decision-making process if you understand that it results from the "ringi" procedure (a process requiring the approval of many people when making decisions).

LOW-CONTEXT AND HIGH-CONTEXT CULTURES

Anthropologist Edward T. Hall identified two levels of cultural context—high and low. According to Hall, differences in the message that high- and low-context cultures communicate can be summarized in the following way: *Low-context cultures* (Germany, Switzerland, Northern Europe, the Scandandinavian countries, and the United States) depend on explicitly written or verbalized messages. *High-context cultures* (China, Korea, Japan, Mediterranean, and Arab countries), on the other hand, depend on the explicitly written or verbalized message, as well as everything surrounding the message, including nonverbal aspects of the message.[1]

Low-context peoples tend to compartmentalize their lives, including their personal relationships, their work, and various aspects of day-to-day living. This results in their increased need for more detailed information when they interact with others, including specific wording in correspondence and written agreements. In contrast, high-context countries make extensive use of information networks encompassing their family, friends, colleagues, and clients. Because of their close personal relationships, people in these cultures do not require much in-depth background information; therefore, written correspondence and agreements often seem far less important.[2]

Cultural characteristics that have a great impact on international communications include customs, values, language barriers, decision-making processes, status, and manners.

Customs

What customs in other countries differ from American customs?

International business is increasingly transacted in social situations. Therefore, awareness of customs common to other cultures is essential in international relationships. European countries accept the exchange of gifts as customary; however, in certain Far East cultures, such as Korea and Japan, gift giving—especially during the first visit—may be interpreted as bribery. Also, Europeans may prefer that you open a gift in the presence of the giver, but doing so in Japan or Korea is considered bad taste.

Some world religions prohibit the intake or use of certain food or drink items. The Muslims, for example, avoid tobacco, alcohol, and meat. Arabs do not use the left hand to remove food from a serving dish because they consider that hand to be unclean. Countries and areas of similar heritage and geographic location usually will possess similar customs.

Exhibit 17-1 lists countries that would conceivably share common attitudinal dimensions and customs. Conducting business with various countries common to one of the clusters involves an understanding of customs and values that other countries in that particular cluster would, for the most part, accept.

When business dealings require movement from cluster to cluster, the attitudes, beliefs, values, and methods of doing business are typically quite different. In addition, the farther one moves away from a particular cluster, the greater the change in customs and expectation becomes. Through a better understanding of values common to a particular cluster, overcoming common cultural barriers between your company and companies within the cluster become possible. The result is a greater possibility of effective communications. Categorizing countries by clusters is, of course, not a precise

[1] "Excerpts", from THE HIDDEN DIMENSION by Edward T. Hall, Copyright 1966, 1982 by Edward T. Hall, Used by permission of Doubleday, a division of Bantam Doubleday Dell Publishing Group, Inc.
[2] E. T. Hall and M. R. Hall, *Understanding Cultural Differences* (Yarmouth, ME: Intercultural Press, Inc., 1990): pp. 6–7.

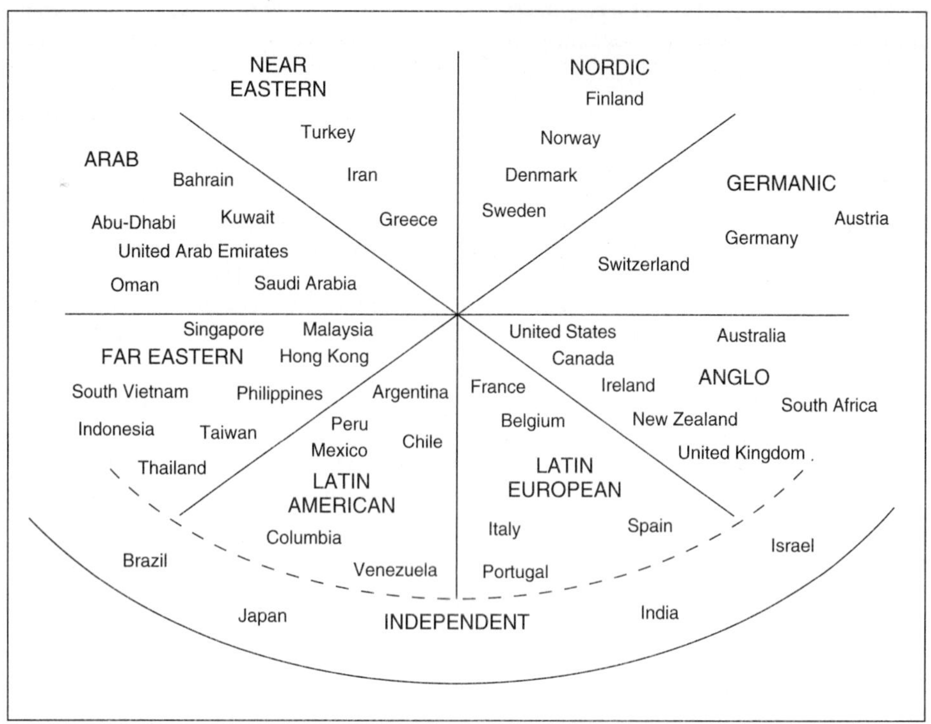

Exhibit 17-1 A synthesis of country clusters. Source: Simcha Ronen and Oded Shenkar, "Clustering Countries on Attitudinal Dimensions: A Review and Synthesis," *Academy of Management Review 10*, no. 3 (July 1985): p. 449.

science. But the authors of the cluster shown in Exhibit 17-1 explain the overall value and effectiveness of clustering as follows:

> Despite these limitations, however, the results available thus far allow one to draw certain conclusions. First, it appears that countries/nations can be clustered according to similarities on certain cultural dimensions. These dimensions typically measure work goals, values, needs, and job attitudes. The discriminate validity of these variables is supported: The resulting clusters consistently discriminate on the basis of language, religion, and geography. The support for the Anglo, Germanic, Nordic, Latin European, and Latin American clusters appears to be quite strong. Clusters describing the Far East and Arab countries are ill-defined and require further research, as do countries classified as independents (e.g., Israel and Japan).[3]

The information in the Ethics Episode will help you avoid creating an ethics dilemma for yourself when you are communicating in the global marketplace.

Values

American *values*—ideals that we believe to be important—are often quite different from those of foreign countries in which we conduct business. Our "melting-pot" type

[3] Simcha Ronen and Oded Shenkar, "Clustering Countries on Attitudinal Dimensions: A Review and Synthesis," *Academy of Management Review 10*, no. 3 (July 1985): p. 452.

ETHICS EPISODE

Proper business protocol and acceptable social graces are important to success and prosperity for the American businessperson. The manner in which one speaks to associates, superiors, and prospective customers is usually learned as a person matures personally and professionally.

Americans commonly conduct business quickly, legally, and with few unnecessary amenities. Business to the American businessperson is just that—business. But American executives operating in an international setting must learn to be patient. In addition, they must modify their normal manner of conducting business to satisfy the needs and expectations of the culture with which they will be dealing. As a Japanese official stated, "You Americans have one major weakness; if we make you wait long enough you will agree to anything!" The key word for successful international business appears to be "Patience"!

Too many times our lack of patience may cause some of our actions to become unethical. The following is an example: Suppose you are trying to negotiate a business undertaking with a Japanese business. You become frustrated because of the characteristically slow Japanese decision-making process. You decide to tell your counterparts that your superiors have told you that a decision must be forthcoming in a week or the "deal is off" when, in fact, your superiors have not set a deadline. Your statement represents an unethical action on your part.

International business requires relentless American executives to slow down and learn to enjoy the finer aspects of the culture in which they are planning to conduct business. The American executive must acknowledge that an Asian firm may refuse to deal with strangers. Rather than ruining the possibility for current and future business contracts, the aspiring international business executive must have the patience to not walk into a Chinese corporation unannounced. Rather, he or she must learn to establish contacts with the appropriate people. This requires a sense of timing that is truly Asian—not American.

of culture has a basically European influence, so the most significant differences occur between Americans and people from cultures in the Middle and Far East.

What values in other countries differ from American values?

The work ethic remains one of America's most basic values. For several reasons, Americans believe in the value of hard work; the harder one works, the more money he or she is likely to earn. The more money one earns, the more comforts he or she can enjoy. In contrast, in some cultures, like Iran, materialism is condemned. Americans also believe in streamlining the workforce and in working as efficiently as possible. In contrast, some cultures, particularly those with high unemployment, such as India and Pakistan, value the creation of jobs more highly than the efficient completion of a job.

Americans also value progress. Nothing is inherently wrong with moving tons of dirt or rocks in building a super highway. Nor is anything wrong with constructing a dam across a river if, as a result, thousands of acres will be irrigated. Conversely, Asian cultures such as India value human adjustment to the physical environment rather than vice versa.

A strong belief in individualism and democratic ideas contributes to less respect by Americans for authority. In contrast, many other cultures put the individual below those in power. Moreover, people from other cultures do not always value the democratic process.

The Japanese consider employment to be for life, and Japanese employers play a more important role in employees' lives than do employers in American companies. Japanese management provides living accommodations for their employees and pay for their weddings. Until fairly recently, losing one's job was considered disgraceful in Japan. Little, in fact, could be more disgraceful for an individual.

American culture is based on competition and free enterprise; however, competition in some Asian cultures, such as Japan, is viewed as destructive because it encourages divisions and challenges rather than cooperation within work groups.

Decision-Making Process

How do decision-making processes in other countries differ from American decision-making processes?

The process by which decisions are made also varies widely from culture to culture. Some cultures, such as Iraq, have a higher authority that imposes decisions on the people. Other cultures encourage decisions that emerge slowly because of the group consensus process, as in Japan. The amount of shared responsibility for decision making also varies widely from culture to culture.

For organizations in the United States, the goal is to reach decisions as quickly and as efficiently as the circumstances allow. Most Western European societies endorse this value; but Latin American countries focus on minute details and lengthy discussions. Failure to discuss a situation in detail tends to arouse suspicion, with "offenders" considered untrustworthy.

Language Barriers

Language is a significant cultural difference that affects international business communication. An ability to read, write, and understand a foreign language does not guarantee the absence of language barriers. Fortunately for Americans, English is the most common language used in business abroad. For the present at least, rather than having to learn a foreign language, Americans must learn how to use English in a manner that will be readily understood by those for whom it is a second language. Americans working in the international arena quickly learn that American speech is not synonymous with the English language.

Americans who work overseas for any length of time find it desirable to learn the native language in the country in which they are living. Learning the language may not be absolutely necessary for their job assignment, but a basic mastery of the language will be necessary if they hope to integrate themselves into their new culture. Many companies provide language training for employees who are designated for foreign travel or work. Other companies reimburse their employees for expenses incurred in arranging for their own language study.

The majority of the international business letters are in English. In large organizations, letters in languages other than English are often translated by professional translators, unless, of course, the recipient is competent in that particular foreign language. Letters written in English by someone for whom English is a second language are generally clear enough to create understanding, even though they may not meet our standards for effective business letters. However, the situation is changing. Increasingly, countries prefer that negotiations and contracts be based on the language native to the country originating the negotiations or contracts.

Written communications that create the greatest number of problems in the international market are advertisements, warranties, and manuals that must be translated from English to another language. In some instances, a major portion of the message is lost in the translation—and sometimes with disastrous results. For example, when Pepsi Cola was introduced to the Asian market, its slogan, "Come alive with Pepsi," was interpreted to mean that Pepsi brings relatives back from the grave!

Why does oral communication in international business present more problems than written communication?

Oral communication presents more problems in international business communication than does written communication. First, many individuals who learn a foreign language develop a greater reading/writing fluency than a speaking/listening fluency. Consequently, they have more difficulty understanding and being understood when communicating orally. Second, *idioms,* expressions peculiar to a certain segment of the world's people, are more commonly used in oral communication than in written communication. American idioms tend to be confusing to individuals for whom English is a second language. Just as foreigners have difficulty understanding English idioms, Americans have equally as much difficulty understanding idioms in other languages. Following is a short list of American idioms, which people in other cultures may find confusing:

"... eat a hot dog."
"... so hungry I could eat a horse."
"... runs for office."
"... shot my idea down."
"... got fired."
"... visit the john" or "head." (meaning restroom)
"... pulling my leg." (meaning a lack of seriousness)
"... threw the book." (meaning convicted)
"... got bumped upstairs." (meaning promoted)

The following suggestions will help you overcome cross-cultural written or oral language barriers:

What suggestions can you offer that will help you eliminate either oral or written language barriers in international business?

1. Use specific, concrete terms rather than abstract words to express yourself.
2. Use short, precise words, sentences, and paragraphs.
3. Avoid idioms, slang, or jargon.
4. Use pointing expressions, such as *for example, furthermore,* and *in addition,* as well as transitional expressions, such as *however* and *therefore.*
5. Avoid the use of abbreviations.

If your job responsibilities eventually require the preparation of letters sent to foreign countries, you should, as much as possible, gear your correspondence to the recipients' expectations. Generally this will require you to be more formal than when you write to Americans. When you write to a Japanese businessperson, remember Japanese tend to be more apologetic and humble than American businesspeople. A fast-start opening may be offensive to the Japanese because they believe that one should begin a letter with a comment about the weather or the season.

For example, during the Japanese growing season, you might begin a letter with "In this season of abundant greenery ..." You may follow with a comment about the reader's health. After expressing other pleasantries, the main point of the letter is finally introduced.

Status

How does status in other cultures differ from status in the American culture?

Cultures vary in the ways they accord status to business employees. In the United States, office placement, size, and furnishings often reveal status. For example, the offices of top-level executives generally will have thicker carpets than do the offices of lower-level executives. Wooden furniture is often provided executives, but lower-level executives generally have metal furniture. Also, the higher your hierarchical level, the more privacy and seclusion you are allowed. Furthermore, an organization's status is enhanced when it names one of its major buildings after itself.

For many other cultures, status is much less important. Offices in Middle Eastern cultures tend to be much smaller and more modest than their American counterparts. In France, privacy and seclusion are not assigned as much significance. French executives are commonly located in large open areas, their subordinates surrounding them. In England, the offices of the highest-ranking people in organizations are sometimes located below ground level; in the United States, the highest status location for top executives is the top floor.

Manners

Before traveling to a foreign country, you should read books and articles about the culture. Visiting with people who have recently had business dealings in this particular country may also be useful. Focus on customs, religion(s), politics, history, national heroes and heroines, attitudes toward education, gambling, drinking, sports, important holidays, and so forth. For business relationships, specifically learn as much as possible about business rules and protocol, how decisions are made, the etiquette of business relationships, and proper dress for informal and formal meetings. The references/sources identified later in this chapter should help you become familiar with other cultures.

How do manners in other cultures differ from manners in the American culture?

The manners considered acceptable in different cultures obviously vary greatly. Introductions and farewells are often more formal in foreign cultures than in the United States. Business executives from an Asian nation often bow during introductions; when saying farewell, they also bow before backing out of a room. Preparing yourself to sit patiently through a three-hour lunch in most European cultures is the sign of "knowing your manners."

Interactions with Middle Eastern cultures—Saudi Arabia, for example—-require some insight into the respect given to elders. A hush usually falls when an older person enters a room filled with younger people. Understanding the reason for this sudden quietness will save you from making embarrassing comments during some business interactions.

Being familiar with the manners considered acceptable in foreign cultures enables you to conduct business more comfortably. Continual anxiety about offending the person with whom you are dealing will not prevent you from concentrating fully on the business at hand.

INTERNATIONAL NONVERBAL DIFFERENCES

Communication in general and international communication in particular requires a keen awareness of nonverbal differences that influence the communication process. Nonverbal communication skill is important for the following reasons: (1) When the verbal and nonverbal messages are not consistent with one another, miscommunication can occur, and (2) nonverbal cues do not have universal international meaning. Communication efforts will obviously be affected when a positive nonverbal cue in one culture has a negative connotation in a different culture. Types of nonverbal differences include posture, movement, gestures, space, paralanguage, eye contact, touching, and time.

Posture

Nonverbal signals that may communicate a relaxed situation (slouching in a chair, crossing one's legs, and arms away from the body) in the United States are often interpreted as a demonstration of disrespect in other cultures. In Saudi Arabia, a visible shoe sole is offensive when one's legs are crossed. And Asian cultures believe that a relaxed appearance during a conversation indicates loss of control over the situation.

Movement

Americans move faster and more abruptly than people from other countries. Perhaps this is because Americans have more space around them and will make use of that space as they communicate. People from the Middle East and Asian cultures prefer a communication situation in which less movement is displayed. The Massai of East Africa carry themselves in a way that shows pride, strength, and self-assurance. In fact, their movements often show superiority over other African tribes.

What differences exist between gestures used in the American culture and gestures used in foreign cultures?

Gestures

Gestures that are acceptable in one culture may be obscene and insulting in other cultures. For example, in India a wink is insulting. Making a circle with the thumb and index finger is a sign of contempt in South American countries. In Japan this same sign depicts money, whereas in the United States it signals everything is "okay." The "V" gesture (formed by raising the index and middle finger) is a sign of disrespect in Western Europe. The American gesture for saying no (moving the head back and forth) is not understood by Japanese who move their right hand to signal no. In Italy, no is signaled by waving a finger in the speaker's face. The gesture used by hitchhiking Americans is considered obscene in Italy.

Americans observe facial expressions to interpret the true meaning of a message. When a discrepancy occurs between the verbal and nonverbal message, the nonverbal message is considered the more accurate display of the communicator's intent. In Japan, however, the face remains impassive regardless of the nature of the conversation. Therefore, you would be misinterpreting an emotionless facial expression by a Japanese businessperson to be a sign of disinterest. You can also easily misinterpret the meaning of a Japanese smile. Americans usually interpret a smile as a sign of agreement, but the Japanese smile can actually mean several different things. It may be used to disguise the individual's real feelings, or to say, "I understand" or conversely, to say, "I don't understand."

Space

Americans value space more than peoples of other cultures. We are uncomfortable when friends or business associates get too close. As shown in Exhibit 17-2, Americans prefer personal space boundaries as they relate to various personal and professional associations and communications.

What differences exist between how Americans view space and how people in other cultures view space?

Exhibit 17-2 Overlap circle drawing showing proxemics: personal space. Source: "Excerpts", from THE HIDDEN DIMENSION by Edward T. Hall. Copyright 1966, 1982 by Edward T. Hall. Used by permission of Doubleday, a division of Bantam Doubleday Dell Publishing Group, Inc.

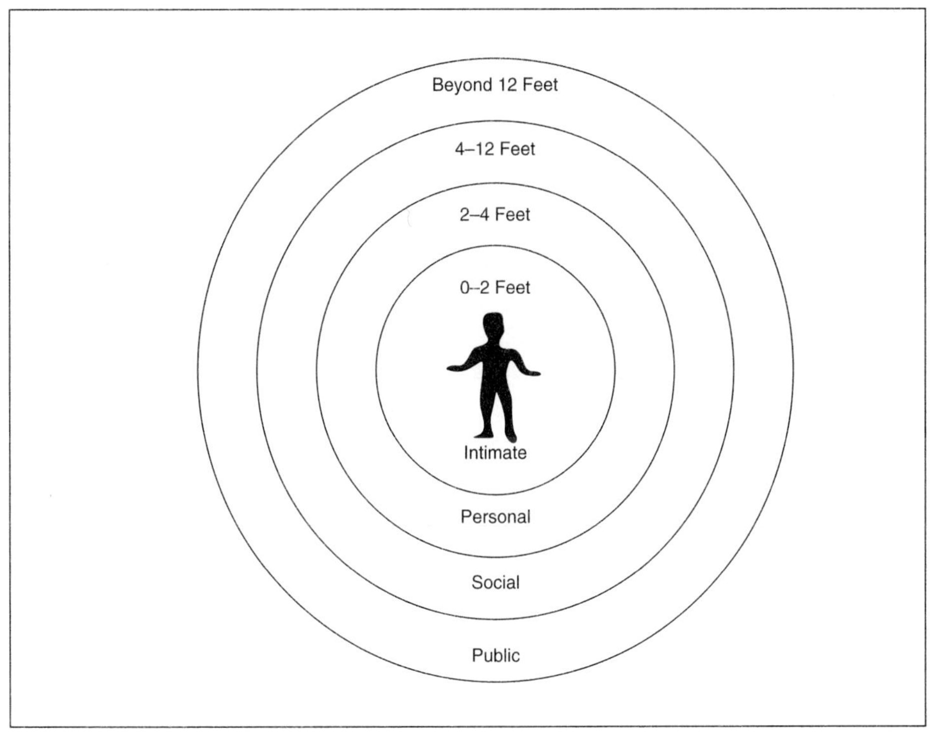

Every culture has its own perception of what is the appropriate personal space for conducting business. Americans consider from zero to two feet to be a person's *intimate space* and, as such, you should not enter it unless invited. But some other cultures, typically in the Middle East, do not recognize the concept of an inviolate intimate space. In these societies, a business transaction may involve a kiss on each cheek from a person of the same gender.

Americans define *personal space* as from two feet to four feet between people. This is the normally accepted space for Americans to conduct business conversations. Latin Americans customarily conduct business in the intimate space, which Americans find uncomfortable. Often, in business conversation, Latin Americans will continually try to enter the intimate space of the person with whom they are conversing. Americans have a tendency to put a barrier (such as a desk or table) between them and the person of another culture as a means of protecting their intimate space.

For Americans, *social space* is defined from four feet to twelve feet between people. Americans are very comfortable in social gatherings when this is the space within small conversation groups. If someone deliberately attempts to close up this space, group members usually exhibit increased signs of uncomfortableness; and should the situation not change, most individuals will probably move to different areas or different groups.

People from Mediterranean countries, southern European countries, the Middle East, and Latin America prefer to position themselves more closely to the persons with whom they are communicating than do Americans conversing with other Americans. An important point to remember is that individuals from these cultures may interpret a desire for greater distance as an indication that we prefer a cold, distant, or even an aloof relationship. In sum, to avoid miscommunication in intercultural communications, you should observe and understand the ways societies define intimate, personal, and social space.

In some cultures, the gender of those communicating also influences the amount of space customarily viewed as appropriate for conducting business. For example, in South America, men feel obligated to position themselves at least five feet from female business associates when communicating with them.

How individuals occupy space also varies from culture to culture. For example, the Chinese prefer to sit side by side when they communicate, whereas Americans offer a face-to-face arrangement. The typical American behavior of attempting to put office visitors at ease by standing when they enter or by moving out from behind the desk has little or no communication significance in other cultures.

Paralanguage

Paralanguage refers to the verbal elements that accompany spoken messages, including such qualities as emphasis, pitch, rate, tone, and volume. Paralanguage appears to have wider agreement among the cultures than the other elements of nonverbal communication. Thus, people from all cultures tend to talk faster and louder when they are excited and to use a higher-pitched voice when communicating happiness. The most significant paralanguage difference among cultures is the meaning assigned to a pause during a conversation. Americans may pause because they are uncomfortable about the situation being discussed, whereas Arabs may use pauses for reflection.

Many businesspeople consider language as the only essential element in successful cultural relationships. But researchers have discovered that actual language is not as crucial to the meaning of the message as are the nonverbal and paralanguage aspects. Albert Mehrabian, a communications expert, concluded that the various elements of communication impact on the communication process as follows: language, 7 percent; paralanguage, 38 percent; nonverbal, 55 percent.[4] People become confused when the

[4]Albert Mehrabian, "Communication Without Words," *Psychology Today 2* (September 1968): p. 52–55. Reprinted with permission from *Psychology Today,* Copyright © 1968 (SUSSEX Publishers, Inc.).

words indicate satisfaction, but the paralanguage reveals displeasure. To illustrate, a supervisor may tell employees he or she is pleased with the manner in which a certain task or project is performed; that they worked together as a team; and that they should take a few minutes off before resuming their responsibilities. However, should the supervisor not join the workers during the break, her nonverbal behavior speaks much louder than her words.

Eye Contact

Americans use eye contact to interpret another person's honesty, genuineness, and sincerity. A break in eye contact is typically viewed as accompanying a lie or an insincerity. In contrast, the Japanese do not place much emphasis on lack of eye contact, to show respect, while Latino Americans avoid it with strangers. However, other cultures where eye contact is rarely broken may make Americans uncomfortable.

What differences exist between the use of eye contact by Americans and eye contact used by people in other cultures?

Touching

Some cultures, especially Middle Eastern, Latin American, and European countries along the Mediterranean, practice more touching than Americans. Frequent touching and hugging are common, and they touch one another more during conversation than do Americans. Other cultures, such as Thailand, avoid touching one another in public. In Malaysia and other Islamic countries, the head should never be touched because it is considered to possess sacred spiritual and intellectual powers.

Time

The way Americans use time differs considerably from other cultures. Americans are schedule-oriented and regimented in their daily lives. Timeliness and promptness are prized, with the result that many people abhor being kept waiting for more than just a few minutes. By contrast, Latin Americans see nothing wrong with showing up forty-five to sixty minutes late for an appointment. Business callers will have as much time as they desire, even if it causes the next caller's appointment to begin an hour late! In these countries, business transactions are prolonged because prolonged discussions are commonplace. To people in these cultures, the result is not as important as the discussions leading to the result—a phenomenon that Americans frequently find quite frustrating. In the Middle East, business dealings also often progress at what Americans consider a snail's pace.

For similar reasons Americans interpret a slow response to their correspondence negatively, but people from other cultures view a slow response in a positive light. After all, the important events in life take much longer than the unimportant ones. Therefore, why not allow events to unfold in their own time?

CULTURAL VARIATIONS IN WRITTEN BUSINESS COMMUNICATION

When Americans prepare business letters for foreign audiences, they need to be aware of common practices within those cultures. In some cases, similarities exist between the way Americans organize certain types of business letters and the way peoples of other cultures organize their letters. However, differences are sufficient that our standard practices can become problematic in the international arena.

Americans who prepare written documents for foreign readers are much more likely to use letters than either memos or reports. Unless Americans are fluent in the language of the message recipient, they should prepare the letter in English. An alternative is to have the letter translated into the reader's language if a skilled translator is available. Large organizations that have considerable international dealings often hire professional translators. Occasional users of translation services generally use such agencies as Berlitz and Corporate Language Services.

You will find the following general suggestions helpful as you prepare business letters to be sent to peoples of other cultures:

1. Avoid jargon, slang, or idioms because such expressions rarely translate well, and their meaning generally will be lost.
2. Avoid acronyms (such as NAFTA for North America Free Trade Agreement) or abbreviations unless the term is spelled out in full before you write its acronym.
3. Choose frequently used short and simple words with the fewest number of syllables as possible.
4. Use short, simple sentences composed of precise, concise words.
5. Use short paragraphs of four to five lines, keeping the information in a paragraph related to only one topic.
6. Use transitional expressions between sentences and paragraphs (examples are *in addition, furthermore,* and *therefore*).
7. Use a more formal writing style than if you were writing to another American.
8. Use either of two date styles on letters: the American style (January 20, 199x) or the European style (20 January, 199x or 1.20.199x).
9. Use a letter format customary for the country to which you are sending your message.
10. Avoid the use of contractions (*it's, here's*).
11. Use concrete expressions rather than abstract expressions.
12. Use a direct approach when writing letters to low-context readers but the indirect approach when writing letters to high-context readers.
13. Use specific action words rather than general action words. For example, say you are "going to hire" a new employee rather than "look for a new employee."
14. Apply the following suggestions when you prepare a business letter to be sent to a reader in a specific culture.

Japanese

Although Americans believe in getting to the point immediately in writing request and good-news letters, Japanese generally show humility in the opening with a statement about the current season, nature, or the weather. An inquiry about the reader, about his or her family, or about health often follows this statement. Only after this is the main idea of the letter presented. In a request letter, Japanese prefer to ask if the reader would consider doing something rather than requesting that the reader comply with the stated request. The following is such an example: "Would you consider sending me an application for employment?" as opposed to "Please send me an application for employment."

Disappointing-news letters in Japan begin with an apology to the reader for causing disappointment. Furthermore, Japanese business letter writers, because of a desire to preserve harmony, use a number of techniques to say no without actually saying it, even when the negative response is unlikely to create hard feelings.

French

Letters written in the French culture are also more indirect than American letters. For example, in a request letter, the French prefer to state the reasons for the request before the request itself. In addition, the openings and closings of French letters tend to use a more formal writing style than Americans consider appropriate. For example, thanking the reader in advance is acceptable to the French, whereas Americans consider that this takes the reader for granted.

German

Compared with American business letters, German letters tend to have a rather formal standard opening, perhaps referring to the reader's letter. Although Americans believe that the opening of a letter containing obvious information (such as referring to having received the writer's letter) is inappropriate, for Germans such an opening is acceptable. Moreover, significant differences exist between the American culture and the German culture regarding the appropriate location for negative news. Germans present negative news in the opening (direct approach); Americans prefer that it be delayed until later in the letter (indirect approach). For this reason, German letters are generally seen as being more terse than letters in many other cultures.

Other Cultural Differences

Italians open their business letters by referring to the reader and his or her family members. Individuals from Spanish-speaking countries write with a more flowery, colorful style than what Americans consider to be needed or appropriate. Including exaggerations in Latin American business letters is common.

A grasp of the special characteristics considered appropriate in preparing business letters for foreign readers will enable you to be a more effective international communicator. Obviously, most Americans do not purposely write business letters to offend foreign readers. Unless, however, Americans are sensitive to cultural preferences, they may be offending a foreign audience without even realizing it.

PREPARING FOR AN INTERNATIONAL ASSIGNMENT

What suggestions can you offer that will be helpful to one preparing for an international assignment?

After receiving an international assignment, preparatory work on your part will be well worth your effort. The extent of your preparation will likely affect the amount of satisfaction you derive from the assignment, at least initially.

Among the most effective ways in which you can prepare yourself are the following: (1) Attain a basic mastery of the language, (2) become aware of the communication differences between American culture and the culture in which you will be living, and (3) learn as much as you can generally about the new country in which you will be living.

Attain Language Mastery

With the increase in international American business and the vast number of American corporations that are becoming multinational, more and more students are studying foreign languages. Nevertheless, unfamiliarity with a country's language should not automatically make you turn down an international assignment. Even if you have studied a foreign language, especially French or German, the odds are good that it is not the language used where you will be assigned. Rather, Japanese and Spanish are the two foreign languages most frequently needed by Americans working in the international arena.

As we explained earlier, English has been and continues to be the universal business language. You most likely will not need a basic mastery of the foreign language as much for your job as for special situations. If you hope to become socially involved, a basic mastery of the language native to that country is imperative.

To attain a basic mastery of a foreign language, you can enroll in college/university language classes, attend classes offered by a private company, or have private language lessons with a tutor. Some companies pay the cost of this training; others require that employees pay.

For planning a meeting to be held in a foreign country, use the information in Communication Capsule 17-1.

Communication Capsule 17-1 Keeping Global Meetings on Familiar Ground

Today's business executives are operating in a global environment where geophysical barriers are disappearing and previously unavailable frontiers are becoming readily accessible. Germany is once again united; the Iron Curtain has fallen. Drastic economic and political changes are sweeping through much of the world. Partly because of these changes, more American workers are traveling abroad for business than ever before. However, planning a business meeting overseas is more than simple logistics.

Both planners and participants should be ready to deal with any possible clash of cultures. The following are suggestions for arranging international meetings.

Allow Ample Time. International meetings require more lead time than domestic meetings. As a meeting planner, spend at least a week to ten days beforehand in the city where the meeting is scheduled to be held. Check for areas of local interest, and pay particular attention to the details of the hotel contract. Do not be alarmed if the hotel requires a substantial deposit in the country's currency.

Obtain a Local Contact. Gaining assistance from a local resident will assist you in knowing what is acceptable and what is not. He or she will also be able to assist your planning by pointing out some less-than-obvious concerns and situations. A good source of information about local contacts is the country's embassy in the United States. Another source is the airline that has been selected as the official airline to carry participants to the meeting city or location.

Take Care of Detail. Learning the customs of the country will help you avoid critical mistakes when dealing with the locals. The local people will appreciate your taking time to study their culture. Your library is a good place to start. Another good source is the international business department at a nearby university.

When traveling to a country where the native language is not English, a worthwhile suggestion is to hire an interpreter through the country's embassy in the United States.

Compile a list of facts and situations that your participants should keep in mind when preparing for their trip. For instance, is a visa required to enter the country? Are vaccinations required? Is the power voltage different from that in the United States? How many pieces of luggage are allowed? You should also include for your participants a brief overview of the country, including the currency used, the religious differences, interesting sights to see, location of the American embassy, and so forth.

Preparation of Your Speakers. Inform speakers about whether they need a working permit to present at the meeting. Also prepare the speaker for an audience that might include non-English-speaking participants. Even though your speakers are experienced and knowledgeable, you might remind them to not use slang and to speak slowly and distinctly.

Be Aware of Communication Differences

The information in this chapter should help you understand the differences between your culture and the one with which you may be conducting business. You will, nevertheless, benefit from a more thorough, in-depth study. A variety of sources will help you develop a more intensive understanding of these differences.

Learn About the Country

The more you know about the country you are relocating to, the less frustration you will experience. As we discussed earlier, visit with others who have worked or lived in the country under consideration.

The information in Exhibit 17-3 should help you prepare for an international assignment.

Organizations to contact and printed information of possible usefulness are the following:

American Society for Training and Development
P. O. Box 5307
Madison, WI 53705

The Business Council for International Understanding
American University
Washington, DC 20016

Intercultural Communications, Inc.
P. O. Box 14358
University Station
Minneapolis, MN 55415

I. Language
   A. Is the English language used? ________
   B. What is the primary language? ________
   C. What are the accepted forms of address for men, women, and officials? ________

II. Communication Styles
   A. What are the country's acceptable communication styles? ________
   B. What are the common gestures? ________
   C. What are the expectations in terms of formal and informal dress? ________
   D. What kinds of personal manners should be avoided? ________

III. Laws, Religion, and Politics
   A. What freedoms can you expect in this country? ________
   B. What business regulations exist? ________
   C. What are the significant religious holidays? ________
   D. What behavior is expected? ________
   E. What are the political customs that you are expected to know and observe? ________
   F. What role do special interest groups play in normal business operations? ________

IV. Customs and Background
   A. What are the national sports? Sports heroes? Heroines? ________
   B. What are the attitudes toward education? Gambling? Religion? ________
   C. What is the length of the expected work day? ________
   D. Are certain colors considered sacred? Positive? Negative? ________

Exhibit 17-3 International communication checklist.

Intercultural Network, Inc.
906 N. Spring Avenue
LaGrange Park, IL 60525

Intercultural Press, Inc.
P. O. Box 700
Yarmouth, MA 04096

Overseas Briefing Associates
210 East 36th Street
New York, NY 10016

The Society for Intercultural Education, Training, and Research
1414 22 Street NW, Suite 102
Washington, DC 20037

Country Updates, published by Intercultural Press, Inc.

The Cultural Environment of International Business, Vern Tepstra, Cincinnati: South-Western Publishing Co., 1978

Living Abroad, Ingemar Tobiorn, Chichester: John Wiley & Sons, 1982

Managing Cultural Differences, Phillip R. Harris and Robert T. Moran, Houston: Gulf, 1979

Survival Kit for Overseas Living, Robert L. Kohls, published by Intercultural Network, Inc., 1979.

Training for the Cross-Cultural Mind, published by The Society for Intercultural Education, Training, and Research, 1980.

Understanding Intercultural Communication, Larry A. Samovar, Richard E. Porter, and Nemi C. Jain, Belmont, CA: Wadsworth, 1972.

SUMMARY

International business communication is increasing in importance as more and more transactions occur in the global marketplace. This means that increasingly American workers and management will have to be comfortable engaging in business in an international context. Being knowledgeable about international business communication not only will enable you to be more successful in your job responsibilities but also will help you experience more satisfaction when you live abroad or make business trips.

Businesspersons involved with international business must be aware of the differences between the culture they are familiar with and the culture to which they are assigned. Important cultural elements include customs, values, language barriers, decision-making processes, status, and manners.

Another important area for those involved with international business is nonverbal communication, which does not have universal meaning. The important elements of nonverbal communication are posture, movement, gestures, space, paralanguage, eye contact, touching, and time.

If you are ever fortunate enough to receive an international assignment, prepare yourself thoroughly for the new experience. The more prepared you are, the more you will enjoy the experience.

REVIEW QUESTIONS

1. As international trade continues to increase, what changes in the study of international communication will become necessary?
2. Explain the concept of "an ethnocentric reaction" in international business communication.
3. Compare the different values of Americans and Asians and people in Middle Eastern countries.
4. What is the typical focus of the business decision-making process in Latin American countries?
5. What suggestions can help someone avoid or diminish written and oral language barriers in international business communication?
6. What are the differences in the body movements of Americans and those of people in many foreign cultures?
7. What is the significance of the smile as a nonverbal gesture in Japanese culture?
8. What does eye contact communicate to Americans, and how does this compare with its meaning in other cultures?
9. How is the American use of time different from that of foreign cultures?
10. Outline several suggestions to increase the effectiveness of your business letters to foreign readers.
11. What are some of the major differences between American and Japanese business letters?
12. Outline points to remember when planning a meeting in a foreign country.

APPLICATION PROBLEMS

1. You have been assigned the task of preparing a list of important behavioral rules for a group of ten Japanese students who will spend next semester on your campus. Prepare an outline of items and information you will include on your list of behavioral rules to help them integrate into the American culture.

2. Assume that you have the opportunity to work in an international branch office of your current employer. After you select the country, prepare a report that includes the following:
    a. A discussion of the stereotyped image of the people of that country. (If you can find a native of that country, discuss with him or her your stereotyped image to determine the accuracy of your perceptions.
    b. A discussion of the stereotyped image you perceive the natives of that country have of Americans. How accurate is that image?
    c. A discussion of the differences between your culture and the culture in the country you selected.
    d. A discussion of the differences between the nonverbal communication commonly used in the United States and the nonverbal communication used in the country you selected.
3. Obtain from an international student a business letter written in his or her native language. Ask the student to translate the letter into English. Prepare a report in which you discuss the differences and similarities between the translated letter and a comparable letter prepared by an American writer for an American reader.
4. Now prepare a letter for the international student you worked with in application problem 2. Either you or your instructor will select the situation about which you are writing. Adapt the content, format, and writing style so it is appropriate for your international reader.
5. Select ten types of nonverbal gestures Americans commonly use. In a conversation with two international students from two different countries, display these gestures and explain their meaning. Then determine whether each gesture means the same thing to each of these students. If the gesture means something else, determine its meaning. Then determine what gesture (if any) is used in the students' cultures to communicate the comparable nonverbal message communicated by each of your gestures.
6. Discuss with an international student how a business writer in the United States would structure a business letter delivering negative news to a reader. Find out from the international student how business letters in his or her country deliver negative news. Prepare a memo for your instructor outlining the similarities and differences identified in your discussion.
7. Ask an international student identify for you several common idioms used in his or her country. Ask the student translate these idioms into English. Determine whether you can give the correct meaning for each idiom. Prepare a memo for your instructor in which you identify the idioms and what they mean in the international student's culture.
8. Interview a business employee who has spent considerable time working abroad. Find out how he or she prepared for the assignment, how adequate he or she felt the preparation was, what he or she might do differently in preparing for another international assignment, and what his or her biggest adjustment was in working abroad. Prepare a memo for your instructor discussing your findings.
9. Select a company in your community that does business frequently with companies in other countries. Interview an employee whose job involves working with business employees in the other country. Ask the interviewee to identify the most significant challenges affecting his or her business dealings, what he or she has learned about working with the employees of the other company, and what kind of training he or she had that helped make this "international relationship" work.
10. Discuss in a memo to your instructor a situation you've experienced in which you could have been accused of being ethnocentric. If an identical situation occurred in the future, would you handle yourself and the situation differently? If so, how?

Pretest

Circle the "C" beside sentences 1–15 that are grammatically correctly and beside sentences 16–30 that are punctuated correctly. Circle the "I" beside any sentence that contains an error.

C I 1. Either John or Mary are available this afternoon.
C I 2. One of the boxes are here.
C I 3. Every person is accountable to his or her supervisor.
C I 4. The committee meet at two tomorrow afternoon.
C I 5. John, as well as his two cousins, are at John's parents for the weekend.
C I 6. Neither the book nor the reports is lost.
C I 7. His main concern at this time are his grades.
C I 8. Every one of the items are here.
C I 9. Either Bill or John will present his report at the meeting.
C I 10. Each student should take his or her completed assignment to the teacher in charge.
C I 11. The class will have their final exam on Monday.
C I 12. Whom is at the door?
C I 13. John is the person about whom I spoke.
C I 14. If I was him, I would go.
C I 15. She is the smarter of the three sisters.
C I 16. The manuscript has been finalized and it has been approved for duplication.
C I 17. I plan to see Bill on Monday, and see Mary on Tuesday.
C I 18. The book is on my desk, you may use it if you wish.
C I 19. Managers, who are aggressive and who work hard, are always assured of promotions in this company.
C I 20. I will call John Smith who is generally willing to help us in situations such as this.
C I 21. My decision, however, is not necessarily final.

C I 22. The report that is due Wednesday will contain some surprising facts.

C I 23. John's plan which he presented at Tuesday's meeting is sure to cause some concern among the office staff.

C I 24. To obtain the best results from your efforts you need to work closely with your supervisor.

C I 25. The company is planning to hire a new enthusiastic, energetic sales manager.

C I 26. I would like to help you with the problem, therefore, will you please see me this afternoon?

C I 27. A well known artist has been commissioned to restore the mural in the lobby.

C I 28. His three goals are the following, to get promoted quickly, to have the best sales performance among his colleagues, and eventually to become sales manager.

C I 29. A new mens' store will open next week.

C I 30. Fifty six years ago, the company nearly went bankrupt.

Answers: Following the correct answer for each item is a sequence of numbers that refers to the rule number pertaining to the sentence. An "A" preceding each number means that the rule can be found in Appendix A (Grammar); and "B" means that the rule can be found in Appendix B (Punctuation).

1. I A-3.5.
2. I A-3.2.
3. C A-3.5.
4. I A-3.1.
5. I A-3.8.
6. I A-3.7.
7. I A-3.1.
8. I A-3.5.
9. C A-4.8.
10. C A-4.8.
11. I A-4.3.
12. I A-4.14.
13. C A-4.15.
14. I A-2.1.3.1.
15. I A-5.3.2.
16. I B-1.3.1.
17. I B-1.3.3.
18. I B-1.3.2.
19. I B-1.6.1.2.1.
20. I B-1.6.1.2.
21. C B-1.6.1.4.
22. C B-1.6.1.2.1.
23. I B-1.6.1.2.
24. I B-1.2.1.
25. C B-1.4.1.
26. I B-2.3.1.
27. I B-4.1.1.
28. I B-3.1.1.
29. I B-5.4.
30. I B-4.3.1.

Posttest

Circle the "C" beside sentences 1–15 that are grammatically correct and beside sentences 16–30 that are punctuated correctly. Circle the "I" beside any sentence that contains an error.

C I 1. Either Bill or David is available to answer your question.
C I 2. One of the files is missing.
C I 3. Every person is accountable for their actions.
C I 4. The board meets tomorrow afternoon.
C I 5. The report, as well as the graphic aids, have been completed.
C I 6. Either the manager or his two subordinates is not telling the truth.
C I 7. David's main concern at this time are his finances.
C I 8. Each of the books are here.
C I 9. Either Mary or Bill will present their data at tomorrow's meeting.
C I 10. Every student is responsible for his/her materials.
C I 11. The subcommittee plans to have their meeting in the morning.
C I 12. The person who you saw in the mailroom is John's brother.
C I 13. Whom are you interested in hiring?
C I 14. If he was an astute manager, that problem would not have arisen.
C I 15. Of the two sisters, Mary is the taller one.
C I 16. The sales report is on my desk, but I have not seen the financial report as yet.
C I 17. The material you requested is out of stock but should be available for shipment next week.
C I 18. His car is at the garage, its transmission is not working properly.
C I 19. Hard-working employees, who toil until the job is completed, are well thought of here.
C I 20. John will call someone, who is familiar with the computer problem we have been experiencing.
C I 21. The report, therefore, should be of considerable help.

C I 22. Last month's sales report which came out yesterday revealed several significant trends.

C I 23. Mary's performance, that is always the best among the sales group, is being recognized by top management.

C I 24. With that thought in mind, will you please prepare a memo about John's latest decision?

C I 25. The company needs an aggressive, astute manager to replace Bill when he retires.

C I 26. My performance is comparable to John's performance, however, he always seems to have a better appraisal.

C I 27. John Smith, who is well-known for his expertise in financial analyses, is to be the keynote speaker.

C I 28. His strengths are the following; loyal, cooperative, and dedicated.

C I 29. The childrens' playground is new.

C I 30. Twenty-two years seems like a long time.

Answers: Following the correct answer for each item is a sequence of numbers that refers to the rule number pertaining to the sentence. An "A" preceding each number means that the rule can be found in Appendix A (Grammar); and "B" means that the rule can be found in Appendix B (Punctuation).

1. C A-3.5.
2. I A-3.2.
3. I A-3.5.
4. C A-3.1.
5. I A-3.8.
6. I A-3.7.
7. I A-3.1.
8. I A-3.5.
9. I A-4.8.
10. C A-4.8.
11. I A-4.3.
12. I A-4.15.
13. I A-4.15.
14. I A-2.1.3.1.
15. C A-5.3.2.
16. C B-1.3.1.
17. C B-1.3.3.
18. I B-1.3.2.
19. C B-1.6.1.2.
20. I B-1.6.1.2.
21. C B-1.6.1.4.
22. I B-1.6.1.2.
23. I B-1.6.1.2.
24. C B-1.2.1.
25. C B-1.4.1.
26. I B-2.3.1.
27. I B-4.1.1.
28. I B-3.1.1.
29. I B-5.4.
30. C B-4.3.1.

Appendix A: Grammar Usage

Correct grammar usage is critical to the success of your writing. Using grammar correctly in the material you write is expected—and essential. The information that follows provides coverage of grammar usage.

1. NOUNS

1.1. *Nouns* name a person, place, or thing.
1.2. Nouns have several properties, including the following:

1.2.1. Singular nouns: Nouns that refer to a single entity.

John's performance is exemplary. (*John's* and *performance* are singular nouns.)

1.2.2. Plural nouns: Nouns that refer to a multiple entity.

The managers are well informed. (*managers* is a plural noun.)

1.2.3. Proper nouns: Nouns that by custom are capitalized.

John went home early. (*John* is a proper noun.)

1.2.4. Common nouns: Nouns that by custom are not capitalized.

John went to the meeting. (*meeting* is a common noun.)

1.2.5. Possessive nouns: Nouns that show ownership; can be either proper or common; singular or plural.

John's office is occupied. (*John's* is a singular possessive noun in the proper form.)

1.2.6. The managers' performance is noted. (*managers'* is a plural possessive noun in the common form; *performance* is a singular noun.)

2. VERBS

2.1 *Verbs* describe an action.
2.2. Tense is the verb element that expresses time in relation to the action stated in the verb.

2.2.1. The three major tenses are present tense, past tense, and future tense. In addition, the three perfect tenses—present perfect, past perfect, and future perfect—are used to indicate a state of being or the state of a completed action. The progressive tenses—present progressive, past progressive, and future progressive—are used to indicate the state of progress on certain actions.

2.2.2. The principal parts of the verb—present, past, past participle, and present participle—are used to form the nine tenses mentioned in 2.2.1.

2.2.2.1. Regular verbs are verbs whose past and past perfect forms are developed by adding a *-d*, or *-ed* to the present form.

Present	Past	Past Participle	Present Participle
work	worked	worked	working
shave	shaved	shaved	shaving
paint	painted	painted	painting

2.2.2.2. Irregular verbs are verbs whose past and present participle forms cannot be developed by adding a *-d* or *-ed* to the present form.

Present	Past	Past Participle	Present Participle
do	did	done	doing
see	saw	seen	seeing
eat	are	eaten	eating
drink	drank	drunk	drinking

2.2.2.2.1. An auxiliary verb (*is*, *are*; *was*, *were*; *can*, *could*; *do*, *did*; *had*, *has*; *shall*, *should*; *will*, *would*) must be used with a verb in the past participle form.

I *did* my part. (past tense)

I *have done* my part. (past participle)

2.2.3. *Present tense* is used (1) to express present time or (2) to make statements that are always true.

I am at home. (statement that expresses present time)

I eat every day. (statement that is always true)

2.2.4. *Past tense* is used to express action that occurred in the past.

I worked yesterday. (past action)

John wrote a letter yesterday. (past action)

2.2.4.1. Using the past participle form of an irregular verb to express an action that should be stated in past tense is not possible.

I swum for an hour. (incorrect because *swum* is a past participle)

I swam for an hour. (correct because *swam* is past tense)

I drunk my coffee. (incorrect because *drunk* is a past participle)

I drank my coffee. (correct because *drank* is past tense)

I had drunk my coffee before they arrived. (correct because past participle *drunk* requires an auxiliary verb—*had*)

2.2.5. *Future tense* is used to express time in the future. The future tense is formed by inserting *shall* or *will* before the present tense of the verb.

2.2.5.1. To express simple future tense in ordinary conversation, use *will* with all three persons.

I will go to town this afternoon.

You will be able to do well on that project.

They will be here shortly.

2.2.5.2. To express simple future time in formal conversation, use *shall* with the first person (I, we) and *will* with the second person (you) and with the third person (he, she, it, they).

I shall be delighted to read your report when it arrives. (first person)

You will be delighted to know that I received your report (second person)

They will be in class until noon. (third person)

2.2.5.3. To express future determination, promise, or threat in ordinary conversation, use *will* with all three persons.

I will arrive at 5 P.M.

2.2.5.4. To express future determination or promise in formal conversation, use *will* with the first person and *shall* with the second or third person.

No matter what circumstances result, I will be there on Friday. (determination)

You shall return by dusk or be prepared to suffer the consequences. (threat)

We shall overcome our barrier. (determination)

2.2.6. *Present perfect tense* is used to refer to action started in the past that is completed at any moment before the present. The present perfect tense is formed by placing *have* or *has* before the past participle form of the verb (done, seen, eaten, drunk, etc.).

I have completed my homework. (*have* plus the past participle form of *complete*)

I have drunk all the coffee that was in the cup. (*have* plus the past participle form of *drink*)

2.2.7. *Past perfect tense* is used to refer to an action that was completed before another past action. This tense is formed by placing *had* before the past participle.

I had eaten my dinner before she arrived.

I had written the answers to the problem before I left.

2.2.8. *Future perfect tense* is used to refer to an action that will be completed before a specific time in the future. It is formed by adding the verb *shall have* or *will have* to the past participle.

We shall have completed the assignment by the time she arrives.

They will have completed the assignment by the time you arrive.

2.2.9 *Present progressive tense* is used to refer to an action that is still in progress. It is formed by adding the verb *am*, *is*, or *are* to the present participle form of the verb.

We are working as rapidly as we can. (present participle of *work*, which is *working*, is added to *are*)

I am doing the assignment now.

2.2.10. *Past progressive tense* is used to refer to an action that was in progress at some time in the past. It is formed by adding the verb *was* or *were* to the present participle form of the verb.

They were sleeping at the time the fire drill was conducted. (present participle of *sleep*, which is *sleeping*, is added to *were*)

2.2.11. *Future progressive tense* is used to refer to an action that will be in progress at some future time. It is formed by adding the verb *shall be* or *will be* to the present participle.

We shall be working on the assignment this weekend when you are in Washington. (present participle of *work*, which is *working*, is added to *shall*)

I will be sleeping when you arrive.

2.1. The mood of the verb is used to indicate the intent of the statement: a fact, a command, or a wish, for example.

2.1.1. *Indicative mood.* This is the mood used to express a fact or ask a question.

They will go home tomorrow. (fact)

When does he plan to leave? (question)

2.1.2. *Imperative mood.* This is the mood used to express a command or to make a request.

Do your assignment before you return to class. (command)

When you come to class, please be prepared. (request)

2.1.3. *Subjunctive mood.* This is the mood used to express a statement that is contrary to fact or to make a wish.

I wish I were going with you. (wish)

I wish it were summer. (contrary to fact; because it is fall)

2.1.3.1. When a verb in the present tense is used, the subjunctive form of the verb *to be* requires the use of *were.*

If I were angry, I would tell you.

2.1.3.2. When the auxiliary (helping) form of a verb is required in the subjunctive mood, *be* precedes the remainder of the verb.

She insisted that she be given a chance to redeem herself.

2.1.3.3. In a sentence that is contrary to fact (which requires the subjunctive mood) and that refers to past time, the correct verb is *had been.*

If they *had been* here yesterday, they would certainly have been proud of you.

2.3. Voice of verbs is used to indicate whether the subject of the verb is (1) performing the action or (2) being acted upon.

2.3.1. If the subject is performing the action, a verb in the *active voice* is being used.

The student prepared the report. (subject, *student*, performed action, *prepared*)

The girl ate the dinner. (subject, *girl*, performed action, *ate*)

2.3.2. If the subject is being acted upon, a verb in the *passive voice* is used.

The report was prepared by the student. (subject, *report*, was acted upon, *prepared*)

The dinner was eaten by the girl. (subject, *dinner*, was acted upon, *eaten*)

2.3.3. The active voice is suited for straightforward, direct, concise writing of a personalized nature. Most business writing should use active voice.

2.3.4. The passive voice is suited for writing of an impersonal nature. It is particularly suited for removing a harsh, blunt tone from writing. Some writers prefer to use passive voice when making suggestions or recommendations as a means of avoiding a dictatorial tone.

I recommend that you take drastic action. (active)

Recommended is that you take drastic action. (passive)

2.3.5. Do not frequently shift back and forth from active voice to passive voice. To do so creates an awkward writing style that is difficult to read.

Poor: John wrote the report. (active)

The report was typed by Mary. (passive)

Sally proofread and duplicated the report. (active)

The various copies were distributed by Tom. (passive)

Improved: After John wrote the report, Mary typed it. (active)

Sally proofread and duplicated the report, and Tom distributed the various copies. (active)

3. SUBJECT-VERB AGREEMENT

3.1. The subject of a sentence and its verb must agree in number and in person.

He is the new professor in the department. (Singular subject *he* and verb *is* agree in number.)

They are planning to arrive at noon. (Plural subject *they* and verb *are* agree in number.)

John and Mary are enrolled in the same class. (Compound subject *John* and *Mary* and verb *are* agree in number.)

You are too kind to him. (Second-person subject *you* always takes a plural verb even though the subject *you* refers to one person.)

3.2. Words that fall between the subject and verb are not considered when determining whether to use a plural verb in the sentence.

One of the professor's books has been returned. (Singular subject *one* agrees with singular verb *has*, although the plural noun—*books*—falls between the subject and verb.)

The contents of the report are questionable. (Plural subject *contents* agrees with plural verb *are*, although a word—*report*—falls between the subject and verb.)

3.3. Two singular subjects, when joined with *and*, form a compound subject and require a plural verb.

John and Bill are roommates in college. (Singular subjects *John*, *Bill* require a plural verb.)

3.4. Two nouns referring to the same subject require a singular verb.

Mr. Brown, our secretary and treasurer, is to sign the document. (Two nouns—*secretary* and *treasurer*—refer to the same subject and therefore require a singular verb.)

3.5. *Each*, *everybody*, *anybody*, *either*, *every*, *neither*, *a*, *an*, and *another* are always singular and require the use of a singular verb even though the subject may consist of two or more singular words.

Neither he nor she is to attend the meeting. (Two singular subjects—*he*, *she*—require a singular verb—*is*—when preceded by *neither*.)

He and she are to attend the meeting. (Two singular subjects—*he*, *she*—joined by *and* require a plural verb.)

3.6. A subject comprised of two plural words and connected by *either, or; neither, nor; not only, but also* requires a plural verb.

Either the presidents or the vice presidents of the student organizations are to file the report. (Two plural words— *presidents, vice presidents*—require a plural verb.)

3.7. If the subject in a sentence is composed of both singular and plural words and the words are connected by *either, or; neither, nor; not only, but also*, the plural word should be placed nearer the verb, which should be in the plural form.

Neither Mary nor her coworkers are planning to leave the building at 5 P.M. (Singular word—*Mary*—followed by plural word—*coworkers*—requires plural verb.)

3.8. The number of the subject determines the number of the verb when phrases such as *including, as well as, in addition, together with,* intervene between the subject and verb.

Your report, including the appendices, is due on Friday. (Singular subject—*report*—followed by intervening phrase that contains a plural word—*appendices*—still requires a singular verb—*is*.)

Mary, as well as her two sisters, plans to go home this weekend. (Singular subject—*Mary*—requires singular verb—*plans*— although a phrase containing a plural word—*sisters*—intervenes.)

3.9. The number of the verb is determined by the number of the noun to which such words as *any, none, most, all* refer.

Do any of the students present have questions? (The word *any* refers to *students*, which is plural; therefore, a plural verb— *do have*—is required.)

All of the class was here. (The word *all* refers to *class*, which is singular; therefore, a singular verb—*was*—is required.)

All of the class members were here. (The word *all* refers to *members*; therefore, a plural word—*were*—is required.)

3.10. The verb agrees with the subject rather than the predicate complement.

His main worry at the moment is his grades. (Singular subject—*worry*—requires singular verb—*is*; *grades* is the predicate complement.)

Their chief goal is to become good students. (Singular subject—*goal*—requires singular verb—*is*; *students* is the predicate complement.)

3.11. To determine subject-verb agreement easily in an inverted sentence, phrase the sentence in the normal order to ascertain the correct number of the verb to use.

Inverted:	Together we will go to the movie.
Rephrased:	We will go to the movie together. (Plural subject—*we*— and plural verb—*go*—agree.)
Inverted:	Of these facts we are sure.
Rephrased:	We are sure of these facts. (Plural subject—*we*—and plural verb—*are*—agree.)

4. PRONOUNS

4.1. A *pronoun* is used in place of or refers to a noun (*she* is used for *Mary*; *he* is used for *John*; *it* is used for *car*).

4.2. Pronouns have qualities of number, person, and gender.

4.2.1. Number refers to—

Singular (I, he, she)

Plural (we, they)

4.2.2. Person refers to—

First person (I)—person speaking

Second person (you)—person to whom you are speaking

Third person (he, she, they, it)—persons or things about whom you are speaking

4.2.3. Gender refers to the sex of the pronoun.

Masculine—he

Feminine—she

Neuter—it

4.3. A pronoun must agree with its antecedent (the noun that is replaced by the pronoun) in number, person, and gender.

Jim said that he could do the assignment. The pronoun *he* agrees with *Jim*, the antecedent, in number (singular), person (first), and gender (masculine).

The members of the organization are to express their views. The pronoun *their* agrees with *members* in number (plural), person (third), and gender (neuter).

The committee presented its report. The antecedent *it* agrees with *committee* in number (singular), person (third), and gender (neuter).

4.4. When the antecedent consists of two nouns joined by *and*, a plural pronoun should be used.

May and Susan plan to take their makeup exams this afternoon. (*their* agrees with plural subject in number.)

4.5. When the antecedent consists of two singular nouns joined by *or* or *nor*, a singular pronoun should be used.

Either Ted or Mary will have to give me his/her book. (*his/her* is required because two singular nouns—*Ted, Mary*—are joined by *or.*)

4.6. When the antecedent consists of two plural nouns joined by *or* or *nor*, a plural pronoun should be used.

Either the Smiths or the Browns will have to use their car. (*their* is required because of two plural nouns—*Smiths, Browns*—joined by *or.*)

4.7. When the antecedent refers to both males and females, a masculine and feminine pronoun should be used.

Everyone should take his/her seat.

4.8. When any of the following indefinite pronouns are used, a third person singular pronoun should be used: *anyone*, *each*, *every*, *either*, *neither*, *no one*, *anybody*, *someone*.

Anyone who has not already done so needs to turn in his/her report soon. (*his/her* agrees with *anyone.*)

Every person who plans to go to the picnic is responsible for finding his/her own ride. (*his/her* agrees with *every person.*)

4.9. When any of the following indefinite pronouns are used, a plural pronoun is required: *many*, *both*, *others*, *several*.

Many of the students have completed their assignments. (*their* agrees with *many.*)

Both of them are ready to return their books. (*their* agrees with *both.*)

4.10. The indefinite pronouns that follow may be either singular or plural, depending on the noun or pronoun to which they refer: *any*, *more*, *most*, *none*, *all*, *some*.

Most of them are ready to turn in their projects. (*their* agrees with plural *them.*)

Most of the report is completed, but it has not yet been typed. (*it* agrees with singular *report.*)

4.11. Case refers to the form of pronouns that show their relation to other words in a sentence. Three cases of pronouns are found: subjective, objective, and possessive.

4.11.1. The following illustrates the three cases for the following pronouns: I, you, he, she, it, we, they, who.

Subjective: I you he she it we they who

Objective: me you him her it us them whom

Possessive: my your his her its our their whom

4.11.2. The *subjective case* is used as the subject of a verb or with a linking verb (form of the verb *be*)

We did our homework. (*we* is used as a subject of the sentence.)

John is the one who called you. (*is* is a linking verb and should be followed by a pronoun in the subjective case.)

4.11.3. The *objective case* is used as an object of a verb, the object of a preposition, and the subject of an infinitive.

They had dinner for my brother and me last night. (object of verb)

Just between you and me, I don't like his decision. (object of preposition)

Professor Jones asked me to stay after class. (subject of an infinitive)

4.11.4. The *possessive case* is used to show possession and to modify a gerund, which is a verb form used as a noun and ends with an *-ing*.

This is my book. (possessive)

I appreciate your talking with him. (*your* modifies the gerund, *talking*.)

4.12. In a clause in which the verb is omitted, the pronoun that precedes the omitted verb should be in the same case as if the verb were present.

She is taller than I. (This sentence is actually saying, "She is taller than I am.")

I have been here longer than they. (". . . than they have been.")

4.13 Pronouns ending in *-self* (myself, yourself, himself, herself, themselves, etc.) are used (1) to refer the verb's actions back to the subject or (2) to emphasize a noun or pronoun expressed earlier in the sentence.

They are putting themselves in a precarious position (*themselves* refers the verb's actions—*putting*—back to the subject *they*)

I will go myself. (*myself* emphasizes *I*)

4.14. *Who* and *whoever* are pronouns in the subjective case. They can be used whenever another pronoun in the subjective case (I, you, she, he, etc.) can be substituted in the sentence for *who* or *whoever*. For example, in the sentence, "Who is there?" *he* could be substituted for *who*. (See 4.15 for the use of *whom* or *whomever*.)

Who is there? (he is there; therefore, *who*)

Who went with you? (he went with you; therefore, *who*)

John is the one who I think should go. (he should go; therefore, *who*)

Whoever succeeds is fortunate. (he succeeds; therefore, *whoever*)

4.15. *Whom* and *whomever* are pronouns in the objective case. They can be used whenever another pronoun in the objective case (me, him, her, us, them, etc.) can be substituted in the sentence for *whom* or *whomever*. For example, in the sentence, "With whom am I to go?," *him* could be substituted for *whom* (I am to go with him).

The manager to whom I referred was Ms. Johnson. (I was referred to *her*.)

Whom do you plan to support? (they plan to support *him*.)

For whom is this report? (this report is for *her*.)

4.16. The use of the relative pronouns, *who*, *which*, and *that* should be guided by the following:

4.16.1. *Who* is used when referring to individual persons.

John is the student who received the highest grade on the exam.

4.16.2. *That* is used when referring to a type or class.

John is the type of person that works well with others.

4.16.3. *Which* is used to introduce nonessential clauses that pertain to objects, animals, or places.

John's paper, which was handed in late, had numerous errors. ("which was handed in late" is a nonessential clause.)

4.16.4. *That* is used to introduce essential clauses that pertain to objects, animals, or places.

The road that I take to work is very rough. ("that I take to work" is an essential clause; and without it, the meaning of the sentence is changed.)

5. ADJECTIVES

5.1. As modifiers of nouns or pronouns, *adjectives* are used to describe, to quantify, or to identify.

A small house—a description

A few pens—a quantity

The man with the red hair—an identity

5.1.1. Adjectives cannot be used to modify verbs, other adjectives, or adverbs. Adverbs are used for this purpose. (See Section 6.)

5.2. An adjective should be used in the following situations:

5.2.1. When the word that follows the verb refers to the subject of the sentence.

That picture is beautiful. (*beautiful* refers to picture, which is the subject of the sentence.)

5.2.2. After a verb referring to one of the senses (sound, look, taste, smell, feel).

She feels bad. (not *badly*, which is an adverb)

John sounds poor. (not *poorly*, which is an adverb)

David looks neat. (not *neatly*, which is an adverb)

5.2.3. After a linking verb (form of *to be*, *become*, *seem*, *appear*, *grow*).

She seems to be well.

He grew tall.

She appears to be sick.

5.3. Adjectives show comparison in three degrees: positive, comparative, and superlative.

Positive	Comparative	Superlative
tall	taller	tallest
small	smaller	smallest
big	bigger	biggest
good	better	best
bad	worse	worst
productive	more productive	most productive
efficient	less efficient	least efficient

5.3.1. The *comparative* form is used when comparing two persons or two things.

She is prettier than her sister.

He is the more efficient of the two workers.

5.3.2. The *superlative* form is used when comparing three or more persons or things.

Of the three sisters, she is the prettiest.

He is the most efficient worker in the department.

6. ADVERBS

6.1. *Adverbs*, which modify verbs, adjectives, and other adverbs, describe how, when, where, or to what degree.

He ran quickly. (how)

She came early. (when)

John scored well on the test. (how much)

6.2. An adverb should be used when the word that follows the verb refers to the action of the verb.

He talks slowly. (not slow)

She works rapidly. (not rapid)

6.3. Although most adverbs end in *-ly*, an *-ly* ending is not a definitive characteristic of all adverbs, because some adjectives also end in *-ly*. Examples are costly, timely, matronly, lively, lovely, and friendly.

Her accident was costly. (*costly* modifies *accident*, which is the subject of the sentence, and, therefore, *costly* must be an adjective.)

John's advice was timely. (*timely* modifies *advice* and, therefore, is an adjective.)

John's advice was very timely. (*very* is an adverb modifying the adjective *timely.*)

6.4. As with adjectives, adverbs show comparison in three degrees: positive, comparative, and superlative.

Positive	*Comparative*	*Superlative*
well	better	best
soon	sooner	soonest
bright	brighter	brightest
often	more often	most often
hard	harder	hardest

He arrived sooner than she. (comparative)

The sun shone more brightly today than yesterday. (comparative)

Of all the students in the class, he works the hardest. (superlative)

6.5. Although the adverb typically follows the verb it modifies, it may be placed before the verb. A guiding rule is to place the adverb where it clearly conveys the meaning that was intended. In the following examples, the adverb is placed in several locations in the sentence.

Only I did the assignment.

I only did the assignment.

I did only the assignment.

I did the assignment only.

6.6. The word *real* should not be used when *very* is required.

She is real beautiful. (incorrect)

She is very beautiful. (correct)

7. CONJUNCTIONS

7.1. *Conjunctions* connect verbs, phrases, or clauses to other parts of the sentence. In certain instances, conjunctions are used to show the relative importance of the ideas conveyed in the words, phrases, or clauses.

7.2. Conjunctions appear as coordinating conjunctions, subordinating conjunctions, or correlative conjunctions.

7.2.1. *Coordinating conjunctions* are used to convey a relationship of equal importance. They include *and, but, or, for, nor, yet,* and *so.*

Their book is here, but their workbook is missing.

7.2.2. *Subordinating conjunctions* are used to convey a relationship of unequal importance. They include *when, where, how, since, because, although.* A subordinate conjunction joins a subordinate clause and a principal clause.

I have to hurry because I am behind schedule.

7.2.3. *Correlative conjunctions* are used in pairs, with the first conjunctions introducing and the second conjunction connecting the elements. They include *both, and*; *not only, but also*; *either, or*; *neither, nor.*

8. PREPOSITIONS

8.1. *Prepositions* are used to join a noun or pronoun to some other word in the sentence in order to show a relationship. Examples of prepositions are *by, for, in, to, of, before, at, up, with, from.*

8.2. Prepositional phases, which consist of a preposition and its object, should be placed as closely as possible to the words they modify.

8.3. Generally, you should avoid ending a sentence with a preposition.

What play is she appearing in? (incorrect)

In what play is she appearing? (correct)

8.4 *Like* and *as* have specific uses in sentences, and their uses are not interchangeable.

8.4.1 *Like* is a preposition and is followed by a noun or pronoun, not followed by a verb.

His father looks like his grandfather.

8.4.2 *As* is a conjunction and is used to join clauses or phrases containing verbs.

It looks as if it will snow. (correct)

It looks like it will snow. (incorrect)

Appendix B: Punctuation

Punctuation marks arc of two types: internal and terminal. The most common internal punctuation mark is the comma, with the period the most common terminal mark. Punctuation marks facilitate the ease with which material is read.

1. COMMA

1.1. Appositives

1.1.1. An *appositive* is composed of one or more words that provide additional information about the noun(s) it(they) immediately follow(s).

1.1.1.1. Nonessential appositives (appositives that can be eliminated from the sentence without changing its meaning) are separated from the remainder of the sentence by commas.

John's youngest brother, Bill, will be here for the holidays. (John can have only one youngest brother; therefore *Bill* is not essential to the meaning of the sentence.)

Mr. Jones, my favorite professor, is moving to California.

1.1.1.2. Essential (or restrictive) appositives (appositives that cannot be eliminated from the sentence without changing its meaning) are *not* separated from the remainder of the sentence by commas.

My friend Mary is going to help Susan. (You have more than one friend; therefore, you have to identify which friend is going to help; consequently, *Mary* is an essential appositive.)

My grandmother Susan is spending the holidays with us.

1.2. Complex sentences

1.2.1. In a *complex sentence*, a comma is used to separate an introductory dependent clause from the independent clause.

If you plan to attend the meeting, please call John. (Because the sentence contains an introductory dependent clause, it is separated from the independent clause by a comma.)

When you see Bill, please give him a message for me.

Please call John if you plan to attend the meeting. (Because the independent clause precedes the dependent clause, the two clauses are not separated by commas.)

Will you please give Bill a message from me when you see him?

1.3. Compound sentences

1.3.1. In a *compound sentence*, the two independent clauses are separated by a comma when the two clauses are joined by a coordinating conjunction (*and, but, or, nor, for, yet*).

The office has been painted, but the floor has not been cleaned. (A coordinating conjunction separates the two independent clauses; therefore, a comma is needed.)

Mary has been in San Antonio for three days, but I expect her in the office tomorrow.

1.3.2. In a compound sentence in which the coordinating conjunction is missing between the two independent clauses, use a semicolon to separate the two clauses. To use a comma in this situation results in a comma splice (separating two independent clauses with a comma when the conjunction is missing).

The office has been painted; the floor has not been cleaned. (The coordinating conjunction is missing; therefore, use a semicolon in place of a comma.

Mary has been out of the office for three days; I expect her here tomorrow.

1.3.3. Do not place a comma before a coordinating conjunction in a simple sentence that contains a compound predicate.

I will be in Dallas tonight and in Houston tomorrow. (This is a simple sentence with a compound predicate; therefore, do not put a comma before the conjunction.)

Bill went to the movie and will not return until 11.

1.4. Coordinate adjectives

1.4.1. *Coordinate adjectives* involve the use of two adjectives that equally modify the same noun. When the word *and* is removed from between them, the two adjectives are separated by a comma. An effective means to determine whether the comma is needed is to insert *and* in the sentence; if the sentence makes sense with *and*, then the comma is needed in its place when *and* is omitted.

She is a dedicated, well-liked employee. (The comma is needed because this sentence will make sense when *and* is inserted between *dedicated* and *well-liked*.)

John's cheerful, fun-loving personality is appreciated.

1.4.1.1. If the sentence does not make sense when you insert *and*, then the comma is not used when *and* is omitted.

He was driving a beautiful red car. (To put *and* between *beautiful* and *red* does not make sense; therefore, a comma should not be placed between *beautiful* and *red*.)

She has straw blond hair.

1.5. Direct address

1.5.1. When you use in a sentence the name of the individual whom you are addressing directly or another noun to refer to that individual, the individual's name is separated from the remainder of the sentence by a comma.

John, will you please help me? (Because you are addressing *John*, his name is followed by a comma.)

Will you please answer the phone for me, Mary?

Yes, sir, I will be glad to help you. (The word *sir* is used as a substitute for the name of the individual being addressed; therefore, the word is separated from the remainder of the sentence by commas.)

I will be glad to help you, Father.

1.6. Nonessential expressions

1.6.1. *Nonessential expressions* are those that can be eliminated from the sentence without changing the meaning of the sentence. They can appear at the beginning of the sentence, in the middle of the sentence, or at the end of the sentence. They can also be composed of a word, a phrase, or a clause.

1.6.1.1. *Nonessential words, phrases, or clauses* (at the beginning, in the middle, or at the end of the sentence) are separated from the remainder of the sentence by commas.

No, Mr. Johnson will not be able to see you this afternoon. (The introductory word, *no*, is not essential to the meaning of the sentence; therefore, it can be removed from the remainder of the sentence.)

Yes, he plans to be here at noon.

Before its submission, will you please verify the numbers in the data section? (The introductory phrase, *before its submission*, is not essential to the meaning of the sentence; therefore, it is separated from the remainder of the sentence by commas.)

Prior to your leaving, will you please turn off the lights?

1.6.1.1.1. Exception: When the introductory nonessential phrase makes reference to time and is short, the comma can be omitted.

By morning he will be in Dallas. (The introductory phrase, *by morning*, is not essential and makes reference to time; therefore, the comma can be omitted.)

In time he will be knowledgeable about the process.

Chisolm House, which is the oldest restaurant in Flagstaff, caters to young professionals. (The phrase, *which is the oldest restaurant in Flagstaff*, is a nonessential expression, which is separated from the remainder of the sentence by commas.)

John's car, which is an import, is his pride and joy.

John's pride and joy is his new car, which is an import. (The phrase, *which is an import*, is a nonessential expression that is separated from the remainder of the sentence by commas.)

Mary's house is unique, because it is built on the side of a hill.

1.6.1.2. Nonessential clauses, which are often preceded by either *which* or *who*, can be removed from the sentence without changing its meaning. Therefore, nonessential clauses are set off by commas.

Mary's book, which I put on your desk, will be quite helpful. (The clause, *which I put on your desk*, can be removed without changing the meaning of the sentence; therefore, it is set off by commas because it is not essential.)

David's new car, which is green, cost nearly $22,000.

Bill Johnson, who is Bob's supervisor, has had twenty years of managerial experience. (The clause, *who is Bob's supervisor*, can be removed without changing the meaning of the sentence; therefore, it is not essential and is set off by commas.)

My brother, who is governor of South Dakota, has always been interested in politics.

1.6.1.2.1. Essential clauses are those that if removed will change the meaning of the sentence. Therefore, they are not set off by commas. Essential clauses are often preceded by *that*.

The house that burned this morning has historical significance. (The clause *that burned this morning* is essential; therefore, it is not surrounded by commas.)

The boat that left the dock earlier will sleep eight adults.

1.6.1.3. *Parenthetical expressions*, which are set off by commas, are words or phrases that interrupt the flow of a sentence.

You will, of course, be compensated for your expenses. (The expression *of course*, interrupts the flow of the sentence; therefore, it is set off by commas.)

Ms. Johnson, the individual whom you recently recommended for the opening, was just hired this morning.

1.6.1.4. Transitional expressions include such words or phrases as *therefore, moreover, however, namely, as a result, of course.* When they separate two independent clauses in a compound sentence, they are preceded by a semicolon and followed by a comma. When they appear in the middle of an independent clause, they are surrounded by commas.

He will be in the office tomorrow; therefore, I will be able to talk to him then. (The two independent clauses are separated by the transitional expression *therefore*; consequently, it is preceded by a semicolon and followed by a comma.)

John wants to help you; however, he will be unable to do so.

His schedule, therefore, has been changed. (The transitional expression appears in the middle of the sentence; therefore, it is surrounded by commas.)

He will, of course, be available to help you.

1.6.1.5. When words, phrases, or clauses interrupt the flow of the sentence, they are always considered as nonessential and are separated from the other parts of the sentence by commas.

I can help you tomorrow, if that is convenient for you. (The clause *that is convenient for you* interrupts the flow of the sentence; therefore, it is separated from the remainder of the sentence by commas.)

Your partial order can be sent immediately or, if you prefer, next week when the backordered items are available.

1.7. Omission of verb

1.7.1. When a sentence is composed of two clauses, with the same verb appearing in both clauses, the verb can be omitted from the second clause, with a comma used in its place. In some instances, both the subject and the verb are omitted from the second clause.

The girls will leave in the morning, and the boys, in the afternoon. (The verb *will leave* appears in both clauses; however, in the second clause, it can be omitted and replaced by a comma.)

In English, he earned an A; in Spanish, a B.

1.8. Series

1.8.1. When three or more words, phrases, or clauses compose a unit, the various items of the unit are separated by commas. Normally, the word *and* or *or* is used between the last two items in the unit.

John, Bill, and Susan plan to be here for the holidays. (Because three words compose the series, the various elements in the series are separated by commas.)

Yellow, white, and green are the colors in her new dress.

1.8.2. When the word *and* or *or* is used between each of the items in the unit, the commas are omitted.

Red and blue and white are patriotic colors. (Because *and* appears between each item in the unit, the commas are not used.)

Yellow and white and green are the colors in her new dress.

1.9. State

1.9.1. When the city and state are used together in a sentence, the name of the state is surrounded by commas.

Chicago, Illinois, is the location of O'Hare Airport. (The use of the city and the state requires that the state be surrounded by commas.)

The meeting will be held in New Haven, Connecticut, the home of Yale University.

1.10. Year

1.10.1. When a sentence contains a date composed of the month, day, and year (in that order), surround the year by commas.

John plans to retire on January 1, 2000, which will mark the end of his thirty-fifth year at Arco. (Because the sentence contains an expression with the month, day, and year, the year is surrounded by commas.)

July 4, 1776, is an important day for Americans to remember.

John plans to retire January 2000 from his position at Arco. (Because the date is missing one of the elements, the year is not surrounded by commas.)

March 199x is eagerly awaited.

2. SEMICOLONS

2.1. Compound sentence

2.1.1. When the coordinating conjunction is missing between the two independent clauses in a compound sentence, a semicolon separates the two independent clauses. To use a comma in this location results in a comma splice.

John was here this morning; he will not be here this afternoon. (Because the coordinating conjunction—*but*—is missing, a semicolon is needed in place of a comma.)

The books have arrived; the reports have not arrived.

2.1.2. When a coordinating conjunction is used to separate the two independent clauses in a compound sentence but one or both of the independent clauses contains a comma, then a semicolon is used before the coordinating conjunction.

I will, however, be glad to help you tomorrow; but I am not able to help you today. (Because the first independent clause contains commas, then a semicolon is used to separate the two independent clauses.)

John, will you please send the report immediately; you need not be concerned about the production data.

2.2. Series

2.2.1. When commas are found in a series, then the items composing the series are separated by semicolons.

He has lived in Denver, Colorado; Austin, Texas; and Tulsa, Oklahoma. (Because the various items composing the series have commas, semicolons are used to separate the items.)

The following individuals have been invited to the seminar: Pat Jones, president; Sally Brown, vice president; and Mary Johnson, treasurer.

2.3. Transitional expressions

2.3.1. When a transitional expression separates two independent clauses, use a semicolon before and a comma after the transitional expression. Examples of transitional expressions are *therefore*, *moreover*, *however*, *consequently*, *hence*, *accordingly*, *namely*, *nevertheless*, *furthermore*, *for example*, and *otherwise*.

He will be out of the office tomorrow; therefore, you will be able to use his parking space. (Because this sentence is composed of two independent clauses and a transitional expression, a semicolon is placed before and a comma after the expression.)

Your report was well written; furthermore, it was well organized.

2.3.2. To use a comma rather than a semicolon before the transitional expression results in a comma splice.

3. COLON

3.1. Lists, explanations, or examples

3.1.1. When a list, an explanation, or an example follows a clause in which *the following*, *as follows*, or *follows* appears, a colon separates the two elements.

His reasons are as follows: The company cannot afford to hire additional people at this time nor can it afford to replace equipment. (The expression *as follows* requires the use of a colon.)

The following are his favorite colors: red, blue, and green.

His reasons are that the company cannot afford to hire additional people at this time nor can it afford to replace equipment. (The colon is not needed because the word *follows* or *following* is not present.)

His favorite colors are red, blue, and green.

The following three items are needed: money, equipment, and raw materials. (Because of *the following*, a colon is needed.)

The following three colors are his favorite: red, blue, and green.

3.1.1.1. Note that when an independent clause follows the colon, then the first word of the clause is capitalized. When a list of words or a dependent clause follows, then the first word of the list or clause is not capitalized.

3.1.2. When the words, phrases, or clauses that follow such expressions as *for example*, *namely*, and *that is* explain the first part of the sentence, place a colon before the expression.

John has several favorite responsibilities: namely, evaluating personnel, preparing year-end reports, and compiling employment data. (Because the words that follow *namely* explain the first part of the sentence, a colon is placed before *namely*.)

Mary prefers earth-tone colors: for example, taupe, rust, and beige.

3.2. A colon should not be placed after such expressions as *are* or *were* when doing so separates a verb from its complement or object.

Bill's favorite hobbies are coin collecting, reading, and fishing. (A colon is not used after *are*; placing a colon here will result in the separation of a verb from its complement.)

4. HYPHENS

4.1. Compound words

4.1.1. When two or more words are used as a one-word modifier and they precede the word being modified, the two words are joined by a hyphen.

A well-known author will be our keynote speaker. (Because *well* and *known* both modify *author*, they are hyphenated.)

Eating too much fat presents a high-risk factor.

An author who is well known will be our keynote speaker. (Because *well* and *known* follow *author*, the words are not hyphenated.)

Eating too much fat presents a high risk.

4.2. Prefixes and suffixes

4.2.1. A number of prefixes and one suffix (*elect*) are hyphenated.

John, a self-motivated employee, will have a productive career. (The prefix *self* is followed by a hyphen.)

The semi-indirect approach is best.

Mr. Jones, the individual who hired me, is president-elect of the Dawkins School Board. (The suffix *-elect* needs to be hyphenated.)

The treasurer-elect plans to attend the meeting.

4.3. Compound numbers

4.3.1. Hyphenate compound numbers twenty-one to ninety-nine when they appear as words.

Forty-two books are on order. (Because *forty-two* is a compound number, it is hyphenated.)

Twenty-three is the magical number.

4.4. Words than end in *-ly*

4.4.1. Words ending in *-ly* that precede a participle and a noun are not hyphenated.

His rapidly completed assignment was well done. (Because *rapidly* is followed by a participle and a noun—*completed assignment*—*rapidly* is not hyphenated.)

The newly hired employee is excellent.

5. APOSTROPHES

5.1. To form the possessive of a singular noun not ending in an *s* or *s* sound, add an apostrophe and an *s*.

John's car is two years old. (Because *John* is a singular word not ending in an *s* or *s* sound, an apostrophe and an *s* are added to form the possessive.)

Mary's book is overdue.

5.2. To form the possessive of a singular noun ending in an *s* or *s* sound when an additional syllable is formed by pronouncing the possessive, add an apostrophe and an *s*.

Chris's office is on the third floor. (Because an additional syllable is formed when pronouncing *Chris's*, the apostrophe and *s* are added.)

This is the Harris's house.

5.3. To form the possessive of a plural word ending in *s*, add only the apostrophe.

The customers' accounts are up to date. (Because *customers*, which is a plural word, already ends in *s*, only the apostrophe is needed.)

The dogs' leashes are wearing thin.

5.4. To form the possessive of a plural word not ending in *s*, add an apostrophe and an *s*.

The Men's Department is on the second floor. (Because *men* is a plural word that does not end in *s*, the possessive is formed by adding an apostrophe and *s*.)

The children's area is on the second floor.

6. DASH

6.1. The dash rather than commas is used to set off nonessential expressions that need special emphasis.

John's report—which arrived this morning—will be quite helpful. (The phrase *which arrived this morning* is nonessential. To give it special emphasis, it can be separated from the remainder of the sentence by dashes.)

Bill, John, and Susan—my sister's three children—will be here for the holidays.

6.2. The dash can be used to set off a nonessential expression that contains internal commas.

Bill Jones—who is a loyal, trusted employee—will retire on June 1. (Because the nonessential expression contains an internal comma, dashes are used to separate the expression from the remainder of the sentence.)

Mary—who is my longtime, dedicated assistant—is to be promoted in the next two weeks.

7. PARENTHESIS

7.1. Place the terminal punctuation mark (period, question mark, exclamation mark) outside the parenthesis when only the last part of the sentence contains parentheses; otherwise, place the terminal punctuation mark inside the parenthesis.

What are your plans for tomorrow (Wednesday)? (Because only a part of the sentence involves the use of parentheses, the parenthesis is placed inside the question mark.)

John lives in Lincoln (Nebraska).

7.2. Place commas, semicolons, and colons outside the parenthesis.

John lives in Lincoln (Nebraska), but Susan lives in Kansas City. (Commas are placed outside the parenthesis.)

John lives in Lincoln (Nebraska); Susan lives in Kansas City.

8. QUOTATION MARKS

8.1. Commas and periods are always placed inside quotation marks, but colons and semicolons are always placed outside quotation marks.

"She will be glad to help you," replied Mary. (Commas are always placed inside quotation marks.)

I said, "I will be glad to help you tomorrow"; however, I am not able to help you today. (Semicolons are always placed outside quotation marks.)

8.2. Question marks and exclamation marks are placed inside quotation marks when the question or exclamation mark pertains to a portion of the sentence. But when the question or exclamation mark pertains to the entire sentence, the mark is placed outside the quotation marks.

He yelled "Run"! (Because the exclamation mark pertains to the entire sentence, the exclamation mark is placed outside the quotation marks.)

My supervisor said, "This is excellent!" (Because the exclamation mark pertains to a portion of the sentence, the mark is placed inside the quotation marks.)

Appendix C: Letter and Memorandum Format

USE THE RIGHT PAPER

High-quality paper should be used for letterheads as well as for envelopes. To save money, purchase letterhead paper in a lighter weight for use as envelopes. Therefore, you may use a 20-pound or 24-pound bond paper for letterhead and a 16-pound paper for mailing envelopes. The use of good-quality paper is important because the print stands out more clearly.

Most business letters are typed on 8½- by 11-inch stationery, imprinted with the company's name, address, and phone number, as well as the division or the branch office. This is known as letterhead stationery. Most companies use white stationery, although ivory and light gray tones are also acceptable.

If a letter is longer than one page, plain paper is used for the extra pages. This paper should be of the same size, color, and quality as the letterhead.

For writing memos within an organization, a smaller-sized letterhead can be used. Such paper may be 8½ by 5½ inches or 5½ by 8½ inches but is sometimes as large as 8½ by 11 inches.

PARTS OF A BUSINESS LETTER

Business letters contain the following parts: dateline, mailing notation, inside address, salutation, subject line, body, complimentary close, signature line, reference initials, copy notation, and postscript.

Dateline

When letterhead is used, type the dateline 2½ inches from the top edge of the sheet of paper. Some individuals prefer to locate the dateline a double space below the last line of the letterhead. If you are using plain paper (not letterhead), type the dateline about twelve or fourteen lines from the top of the paper.

The dateline in full-block and simplified letters is typed on the left margin. The dateline in modified block letters begins at the center or is centered.

Mailing Notation

If a letter is to be delivered by messenger or by registered, certified, or special-delivery mail, the appropriate notation is to be typed on the letterhead. The notation should begin at the left margin, one double space below the dateline. This notation is generally typed in all caps and underlined.

Inside Address

The name and address of the person or company receiving the letter are identified in this section of the letter, which appears after the last immediately preceding element—either the dateline or mailing notation. The inside address begins at the left margin of the letter and is single-spaced. Four to six lines are commonly left between the dateline (or mailing notation) and the inside address.

Unless the inside address is unusually long, you may type the addressee's title on the same lines as his or her name. Otherwise, it may be typed on a separate line.

When the letter is addressed to an individual, a personal title such as Mr., Miss, Ms., or Mrs. must be used.

Salutation

The salutation—the official greeting—is typed two lines beneath the last line of the inside address. A colon follows the salutation if you are using mixed punctuation. The colon is omitted when open punctuation is used. In addition,

1. The salutation must agree with the first line of the inside address.
2. Only the first word and all nouns in the salutation are capitalized.
3. The salutation is omitted when the simplified letter style is used.
4. If an "Attention" line is used, the salutation is typed on the second line after the attention line.

Following is a list of preferred salutations:

Singular	*Plural*
Dear Mr.	Ladies and Gentlemen
Dear Miss	
Dear Mrs.	
Dear Ms.	

Subject Line

The subject line, which summarizes the main topic of the letter, usually appears on the second line (double space) below the salutation. When the paragraphs are blocked on the left margin, the subject line is also likely to be blocked. When paragraphs are indented, you may center the subject line horizontally on the page.

You may capitalize all of the word *subject* or only the initial letter of each word. A colon should follow the word subject, as the following examples show.

SUBJECT: Year-End Report
Subject: Year-End Report

In a simplified letter format, the subject line begins a triple space below the address and a triple space above the body. The word *subject* is omitted, and the entire subject line is capitalized, as in the following.

REQUEST FOR INFORMATION

Body of the Letter

The body of the letter, which consists of the message, starts on the second line (double space) beneath the salutation. When a subject line is used, the body begins a double space below the salutation. Paragraph indentation—usually five, seven, or ten spaces—is consistent with the letter style you are using.

Complimentary Close

The complimentary close is typed on the second line (double space) below the body of the letter. Only the first word of the complimentary close is capitalized. A comma follows the complimentary close when mixed punctuation is used but is omitted with open punctuation. Information about punctuation styles appears later in this appendix.

In full-block letters, the complimentary close appears flush left; but in left modified block letters, it begins at the horizontal center of the page. The complimentary close is omitted in the simplified letter.

The Signature

Much variation appears in the style of the signature. The full signature includes the company's name, which is presented two spaces directly below the complimentary close. If the name is so long that it would overrun the right margin, it is centered below the complimentary close. The name, the name and title, or only the title of the originator is typed three or four spaces below; the department affiliation may be indicated. The letter writer signs his or her name in the space between the lines. Many firms omit the company name in the signature. The name on the letterhead is considered sufficient for purposes of identification and responsibility. Shown next is the customary way of presenting the signature.

Sincerely yours,

Karen Flock, President

Reference Initials

Reference initials identify the persons who dictated and typed the letter. They usually appear at the left margin a double space below the typed name and title. In long letters, however, they may appear on the same line with the official title. If you wish, you may use only the typist's initials, as the second example shown below illustrates.

JD/bd

bd

Enclosure Notion

If an item is included in the envelope with the letter, type the word Enclosure at the left margin on the line below the reference initials. If more than one item is to be enclosed, use the word Enclosures and indicate the number of items. Another alternative is to identify the enclosure. Four alternative styles are shown here.

Enc.
Enclosures
Enclosures (2)
Enclosures: Contract
Check

Copy Notation

If the writer wishes the addressee to know that other people will be receiving a copy of the letter, he or she should place a "pc" (photocopy) or "xc" (xerox copy) notation flush left on the line below the enclosure notation. If several persons are receiving copies, their names should be listed according to their rank, or alphabetically, if they are of equal rank.

If the addressee is not to be informed about another person receiving a copy of the letter, type a "bpc" (blind photocopy) notation in the upper left corner of the copies sent to blind-copy recipients and the file copy—but never on the original.

Postscript

A postscript expresses an idea that has been deliberately withheld from the body of the letter or an afterthought. But including an afterthought may not be effective if it suggests that the body of the letter is badly organized.

Start the postscript on the second line below the copy notation (or whichever notation was last typed). If your previous paragraphs are indented, indent the first line of the postscript; otherwise, begin it at the left margin.

You may type PS, P.S., or begin with the first word of the postscript, omitting the PS notation.

Exhibit C-1 shows these letter parts.

Multiple-Page Letters

Use plain paper of the same quality as the letterhead, but never letterhead, for the second and each additional page of a long letter. Use the same left and right margins as on the first page.

On the seventh line from the top of the page, type a continuation-page heading consisting of the following: the name of the addressee, the page number, and the date. Either of the following styles is acceptable.

Mrs. C. P. Canady 2 March 1, 199x

or

Mrs. C. P. Canady
Page 2
March 1, 199x

ABC Corporation

111 Main Street (406) 422-2682 Johnson, IA 47631-0962

January 30, 199x

(3-4 spaces)

REGISTERED

(3-4 spaces)

Mr. Grant Green
Delvin Equipment Company
8907 South Street
Yukon, IA 48984-3624

(double space)

Dear Mr. Green

(double space)

SUBJECT: Transparency Maker

(double space)

The Transparency Maker we purchased from you on December 21 is being returned, and we are requesting that it be replaced with a new Maker.

(double space)

On five occasions during the month that we have had the Maker, it was inoperable at critical times. Because we bought the machine primarily to make transparencies on very short notice, several of our executives were severely inconvenienced when they were unable to make transparencies for use in their presentations. When the Maker is inoperable, we either have to use an outside service or do without the desired transparencies. You can see by examining the enclosed transparency that the machine is not working properly.

(double space)

The concern your company has for its customers leads me to believe that you will want us to own a Maker worthy of its excellent reputation.

(double space)

Your replacing the machine soon so we can provide a fast, efficient transparency-making service for our executives will be appreciated.

(double space)

Sincerely

(3-4 spaces)

Jason Brown
Executive Vice President

JB:cm
Enclosure
pc: William Doe

The Transparency Maker was shipped to you this morning.

Exhibit C-1 Business letter parts.

Resume typing the message on the third line below the last line of the continuation-page heading.

Always type at least two lines of a paragraph at the top of a continuation page, and leave at least two lines of the paragraph at the bottom of the previous page. Do not divide a paragraph that contains three or fewer lines.

Never use a continuation page to type only the closing section of a business letter. (The complimentary closing should always be preceded by at least two lines of the message.)

Leave a bottom margin of at least 1 inch at the foot of each page of a letter (except perhaps the last page), and keep the bottom margin as uniform as possible on all pages except the last.

LETTER STYLES

Four basic business letter styles are commonly used in business offices: full block, modified block with blocked paragraphs, modified block with indented paragraphs, and simplified.

Full Block

Each line of a full-block letter begins at the left margin. This letter style saves typing time and diminishes the opportunity for error. This letter style should not be used unless it compliments the letterhead. (See Exhibit C-2.)

Modified Block with Blocked Paragraphs

The modified block with blocked paragraphs letter style is more streamlined than the modified block with indented paragraphs. The modified block with blocked paragraphs style is gradually becoming the preferred business letter style. The date line begins at the center, as do the complimentary closing and originator's name and title. (See Exhibit C-3.)

Modified Block with Indented Paragraphs

The modified block with indented paragraphs letter style differs from the modified block with blocked paragraphs style in that the paragraphs are indented five, seven, or ten spaces. The date line and closing lines begin at the same locations as they do with the modified block with blocked paragraphs letter style. (See Exhibit C-4).

Exhibit C-2 Full block; mixed punctuation.

ABC Corporation

111 Main Street (406) 422-2682 Johnson, IA 47631-0962

January 30, 199x

(4-8 spaces)

Mr. John Grant
Arcom Office Products Company
1243 Main Street
Jefferson, MI 48832-2947
(double space)
Dear Mr. Grant:
(double space)
Will you please send me the illustrated promotional packet mentioned in a Delta Max office copier ad you recently ran in the *Detroit News*?
(double space)
The feasibility of purchasing a copier for use in an office that makes between 350 and 500 copies per month is being investigated. The copier will also need to be capable of reducing and enlarging material.
(double space)
Your sending the requested material by February 18 will be appreciated as I plan to make a purchasing decision within the next few weeks.
(double space)
Sincerely,

(3-4 spaces)

William Doe
President

blt

Exhibit C-3 Modified block with blocked paragraphs; mixed punctuation.

ABC Corporation

111 Main Street (406) 422-2682 Johnson, IA 47631-0962

January 30, 199x

Mr. John Grant
Arcom Office Products Company
1243 Main Street
Jefferson, MI 48832-2947

(double space)

Dear Mr. Grant:

(double space)

Will you please send me the illustrated promotional packet mentioned in a Delta Max office copier ad you recently ran in the *Detroit News*?

(double space)

The feasibility of purchasing a copier for use in an office that makes between 350 and 500 copies per month is being investigated. The copier will also need to be capable of reducing and enlarging material.

(double space)

Your sending the requested material by February 18 will be appreciated as I plan to make a purchasing decision within the next few weeks.

(double space)

Sincerely,

(3-4 spaces)

William Doe
President

blt

Exhibit C-4 Modified block with indented paragraphs; open punctuation.

ABC Corporation

111 Main Street (406) 422-2682 Johnson, IA 47631-0962

January 30, 199x

Mr. John Grant
Arcom Office Products Company
1243 Main Street
Jefferson, MI 48832-2947

(double space)

Dear Mr. Grant

(double space)

Will you please send me the illustrated promotional packet mentioned in a Delta Max office copier ad you recently ran in the *Detroit News*?

(double space)

The feasibility of purchasing a copier for use in an office that makes between 350 and 500 copies per month is being investigated. The copier will also need to be capable of reducing and enlarging material.

(double space)

Your sending the requested material by February 18 will be appreciated as I plan to make a purchasing decision within the next few weeks.

(double space)

Sincerely

(3-4 spaces)

William Doe
President

blt

Simplified Letter

A simplified letter style omits the salutation and closing and includes a subject line in capital letters. All lines begin flush left. The simplified letter is an interesting example of the movement toward simplifying letter formats. (See Exhibit C-5.)

BUSINESS LETTER PUNCTUATION

Two types of punctuation, open and mixed, are used in letters presented in the full block, modified block with blocked paragraphs, and modified blocked with indented paragraph letter styles.

Open Punctuation

Marks are omitted from the lines of the return address, salutation, and complimentary close, unless an abbreviation is used. In that case, the period is typed as part of the abbreviation. Exhibit C-4 is presented with open punctuation.

Mixed Punctuation

In business, mixed punctuation is the style commonly used. A colon is used after the salutation and a comma after the complimentary close. Exhibits C-2 and C-3 are presented with mixed punctuation. No other end-of-line punctuation is used in the opening and closing lines. However, a period must follow any abbreviation that ends a line.

Although punctuation in other parts of the letter is no different, a colon after the salutation and a comma after the complimentary close may be used or omitted in the full block, modified block with block paragraphs, or modified block with indented paragraph letter styles.

Exhibit C-5 Simplified letter.

ABC Corporation

111 Main Street (406) 422-2682 Johnson, IA 47631-0962

January 30, 199x

Mr. John Grant
Arcom Office Products Company
1243 Main Street
Jefferson, MI 48832-2947

(triple space)

REQUEST FOR PROMOTIONAL PACKET

(triple space)

Will you please send me the illustrated promotional packet mentioned in a Delta Max office copier ad you recently ran in the *Detroit News*?
(double space)
The feasibility of purchasing a copier for use in an office that makes between 350 and 500 copies per month is being investigated. The copier will also need to be capable of reducing and enlarging material.
(double space)
Your sending the requested material by February 18 will be appreciated as I plan to make a purchasing decision within the next few weeks.

(3-4 spaces)

WILLIAM DOE - PRESIDENT

blt

ADDRESSING ENVELOPES

Generally you will use single spacing and blocked style when addressing an envelope. Type the city, state, and zip code on one line. Leave one or two spaces between the state and the zip code. The U.S. Postal Service recommends that the information be typed in all capitals with no punctuation.

MR KEITH CARRADY
JOHNSON PRODUCTS DIVISION
1383 MAIN STREET
LITTLE ROCK AK 43312-0322

When addressing a large (No. 10) envelope, begin the address on line 14 from the top and about 4 inches from the left edge. When using a small (No. 6) envelope or when addressing a postcard, begin the address on line 12 about 2 inches from the left edge.

If the return address is not imprinted on the envelope, type a return address in the upper-left corner of the envelope. The return address should contain the following information arranged in three lines: (1) the name of the writer or company, (2) the street address, and (3) the city, state, and zip code. The following example illustrates the appropriate format for a return address.

Ms. Caroline Brown
1288 Liberty Avenue
Tempe, AZ 98744-0342

Type an attention line or a notation, such as personal or confidential, below the return address. It should begin on line 9 or at least two lines below the return address. Begin each word with a capital letter and use underscoring.

If a special mailing procedure is used, type the appropriate notation, such as SPECIAL DELIVERY or REGISTERED, in capital letters in the upper-right corner of the envelope, beginning on line 9. The notation should end about ½ inch from the right margin.

INTEROFFICE MEMORANDUM

The interoffice memorandum, shown in Exhibit C-6, is used when one writes to another employee in the office. The inside address, salutation, and complimentary closing are omitted to save time and effort.

Exhibit C-6 Interoffice memorandum.

Interoffice Memorandum

January 30, 199x

TO: John Brown
FROM: Dick Smith
SUBJECT: January Sales Figures

(triple space)

The January Sales figures are attached that you requested during our phone conversation this morning.
(double space)
Please let me know if you would like for me to provide you with additional information that might be helpful as you prepare your report.

blt

Attachment

Appendix D: Legal Aspects of Business Communication

Each person who composes business messages must carefully guard against statements that may generate unnecessary legal action. Written and verbal attacks against the reputation of another person may be very costly in time and money, even if they are true. Covering all the legal constraints that affect communication is impossible; but the following discussion reveals several of the legal risks and complications common to business communication. For advice on specific details about complicated situations, we suggest you consult legal counsel. Remember: Ignorance of the law is not an acceptable defense.

DEFAMATION

Every person has the right to be free of malicious gossip and unjustified attempts to undermine his or her reputation. Any breach of this right is referred to as defamation. When the defamation is spoken, it is slander; when it is written, it is libel.

Before legal action is encouraged, the statements must be (1) untrue, (2) communicated to another person, and (3) cause some personal injury, such as contempt, ridicule, or disrepute.

In a legal sense, any means of communicating a defamatory statement to a third party is considered a defamatory action. The third-party element is interesting because it emphasizes the point that statements made to someone's face are not defamatory. But repeating the statement to just one additional person may be considered as defamation.

Case Point

Mr. Jones tells Mr. Smith that he considers him to be an incompetent architect. This is an opinion, and, as such, a successful legal action would be very rare.

However, Mr. Jones tells Mr. Strong the same thing, and now Mr. Smith may be legally justified and perhaps successful in challenging Mr. Jones's statement. In the process, Mr. Smith would have to prove personal injury, but that is often not difficult to do.

Libel versus Slander

Libel (written defamation) is naturally more permanent than slander (spoken defamation) and also easier to prove, so the laws pertaining to libel are more severe than those relating to slander. Libelous statements may appear in all permanent-type communications, such as letters, memos, circulars, pictures, newspaper stories, and published articles. Even letters marked "personal" or telegrams may become grounds for libel if the receiving party can prove that you were aware of the possibility of the message's being intercepted.

If a third party receives information by eavesdropping or reading other people's mail, the writer would normally not be held liable unless he or she knew of such possibilities.

Defamatory Terms

Successful libel cases show that judges may consider the following words libelous. Therefore, avoid them or use them with extreme caution:

bankrupt	forger	profiteer
communist	fraud	quack
corrupt	hypocrite	shyster
crook	incompetent	swindler
dishonest	inferior	thief
disreputable	insolvent	unchaste
drug addict	kickbacks	unworthy of credit
falsified	misappropriation	worthless

When composing letters about overdue accounts, you should write like a prudent person and not harass, oppress, or abuse a person unreasonably. Harassment could include abusive language, anonymous communication, and use of the telephone in an abusive manner.

Defamation is considered to apply when the statements affect an essential characteristic of a person's work. For instance, saying that a teacher is addicted to a drug may be much more slanderous than saying the same thing about a popular singer. As you write, remember that statements which chastise the ability of a person to do his or her job are libelous.

If what you write is true, your defense in a libel suit is probably adequate. But if no evidence of truth or good reason exists for your statements, you may have to pay large money damages.

Invasion of Privacy

A person's name, picture, or other identifying information may represent excellent material for sales and promotion letters. But if this material is used without permission, a person may have cause for legal action, based on invasion of his or her privacy.

Fraud

The basis of fraud is false representation or concealment. Fraud is, however, not that cut and dried. For fraud to exist, the following circumstances must be present:

1. *False representation or deliberate concealment of a present or past fact must exist.* To constitute fraud, misrepresentation or concealment must be deliberate and result from a definite action on the part of the accused party. Facts or material that fall into the area of opinions, judgments, or prediction of the future normally do not constitute fraud. You may honestly claim that something "is a bargain" or "is the best on the market" with little fear of your remarks being fraudulent.

2. *Misrepresented or concealed facts must be material facts.* A fact is considered material if knowing the true or complete facts would have allowed the defrauded party to avoid entering into the agreement. Whether the fact is actually very important or

only of minor importance is of little consequence. The action encouraged by the misrepresentation or concealment is the major point.

3. *The person who makes the false representation must know it to be false or initiate it recklessly without regard to its truth.* Fraud is clearly existent when a person deliberately makes a false statement, conceals a material fact, or intentionally acts in such a way as to mislead another person into an agreement or contract. Fraud also exists when a person makes a statement without determining its truth or falsity, especially if he or she happens to know the facts.

Example

McElroy, a registered firearms dealer, represented to a prospective buyer, Wetzel, that a Winchester rifle was an authentic 1906 model previously owned by one person. McElroy had purchased the rifle at a Southern gun show and wanted to sell it as soon as possible. To ensure the sale, he told Wetzel what he thought he wanted to hear. When Wetzel checked the serial number, he discovered the gun was sold in 1904 to the military. Wetzel successfully sought to have the sale set aside on grounds of fraud.

McElroy had made statements concerning the rifle with reckless disregard of the truth. As a registered firearms dealer, McElroy was expected to know the facts about the rifle, so his statements were considered to be fraudulent in nature.

4. *Misrepresentation must be made with the intention of influencing the other person to act on it.* For a statement to be fraudulent, the person making it must intend that the fact will be relied upon and acted upon.

5. *The misrepresentation or concealment must induce action and cause injury to the other party.* Fraud does not actually exist until the person who was supposed to be misled actually is convinced and enters into the agreement or contract. Even then, the defrauded party must be able to prove injury, or no legal right or need to recover damages exists.

You can avoid fraud in business communication if you are direct, careful, and honest. People who find themselves in court because of their statements should have previously weighed the chance of such an occurrence or paid more attention to the actions constituting fraud.

Warranties

A seller usually assumes certain obligations concerning the goods being sold. These obligations may involve the quality of the goods, clear title, or other information about the nature of the goods.

Express warranties refer to an assurance of quality or promise of performance explicitly stated by the seller of goods. *Implied warranties* may consist of an obvious fact, such as conveying clear title to goods that were sold. They may also refer to quality and performance standards required by law. Express warranties are usually easier to prove in a legal action; but any warranty, express or implied, should be avoided if it cannot be substantiated.

If sellers simply exaggerate the merits of goods as part of a sales talk, this is referred to as *puffing* but does not constitute a warranty. These kinds of statements are considered personal opinions or value judgments, and buyers are not justified in relying on them. If, however, the buyer asks the seller's opinion as an expert, the seller's remarks about quality become part of the bargain and may be considered a warranty.

Some of the more obvious "business" activities that often lead to legal problems are letters and printed matter concerning lotteries, obscene literature, extortion, and solicitation of illegal business. In addition, copyright laws must be honored when material is duplicated, and other legal constraints (avoidance of libelous material) should be considered when preparing written messages.

Write, act, and promise as you would like to receive. In other words, in business communication, always act like a prudent person.

Appendix E: Technology and Business Communication

Much of the electronic equipment in today's offices impacts business communication by enhancing the efficiency of creating and distributing documents and by improving the quality of the communication product. The invention of the computer microchip has made possible the vast majority of the technological advances that have revolutionized various communication processes.

The components of the electronic office that affect business communication are word processing, facsimile machines, telecommunications, and electronic mail.

WORD PROCESSING

Although a number of the components of the electronic office have transformed written and oral communication, perhaps none has had a greater impact than *word processing*, a computerized system used in preparing text material. As more and more employees use desktop computers capable of performing word processing functions, those with good keyboarding skills are preparing their own written communication. That is, these people use a simultaneous originating-keyboarding process to prepare their own written communication rather than ask an office employee to keyboard the material they dictate. Some employees use the equipment to draft the message and then have their administrative assistant edit the message to ensure the correctness of the format, grammar and punctuation usage, and so forth.

Word Processing Equipment

Equipment used to perform word processing operations provides several capabilities. In addition to its use in keyboarding material, the equipment is used in the editing process to change draft copy. The equipment is also capable of electronically capturing and storing keyboarded material.

The types of equipment now commonly used to perform word processing operations include the following:

1. *Text-editing devices* (also called text editors and word processors). They perform word processing operations but very few, if any, additional operations. In some instances they are used to sort and/or alphabetize material.

2. *Desktop computers* (also called personal computers or microcomputers). This equipment can perform a variety of functions, including word processing and data manipulation, such as that found on spreadsheets and databases. Most word processing tasks performed today on desktop computers are as efficient as those performed by text-editing devices dedicated only to performing word processing functions. The multifunctional capability of desktop computers, however, often makes them at least as attractive, and perhaps more so, than dedicated word processing devices.

3. *Desktop terminals* are generally interconnected to a computer mainframe or to a small business computer. Because the desktop terminals most likely do not possess their own intelligence (they are, therefore, often called "dumb" terminals), this equipment is inoperable whenever the main system is inoperable. Depending on the type of equipment, desktop terminals may perform word processing operations as efficiently as dedicated devices.

Functional Capabilities of Word Processing Equipment

The equipment used in word processing operations is capable of performing a number of functions, including those identified in Communication Capsule E-1.

Communication Capsule E-1 Functions Performed by Word Processing Systems

Among the various functions word processing systems are capable of performing are the following:

Arithmetic function: The system is capable of performing addition, subtraction, multiplication, and division on numerical data.

Block move and insert: The system can move a block of material from one location and insert the material at another location.

Copy: The system can copy a block of material, making it simpler and easier to insert in different locations in the same document. The blocking function eliminates the extra effort of having to rekeyboard the same material several times.

Dictionary: The system can store in coded form words or phrases used repetitively, which makes these words/phrases available for later retrieval and use. To retrieve a word, its coded version is keyboarded and the word is automatically inserted at the desired location.

Footnote placement: The system can automatically move footnotes from one page to another, which is necessary when the material to which a footnote refers is moved from one page to another.

Global search and replace: The system can automatically search a document for each occurrence of a word or phrase. Some equipment will automatically replace upon command a word or phrase with another word or phrase. Other equipment requires the manual keyboarding of the replacement word at each location.

Macros: The system, using a stored macro, can upon command perform a desired function. To illustrate, when you access the macro for your name and job title, the system will automatically insert at the desired location your name and job title. This feature is especially well suited for repetitive functions.

Page numbering: The equipment can automatically number the pages. When the number of a page changes because you have added or deleted material, page numbers are automatically corrected.

Pagination: The equipment can automatically place the prescribed number of lines on a page and then automatically start the next page. The system can automatically prevent the occurrence of widow (one line of a paragraph left at the bottom of a page) or orphan lines (one line of a paragraph left at the top of the page).

Repagination: The equipment can repaginate with the prescribed amount of material on each page after material is added to or deleted from a document.

Right-hand justification: The equipment can automatically produce printed material that has an even right margin.

Spelling dictionary: The equipment can automatically compare the spelling of keyboarded words with the spelling of words contained in the system's dictionary. Words that are not comparable because they are not stored in the dictionary, are misspelled, or are proper nouns, are highlighted on the screen, which facilitates proofreading.

Word wraparound: The equipment can automatically wrap a word keyboarded at the end of one line around to the beginning of the next line when the word is too long to fit on the previous line.

Other Equipment Used in Word Processing Systems

Word processing systems also extensively use dictation equipment and copier equipment. The business writer may use dictation equipment at the beginning of the production cycle while copier equipment comes into play at the end of the production cycle.

In most word processing systems, employees generally can either: (1) perform their own keyboarding tasks or (2) use dictation to input their material into the word processing cycle. Especially for routine correspondence, most organizations discourage using handwriting to originate material, although some organizations do permit handwriting when originating technical reports. Because word processing operators can transcribe dictation faster than handwritten material and because people with a little practice can dictate material faster than they can handwrite, dictation makes sense from an efficiency and productivity standpoint. When dictating, follow the recommended procedures presented in Chapter 4.

FACSIMILE MACHINES

Although facsimile technology is nearly as old as telephone technology, the facsimile process did not receive much attention until the 1980s. *Facsimile machines* (or *fax machines*) are electronic devices that transmit identical duplicates of documents from one location to another. The signals depicting the images on the documents are transmitted over telephone lines. To transmit a document—a form, a letter, a chart, a photograph, or a report—place it on the facsimile device. Then dial the phone number of the message recipient (most likely the number for a dedicated fax line). After the sender's and the receiver's fax units are interconnected, the transmission process begins. An increasing number of companies now leave their fax machines operational twenty-four hours a day.

Some of the more advanced fax machines are capable of operating unattended, and they can automatically dial up to fifty telephone numbers prestored in the unit's memory. These devices also transmit a page of material in approximately six seconds. When such equipment is available, it is often used later at night when long-distance toll charges are the lowest, especially if multiple-page documents are being transmitted to various receivers.

Fax machines are especially useful for the fast transmission of business documents. Increasingly, they are used in-house as well as nationally and internationally. Because of the unreliability of international mail, fax machines are especially useful when a business deal may "fall through" simply because of a slow, unreliable mail delivery system.

As more people install fax/modem cards in their desktop computers, they are able to send to the locations by facsimile process the materials they originate on their computer. Assume you keyboard a letter to be sent to an employee in another company, located either in the same city or 2,000 miles away. Depending on the type of fax, communication, and word processing software you are using, you will likely be able to "fax" the message by accessing the print function of your word processing software. Most likely, fax capability is identified as one of your printer choices. If so, then all you have to do is switch from the default printer to the fax function. In a few seconds, you should be asked to input the recipient's name and his/her fax telephone number. After this has been completed, you can activate the transmission process.

With a fax/modem card to transmit your messages, you may consider having your company's letterhead and your signature digitized to make it easier to store material permanently and retrieve it when necessary. Through this process, you are able to have your company's letterhead and your signature appear on each letter you send by this process. Otherwise, only the keyboarded text is transmitted.

Portable fax machines are now available that can be used with cellular phone equipment. This new technology enables travelers to transmit messages from their cars or from remote work sites. Another innovative use of fax technology is during videoconferences. Thus, participants are able to share—almost instantly—documents with one another.

TELECOMMUNICATIONS

Most employees, regardless of their job title, make extensive use of telecommunications in carrying out their job responsibilities. Telephone systems are an integral part of telecommunications.

Today, *telecommunications* involves the transmission of voice, data, and images by means of telephone lines, microwave systems, earth-orbiting communication satellites, fiber optics, and airwaves used by cellular phone technology. Telecommunications is also used extensively in electronic networks, which provide the link between various types of office equipment, enabling these devices to communicate with one another.

Telecommunications supports the following specialized communication functions: teleconferencing, videoconferencing, transmitting e-mail (electronic mail).

Teleconferencing

As an alternative to holding face-to-face conferences, *teleconferencing* is a communication process that facilitates discussion among the members of an executive group who are in different locations. Executives remain in their respective locations but "teleconference" with one another via telephones. Teleconferencing allows the executives to communicate with one another by voice only.

Videoconferencing

A communication process that allows conference participants to see one another's images on television monitors as they communicate, *videoconferencing* adds another dimension to the communication process. Besides their own images, participants can view images of charts and graphs. Data can also be transmitted to each of the conference sites.

Television equipment is used extensively in videoconferencing. First, television cameras input the images into the system; next a telecommunications link (fiber optics or communications satellite, typically) transmits the image to the various destination sites, and then a television monitor receives incoming images.

For many companies, teleconferencing and videoconferencing are cost-effective ways to hold remote-site executive conferences. In addition to reducing traveling costs and improving employee productivity, they allow remotely located executives to interact more often than if they all had to travel to a common site.

Electronic mail

Electronic mail, or e-mail, is technology used to transmit messages electronically from one location to another. E-mail usage is rapidly expanding with all employees in many organizations now being electronically interconnected. E-mail messages can be sent to other employees within the same organization or to individuals living in other parts of the world.

Receiving or sending e-mail requires access to a communications service, such as that provided on a local area network (LAN), the Internet, (discussed in a later section of this appendix), or a commercial communication service, such as America Online or Compuserve. Appropriate software is also needed to operationalize the e-mail function. A widely used software package used on local area networks is cc:Mail. It also enables the user to transmit e-mail beyond the local area network.

Desktop computers equipped with modems commonly transmit the documents and messages. Electronic codes representing alphabetic and numeric information are transmitted over a telecommunications line. Equipment at the sending location encodes the material into signals that can be electronically transmitted. At the destination location, the receiving equipment decodes these signals so the material can be reconfigured into a format people are capable of reading. Depending on the available technology, you will likely be able to access your e-mail from off-premise computers, day or night.

Users of e-mail need to be cautioned that although a personal password is needed to access the e-mail function, message security is often a concern. The best rule of thumb is to avoid sending anything through the e-mail system that you do not want people other than the designated recipient to read.

E-mail messages resemble the memo format, with a "to" line, a "from" line (which the communication service's software may automatically insert for you), and a "subject" line. If you wish, you can send the same message to other people simultaneously as the more-sophisticated e-mail systems also have a "carbon copy" capability. This simply means that the same message will be sent to the person for whom it was intended as well as to other individuals listed as carbon copy recipients. In addition, the date and time of transmittal are also automatically provided on the message.

In most cases, if you wish to prepare a paper copy of your message, you can easily do so with the print command. You can originate the text of the e-mail message just as you would if you were using word processing to originate a document that will be prepared as a paper copy.

With laptop computers, a modem, and a cellular phone, you can transmit e-mail from your car and a remote work site. From a hotel room or your home, a regular telephone rather than a cellular phone can be used to transmit e-mail.

Several other features commonly available on the more sophisticated e-mail systems are the ability to

1. edit messages.
2. check the spelling of your work.
3. import material from other sources (from material prepared using word processing, for example).
4. file messages by categories in electronic file folders.
5. archive messages for permanent storage.
6. search all of your stored messages by key word to find desired information.
7. forward messages to other e-mail users.

When you prepare e-mail messages, you need to exercise as much care as when you are transmitting hard-copy messages. Some people believe they don't need to exercise as much care when preparing e-mail messages, often resulting in the transmittal of messages with typographical errors, grammatical errors, and punctuation errors. For readers who are offended by these types of errors, you may be communicating the hidden message that you do not have sufficient respect for them to transmit error-free work. Moreover, errors in your e-mail messages discredit you as a writer. Furthermore, if your message is electronically filed—perhaps for years—the negative impression it makes may also reflect, in the view of others, on your overall communication ability.

E-mail messages should be structured as you would the same messages for presentation as paper copies. Just as you avoid venting your anger in paper documents, you should avoid doing so in e-mail messages. Furthermore, the use of e-mail is not appropriate for communicating gossip or small talk.

Internet

In increasing numbers of organizations, employees have access to the Internet, which allows them to access information and/or communicate with other Internet users worldwide. The *Internet*, which is basically a network of networks, comprises thousands of networks and millions of users. Because the Internet is not owned by anyone, although it was originally managed by the National Science Foundation, being able to determine accurately how many networks compose the Internet or how many users it has is virtually impossible. The number of networks and users changes by the hour, as hundreds of thousands of colleges, research companies, government agencies, and other entities connect their computer systems to this worldwide network.

To use the Internet either at work or at home, you need a computer, a modem, a phone line, and telecommunications software. Access to Internet is attainable in two basic ways: (1) through a college/university or an organization (company, public library, and so forth) whose computer system is connected to the Internet or (2) through a commercial subscription service, such as Compuserve or America Online.

The Internet is used in a variety of ways, including the following: to transmit e-mail messages, access file libraries, access library card catalogs, retrieve weather reports and news reports, access a variety of databases, participate in live keyboard chats with people worldwide, access helpful information on a variety of topics through the use of electronic bulletin boards, access journal articles, and play on-line games with people from around the world.

Index

A

B

C

H

I

J

K

L

M

N

O

P

Q

R

S

T

U

V

W

Y

Exercise 1

Name ______________________ Section ______________ Grade ______________

Edit the following paragraphs, paying particular attention to the goals set for each paragraph. In addition, correct any other errors you find in punctuation, grammar, or writing style. For example, in the first paragraph, you are to identify long and difficult words and substitute short and simple words for them.

Correctness

Goal: Use short, simple words.

It was the financial advisors recommendation that the company diversify its investments portfolio. The principle objective in diversifying, according to the financial adviser, is to definitely assure that the company does not violate it's own investment philosophy.

Goal: Use variety in sentence structure.

Mrs. Darlington appointed a committee to examine the merits of the proposal. The committee subsequently conducted a thorough search of the literature. It was the purpose of the literature search to provide a basis for decision making. The final results of the committee's actions will be known shortly. The proposed program is projected to result in a savings of approximately $20,000 a year.

Goal: Avoid expletives.

There are several things you must remember about being employed as a research assistant. It is your responsibility to complete your work on time. Furthermore, you need to be loyal, and it is important to be cooperative. There is also a need to work as a team player. Finally, there is no reason to not do you best work at all times.

Exercise 2

Name ______________________________ Section ________________ Grade______________

Edit the following paragraphs, paying particular attention to the goals set for each paragraph. In addition, correct any other errors you find in punctuation, grammar, or writing style.

Correctness

Goal: Use correct modifiers and agreement.

It is my understanding that the data in the report was incorrect. Due to the fact that the data was incorrectly used, the conclusions were faulty based on the data. Having worked long and hard on the report, the recommendations that Mr. Jones presented were not valid.

Goal: Use correct pronoun agreement.

Everyone at the next meeting is invited to present their recommendations. Neither the president nor the vice president will attend the meeting, but each department head will attend to obtain the recommendations for their respective departments. There is widespread belief among each department head that most of the recommendations is going to help their departments.

Goal: Use correct pronoun case and active voice.

The report will be presented by Mrs. Jones, Mr. Green, and I. Mrs. Jones has indicated that the research methodology section will be presented by her but that the findings section that Mr. Green wrote will be presented by he. Both of them will let I present the recommendations and the implications section that was written by me.

Exercise 3

Name ______________________________ Section ________________ Grade ______________

Edit the following paragraphs, paying particular attention to the goals set for each paragraph. In addition, correct any other errors you find in punctuation, grammar, or writing style.

Correctness

Goal: Use correct subject-verb placement.

In order to help you with the situation you outlined in your recent letter, additional information that you will be able to provide us is needed. The information listed on the attached card is what we need. You will be glad to know that since your stereo is still under warranty, any new parts that we might have to install will be free.

Goal: Use words correctly.

The individual who you told me about yesterday lay the report on Johns desk this morning. The report was concerned with the affects of mastery of writing principals on one's promotion. The report lay the blame for writing weaknesses of employees squarely on the environment people were raised in. The report says people master writing principals when the family demanded it.

Goal: Use correct punctuation.

When the committees decision was announced by Mr. Brown he indicated that the decision was thoroughly considered. The committee recieved considerable input from many people, the committee also tried to carefully weigh the affect of it's decision on each and every employee. However in the final analysis, managements' decision is the only one that will count.

Exercise 4

Name ________________________________ Section ________________ Grade ______________

Edit the following paragraphs, paying particular attention to the goals set for each paragraph. In addition, correct any other errors you find in punctuation, grammar, or writing style.

Correctness

Goal: Use clear pronoun antecedents.

Sandy Grant asked Jill Hopper if the rough draft of her report was ready for examination. She indicated that she thought some of the data that was collected earlier would have to have its accuracy verified. However, when Jill indicated that several pages of her report remained to be typed, Sandy indicated that she would have to have it completed within two days.

Goal: Use correct punctuation.

As I was walking to the building this morning. John yelled "Congratulations"! I said, "For what"? He asked, "Haven't you heard"? I asked him what he was talking about, he then told me that I had been selected as "Employee of the Month". I am very pleased to have been selected, and will enjoy the privileges of the award for one month.

Goal: Use correct grammar.

To quickly master the written business communication elements are his goal. Since he has accepted a position that will require considerable writing, him mastering this material is of considerable importance. However he will probably not know if he has accomplished his goal until he has been on the job for several months.

Exercise 5

Name ______________________________ Section _______________ Grade _____________

Edit the following paragraphs, paying particular attention to the goals set for each paragraph. In addition, correct any other errors you find in punctuation, grammar, or writing style.

Correctness

Goal: Use correct grammar and pronouns.

John asked Bill if he knew where his reference manual was. Bill questioned John which reference manual he was talking about because he had three. He went on to say that the Johnson manual was the better of the three in his mind. When he asked why he felt this way, he indicated that the breadth of the material made it the better one.

Goal: Use "that" and "which" correctly.

Following is the information, which you requested. The pamphlet, which is concerned with fringe benefits, is out of print. The new pamphlet on employee stock option plans, that Bill Murray wrote, will be available next month. Another new pamphlet approved by the committee, that is being written by Sally Brown, should also be available next month.

Goal: Use correct verb forms.

The criteria you should use in evaluating the students reports is enclosed. The use of the criteria will help assure that everyone are treated equally. Of special significance is the fact that the data in the report is accurate and the conclusions reflect the findings. Upon completion of the grading process, will you please tell me if you believe the criteria was helpful.

Exercise 6

Name ______________________ Section ______________ Grade ____________

Edit the following paragraphs, paying particular attention to the goals set for each paragraph. In addition, correct any other errors you find in punctuation, grammar, or writing style.

Correctness

Goal: Use correct punctuation.

Mr. Jake Hidea who is a well known author in the finance field will be the keynote speaker at the convention. His topic is "Investing in the Future". Given Mr. Hideas expertise and the members interest in this topic, I am sure this session will be very-well attended, for that reason it needs to be scheduled for a large room.

Goal: Use courteous tone and avoid expletives.

It is with regret that I must inform you that there is no way Arcam can comply with your request that we replace the malfunctioning CD player in your auto. Our service technician found there is evidence that the CD player was tampered with. Of course, this voids the warranty and therefore it is not reasonable to expect us to replace the CD player.

Goal: Use words correctly.

John Brown our service technician feels that the problem you have been having with your new carpet lays with the manufacturer, not with us. The "ripple effect" you see is not a result of the manner in which the carpet was lay down but rather because of a manufacturing defect. Because the problem lies with the manufacturer, we have asked the zone manager to contact you.

Exercise 7

Name ______________________ Section ______________ Grade ____________

Edit the following paragraphs, paying particular attention to the goals set for each paragraph. In addition, correct any other errors you find in punctuation, grammar, or writing style.

Correctness

Goal: Use correct subject-verb placement.

The new plant manager in carrying out the directives of his superiors will have to make several important decisions. Since the new manager is experienced, the decisions that he will be expected to make during his first month on the job will have a long term impact on company. When President Brown announced the hiring of the new manager, he indicated that he, in anticipation of the impact of these decisions, will be supportive.

Goal: Use short, simple words.

Being cognizant of the perpetuance with which Mr. Brown has persevered in his position as confidant of the president, I am skeptical if he will have a proclivity to assist us in dispensing with the presidents autocracy and his expectation that all subordinates operate as automatons. Because of Mr. Brown's avarice, he will not likely do any thing to jeopardize his position.

Goal: Use correct grammar.

John indicated that if he was me, he would not delay reporting the rule infraction to the compliance committee. However, he is not I. It is my belief that we need to verify whom is at fault, before we report the incident. Us reporting the incident to early may result in the guilty party never being brought to justice.

Exercise 8

Name ______________________________ Section ________________ Grade ______________

Edit the following paragraphs, paying particular attention to the goals set for each paragraph. In addition, correct any other errors you find in punctuation, grammar, or writing style.

Correctness

Goal: Use correct punctuation.

When you have good news to report in a business letter it is advisable to report the good news in the opening paragraph, however when you have bad news to report it is best to delay it's presentation until a latter paragraph. These suggestions are consistent with the direct, and indirect organization approach which has been the recommended business letter structure for several decades.

Goal: Use pronouns correctly.

It is her whom is primarily at fault for the department not getting the increased funding they requested. The problem arose when she reported to the president recently that the department was overstaffed and that they were purchasing unecessary items. It was the presidents decision therefore to not increase the departments funding for this year because the individuals that are responsible for this situation need to be more fiscally responsible.

Goal: Distinguish between "that" and "which."

John' decision that he made last week to increase the size of the accounting staff was a prudent one. The accounting department that has been understaffed now for several years, was grateful for his recommendation. The outcome, which will be noticed immediately, is a reduction in the work backlog. It is the manager's intent to reduce the backlog within six months' that will result in greater company wide efficiency.

Exercise 9

Name ______________________________ Section ________________ Grade ______________

Edit the following paragraphs, paying particular attention to the goals set for each paragraph. In addition, correct any other errors you find in punctuation, grammar, or writing style.

Correctness

Goal: Use pronouns that relate to antecedents.

Bill told John that he was to be named as the departments representative to the computer resource committee. He indicated that he did not know if he should accept the assignment since he had to spend most of the month of June at the Paris branch office. He went on to say that the president knew of his plans to be gone when he talked with him about the appointment.

Goal: Use "lie" and "lay" correctly.

When I stepped into Johns office he asked me if I was the one whom had lain the marketing report on his desk. I indicated that I was not the one who lay it there but that I believed Susan had laid the report there. I then asked him why he wondered if I was the one who lay the report on his desk. He indicated that he wanted to thank whomever was responsible for lying the report on his desk.

Goal: Use correct punctuation.

The new sales manager who has had ten years experience with ABD Company came to us with excellent recommendations. He is a well known sales manager, who is credited with helping ABD recover its latest financial crisis. I know he will do good here, he has excellent qualifications, and a keen mind when designing marketing strategies for new products.

Exercise 10

Name ______________________________ Section ________________ Grade ______________

Edit the following paragraphs, paying particular attention to the goals set for each paragraph. In addition, correct any other errors you find in punctuation, grammar, or writing style.

Conciseness

Goal: Avoid trite and redundant expressions.

By and large, each and every employee has availed himself/herself of the opportunity to take advantage of the new employee assistance program. Inasmuch as the company has invested heavily in this program, top management is more than happy to see the final results of the first year of the program's operation.

Goal: Use active voice.

The letter was written by Mr. Johnson. However, the ideas he presented in the letter were based on the data that was collected by Mr. Green. After the substance of the letter has been approved by the executive committee, it is the committees intent that the various ideas will be implemented by the unit supervisors.

Goal: Eliminate unneeded words.

By and large, the employees were found to be quite pleased with the new program for the most part. However, there were a few things that the employees indicated that should be changed. Namely, the procedure the employees have to follow in order to get reimbursed for the cost of the tuition of the college level courses they complete.

Exercise 11

Name ______________________ Section ______________ Grade ______________

Edit the following paragraphs, paying particular attention to the goals set for each paragraph. In addition, correct any other errors you find in punctuation, grammar, or writing style.

Conciseness

Goal: Avoid trite and redundant expressions.

By and large, our goal is to significantly increase our departments output. Since we are unable to avail ourselves of new equipment, the goal will be achieved first and foremost by employees' who learn to become more efficient, effective workers. If and when the department achieves their goal, then we will be in a better position to seek increased financial funding.

Goal: Eliminate unneeded words.

For the most part, we have generally been pleased with the quality of the services we have been obtaining from the Johnson Corporation. Although the Johnson Corporation generally has been providing us with good service, we have had a problem with them in two areas: in the data analysis project they did for us as well as in the data collection project. However, once our expectations were clearly communicated to them, we have not experienced further problems.

Goal: Use active voice.

The data for the year-end report was compiled by John Smith but it was Bill Jones who actually performed the calculations on it. It was not discovered until the data were being analyzed that a serious error on several calculations had been made by Bill. Fortunately, the error was caught by Mary Jones before the report was distributed to our stockholders. In the final analysis, being more careful is a skill that Bill needs to learn.

Exercise 12

Name ______________________________ Section ______________ Grade ____________

Edit the following paragraphs, paying particular attention to the goals set for each paragraph. In addition, correct any other errors you find in punctuation, grammar, or writing style.

Clarity

Goals: Use parallel construction.

The idea he presented is not workable not is it going to get managements approval. The idea has three problems: (1) it is not financially sound, (2) is going to have a negative impact on employee morale, (3) to invest in the idea means that other programs would have to be neglected.

Goal: Create sentence unity.

The book that you inquired about is out-of-stock but the membership list is up-to-date. The list you requested will be sent under separate cover, and the book has been placed on back-order status. Attached to the membership list is an explanation of the code that appears before each members name, you will want to be selective in choosing the person's that you send your survey to.

Goal: Use logical development.

The location of the graphic aid must be determined. But before you can do that you must determine what type of graphic aid you will be using. The importance of the information one is presenting is often considered in determining if a graphic aid should be used. The more important the information, the more likely a graphic aid will be used.

Exercise 13

Name ______________________________ Section ________________ Grade ______________

Edit the following paragraphs, paying particular attention to the goals set for each paragraph. In addition, correct any other errors you find in punctuation, grammar, or writing style.

Clarity

Goal: Create effective transition between sentences and sentence coherency.

John indicated that he will be happy to help us tomorrow. He will not be able to help us today since he has to attend a committee meeting most of the afternoon. John is anxious to help because he has several ideas for solving the problem. He feels the problem can be easily managed. He had experience dealing with this same problem when he worked at ABC Company.

Goal: Use modification and conciseness.

John indicated that the sick-leave policy only would be discussed at the committee meeting that was called on an emergency basis. However, of those attending the meeting, the majority also asked that the committee review the new employee handbook section on maternity leave. John ruled that the sick-leave policy only could be discussed according to the pre-arranged agenda.

Goal: Create paragraph coherence and logical development.

If you would like to go to the meeting with me, please let me know. The meeting on Fringe Benefits has been scheduled for next Thursday. One of the speakers is John Brown. John Brown is a well-known authority on fringe benefits. John is a well known authority also on the use of the cafeteria approach to fringe benefits.

Exercise 14

Name ________________________________ Section ________________ Grade ______________

Edit the following paragraphs, paying particular attention to the goals set for each paragraph. In addition, correct any other errors you find in punctuation, grammar, or writing style.

Clarity

Goal: Use parallel construction.

John has two primary goals: to help the company succeed and eventually becoming president. Not only is he a dedicated employee but he is also loyal. His work is always well done and the care and thought that goes into it is clearly reflected. The quality of the work John does when considering his two primary goals should enable him to succeed.

Goal: Use logical development.

One of the first steps in writing a business report is to determine its purpose. However, before you can do that, you must consider your reader. The failure of the writer to consider the reader often results' in the preparation of a report with a diminished usefulness. After you have determined your purpose and considered your reader, then you begin writing the report after you have prepared a general outline that the writer will follow.

Goal: Use modification correctly.

The book I have become quite dependent on on financial ratios has helped me on numerous occasions. One of the reasons I like this book is because of it's thorough discussion of what each ratio is used for as well as how the ratios are calculated to get the desired results by the financial analyst. This book on financial ratios have been a life saver many times for me.

Exercise 15

Name ______________________________ Section ________________ Grade ______________

Edit the following paragraphs, paying particular attention to the goals set for each paragraph. In addition, correct any other errors you find in punctuation, grammar, or writing style.

Courtesy

Goal: Use positive language.

Not only did Mr. Jones apologize for the serious error made in the data he presented, but also he went out of his way to provide correct data. Unless Mr. Jones is careless again in the future, we probably do not need to worry about this situation's having a detrimental impact over the long run. It is our hope that it will not have a detrimental impact.

Goal: Establish confident tone.

You will likely agree that the data would seem to show that the implementation of the program is probably a necessity. The executive committee most likely will agree with this supposition. If the executive committee decides to support the implementation of the program, it is the intent that a committee should probably be appointed to plan the program.

Goal: Use you-attitude.

I am confident of my belief that the program is working better than any of us expected, myself included. I believe the success of the program is largely the responsibility of the supervisor, Mrs. Carter. I know several others who share my belief about the role that Mrs. Carter plays in assuring the success of the program.

Exercise 16

Name ______________________ Section ______________ Grade ______________

Edit the following paragraphs, paying particular attention to the goals set for each paragraph. In addition, correct any other errors you find in punctuation, grammar, or writing style.

Courtesy

Goal: Use gender-neutral language.

The success of the employee is due largely to the amount of effort he expends in carrying out his job duties. An employee who works as hard as he would if he were the owner of the company will be more valuable to the company. He will also be promoted more quickly and receive higher salary increases as a result.

Goal: Use courteous tone.

It is difficult for me to believe how you could possibly feel that you have been treated unfairly. You must remember that you are the one who failed to follow the directions regarding the use of your camcorder. You must also remember that we are not obligated to cover under warranty any intentional or unintentional misuse of the products we manufacture.

Goal: Use positive language.

Mary reported that she would not be able to attend the meeting until 4:30. Unfortunately, her assistant is currently on vacation, and will not return to the office until next week. Therefore, Mary is not able to leave her work area until after the office is closed to the public at 4:30. She indicated that her not being there at the beginning of the meeting should not be a problem, however.

Exercise 17

Name ______________________ Section ______________ Grade ____________

Edit the following paragraphs, paying particular attention to the goals set for each paragraph. In addition, correct any other errors you find in punctuation, grammar, or writing style.

Courtesy

Goal: Use you-attitude.

I know you indicated that I should attend the meeting, but I will be unable to do so because I am scheduled to be in Denver that day presenting a paper on the research project I completed last summer. If you wish, I can contact Ray Smith to determine if he could attend the meeting in my place. I believe he is familar with the Harris situation that will be discussed at the meeting.

Goal: Use positive language.

Notwithstanding your belief that we should not sign the contract until we obtain the additional information from Brown Company, I do not believe that we should wait to sign. I do not think we will have the needed information by the last day we can sign the contract. Rather than risk having the contract expire, I do not believe we should be afraid to attach an amendment to the contract.

Goal: Use nonoffensive language.

You claimed that we did not seem to want to help you in your recent letter. However, I do not believe that you have the right to say that since you failed to send us a full explanation of the problem that you assert you are having with the Model 10 fan. If you expect us to help you once again we request that you send us the requested information.

Exercise 18

Name ______________________________ Section ________________ Grade ______________

Edit the following paragraphs, paying particular attention to the goals set for each paragraph. In addition, correct any other errors you find in punctuation, grammar, or writing style.

Courtesy

Goal: Use you-attitude.

I recall a recent discussion I had with you in which I asked you to look over the third quarter report I had just completed when I sent it to you. I decided to seek your help because I knew you were the one whom had compiled the financial data. Since I have not yet received your reactions to it, I am concluding that either you did not receive it or you have not had time to look at it.

Goal: Use positive language.

It is not uncommon to find at least 30-40 percent of the employees who do not agree with any new changes we try to implement. For the most part, these are employees whom are opposed to change because of a fear of the unknown or they are employees approaching retirement age and they believe they will have difficulty learning anything new. Sometimes I have difficulty accepting this type of attitude among employees.

Goal: Use nonoffensive tone.

It seems to me that if you would take your bill paying as seriously as you take finding fault with others that this would not have happened. Then after it did, you seem to think that the entire matter is all our fault. Let me remind you that we had a good working relationship until you tried to rip us off by claiming an error on your bill. Surely, you do not think that we wouldn't have procedures designed to catch people like you whose actions are of a very questionable nature.

Exercise 19

Name ______________________________ Section ________________ Grade______________

Edit the following paragraphs, paying particular attention to the goals set for each paragraph. In addition, correct any other errors you find in punctuation, grammar, or writing style.

Concreteness

Goal: Use specific, concrete words.

The scores of the students on the achievement test increased significantly when compared with the scores attained by those students' taking the test during the last several years. Approximately half of the students increased there percentile rankings by an average of several points over their scores on the test when they took it the last time.

Goal: Use specific, concrete words.

In the near future, will you please compile for me a list of the things you believe they would like to have in a benefits package. When we have a composite list, management can examine the items on the list to determine which ones might be feasible. Getting input will give us a better idea of what to recommend.

Goal: Use specific, concrete words.

Bill told me recently that my sales figures during the last several months have increased significant. He asked me what I attributed this to. After pondering his question for a while, I indicated that I didn't know for sure sure but I suspect it is due to hard work and a quality product more than anything else. He also told me that he was going to recommend me for a significant pay increase the next time he has the opportunity to do so in a few weeks.

Exercise 20

Name ______________________________ Section ________________ Grade ______________

Edit the following paragraphs, paying particular attention to the goals set for each paragraph. In addition, correct any other errors you find in punctuation, grammar, or writing style.

Concreteness

Goal: Use specific, concrete words.

The financial picture of that branch has improved considerably during the last fiscal period. Perhaps more than anything, this improvement can be attributed to perserverance and a "stay the course" attitude of management. Although no one will know for sure until the end of the next fiscal period, there is a good possibility this trend will continue for the foreseeable future.

Goal: Use specific, concrete words.

John's overall improvement the last few weeks is nothing short of a miracle given the condition of his health before he began the treatment program. All of his friends have mentioned a significant contrast in several before-after areas of comparison. If all goes as predicted, he should make a total recovery.

Goal: Use specific, concrete words.

The new branch is located a few miles from here. Several new employees had to be hired to staff the branch when it opened a short time ago. The majority of these employees were hired when the Hearthland Savings and Loan closed its doors recently. Several here believe we were fortunate to be able to hire such a well trained staff in such a short time.

Exercise 21

Name ______________________________ Section ________________ Grade ______________

Edit the following paragraphs, paying particular attention to correcting errors in punctuation, grammar, and writing style as well errors of substance.

Inquiry Letter—A

Part A describes a situation that elicits the letter shown in Part B. After reading the material in Part A, edit/rewrite Part B, making sure you accomplish in your revision of each section what you have been asked to accomplish. Correct in your revision other errors in style, structure, grammar, or punctuation. Add any information that might be needed.

Part A: The Situation

John Brown recently saw an advertisement in *Consumer Computer Products* about a new graphics/presentation software package, called Graphit. Some of the claims for this new product are (1) it is the easiest one on the market to use, (2) it is versatile, and (3) a variety of word processing software packages facilitate the importation of graphics prepared using Graphit into a variety of word processing packages, including the one you currently use (WordProcess). Mr. Brown has several questions about Graphit, including how much memory it needs, if it can be used on an IBC computer, if it accommodates color printing on a color printer, if it comes with a tutorial, and how much space it requires on a hard drive. Mr. Brown's goal in writing the letter is to obtain answers to his questions and any other information Computer Associates has about Graphit.

Part B: John Brown's Letter

Opening Paragraph

I recently saw advertised in *Consumer Computer Products* your new Graphit software package, I am interested in obtaining additional information about Graphit as I feel it might be just the type of software package I am looking for.

Revision: In the space below, provide your revised version of the opening paragraph, making sure it captures a you-attitude. In addition, correct other errors you find in style, structure, content, grammar, and punctuation. Add any information you believe should be included.

Middle Section

I have several questions I need answers to. What kind of memory does the package require, can it be used on an IBC computer like mine? If you have a color printer, can you get the output to print in color? Does Graphit come with a tutorial? What kind of space on a hard drive does it require?

Revision: In the space below, provide your revised version of the middle section of John Brown's letter, making sure it contains the content and structure appropriate for this type of letter, especially the inclusion of reader-benefit material. Correct other errors you discover in style, grammar, or punctuation. Add any information you believe should be included.

Closing Paragraph

I wish to take this opportunity to thank you for sending me material I've requested in addition to any other information you feel might be helpful to me.

Revision: In the space below, provide your revised version of the closing paragraph of John Brown's letter, making sure it is consistent with an effective closing for this type of letter. Correct any errors you find in style, grammar, or punctuation. Add any information you believe should be included.

Exercise 22

Name ______________________ Section ______________ Grade ______________

Edit the following paragraphs, paying particular attention to correcting errors in punctuation, grammar, and writing style as well as errors of substance.

Adjustment-Request Letter—A

Part A describes a situation for the letter shown in Part B. After reading the material in Part A, edit/rewrite Part B, making sure you accomplish in your revision of each section what you have been asked to accomplish. Correct in your revision other errors in style, structure, grammar, or punctuation. Add any information that might be needed.

Part A: The Situation

From your company six weeks ago James Smith purchased as a gift for his teen-age son a personal stereo unit (Model 8744) that contains a CD player, a dual tape deck, and an AM-FM stereo radio. The store from which he bought it is no longer in business, so he sent you the claim letter found in Part B. The letter indicates that sound no longer comes out of the speakers but that one can hear sound through earphones attached to the speaker jack. As you will notice, Mr. Smith was obviously not in a good mood when he wrote the letter. He wants to find out if he should return it to the company for a replacement or if it should be taken to a service center where it can be repaired.

Part B: James Smith's Letter

Opening Paragraph

I haven't been as upset for a long time as I was when my son told me your Model 8744 personal stereo that I had purchased for him not more than six weeks ago was no longer working. I was even more upset to learn that the store where I bought this piece of junk is no longer in business. I guess one might wonder if selling shoddy merchandise like your Model 8744 was responsible for it going out of business, what do you want me to do with this piece of junk?

> Revision: In the space below, provide your revised version of the opening paragraph, making sure it captures you-attitude, eliminating the negative tone, and restructuring the content to conform with a suitable opening of an adjustment-request letter. Correct any other errors you find in style, structure, content, grammar, or punctuation. Add any information you believe should be included.

Middle Section

Let me tell you what happened, and it isn't because of negligence on his part since he is very careful with his property and would never misuse or damage it in any way. You can not hear anything come from the speakers but one can hear sounds from an earphone plugged into the speaker jack. Obviously, something is seriously wrong with this personal stereo. Do you know why it would be doing this.

Revision: In the space provided below, provide your revised version of the middle section of Mr. Smith's letter, making sure it contains the content and structure appropriate for this type of letter and an appropriate tone. Correct any other errors you find in style, grammar, or punctuation. Add any additional information you believe should be included.

Closing Paragraph

I will expect your immediate attention to this matter. How well you handle it will determine if I ever buy another product from your company.

Revision: In the space provided below, provide a revised version of the closing section of Mr. Smith's letter, making sure it contains the content and tone appropriate for this type of letter. Correct any other errors you find in style, grammar, or punctuation. Add any additional information you believe should be included.

Exercise 23

Name ______________________________ Section ________________ Grade ______________

Edit the following paragraphs, paying particular attention to correcting errors in punctuation, grammar, and writing style as well as correcting errors of substance.

Favor-Request Letter—A

Part A is the situation that elicited the letter shown in Part B. After reading the material in Part A, edit/rewrite Part B, making sure you accomplish in your revision of each section what you have been asked to accomplish. Correct in your revision other errors in style, structure, grammar, or punctuation. Add any information that might be needed.

Part A: The Situation

Linda Graystone is a fourth-grade teacher in Highwood Elementary School in Dickinson, Nebraska. Her class has been studying a unit on various types of careers, including careers in banking. To help her students better understand the role and function of banking in our society, she decided to write you, the executive vice president of First National Bank in Dickinson, Nebraska, asking you for a favor: to provide her students with a field trip through the First National Bank. She also desires that her students learn as much as is appropriate about the various positions found in First National Bank. Following is her favor-request letter.

Part B: Linda Graystone's Letter

Opening Paragraph

I am a fourth-grade teacher at Highwood Elementary School here in Dickinson. My students have been studying a unit on careers, including careers in banking. As a favor to my students and me, would you be willing to provide us with a field trip of First National Bank. We are most interested in obtaining a better understanding of the role and function of banking. I hope so.

> Revision: In the space below, provide a revised version of the opening paragraph of Ms. Graystone's letter, making sure it conforms with the content, style, and tone appropriate for a favor-request letter. Correct any other errors you find in grammar or punctuation. If you need to add more information, do so.

Middle Section

I have two or three students in this class who tend to be class clowns. I will point them out to you before we start the trip so you can keep your eyes better on them, perhaps this way you will be able to control them well. I've found that if I keep them preoccupied then I am better able to keep them under control.

Revision: In the space below, provide a revised version of the middle section of Ms. Graystone's letter, making sure it conforms with the content, style, and tone appropriate for a favor-request letter. Correct any other errors you find in grammar or punctation. If you need to add additional information, do so. If you decide to delete information, do so.

Closing Paragraph

I realize I am not giving you much time to arrange this, but I am wondering if you could possibly do the field trip on Friday of this week. It would sure help me out if you could possibly do it on Friday. I will call you tomorrow to learn of your response to my favor request. If I can ever return the favor, I will be happy to try to do so.

Revision: In the space below, provide a revision of the closing section of this paragraph. Please make sure it contains appropriate content, style, and tone. Correct any other errors you find in grammar or punctuation.

Exercise 24

Name ______________________ Section ______________ Grade ____________

Edit the following paragraphs, paying particular attention to correcting errors in punctuation, grammar, and writing style as well as errors in substance.

Letter Responding to an Inquiry—A

Part A describes a situation that elicits the letter shown in Part B. After reading the material in Part A, edit/rewrite various sections found in Part B, making sure you accomplish in your revision of each section what you have been asked to accomplish. Correct in your revision other errors in style, structure, grammar, or punctuation. Add any information that might be needed.

Part A: The Situation

Jim Gardiner, a customer service representative for Software, Inc., recently prepared a response to a letter the company received from John Brown. Mr. Brown asked several questions about Graphit, a new graphics/presentation software package he saw advertised in *Consumer Computer Products*. Software, Inc. is promoting this product as the easiest to use of its type on the market, its versatility, and its ease in importation of graphics created by it into documents being originated by a variety of word processing software packages. In his letter, Mr. Brown asked a number of questions about Graphit, including the amount of memory it requires, if it can be used on an IBC computer, if it accommodates color printing on a color printer, if it comes with a tutorial, and how much space it requires on a hard drive. Following is the letter Mr. Gardiner prepared in response to Mr. Brown's inquiry.

Part B: The Response

Opening Paragraph

I have received your letter of March 7, 199x, and am glad to provide you with the answers to the questions you asked in your letter. Having the opportunity to help interested customers is always a pleasure for me.

> Revision: In the space below, provide your revised version of the opening paragraph, making sure it captures a you-attitude, has a fast-start opening, and corrects any other errors you find in style, structure, content, grammar, and punctuation. Add any information you believe should be included.

Middle Section

There are several things that make Graphit a desirable product for you, it runs on IBC and IBC compatible computers. It requires 640K of memory, and consumes 6MB on your hard drive. Furthermore you will find the tutorial that comes with it very easy to use. You also asked if it accommodates color printing on a color printer, it does.

I know you will be very pleased with Graphit just as the vast majority of our other customers are. Most that I have talked with cannot believe how easy it is to use.

Revision: In the space below, provide your revised version of the middle section, incorporating resale material and perhaps some sales-promotion material. Correct any other errors you find in style, tone, structure, content, grammar, and punctuation.

Closing Paragraph

I want to take this opportunity to thank you for your inquiry about Graphit. I hope I have answered your questions in a way that you will find useful.

Revision: In the space below, provide your revised version of the closing paragraph, creating a you-attitude and an action orientation. Correct any other errors you find in style, tone, structure, content, grammar, and punctuation.

Exercise 25

Name ______________________________ Section ________________ Grade ______________

Edit the following paragraphs, paying particular attention to correcting errors in punctuation, grammar, and writing style as well as errors of substance.

Letter Granting an Adjustment—A

Part A describes a situation that elicits the letter in Part B. After reading the material in Part A, then edit/rewrite Part B, making sure you accomplish in your revision of each section what you have been asked to accomplish. Correct in your revision other errors in style, structure, grammar, or punctuation. Add any information that might be needed.

Part A: The Situation

Janet Snyder works in the adjustment section of Quality Electronics Company, a manufacturer of radios, stereo equipment, and cellular telephones. The companies that sell your products handle Quality's warranty work, for which it reimburses them. Ms. Snyder recently responded to a curt letter received from James Smith regarding a personal stereo unit (Model 8744) he purchased for his teen-age son six weeks ago. Because the store where he bought the personal stereo is no longer in business, Mr. Smith had to contact Quality to let it know about the problem with the unit: The speakers no longer work although one can hear sound when using the speaker jack and a set of earplugs. Following is Ms. Snyder's reply in which she grants a favorable adjustment.

Part B: Ms. Synder's Letter

Opening Paragraph

Mr. Smith, I sensed from your letter that you are quite upset about the malfunctioning of the personal stereo unit (Model 8744) that you purchased for your son six weeks ago. I discussed this situation with one of our engineering technicians, who believes that the problem is probably caused by one or more wires that have come lose.

Revision: In the space below, provide your revised version of the opening paragraph, making sure it conforms with an appropriate opening for a letter granting a favorable adjustment. Correct any other errors you find in style, structure, content, grammar, or punctuation. Add any information you believe should be included.

Middle Section

I'm sorry that the store where you purchased this unit is no longer in business and that you had to take the trouble to contact us. Let me assure you that we have very, very few problems with the products we manufacture, except when the customer has misused them. Although we believe that may have happened in this case, we will give you the benefit of the doubt. Accordingly, we are sending you a Model 8744 to replace the one that is no longer working. On the warranty that is enclosed, I have underlined the sentences that address the issue of customer misuse, just so you are aware that it will void the warranty on your replacement unit. Please return the malfunctioning unit to us using the mailing labels enclosed with this letter.

Revision: In the space below, provide your revised version of the middle section of the letter, making sure it conforms with an appropriate middle section for this type of letter. The inclusion of appropriate resale material is suggested. Correct any other errors you find in style, structure, content, grammar, or punctuation.

Closing Paragraph

Mr. Smith, you should consider yourself lucky, that we granted your request as we generally deny requests of a questionable nature. I hope your son enjoys the use of his new personal stereo unit.

Revision: In the space below, provide your revised version of the closing paragraph, making sure it conforms with the content appropriate for the closing paragraph of this type of letter. Correct any other errors you find in style, structure, content, grammar, or punctuation.

Exercise 26

Name ______________________________ Section ______________ Grade ____________

Edit the following paragraphs, paying particular attention to correcting of errors in punctuation, grammar, and writing style as well as errors of substance.

Letter Granting a Favor Request—A

Part A describes the situation that elicits the letter shown in Part B. After reading the material in Part A, edit/rewrite Part B, making sure you accomplish in your revision of each section what you have been asked to accomplish. Correct in your revision other errors in style, structure, grammar, or punctuation. Add any information that might be needed.

Part A: The Situation

As the executive vice president of the First National Bank in Dickinson, Nebraska, you receive the requests from schools and groups regarding field trips through the bank's facilities. Generally, you ask your administrative assistant, Sally Grant, to write responses. The following letter is the one that Mrs. Grant recently sent to Linda Graystone, a fourth-grade teacher in Highwood Elementary School in Dickinson about a field trip of the bank. Mrs. Graystone indicated in her letter that her class had just completed a unit on careers, including banking careers. You are agreeable to accommodating her request for the field trip that you are suggesting take place a week from Wednesday at 2 P.M. You are recommending that it last approximately 45 minutes.

Part B: Sally Grant's Letter

Opening Paragraph

Your letter to Mr. David Greenfield, the executive vice president of First National Bank here in Dickinson have been received and he has asked that I reply to it. He also asked that I commend you on teaching a unit on careers.

> Revision: In the space below, provide a revised version of the opening paragraph of Mrs. Grant's letter, making sure it conforms with the content, style, and tone appropriate for such a letter. Correct any other errors you find in grammar or punctuation. Include any additional information you believe should be added.

Middle Section

Mr. Greenfield has given many tours through our premises and he seems to have a special way of working with students considered by their teachers to be trouble makers. Because your letter did not suggest a day or time, he is recommending the field trip take place a week from Wednesday at 2 P.M. and last for 45 minutes. We hope this will work for you.

> Revision: In the space below, provide a revised version of the middle section of the letter, making sure it conforms with the content, style, and tone appropriate for such a letter. Correct any errors you find in grammar or punctuation. Add any additional information that you believe should be included.

Closing Paragraph

Both I and Mr. Greenfield look forward to seeing you at the field trip.

> Revision: In the space below, provide a revised version of the closing paragraph of the letter, making sure it conforms with the content and style appropriate for a letter in which a favor request is granted. Correct any errors you find in grammar or punctuation. Add any information you believe should be included.

Exercise 27

Name ______________________________ Section ________________ Grade______________

Edit the following paragraphs, paying particular attention to correcting errors in punctuation, grammar, and writing style as well as errors of substance.

Negative Response to an Inquiry Letter—A

Part A describes the situation that elicits the letter shown in Part B. After reading the material in Part A, edit/rewrite Part B, making sure you accomplish in your revision of each section what you have been asked to accomplish. Correct in your revision other errors in style, structure, grammar, or punctuation. Add any information that might be needed.

Part A: The Situation

Martha Atchinson, a customer service representative for Bleufort Corporation, recently received from David Joseph a letter in which he requested answers to several questions about a new mulching lawn mower (Model A-12) manufactured by Bleufort. He was interested in learning if the A-12 came with a grass-catching bag so that the mower could be used either as a conventional mower or as a mulching mower (the answer is no); if the A-12 is available with a 5-horsepower engine (no; a 4.5 horsepower engine is standard); if the mower is available with an electronic starting mechanism (no; it is only available with a manual start); and where the nearest dealer is located (in Denver, Colorado). Mr. Joseph lives in Alva, Oklahoma. Following is Ms. Atchinson's response to Mr. Joseph's letter.

Part B: Ms. Atchinson's Letter

Opening Paragraph

Your recent letter asking about our A-12 mulching lawn mower has arrived, and I regret to have to inform you that our dealer who lives nearest you is in Denver, Colorado. We are currently working on getting dealers lined up in Oklahoma but so far none has been selected to carry our lawn care products.

> Revision: In the space below, provide your revised version of the opening paragraph, incorporating an appropriate buffered opening and eliminating the trite, negative material. Correct any other errors you find in style, structure, content, grammar, or punctuation. Add any information you believe should be included.

Middle Section

You asked several other questions about our A-12. You wondered it it can be equipped with a grass-catching bag so it can be used as a conventional mower. The present model cannot be so equipped but our engineers are working on this for next year's model. It does not come equipped with a 5-horsepower engine, although the standard 4.5 engine seems to have ample power. You also asked if it comes equipped with an electronic starting mechanism. The A-12 only has a manual start. Mr. Joseph, I wish I was able to give you positive answers to your questions but I simply cannot. However, please be assured that we have many satisfied users of this mower even though it doesn't seem to have the features you are interested in.

Revision: In the space below, provide your revised version of the middle section, removing the negative tone, adding appropriate resale material, and correcting any errors in style, structure, grammar, or punctuation.

Closing Paragraph

Perhaps you should wait until next year when our new line of mowers are available as I believe they will contain more of the features you are interested in.

Revision: In the space below, provide your revised version of the closing paragraph, making sure it is consistent with an effective closing for this type of letter. Correct any errors you find in style, grammar, or punctuation. Add any information you believe should be included.

Exercise 28

Name ______________________ Section ______________ Grade ______________

Edit the following paragraphs, paying particular attention to correcting errors in punctuation, grammar, and writing style as well errors of substance.

Negative Response to an Adjustment Request—A

Part A describes a situation that elicits the letter shown in Part B. After reading the material in Part A, edit/rewrite Part B, making sure you accomplish in your revision of each section what you have been asked to accomplish. Correct in your revision other errors in style, structure, grammar, or punctuation. Add any information that might be needed.

Part A: The Situation

Kenneth Mason, the manager of the adjustment unit in DeArco Products, Inc., a manufacturer of exercise equipment, recently received a letter from Jon Grant who requested that his three-month-old rowing machine be replaced because several of the moving parts are showing excessive wear. DeArco Products, Inc. has a one-year warranty on all of its products. However, the warranty does not cover equipment purchased for commercial use. In checking the serial number of his rowing machine (he included the unit's number in his adjustment request letter), you discover the unit was shipped by your company four years ago to Be-Trim Exercise Center located in the same city in which Mr. Grant lives. Because of the circumstances under which Mr. Grant made the request (he was dishonest in reporting the age of the equipment as well as in indicating that he was not the original purchaser), you decide to deny his request for an adjustment. Following is the letter Mr. Mason sent Mr. Grant.

Part B: Mr. Mason's Letter

Opening Paragraph

I have to deny your request for a replacement of your rowing machine for two reasons: (1) the device is actually four years old, not three months as you indicated in your letter; (2) the device was originally sold to the Be-Trim Exercise Center, which voids the warranty because the warranty does not cover our products used commercially.

> Revision: In the space below, provide your revised version of the opening paragraph of Mr. Mason's letter, incorporating a buffered opening, including you-attitude, and deleting the negative tone. Correct any errors you find in style, grammar, or punctuation. Add any information you believe should be included.

Middle Section

Mr. Grant, it is perturbing to me that you would try to deceive us in order to obtain something to which you are not entitled. People who do this cost American companies millions of dollars each year. This cost in turn has to be past on to our honest customers.

You perhaps are not aware that DeArco has a restoration program for people in your situation who want their equipment restored to a like-new condition. The cost is $84 which includes shipping, handling, repairs, and labor. Please let me know if you would like to take advantage of this program.

> Revision: In the space below, provide your revised version of the middle section, making sure it is consistent with an appropriate middle section of this type of letter. Incorporate an implied refusal, along with resale material.

Closing Paragraph

I hope you understand why we have had to deny your request, for a replacement rowing machine.

> Revision: In the space below, provide your revised version of the closing paragraph, making sure it is appropriate for this type of letter. Correct any errors you find in style, grammar, or punctuation. Add any information you believe should be included.

Exercise 29

Name ______________________ Section ______________ Grade ____________

Edit the following paragraphs, paying particular attention to correcting errors in punctuation, grammar, and writing style as well as errors of substance.

Negative Response to Credit Request—A

Part A describes the situation that elicits the letter shown in Part B. After reading the material in Part A, edit/rewrite Part B, making sure you accomplish in your revision of each section what you have been asked to accomplish. Correct in your revision other errors in style, structure, grammar, or punctuation. Add any information that might be needed.

Part A: The Situation

David Murray is the credit manager for the Grantham Department Store, which has its own credit program. The Credit Department is quite strict in granting credit. When a credit applicant is denied credit, Mr. Murray sends the applicant a letter, a copy of which is found in Part B. Mr. Murray has decided the best policy is to be honest in telling each applicant just why he/she was denied credit.

Part B: Mr. Murray's Letter

Opening Section

I regret that it is necessary for us to have to deny your recent credit application. Having to tell individuals like you who have been a faithful customer for several years is hard to do. If you are like many of our credit denials, however, this is not the first time you have been denied credit.

> Revision: In the space below, provide your revised version of the opening paragraph, incorporating an appropriate buffered opening and eliminating the negative material. Correct any other errors you find in style, structure, content, grammar, or punctuation. Add any information you believe should be included.

Middle Section

I tried many different ways to get you qualified for credit. None of them worked, however, because quite simply you just aren't qualified. Your biggest problem is that you have too much debt for the amount of income. When this happens, a person becomes a credit risk that we just cannot afford.

I hope our denying your credit application will not cause you to quite shopping with us. Please remember that we are just as concerned about your situation as you are.

Revision: In the space below, provide your revised version of the middle section of Mr. Murray's letter, making sure it contains the content and structure appropriate for this type of letter. Include sales-promotion material, and correct any other errors you find in style, grammar, or punctuation. Add any information you believe should be included.

Closing Paragraph

When and if your financial background improves to the point where you believe you might qualify for a credit account, please do not hesitate to re-apply.

Revision: In the space below, provide your revised version of the closing paragraph of Mr. Murray's letter, making sure it is consistent with an effective closing for this type of letter. Correct any errors you find in style, grammar, or punctuation. Add any information you believe should be included.

Exercise 30

Name ______________________ Section ______________ Grade ______________

Edit the following paragraphs, paying particular attention to correcting errors in punctuation, grammar, and writing style as well as errors of substance.

Request Collection Letter—A

Part A describes the situation that elicits the letter shown in Part B. After reading the material in Part A, edit/rewrite Part B, making sure you accomplish in your revision of each section what you have been asked to accomplish. Correct in your revision other errors in style, structure, grammar, or punctuation. Add any information that might be needed.

Part A: The Situation

As the collections manager in the Credit Department of Armitage Petroleum Company, Mr. John Smith has to prepare a number of collection letters that are sent to individuals who have allowed past-due balances to accumulate on their charge accounts. The letters are designed to become more aggressive in their request for payment as the length of a customer's delinquent period increases. Following is the form request collection letter sent by Armitage to its customers whose payment delinquency merits the letter.

Part B: Mr. Smith's Letter

Opening Paragraph

I would have thought that you would have gotten the message by now that you need to pay the past-due balance of your account, the amount of which is now $xxxxx.xx. You simply cannot afford to let this situation continue without doing something about it.

> Revision: In the space below, provide your revised version of the opening paragraph, making sure it captures you-attitude and is appropriate for the opening of this type of letter. Correct any other errors you find in style, structure, content, grammar, and punctuation. Add any information you believe should be included.

Middle Paragraph

Your continued inattention to this situation will put us in the unpleasant position of having to report your delinquency to the appropriate individuals, an action that will virtually destroy your creditworthiness. While I am sure you do not want this to happen, your continuing to ignore our requests for payment or even an explanation why you are unwilling to pay on this account will put us in a position where we have to take drastic actions. The next time we have to contact you about this situation will be the last time. If you fail to do as we request at that time, your account will be turned over to a collection agency, an action that becomes a permanent part of your credit records.

> Revision: In the space below, provide your revised version of the middle section of this letter. Pay particular attention to the tone of your revision, making sure it is forceful but not tactless. Correct any other errors you find in style, structure, content, grammar, and punctuation. Add any information you believe should be included.

Closing Paragraph

I hope you will sit down right now and either write us a check for the amount you owe or let us know why you have ignored our previous requests for payment. Only then will we be able to improve our relationship.

> Revision: In the space below, provide your revised version of the closing paragraph of this letter, making sure it conforms with the content appropriate for this type of letter. Correct any other errors you find in style, structure, content, grammar, and punctuation. Add any information you believe should be included.

Exercise 31

Name ______________________________ Section ________________ Grade ______________

Edit the following paragraphs, paying particular attention to correcting errors in punctuation, grammar, and writing style as well as errors of substance.

Letter of Application—A

Part A describes the situation that elicits the letter shown in Part B. After reading the material in Part A, edit/rewrite Part B, making sure you accomplish in your revision of each section what you have been asked to accomplish. Correct in your revision other errors in style, structure, grammar, or punctuation. Add any information that might be needed.

Part A: The Situation

Jason Brownlee, a management information systems major at Oklahoma State College, will be receiving his bachelor's degree (with distinction) in a few months. Accordingly, he has begun the process of looking for a position to assume once he is graduated. His immediate career choice is to work as a systems analyst. At the time Jason wrote the following letter of application, he had a 4.0 overall grade point average, was president of the student council, was president of the Management Information Systems Association (membership comprised of management information systems majors), was vice president of the Young Republicans at OSC, vice president of his social fraternity, and had held several committee chair positions in his church's youth group. As a junior, Jason was selected by the faculty in the School of Business as the recipient of the Melvin Smith award, which is presented annually to the outstanding junior business major. Furthermore, between his sophomore and junior years and between his junior and senior years, Jason had internships in the data processing centers of two large companies in his hometown of Tulsa. Following is the letter Jason Brownlee has been sending with his resume.

Part B: Jason Brownlee's Letter

Opening Paragraph

I am interested in learning if your have any openings for a systems analyst? I will be graduated with distinction by Oklahoma State College at the end of the current semester. Given my background of service, leadership, and scholastic achievment I am confident of my ability to be an excellent employee for you. I will appreciation your giving me a chance to prove myself to you.

> Revision: In the space below, provide your revision of the opening paragraph, creating a you-attitude, deleting any traces of an arrogant tone, adding any additional material that is needed, and removing any unnecessary material. Correct any other errors you find in style, structure, content, grammar, or punctuation.

Middle Section

I am enclosing a resume with this letter that mentions a number of my accomplishments, many of which are indicative of my leadership potential. You will notice that the leadership positions I've held provide a nice balance in that some are professional and others are personal. I always strive to be able to prove that my background is balanced, yet diverse.

I am the only one of the graduating seniors in management information systems who had an internship at both the end of the sophomore year and the junior year. Perhaps this also reveals something about my background. I found both internships to be excellent in giving me an opportunity to apply in a realistic setting what I've learned in the classroom. Most of my fellow majors are not able to do that. I've been told by several people that the nature of my internship experiences will make me a more valuable employee.

> Revision: In the space below, provide your revision of the middle section of this letter, making sure it conforms with the content and style desirable for letters of application. Add any needed material and delete any unneeded material. Correct any other errors you find in style, structure, content, grammar, or punctuation.

Closing Paragraph

I would like to have the opportunity to better sell you on my qualifications through an interview. Please contact me at (410) 844-8844 to let me know a time that is convenient for you to talk to me about this position. Because I am rather hard to get ahold of, please feel free to leave messages on my answering machine.

> Revision: In the space below, provide your revised version of the closing paragraph of Jason Brownlee's letter, making sure it is consistent with an effective closing for this type of letter. Correct any errors you find in style, content, grammar, or punctuation. Add any information you believe should be included.

Exercise 32

Name ______________________________ Section ________________ Grade______________

Critique the following paragraphs, paying particular attention to the identification of errors in punctuation, grammar, and writing style as well as substance. Rewrite each paragraph.

Speaking Invitation—B

Part A describes a situation that elicits the letter shown in Part B. After reading the material in Part A, prepare in the space provided a written critique of each section of the letter, identifying weaknesses in content, style, structure, grammar, or punctuation. Following your line-by-line critique, rewrite each section, eliminating these weaknesses. Add any information that may be needed.

Part A: The Situation

David Ramariz is the convention program cochair for the Ohio Materials Manufacturing Association, an organization whose members include approximately 1,500 materials manufacturing managers. The convention he is helping plan will be held May 16-18 next year at the Hotel Mariwell in Cincinnati. One of the tasks for which he is responsible as program cochair is to obtain speakers for eight sessions, each lasting an hour. The following letter was sent by Mr. Ramariz to eight individuals on his initial speakers' list, inquiring into their availability/willingness to speak at the convention.

Part B: David Ramariz's Letter

Opening Paragraph

I am the convention program cochair for the Ohio Materials Manufacturing Association. We will hold our annual convention May 16-18 next year at the Hotel Mariwell in Cincinnati. Our organization has approximately 1,500 members, most of who are materials manufacturing managers.

Critique:

Rewrite:

Middle Section

This letter is your cordial invitation to be one of our session speakers at this convention. You are being invited since you are known throughout our industry as a very dynamic, knowledgeable speaker who would probably be willing to speak for nothing. Unfortunately, our association doesn't have the budget to pay their speakers an honorarium. Only expenses they incurr in getting too the convention and back home.

Critique:

Rewrite:

Closing Paragraph

I hope you will give serious consideration to this offer, please let me know your decision.

Critique:

Rewrite:

Exercise 33

Name ______________________________ Section ________________ Grade ______________

Critique the following paragraphs, paying particular attention to the identification of errors in punctuation, grammar, and writing style as well as substance. Rewrite each paragraph.

Reservation Letter—B

Part A describes a situation that elicits the letter shown in Part B. After reading the material in Part A, prepare in the space provided a written critique of each section of the letter, identifying weaknesses in content, style, structure, grammar, or punctuation. Following your line-by-line critique, rewrite each section, eliminating these weaknesses. Add any information that may be needed.

Part A: The Situation

Jonathan Miller, his wife, and their three small children (Amy, age 5; Brent, age 3; and Nicole, age 6 months) are planning a three-week vacation June 7 to June 28. Because of the ages of their children, the Millers have decided to spend two or three nights in the same facility in several locations rather than long days in their car traveling daily from one location to another. They have decided to book their motel/hotel reservations several months before they actually begin their vacation. Following is a letter that Mr. Miller used in booking reservations at one motel.

Part B: Mr. Miller's Letter

Opening Paragraph

My wife, three small children, and I are planning a vacation this summer, first in several years. Since we want everything to be flawless, we have decided to make our motel reservations several months ahead of the time we will be needing them.

Critique:

Rewrite:

Middle Section

Will you be good enough to reserve a room for us for the nights of June 10, 11, and 12? Our preference is to be on ground floor away from the pool. I liked the looks of the room I saw in the brochure our travel agent gave us.

Critique:

Rewrite:

Closing Paragraph

I will appreciate your letting me know the status of this request as soon as possible.

Critique:

Rewrite:

Exercise 34

Name ______________________ Section ______________ Grade ______________

Critique the following paragraphs, paying particular attention to the identification of errors in punctuation, grammar, and writing style as well as substance. Rewrite each paragraph.

Letter of Congratulations—B

Part A describes a situation that elicits the letter shown in Part B. After reading the material in Part A, prepare in the space provided a written critique of each section of the letter, identifying weaknesses in content, style, structure, grammar, or punctuation. Following your line-by-line critique, rewrite each section, eliminating these weaknesses. Add any information that may be needed.

Part A: The Situation

Daniel Williams was recently promoted from executive vice president of the Merrick Corporation, a manufacturer of heavy-duty earth-moving equipment, to president. A friend of his, Bill Johnston, upon hearing the announcement, sent him the letter of congratulations that follows.

Part B: Bill Johnston's Letter

Opening Paragraph

I was very pleased Dan when I heard the good news about your being promoted to president of Merrick. I know we have talked often about your hoping this would some day happen. I also know the board of directors could not have found a better person to serve as president.

Critique:

Revision:

Middle Section

I know you will do very well as president. Given your vision of where the company should go at this time, I know many people believe as I do that the best lays ahead for Merrick. I have always been impressed with your leadership skills, the immediate respect you command from those with who you work, and your keen ability to stay several steps ahead of the competition.

Critique:

Revision:

Closing Paragraph

I have no doubts whatsoever, Dan, that when you retire as president of Merrick, you will be the one who is generally credited with "putting Merrick on the map." Congratulations!

Critique:

Revision:

Exercise 35

Name ______________________________ Section ________________ Grade ______________

Critique the following paragraphs, paying particular attention to the identification of errors in punctuation, grammar, and writing style as well as substance. Rewrite each paragraph.

Letter Accepting an Invitation—B

Part A describes a situation that elicits the letter shown in Part B. After reading the material in Part A, prepare in the space provided a written critique of each section of the letter, identifying weaknesses in content, style, structure, grammar, or punctuation. Following your line-by-line critique, rewrite each section, eliminating these weaknesses. Add any information that may be needed.

Part A: The Situation

Marvin Grimsley has been invited to make an hour-long presentation at the Ohio Materials Manufacturing Association convention to be held May 16–18 next year at the Hotel Mariwell in Cincinnati. Around 1,500 members of the association are expected to attend the convention. Following is Mr. Grimsley's letter that was sent to David Ramariz, the convention program cochair, in which he accepted the invitation.

Part B: Mr. Grimsley's Letter

Opening Paragraph

The invitation you recently sent me inviting me to speak at the Ohio Materials Manufacturing Association was gratefully received. I am pleased to have been considered for such an honor as addressing the members who will be attending this convention.

Critique:

Revision:

Middle Section

Since you didn't mention the topic you want me to speak on, I assume I have the flexibility to choose the topic myself. At this time, I don't have the slightest idea what I might speak on but I am sure that as I think about it in the days ahead, a topic will come to mind. Also, if you would care to make any suggestions regarding a topic, feel free to do so.

Critique:

Revision:

Closing Paragraph

It was great to be thought of as a person who could make a contribution to the success of your convention.

Critique:

Revision:

Exercise 36

Name ______________________ Section ______________ Grade ______________

Critique the following paragraphs, paying particular attention to the identification of errors in punctuation, grammar, and writing style as well as substance. Rewrite each paragraph.

Letter Declining an Invitation—B

Part A describes a situation that elicits the letter shown in Part B. After reading the material in Part A, prepare in the space provided a written critique of each section of the letter, identifying weaknesses in content, style, structure, grammar, or punctuation. Following your line-by-line critique, rewrite each section, eliminating these weaknesses. Add any information that may be needed.

Part A: The Situation

Mr. James Brown was recently invited to be the after-dinner speaker at the Marcy, Nebraska, Chamber of Commerce annual banquet. Mr. Brown is well known for his worthwhile presentations that are delivered in a light, humorous manner. In looking at his calendar, he discoverd that he will be out of town attending his daughter's college graduation on the evening of the banquet. Consequently, he has to decline the invitation, which he did in the letter that follows.

Part B: Mr. Brown's Letter

Opening Paragraph

Your kind invitation to speak at the Marcy Chamber of Commerce annual banquet has been received but unfortunately I will have to decline because I will be in Michigan attending my oldest daughter's graduation from Michigan State College. Being able to speak before this esteemed group would have been a distinct honor that regrettably I shall have to turn down.

Critique:

Revision:

Middle Section

I recently had the opportunity to hear Sandra Grant, executive vice president of Daniels State Bank in Wood River, and she did an excellent job. If you are needing a recommendation for another speaker, I would recommend her to you. She handles herself very well before a group perhaps because of her background as Miss Nebraska. Needless to say, she is also pleasant to look at.

Critique:

Revision:

Closing Section

It would be a pleasure for me to speak to your group at a later date. All you need do is ask. Perhaps I won't have a scheduling conflict the next time.

Critique:

Revision:

Exercise 37

Name ______________________________ Section ________________ Grade ______________

Critique the following paragraphs, paying particular attention to the identification of errors in punctuation, grammar, and writing style as well as substance. Rewrite each paragraph.

Favor-Refusal Letter—B

Part A describes a situation that elicits the letter shown in Part B. After reading the material in Part A, prepare in the space provided a written critique of each section of the letter, identifying weaknesses in content, style, structure, grammar, or punctuation. Following your line-by-line critique, rewrite each section, eliminating these weaknesses. Add any information that may be needed.

Part A: The Situation

Marilee Taylor, executive vice president of the Jackson Furniture Company, a manufacturer of fine home and office furnishings, occasionally receives from college students requests that they be given an opportunity to do a spring-break internship with various executives and managers within the company. Although the company used to do this as a favor to local college students, it quit doing so several years ago when one of the student interns removed several confidential files from the premises. At that time, a decision was made to refuse all future internship requests. Following is a letter Ms. Taylor sent to Diedre Martin in response to her request for a spring-break internship.

Part B: Ms. Taylor's Letter

Opening Section

An unfortunate situation several years ago that involved a spring-break intern has caused us to put a total ban on accepting interns. For that reason, I am unable to grant your request.

Critique:

Revision:

Middle Section

It is unfortunate that one college student several years ago caused us to have to quite accepting spring-break interns. This particular student removed from the premises several confidential files. Since we have to maintain the integrity of all company information, I am sure you can understand why we no longer are able to accept spring-break interns.

Critique:

Revision:

Closing Paragraph

I wish I was in a position to accommodate your request; however, now that I've explained the situation, perhaps you can understand the need to refuse your request.

Critique:

Revision:

Exercise 38

Name ______________________ Section ______________ Grade ______________

Critique the following paragraphs, paying particular attention to the identification of errors in punctuation, grammar, and writing style as well as substance. Rewrite each paragraph.

Ultimatum Collection Letter—B

Part A describes a situation that elicits the letter shown in Part B. After reading the material in Part A, prepare in the space provided a written critique of each section of the letter, identifying weaknesses in content, style, structure, grammar, or punctuation. Following your line-by-line critique, rewrite each section, eliminating these weaknesses. Add any information that may be needed.

Part A: The Situation

When a credit customer of Okla-Ark Gas Company has allowed his charge account to develop a "problem" status because of a long-term past-due balance, the customer is sent an ultimatum letter. The purpose of this letter is to communicate that he must pay the past-due balance of the account by the stated due date, or the account will be turned over either to a collection agency or to an attorney. Following is the letter prepared by Ms. Janet Jones, the collection manager.

Part B: Ms. Jones Letter

Opening Paragraph

If you thought we were bluffing in earlier letters about your need to pay the past-due balance of $xxxxx.xx on your Okla-Ark Gas Company charge account now is the time to take our request seriously. Unless we have full payment of your account by xxxxxxxxx xx, we have no options left but to turn your account over either to a collection agency or an attorney.

Critique:

Revision:

Middle Section

Surely you know the outcome of not paying your bills on time and how that can destroy your ability to obtain credit in the future. From our standpoint, money owed us that we cannot collect causes us financial difficulty. Please be fair to yourself and to us and pay us by the deadline the amount you owe. Doing so will benefit you more than you will probably ever know.

Critique:

Revision:

Closing Paragraph

I suggest you do what is right and fair and pay the amount of your past-due balance by the deadline. This is the last opportunity you will have to do so in a nonlegal environment.

Critique:

Revision:

Exercise 39

Name ________________________________ Section ________________ Grade ______________

Critique the following paragraphs, paying particular attention to the identification of errors in punctuation, grammar, and writing style as well as substance. Rewrite each paragraph.

Interview Follow-Up Letter—B

Part A describes a situation that elicits the letter shown in Part B. After reading the material in Part A, prepare in the space provided a written critique of each section of the letter, identifying weaknesses in content, style, structure, grammar, or punctuation. Following your line-by-line critique, rewrite each section, eliminating these weaknesses. Add any information that may be needed.

Part A: The Situation

Mary Dickinson, an accounting major at State College of Kansas, will be receiving her bachelor's degree in a few months. She began looking for a job following graduation several weeks ago. Her efforts have paid off as she has had several home-office (or second) interviews. Following is the letter she sent to one of the partners in a CPA firm in which she recently interviewed.

Part B: Mary Dickinsons's Letter

Opening Paragraph

Now that I have had several home-office interviews, I can honestly say that the one I had with you last week was by far the best. I believe this for two basic reasons: the cordiality with which I was treated and the nature of the position I would fill should I be lucky enough to be hired by your firm.

Critique:

Revision:

Middle Section

Several things particularly impressed me about your company. Obviously, the salary you pay and the benefits you provide are very impressive. In addition, the training program you provide new hires appears to be an excellent one. I also especially appreciate that you give new hires considerable flexibility—more so than any other firm I have interviewed. I believe this is good because after all we have completed a bachelor's degree in accounting. I also like the fast-track promotion program you have been using for several years.

Critique:

Revision:

Closing Paragraph

Mr. Perry, no words can describe how honored I would be to be given an opportunity to work for your accounting firm. I shall anxiously await what I hope will be a positive decision on your part.

Critique:

Revision:

Exercise 40

Name ______________________ Section ______________ Grade ______________

Critique the following paragraphs, paying particular attention to the identification of errors in punctuation, grammar, and writing style as well as substance. Rewrite each paragraph.

Letter of Resignation—B

Part A describes a situation that elicits the letter shown in Part B. After reading the material in Part A, then prepare in the space provided a written critique of each section of the letter, identifying weaknesses in content, style, structure, grammar, or punctuation. Following your line-by-line critique, rewrite each section, eliminating these weaknesses. Add any information that may be needed.

Part A: The Situation

William Brown has been employed by the Garner Communications Consulting Group for four years. Because of his academic background (communications) and his expertise as a consultant in helping companies improve the quality of their communication programs, he has decided to quit Garner so he can become a consultant working on his own. During the four years Mr. Brown has worked for Garner, he has developed a reputation for helping his client companies vastly improve the quality of their communications programs as well as a reputation for frequently faulting Garner's management team for some of the decisions/actions it has taken during the last four years. Some of the management team is glad to see him leave; others are disappointed. Following is the letter of resignation he submitted.

Part B: Mr. Brown's Letter

Opening Paragraph

I am hereby requesting in this letter that my resignation from Garner Communications Consulting Group be accepted by the partners immediately.

Critique:

Revision:

Middle Section

I wish I could say that I have really enjoyed working here. While I enjoyed the work with the clients and learned much about communications consultancy from these project, I felt the restrictions placed on me by certain partners definitely hampered some of my creativity. Because of the rather hostile atmosphere I found myself in the middle of from time to time, I have decided to leave the employ of the Garner Communications Consulting Group. I guess it is quite obvious and I will readily admit that some of you definitely "got the last laugh." I hope you are satisfied.

Critique:

Revision:

Closing Paragraph

I will look forward to your tendering this resignation request immediately and your sending whatever I am owed to my home address.

Critique:

Revision:

Exercise 41

Name ______________________ Section ______________ Grade ____________

In each of the following sentences, determine if the underlined portion is correct or contains an error in word usage, grammar, or punctuation. When you rewrite each sentence in the space below the sentence, correct any errors in the underlined portion(s) as well as edit each sentence for courtesy, conciseness, concreteness, and clarity.

1. One of the books are missing from the office occupied by Mr. Johnson.

2. The person who you wish to speak to will not be available until 2 o'clock this afternoon, he will be able to talk with you then.

3. I wish it was time to graduate; however, that will not happen for six more weeks.

4. The report on intercultural communication was prepared by Jason Mellon, but was typed by Melinda Green.

5. Bill wanted me to ask Randy where his book is, however, I am not sure that he ever received the book.

6. Neither Bill nor Mary is ready to give their presentations this afternoon but each should be ready to present by tomorrow afternoon.

7. Of the three students whom are making plans to attend the convention that will be held next month, John is the brighter one.

8. Since you are planning to attend the meeting tomorrow; will you please check with Mr. Smith to determine if he wants to visit with you today?

9. John did his work quick this morning due to the fact that he was to leave for Chicago at noon.

10. The clouds look like it will rain at any moment, but today's forecast did not indicate that it was to rain today.

11. Bill's suggestion to implement a training program, that was well received by management, is needed bad because in the event that we need to hire new employees, training will be crucial.

12. Due to the fact that your unit was singled out by top management as the unit with the best productivity in the company, I do not think you have to be concerned about cutbacks in the number of employees in your unit.

13. John is not sure at this time if he should plan to attend the meeting in Dallas because it appears that Mr. Jones is planning to take his vacation at that time.

14. Please lie your report on my desk, so that I will be sure not to miss it when I gather the documents to take home this weekend that need my attention.

15. Mary, as well as her two brothers, are planning to spend the holidays with their parents, who live in a small town on the outskirts of Boston.

Exercise 42

Name ______________________________ Section ________________ Grade ______________

In each of the following sentences, determine if the underlined portion is correct or contains an error in style, word usage, grammar, or punctuation. When you rewrite each sentence in the space below the sentence, correct any errors in the underlined portion(s) as well as edit each sentence for courtesy, conciseness, concreteness, and clarity.

1. If I was really concerned about Johns' well being, I would be glad to help him, but I do not think we have anything to worry about regarding his ability to perform well in his new job.

2. David and Mary plan to take his/her vacation at the end of the month, they want to do their best to avoid the crowded conditions that will likely prevail in Washington later in the summer.

3. Either Ms. Johnson or one of her subordinates plans to serve as tour guide when you bring your class to our company for their field trip through our premises.

4. All 120 pages of Al's report has been edited; but Mary is not expected to complete typing it until tomorrow.

5. Whom is to help you with the Jackson proposal, or has that not yet been decided by Mr. Bailey?

6. My thinking is that we should involve the systems department in this project, there are several parts of the project they could help us with.

7. John plans to fly to Houston this afternoon, and on to Phoenix tomorrow, he does not plan to be back in the office until Friday morning.

8. One of the pages of Bills report are missing in the final draft of my copy, please see if other's are also missing page 12.

9. None of the students in my morning class has any incomplete assignments, however, that is not the case with my afternoon class as five of them has incomplete assignments.

10. I wish it was possible for me to help you with the program on Friday, but I will not be here as I will be St. Louis.

11. Chris' goals are real ambitious, but knowing Chris as I do, I do not think he has a thing to worry about regarding their accomplishment.

12. Mary said that after she lay down for an hour, she felt better, she is not as pale as she was this morning.

13. Of the three books you are considering, I believe you will find David Browns book to be the better choice of the three.

14. Although Jim believes he knows who he wants to serve on the committee with him, I suspect that before all is said and done, Mr. Jones will also want to make several recommendations as to who should serve on the committee.

15. The guests drunk all of the coffee before I had a chance to make more coffee, never before had we not been able to keep up with the demand.

Exercise 43

Name ______________________ Section ______________ Grade ______________

In the space below each sentence, rewrite the sentence, correcting errors in writing style, word usage, grammar, or punctuation.

1. Neither David nor his parents plans to attend the Brown family reunion, that is held each year.

2. In Jim's office one of the ceiling panels need to be repainted since it was stained when the roof leaked.

3. Due to fact that the mens' department is moving from the second floor to the third floor, our plan at the present time are to move home furnishings to the second floor where the mens' department was.

4. It is a well known fact that Mr. Crandell plans to announce his retirement as president of the company by the end of the year.

5. John remembers that Bill lay the Samuelson report on the top of the file cabinet this morning, but it is nowhere to be found.

6. I wish I was going to New Orleans with you but I am unable to do so because I have to make a presentation on Friday to the sales managers.

7. I have often found that when one has to question if you should do something, then you probably should not.

8. You helping Jim with his work is greatly appreciated by both of his parents.

9. Stephen Mattehson's latest book, that I make reference to in my presentation, is going to be invaluable for individuals calculating financial ratios.

10. One of his greatest fears are flying in an airplane, a problem he has tried to overcome many times.

11. In the event that you are unable to attend the meeting from the beginning, will you please send someone to represent the department until your arrive?

12. When she was asked if she was planning to help finalize the report tomorrow she replied in the affirmative.

13. Each and every person is accountable for their actions.

14. John should plan to attend the morning session, however, he does not need to attend the afternoon session.

15. Is he the person who you had in mind when your made your recommendation last week?

Exercise 44

Name ______________________________ Section ________________ Grade ______________

In the space below each sentence, rewrite the sentence, correcting errors in writing style, word usage, grammar, or punctuation.

1. To be successful in life one needs to have a strong work ethic; you also need to work good with others.

2. My immediate goal is to finish college in the spring; then moving to Houston is something I would look forward to doing.

3. The order of 12 books have arrived but the video tapes will not be shipped until next week.

4. Every student must be concerned about their overall academic performance.

5. Neither the president nor the vice presidents was aware of the financial situation until this morning.

6. There are several things one needs to keep in mind if you are to be considered for promotion to a management position.

7. Do you know if the outcome of Johns decision is likely to effect the overall performance of the auditing section?

8. Among the two work units being considered for top honors I believe Sally's unit is most deserving.

9. Will you please join the two groups together since the greater the number of individuals whom can help, the better.

10. I wish to take this opportunity to thank you for you assisting me with my presentation last week.

11. I will not be able to see him until tomorrow morning because my plans are to spend the afternoon at Jackson Street branch.

12. The presentation was made by her due to the fact that she is the one who was most familiar with the data being presented.

13. All of the staff were present to hear John assessing the affect of the unfriendly takeover of Martin Company by Williams Company.

14. Less opportunities are available for promotion to the employees in the accounting department now than were available several months ago.

15. The analysis of the situation by Gordon revealed several benefits which the employees need to be made aware of.

Exercise 45

Name ______________________ Section ______________ Grade ______________

In the space below each group of sentences, combine the sentences into the type of sentence indicated above each group. In the process of combining the sentences in each set, pay particular attention to conciseness, clarity, correctness, and so forth. The following is an example:

(Simple sentence)
I am a systems analyst.
The company for which I work is Acme Manufacturing Company.
I have worked there for three years.

I have worked as a systems analyst for three years at Acme Manufacturing Company.

1. (Simple sentence)
John is my brother.
He has lived in Houston for the last two years.
He works for an oil company.

2. (Complex sentence)
Your report contained data.
The data were requested by the president.
Therefore, I gave him your entire report.

3. (Compound sentence)
Our office has been newly carpeted.
It also has had its walls painted.
The new office furniture has not arrived.

4. (Compound sentence)
You ordered booklets that have been sent.
The technical manual is on backorder.
It will be sent soon.

5. (Compound sentence)
The report was written by Mary.
It contained various statistical tables.
The information in these tables was compiled by Bill.

6. (Simple sentence)
You expended effort in obtaining the approval of the expansion project.
This effort is appreciated.
You provided expertise in the preparation of the proposal.
That effort is also appreciated.

7. (Complex sentence)
You are writing the annual sales report.
You have not yet completed writing it.
When you do, you are to give John a rough draft of it.

8. (Simple sentence)
John works in a department.
His department is no longer vital to the success of the company.
As a result, it is being merged with the Accounting Department.

9. (Compound sentence)
The president will soon inform the employees about the new fringe benefits program.
The employees are eager to hear these recommendations.
The salary increase program is a concern of the employees.

10. (Complex sentence)
Mr. Jones is now at lunch.
He plans to return to the office after lunch.
Mrs. Smith would like to visit with him after he returns.
She would like to visit with him about the new employee training program.

Exercise 46

Name ______________________ Section ______________ Grade ______________

In the space below each group of sentences, combine the sentences into the type of sentence indicated above each group. In the process of combining the several sentences in each set, pay particular attention to conciseness, clarity, correctness, and so forth. The following is an example:

(Simple sentence)

I am a systems analyst.
The company for which I work is Acme Manufacturing Company.
I have worked there for three years.

I have worked as a systems analyst for three years at Acme Manufacturing Company.

1. (Simple sentence)
The company has two main goals.
One goal is to increase employee productivity by 10 percent.
The other goal is to decrease operating expenses by 5 percent.

2. (Simple sentence)
Getting along with people on the job is critical to one's success.
This can be done by treating them with respect.
It can also be done by showing them courtesy.

3. (Compound sentence)
The company has installed a new computer system.
We believe it has increased the productivity of all employees.
We will know at year's end if it has increased employee productivity.

4. (Complex sentence)
Employees need several skills.
One skill they need is the ability to communicate their ideas effectively to management.
This skill will enable them to be promoted more quickly than their counterparts.

5. (Compound sentence)
Mr. Johnson is the executive vice president.
He wrote a proposal that adequately documented the need for the 10,000-square-foot addition.
He did not adequately document the need to purchase for this project 2.5 acres from Smith Company.

6. (Compound sentence)
We have a new computer systems analyst.
She is impressed with the power of our computer system.
She is also impressed with the amount of software we have made available to our employees.
She is not equally impressed with the administrative computer systems we have developed over the years.

7. (Complex sentence)
Jim is job hunting.
He has had two interviews with banks.
He would like to work in a loan department.

8. (Compound sentence)
The vote on the new fringe benefits package took place yesterday.
The employees in the sales department voted to approve the package.
The employees in the marketing department voted against the package.

9. (Simple sentence)
Both Mary and Bill have ideas for solving the deficit situation in the research unit.
Mary's ideas for solving the situation seem much better than Bill's ideas.
Bill's ideas for solving the situation seem much weaker than Mary's ideas.

10. (Compound sentence)
We have ordered several reports from Investments, Inc.
The reports on equity mutual funds have arrived.
The reports on bond funds have not arrived.

Exercise 47

Name ______________________________ Section ________________ Grade ______________

In the space below each group of sentences, combine the sentences into the type of sentence indicated above each group. In the process of combining the several sentences in each set, pay particular attention to conciseness, clarity, correctness, and so forth. The following is an example:

(Simple sentence)
I am a systems analyst.
The company for which I work is Acme Manufacturing Company.
I have worked there for three years.

I have worked as a systems analyst for three years at Acme Manufacturing Company.

1. (Two sentences)
Mr. Smith is getting new bookcases for his office.
They have been ordered.
They should arrive in two weeks.
The new file cabinets are on back order.
They will be on back order for at least a month.

2. (Two sentences)
Mrs. Jones and Mr. Smith are swapping offices.
They are swapping offices because of recent changes in their work assignments.
Mr. Johnson and Mr. Brown also have had recent changes in their work assignments.
They are not swapping offices.

3. (Two sentences)
Mrs. Swanson has served for twenty years as the president's secretary.
To recognize her for this accomplishment, a reception will be held in her honor next month.
The reception is to be a surprise to her.
She has three children.
All three children plan to attend the reception.

4. (Two sentences)
Mary Blackstone served as convention chairperson.
She is to be commended for her efforts as chairperson.
Her efforts helped ensure the success of the convention.
Several who attended the convention mentioned that it was the best convention they have ever attended.

5. (Two sentences)
The last two weeks of weather have been unusual.
It has been unusual because of the number of cool days.
It has also been unusual because of several nice rains.
Neither the cool days nor the rain are typical for this month.

6. (Two sentences)
John's parents live in Denver.
He plans to spend the Christmas holidays with them.
On January 2, John plans to go to Vail.
He will meet several friends there for a week of skiing.

7. (Two sentences)
William is in charge of a sales group.
His sales group led the company during the fourth quarter.
This is because his group had a 12.4 percent increase in sales.
William will be quite surprised about this.
This is the first time his group has led the company in quarterly sales.

8. (Two sentences)
Jim was not aware that Mary Brown has been promoted.
Mary has been promoted to executive vice president.
A memo was sent announcing her promotion.
Apparently Jim did not get the memo.

9. (Two sentences)
The football team had a winning season last year.
This accomplishment seems remarkable.
This is because the coach accomplished this feat as a new coach.
This is only his second year as head coach of the team.

10. (Two sentences)
Three times yesterday the printing press broke down.
This is disturbing.
The press is only three years old.
It breaks down as often as a press fifteen years old.

Exercise 48

Name ______________________ Section ______________ Grade ____________

In the space below each group of sentences, combine the sentences into the type of sentence indicated above each group. In the process of combining the several sentences in each set, pay particular attention to conciseness, clarity, correctness, and so forth. The following is an example:

(Simple sentence)
I am a systems analyst.
The company for which I work is Acme Manufacturing Company.
I have worked there for three years.

I have worked as a systems analyst for three years at Acme Manufacturing Company.

1. (Three sentences)
The accounting division needs a new manager.
It got permission from the executive committee to begin looking for a new manager.
The new manager will replace Harry Brown.
Mr. Brown retired after working for the company 18 years.
The new manager is to be on the job within three months.

2. (Three sentences)
The carpet for the new addition has been backordered.
This will result in our missing our goal of occupying the new addition by July 1.
We will not be able to take receipt of the new furniture for the addition until the carpet has been installed.
Streamdean Furniture Company has been notified to delay shipping the furniture.
We will ask it to ship the furniture when we have a firm occupancy date.
The project manager believes we should be able to move in by August 1.

3. (Three sentences)
I had a recent discussion with John.
He told me he has three long-range goals.
By the time he is 35, he hopes to become manager of his department.
He also wants to become section head by the time he is 45.
He also said that he wants to serve on the state's Tourist Council.

4. (Three sentences)
Mary Baker submitted an impressive report.
It was impressive because it provided a critical analysis of the problem.
It also analyzed the factors that created the problem.
It also suggested three alternative solutions.
Each alternative solution is worthwhile.

5. (Three sentences)
The new computer system we recently installed is working well.
It did not work well initially.
Among the problems was one with the local area network.
The problem with the network primarily involved software.
To a lesser extent the problem involved hardware.

6. (Three sentences)
Oral and written business communications essentials are important to learn.
Employees with well-developed communication skills are often promoted more quickly than their counterparts.
Those with less well-developed communication skills are often promoted less quickly than their counterparts.
Paying rich dividends is putting forth the effort to master communication skills.

7. (Three sentences)
The Senate recently passed legislation.
One piece of legislation will have important implications for our company.
Our company can now offer a new deferred income package for certain employees.
These are employees making more than $50,000.
These employees can now shelter up to 8 percent of the gross salary.

8. (Three sentences)
We hired a consultant.
This consultant was hired to examine our administrative procedures.
He has finished with the data collection.
In collecting the data, he talked with 85 percent of employees who work in administrative offices.
The consultant is writing a final report.
His report is due in three weeks.